SCIENCE FICTION
TELEVISION SERIES,
1990–2004

THE EARLIER VOLUME

Science Fiction Television Series:
Episode Guides, Histories, and Casts and
Credits for 62 Prime-Time Shows, 1959 through 1989
(McFarland, 1996; paper 2006)
by Mark Phillips and Frank Garcia

SCIENCE FICTION TELEVISION SERIES, 1990–2004

Histories, Casts and Credits for 58 Shows

by FRANK GARCIA *and*
MARK PHILLIPS

with a foreword by BRAD WRIGHT

McFarland & Company, Inc., Publishers
Jefferson, North Carolina, and London

LIBRARY OF CONGRESS CATALOGUING-IN-PUBLICATION DATA

Garcia, Frank, 1961–
Science fiction television series, 1990–2004 : histories, casts
and credits for 58 shows / by Frank Garcia and Mark Phillips ; with a
foreword by Brad Wright.
p.   cm.
Includes bibliographical references and index.

ISBN 978-0-7864-2483-2
illustrated case binding : 50# alkaline paper ∞

1. Science fiction television programs— United States— History
and criticism.   I. Phillips, Mark, 1959–   II. Title.
PN1992.8S35G37   2009   791.45'615 — dc22   2008029425

British Library cataloguing data are available

Cover image ©2009 Blend Images.

Manufactured in the United States of America

McFarland & Company, Inc., Publishers
Box 611, Jefferson, North Carolina 28640
www.mcfarlandpub.com

For science fiction television
series fans everywhere

ACKNOWLEDGMENTS

The following people graciously agreed to be interviewed for this book, talking about their work in science fiction television, or offering us help in other ways. This book would not have been possible without their continued friendship, support and assistance.

The authors would like to extend their thanks to Brad Wright for writing this book's foreword and for his interview.

The authors also wish to thank writers Greg Cox and Michael Cassutt for their advance preview reviews.

Frank Garcia interviewees: Enid-Raye Adams, Steven Barnes, Hans Beimler, Gretchen Berg, Bruce Boxleitner, Alan Brennert, Julie Caitlin Brown, Laura J. Burns, Trey Callaway, James Cameron, Michael Cassutt, Garry Chalk, Lewis Chesler, Kevin Conway, Manny Coto, Nicole DeBoer, Robert DeLaurentis, Pen Densham, Chris Dickie, Holly Elissa Dignard, Tony Dow, Alisen Down, Ellen Dubin, Sam Egan, Erica Ehm, Neill Fearnley, Jonathan Frakes, Brent V. Friedman, Paul Gertz, Jonathan Glassner, Bruce Seth Green, Bruce Greenwood, Anthony Michael Hall, Aaron Harberts, Jeff Hayes, Torri Higginson, Marjean Holden, Barclay Hope, Joan Horvath, James Hudnall, Kenneth Johnson, Jeff F. King, John Kretchmer, Robert Leeshock, Richard Barton Lewis, Melinda Metz, Art Monterastelli, Bill Mumy, James Nadler, Joe Napolitano, Kathrin Nicholson, Adam Nimoy, David Nutter, Rockne S. O'Bannon, Peter O'Fallon, Luke Perry, Michael Piller, Shawn Piller, Kim Poirier, Deborah Pratt, Larry Raskin, Stephen Roloff, Grant Rosenberg, Scott Mitchell Rosenberg, Lisa Ryder, Daniel Sackheim, Alan Scarfe, Melinda Snodgrass, Mark Sobel, Joseph Stefano, Mark Stern, David Ogden Stiers, Kristoffer Tabori, Rachael Talalay, Tracy Torme, Keegan Connor Tracy, Ken Tremblett, Jesus Salvador Trevino, Justina Vail, Alan Van Sprang, Malcolm Jamal Warner, Robert K. Weiss, Robert Wertheimer, Peter Williams, David Winning, Robert Hewitt Wolfe, Monica Wyatt, Bryce Zabel, Alex Zahara, and Marc Scott Zicree.

For generously providing the use of materials they owned: Robert T. Garcia for the Andreas Katsulas interview. Mark Leiren-Young for making available his interview with Stephen Roloff on *TekWar*.

Thanks to all those with unique talents who helped: to Anna Kaplan for her continued and consistent support throughout the project's life. Also special thanks to M.D. Jackson for his assistance with the cast biographies. Peter Jurasik for generously contributing his tribute to Andreas Katsulas. Gilla Nissan for her permission to use the Andreas Katsulas interview. Julie Caitlin Brown for her help in making the important connections. Dan Forcey and Adam Rosenblum at Platinum Studios for help with *Jeremiah* matters. Alex Daltas at Trilogy Entertainment Group for help with *Space Rangers* matters. Brian Millikin at Piller2 for help with *Dead Zone* matters. Bill Wanstrom for opening up Gatecon where many interviews were obtained. Eric Stillwell for making yet more important connections. Juleen at Shelter Entertainment for making the *Babylon 5* connections. Melanie Turner at Pacific Artists for *Mysterious Ways* connections. Lois Holmlund for her help in making *Earth: Final Conflict* connections. Susan Sussman at Diverse Talent for her help in multiple important connections. Dennis Kristos for his expertise in *Babylon 5* and *Andromeda*. Melanie Paull for help with *Harsh Realm* access. Lynn Hockenbery for help with *Odyssey 5*.

Mark Phillips Interviewees: Vaughn Armstrong, Stefan Arngrim, Steve Aspis, Mike Bailey, Dr. Robert Ballard, Greg Bear, Hans Beimler, Paul Ben-Victor Dr. Barry Beyerstein, Tony Bill, Meghan Black, Jacquelyn Blain, Chris Brancato, Allison Liddi Brown, Billy Brown, David Carren, Lanai Chapman, Kristen Cloke, William Corcoran, Manny Coto, Roger Cross, Holly Dale, Janet Davidson, William B. Davis, Joel de la Fuente, Aaron Douglas, Brian Downey, Ellen Dubin, Michael Duggan, Carleton Eastlake, Jane Espenson, Joseph Patrick Finn, Isabelle Fox, Jerry Freedman, Robert Ginty, Marita Grabiak, Christopher Graves, Javier Grillo-Marxauch, Olivier Gruner, Tim Guinee, Dean Haglund, Janet Muswell Hamilton, Patrick Hasburgh, Richard Herd, Steve Howarth, Philip Jackson, Rick Jacobson, Andre and Maria Jacquemetton, Kevin Kerslake, Jeff King, Rob LaBelle, Eleanore Lindo, Chris Long, Rena Lundigan, Nancy Malone, Richard Manning, George Mendeluk, Joe Menosky, Peter Mohan, James Morrison, David Nutter, Rockne S. O'Bannon, Michael Pare, P.J. Pesce, Stephen Posey, Burt Prelutsky, William Rabkin, Kathryn Reindl, Faryl Saliman Reingold, Tucker Smallwood, Sebastian Spence, Jeri Taylor, J. Miller Tobin, Tracy Torme, Jesus Salvador Treviño, Ethlie Ann Vare, Vincent Ventresca, Mark Verheiden, Leanne Wilson, S.S. (Steve) Wilson, Paul Woodmansee and Ed Zuckerman.

Thanks also to the following: Kate Duncan of the excellent and comprehensive site, *Space: Above and Beyond* Alumni News & Reviews. Kate secured exclusive quotes from the cast and provided invaluable editorial help with the *Space: Above and Beyond* chapter. Amanda Rogers, of Shoom Zone Productions (www. shoomzone.com), provided information for the *Invisible Man* chapter and made the interviews with Vincent Ventresca and Paul Ben-Victor possible. Diana Ford, president of the Official Vaughn Armstrong Fanclub U. K. (www.theadmiralsclub.com), for arranging the interview with Vaughn Armstrong. Sandra Chalmers of The Narrow Road Company agency in London for arranging the Leanne Wilson interview. The people at www.stampede-entertainment.com (creators of *Tremors*) who arranged the interview with S.S. Wilson. Yohko Kaneko of The Official Michael Pare fan club who kindly arranged the Pare interview. Wendy Shobe of The Characters Talent Agency in Vancouver for setting up the chat with Meghan Black. Lee Goldberg for connecting us with several of the *seaQuest* writers. Karen Myatt for background information on *Star Trek: Voyager* (as well as her continued help and encouragement over the years). David McDonnell, editor of *Starlog*. Mike Bailey for the excellent *Firefly* essay and to his wife Beverly for her editing of same. (Mike, a radio personality and writer in Portland, Oregon, has a marvelous web site devoted to the *Voyage to the Bottom of the Sea* motion picture and TV series, http://www.vttbots.com, which includes cast interviews, rare production photos and a fantastic episode guide that identifies even the nameless *Seaview* crewmen.) Dennis Kristos for co-writing portions of the *Andromeda* essay and for his input on *Firefly*. Anna L. Kaplan for her invaluable help and information on the various *Star Trek* chapters and reading over all of the other chapters in this book. Steve Howarth (a modelmaker for the *Space Precinct* series) for helping with information and photos. His web site, www.fingertipfabrications.com, is devoted to modelmaking and sculpting for Industry, Film and Television. Deborah Liddi Brown for arranging the Allison Liddi Brown interview. Meg Furihata for arranging the Tim Guinee interviews. Julia Houston at http:/www.sci fix-ile.com (a great place for SF buffs) for information on *Star Trek: Voyager*. People who helped with advice and information: illustrator Tom Holtkamp (www.tomholtkamp.com), Dan Borgman, Candy Krause, Laurie Close, Cindy Baker, Maria Tereza Pinho Gomes da Silva, William Lenihan and Montreal film historian Alain Bourassa. And special thanks to Elizabeth Phillips (Mark's Mom) for her invaluable help in assembling the Index.

TABLE OF CONTENTS

FOREWORD BY BRAD WRIGHT

I love science fiction. Always have. I was six years old when the original *Star Trek* aired, and I beamed aboard right away. I had no problem at all believing "warp" speed was possible if you had the right kind of crystals, or for that matter, that Sulu could drive a ship across the galaxy with three rocker switches. And don't even get me started on how cool *The Twilight Zone* and *The Outer Limits* were back in the day. *"To Serve Man... It's a cookbook!"* That there's gold. The days of giant-eyeballed rubber-suited aliens are behind us but if a science fiction series comes on the air, I give it a chance. Sometimes it's gold ... sometimes it's kryptonite. But it's always more interesting to me than the usual television fare like *Medical Hospital Doctors* or *Police Cops* or ... okay, I made those titles up, but you get the idea. Good SF is as good as it gets. You obviously feel the same way, otherwise you wouldn't be reading this.

I'm not one of those screenwriters who happened to get work in the genre and then got stuck there, I'm one who went into the business so that I could write an episode of *Star Trek: The Next Generation* one day. Sure, I never got to do that, but that was only because I joined the writing staff of the new *Outer Limits* at MGM's studios in Vancouver and haven't left the lot since. I don't regret it. *Outer Limits* was a writer-producer's dream. Every week a movie. Sometimes great, sometimes not so much. Anthology is great fun for a science fiction writer, since it keeps open the possibility of the heroes failing and the world coming to an end after all (which, in retrospect, I did perhaps a few too many times). Then there was

Stargate SG-1 and *Stargate Atlantis*, and my next project will probably be SF too. I love it.

SF writers are often asked why they don't want to write and produce some other genre like a drama, comedy, mystery, or action, but my answer is simple. Science fiction isn't a single genre. It's all of them. We're able to write suspense shows, medical shows, war stories, every genre there is ... all under the guise of science fiction. It's like cheating, really. And the beauty of it is, we can make a medical drama one week and an action-adventure the next. (In fact, I probably have to make the medical drama in order to afford the action-adventure.) That isn't to say you can just set up a hospital in space and call it science fiction (although *Firefly*, more or less a western, was a truly brilliant exception to that rule); there has to be something about the story and the milieu that makes it science fiction as opposed to a story that could happen anywhere but just happens to be set on Ceti Alpha 5. (I know, I know, *there is no Ceti Alpha 5!*) If I ever found myself writing for a straight-up cop show or medical drama, I'm sure I'd eventually pitch a story where the suspect is not human or the patient is *patient zero*.

Science fiction television lets us go places that ordinary television can't hope to take us. And I'm not just talking about the Pegasus Galaxy. Heroic acts can take on a completely new meaning. It's one thing to run into a burning building, but it takes a real hero to fly his starship — set to explode, mind you — into the maw of a doomsday device. (If you're reading this book, you get the reference.) SF also allows us to tell cautionary tales about the environment, war, and politics—any of our planet's current problems—under the guise of someone else's planet's problems. Above all, SF gives us a look into our own future, sometimes with hope, sometimes with dread, even if sometimes it gets a little ahead of itself. (It's well past 2001 and we still can't fly the Pan Am shuttle to the orbiting hotel on our way to the moonbase. *Space: 1999* was a little off the mark in the prediction department too.)

I think the best years of SF television are still ahead of us. The state of the art of visual effects is opening up possibilities for a whole new range of stories. True, there have been a few recent series that have come and gone before they could fulfill their promise, but it has always been that way. There will be another *Star Trek*, just as I'm sure there will be another *Star-*

gate and dozens more series, good and bad, and I'll give them all a chance. I hope you do too.

Through hundreds of interviews with producers, writers, directors and actors, this book's authors offer their perspectives on how and why your favorite SF shows came together, and, sometimes (most intriguing) how they came apart. It's a gift to anyone who wants a unique, behind-the-scenes look at all 58 SF series made between 1990 and 2004; a herculean effort, by any standard. I just hope another 58 shows get made in the next fifteen years.

Brad Wright
British Columbia, Canada
Fall 2008

Brad Wright is the co-creator and executive producer of Stargate SG-1 *and* Stargate: Atlantis. *He was also co-executive producer and writer on* The Outer Limits *(1995–2002).*

INTRODUCTION

If there was a moment in the last 22 years that was pivotal to the life and future of the science fiction television series genre, it occurred in November 1986. The place: the commissary of Paramount Studios in Los Angeles. There, two men sat down and had lunch together. One of them, a producer, was eager to hire the other, a studio executive, to work on his brand new and very risky television series.

Star Trek creator Gene Roddenberry first met Paramount executive Rick Berman in a boardroom and invited the vice president of longform and special projects to lunch. Berman was so impressed with Roddenberry that he quit his job in the television division at the studio and joined Roddenberry's team. Because of Berman's involvement in the rebirth of *Star Trek*, a total of four TV series from 1987 to 2005 would be created. Additionally, *Star Trek: The Next Generation*'s success in first-run syndication helped spawn many other TV series documented in this book. We can draw a direct line from the *Star Trek* shows to *Earth: Final Conflict* and *Andromeda* and find tangential influences in *Babylon 5, Farscape, Lexx*, and the *Stargate* franchise.

Had Roddenberry and Berman not liked and respected one another and agreed to work together, the television landscape over the next 19 years would have played out very differently. Because it did happen, we are all beneficiaries of their talents.

In this book you'll find essays that painstakingly collect documentation for 58 science fiction television series with voices from more than 150 interviewees. Each and every one of these speakers was intimately involved in the creation of their shows, as executive producers, writers, directors or actors. Each generously shared with us their thoughts and memories of creating entertainment that has resulted in, variously, groundbreaking TV series, memorable TV series, series that had strong merits but were blunted by some flaws, or series that are just as well forgotten.

In this book we've strived to give everyone his due. As authors and journalists, we decided that it was you, the reader, who should tender final judgment.

A LOOK AT SCIENCE FICTION ON TELEVISION

Robert Hewitt Wolfe, who developed Gene Roddenberry's *Andromeda* series, admits that the pioneers of SFTV, such as Rod Serling, Joseph Stefano and Roddenberry, had it harder than he did; these legendary creator-producers faced strange network edicts, little fan support, skepticism of the genre by mass audiences, lower TV budgets and no computer generated effects. "I had a much bigger helping hand than Gene did," Hewitt says. "There's more of a tradition of doing these shows now. Gene was breaking new ground. I didn't have to fight those battles."

Debuting in 1987, Roddenberry's aforementioned *Star Trek: The Next Generation* was the show that opened up a robust, new world for first-run SF series in syndication. But even *Next Generation* had its own barriers to break through. It was criticized for being too mild in a modern era where its writers had free rein without network interference. However, it did take an unusual step by killing off one of its major characters, Tasha Yar (Denise Crosby), a first in *Star Trek* history. It also featured stories dealing with Alzheimer's disease and drug addiction, as well as a mature and sensitive handling of Starfleet's Prime Directive (non-interference with alien cultures).

In the 1990s, certain SFTV series began to dominate the airwaves. The *Trek* series *The Next Generation, Deep Space Nine* and *Voyager*, as well as *The X-Files* and *Babylon 5*, were enormously popular. Four of these were space-based TV series whereas *The X-Files* explored the hidden, dark regions of our world. *The X-Files* developed its own complex mythology and transcended its genre roots by exploding into an iconic phenomenon. The series made major stars of the previously unknown David Duchovny and Gillian Anderson. It was a hip show that generated a flood of merchandising and magazine covers and received the respect of the mainstream audience and press.

As other shows premiered, there was a further move away from the episodic form: the five-year story arc of J. Michael Strazynski's *Babylon 5*, for example, and the increasingly character-oriented plotting of *Star Trek: Deep Space Nine*, which also later engaged in deliberate serialization.

Lexx: The Dark Zone took the noisy and rude route, with anti-heroes who didn't give a rat's whisker about saving the world. They were hedonistic space travelers, each of them bullied by their hormones and nuttier than a fruitcake, flying around the universe in a giant bug, satiating their own primitive needs before considering the worlds around them.

The protagonists of *Firefly* and *Starhunter* were engulfed in bleak, grubby galaxies, beset by collapsed alliances and corrupt conglomerates but often perceptive enough to sort things out with a battered sense of morality.

Century City, set in 2030, addressed adult themes that included virtual rape, genetic manipulation and the administration of drugs that could wipe out memories of abuse. It truly defined SF storytelling, dealing with technology's impact on human lives.

The officers, crew and civilians of *Bat-*

tlestar Galactica (2003–2008) have been put through the interstellar wringer like no other SF characters, with near-assassinations, terrorist attacks, betrayals by loved ones, paranoia, food shortages and sacrifices by leaders who have the responsibility of keeping the last remnants of humanity alive. Humor need not apply; these are stories of life and death, dark and unpredictable.

Other shows just want to have a good time. Those who can decipher the plotting of *Andromeda* may laugh (or cry) at the somersaulting antics of its bizarre crew. And there must be bleary eyes somewhere, tracking *Tracker* at 2 or 3 A.M., as a European-accented alien hunts down naughty ETs while solving kidnappings and beating up art thieves.

Sometimes old shows return, philosophically changed. The original *Outer Limits* (1963–1965) encouraged viewers to push the envelope of their knowledge by challenging the human mind with science. The new *Outer Limits* was more cautious, suggesting that scientific ambitions ought to be tempered in favor of submitting them to a higher power.

The key to what makes an SF show successful remains elusive. Such high-powered series as *Surface, Threshold* and *Invasion* all died after a single (2005–2006) year. Many producers state that a good time slot is crucial but there are other factors. Greg Bear, the Hugo and Nebula award-winning author whose novels include *The Forge of God* and *Blood Music*, offers his perspective: "Even a great ensemble cast and terrific characters can't save shows that are poorly formulated or unconvincing. New worlds, future or otherwise, must have their own logic, not too far from our own logic — but also their own history, myth and technology. What audiences expect includes startling ideas and stimulating controversy but they also want to be comfortable within that world. That comfort level will allow viewers to accept additional challenges from a position of trust."

Whether shows are good or bad, it's clear that technology has allowed SFTV to flourish. In the 1960s and 1970s, the SFTV experience was limited to watching episodes of *Star Trek* or *The Six Million Dollar Man* on channels and at times dictated by broadcasters. Some fans audio-taped episodes from television. Then, many fans were unaware there were thousands of other fans out there. Today, episodes are on DVD or available for downloading from the Internet, reruns are on the Sci-Fi Channel (a cable network that *TV Guide* once called doomed, claiming its audience was too limited) and the Internet teems with chat rooms and bulletin boards, where practically every SF show has a topic header. There are web sites, magazines and fan clubs that saturate shows in coverage. And whereas in the past, many fans were often reticent about speaking out publicly, or had to listen passively as critics rapped their favorite shows, viewers are now as vocal as media critics. One woman wrote *TV Guide* to angrily announce that she and her husband were giving up on *Invasion* because "the constantly shifting cameras and quick cuts are making us seasick." Other fans rave over how these same techniques have made *Battlestar Galactica* a great-looking show. In the world of SF, differences of opinion are always encouraged and vigorously debated.

Today's SF creators, such as Chris Brancato (*First Wave*) and Ron Moore (*Battlestar Galactica*), have personally engaged and discussed their shows with fans online, welcoming viewer feedback.

THE SFTV NUTS 'N' BOLTS

Despite the genre's popularity, SFTV still attracts a niche audience. Ratings tend to reflect this, and the industry treats it that way. But marketing has to do better. We never saw Bruce Boxleitner on *The Tonight Show* but we did see him on *Regis & Kathie Lee*. *The X-Files* was the show that garnered the greatest mainstream media attention and David Duchovny and Gillian Anderson received better media exposure. Various flavors of *Star Trek* have enjoyed mainstream media attention while many other genre shows rarely warranted a blip of coverage. Despite the expansion of the genre, SFTV shows remain niched and struggle to survive. The Sci-Fi Channel's modest ratings tend to bear this out even with a popular se-

ries such as *Battlestar Galactica*. We also see this reflected in Emmy awards. Usually genre shows gain attention only in the technical categories and rarely for writing, directing or acting. However, *Quantum Leap* and *The X-Files* are two shows that have received major Emmy recognition.

In spite of this "niching," shows do survive and *Stargate SG-1* holds the current world record for the most successful SFTV show in American history, running for 10 consecutive years (214 episodes). (The UK's *Doctor Who* holds the international record with 30 years of the same title but with different casts.) *The X-Files* had a similar track record with nine consecutive years and 202 episodes. But, as a franchise title, *Star Trek* remained popular with four consecutive TV series exploring the United Federation of Planets universe. *Star Trek: Enterprise*'s truncated journey, however, was evidence that the *Star Trek* audiences were dwindling and needed a rest.

A major reason that some shows do well is because the creative artists behind the scenes stay with it and organically evolve and guide it. Creative consistency is one of the hallmarks of a long-lasting series. A raft of new producers didn't come and go, shunting the series to and fro, as was done on *seaQuest* DSV and *Sliders*.

Surprisingly, there is a new trend in the creative management of a TV series today. Many leading actors are now participating as producers, writers and directors. There are actually seven shows on our list that had stars who participated as producers: *Andromeda* (Kevin Sorbo), *The Dead Zone* (Anthony Michael Hall), *Jeremiah* (Luke Perry), *Psi-Factor* (Matt Frewer), *Sliders* (Jerry O'Connell), *Stargate SG-1* (Richard Dean Anderson) and *TekWar* (William Shatner). Ben Browder wrote two episodes of his series *Farscape* and numerous cast members of *Star Trek: The Next Generation* made their directorial debut with episodes of that show. Actor Jonathan Frakes has been the most prolific and successful of this group, having directed the *Star Trek* features *First Contact* and *Insurrection*. These are examples of actors stepping out and taking their work very seriously and, depending on the degree of involvement, carrying the show's quality on their shoulders.

When a show isn't working, networks and producers still have the impulse to "change the cast!" as a course correction. It's sometimes successful (for example, *Babylon 5*: Michael O'Hare departed after the first season and Bruce Boxleitner arrived as the new commander of the space station). But more often it's a sign of desperation to attract their viewers (for instance, *seaQuest*, where the cast was broken up each season).

Casting is a tricky roll of the dice in any TV series and when there's a change in the cast, the event can sometimes have the impact of an earthquake in the life of the series. There are three types of cast changes:

(1) When a producer says, "We want to evolve the series!" which is a sincere, honest attempt to change for story purposes and provide some turnaround so the show stays fresh.

(2) When a performer announces, "I want to leave the show!" When that happens, producers are forced to create a new character. This can wreak havoc with cast chemistry or enhance it depending on the newcomer chosen. It can also divert storylines previously planned or open new roads. The method in which a character exits a series can sometimes be spectacular. It can be a fiery death or a simple walkout with an open door for a return in future episodes.

(3) When a producer or broadcaster says, "The show isn't working! We need to change the cast or actor so we can attract a bigger audience!" This one is the most agonizing. It's a purposeful course correction. A performer is forced out and a replacement must do better. It is also the most risky because the series creators must make good decisions to improve a show. If the audience doesn't like the new player(s), their loyalty can go down and affect the show's ratings and therefore whether it continues.

As you read the chapters, look for examples of series that exemplify these course-changing events.

Thirty of our shows ran for multiple seasons and 28 were "one-season wonders." That's almost a 50 percent failure rate. The shortest lived shows were *Space Rangers* with six episodes, *Mercy Point* with eight episodes, and *Harsh Realm* and *Sleepwalkers*—both with nine episodes produced.

But there can be many reasons for a show to be short-lived. It could be a bad timeslot, poor network support or programming, budgetary issues—or it could simply be that the audiences didn't like a show's premise, characters or cast.

To attract their audiences, creators and producers are being more innovative. They're actually "blending" the genres beyond core staple SF ideas to give series that extra edge. In a simplified, face-value evaluation, some of these "blended shows" include *The X-Files*, as a law enforcement-detective procedural blended with SF. *Century City*, as *L.A. Law* pushed into the future. *Harsh Realm*, as military adventure placed in a virtual game environment. *Mercy Point*, as *St. Elsewhere* at a space station. *Roswell* as a teenage soap opera infused with an SF component.

On the other end of the spectrum, SFTV shows are becoming incredibly sophisticated and complicated and can be difficult to explain in just a paragraph. *Babylon 5*'s premise may have started out as "*Casablanca* in space" but it evolved, each season, into different plot thrusts, building on what came before. *Babylon 5* was, by design, "a novel for television" with a beginning, middle and end. It's probably the only TV show with a built-in endpoint that was conceived by its creator, J. Michael Straczynski, even before the show was bought. All other television is your standard "make-it-up-as-you-go-along" plot and character-building methodology. (This style has its own advantages, primarily spontaneous invention and tangents.) As *Jeremiah* star Luke Perry notes, "Television is a living, breathing organism."

Among the many series that are difficult to explain succinctly because of their dense plot and character arcs are *Andromeda, Earth: Final Conflict, Farscape, Star Trek: Deep Space Nine,* and *The X-Files*. And this sophistication is a double-edged sword for viewers. It gives them a lot to mull over, providing "water cooler" discussions and/or extended threaded conversations on Internet message boards about each episode's events. The other side is that the sophistication can be confusing and demanding. It forces viewers to watch every episode to keep up with the machinations of the plot and character events often cloaked in dense, mysterious layers to be deciphered. This rewards viewers for their dedication and, if producers and writers do their jobs properly, is satisfying and thrilling.

What do we look for when we watch and enjoy science fiction television shows? What is that aspect that stimulates us to go back each week and spend an hour watching? That "It Thing" is the show's unique and exciting premise—the presentation of a fresh, original science fiction *idea*. It's too simplistic to say a series' premise is what can make a show live or die, so perhaps the revision is to say "the greatest thing about a science fiction show is a *well-executed*, fresh and original science fiction idea." We can point to programs such as *Babylon 5, The Dead Zone, Quantum Leap, Star Trek: TNG* and *The X-Files* as examples. Such shows resonate with an audience and live a good life. A show such as 1973's *Starlost* had a fantastic and incredible premise: Earth's remaining civilizations traveling through the depths of space in a spaceship consisting of self-contained domes. But it was an idea that was hampered by an incredibly low budget, contrived writing and poor visual effects.

In a related topic, there are two distinct approaches to dramatic science fiction on television: There is the "viewer-friendly," accessible variety such as *Star Trek* and *The X-Files*, but there is also the more serious literary thrust of series like *The Ray Bradbury Theater* (1986), which are short stories taken from the Master's books. The more recent series *Total Recall: 2070* was heavily influenced by the works of Philip K. Dick and the 1982 film *Blade Runner*, which was based on his novel *Do Androids Dream of Electric Sheep? Babylon 5* was also a serious attempt at developing "a novel for television," achieving something grand that hadn't previously been tried in the medium.

The emergence of high-quality visual effects has given us the opportunity to enjoy great eye-candy. When *Star Trek: The Next Generation* premiered in 1987, it used the latest in effects technology to present the 24th century. In 1993, *Babylon 5* pioneered the use of computer-generated visual effects to depict the rotating, three-mile-long space station. That breakthrough was later followed by *Sliders, Stargate SG-1, Lexx, Earth: Final Conflict,* and other shows. Each program brought its own unique vision to the tube.

CGI effects technology is now so advanced, its use has come full circle. CBS Paramount has gone back to the original *Star Trek* and refurbished it with new, state-of-the-art effects in preparation for High Definition TV and DVDs. In the fall of 2006, the series was rebroadcast with those new effects in syndication on U.S. stations.

THE STATE OF THE ART OF SFTV

"With its darkly veiled view of terrorism and its almost prism-like window into how ordinary people live their lives during anxious times, it might be one of the most important television series of its time—this generation's version of Rod Serling's *The Twilight Zone*." That's the assessment of Alex Strachan, TV columnist for *The Vancouver Sun*, about the reimagining of *Battlestar Galactica*, which premiered on the Sci Fi Channel as a mini-series in 2003. Slightly more than a year later it became a weekly series, with Edward James Olmos (as Commander Adama) and Mary McDonnell (as President Laura Roslin) leading the last bits of humanity (survivors of a robotic Cylon attack) through space. Their purpose: to find sanctuary on a mythical planet known as Earth.

The show's driving force, writer Ronald D. Moore, was intrigued by the original *Galactica*'s premise, with its dark story of humanity facing destruction at the hands of their machine-made Cylons. Moore dropped the campy elements that overwhelmed the original and redid the show for modern audiences. This meant changes that angered its loyal fans: changing

Starbuck to a female pilot and transforming Boomer into a Cylon. There was also President Roslin facing terminal cancer and Adama's bitter estrangement from his son, Apollo. While *Star Wars* and *The X-Files* had broadened the appeal of science fiction, the genre still suffered from a dubious reputation. "The minute they bring on any four-eyed monsters, I'm gone," said Olmos. Executive Producer David Eick reflected years later, "We wanted to avoid those kind of outer space conventions. The big mistake for us would be to become an SF show first. Our job is to tell a good story, not to tell a good SF story."

A constant theme was the examination of the moral and political fallout of war, as Adama and Roslin are heatedly criticized by their own people for their wartime decisions. Reflective of our post 9/11 existence, *Galactica* became the primary SF show of recent years that drew story material from current events and addressed those issues unflinchingly. Indeed, as Strachan noted, it is reminiscent of *Twilight Zone*, which also dealt with topical subjects in the 1960s. (The creators of *Lost* also called *Twilight Zone* a big inspiration, but that was more for its quirky ambiance.)

Some fans noted that *Galactica*'s method of addressing hot political and social themes via futuristic stories made it bravely topical without being subjected to nervous censorship. However, the TV world has changed dramatically since Serling did the same with *Twilight Zone*. The once admired process of camouflaging important themes as *Twilight Zone* and *Star Trek* once did, and as *M*A*S*H* did in the 1970s (its vintage Korean War setting a safe arena to make dramatic stabs at the then-current and controversial Vietnam War), was once a creativity necessity but that's no longer required. Nor is it as daring. In this Internet-driven world, viewers are deluged from all directions by every point of view. And in recent years, shows such as *Law and Order*, *Grey's Anatomy* and *The West Wing* have taken topical issues head-on while the cable channels have offered a variety of topical fare, free of network edicts. Even Rod Serling said, shortly before he died in 1975, that contemporary issues had become too pressing to

cloak them in SF prose; they now had to be "attacked directly" by writers. On that level, SFTV's power has been marginalized.

But dramatically, *Galactica*'s veiled allusions to real-life events have made it one of the most complex SF shows ever made. It's a long way from the warm but simple stories of 1980s SF. An episode of *Starman* (1986–1987) dealt with the alien saving an endangered falcon. The ET of *Hard Time on Planet Earth* (1989) became a contestant on *The Dating Game* to turn a beautiful woman's life around. *War of the Worlds* (1989–1990) defined its heroes and aliens mainly by the kinds of weapons they could devise to destroy one another. Much of *Star Trek: The Next Generation*, with its renegade or misunderstood aliens of the week, now seems safely ensconced in compartmentalized clean storytelling, compared to the edgy, uncompromising scenarios of *Galactica*. *Galactica*'s biggest challenge was re-imagining an old show that had such a dubious reputation. The 1978–1979 ABC series was slaughtered by critics and was number five on the list of worst SF series ever, as selected by over 100 writers and critics in John Javna's book, *The Best of Science Fiction TV* (1987). Making a better *Galactica* may not have been hard but Moore and his writers had to convince wary viewers to accept a show with the original's basic premise and characters, re-aligned with adult situations.

"Don't assume a remake of a cruddy show has to be cruddy," Chuck Barney of *The Contra Costa Times* urged. "Yet despite the critical raves, *Battlestar Galactica* remains prime time's quietest sensation. Its producers and supporters hope it will finally break out into the mainstream."

The show's Sci Fi Channel ratings have been comparatively modest: It averages a 1.7 rating, compared to 18.0 for *CSI Miami*, a network show. Despite many strides, SFTV still remains a niche product. "I do worry that there are people who are never going to turn on a show called *Battlestar Galactica*," admits David Eick. "I'm talking about the same people who enjoy hits like *24* or *E.R.* That's a challenge, to break out of the genre and appeal to mainstream audiences."

This, despite such hip praise from magazines such as *Rolling Stone* ("The smartest and toughest show on TV"). A time slot change for *Galactica* in early 2007 (from Fridays to Sundays) was designed as a ratings booster but the numbers remained the same. "*Battlestar Galactica* will always be limited by its title," laments Eick. But the series has been nourished by the critical acclaim (including a prestigious Peabody Award) and by an incredibly loyal fan base.

All of this underscores a critical challenge that has faced SFTV creators from the beginning: getting an audience. Before today's genre shows entered modern syndication, and cable, where they often flourished with conservative but profitable ratings, survival for a network SF show meant attracting the fickle mainstream audience. This meant grabbing viewers who were baffled or turned off by the genre unless the show had a popular star (Lindsay Wagner as *The Bionic Woman*) or if the premise doubled as an adventure show (*The Six Million Dollar Man*, *Voyage to the Bottom of the Sea*) or if it had famous comic-book origins (*The Incredible Hulk*).

When *Twilight Zone* began to fade in the ratings in 1963, Rod Serling was forced by CBS to tour the country with a UCLA student (who had a genius IQ) to promote the series. Serling was reluctant, considering the tour a lowbrow gimmick, but he understood it was a necessity to drum up numbers.

There have been recent instances where the SF audience doesn't turn up for a genre show but the mainstream audiences welcome it without hesitation. *The 4400*, a USA Network series that premiered in 2004, stars Joel Gretsch and Jacqueline McKenzie as federal agents who are investigating the mysterious abduction of 4400 people over the past 60 years. When the abductees are returned to present-day Earth, they have confused memories, subtle powers and a secret mission, dealing with the future of mankind. It's an imaginative premise that comes without spaceships and aliens. The special effects are used sparingly in storylines that emphasize drama over spectacle.

"It shocked the shit out of us when we found out we had a more mainstream audience than an SF one," remarks executive producer Ira Steven Behr. "In fact, *The 4400* hasn't been embraced by the SF base. The buzz for the show from genre fans is very low."

Created by Scott Peters and Rene Echevarria, *The 4400*'s stories focus on government agendas and corruption (out to exploit the abductees' powers for military purposes), prejudice (the 4400 are ostracized and targeted by fearful people) and the dangerous power of cults. As in *Battlestar Galactica*, the characters are a varied lot, who evolve, disappear and die, and whose motives can shift from good to evil or vice versa. The series also has one of the most haunting title sequences ever created, its moody music theme sung by Amanda Abizaid.

CHANNELING THE SCI FI

The date September 24, 1992, was a very special one for SF fans everywhere. That's when the Sci-Fi Channel arrived in the homes of U.S. cable subscribers. Because there was now a cable (and satellite) channel that devoted its programming to SF, fantasy, horror and the paranormal, a galaxy of TV series, movies and non-fiction documentaries were seen by millions of viewers. For the first time in the medium, science fiction's popularity grabbed a network it could call its own. The significance of the channel was validated when it began to create its own original series programming with fare such as *Mission: Genesis*, *First Wave*, *Stargate SG-1*, and *Farscape*, and successful mini-series such as Frank Herbert's *Dune*, *Children of Dune* and Steven Spielberg's *Taken*. Later, Sci-Fi also greenlighted the *Battlestar Galactica* remake which became a hit series.

There continues to be a stigma to being "a science fiction TV series." Some people continue to regard SF as a genre for children to enjoy. But that's no longer fair. There's plenty of serious, adult SF. The genre has grown up. Complex fare such as *Babylon 5*, *Dark Angel*, *The Outer Limits*, and *The X-Files* demonstrated the field's maturity on television. And the genre's popularity has increased tremendously as we go deeper into the 21st century.

People in generations past once considered the 21st century as "the age of the future." Well, we're here. We're quite past Stanley Kubrick's epoch *2001* but we don't have a moonbase yet.

The genre's popularity is evident when you consider that in our first book, *Science Fiction Television Series: Episode Guides, Histories, and Casts and Credits for 62 Prime-Time Shows, 1959 through 1989*, we found 62 TV series over 30 years. In this volume we found 58 TV series in just 14 years. That's a remarkable increase in density and popularity. And in content, more complex than ever.

We are dreamers. And we always will be. That's what science fiction on television is all about — dreaming our way into the unknown frontiers of science and ourselves. And we're having so much fun in doing it.

OUT OF THE SFTV VORTEX

For this book to be possible, and to shape and grade it to a practical level, it was necessary to eliminate certain subcategories of the science fiction, fantasy television history. We decided to eliminate four distinct categories:

(1) **Superheroes:** *Birds of Prey*; *Black Scorpion*; *The Flash*; *Human Target*; *Lois & Clark: The New Adventures of Superman*; *MANTIS*; *Mutant X*; *Nightman*; *Smallville*; *Swamp Thing*; and *Witchblade*.

(2) **Comedy, fantasy and horror:** *Alienated*; *Angel*; *Beastmaster*; *Brimstone*; *Brisco County, Jr.*; *Buffy the Vampire Slayer*; *Charmed*; *The Chronicle*; *Crow: Stairway to Heaven*; *Dark Shadows*; *Deadly Games*; *Forever Knight*; *G. vs. E*; *Highlander*; *Hercules*; *The Immortal*; *Joan of Arcadia*; *Jules Verne's The Lost World*; *Legend*; *Poltergeist: The Legacy*; *Relic Hunter*; *Roar*; *The Secret Adventures of Jules Verne*; *Strange Luck*; *Tales from the Crypt*; *Third Rock from the Sun*; *Tru Calling*; *Wolf Lake*; and *Xena: Warrior Princess*.

(3) **Children's shows:** *Hypernauts*; *Mission: Genesis* (a.k.a. *Deepwater Black*); and *Space Cases*.

(4) A category of shows that has an "SF component" in its premise and doesn't quite rise to the level of true SF because of the show's dramatic focus. For example, on this subcategory list is *The Sentinel*, which is about a police detective who gains superenhanced sensory powers as a result of a harrowing experience in the jungles of Peru. The series allows the detective to use these powers in the course of his daily job in a major metropolitan city. Although it has that SF component, the show is clearly, and thoroughly, a gritty, real-world crime drama adventure. In a similar vein, *Level 9* is a show about future tech crimes and how a band of criminal and tech experts join forces to keep the bad guys at bay. At its core this is a crime drama with future tech as the SF conceit wrapping around the drama. Some of these series were successful high-quality television, while others sputtered out at 13 episodes or less. The shows in this category are: *Level 9, Now and Again, Nowhere Man, The Sentinel* and *Viper*.

It would take another whole book to document these shows in the present format.

When it comes to credits in our chapters, we've taken pains to sort producers in chronological order and we notate this, but if the person stayed with the series all the way through, we omit the years. These are listed farthest to the left. Those listed farthest to the right of the listing without years means we were unable to identify a time period of their tenure on the series. Otherwise, we sort and group names with the years they served as best as we can, and without repeating "same year entries" repeatedly. Listing of all production credits are not possible due to space restrictions.

It has been a long journey to assemble the histories of science fiction television series from 1990 to 2004 and we thank everyone who has participated and the fans who have kept interest in these shows alive.

SCIENCE FICTION TELEVISION SERIES, 1990–2004

Andromeda
2000–2005

Captain Dylan Hunt and his spaceship, the Andromeda Ascendant, *are transported 300 years into the future. He and his new crew, an eclectic group of humans and aliens, now attempt to unite and bring order to a chaotic and malevolent universe.*

Cast: Kevin Sorbo (Dylan Hunt), Lisa Ryder (Beka Valentine), Keith Hamilton Cobb (Tyr Anasazi) *Year 1–3*, Laura Bertram (Trance Gemini), Gordon Michael Woolvett (Seamus Harper), Lexa Doig (Andromeda), Brent Stait (Rev. Bem) *Year 1–2*, Steve Bacic (Telemachus Rhade) *Year 4–5*, Brandy Ledford (Doyle) *Year 5*

Created by: Gene Roddenberry; **Developed by:** Robert Hewitt Wolfe; **Executive Producers:** Allan Eastman *Year 1*, Adam Haight *Year 1–5*, Majel Barrett (Roddenberry) *Year 1–4*, Jay Firestone *Year 1–4*, Robert Hewitt Wolfe *Year 2*, Kevin Sorbo *Year 2–5*, Josanne B. Lovick *Year 2–5*, Robert Engels *Year 3–5*; **Co–Executive Producer:** Robert Hewitt Wolfe *Year 1*; **Supervising Producer:** Karen Wookey *Year 1*; **Line Producer:** Robert Simmonds; **Producers:** Sherry Gorval *Year 1–5*, Keri Young; **Co–Producers:** Josanne B. Lovick *Year 1*, Ethlie Ann Vare *Year 1–3*; **Associate Producers:** Louisa Rees *Year 4*, Karen Smith *Year 5*; **Consulting Producers:** Emily Skopov, Karen Wookey; **Creative Executive:** Seth Howard *Year 1*; **Senior Consultants:** Matt Kiene, Joe Reinkemeyer *Year 1*, Paul Barber & Larry Barber *Year 4–5*; **Creative Consultant:** Karen Corbin *Year 1*; **Consultants:** Eric Gold *Year 1*, Naomi Janzen *Year 4*; **Executive in Charge of Production for Global:** Anne Frank; **Writers included:** Naomi Janzen, Steven Barnes, Richard B. Lewis, Ashley Miller, Matt Kiene, Joe Reinkemeyer, Zack Stentz, Ethlie Ann Vare, Emily Skopov, Michael Cassutt, Robert Hewitt Wolfe, Gordon Michael Woolvett, Gillian Horvath, Larry Barber, Paul Barber; **Directors included:** Allan Kroeker, Richard Flower, Brenton Spencer, Brad Turner, Allan Eastman, TJ Scott, George Mendeluk, David Winning, Phillip Segal, Michael Robison, Jorge Montesi, Martin Wood, Allan Harmon, Peter DeLuise; **Guest stars included:** Marjorie Monaghan, William Katt, Leila Johnson, Jayne Heitmeyer, Sam Jenkins, Maya O'Connell, Nigel Bennett, Michael Shanks, Maury Chaykin, Bruce Harwood, Roger R. Cross, Kristina Copeland, Kristen Lehman, Christopher Judge, Paul Campbell, Krista Allen, Christina Cox, Michael Ironside, Carmen Moore, Sebastian Spence, Nicholas Lea, Gary Jones, Don S. Davis, John de Lancie (as Uncle Sid); **Production Designer:** Richard B. Lewis; **Special Effects Supervisor:** Darren Marcoux; *Andromeda* Theme "Andromeda Invictus" **Composed and Conducted by:** Matthew McCauley

An Andromeda (IV) Productions Ltd. production; Produced in Association with Global — A CanWest Company; BLT Productions LTD; Tribune Entertainment; MBR (Majel Barrett Roddenberry) Production; Fireworks— A CanWest Company; Syndicated: October 2000–2004, Sci-Fi Channel: 2004–2005; 60 minutes; 110 episodes; DVD status: Complete series

> He is the last guardian of a fallen civilization, a hero from another time, faced with a universe in chaos. Dylan Hunt recruits an unlikely crew and sets out to reunite the galaxies. On the starship *Andromeda*, hope lives again.— Year Two Narration

Gene Roddenberry's Andromeda, despite many cast and story changes, prevailed as one of television's most resilient shows. Years after cancellation, it's still a fixture on cable and syndication across North America. Kevin Sorbo only regrets it didn't become a feature film franchise like *Star Trek.*

Sorbo was disappointed over the lack of promotion, but *Andromeda* ran five years, confounding some critics, who slammed it as campy space chaos. It triumphed as the top-rated drama in syndication for most of its run.

The story centers on Captain Dylan Hunt, in a galaxy where humans and aliens co-exist in the Systems Commonwealth. But the power-hungry Nietzschean warriors plot to overthrow the Commonwealth with a sneak attack. Dylan tries to warn the Commonwealth but his ship, the *Andromeda Ascendant*, becomes trapped and frozen in the gravity well of a black hole's main horizon.

Three hundred years later, another ship, the *Eureka Maru*, commanded by Beka Valentine, a feisty blond-haired mercenary who salvages old derelicts, finds Dylan's ship and breaks it out of its frozen cocoon. Beka demands Dylan's ship. He refuses and after some scuffling, Beka agrees to join Dylan as his first officer aboard the *Andromeda Ascendant*, along with her crew: Harper (an engineer from Earth with a penchant for wisecracks), Trance Gemini (a purple-skinned medic with a tail), Rev. Bem (a reformed Magog, a devout follower of the Wayist religion, resembling a cross between a bat-faced demon and hell hound, who has eschewed the savagery of his Magog brethren) and Tyr (an imposing Nietzschean warrior and weapons guy). There's also the *Andromeda Ascendant*'s resident artificial intelligence system, nicknamed Rommie. A sentient ally of Dylan's, she appears in three forms: as a hologram, an on-screen display and, most fetchingly, a beautiful android.

It takes Dylan time to get used to this new world. "Everyone I knew, my entire world, is gone," he says in disbelief. During these past 300 years, the Commonwealth has been fractured by intergalactic civil war, allowing an invasion by the Magog (a savage, predatory species who both feed on and use their victims as hosts for the eggs of their parasitic young). The Commonwealth's fall has fostered rivalries and genocidal wars among factions of the genetically superior Nietzcheans.

The *Andromeda Ascendant*, despite its age, remains a formidable High Guard warship, equipped with Nova bombs powerful enough to destroy planets. Dylan and his new crew set out to unite the 50 planets of the Commonwealth and fight bad guys along the way. As the series progressed, it is revealed that the human contingent of *Andromeda*'s new crew, though appearing loyal to Dylan, are harboring secret agendas.

The series was based on a mid–1970s starship storyline by Gene Roddenberry. The name Dylan Hunt was lifted from his TV-movie *Genesis II* (1973). Roddenberry died in 1991 but after his posthumous *Earth: Final Conflict* series (1997–2002) was a hit, Tribune Entertainment looked to start another Roddenberry-inspired series. Roddenberry's widow, Majel Barrett-Roddenberry (one of *Andromeda*'s executive producers), approached Kevin Sorbo and Sorbo, a classic *Star Trek* fan best known as TV's *Hercules*, signed on as captain.

The job of developing the series was left to Robert Hewitt Wolfe. "Reestablishing and protecting civilization" was how Wolfe defined Dylan's future mission.

"Originally, I think Tribune had gone to Rene Echeverria," says Wolfe today. "He wasn't available and recommended me. I had a nascent idea of what I would like to do in a starship-type series and my ideas meshed well with material that Gene had developed. I wrote a proposal, Tribune ordered a bible and bought the series off the bible. They ordered 44 episodes, which was an amazing commitment."

The show's original title was *Phoenix Rising*. "I wanted stories of heroic people achieving amazing things," he says. "And to convey the emotional cost of that, as well as have some fun and drama. It was a great opportunity to not only extricate some of Gene's philosophy but lay out some of my own."

While there was an early plan to make Dylan and Beka into a *Moonlighting*-like couple, butting heads to hide their mutual attraction, it was decided that Kevin Sorbo and Lisa Ryder had natural chemistry as allies. Sexual tension would ruin things.

"I felt good about the cast," says Wolfe. "Kevin was already attached to the project, so was Keith, but I took time to find the other actors. It was a terrific group."

Lisa Ryder, who played Beka Valentine, says today, "I enjoyed the opportunity to play a strong, physical woman who was irreverent, sarcastic and fallible." But she was nervous early on. "My very first shot was on the bridge with Keith [Hamilton Cobb]. I was trying to make small talk with him between takes and he wouldn't talk! He wouldn't say anything. That was funny and awkward," she laughs. "As characters, we were supposed to have known each other forever but as actors, we didn't know each other at all. That was difficult. But it ended up as a great, happy set, with a lot of laughs. It was a very professional, bright group of actors. Kevin was the big kid on set, [and] he would do outtakes just to make the blooper reel."

Filmed in Vancouver, the first-year stories had Dylan link up with his old flame, travel back to his own time for a brief visit, and receive a life prison sentence. The show was an immediate ratings hit. "Comedy, action, philosophy, cybersex — all of these and more seem to have found their way into *Andromeda*'s largely impressive first season," raved Britons' *TV Zone* magazine.

Trance Gemini was one of the strangest humanoids concocted for TV. Her long animal tail got a lot of attention but it caused consternation on the set. The plan was to move the tail through animatronics but that didn't work. "It was supposed to be like a monkey tail and wrap around

Andromeda star Lisa Ryder, left, director Jorge Montesi, and Ken Tremblett (courtesy Ken Tremblett).

her neck but it just sat there," observed Sorbo years later. When a stuntman kept accidentally stepping on her tail, actress Laura Bertram admonished him, "Hey, watch the tail!" That phrase became so popular on set that it was used by Trance on the show. Occasionally, CGI effects made her tail come alive, but it became too troublesome. In year two's "Last Call at the Broken Hammer," her beloved tail was shot off. "I got hate mail about that for a year!" laughs director David Winning.

Producing the show was a big challenge. "Production was our Achilles heel," says writer-executive story editor Ethlie Ann Vare, who also coproduced. "We had a very low budget compared to, say, a *Star Trek* franchise. Some ideas looked great on paper but looked limp onscreen. And *limp* was an appropriate description for Trance's tail, an excellent concept that couldn't be properly realized."

Wolfe agrees. "We were horribly under-budgeted. That was a primary weakness of the show and created an inability to execute the show's vision. We had good and talented people but un-

fortunately, due to the economics of syndication at the time, the money to do a space-based show wasn't there. We had big ideas that required significant budgets. It was less than satisfying to arrive on these less than populated worlds, mostly full of humans, because that's all we could afford. Had I known the lack of money would affect us so strongly, I would have developed the show in such a way to avoid those limitations. Unfortunately, we ended up being criticized as cheesy. The stories weren't cheesy, the actors weren't cheesy, but some of the execution was, the same way the old *Doctor Who* was cheesy. I've never encountered that level of economic restriction before or since *Andromeda*."

Tribune Entertainment demanded that the show be top-loaded with action. "There was always a push for the show to be incredibly ambitious," explains Wolfe. "Things like, 'We want bigger fight scenes, we want more action, we want more space battles.' There was a desire for more screen value without the commensurate commitment of finance."

The actors coped with dialogue crammed with technical jargon. Even Sorbo, a life-long astronomy buff, admitted, "We went crazy with some of the terminology. I would say, 'Give it to Gordie!' because he was very good about spouting that stuff. So was Lexa."

In terms of relating to the characters, Sorbo praised the show's writers as being very smart. "They learned the cadence of each of us and what we could do. Everyone cared about the show. People were always prepared and ready to go."

David Winning agrees. "Some of the best actors today are working in SF. They have to act opposite green screen or with big rubber dragons and manage a straight face!"

Ethlie Ann Vare was excited to join that first year. "I had written for Gene Roddenberry's *Earth: Final Conflict* and done an episode of *Beastmaster* for Tribune Entertainment. When they were developing *Andromeda*, they asked me to meet with Robert Hewitt Wolfe and read the show's bible. I was mightily impressed with both and was delighted to be the first writer hired for the show."

She particularly enjoyed writing scenes for Beka. "Beka Valentine was my kick-ass alter ego, not that I can't kick the occasional ass my own self," she says. "I loved writing her and loved how Lisa Ryder brought so many layers to the portrayal. Beka could be thorny and sometimes alienated even humans. They Who Must Be Obeyed [the powers-that-be] did soften her up over time. But you always knew where you stood with Beka. I wrote a whole novel, *Gene Roddenberry's Andromeda: The Broken Places*, concluding her story."

Sometimes real-life events dictated changes in stories. "Here's a last-minute story change that only happens once in a lifetime — I hope," Vare says. "The script was 'Be All My Sins Remembered,' in which Beka's first love returns as a social activist-turned-terrorist. He hijacks the *Eureka Maru* [Beka's ship] to ram it into the capital city of a war-torn planet on behalf of the underdogs. The spacecraft would become a kinetic missile, with her crew still aboard. I finished the script in late August of 2001. On September 11, I ripped it up and started over."

"In Ties That Bind," Beka's swindler brother Rafe Valentine (played by Cameron Daddo) makes an appearance. Vare reveals, "There was such chemistry between the two actors and characters that I seriously toyed with the idea of revealing Rafe Valentine to have been adopted. That way, the two of them could hook up." In "Star Crossed," Michael Shanks of *Stargate SG-1* appeared as an android who boards the *Andromeda*. "This time the actors *did* hook up!" she says. "I like to think it was my romantic dialogue that made actress Lexa Doig fall for Michael Shanks. Today, they are married and have a gorgeous baby."

"A Rose in the Ashes," where Dylan is sentenced to life in prison, was less successful. "Xax, the schizophrenic, alien mass murderer, came out looking like he was wearing my Aunt Fanny's fur coat," says Vare. "Definitely a case where execution did not meet expectation." John de Lancie guest-starred as Beka's Uncle Sid, who pays a visit, in "Pearls That Were His Eyes." "We first offered the role to William Shatner," Vare recalls. "No offense to Mr. de Lancie, who was wonderful, but I can really see Mr. Shatner in his *Boston Legal* persona as Uncle Sid."

In "It Makes a Lovely Light," Beka believes a faster-than-light slipstream route could lead to Dylan's home planet. "It won a Prism Commendation [the Entertainment Industries Council award, recognizing the accurate depiction of drug use and addiction in entertainment] for the way it handled drugs realistically. They Who Must Be Obeyed toned down some of the drug references, but bless them for leaving in Tyr's excuse for not taking Beka's flash away from her: 'It was working.'"

In "A Heart for Falsehood Framed," the search is on for a stolen, priceless Hegemon Heart. "This gave us a taste of the carefree rogues that the *Maru* crew had been *before* they met Dylan and got religion," Vare points out. "Beka always did like hot men. As Ted Sturgeon once said to me about writing 'Amok Time' for *Star Trek* [the original series]: 'I just wanted to get Spock laid.'"

In "Home Fires," Dylan finds a message from his late fiancée, Sara. "Kevin's wife [Sam Jenkins] played his dead fiancée. Those were real tears being shed in that show," says Vare.

When budget crunches occur, TV series save money by re-using old footage. In Vare's year two script, "The Things We Cannot Change," Dylan suffers hallucinations and flashbacks while trapped in a spacesuit. "That was me making lemons into lemonade," she explains. "We had to do a clip show for budgetary reasons, so I made flashbacks part of the story. Boy, could you see the way hair, makeup and wardrobe had evolved over the past two years!"

After two years, *Andromeda* had, in addition to Wolfe and Vare, an impressive cadre of writing talent to draw from. Staff writers included the duos of Ashley Miller–Zack Stenz and the former *Buffy, the Vampire Slayer* team of Matt Kiene–Joe Reinkemeyer. SF novelists Walter John (WJ) Williams and Steven Barnes also contributed scripts. Wolfe wanted an arc story that would follow Hunt and his crew's attempt to reestablish the Commonwealth while still leaving room for stand-alone episodes. But at the beginning of the second year, Tribune promoted Kevin Sorbo to co-executive producer. Sorbo insisted on changes, mostly cosmetic ones, and got them. The character's costumes were redesigned and the look of the Magog and Trance Gemini were reinvented. New companies were engaged to do prosthetic makeup and CGI special effects, once the original companies' contracts expired.

There was also pressure on Wolfe to increase the number of stand-alone episodes. Sorbo had received mail from ex–*Hercules* fans, complaining that *Andromeda* was getting too hard to follow, confused by Wolfe's Commonwealth arc. When Wolfe was dropped during year two, fans suspected Sorbo had executed a coup, ousting the series developer. Wolfe admits he preferred the character-arced storylines, while Sorbo wanted more stand-alone plots. Sorbo also wanted Dylan looser and more unpredictable, with more romance. "I always put in my two cents," Sorbo admitted during year one, saying he read every script and made extensive notes on them. Now as co-executive producer, he was able to flex more creative muscle.

Wolfe says, "I got to do mostly what I wanted to do, until I got fired." He adds that Tribune also wanted the changes Sorbo pushed for. "As a producer, you're always negotiating with the buyer of a series, trying to figure out what they want and how to be compatible without compromising the show's overall artistic vision. There were a few things they wanted that I wasn't enthralled about."

Nevertheless, Wolfe was surprised by his firing. "They never gave me a reason, aside from creative differences. I always suspected they would be more comfortable if I was gone, so they could do the sort of things they wanted to. I did think they would have waited until the end of the season!"

There were rumors that Sorbo and Wolfe had clashed over the show's direction. "There was always a bit of creative tension between us but we had a reasonably good relationship," explains Wolfe. "Kevin's vision of the show and my vision were slightly different. He saw Dylan as more of a straight-ahead hero. I saw Dylan as more of a troubled character, who did the right thing but was more fallible. Kevin can do very good work when he's focused. He really believed in the character and he did a good job as Dylan." Once he left, Wolfe rarely looked back. "I saw a bit of the later shows but I never watched an entire episode, so I can't say whether they were good or bad."

The series continued without a head writer for several weeks until former *Twin Peaks* head scribe–script supervisor Robert Engels was announced as Wolfe's replacement.

Some fans felt Engels was the wrong choice, creatively. The show drew away from the Commonwealth arc and offered a series of stand-alone episodes. Shortly afterward, the Commonwealth returned to the storyline in an inexplicably restored state. Stories concentrated on Dylan and his crew's exploits and their relationship to the rebuilt Commonwealth. Engels also introduced another alien race, a cross between *Alien* and *Predator* creatures, who were able to bridge dimensions and threatened the Commonwealth. This storyline's twists and turns left a lot of fans scratching their heads. These dimension-hopping creatures made a repeat appearance later in the third year, resolving that nascent storyline and then permanently disappeared. But to critics, that was an example of unfocussed and confusing storytelling under Engels' aegis.

Stories began to lighten up, with more emphasis on Dylan Hunt. It was a universe where moral, thought-provoking and perceptively adept observations need not always apply. When faced with an hostile alien ship, Beka yells, "Let's blow the crap out of it!"

This change in direction was the major cause of controversy. Sorbo held fast that Wolfe's story vision had become too complicated and there had to be a change. At Vancouver's Gatecon convention in 2005, Sorbo clarified: "I liked Robert Wolfe and his episodes were smart and intelligent. He understood the genre very well. But his writing was too dark. On the flip side, Bob Engels was, as a guy on the set, very warm and jovial. He listened to everyone's ideas."

"The first season was very formal," director David Winning notes. "Everyone was nervous, trying to keep it going. The later seasons were more relaxed and lighthearted. There was more of a *Star Trek* feel to the shows. But when [Wolfe left], it did suffer from a lack of focus. It lost a lot of viewers, who expected story arcs to play out.

They felt cheated. But Bob Engels was a great producer and he gained us new fans. Everyone continued to enjoy the interaction of the characters and Trance remained my favorite character. In a good sense, *Andromeda* was more soap opera than SF."

Lisa Ryder preferred Wolfe's vision. "Robert Wolfe reflected more of Gene Roddenberry's old school, where stories were more complex and SF-based," she says. "He was creating this complicated, interwoven storyline and I preferred that. I loved Bob Engels as a person but the second half of *Andromeda* was more fantasy. And Kevin was interested in doing a show with a lot more humor, more action and more stand-alone stories. His big complaint was, 'I don't want people to have had to watch the previous year to understand what's going on.' There were two schools of thought: the long-time viewers, who loved the creation of a story lore, and the 18–25 demographic, who didn't feel rewarded by serialized storytelling."

Some fans felt Dylan was monopolizing the stories. "It started out as an ensemble show," says Ryder. "Dylan was more of a fallible, vulnerable everyman of great integrity in this chaotic, crazy world, fighting to make a difference. But as the years went on, it was revealed that Dylan was a Paradine, a kind of immortal, infallible being, and that was a big change to the core character. The rest of us went from being caught in this world of chaos to being soldiers of the Commonwealth."

By the fourth year, much of Dylan's crew had grown disillusioned with the Commonwealth and they left Dylan to go their own ways.

"That was another big change, 'Screw the Commonwealth!'" says Ryder. "We all went back to square one, each of us looking out for himself or herself and Dylan had to rein us back in. Some of these changes were for the good and some I didn't agree with, but that's the nature of doing a television show."

Actor Brent Stait (Rev. Bem) voluntarily left the series during year two because of his allergy to the grueling makeup. And Keith Hamilton Cobb (Tyr) officially left the show at the end of year three. He agreed to make a few guest appearances in year four, as Tyr joins the sinister Abyss entity which is dedicated to destroying the Commonwealth. Dylan prevails and Tyr is killed off. "To be honest, Keith wasn't very happy," explains Sorbo. "I liked him on the show, he created a great dynamic between our characters. But he wanted to do something different with his life and so his character's exit was expedited."

Steve Bacic had played the traitorous Gaheris in the pilot, where he was killed off. When Keith Hamilton Cobb left the show, producer Seth Howard, who had worked with Bacic on *Earth: Final Conflict*, brought Bacic back as Telemachus Rhade, a Nietzschean warrior and lieutenant commander of the *Andromeda Ascendant*.

Before Bacic had been cast, Mark Conseulos, talk show host Kelly Ripa's husband, had been considered as a new character, but Bacic was the right choice.

"Steve was perfect as Telemachus," says Lisa Ryder. "He had worked with us before and had a relationship with the cast and crew. Everyone liked him. It made sense to have him return, rather than casting a new person."

The show's smirky boys-of-all-ages humor continued but it wasn't always appropriate. In "Broken Hammer," the guest villain is killed off by the heroes and Lisa Ryder felt the bad guy's demise was tasteless. "We shot this dude full of holes and then we made a flip comment, 'Now he'll make a good pin cushion.' We all balked at that line. It was offensive. So there were some missteps."

The director of the episode, David Winning, says, "I take the blame there. I made the villain more lovable than he had been written. He was a spy but the actor [John de Santis as Hsigo] played him kind of lovable. In retrospect, we should have had him play it more sinister."

There were still laughs. "We were shooting an episode called 'A Heart for Falsehood Framed,'" recalls Winning, "and the leader of an alien race was fighting to get a diamond. A Vancouver actress, Nicole Parker, was a last-minute replacement for another actress. She didn't fit that well into the costume and when we put a head piece on her, she couldn't see a thing. We filmed this in the *Andromeda* board room for two hours and because of the wet glue inside the costume head, she began to get dizzy. Plus, she couldn't see. When the scene ended, she was supposed to exit the room, but instead, she walked right into the wall. My assistant director Richard Flower ran out and took care of her. But it was a funny moment and it ended up in the blooper reel."

The fan mail sometimes surprised the actors. "I received a letter from a girl who was having a hard time," Ryder recalls. "She was inspired by my character, a strong woman, and she said she wanted to be a writer. I encouraged her to stick to writing because it was an outlet for the emotion and turmoil she was going through. Her letters were so heartwarming, they really moved me and reminds you there is an audience out there!"

The series continued with its signature moves, such as sparks flying from control consoles, stuntmen doing somersaults through the air and Dylan always making quips when facing danger. "I know who has been naughty and who has been nice," he chides a hostile hologram.

Andromeda also had the most complete screen credits of any show in history, identifying everyone in its crew, from the tool maintenance man to assistant chef to the car drivers for its cast.

There was also an acknowledgment to real science. Science advisor Paul Woodmansee recalls suggesting that the spaceships in the series use anti-protons as their power source. And the episode "All Too Human," where the *Eureka Maru* sinks into an alien ocean, called for his expertise. "Ashley Miller told me he needed a way for the spaceship, which was deep underwater, to get to the surface. I suggested flooding the ship [with the crew using EVA suits] and using its ventilation to slowly provide thrust to move the spaceship upward. I'm particularly proud of that unique suggestion, especially since Ash and Zack Stentz did such a good job with that episode."

In another instance, Harper was supposed to use a welder to attach two pieces of metal. "My comment wasn't as polite as it could have been," Woodmansee admits. "I said, 'A welder? Why not use an antelope bone?' The use of a welder was primitive, since the *Andromeda* had Nanobot technology." Woodmansee suggested that Nanobots be used to knit the metal together.

Woodmansee had been a engineer at JPL (Jet Propulsion Laboratory), working on propulsion systems for interplanetary spacecraft. He gave notes on the science, engineering and military aspects of *Andromeda*'s scripts. Woodmansee was five years old when he watched Neil Armstrong walk on the moon in 1969 and that helped spark his interest in real science. "I especially enjoyed working with Robert [Wolfe], Ash and Zack to create a working technology of the universe for *Andromeda*. I'm glad the writers tried to be more scientific and technically accurate. The series also had fast action and good character stories. The interplay between the crew was crucial to the show's popularity."

In addition to its stand-alone adventures, the series' fourth year attempted to retrieve the threads of Wolfe's original story arc, an apocalyptic scenario about the coming of the Spirit of the Abyss and its Magog Worldship, which will destroy all civilization unless the Commonwealth stands in its way.

Sorbo was now pleased with the series and marveled, "Our visual effects get better every year. They're awesome!"

But when year four looked to be *Andromeda*'s end, a confusing cliffhanger was devised. A Magog Worldship attacks peaceful citizens aboard a space station and as Dylan tries to protect them, all of his friends seem to perish in the confrontation. End of series?

No. A last-minute renewal brought a fifth year. The series moved from syndication to The Sci-Fi Channel's schedule. Some fans and critics weren't happy. "Suddenly the lovable misfits of *Andromeda* are no longer lovable," winced *TV Zone*'s Sharron Hather. "A deep, dark strategy designed to increase Dylan's popularity by decreasing that of his supporting characters has backfired spectacularly."

Year five began with the two-parter "The Weight," as Dylan and his ship are transported to another star system called Seefra, where he gathers back his crew. Dylan adjusts to this new world, whose inhabitants exist on drought-ridden planets. He also tries to energize his ship for a leap back home. Time is of the essence, since one of the Seefra Systems stars is heading towards a supernova. Unless its regress is reversed, it will result in the apocalypse of the entire system.

A new cast addition was the android Doyle, played by Brandy Ledford. She was brought in after the Rommie android was destroyed (allowing Lexa Doig, who was pregnant, to be temporarily written out of the series). Harper created this beautiful mechanical woman, who wanted to experience human emotions, and dressed her in a pink Barbie spandex outfit. Harper had also placed Rommie's consciousness into Doyle. Ledford was stunning, unwittingly stealing any scene she was in. A dancer and kickboxer, she jumped right in to do her own fighting and stunts.

Actor Ken Tremblett guest-starred as Beka's love interest in "The Weight." He recalls some irony in auditioning for the role of Jonah. "The guy who had gone in [to audition] just before me was Lisa Ryder's real-life husband, a good-looking actor named Ari Cohen. They had just gotten married. I thought, 'Oh no, I can't get this. It's a waste of time...' But I was told later that the two of them didn't look right as a couple for the episode. When I got the job, I couldn't believe it.

They wanted someone who was physically bigger, a more ominous-looking person, for the character." Tremblett also had to contend with the space-age technobabble. "The language in these SF auditions is not normal conversation, it's either very technical or an alien language. You have to make it real. Being Lisa Ryder's love interest in the episode was wonderful. But then I learned her character had a new love interest every week! Ha!"

As for the rest of the cast, he says, "Kevin Sorbo was fun. He was jovial, jokey and relaxed. Everyone was very loose. I thought because of the massive amount of dialogue and special effects that it wouldn't be like that. But they were all very comfortable with each other. I enjoyed working with them."

For year five, Engels and his writers revived an earlier Perfect Possible Future concept, a world that Trance had visited in year two and, upon her return, was her future, more mature self. But increasingly, many ideas in *Andromeda* were overambitious, underdeveloped and poorly explained. Some critics called the storylines incomprehensible.

For the two-part *Andromeda* finale, "Heart of the Journey," Engels delivered a resolution to Robert Wolfe's original premise. The crew is still in the Seefra System, a nine-planet binary star system where civilization has long collapsed and superstitious locals have outlawed certain technologies. This is also where Dylan Hunt's ancestral home, the planet Tarn Vedra, is located and he realizes his true nature of being a Paradine. With the help of fellow Paradine Flavin (Alan Scarfe), he discovers who and what he is, restoring both *Andromeda* (the ship and Rommie, the AI) back to working order.

Viewers also learned that Trance Gemini was a member of the Nebula, a race of stellar avatars with incredible powers, able to break people down into molecules and reassemble them. Trance doesn't share the Nebulas' dark willingness to allow the Commonwealth and its universe to fall to the evil Abyss (the avatar of a black hole) and Magog minions.

It all ends with a square-off between Dylan and a devious entity known as Maura (Emmanuelle Vaugier). She is determined to destroy Dylan because he's the last of the Paradines. Her ships surround the *Andromeda* and Dylan and his crew vow to fight to the death. In the midst of space battles, sparks, flashbacks, more sparks and stunt somersaults, Trance destroys Maura and the *Andromeda* rips through the Abyss entity in a sacrificial move, only to reappear safely back home, with all hands accounted for. The crew departs the bridge one by one, until only Dylan is left on the darkened bridge. He sadly turns and walks away. Fade out. Sorbo called that entire fifth year his favorite.

"Those final days of filming were pretty sad," recalls Ryder. 'There was lots of pressure and it was very emotional. The cast and crew had become family. We had had lots of births, deaths, divorces and marriages over those five years. We did this one shot, where Dylan and Rhade are walking down the ship's corridors, and the rest of us, including all of the crew, decided to surprise them by quietly filing in behind them. It was very touching."

"*Andromeda* was a damn good show," says Sorbo, "but it was one of the best kept secrets on TV. For whatever reasons, it didn't get the promotion it deserved. It's amazing it went on for five years. Even the original *Star Trek* and *Lost in Space* didn't run that long."

"It was one of my most enjoyable writing gigs," states Ethlie Ann Vare. "I still keep in touch with many of my *Andromeda* colleagues. They were and are a remarkable and talented crew. We cared about the show and that made the viewers care, too. The strength of the show was that its universe was so rich and internally consistent. What you saw onscreen was only the tip of a huge iceberg of story. That invisible 90 percent made an incredible foundation."

"The show's overall idea, of rebuilding civilization, had a strong resonance," says Robert Wolfe. "We had a charismatic lead, a wonderful cast and, during my administration, which is all I can speak for here, a very strong writing staff. We also had some very good directors. I was very happy with the writing for the first 30-odd episodes. And when we could afford it, we had some interesting set design and alien races. The space effects were also great, although we re-used a lot of shots. It's incredibly difficult to get a show to last five years. Despite the difficulties and the fact that I didn't make it to the end, I'm proud of the series."

Many fans were curious as to how Wolfe would have ended the saga had he been in charge, so he wrote his own abridged version in April 2005, after the series ended. Wolfe wrote this purely as his own fan fiction. Titled "Coda," it has Harper encounter Trance, now in her purple-colored, tail-twisting form from the early days. She tells him that their last two years of adventure have been only one possible future for them. She's dismayed that she can't see a happy future for anyone. In the one alternate future that she sees most clearly, the Abyss figures prominently. If it's destroyed, balance in the universe will be forever disrupted. If the Abyss prevails, everyone on the *Andromeda* except Beka will perish and Beka will have to make a tough decision. Whatever scenario plays out, it's certain the characters will face poetic oblivion for the greater good. To summarize any more of Wolfe's deep, rich dialogue between the two characters would be to dilute his work and cheat loyal viewers. His full version is on the web at http://www.rhwolfe.com/Insider%20Info. htm

"Some fans loved it, some were horrified," chuckles Wolfe over that finale. "I wasn't writing it to say this is necessarily the right way for it to end. It's just an incredibly condensed version of what I would have done."

Looking ahead, Lisa Ryder says, "Twenty years from now, I hope people will remember *Andromeda* as bringing a bit of levity to the genre and that they remember the relationships of the characters. The very special friendships that developed between those diverse characters really worked. As actors, we worked hard to maintain that."

CAST NOTES

Kevin Sorbo (Dylan Hunt): The Minnesota-born actor did over 150 TV commercials before landing the role in *Hercules: The Legendary Journeys* (the 1995–1999 New Zealand–filmed series). That was a huge success, broadcast in over 115 countries. Sorbo played football, basketball and baseball in high school, and grew up being the campus jock, a persona well-suited for his later roles of heroism. An astronomy buff, he's read countless books about space. He was also a big fan of the original *Star Trek* and *Twilight Zone* series. He wasn't hesitant about suggesting changes for his Dylan Hunt character, whom he saw as being similar to Bruce Willis's character in *Die Hard*. One of his earliest TV guest shots was in *Murder, She Wrote* (1984) and in 1993 he was up for the role of Mulder for *The X-Files* and Clark Kent in *Lois and Clark: The New Adventures of Superman*. He had a recurring role on TV's *The O.C.* in 2006. The actor is known for heading a mentoring program for inner-city youth and participating in charity golf tournaments.

Lisa Ryder (Beka Valentine): According to Ryder, one actress who auditioned for the Beka role was Nancy Ann Sakovich (previously a star of *PSI Factor: Chronicles of the Paranormal*). A graduate of the University of Toronto's drama program, Ryder also studied dance at Edmonton's School of Ballet and Toronto's Metro Movement. She guest-starred as Boone's wife in *Earth: Final Conflict* in 1997 and had guest shots on *Total Recall 2070*, *Jason X*, *Forever Knight* and *Kung Fu: The Legend Continues*. She co-starred in the TV film *Secret Lives* (2005). She is also an accomplished playwright whose credits include the one-woman play "Put Me Away!"

Keith Hamilton Cobb (Tyr Anasazi): Born in North Tarrytown (now Sleepy Hollow), New York, his education included New York University Tisch School of Arts. He loves the works of William Shakespeare and his stage credits include *Othello* and *Hamlet*. He became well-known on *All My Children* (1994–1996) and *The Young and the Restless* (2003–2005). In 1996, *People* magazine called him one of the 50 most beautiful people in the world. He also had a recurring role in the TV series *Noah's Arc* (2006).

Laura Bertram (Trance Gemini): From the age of four, this Toronto-born actress wanted to be a ballet dancer. She had seven years' study with the Canadian Children's Opera Chorus. Her first TV series, the Canadian-made *Ready or Not*, about teenagers, ran from 1993–1997. She also appeared in TV's *Are You Afraid of the Dark?*, *Road to Avonlea* and *Street Legal*. After *Andromeda*, she had a recurring role in *Robson Arms* (2007).

Brent Stait (Rev. Bem): The Manitoba-born actor began appearing in 1980s Canadian series such as *Captain Power and the Soldiers of the Future* and *Night Heat*. He later guested on *Cold Squad*, the new *Outer Limits*, *The X-Files* and *First Wave*. He also appeared in Steven Spielberg's mini-series *Taken* (2002). After *Andromeda* he showed up on *Battlestar Galactica*, *The 4400*, *Supernatural*, *Blade: The Series* and *Stargate: Atlantis*.

Gordon Michael Woolvett (Seamus Harper): Born in Hamilton, Ontario, he was nominated for a Canadian Gemini award for his role in the TV film *Princes in Exile* (1990). In the mid–1990s he was a YTV kiddie show host known as P. J. Gord. He co-starred in the 1997 kiddie show *Mission Genesis* (with Nicole deBoer), a series he laments as not having enough of a budget to continue. Laura Bertram (Trance on *Andromeda*) played his girlfriend. He also appeared in the film *Bride of Chucky* (1998) and episodes of *Mysterious Island*, *Sliders* and *Forever Knight*. His character of Harper in *Andromeda* was like a space-age frat boy in love with himself. Harper was also politically incorrect when it came to space chicks ("Man, she's got nice toys!"). Harper also had a Magog larvae in him and was always asking someone to remove the eggs. A self-confessed SF fan, Woolvett once admitted he could name any *Star Trek: The Next Generation* episode within ten seconds of seeing any part of it.

Lexa Doig (Andromeda): Her father is Scottish, her mother Filipina. Her character on *Andromeda* was described by Robert Hewitt Wolfe as "a hot chick who also happens to be an incredibly cool piece of machinery." Along with Gordon Michael Woolvett, Doig was adept at delivering the shows' convoluted technobabble. She originally read for the Beka Valentine role and even wore big army boots to add to her height during the audition. Born in Toronto, Doig saw the play *Porgy and Bess* when she was nine and that got her interested in acting. She did commercials and was host of YTV's *Video and Arcade Top 10* in 1991, with future *Andromeda* co-star Gordon Michael Woolvett. She made her acting debut in a *TekWar* segment (1994). Her husband is actor Michael Shanks (*Stargate SG-1*). The *Stargate* connection doesn't end there: She was also cast in *Stargate SG-1*'s final two years (2005–2007) as new medical chief, Dr. Carolyn Lam. Her movies include *Killer Eyes* (2007).

Steve Bacic (Telemachus Rhade): Born in Croatia, he grew up in Windsor, Ontario. He made his TV acting debut on *21 Jump Street* in 1991. After *Andromeda* he guest-starred on *ER*, *Blade: The Series* and, in 2007, *Flash Gordon* and *Blood Ties*.

Brandy Ledford (Doyle): See the chapter *The Invisible Man*'s Cast Notes.

SOURCES

Hather, Sharron. Review of *Andromeda*. *TV Zone* no. 142, September 2001.

_____. Review of *Andromeda*. *TV Zone* no. 186, 2005.

Hines, David Z.C. "Gene Roddenberry's *Andromeda*—Writer/producer Robert Hewitt Wolfe on Breathing Life into Roddenberry's Concept." *Cinefantastique*, December 2000.

Nazzaro, Joe. "Golden Girl." *Starlog* no. 295, February 2002.

_____. "*Andromeda* Strains." *Starlog* no. 279, October 2000.

Spelling, Ian. "Space Shuffle—Kevin Sorbo Captains the Renovated *Andromeda* Through a Stormy Second Season." *Starlog* no. 298, October 2002.

Babylon 5

(1994–1998)

A grand saga in a 23rd century universe where humans and aliens attempt to work out their differences peacefully aboard a five-mile-long space station called Babylon 5. *It's a port of call for Commander Jeffrey Sinclair and, later, Captain John Sheridan. Denizens of the station must fight against an awakened alien species called The Shadows, a corrupt faction of Earthforce military and sinister telepaths with their own agenda.*

Cast: Michael O'Hare (Commander Jeffrey Sinclair) *Year 1*, Bruce Boxleitner (Captain John Sheridan) *Year 2–5*, Claudia Christian (Commander Susan Ivanova) *Year 1–4*, Mira Furlan (Ambassador Delenn), Peter Jurasik (Ambassador Londo Mollari), Andreas Katsulas (Ambassador G'Kar), Richard Biggs (Dr. Stephen Franklin), Jerry Doyle (Michael Garibaldi), Andrea Thompson (Talia Winters) *Year 1–2*, Patricia Tallman (Lyta Alexander) *Pilot, Year 3–5*, Johnny Sekka (Dr. Benjamin Kyle) *Pilot*, Tamlyn Tomita (Laurel Takashima) *Pilot*, Robert Rusler (Warren Keffler) *Year 2*, Jason Carter (Marcus Cole) *Year 3–4*, Caitlin Brown (Na'Toth) *Year 1*, Bill Mumy (Lennier), Stephen Furst (Vir Cotto), Jeff Conaway (Zack Allen) *Year 3–5*, Tracy Scoggins (Capt. Elizabeth Lochley) *Year 5*

Recurring Cast: Ardwight Chamberlain (Kosh's voice), Jeffrey Willerth (Kosh), Julia Nickson (Catherine Sakai), Mary Kay Adams (Na'Toth), John Shuck (Draal), Denise Gentile (Lise Hampton), Efrem Zimbalist, Jr. (William Edgars), Mar-

Director Jesus Salvador Trevino is surrounded by four aliens in a scene for a *Babylon 5* episode (courtesy Jesus Salvador Trevino).

jorie Monaghan (Number One), Wayne Alexander (Lorien), Joshua Cox (Corwin), Wortham Krimmer (Cartagia), Tim Choate (Zathras), Melissa Gilbert (Anna Sheridan), Walter Koenig (Alfred Bester), Robin Atkin-Downes (Byron) *Created by:* J. Michael Straczynski; *Executive Producers:* J. Michael Straczynski, Douglas Netter; *Producers:* John Copeland, Richard Compton *Year 1; Co-Producer:* Skip Beaudine; *Associate Producers:* George Johnsen, Susan Norkin; *Writers included:* J. Michael Straczynski, David Gerrold, D.C. Fontana, Neil Gaiman, Lawrence G. DiTillio, Peter David, Harlan Ellison; *Directors included:* Richard Compton, Adam Nimoy, Tony Dow, Michael Vejar, Jim Johnston, John C. Flinn, Kevin G. Cremin, Jesus Salvador Trevino, Janet Greek, David J. Eagle, Goran Gajic, Stephen Furst, J. Michael Straczynski; *Directors of Photography:* John C. Flinn III, Fred Murphy; *Production Designer:* John Iacovelli; *Costumes:* Anne Bruice; *Special Makeup FX:* Optic Nerve Studios; *Visual Effects by:* Foundation Imaging, Ron Thornton, Paul Beige-Bryant, Netter Digital; *Conceptual Consultant:* Harlan Ellison;

Guest Stars included: Penn and Teller, June Lockhart, Michael Ansara, Malachi Throne, Michael York, Carrie Dobro, Harlan Ellison, Robert Englund, Robert Foxworth, David McCallum

PTEN Network ("Prime Time Entertainment Network")/Syndicated/Warner Bros. Television/Babylonian Productions/TNT Network *Year 5*; 1994–1998; 60 minutes; 110 episodes; DVD status: Complete series

When producer-writer J. Michael Straczynski had his epiphany in the shower for a brand new science fiction show, he was so excited that he just had to jump out and dash immediately for a notepad and write it all down. The year was 1986. It was the dawn of a new age for science fiction television. It would become a five-year saga with a large cast of humans and aliens. But first, the words had to be put down. The first title typed on a sheet of paper was "The Babylon Project."

The ambitiousness of the proposed series' premise and goals would also become a double-edged sword. Would studios and networks be willing to accept a series premise with such a large scope for a limited budget? As Straczynski worked out the details, he promised himself that this would be different. All the stories would be pre-planned and it would be "a novel for television." Unlike any other television series made, this would be an SF show that had a beginning, a middle and an end, unlike typical television-making where it was "make it up as you go along" plotting and writing.

By spring 1987, with a writer's bible and a full series treatment in hand, Straczynski took the materials to John Copeland and Douglas Netter, producer colleagues with whom he had worked on *Captain Power and the Soldiers of the Future*, a live-action children's SFTV show.

The property was shopped to HBO, ABC, CBS, but landed finally, in March 1989, at Chris-Craft Television, a consortium of independent television stations across the U.S. One of their business deals was coaxing Warner Bros. into creating a new network, and so they were eager to accept *Babylon 5*. But it would take three years for the wheels to turn.

In the summer of 1989, *Babylon 5* was pitched to Paramount, but was turned down. It was in December 1989, that Warner Bros. started up the syndicated Prime-Time Entertainment Network (PTEN) consisting of three TV series: *Kung Fu: The Legend Continues*, Harve Bennett's *Time Trax* and *Babylon 5*.

Babylon 5 was sold because of two appealing items: Straczynski's concept and story plus special effects wizard Ron Thornton's groundbreaking visuals generated on a desktop computer.

A series pilot, "The Gathering," was filmed in August and September 1992 and aired on February 22, 1993, as part of the newly formed PTEN network consortium. Reception for the pilot was good in ratings and fan word-of-mouth feedback. Because of the network's faith in the show's promise, the series was ordered. The producers needed soundstages and found warehouse space in Sun Valley, California.

Straczynski weaved an intricate tapestry of character and plot stories that was, in its first season, mostly stand-alone stories, but planted seeds and portents for future stories. Subtly, single lines of dialogue would later become an entire episode. The series' major story arcs, affectionately termed by faithful fans as "wham" episodes, were the ones that advanced the plotting significantly. Another aspect of the show that was often rare in series television was that in every season the status quo changed. This show was not "static" in its premise.

Actor Bruce Boxleitner, who signed on in the second season, says that it was this aspect of the show that intrigued him. "It has its own uniqueness. You don't get that in a lot of television programming with a normal series," he says. "It's the uniqueness that we created; this very specific universe and a very specific history. And that's what attracted me when I read the first script. When I saw it and said, 'Wow! It's very different!' It's different from *Star Trek*— enough. And has its similarities so it has attractions that way."

Co-star Andreas Katsulas agrees. When he was cast as G'Kar, ambassador from the Narn, one of four intergalactic diplomats aboard the station, Katsulas says that despite the rigorous requirements for elaborate, full-head prosthetic makeup in the role, what he saw was an opportunity. "My attraction from the beginning was that script— that character," says Katsulas. "You have to play that character whether he's got a ton of makeup on or whether you just play it with nothing."

Had the character not been fleshed out and given a multi-dimensional range, Katsulas said he would have rejected the role outright. "If they gave me a character that was one-dimensional and asked me to go through that, I probably wouldn't do it. Not for anything. Not for money, for fame or anything else."

Babylon 5 the story picks up ten years after the Earth-Minibari war, in the year 2258. The space station was situated "in neutral territory" so that all of the alien races could come together for commerce and diplomatic affairs. The first season was focused primarily in expositional stories, so that we could come to know Commander Jeffrey Sinclair and the four alien ambassadors: Kosh from the Vorlon Empire, Londo from Centauri Prime, Delenn from the Minibari Federation and G'Kar from Narn. They all had their own distinctive cultures and personalities. Also plaguing Sinclair was Earth's Psi-Corps, the police branch of human telepaths, and Alfred Bester, one of its agents. Talia Winters joined the station as its resident commercial telepath.

An important aspect of Sinclair's life was trying to understand what happened to him in the final day of the Earth-Minibari war. He had blacked out in battle and, just on the cusp of the Minibari victory over Earth, they surrendered. Why? For ten years the Minibari refused to explain. And the reason eventually was disclosed in "Revelations," in the series' second season.

But many other mysteries were planted in this first season. Who built "The Great Machine" that was discovered deep in Epsilon 3, a nearby planetoid where the station was parked? Why did Babylon 4, after having disappeared years ago, suddenly appear again and where did it go after all the people aboard her were evacuated? In the season finale, Londo began to make some bad choices in his alliances and this would have enormous repercussions in his future.

Director Bruce Seth Green, who directed four episodes in this first season, recalls being impressed with the show's efficiency. Scripts actually were available several days ahead of time. "That was one of the things I wasn't used to and I remember being very, very happy about. Joe had such a strong idea of what he wanted to do with the entire series," says Green. "The plot line was pretty delineated and the scripts well written by the time I got there. And that wasn't always the case in other shows."

Another director, Adam Nimoy, agreed: "It's really helpful for a director to kind of read it and re-read it and let it sink in for a while before you start to really break it down."

Although the series was gaining popularity with audiences, B5 was still a cast of relatively unknown actors. By mutual agreement with the producers, Michael O'Hare departed from the series. The PTEN network and Warner Bros. asked for a bigger "name" actor to better market the show. Straczynski says he always had Sheridan planned but just moved his introduction earlier in the story arc. O'Hare was a theatrical actor and was willing to move on to other roles, and return later to pick up on the character. While fans did like Commander Sinclair, not everyone liked O'Hare's personality. Initially, this sudden move was controversial amongst fans, and there was much Internet discussion about it.

For those reasons, a call went out for a new station commander and Bruce Boxleitner was cast as Captain John Sheridan. Sinclair was "taken off the chessboard" and diverted to become the first Earth ambassador to Minibari. His role would be pivotal later in the third season.

"When I first came on, they made it very easy," said Boxleitner. "Everyone extended themselves a lot! We're all professional actors and that's very much part of what goes with the package when you do a show."

When Sheridan arrived on the station, he was startled that Ambassador Delenn's mysterious procedure, "the Chrysalis," had transformed her into a human–Minibari hybrid. Also, as the season developed, G'Kar began to realize that the universe had a new, mysterious enemy. They were called "The Shadows," large black, alien vessels with powerful laser beams—an enemy from a thousand years ago.

War between the Centauri and the Narn was declared when the Shadows destroyed a Narn outpost and let the Centauri take the victory. Later, Londo's Centauri forces nakedly bombarded and invaded Narn, leaving G'Kar to request asylum on *Babylon 5*. Sheridan also grew to suspect that Earth President Santiago's death might not have been an accident.

At the request of actress Andrea Thompson (who didn't feel she had enough to do), Talia was written out of the show in "Divided Loyalties" and Patricia Tallman, as Lyta Alexander, the ship's original telepath (in the pilot "The Gathering"), returned. The second season ended when the mysterious Vorlon, Kosh, revealed his true appearance while in the act of saving Sheridan, who had jumped from a transport tube to avoid a bomb. The Vorlons use a psychic cloak that disguised their true form and allowed them to manipulate races by appearing in different forms, including posing as messengers of various religions.

In the space of one day, in the limbo between seasons, Warner Bros. warned that the show might not be renewed, because of an impasse between Warner Bros. and PTEN over reruns, but it was saved on June 8, 1995.

The main thrust of the third season was basically "pulling the trigger" on many of the mysteries and plot thread that had thus far been laid down.

Because of the Shadows' renewed presence, an intergalactic war was imminent, so Draal, keeper of the Great Machine inside the planetoid, warned Sheridan and Ivanova that it was time to gather allies—an Army of Light. But first, Sheridan had to contend with darker matters closer to home: Earth President Morgan Clark's regime was becoming totalitarian and he created an insidious paramilitary organization called the Nightwatch, whose members were ordered to report anyone suspected of being an alien infiltrator. Later, captains of various Earth Alliance battlecruisers openly revolted against Clark's orders and other colonies followed. EarthForce was now splintered between those working for Clark and those who believed he was an insidious leader. Clark attempted to capture *Babylon 5* for himself as a base of operations. A great battle ensued between Clark's EarthForce battlecruisers and the defensive B5 station forces. *Babylon 5* was saved from an

Babylon 5 cast members Bill Mumy, left, Jeff Conaway, Tracy Scoggins, Bruce Boxleitner, Mira Furlan, and Jerry Doyle (©Warner Bros. Television).

invasion by Clark's forces when Delenn, commanding a fleet of Minibari battlecruisers, arrived at a critical moment, protecting the station. Overwhelmed by the opposition, Clark's invading army retreated back into hyperspace.

Babylon 5, as a station, seceded from the Earth Alliance and became independent. Later, after direct confrontations with the Shadows, a War Room was set up to manage the conflict.

In the events of "War Without End," Ambassador Sinclair returned to *Babylon 5* when he received a mysterious letter. With *B5*'s command crew and Delenn, and with Draal and the Great Machine's help, Sinclair traveled back in time and snatched *Babylon 4* to use again as a base against enemies. Many secrets were revealed in this two-parter, bringing to light a number of different plots.

The season ended when the Army of Light confronted the Shadows openly and then Captain Sheridan received a very surprising visitor when his wife Anna Sheridan, previously believed to be dead, showed up on the station. With her, he traveled to Z'ha'dum, the Shadows' homeworld, and there, he came to understand that the Shadows' motives were to create chaos on a galactic scale.

Katsulas, like many of the other cast members, lucked out in being hired for the show. He found a great friend in Peter Jurasik, who served as the yang to his yin. The acrimonious, and at times volatile, relationship that G'Kar and Londo had was almost a bedrock foundation for the series. At one point, on completing three seasons and 66 episodes, Katsulas realized that the number of times that the two characters had scenes with each other "was not that many!"

"That's what I find so intriguing—the power of these two characters when, in fact, Joe uses us very sparingly," noted Katsulas. "And wisely so, because when you have a good thing you don't want to overdo it... Better to leave the fans waiting for the next time the two of them confront each other. So it's pretty amazing."

Tensions regarding the show's future resurfaced because PTEN was dissolving. But while in Blackpool, England, Straczynski read a telegram to faithful *B5* fans that the show had been renewed. Filming recommenced on August, 1996.

Stories quickly moved to serialization and every single episode was written by Straczynski, a writing marathon streak that began in the middle of the second season.

As the fourth year opened, the *B5* command crew discovered that "it was a year of joy, a year of pain, the year everything changed...." Sheridan, trapped on Z'ha'dum, found an unlikely, surprising ally in a very old alien being named Lorien. Meanwhile, without Sheridan, Ivanova nervously held down the fort aboard the station. Upon return to *B5*, Sheridan rallied all the alien races in an alliance to fight against the Shadows. Later, the Vorlons engaged in their own combat with the Shadows, unleashing intergalactic chaos. Elsewhere, Londo found that he had to take steps to make sure that the insane Centauri emperor, Cartagia, did not put Centauri Prime at risk by an alliance with the Shadows. The Army of Light marshaled their forces and stopped the Shadows and the Vorlons.

The resulting picture became clear: The Vorlons represented order. The Shadows represented chaos. Their never-ending battle, which stretched as far back as 1,000 years ago, depicted two races fighting for their beliefs. And now the younger races, with Sheridan as their focal point, ordered them all to "Get out of our galaxy!" And so they did. It was time for the younger races to be the new shepherds.

In their return home, Sheridan and his team came to realize that there was one more problem to solve: EarthGov's determination to rip away *Babylon 5*'s independent status. Believing that EarthGov's President Clark was a puppet of the Shadows, Sheridan pulled together a combined attack force consisting of splintered Earthforce battlecruisers and prepared for an attack against the home world—Earth itself. On one side of the conflict was President Clark; on the other, Sheridan's allies, who were determined to take back Earth from the president. At the battle's climax, Sheridan's forces prevailed but at a great cost of lives and ships. A new Interstellar Alliance between the humans on Earth and the aliens was born and Sheridan resigned from Earthforce, only to become the new Alliance's elected president.

When director Tony Dow, who initially joined the show as a visual effects producer for Netter Digital, began directing episodes in this season, he came to realize how different *Babylon 5*'s production methodology was from other Hollywood shows. For every episode Straczynski and the production staff would get together and have a "tone meeting," which is a meeting of minds between them and the director of the week. "The tone meetings were one of my favorite aspects of doing the show," said Dow. "I don't understand why more shows don't use this invaluable tool. Where I found the meetings helpful, was explaining call-backs to previous stories and how a unique character or scene fit into the overall thread of the five-year story line. It was also beneficial to run technical ideas by Joe and John [Copeland, the producer], such as complex camera shots, lighting effects, special props, etc. They ran a tight ship and it was always better to check with them about new ideas, suggestions for changes or approaches to scenes. The way the meetings proceeded was that Joe would go through the script page by page explaining anything out of the ordinary. If I had a note or question, it would be addressed. It was very give and take with Joe doing most of the giving."

By December 1996, however, Straczynski began shifting the story so that it was possible to fold the five-year saga into four, because there was great concern that a fifth season would not find a slot in the crowded television marketplace. The number of hours devoted to syndicated programming were decreasing. So great was this concern that the show's final episode, "Sleeping in Light," was filmed as the last episode of the season.

It was executive producer Douglas Netter who fiercely hunted for a broadcast venue for the fifth season and he found it in TNT, the Turner Network, who purchased the series reruns and also commissioned two movies of the week, "Thirdspace" and "In the Beginning," filmed immediately following "Sleeping in Light." They also commissioned a "special edition" release of the series pilot, "The Gathering." In retrospect, Straczynski was unhappy with the way the film was edited by director Richard Compton. After five years on the series as executive producer and writer, Straczynski had strong opinions on how the film should have been assembled. Many scenes of interesting character development that was left on the cutting room floor were reinstated. A new music score by series composer Christopher Franke was laid in along with some enhanced special effects. Both Straczynski and B5 fans were happier with this refined cut.

But behind-the-scenes business reality boiled over. In July 1997, all the actors had to renegotiate their contracts and there was a casualty among the ranks. Because of a contractual and scheduling dispute, Claudia Christian, as Susan Ivanova, did not return for the fifth year. In the retelling of the incident, Christian and Straczynski had differing views over whether she was fired or if she quit. She had signed to do a film, but Warner Bros. wouldn't allow her the time she needed and Christian says that she was fired. Straczynski disputes that she was fired; that in truth she quit the series. Consequently, he was forced to write her out.

Events such as this, and the previous removal of Psi-Corp's telepath Talia Winters (actress Andrea Thompson), required Straczynski's "master plan" to be adjusted accordingly. He tried to stay with the roadmap as much as possible, but filmmaking realities had to be acknowledged.

Enter Christian's fifth season replacement: actress Tracy Scoggins as Captain Elizabeth Lochley, in command of the space station while President Sheridan dealt with the enormous task of "empire building."

Three story arcs dominated the season: Sheridan's struggle to manage and build consensus among the Alliance members; as they fought amongst themselves, unknown raiders attacked Alliance ships. It became his mission to discover whether the Centauri were responsible or if they were being framed for the atrocities.

With regard to portraying Sheridan, Boxleitner recalled that one of Straczynski's tips to him was to look at real-life wartime commanders, especially General Dwight Eisenhower and General Douglas MacArthur. "These men were our great leaders during World War II," said Boxleitner. "Especially Eisenhower — here was a man who [became] supreme commander of an entire armada. He had to try and keep together the various allies who were bickering amongst themselves, which certainly fits into our saga. We have to keep them together in some kind of order to fight against the common enemy. So there is a very Eisenhower-ish character. MacArthur — there was another great commander of World War II. Command doesn't necessarily mean shouting out orders. There is a certain carriage of command. So Joe kept giving me those various types of images.... Sinclair is more [like] General George Marshall of World War II. Sheridan is more like MacArthur, the guy out there in front."

Adding to Sheridan's burden, a telepath named Byron sequestered himself and his telepathic acolytes aboard the station, looking for a home for themselves. Psi-Corps' Bester demanded their arrest. The confrontation ended in a tragedy for the telepaths.

The final five episodes were a novelistic page-turner, many of the characters moving on to different positions in the B5 universe. Londo returned home to Centauri Prime where he found himself made emperor, but under the darkest of circumstances. In "Objects in Motion," Sheridan and Delenn left the station for Minibari, the new, permanent seat of the Alliance. In "Objects at Rest," the true final episode of the series, all the actors reacted to the series' conclusion in different ways. Some felt they were ready, others were angry, but most just felt sad. In the final moment filmed, Sheridan and Delenn are just about to leave, and they gave a speech to everyone. Many of the extras were *B5* crew people. "A lot of the crew members wanted to be in it," recalled Boxleitner. "We had a very busy morning that day at the Optic Nerve makeup trailers because most of them wanted to be aliens. A lot of them were Minibari and Narns. It was kind of fun."

Those final moments were spent, said Boxleitner, "signing a lot of memorabilia, signing a lot of pictures to each other and saying goodbyes."

To emphasize how strongly attached the actors were to the show, and playing their characters, Bruce Boxleitner joked, "Andreas Katsulas will walk out in full G'Kar makeup and never take it off. That'll be it. They'll put him in a looney home. The people dearly love their characters and the show!"

Boxleitner's joke was appreciated by everyone on the production. Notoriously, Katsulas maintained a "G'Kar persona" during shooting. He was so dedicated to staying in character that all his workmates got used to it. Peter Jurasik joked that if anyone wanted to address personal matters with Andreas, they'd have to get him either before or after shooting. "Peter and I are probably as different as night and day in this regard," said Katsulas. "Peter can go off and do schtick and tease and play and joke around and he still knows how to then in one second get back into Londo. I'm worried that if I let myself get too far away from my focus on the character that the second it takes to get it back I'll lose it, and the camera will be rolling and I'll be lost. It's just temperament. Sometimes I do play around. Then suddenly a voice says, 'Andy, don't get too far away from this or you'll never find it again.' It's almost superstitious. Like there's a place inside where I need to be to do G'Kar and I don't want to get too far away from it."

Aside from being strict about staying in character, Katsulas studiously worked from the script given to him, and didn't want to know about the future of the character.

"When people start talking about what's going to happen, I run away," said Katsulas. "I don't want to know. If in the first year Joe had said, 'I'm going to start you out as a bad guy. This G'Kar is a real stinker and then around the middle of season two and into season three he's going to go through a change and become a good guy,' I would have started playing the end already in the first [season]—so it's good not to know."

In the series final episode, "Sleeping in Light," directed by Straczynski, "the Great Maker" himself, Sheridan, realized he was dying. He called in his best friends for a final dinner and it was then that *Babylon 5* was purposely destroyed by carefully planted explosives. (The final lights switch was turned off by Straczynski himself!) The station had outlived its usefulness.

"I thought, 'Wow, this is some of the best stuff I was able to do on the show.' It's the end," noted Boxleitner. He praises the producers for having done their job, and packaging *Babylon 5* as a series for television. "I think they quite seriously set up the proper atmosphere and they got the right team together to do it," he says. "They were always available if you needed to talk to them, if you had a problem."

But Boxleitner also realized that, as well organized as was Straczynski's "master plan" for the series was, there were further story threads or tangents that could have been explored. One example, he says, was the suggestion of a war between humans and the telepaths. And then, there was the son of Sheridan and Delenn. "Certainly people have asked 'What about David Sheridan?' That got dropped. I don't think Joe ever intended to see him. I think he was going to be talked about much more, but I guess those were some of the things that had to be dropped. Joe changes his mind quite often, too. He had to weigh the more important points that he wanted to get to rather than something more insignificant."

Babylon 5 didn't end with the series. Two more movies of the week was commissioned by TNT, as they had already bought the spin-off series *Crusade*. "River of Souls" was a TNT film that revisited a mysterious alien race we glimpsed in the first season episode "Soul Hunter" (with Martin Sheen as the title character). The Soul Hunters captured "the life essence" of a person at the moment of their death, and for the second time, one of those Hunters arrived on *Babylon 5*.

"A Call to Arms" was the second TNT-commissioned movie and served as a transition film into *Crusade* the series.

J. Michael Straczynski holds a record for the longest unbroken period of banging out scripts. In total he wrote 91 of the 110 episodes, going from the middle of the second to the final season uninterrupted except for a script by novelist Neil Gaiman in the fifth season. *Babylon 5* made strong science fiction literature connections when it hired Gaiman and others such as screenwriter-novelist David Gerrold and Peter David to write episodes. Plus, author Harlan Ellison was a conceptual consultant on the show. He even showed up as a Psi-Corp officer and was a computer's voice.

Babylon 5 was remarkable for overcoming enormous odds at the end of each season by getting renewed and for having faithful fans who congregated on the Internet as a community. More than that, it set the bar high on visual effects, budget-conscious production techniques, and "big scope" storytelling with strong underlying themes and philosophies.

Boxleitner summed up the experience by remarking, "We got to finish it. Then we got to walk away! That's all I wanted. Tell the story as best we could and hope we meet everyone's expectations."

The *B5* universe lived on in various merchandising spin-offs: soundtrack albums from composer Christopher Franke, comic books and *B5* universe "canon" novelizations from Dell and DelRey Books.

"*B5* will have no problem with the test of time," agreed Tony Dow. "The show is timeless in concept and deals with issues that will be around in the 'real world' for a long time. The only negative I can think of is the complexity of the show and the commitment the viewer must make to get involved. Herein lies the yin and the yang, the positive and the negative, the reason why the show should, but may not, live into the future."

In 2002, *Babylon 5* returned to the airwaves as a made-for-TV movie for the Sci-Fi Channel. Titled *The Legend of the Rangers: To Live and Die in Starlight*, it had a brand new premise and cast with only Andreas Katsulas acting as connective tissue from the *B5* universe, reprising his role as the Narn G'Kar. The story focused on The Rangers, a small team of the galactic force, aboard an old Minibari spacecruiser, the *Liandra*. It was helmed by Captain David Martell (Dylan Neal) and run by a multi-species crew that included Minibari first officer Dulann (Alex Zahara), human combat specialist Sarah Cantrell (Myriam Sirois), covert and intelligence expert Malcolm Bridges (Dean Marshall), navigator Kitaro Sasaki (Warren Takeuchi), Minibari medical specialist Firell (Enid-Raye Adams), Narn engineer Na'Feel (Jennie-Rebecca Hogan) and a Drazi named Tirk (Gus Lynch).

The movie's plot had the *Liandra* on a diplomatic mission, ferrying dignitaries to an important conference, when they encounter a never-before-seen villain, The Hand. Martell finds a traitor onboard and, because of the crew's ingenuity, the *Liandra* escapes unharmed from a planted bomb. *Rangers* was a pilot for a proposed series, but on January 19, 2002, when the film premiered, it was opposite an NFL/AFC football game and got trounced on the East Coast feed since *B5* male demographics are the same as football. On the West Coast feed, which was after the game, the demographics ratings exceeded expectations. However it was the 1.7 average rating that counted and the Sci-Fi Channel did not pick up the series due to financial considerations.

In 2004 and 2005, there was an attempt at making a feature film, its tentative title *Babylon 5: The Memory of Shadows*. It would have focused on the Technomages (first introduced in the *B5* episode "The Geometry of Shadows" and later seen in the "A Call to Arms" TV movie and *Crusade* the series). The effort got as far as pre-production, with an intent to film in England, but ultimately the project did not come together.

B5 fans rejoiced in November 2006 when Warner Bros. issued a press release announcing a direct-to-DVD project titled *Babylon 5: The Lost Tales*, targeted to the rabid *B5* fans who bought up the DVD boxsets of all five seasons, the TV movies and *Crusade*. The Vancouver-made *B5: TLT* consisted of two new stories under the umbrella title "Voices in the Dark." Straczynski shepherded the project as writer, producer and director. This project marked the second time that he stepped behind the cameras and called "Action!" after debuting in "Sleeping in Light." Actors signed to the project were Bruce Boxleitner, Tracy Scoggins and Peter Woodward, reprising their roles as Sheridan, Lochley and Galen respectively. Other actors cast in guest-starring roles were *Stargate SG-1*'s Teryl Rothery (as an ISN reporter) and *Seven Days*' Alan Scarfe (as a priest). (Initially three stories were planned, but it was decided that a Garibaldi story which would have featured Jerry Doyle was too complicated to be included in this volume.) If the DVD sold well, more movies were possible.

Only rarely has so much time passed between the ending of an SFTV series and a reunion for further adventures with members of the original cast and crew. The *Bionic* team did it three times as MOWs after a nine-year hiatus, *Alien Nation* as five MOWs after five years, and famously *Star*

Trek with six feature films and four TV spin-offs after a ten-year shore leave. *Babylon 5* returned to the cameras (notwithstanding 2002's *Legend of the Rangers*) after a nine-year fade to black.

For many fans, returning to *Babylon 5* is like revisiting an old friend or, perhaps more aptly, stepping up to a bookshelf and reaching for a series of five favorite novels and each book contains 22 chapters, totaling 110 parts. Turning the pages is a chance to relive the adventures all over again.

CAST NOTES

Michael O'Hare (Commander Jeffrey Sinclair): A theatrical actor by trade, O'Hare appeared in Broadway productions of Aaron Sorkin's *A Few Good Men* as Col. Jessup, *Man and Superman*, and *Players*. Off-Broadway credits include *Galileo*. He was the first white actor to be nominated by the black theater community for best actor for his performance in *Shades of Brown*. Michael has many film credits, including *The Promise* (1979), *By a Thread* (1990) and *Ambulance* (1990). For television he's guest-starred on *Trapper John M.D.*, *TJ Hooker*, *L.A. Law* and *Law & Order*.

Bruce Boxleitner (Captain John Sheridan): Long before B5, Boxleitner gained fame in Hollywood in a number of film and television roles. He was the spymaster in *Scarecrow and Mrs. King* (1983) with Kate Jackson, and starred in the *How the West was Won* (1977) series. He is forever known as the title character in the groundbreaking SF film *Tron* (1982). He is also the author of two SF-Western hybrid novels, *Frontier Earth* and its sequel *Frontier Earth: Searcher*. He's married to actress Melissa Gilbert, who played his wife Anna Sheridan on *Babylon 5*.

Claudia Christian (Cmdr. Susan Ivanova): Prior to *Babylon 5*, Christian made appearances in features such as *The Hidden* (1987) and *Hexed* (1993). She also guest-starred on *Space Rangers*. After *Babylon 5* she did a "backdoor pilot" on *Highlander*, "Two of Hearts," when they were looking to do a series spin-off but Elizabeth Gracen got the role on *Highlander: Raven*. Christian has also done extensive voice work in *Atlantis: The Lost Empire*, both the 2001 animated film and companion video game. In recent years Claudia moved to England and has focused on stage and film there. She appeared in the BBC comedy *Broken News* (2005) and a SF spoof, *Starhyke*. On stage, she appeared in *Killing Time* at the Edinburgh Fringe Festival in 2006.

Mira Furlan (Ambassador Delenn): Originally from Zagreb, Croatia (formerly Yugoslavia), Furlan was a member of the Croatian National Theater and has extensive Croatian film credits. *Babylon 5* was one of her earliest roles in Hollywood. Her husband Goran Gajic, a film director, directed her in B5's "And All My Dreams, Torn Asunder." Later, she did voice work for *Spider-Man* the animated series (as Silver Sable). More recently she had a recurring role as Danielle Rousseau in the monster ABC hit series *Lost*.

Andreas Katsulas (Ambassador G'Kar): Katsulas was a prolific Hollywood and theatrical actor. In his early days, he toured with Peter Brook's International Theater Company, performing in venues all over the world. He was the one-armed man in *The Fugitive* (1993) starring Harrison Ford. He was also Romulan Commander Tomalek in *Star Trek: The Next Generation*. Other guest appearances included *Alien Nation*, *The Equalizer*, *Max Headroom* and *Star Trek: Enterprise*. He reprised his role as G'Kar in the Sci-Fi Channel MOW *Babylon 5: Legend of the Rangers* (2002). He died in February 13, 2006 of lung cancer.

Peter Jurasik (Ambassador Londo Mollari): He began his career working in New York City and in theaters up and down the East Coast. Later, after moving to Los Angeles, he began an extensive film and TV career but is best known for his work as Sid "The Snitch" on the 1980s police drama *Hill Street Blues*. Before B5, he also appeared with Bruce Boxleitner in *Tron* (1982). After B5, Peter guested on several episodes of *Sliders*. He's also an SF novelist, co-authoring *Diplomatic Act* with William H. Keith Jr. for Baen Books; the storyline is a bit of a spoof of his role as Londo, following an actor in a science fiction television series who is kidnapped by aliens looking for help from an intergalactic diplomat. In 2003 he left Los Angeles and retired with his family to a small town near the Atlantic Ocean. He continues to act in various film and TV projects and teaches in the film student department at the University of Wilmington, North Carolina.

Richard Biggs (Dr. Richard Franklin): Before B5, Biggs starred in *Days of Our Lives* for five years (1987–1992). After *Babylon 5* he reprised his role as Dr. Franklin in the *Crusade* episode "Each Night I Dream of Home." He had a recurring role in the daytime soap *Guiding Light*. On stage, he performed in Shakespeare's *The Tempest*, *Taming of the Shrew* and *Cymbeline*. Richard died on May 22, 2004, as a result of a torn cardial aorta.

Bill Mumy remembers Biggs:

I miss Rick. He was always fun to be around. He was in fantastic shape and I used to tease him all the time and ask him where his cape was, since he looked like a superhero. Rick not only talked the talk, but he walked the walk. He organized events to help raise money for charity and he motivated others in the *Babylon 5* cast to participate and help and we all did. No one could refuse Rick. At convention appearances, he always acted like the master of ceremonies during Question and Answer sessions. He had a great sense of humor. He was a fine actor, a fun man to hang out with and he had a beautiful family. He had a lot to live for. Just shows you, you never know what's right around the bend. I hope he's in a better place.

Jerry Doyle (Security Chief Michael Garibaldi): Before *B5*, Doyle was a salesman for a corporate jet company. He spent many years as a stockbroker before turning to acting. After *B5*, Jerry unsuccessfully ran for the U.S. House of Representatives in California during the 2004 elections as a Republican. He resides in Las Vegas and works as a host on the Talk Radio Network. He was briefly married to actress Andrea Thompson.

Andrea Thompson (Talia Winters): Thompson has appeared in numerous TV series such as *Falcon Crest, Spenser: For Hire, Silk Stalkings* and *Murder, She Wrote*. After leaving *Babylon 5* at the end of the second season, Andrea landed a major role in *NYPD Blue* as Det. Jill Kirkendall for three seasons before dropping acting to pursue a career in television journalism. After she worked for a year as a reporter at a CBS affiliate in New Mexico, CNN recruited her as a news anchor for Headline News. But that only lasted for several months and then she moved on to Court TV as an announcer. She returned to acting and had a role in *24* (2003).

Patricia Tallman (Lyta Alexander): Working in Hollywood as both an actress and as a stunt artist, Tallman has garnered diverse experiences. She's appeared in the soap opera *Generations* and guest-starred on *Star Trek: The Next Generation, Sheena* and *Dark Skies*. She's appeared in the horror films *Knightriders* (1981), *Monkey Shines* (1988) and *Army of Darkness* (1992). In 2008 she starred in *Dead Air* directed by actor Corbin Bernsen and in a short film titled *Waiting*. As a stunt artist, she's participated in major feature films: Tallman has doubled for Laura Dern in *Jurassic Park* (1993) and performed various stunt duties in *Godzilla* (1998), *Austin Powers* (1999), *The General's Daughter* (1999) and *Bewitched* (2005). Most re-

cently she's guest-starred in *Valentine and Without a Trace*.

Jason Carter (Marcus Cole): A British actor, Carter has appeared in *Beverly Hills 90210, 3rd Rock from the Sun, Diagnosis Murder* and *Lois & Clark: The New Adventures of Superman*. He's also appeared in TV movies and mini-series: *Forever Young* (1983), *Ellis Island* (1984) and *Taking Liberty* (1993). In the end credits of *Babylon 5*'s "Atonement," he sang "The Major-General's Song" from Gilbert & Sullivan's *The Pirates of Penzance*.

Bill Mumy (Lennier): Perhaps the most experienced actor in the cast, Mumy began acting at the age of five. He's appeared in over 400 TV episodes, 18 features and many commercials. In addition to being an actor, he is also a musician, composer and writer. He's also worked extensively in voice work, narrating A&E's *Biography*. He was Will Robinson on CBS's *Lost in Space* (1965–68), and appeared in three episodes of the original *Twilight Zone*: "It's a Good Life," "In Praise of Pip" and "Long Distance Call."

Stephen Furst (Vir): Many people still remember Furst for a prominent role in *Animal House* (1978) as the character "Flounder." But he also did well in *St. Elsewhere* as Dr. Axelrod. For *B5*, Stephen directed three episodes, "The Illusion of Truth," "The Deconstruction of Falling Stars" and "The Corps Is Mother, the Corps Is Father." After *B5*, Stephen stepped up the directing career and helmed three television films, *Title to Murder* (2001), *Dragon Storm* (2004) and *Path of Destruction* (2005).

Jeff Conaway (Zack Allen): Conaway achieved fame in two *Grease* (1978) as Kenickie and in the 1980s TV series *Taxi*. He starred in the short-lived fantasy series *Wizards and Warriors* (1983). He also works as an acting teacher and coach.

Caitlin Brown (Na'Toth): Julie Caitlin Brown came to producing after a 20-year career as a performer, which included stage, television and film. Among her most memorable credits are Raffaela Ottanio for Tommy Tunes' Tony Award–winning Broadway musical *Grand Hotel* and a turn as Gymnasia with George Wendt in *A Funny Thing Happened on the Way to the Forum* for Williamstown Theatre Festival. Guest star appearances include *Star Trek: TNG, Deep Space Nine, Sliders, Becker,* and *JAG*; she was a series regular on *Babylon 5*; and along the way produced, wrote and performed on two original music CDs. Brown starred in and produced *Lifeblood* (year) and co-starred and produced *Bridge of Souls* (year), a feature film based on the work of Marc Zicree, Michael Reaves and Kenneth Mader.

The author of two books, *Love First, the Beginning* on audio CD and the soon-to-be-released *Love First and the Artist,* Brown launched her motivational speaking career in 2006.

Robert Rusler (Keffler): Rusler was an athlete living in Waikiki Beach, Honolulu, Hawaii, as a surfer and skateboarder. When he moved to Los Angeles, he embarked on a martial arts career in the competition circuit. His first starring role was in *Weird Science* (1985) with Anthony Michael Hall and Robert Downey Jr. Later, he appeared in *A Nightmare on Elm Street Part 2: Freddy's Revenge* (1985). His first television series was Francis Ford Coppola's *The Outsiders* (1990). After *Babylon 5* he starred in *The Underworld* (1997) and *Wasted in Babylon* (1999).

Tracy Scoggins (Capt. Elizabeth Lochley): Scoggins started out as an athlete before turning to modeling and then moved into acting. She's appeared in a variety of prime-time TV series such as *TJ Hooker, The Colbys, Remington Steele,* and *The Dukes of Hazzard.* She was in the cast of *Lois & Clark: The New Adventures of Superman* in its first season as Cat Grant, the society gossip columnist.

TRIBUTE: "THE GOOD LUCK OF ANDREAS KATSULAS" BY PETER JURASIK

These days whenever I have occasion to speak about my friend, Andreas Katsulas, I find myself insisting on putting his life in a context and perspective of a *whole life lived.* I remind myself that before I ever met Andreas, way back in 1992 in a quiet waiting room at the auditions for a TV movie called *Babylon 5,* he was already a complete person with a full life. He was a husband with a long marriage, a father raising two terrific children, a son who had lost his own father to a long slow battle against Alzheimer's, and later in life, the sole giver of constant care for his mother, who lost her life to the same disease. He carried himself with a quiet, easy confidence but had a rich and dynamic personality; he stood out in any crowd without effort. He was proud of his hardworking "salt of the earth" Greek-American heritage and sentimental about the people and the traditions of his extended family in their hometown of St. Louis, Missouri. He was then, as always, completely private about his spiritual beliefs but had a strong devotion to his church,

putting in hours of work every week for his religious community.

I try not to forget that long before the wonderful mind of J. Michael Straczynski ever imagined the superb character of G'Kar, Andreas already had a full and successful life in his art. His acting career rested confidently on a seventeen-year working relationship with the British theater icon Peter Brook and his amazing acting troupe in which Andreas distinguished himself in live performances worldwide. Audiences had watched Andreas' acting magic all over the world: from the shadows of the Pyramids of Egypt to the formal theaters of Paris, in empty dirt fields and open marketplaces of remote African villages and back again to command performances for royalty in the Persian palaces of Iran. Anyone who was "in the know" and had been around world-class theater knew Andreas Katsulas and his work. Further, I'm reminded that by the time he treated us to his work on the sound stages of *Babylon 5,* he had already made a significant mark in Hollywood in many films and lots of fine TV. Who can forget his unforgettable portrait of the troubled one-armed man in *The Fugitive,* so carefully and beautifully drawn, leaving a completely unnerving effect on everyone who saw it? We were lucky to have Andreas in our cast and we all knew it.

As far as his work as G'Kar goes, I suspect that you may have a better perspective than I do on his contributions to that character, to *Babylon 5* as a whole and even more so, on his historical place among the actors and creators of science fiction's amazing array of characters; as the saying goes, I'm blind to the forest for the trees. I looked into the eyes of G'Kar more than anyone else; I worked day to day with Andreas in the rare relationship actors share. I know the love, the life and the light he poured into G'Kar. My view is skewed by intimacy. Therefore, I'll leave these more public opinions and conclusions to you, the readers, his fans.

For my part, I will remember him as a simple, strong-willed man who lived his life on his own terms; a true *lover* of life with an enormous appetite for all of its pleasures and an easy open laugh regarding its mysteries and absurdities.

He was a serious and devoted actor who shared the passions of his heart, soul and mind generously in his work and a person I adored working side by side with throughout the days, weeks and years of that graceful time ... and in the end, most importantly for me, a good friend gone away. I miss him often. I look forward to sharing the good luck of his light again — someday, some-where, soon.

Sources

Garcia, Frank. "*Babylon 5*: Legend of the Rangers: Life after Crusade — The Sci-Fi Channel Gives Straczynski Another Shot." *Cinefantastique* 34:1, January 2002.

_____. "*Babylon 5* — The story behind J. Michael Straczynski's Epic Five Year SF Novel for Television." *Cinefantastique* 31:12/32:1, June 2000.

_____. "*Babylon 5* — Straczynski's Prototype for Future TV Creations." *Cinefantastique* 29:9, January 1998.

Garcia, Robert T. Interview with Bruce Seth Green. Used with permission.

_____. Interview with Andreas Katsulas. Used with permission.

_____. Interview with Adam Nimoy. Used with permission.

Beyond Reality

(1991–1993)

Researchers at a private university's Department of Parapsychology investigate telekinesis, UFOs, ghosts and other extraordinary phenomena.

Cast: Shari Belafonte (Laura Wingate), Carl Marotte (JJ Stillman), Nikki deBoer (Celia Powell, later episodes)
Created by: Richard Manning, Hans Beimler; *Executive Producers:* Ron Ziskin, Jon Slan, Shukri Ghalayani; *Co-Executive Producers:* Hans Beimler, Richard Manning; *Supervising Producer:* Janet E. Cuddy; *Producer:* Richard Borchiver; *Line Producer:* Lina Cordina; *Writers included:* James Kahn, Melinda Snodgrass, Richard Manning, Hans Beimler, Melinda Bell, Marc Scott Zicree, Robin Jill Bernheim, Durnford King, Alan Fine, David Bennett Carren, Ira Steven Behr; *Directors included:* Eleanore Lindo, Mario Azzopardi, Graeme Campbell, Randy Bradshaw, Bruce Pittman, Allan Kroeker; *Guest stars included:* Ashley-Ann Wood, Jennifer Griffith, Lawrence Bayne, David Hewlett, Scott Hylands, John Colicos, Errol Slue, Joel Bissonette, Lynda Mason Green, Tom Cavanaugh, Richard Chevolleau, Peter MacNeill, Gordon Pinsent, Michael Hogan, Nigel Bennett, Gwynyth Walsh, Nicholas Campbell, Chris Makepeace

Produced in cooperation with the USA Network and Glen Warren productions; October 1991–March 1993; 30 minutes; 44 episodes; DVD status: Complete series

"A world where anything is possible": These words were spoken by Professor JJ Stillman to a group of kids at a magic show. Professor Stillman started out as a skeptic but the experiments in parapsychology that he and Laura Wingate conducted soon revealed that our world can be shifted just a few degrees out of focus, revealing supernatural doorways.

Research at the university uncovers parallel worlds, ghostly possession and people with healing powers. It's where human minds can astral-project into the body of a killer wolf and where devious doppelgangers and confused phantoms are common.

Laura and JJ use their state-of-the-art laboratory to help ordinary people unravel the unexplained. *The X-Files*, which debuted in 1993 (months after *Beyond Reality* had ended), made the bizarre palatable to mainstream audiences. *Beyond Reality* never had the charisma or promotional muscle of *The X-Files* but had an earnest, believable quality.

Beyond Reality was actually reminiscent of ABC-TV's *The Sixth Sense* (1972) where Gary Collins played a university professor who communicated with poltergeists, living skeletons and witches.

Filmed in Toronto, Canada, the first 13 episodes of *Beyond Reality* averaged a sizable (for cable) rating of 2.3. The series, playing on the USA Network's Friday night schedule, was commissioned for another 11 episodes, and then immediately renewed for a second year.

Richard Manning and his writing partner Hans Beimler created the show. "It was the first show Hans and I created and ran, so we look back on it with a mixture of fondness and, 'Yikes, we sure had a lot to learn,'" says Manning today. "The low budget was a constant challenge, as was the half-hour format. Scripts had no time to waffle or digress, so writers had to dive in quick, tell the story, and wrap up fast. Still, the show was terrific fun to do. We did horror, fantasy, comedy, science fiction, drama … you name it. A vampire story set in 19th century London. A World War II thriller in a submarine. A mad farce in a mythical 1950s *Ozzie and Harriet*–type TV universe. A surreal black-and-white drama, part *Twilight Zone*, part *1984*. A near-death experience seen as a 1930s musical. We were all over the map and we had a ball."

"The executive in charge of the show was Bonnie Hammer," says Hans Beimler. "She was later a big shot at Sci-Fi Channel. She was great to work with, supportive when she needed to be and a straight shooter. Bonnie believed in the show and was always willing to fight for more money when we needed it. That was a big strength because our pilot sucked. An early show called 'Mirror, Mirror,' written by Robin Bernheim, crystallized what was good about our format and how best to use it. Had we been at CBS or NBC, we would've been canceled halfway through the broadcast of our pilot."

He stresses that the shows' heroes were unique. "Our leads were not cops, they were professors," he notes. "They investigated paranormal activity from a scientific, scholarly perspective. Are you yawning yet? They're not cops! They don't carry guns! Oh, my god! What the hell were we thinking?! Chris Carter didn't make that mistake."

Indeed, the characters were very low-key. Laura Wingate had traveled the world, studying different cultures and religions and came away believing in other dimensions.

Professor JJ Stillman, on the other hand, was a clinical psychologist who believed that seeing is believing. "My character likes to make sure each step is properly taken, analyzed and categorized before moving on to the next thing," Carl Marotte said at the time. "Laura is more adventurous. Our differences help us find answers and also makes for some interesting clashes."

Cases included a boy who was contacted by the ghost of his father, a woman abducted by a UFO and a lonely girl who passed through a portal into another dimension. But again, the show's running time got in the way.

"*Beyond Reality* was supposed to be a companion piece to USA's *The Hitchhiker*, which was also a half-hour," says Beimler. "A half hour is not a good format to tackle these kind of subjects. By the time you've engaged the audience in a story, it's time to wrap it up. Often our stories felt short-shifted."

In terms of subject matter, Shari Belafonte felt right at home. "Quite a few people have had experiences with the paranormal," she says. "The first house we lived in, after my mother married my stepfather, had poltergeists in the attic. We never saw them but things moved around quite a bit. Our series showed people what can be, 'beyond our reality.'"

Carl Marotte never met any ghosts but admitted, "This isn't crazy stuff. Some of the situations might have happened or could happen. The proof is always in the gray area."

Writer David Bennett Carren also appreciated the premise. "I've always been interested in the paranormal and this series made a brave attempt to deal with the subject under difficult circumstances. The episodes were shot in four days or less for very little money, which meant we could afford no celebrity guest cast, only one or two swing locations, and very few special effects or stunts. Considering all that, we did some amazing episodes. The leads were appealing and had chemistry, which always helps."

The early episodes were preceded with the note, "The following story of paranormal activity is based on reported incidents." This was later dropped, allowing the series to go off in fanciful directions. The media reviews grew more encouraging. "It's a cheesy but improving drama," noted *People* magazine.

One highlight was "Mirror, Mirror," where a plain-looking young student named Anna (Nikki deBoer) develops a crush on JJ and soon astral-projects herself through a mirror, where she finds a parallel world. She appears as a glamorous, more aggressive personality, where a parallel image of JJ returns her affection. The real JJ astral-projects after her and pulls Anna back to reality before the mirror cracks and the doorway is permanently closed. Grateful to JJ for caring, Anna gains a new appreciation for the real world.

Nikki deBoer, who later joined the casts of *Star Trek: Deep Space 9* and *The Dead Zone*, made such an impression with her fragile performance as Anna that she was later cast as a regular on *Beyond Reality*, as the outgoing Celia Powell.

"We loved Nikki," says Beimler. "We immediately discovered her talent and made her a regular. She literally filmed her own audition tape while in some forsaken, isolated, middle-of-nowhere town in Canada, which is where we reached her. We all had mad crushes on her. She is one of the most pleasant, professional and gifted actresses I've had the pleasure of working with."

Another episode driven by a strong performance was "Asylum," written by the show's executive story consultant, Marc Scott Zicree. Errol Slue played a slave running for his life through a dark forest in 1858. He's killed by his white pursuers and his spirit takes over the body of Mitchell, a black businessman, in 1991. Mitchell is at first thought to be suffering from multiple personalities but it soon becomes clear that he is trying to fight off the aggressive spirit of the slave. The ghost likes the 20th century and doesn't want to give up Mitchell's body. Laura convinces the spirit to release Mitchell but the spirit gasps, "I can't go back and live as a slave," to which Laura replies, "You're doing it to him."

Realizing that his spirit is subjugating an innocent man's body, the ghost returns to his 19th-century fate and Mitchell regains his body. The episode received two Gemini nominations (the Canadian Emmy Award) for director Bruce Pittman and composer Fred Mollin.

"I had just listened to a wonderful audio documentary on National Public Radio, where writers in the 1930s had orally recorded several elderly people who had been slaves prior to the Civil War," recalls Marc Scott Zicree. "I was extremely moved by it, so I came up with a story on the spot, one that would also utilize Shari Belafonte's dramatic skills."

But there was some controversy about Zicree writing the script. "The network was a little concerned. They said, 'You're a white guy and this could be very touchy racial material.' I said, 'Don't worry, I can handle this.' I had grown up in a racially mixed environment and I'm also Jewish. A lot of my family were killed in the

Shari Belafonte (as Laura Wingate) and Carl Marotte (as J.J. Stillman) in *Beyond Reality* (© USA Networks).

Holocaust, so I could absolutely identify with racial persecution."

The producers needed the script quickly, but Zicree says, "The speed with which I had to write it actually made it stronger. Everyone loved the episode. The acting was wonderful and the execution of it was great."

Another memorable segment was "Nightfall," also written by Zicree. While doing a magic show for youngsters, JJ is suddenly transported into a surrealistic park of purple-colored rivers and pink mist, where malevolent vines crawl through the tall trees. He encounters a terrified little girl named Miranda (poignantly played by Ashley-Ann Wood) who instantly trusts him. She confides that she's frightened of the approaching nightfall.

His efforts to calm her remind him of his own guilt over being unable to save his wife from a fatal accident. JJ and Laura realize the girl's appearances are telepathic cries for help; the duo tries to track down Miranda and instead finds a bedridden old woman in a house. It's the real Miranda, on the threshold of dying and scared to let go. JJ takes her hand and for the last time, he returns with her to the strange world where the river is now a gentle turquoise and the moon has risen over a stilled forest. As he sits with young Miranda, he calms her fears of the approaching night and he lets her rest her head on his shoulder so she can sleep ... and the old woman passes away, unafraid. Sensitively directed by Eleanore Lindo and featuring a imaginative, ethereal world, "Nightfall" is a disarming story on the universal fear of dying.

"Originally, the storyline was about a little girl who had psychic power and was a fugitive from the CIA," says Zicree. "But there was nothing original about it." With Richard Manning's encouragement, Zicree was allowed to do another story, "something that had an emotional truth from my life," he says.

A large Toronto park was used for the early scenes of JJ performing magic tricks for his sister-in-law's child. "JJ's wife had died and he had never dealt with his grief," Zicree says. "Since he wasn't there when she died, he never got to say goodbye. Suddenly this little girl reaches out to him mentally and she appears in danger. He tries to save her and finds out that she's really this frightened old woman. He can't save her, he can only gently guide her into death. In this way, he also reaches closure over his own wife's death. I was thrilled by how it turned out."

And there was Zicree's own emotional connection to the story. "My mother had died very suddenly and I hadn't been able to come to terms with that. This episode allowed me to write about that tremendous loss. The whole metaphor of night falling is that it's death approaching. When the girl asks JJ, 'Why does it have to be night?' she's really asking, 'Why do I have to die?' The whole point of the episode is what JJ says to her: 'Maybe when it's night, we slow down and look around and see all of the things we can't see in the daytime.' Without death over our shoulder, we may not value life as much. As a writer, I was trying to come to grips as to why my mother had died, and why we have to undergo these tragedies in life. I was very grateful to Richard for giving me the opportunity to write it. And when we shot it, we had the absolute best effort from everyone. The little girl they cast in the role of Miranda was very good. The music and the spe-

cial effects were also solid. I'm very proud of that show."

Director Eleanor Lindo agrees. "It is one of my favorites of all the work I've done. The particular challenges were working with a child in a demanding dramatic role, one that required a lot of looping, and creating an alternate universe for a low-budget TV episode that was shot in three and a half days. This required a lot of creativity on the part of director of photography Maris Jansons and production designer Harold Thrasher. Because of the schedule, both universes had to be shot at the same locations. We struggled to come up with a look that would differentiate the worlds that could be done 'in the camera.'"

Lindo and her team used special lighting techniques to create Miranda's strange world. "We wanted to heighten the scariness of the dying old woman's inner world and it turned out very well." "'Nightfall' was the very best episode," says David Bennett Carren. "It's one of the best pieces of fantasy television I've ever seen. Marc is a brilliant writer, but he glowed on this one."

Beyond Reality ended unceremoniously in 1993. "We made 44 episodes with little interference from the network," says Beimler. "That was a big strength. We flew under the radar, so to speak. Nobody was paying much attention to the USA Network at the time. And that was a weakness, too. Nobody was watching. We went off for the same reason most shows die an early death. Low ratings."

The X-Files broke new ground into the supernatural and remains the gold standard for televised supernatural. But *Beyond Reality* made its own humble inroads into the TV world of the paranormal. "I wish *Beyond Reality* were in reruns more," Zicree laments. "We were all very proud of what we did. Some of the episodes were very moving, others were really scary. It was before *The X-Files* and it blazed a trail that *The X-Files* would later pursue."

Cast Notes

Shari Belafonte (Laura Wingate): The daughter of acclaimed entertainer Harry Belafonte, she first attracted attention in a series of Calvin Klein TV commercials. As a singer and model she appeared on over 300 magazine covers. She was also seriously considered as a replacement for Kate Jackson when Jackson left *Charlie's Angels* in 1979. Producer Aaron Spelling later cast her in his series, *Hotel* (1983–1988). As star of *Beyond Reality*, Belafonte felt she and Laura Wingate had a lot in common. "We've both traveled around a lot and picked up knowledge that way. I spent my ninth birthday in Africa, my tenth in Japan, my fifteenth in Paris and my sixteenth in Hawaii." She later co-starred in the *Babylon 5* TV movie *Thirdspace* and the theatrical film *Mars* (both in 1998).

Carl Marotte (JJ Stillman): The Canadian-born actor recalled paying his dues as an actor. "I lived in New York for awhile, I had $5,000, which lasted a year. Eating was a luxury." His film debut was in the Canadian-made film *All The Years of Her Life* in 1974. Marotte had a terrifying experience in 1997 as one of the passengers of Air Canada Flight 646, which crashed near an airfield in New Brunswick. A tree ripped into the passenger cabin but miraculously, all of the crew and passengers survived. His later TV credits included *Highlander*, *TekWar* and *PSI Factor* and the TV films *Pentagon Papers* (2003) and *Abducted: Fugitive for Love* (2007). Fans often asked him if the characters of JJ and Laura would fall in love on *Beyond Reality*. "It would have been wrong to let their relationship be anything but platonic," he says. "I liked the fact they were just friends. JJ was married once to the love of his life and she died. Now it's his work that interests him."

Nikki deBoer (Celia Powell): Born in Toronto, Canada, she was a shy girl who was selected to play the lead in her school production of *The Wizard of Oz*. It was quickly apparent she had a natural acting ability. She made her TV debut with Red Skelton in a Christmas special and did many commercials as a youngster. At age 17 she was cast in the CBC drama *9B* (1986). After *Beyond Reality*, she changed her name to Nicole deBoer and co-starred with Robert Patrick in the *Outer Limits* episode "A Quality of Mercy" (as a tortured prisoner of cruel aliens). She also appeared in the SF cult film *Cube* (1997) and replaced Terry Farrell in the last season of *Star Trek: Deep Space 9* (1998–1999). In 2002, she became a regular on *The Dead Zone*, with Anthony Michael Hall.

SOURCES

Beyond Reality review. *People*, 1992.

Century City

(2004)

The Los Angeles law firm of Crane, Constable, McNeil and Montero deal with issues of law and technology that impact human beings (including embryo selection, cloning, artificial intelligence and surveillance cameras) in the year 2030.

Cast: Ioan Gruffudd (Lukas), Viola Davis (Hannah), Nestor Carbonell (Tom), Eric Schaeffer (Darwin), Kristen Lehman (Lee May), Hector Elizondo (Martin)

Created by: Ed Zuckerman; Executive Producers: Ed Zuckerman, Paul Attanasio; *Producer:* Gerrit Van Der Meer; *Co-Producer:* Barbara H. Wall; *Associate Producers:* Katie Jacobs, Marcy G. Kaplan, Chad Savage; *Consulting Producers:* Ellie Herman, David Shore, Ben Queen; *Director of Photography:* Marshall Adams; *Production Designer:* Mark Hutman; *Writers included:* Ellie Herman, Ben Queen, Ed Zuckerman, David Gerken, Roger Wolfson; *Directors included:* Jerry Levine, Peter Markle, Michael Lehmann, David Straiton, J. Miller Tobin, Ron Lagomarsino; *Guest stars included:* Richard Thomas, Lawrence Pressman, Adrienne Barbeau, Megan Ward, Donnelly Rhodes, Judith Hoag, Robert Guillaume, Shannon Walker Williams, Donny Most, Nancy Lineman Charles, Kevin J. O'Connor, Alan Blumenfeld, Danica McKellar

CBS/Universal Network Television/Heel and Toe Productions; March 2004; 60 minutes; 9 episodes

"The Future is in session." That was the motto for this series' ad campaign. But the critics didn't all reach a happy verdict. "I have seen the future and I'm past it," said *USA Today* critic Robert Bianco.

Century City was set in Los Angeles in 2030, a world where a rejuvenated Mick Jagger is making music at age 87, where pre-programmed refrigerators tell people when they're out of milk, and where pillows snore like an absent spouse, bringing comfort. Refreshment dispensers read your body functions and supply a drink that meets your nutritional needs. The drink tastes awful, but this is only 2030, it isn't Nirvana. The futuristic City of Angels has its own legal problems that occur when people use cutting-edge science for their old-fashioned needs.

It postulates an ethnically diverse future where Oprah Winfrey is president, there's a gay vice-president and Britney Spears and Jessica Simpson are nostalgia. The series centers on the law firm, Crane, Constable, McNeil and Montero, whose lawyers are passionate, witty, and occasionally argumentative as they examine both sides of an issue.

Cases are defined by uncomfortable questions: Should a doctor be sneaking embryos (that have a 95 percent chance of being gay) to unsuspecting couples because he fears homosexuals are being genetically deleted by picky couples? How do you handle a child actor who fears puberty will turn him into a has-been and demands prepubescent chemicals to continue his pint-sized career? Or consider the circumstances of a 70-year-old rock singer (Anthony Zerbe) who is fired by his rock mates because he's old. His bandmates, meanwhile, enhance themselves with plastic surgery and chromosome enzymes to maintain their past vigor.

Created by former *Law and Order* writer-producer Ed Zuckerman, *Century City* showed restraint by featuring only six principal characters every week. "Even with six characters, that was a lot," Zuckerman says. "That's a lot of balls to keep in the air. But it was a good group of people, a good dynamic."

The lawyers' personalities are varied. The comically edged Darwin McNeil is constantly on the make, but is often hoisted on his own petard. Hannah Crane, the tough young black lawyer, began the law firm to affirm justice. She has lots of emotional baggage — her own father robbed her of a childhood because he was a workaholic. Lee May Bristol is blonde and beautiful but unattached and deeply unhappy, despite a genetically perfect body. She wears a "Happy Patch" behind her ear, which releases brain opiates to soothe her past heartbreaks. Lukas Gold is a married lawyer who is attracted to Lee May but keeps focused on his work. Tom Montero is a former politician who comes out swinging for a girl who hungers for privacy in the waning years of her adolescence. Then there's Martin Constable, the legal firm's soothing elder, who makes sure cases are examined from both sides.

"We had a terrific cast and they all went on to bigger and better things," says Zuckerman. In particular, he was amused by Eric Schaeffer's portrayal of the eccentric Darwin. "Eric was simply terrific. He was hilarious in that role. I liked the cast and, had the show continued, they could have really grown and flourished."

Director J. Miller Tobin was cautious when he was approached to work on the series. "Initially I was a bit skeptical about the premise. After seeing the pilot and talking to Ed Zuckerman, I was sold. *Century City* was an imaginative way to address pending legal issues based on advances in science and technology."

Despite its novel twists on the law, only four episodes of *Century City* aired on CBS in March 2004. Lost in the shuffle of contemporary law shows such as *Law and Order* and *CSI*, the series didn't make a dent in the competition, never garnering a rating higher than a 6.0. It also wasn't flashy enough to attract science fiction fans, who were glued to pulp SF shows such as *Stargate SG-1* and *Andromeda*.

Instead, *Century City* presented stories of morality and law in the 21st century.

The series adhered to Isaac Asimov's definition of true science fiction: "Science fiction is that branch of literature which is concerned with the impact of scientific advance upon human beings." "These were people very much like ourselves, being confronted with very novel and very difficult choices in the future," says Zuckerman.

When you consider that Los Angeles of 1975 looked pretty much the same in 2005, it makes sense that this Los Angeles in 2030 didn't look much different than it does today.

"Originally, the show was set 50 years in the future," reveals Zuckerman. "We had already shot all of the episodes when somebody said, 'This show doesn't look like its 50 years from now.' Some of that was because we had made some overly conventional wardrobe decisions but it was also hard to stay ahead of what's happening today. I would come up with a brilliant idea and then pick up a newspaper and see it was *already* happening. At the last minute, we ended up changing it to 26 years in the future. We had to go back and dub the actors' dialogue to reflect that change. If I were doing the series over again, I would make it 10 years in the future. That would have been more realistic and simpler, in terms of production."

But the primary focus of the series was issue-oriented drama. This included stories of clones being created to harvest organs for ill people, human personalities being digitally pressed into computers and a teenager suing her parents because they had her injected with an implant which kept her under surveillance. Her privacy crippled, her conversations monitored, she refuses to let her lawyers know her dreams and thoughts. "They're the only things I have left that can't be spied on," says the anguished girl.

Century City came about when Zuckerman, his partners Paul Attanasio and Attanasio's partner and wife, Katie Jacobs, were talking about various ideas. "I had an idea about a law firm that specialized in cutting edge, high technology," says Zuckerman, "and Paul said, 'Oh, like a law firm of the future.' And we began talking about other things and then Paul suddenly said, 'Wait, what about, literally, a law firm of the future?' I said, 'That's a great idea,' and I wrote the pilot."

Unlike some TV law series, which end with ambiguous and nasty verdicts, *Century City*'s lawyers strived to do the decent thing and the judges tempered their legal decisions with compassion. A boy in mental anguish is allowed to have memories of his abusive mother erased so that he can begin a productive life; a teenage girl is granted permission to have a surveillance monitoring chip removed from her body so she can have some privacy. In one episode, a baseball player with a mechanical eye has been banned from playing in the big leagues because his artificial eye may give him an advantage; his defense lawyers argue that his skill and not a state-of-the-art eye will determine his ability. As Martin Constable says, "Do we also ban players who wear glasses and contact lenses next?" The judge raises his eyebrows in agreement and the verdict is for the baseball player.

Sometimes old storylines were moved in new directions. The "husband murders his wife" theme took a twist when the husband was arrested after police confirm that his gun (the murder weapon) had his DNA lock. No one else could have fired it. The denouement is 2030 style: It turns out that the defendant's jealous girlfriend sought out the man's embryonic twin and convinced the criminal twin to shoot the murder weapon, thereby framing the husband with identical DNA. Even in *Century City*, some motives are as ancient as Cain and Abel.

For Zuckerman, the best episodes and most intriguing issues didn't always mesh. "The dichotomy was that some of the most interesting issues were in episodes that weren't executed as well as some of the others," he explains. "I wrote one episode about a boy whose memories of his mother are removed from him because she was abusive. The idea was intriguing but it didn't turn out that well. On the other hand, we did a fantastic show about a [mentally slow] guy who was going to have this implant taken out of his head and that would make him stupid again. It wasn't an idea I found particularly interesting but the woman who wrote it [Ellie Herman] was really passionate about it and it turned out wonderfully. Another show ["To Know Her"], about someone virtually raping a woman long-distance, by piggybacking on the sensations of someone else as they were having sex, was also interesting."

Tobin directed that segment and says, "We addressed the issues of personal privacy. All of our technology is moving towards recording vast amounts of personal data every second — what shows we watch, what numbers we dial, etc. What happens when we record personal experience the way we shoot home videos? What happens when that medium is abused? It's a logical extension of web casting someone's home sex tape, *à la* Paris Hilton, but in this episode, the technology allows for a full sensory experience of the recording, At what point does the technology move from a recording to a physical intrusion — or in the case of this episode, rape? I very much liked this episode. The actors were wonderful, the script was strong, the issues very credible and powerful."

The show could also be humorous. Anthony Zerbe's 70-year-old rock star proved he still had the moves by doing an incredible (and hilarious) break-dance at the end of his trial. And when Miss Bristol explains to a judge, "I'm asking for a directed verdict based on a finding of fault against the applicant as having terminated the marriage without grounds," the exasperated judge snaps, "Stop talking like that!"

The little tidbits about the future are also imaginative — carpets will detect a person's weight, sound systems will play music that best suits a homeowner's mood, and kitchen appliances will automatically cook a favorite dish. Some of *Century City*'s future is already here — tofu prevails as a health snack, men take birth-control pills, and computers respond to voice commands. Computers are omnipresent and solar panels are common. Most of the series takes place indoors and action sequences are non-existent. Long-distance meetings occur with guest lawyers appearing as ghostly holograms. This is a world drenched in technology.

"It was an expensive series because of the effects," notes Zuckerman. "We had to create the virtual courtroom, where you had a holo-room in your office and you could see the judge at her bench. Those floating, 3-D holographic images were very time-consuming and expensive. If we had done 100 episodes and had more experience at creating those effects, we would have gotten them done faster."

Tobin had his own challenges. Compared to motion pictures, Century City's TV budget may have seemed challenging to some, "My main difficulty as a director was to visually portray the 'futuristic' elements of the stories on the extremely limited schedule and budget. There was the issue of creating the 'world' of the show — an office fifty years from now. What do computers look like, will people still use paper, are there still cars? The offices were designed to be open and fluid. However this created the problem of seeing the entire set in every office as well as having to fight reflections in the glass of the office walls. More that one person walked right into a glass 'door.' We also worked a lot on the 'holoroom,' a video conferencing system that used holograms instead of monitors. It was enormously time-consuming to shoot. Each shot needed two, if not three or four elements, that would be composited together."

The show aired on CBS with little fanfare. "There were ads for it when it was launched," says Zuckerman, "but the ratings just weren't there. It was a great idea for a series but after four shows, we were pulled off the schedule."

Tobin liked what he saw. "Century City was most effective, as is most good science fiction, when the conundrum of the episode was a plausible and natural extension of a current social issue. Cloning, surgical enhancement, nanotechnology, pharmaceuticals, privacy, etc. These are all very real and very current sciences that carry unforeseen complications, legally and morally. And any good series is based on believable characters whom you either root for or disagree with. It succeeded wonderfully in creating an ensemble of characters in the law firm that you both liked and respected. Lawyers by nature are negotiators and on this show, there were no clear answers. Our lawyers were put in the situation of having to sort out the complexities of any given problem and trying to address some fair solution."

A real-life lawyer, Michael Asimow, liked how the show presented a balanced view of law firms when he wrote about the series for *Picturing Justice*,

an on-line journal of law and popular culture. "The idea of focusing on cutting-edge bio-tech issues is promising," he noted of the first episode. "There's a lot of neat futuristic tricks like virtual reality pretrial conferences with the judge, much better video games and cosmetic surgery, super-duper genetic technology and cherries without pits. The only implausible premise is that L.A. has a cool monorail system. Dream on."

Media reviews of *Century City* were mixed. Robert Bianco of *USA Today* found it "gratingly preachy" and added, "It is a fairly original idea yet nothing about its vision of the future rings true." Lisa Beebe of *PopCrazy.com* said the show disappointed her sense of wonder. "Come on, have some fun!" she urged. "Add a cranky robot to the cast!" *The Boston's Globe*'s Matthew Gilbert liked the show's unique format but concluded, "The show is so completely taken with its meaty futuristic issues that it forsakes the importance of basic dramatic storytelling." One of the more positive reviews was from Tim Goodman of *The San Francisco Chronicle*, who noted, "It's a guilty pleasure. Not only is it wonderfully cast but enjoys the advantages of dreaming up legal issues that don't currently concern us."

But they will. *Century City* did a good job of raising some complex moral issues that will face society in the near future. Tobin says, "Technology itself is neither 'good' nor 'bad.' How it is used or misused by the humans that employ it is the key issue. All technical advances bring with them great benefit unless there are people that would abuse the power of that development. *Century City* tried to get at the heart of this dilemma. It was most effective when the issues had real impact on the lives of the clients. The show succeeded best when there was a strong political overtone — for example, the show about genetically selecting the sex and attributes of your child. Not quite the abortion debate but frighteningly close. Although the show often lacked in special effects, the central debate about technology and evolution, legal and moral, was extremely strong."

Nine episodes of *Century City* were made, and later rerun to good ratings on Canada's *Space: The Imagination Station* channel in 2005. Chances are the series will be examined by someone in 2030 to see just how closely they hit the mark.

CAST NOTES

Ioan Gruffudd (Lukas): Born in Cardiff, Wales, he studied acting at London's Royal Academy of

Dramatic Arts. He later had a small role in the epic *Titanic* (1998). It was his breakout role in the title role in *Horatio Hornblower* (the British TV series) that brought him to the attention of Hollywood. He starred as Reed Richards in the films *Fantastic Four* (2005) and its sequel, *Fantastic Four: Rise of the Silver Surfer* (2007).

Viola Davis (Hannah): A Tony award winner in 2001 for her stage role in *King Hedley II*, she also appeared on several *Law and Order* segments as Donna Emmett during 2003–2004, and episodes of *The Traveler* in 2007.

Nestor Carbonell (Tom): This New York City–born actor began his career in theater at Harvard and later played Luis on TVs *Suddenly, Susan* (1996–2000) and Batmanuel in the superhero spoof *The Tick* (2001–2002). He also appeared in the film *Lost City* (2005) and guested on TVs *House, Strong Medicine* and *Lost*.

Eric Schaeffer (Darwin): He earned his living early on as a New York City cab driver for nine years. He's also a writer, director and producer. His previous law series, *First Years*, about San Francisco law graduates, lasted for just one month in 2001. He later appeared on several episodes of the TV series *Starved* (2005).

Kristen Lehman (Lee May): See *Strange World* cast notes.

Hector Elizondo (Martin Constable): New York City–born, Elizondo played one of his earliest roles in the 1960s daytime drama *The Edge of Night*. He also starred in a classic *All in the Family* episode (in 1972) as one of the people trapped in an elevator with the always politically incorrect Archie Bunker. Later he played Dr. Phillip Watters on *Chicago Hope* (1994–2000) and appeared in films such as *Celestine Prophecy* (2005).

SOURCES

Beebe, Lisa. *Century City* Review. "The Verdict: This Futuristic Courtroom Drama is Guilty of Wasting my Time. But I Haven't Given Up Yet." Popcrazy.com, March 23, 2004.

Bianco, Robert. *Century City* Review. "Silly 'Century City': The Future is Shallow." *USA Today*, March 2004.

Gilbert, Matthew. *Century City* review. "Issues-Driven Century City Suffers from a Lack of Drama." *Boston Globe*, March 16, 2004.

Goodman, Tim. *Century City* review. "CBS Might Score with Nanopants." *San Francisco Chronicle*, March 15, 2004.

Pierce, Scott D. "This Century City Looks to the Future." *Deseret Morning News*, March 16, 2004.

Yakir, Dan. "Future Law." *Starlog* no. 321. 2004.

Cleopatra 2525
(2000–2001)

A young stripper named Cleopatra undergoes breast augmentation surgery in 2001. When she doesn't awake from anesthesia, she's placed in a cryogenic deep freeze in hopes she can one day be revived. She awakens in the year 2525 and finds that humanity has been forced to move underground. Flying robots called Baileys rule the surface by attacking all humans. Cleo teams up with two female warriors, "Hel" and "Sarge," in the battle to rid the Earth of the mechanical invaders.

Cast: Gina Torres (Helen Carter), Victoria Pratt (Rose "Sarge"), Jennifer Sky (Cleopatra), Patrick Kake (Mauser), Joel Tobeck (Creegan), Elizabeth Hawthorne (The Voice)

Created by: Rob Tapert, R. J. Stewart; **Executive Producer:** R. J. Stewart; **Co-Executive Producers:** Rob Tapert, Sam Raimi, Eric Gruendemann; **Producer:** Chris Black; **New Zealand Producer:** Janine Dickson; **Co-Producer:** Michael McDonald; **Associate Producer:** Sam Clark; **Writ-**

ers included: Hilary J. Bader, Nora Kay Foster, T.J. Scott, Kevin Lund, Carl Ellsworth, Jessica Scott, Zoe Finkel, Melissa Blake; **Directors included:** Greg Yaitanes, Andrew Merrifield, Rick Jacobson, John Laing, Chris Graves, Mark Beesley; **Guest stars included:** David Press, Danielle Cormack, Kate Elliot, Calvin Tuteao, Latham Gaines, Bruce Hopkins, Kirk Torrance, David Telford, Judy McIntosh, Stephen Finch, Tamati Rice

USA Network/Renaissance Pictures; January 2000-March 2001; 30 minutes (the last six episodes of Year 2 were 60 minutes); 28 episodes; DVD status: Complete series

The Zagar and Evans pop song "In the Year 2525," which zoomed to number one in July 1969, was a cautionary tune about how technology could desensitize and mechanize mankind. It questioned whether women could survive in the future. The lyrics were reworked for *Cleopatra 2525*'s title sequence as to say women had the will to survive.

Rob Tapert had produced the earlier TV hit, *Hercules: The Legendary Adventures*, and he and R.J. Stewart co-produced another smash, *Xena: Warrior Princess* (starring Lucy Lawless). They expected their next production, *Cleopatra 2525*, to be similarly successful. Patrick Kake, who played the girls' bio-droid ally, defined the series as "a modern-day *Charlie's Angels*."

It all starts in 2001 when a boob job goes terribly wrong for a stripper named Cleopatra. She plunges into a coma and is placed in deep freeze by doctors. She awakens over 500 years later, after an apocalyptic war. Humans have been forced underground and alien machines called Baileys (giant flying gargoyles) soar above the surface, shooting laser beams at humans who venture above.

Cleopatra is a sweet, innocent girl, filled with 20th century pop-culture references that mean nothing to her warrior friends. "Hel" is a tough-looking woman whose family was killed years ago. "Sarge," the blonde sex symbol, was forced to leave her family after they were brainwashed by the Baileys. Both women shoot laser beams from devices on their wrists and protect themselves with body force fields.

The actresses, Gina Torres and Victoria Pratt, insisted on doing their own stunts. Both women were in great shape, but suffered gashes, pulled muscles, bruises, and bumps during production. They never wavered as they threw themselves into the video game-like action.

The low-budget series was filmed in Auckland, New Zealand. CGI effects depicted the giant Baileys blasting away at humans every week. There was some interesting subterranean set design, including sleek corridors, holograms and computers. Human guards, who looked like storm troopers from *Star Wars*, monitored the underground against subversive cyborgs, who were working with the Baileys to destroy mankind.

In the first episode, "Quest for Firepower," the first thing Cleopatra does after being revived is to look down at her pumped-up breasts and mutter, "Good job!" When Hel and Sarge question her, Cleopatra warns them that she's agent 008 and threatens them with a camcorder, trying to trick them into thinking it's a weapon. Sarge thinks Cleopatra is crazy but Hel sees beyond her facade and gains the girl's trust.

In this episode, Hel ventures to the surface for the first time. Born and raised underground, she is uncharacteristically pensive about going to the surface but is accompanied by Sarge and Cleopatra. When the Baileys swoop down from the skies, the two warrior women blast the flying machines, while Cleopatra cowers with fear and gives a little scream. "Don't ever scream like that again!" an annoyed Hel yells at her, but Cleo's frightened yelps became an annoying mainstay of the show.

J. D. Biersdorfer, critic for *The New York Times*, admitted he was searching for signs that TV science fiction was growing up. Upon seeing *Cleopatra 2525*, he lamented, "It's about three tightly dressed women battling aliens. Even though it weaves a bit of ironic humor in with exposed midriffs, there's still far more eye candy than brain benders on screen."

But there were occasionally stabs of realism. Realizing that she's permanently marooned 500 years in the future, Cleo quietly reflects, "Everyone I loved is gone. My whole world has been destroyed." At the end of the first episode, Cleo has had enough. "Freeze me again," she poignantly asks her two new friends. "Can you wake me when the world is better?" But Hel tells her that the battle to renew humanity is now part of Cleo's fight and asks her to join them. Cleopatra agrees, with a tentative, "All for one and one for all," a motto that inspires both Hel and Sarge.

"I first heard about *Cleopatra* when I was working on *Xena*," recalls director Rick Jacobson. "The idea of the lead character waking to find herself living in the future was a great concept. It was fun for me, and for the audience, to explore the future along with Cleo. There were great situations for the heroines to deal with, including the fate of mankind and its struggle to exist."

Jacobson directed a total of six episodes. "Probably my biggest challenge was shooting my first two episodes," he says. "We had something like 192 effects shots in these two episodes alone. Combine that with a crew, cast, wardrobe, explosions, fight scenes, etc., and it was quite a challenge, but great fun."

Director Christopher Graves, who had also helmed episodes of *Hercules* and *Xena*, says, "*Cleo* was challenging in that we were attempting to create a futuristic world using international stars and visiting guests on a television budget. The result of the financial challenges brought out the best in what the New Zealand film industry has to offer — lateral thinking when it comes to problem solving. For example, our designer and art department were constantly recycling sets, the special effects team pre-wired many of our 'hits' within those sets, stunties pre-rigged pick points for our bigger fights, our lighting team developed a look that could be pre-set in most studios and we, as directors, had to be most efficient during prep. Within a shooting day we utilized two cameras to maximum advantage and knew exactly what we could delegate to the second unit, such as ... visual effects, in order to 'make our day.' We often shot up to nine script pages a day and seven was the norm — challenging in anyone's book when it comes to action-drama. It made a pretty organized director out of me!"

This learning curve had its fill of challenges for Graves. "As all of the crew were working such a tight timetable, every second on set was precious, so we expected the same level of professionalism from our cast. This wasn't always forthcoming, as Jen liked to 'live a little' which sometimes meant she arrived on the set without knowing her lines. This frustrated the hell out of her co-players and presented another challenge for all of us. I remember breaking up a scene into tiny bits in order to help her through a rather wordy passage, while directing her attention away from the rolling eyes of both Gina and Victoria."

But he stresses he enjoyed working with all three actresses. "Gina was a gem to work with — a true professional and easy on the eyes as well. We all loved Gina and if her boyfriend [and future husband, Laurence Fishburne] hadn't been so famous and respected, I'm sure she would have had lots of New Zealand suitors. She maintained her level of professionalism throughout and brought some class to the series. She also had beautiful skin so the makeup department loved her. Victoria was also very professional — easy to work with, fit and physical. She brought the 'punch' to the triad. Vic was fairly forward and did get to know certain members of the crew pretty well. She wasn't afraid to speak her mind when it came to appreciating men."

And then there was the actress who played the title character. "Jen was our wild card," says Graves. "Always bubbly and full of energy, she inspired both adoration and frustration in us all. There was a scene where the three heroes escape out a sliding door into the ether beyond, bidding farewell to a particularly evil baddie, and Jen insisted on sticking out her tongue at her. Vic and Gina both thought it was inappropriate under the circumstances and were less than impressed when I backed Jen and we went with the tongue action. For all her loopiness, Jennifer Sky *was* Cleopatra and, in the end, it was that irreverence that made her character what it was and ultimately gave the show its humanity."

Jacobson also has fond memories of the three actresses who played the futuristic warriors. "Gina had the most work experience," he notes. "She had spent time filming in New Zealand on *Hercules* and *Xena*, so she was a more natural leader of the three. She was mature, sensitive and cerebral, which defined her character of Hel. Vicki had a very physical, strong-willed, dedicated and 'get the job done' type of personality that fit Sarge. Jennifer, the youngest of the three, was an outgoing, carefree type who was willing to do or try anything. Her energy and enthusiasm made Cleo the character that fans enjoyed watching and learning through. All three had great talent and brought great depth to each of their characters."

Recurring characters included the friendly Mauser, a cyborg in human form, who helps with information. Patrick Kake, who was Kevin Sorbo's body double on *Hercules*, said he used Mr. Spock from *Star Trek* as a template on how to play the efficient Mauser. There was also The Voice, a maternal female voice that helps direct Hel against the approaching Baileys.

The villainous Creegan, Hel's nemesis, looks like the Joker from *Batman* with his red hair and lips and white skin. He was responsible for the death of Hel's family when she was a child and is an evil ally of The Baileys. He's originally from the 20th century, where he was known as George Bailey, who created environmental control units to protect Earth. But these machines gained a consciousness and decided that mankind must be destroyed to save Earth from pollution. Bailey sided with the machines and has led their battle against man ever since. He feels pre-ordained to dispose of humanity in a holocaust and tries to find The Voice, so he can neutralize the human resistance. He considers anyone who opposes him "insolent thugs."

With its bright colors, *Cleopatra 2525* truly

was a comic-strip come to life. Jacobson recalls, "*Cleopatra* offered visual eye candy — lots of flash and visual cues. We tried to create a 'working' world. Sci-fi fans like details so every effort was made to create a believable setting. We used pretty much standard bluescreen/element type effects. The challenge was our limited production time frame. We shot two episodes at once, in six to seven days, so we didn't have time to tweak and perfect things."

Jacobson directed "Flying Lessons," an early episode where Cleo is taught to fly in the subterranean shaft. "Those flying scenes were always a challenge," he says. "Trying to get the angles right, working with wind machines and harnesses and listening to Cleo's constant screaming will test anyone's nerves. The wirework [where the heroines would fly through the air] also took time. Working with the stunt coordinator, I tried to create flying moves that were 'inhuman' in nature but still had a natural feel. The last thing I wanted was some cheesy wire-looking shot that called attention to itself."

A lot of the series was filmed outdoors. "Shooting effects outside was also a challenge, mostly due to the elements. The weather in New Zealand changes quickly. Clouds, then wind, then sun, then rain! That always tested the crew."

To the surprise of many, in its first season *Cleopatra* was the highest rated show in syndication (until the new *Andromeda* series came along) and the reviews were generally encouraging. Fans at conventions wore costumes that perfectly replicated that of the three heroines.

The series had a lot of running and explosions as the women blasted away at cyborgs and the flying Baileys. But there was some subtext to the stories.

"Reality Check" begins with an elderly scientist giving the three women a chance to experience VR adventures while sealed in experimental tubes. But Cleo, trapped in her chamber, is transported to a virtual world of 2001. It's the world she left, working in a strip club and romanced by her boyfriend, Johnny (Kieren Hutchison). Johnny admits to her that he created this virtual world to keep Cleo with him forever, but she wants to return with her friends to 2525 and urges him to join her. He can't and sadly bids her farewell. Back in the future, the old scientist admits that *he's* Johnny. He had frozen himself as a young man in 2001 so he could one day awaken with Cleo but was accidentally revived 50 years too early. He therefore created a virtual world

where he and Cleo could have a last visit. The exertion of the VR trip kills him, and as Cleo cries she says, "I need a little help with this one, guys." Hel and Sarge comfort her as Cleo mourns Johnny's loss.

When *Cleopatra* faltered early in its second year, there was a decision to turn the show into a 60-minute adventure. The last six episodes were an hour long, with more time for character development. While ratings were satisfactory, the number of markets carrying *Cleopatra* fell. The producers and distributor blamed the increasingly competitive syndication market, where new networks were crowding out time slots for hour-long syndicated shows.

The series was canceled in 2001, the same year that Cleo had gone into her own suspended animation. "From what I know, the producers always had trouble selling the show as a half-hour series," says Jacobson. "Buyers didn't think enough story could be told in such a short time frame, which is ridiculous. Anyone who watched *Cleo* knew engaging stories were being told in that time frame. The show never got a fair chance to find an audience. It switched time slots over and over again, making it impossible to lock down regular viewers. The switch to the one-hour format was a last effort to conform to the buyer's desires. But it was too late for the show and it was canceled."

Chris Graves felt the hour shift was a good move, but too late. "Creatively, one hour gives more scope to telling a fuller story and gives your characters a chance to develop and gain depth. I'd always take an hour over a half-hour. It was great to move to that format, if only briefly."

Critics weren't harsh but neither did they feel the show was worthy of deep critical thought. "It's campy, with a premise that is amusing," noted *The Deseret Morning News*.

Appraising it today, Jacobson says, "Its strengths were great, strong female lead characters, engaging storylines, the sci-fi setting, futuristic technology, and it was entertaining. There was nothing else like it on television at the time." "*Cleopatra 2525* was the victim of unfortunate broadcasting," says Graves. "By being paired with *Jack of All Trades* [the 19th-century spy series starring Bruce Campbell] and screening it straight after *Xena* in the U.S., it never really found its own audience. We had such fun making it and the futuristic story lines allowed such creative freedom. It was a real blow to discover we'd been canned. We all hoped it would go on forever!"

CAST NOTES

Gina Torres ("Hel"): The New York City–born actress, who is married to actor Lawrence Fishburne, is also a noted opera and gospel singer. She was a regular on the TV series *MANTIS* (1994) and later guest-starred on *Alias*, *24*, *Hercules: The Legendary Journeys*, and *The Guardian*. She was also a regular in *Stand Off* (2006–2007). Her film credits include *Matrix Revolutions* (2003). During production of *Cleopatra 2525*, she categorized it as "three great-looking chicks who keep the world safe." She later starred in another series set 500 years into the future, *Firefly* (as Zoe, in 2003).

Victoria Pratt ("Sarge"): Born in Ontario, Canada, she wrote a book on fitness and bodybuilding and is an expert in kickboxing and Shotokan Karate. She studied acting at The Actors Network in Toronto and did guest shots on *First Wave* and *Xena: Warrior Princess*. She was also a regular on *Mutant X* (2001–2004). Her credits include the films *Comedy Hell* (2005) and *House of the Dead 2* (2006) and the TV series *Day Break* (2006–2007). During the *Cleopatra* series, she married one of the show's writer-directors, TJ Scott.

Jennifer Sky (Cleopatra): The Palm Beach, Florida–born actress loved *Cleopatra*'s special effects, especially how real the Bailey machines looked as they zoomed over her. As a child, Jennifer created fantasy worlds with Barbie dolls. She began her career by traveling around the world as a model and made her acting debut in a 1994 *seaQuest* episode, followed by a guest shot on *Buffy the Vampire Slayer*. She was a regular on *General Hospital* (1997–1998) and has done such films as *Never Die Alone* (2004) and *The Helix: Loaded* (2005).

Patrick Kake (Mauser): He made his acting debut in an episode of *Hercules* (after two years of stunt doubling for Kevin Sorbo). His films include *The Hill* (2002) and *The Chronicles of Narnia* (2005).

Joel Tobeck (Creegan): He endured a three-hour makeup job to transform into the colorful Creegan. Born in Auckland, New Zealand, his mother is actress Liddy Holloway. His film appearances include *Lord of the Rings: Return of the King* (2003), *Stealth* (2005) and *Ghost Rider* (2006).

SOURCES

Biersdorfer, J.P. *Cleopatra* Review. "Not-So-Brave New World: Sci-Fi TV Runs Aground." *New York Times*, February 6, 2000.

Nazzaro, Joe. "Apocalypse's Angel — Victoria Pratt Takes No Prisoners Battling Evil as the Sultry Sarge." *Starlog* no. 285, April 2001.

_____. "Blonde Awakening." *Starlog* no. 283, February 2001.

Code Name: Eternity

(1999)

An alien soldier named Ethaniel arrives on Earth to stop an alien named Banning, who plans to destroy humanity by making Earth's atmosphere the same as that of their home world, Theron.

Cast: Cameron Bancroft (Ethaniel), Ingrid Kavelaars (Laura Keating), Andrew Gillies (Banning), Gordon Currie (Dent), Olivier Gruner (Tawrens), Joseph Baldwin (Byder)

Concept by: William Fruet; **Created by:** William Fruet, Jeff King; **Executive Producers:** Peter Mohan, James Margellos, Dimitri Logothetis, Konstantin Thoeren, Jesse Ryder, Miles Dale; **Executive Producers for Protocol:** Paul Bronfman, Steve Levitan; **Executive Producers for Dune:** Robert Nador, Eve Vercel; **Producers:** Steve Levitan, Tony di Marco, Konstantin Thoeren, Robert Nador; **Line Producer:** Kevin Lafferty; **Executive Consultant:** Rick Drew; **Writers included:** Sarah Dodd, Tracey Forbes, Peter Mohan, Jean-Vincent Fournier; **Directors included:** Rene Bonniere, Jon Cassar, Malcolm Cross, Steve Di Marco, William Fruet, Dimitri Logothetis, Larry A. McLean, Donald Shebib, Fred Gerber; **Guest Stars included:** Leila Johnson, Christina Cox, Billy Dee Williams, Wolf Larson, Lynda Mason Green, Polly Shannon, Nigel Bennett, Rochelle Redfield, Carmelina

LaManna, Guylaine St-Onge, Nicholas Campbell, Monika Schnarre, Eva Habermann, Lucy Van Org, Jeff Wincott, Brooke Johnson, Philip Granger, Kristin Booth, Christina Plate, Jayne Eastwood, Cliff Saunders as Gordon, Hannes Jaenicke as Thorber

A Canada-France Co-Production; From Protocol Eternity Productions Inc.; Dune S.A. and Metropole Televisiona; In Association with CanWest Global Broadcasting; Warner Bros./International Television; Filmed in 1999. Originally aired on Sci-Fi Channel in 2004; 60 minutes; 26 episodes

Every alien who lands on TV Earth seems to search for relatives. *The Phoenix* (a 1982 series) had its hero hunt for his wife while Robert Hays' *Starman* (1986) also searched for his wife while being chased by a government agent. And more recently, *The Visitor* (1998) kept one step ahead of a fanatical colonel as he searched for his son.

Code Name: Eternity had a similar premise: An alien soldier named Ethaniel tries to find his brother while clashing with a rogue alien named Banning (who poses as a respectable businessman). Ethaniel takes human form (a good-looking young guy) and befriends a psychiatrist, Dr. Laura Keating, who helps him understand the weird ways of human beings. They live on a yacht, complete with computer equipment (manned by their conspiracy-expert friend, Byder).

"Variations on the idea had been out there in the marketplace before, but at the time, the alien bounty hunter character was pretty original," says co-creator Jeff King. "Add in the memory twist and the 'villain above suspicion,' plus Dr. Keating, and there hadn't been a series made exactly the way I was going to unfold the story in *Code Name: Eternity*."

Producer Peter Mohan added his own creative imprint on the show. "When I came onto the project, director Bill Fruet had already written a script. It was very much in the *Starman* mold. I thought we needed to bring the concept up to date. There had been fascinating advances in the field of genetic research as well as ethical questions about genetic manipulation. This seemed like a natural and fascinating direction in which to steer a series about alien life forms coming into contact with our own. We got to play with the gray area of where humanity begins and ends."

Another question posed in the series is the whereabouts of Ethaniel's older brother, Thorber. He's a friendly alien who was sent to Earth with Banning years ago to do benevolent research. But when he learns Banning is truly evil, Thorber sends a last message to Theron — a warning that Banning has hatched a scheme to use quantumshift technology to change the Earth's axis and turn it into an atmospheric copy of Theron. This would wipe out all human life. Ethaniel and a team of soldiers head to Earth to apprehend Banning but their spaceship crashes. Ethaniel survives but his memory has been erased and Laura helps him regain his identity.

Banning runs The Eternity Group, a powerful research foundation on Earth. He also disrupts Laura's home life by telling her parents that her new friend Ethaniel is a psycho. This helps to estrange Laura from her father, with whom she already has a tenuous relationship. At Banning's disposal is Dent, a *Terminator 2*–like android who can morph himself to look like other people. Dent is also able to repair itself with CGI liquid effects whenever he gets bashed by the good guys. He smirks when he's ordered to destroy people and often displays an annoying, nervous tick.

"When I came aboard, the project had already been in development for some time by Protocol Entertainment," recalls Jeff King. "I was asked to come in at a time when the series development had stalled. They handed me a feature film script which the various parties all liked but they couldn't figure out how to turn it into a series. I put aside the original development, pitched my take and events followed very quickly. I spent quite a while working on the series bible but once I hit on a story the key buyers liked, I wrote the pilot script very quickly."

The pilot was a fast-paced and exciting piece of work, as Dent wages an all-out pursuit of Ethaniel and Laura. But as the series progressed, there were also quiet moments. Ethaniel has a child-like fascination for humans ("Show me flirting so that I can recognize it," he asks Laura). Occasionally, his actions seem more calculated than innocent. When climbing up a ladder with Laura, Ethaniel looks up admiring at her bottom and says, "I'm beginning to like it." She gives him a scowl and he explains with an innocent smile, "That's humor!"

But there was nothing humorous about a TV series that had several different foreign partners. *Code Name: Eternity* had to please everyone and co-creator Jeff King recalls it was a challenge. "There were several different partners, each with their own, sometimes conflicting sensibilities. I was informed that German audiences wouldn't watch a show where stories didn't have a hard science rationale. In other words, *Star Trek* didn't play well in Germany because a phaser requires a certain leap of faith in physics. A French audience wouldn't go for a series where the bad guys were in latex suits! Every time we got the sensibility right for one, there was a note from one of the others. Thank God for the French. They and Warners finally agreed on a concept. I wrote the pilot and then we waited for our Canadian partner to get the sales lined up so we could go to series."

King, however, didn't end up working on the actual show. "Very unfortunately for me, in the intervening time between the pilot and the show being ordered to series, I had to take a real, every-week paying gig. About three months into that series [the underrated *Total Recall 2070*], *Code Name: Eternity* was ordered. I begged Alliance to let me out of my contract but they wouldn't release me and so *Code Name: Eternity* went forward under a different creative team. They redeveloped the series from my concept to what viewers ultimately watched. That was heartbreaking for me, to see it going and not running it."

Unlike other space-age TV aliens, Ethaniel is no fugitive. He's a hunter and he's constantly blocking Banning's plans. Banning's schemes always end up in Wile E. Coyote-like ruins. Banning can't even frame the duo for murder effectively. And yet the very next week, Banning is just as confident and arrogant as ever.

In one show, Ethaniel and Laura fly to New York City ("Why is it called The Big Apple?" Ethaniel ponders) to stop Banning from using perfume that will seduce and control powerful men. A beautiful model, Claire (Monika Schnarre), befriends Ethaniel for her own selfish motives. In a confrontation on a rooftop, Claire is killed by Dent and Banning escapes. Ethaniel at least receives a valuable lesson in how some women use their beauty to betray men.

In "Thief," Carmelina LaManna gives an energetic performance as an incorrigible thief named Mira. She steals a machine that can change Therons into human beings. Banning desperately needs the device back before he turns into a Theron and dies in the Earth's atmosphere. "We must find that device, it is essential to my survival," he fumes to his mechanical man in his British accent. "My body may revert at any time! Find and kill her!" Dent leaves with a smirk and the chase is on.

Ethaniel's best friend, an alien named Tawrens,

falls in love with Mira and he joins her on the run. Cornered by aliens, Mira finally gives up the device and she and Tawrens escape. Tawrens thinks this beautiful thief has reformed but she ends up stealing his wallet and splitting. It was Tawrens' turn to receive a valuable lesson in how some women use their beauty to betray men.

Olivier Gruner, who was a feature-film action star, had the perfect mysterious persona as Tawrens. Although he had appeared in the pilot, as one of Ethaniel's commandos who crash-lands on Earth, Gruner wasn't interested in joining up for the weekly series. The studio, pleased with his performance in the pilot, tried constantly to get Gruner to join as a regular. "They explained they needed more action in the series and wanted a lighter character," says Gruner. "They found me in my gym, where I was training. A Warner Bros. gentleman asked me why my agent was not responding to their calls." Gruner thought it over and decided to take a chance on the show, noting, "They sent me to Toronto for one episode, called 'Tawrens.' After that episode, they kept me all the way through the end."

"Tawrens was a fun character to play," says Gruner. "He liked to adapt himself to any situation and he liked action. I got to do all of my own stunts, we traveled all around Toronto, and every week we went to a different location. I learned a lot about working on a television series, learning a lot of lines, and we had to work as a team to make the scenes work. What a great experience — thanks to Warner Bros.!"

Banning continually underestimated Ethaniel and Laura. Dent the android has similar trouble: Despite having super strength, he prissily throws a flower vase at Ethaniel, who ducks. Throughout the series, Dent is blasted, hit, shot, tossed through an observation window, kicked into the churning waters of Niagara Falls, bonked on the head by a falling oil drum, set on fire, thrown from a speeding train, caught in explosions, run over by a car and even electrocuted by Laura. But he always comes back with a smile, his suit impeccably pressed.

Producer Peter Mohan got a kick out of Dent. "Dent was a Nanotech-based creature who was able to re-form itself at the cellular level. He started out as a one-dimensional killer, but he took on a deeper dimension as the series progressed. In one show, Dent was left incapacitated and Ethaniel was forced to fix him so they could escape. Ethaniel had the power to communicate with machines, and he gave Dent a little something extra as he re-worked Dent's operating system: a soul. This made for interesting byplay with Dent's evil boss as he suddenly sprinkled their conversations with questions about souls and the nature of good and evil. It also opened the question of 'What is really human?' to potentially include artificial intelligence."

Meanwhile, Ethaniel's powers allowed him to tell whether people were lying or not, and he also had super strength. At one point, when he began examining safety locks to break into an installation, Laura said, "Don't tell me — you can pick locks too?" But Ethaniel can explain. "Locks are simply engaged pressure points — pressure adjusts to pressure." And in they go.

Cameron Bancroft and Ingrid Kavelaars in *Code Name Eternity* (© Warner Bros. International Television).

Ethaniel didn't speak pidgin–English; he was articulate, sensitive and quiet, but with a sense of justice and a growing affection for this vulnerable if capable woman who was his best friend.

Laura (winningly played by Ingrid Kavelaars) was no fool or screaming heroine. She held her own in both the smarts and fight categories. The sexual tension between them is kept light, so there are no dopey scenes of affection to bog down the stories (although in the last episode they express love for each other).

Wrestling with guilt and anger, Laura feels her parents never approved of her life. "They felt I never had the right friends, I never studied the right subjects and I didn't get into the right profession," she laments to Ethaniel.

"Working with Ingrid Kavelaars was great. She had very little experience before the show, but she really stepped up," says Mohan. "She gave it her all to improve her skills and she really became an actress over that year." He also enjoyed dealing with the two villains. "Working with Gordon Currie [Dent] and Andrew Gilles [Banning] was always a treat. In some ways the bad guys became the center of the show because they were so compelling to watch and so good together. Every day, both actors watched dailies together and went, 'Oh yeah, I could have done this, you could have done that!' They were always making their material better because they were so invested in it."

Despite a limited budget, the show had striking visual flair. "There was a lot of work put into the look and creating shots on the cheap but not making them look cheap," says Mohan. "We often shot 'exteriors' in the studio with green screen, marrying them into exterior plates. We had a couple of young fellows [including Jason Pennington] from the East Coast, working on visual effects in the back room. These 19-year-old guys, with a lot of Jolt cola, used computers to create visual effects that were just amazing. They really helped give *Code Name: Eternity* that great look. They're working for Disney and other top-flight markets now.

Another eye-catcher was the main title theme, saturated in vibrant color and with a distinctive music theme. "The title theme music was spectacular," Mohan agrees. "It was done by our composer Amin Bhatia and his partner, Trevor Morris. As soon as we heard it, we knew it would be great."

In the last episode, "Shift" (written by Mohan), Banning captures Ethaniel and Laura as he begins to change the Earth's axis. Banning's digital clock counts down Earth's doom. Tawrens smashes into the room and shoots Banning but too late: A green glow engulfs the Earth. Fade out. "If a second season had come, Ethaniel and Tawrens would have prevented Banning's organization from finishing the process," reassures Mohan.

Filmed in 1999, the series didn't show up in the U.S. until much later. "Because the series did not proceed beyond the 26 episodes, it wasn't as attractive a package for a U.S. sale at that point." says Mohan. The reruns later showed up on major channels in Canada and the U.K. When the 26 episodes were picked up by The Sci-Fi Channel in 2004, *TV Guide* was mystified and griped, "The only reason Sci-Fi Channel could have for recycling this clunker from the scrap heap is to fill a gap in its schedule."

From today's vantage point, Mohan has a good opinion of the series. "It was a well-made show with good action and good SF stories. There were some really touching moments in the love story between Laura and Ethaniel. Banning and Dent had an intricate and funny relationship, with Dent as a creature coming to sentience and questioning his evil master and his own behavior. The show would have been even better if the various studios and networks had shared a common vision for the series. It might have been a really groundbreaking look at the real core questions that we set out to address: 'What is it to be human?' and 'How is that affected by the form that being happens to inhabit, be it human, alien or even nano-robotic?'"

Cast Notes

Cameron Bancroft (Ethaniel): He began acting in front of TV cameras as a child. He moved from Manitoba to Vancouver as a teenager and nearly died in 1983 when he fell 200 feet off a cliff in Capilano Canyon. His injuries ended his dream of being a professional hockey player, so he turned to acting and joined the cast of Canada's popular series *The Beachcombers* in 1985. Moving to California, he made 1980s appearances on *General Hospital*, *Tour of Duty*, and *Out of this World*. He also spent a year on *Beverly Hills 90210* (1995–96). He played Charles Ingalls in the 2004 *Little House on the Prairie* mini-series.

Ingrid Kavelaars (Laura): The Toronto-born actress won Miss Teen London, Ontario, at age 15. When she was 18, she moved to New York City to work in theater. She then made TV commercials and appeared in the Canadian shows *Street Legal* and *Kids in the Hall*. Her SF credits include *Outer Limits*, *Jeremiah* and *Stargate SG-1*. She also appeared in the film *Dreamcatcher* (2003). More recently she co-starred in the Canadian-made *Whistler* TV series.

Andrew Gillies (Banning): This English-born actor has done much Canadian theater, including the prestigious Shaw Festival in Ontario. He had a recurring role as Dr. Harrison in *Mutant X* (2002) and played Prime Minister Tony Blair in the TV film *DC/911: Time of Crisis* (2003). His other credits include *Forever Knight*, *Nikita* and *Relic Hunter*.

Gordon Currie (Dent): The Vancouver-born Curry made ends meet early on by being a Ronald McDonald clown in Los Angeles. He made his acting debut in 1987 on *21 Jump Street* and starred as a vampire in *Blood and Donuts*, a 1995 feature. His other genre credits: *First Wave*, *Earth: Final Conflict* and *Outer Limits*. His other films include *Dark Hours* (2005) and *The Sentinel* (2006).

Olivier Gruner (Tawrens): Born in Paris, he joined the French military as a young man. In 1987 he became Kickbox Champion of the World, a title he kept until his retirement from kickboxing. He later became an international action star. His first movie was *Angel Town* (1990). His later films include *Nemesis* (1993), *Velocity Trap* (1997), *Interceptors* (1999), *SWAT: Warhead One* (2005) and *War of the Dead* (2006).

Joseph Baldwin (Byder): A cousin of actor Alec Baldwin, he's also a writer and producer. This New York native's films include *Iceman* (1999) and *It Had To Be You* (2000).

Sources

TV Guide, 2000.

Crusade

(1999)

The crew of the starship Excalibur *streak across the universe looking for a cure for the Drakh plague now present in Earth's atmosphere.*

Stars: Gary Cole (Captain Matthew Gideon), Tracy Scoggins (Captain Elizabeth Lochley), Daniel Dae Kim (John Matheson), David Allen Brooks (Max Eilerson), Carrie Dobro (Dureena Nafeal), Peter Woodward (Galen), Marjean Holden (Dr. Sarah Chambers)
Created by: J. Michael Straczynski; **Executive Producers:** J. Michael Straczynski, Douglas Netter; **Producer:** John Copeland; **Co-Producer:** Skip Beaudine; **Associate Producers:** Susan Norkin, Tracy Yates; **Production Designer:** John Iacovelli; **Director of Photography:** Fred Murphy; **Directors included:** Tony Dow, John Copeland, Stephen Furst, Janet Greek, Michael Vejar, Jesus Salvador Trevino; **Music:** Evan Chen; **Guest stars included:** Maggie Egan, Edward Woodward, Michael Beck, Gary Graham, Brian Thompson, Richard Biggs (as Dr. Stephen Franklin)
TNT Network/Warner Bros. Television/Babylonian Productions; 1999; 60 minutes; 13 episodes; DVD status: Complete series

As a sequel series to *Babylon 5, Crusade* had all the components needed for success. It was based in the *Babylon 5* universe, was written and produced by original series creator J. Michael Straczynski and featured a new, dynamic cast of characters and an exciting science fiction premise. But it only ran for 13 episodes.

Crusade is an interesting case study of the never-ending battle between art and business in filmmaking. *Crusade* failed as a series not because of its concept or because of money. It failed because of a creative control tussle between the producers and the network that ordered it.

Further adventures in the *Babylon 5* universe was made possible because TNT (the Turner network) had saved the show by commissioning *B5*'s fifth season and two TV movies. At the end of the series' run, Turner asked for a spin-off show and two additional movies, one of which served as "a transition film" into *Crusade. A Call to Arms* aired on January 1999.

"There was much discussion going on between Joe Straczynski and TNT," says director Jesus Salvador Trevino. "They wanted a sixth year of *B5*

and Joe felt that the saga had been planned for five seasons and that the story had, in effect, been told. He was not about to be bullied into artificially creating a sixth year of storyline. But with the huge following that *B5* already had, it made sense to develop a franchise linked to it."

In *A Call to Arms*, President John Sheridan (Bruce Boxleitner, who originated the character on *Babylon 5*) oversaw the construction of a pair of new Human-Minibari hybrid battlecruisers. But then he was suddenly contacted by Galen (Peter Woodward), a Technomage who had technology so advanced it appeared magical. (The Technomages made their first appearance in an episode of *Babylon 5*, "The Geometry of Shadows," as a mysterious race of humans who rarely traveled outside their own group.) When the Technomages decided to go into hiding to keep their technology from being used in the Shadow War (a galactic conflict between the humans and the ancient Shadow aliens as seen on *Babylon 5*), one Technomage, Galen, stayed behind to observe the state of galactic affairs. He gave Sheridan a dire warning that Earth was about to be attacked by an alien race known as the Drakh, who were "servants" of the now-vanquished enemy, the Shadows. With the two new battlecruisers at his disposal, Sheridan raced to Earth to prevent the attack. Despite a massive defense, the Drakh succeeded in releasing a biological virus agent into the atmosphere. Every man, woman and child would die in about five years unless a cure was found.

This was the premise of *Crusade* the series. One of the battlecruisers, the *Excalibur*, commanded by Captain Matthew Gideon, was ordered to scour the galaxy for Shadow technology that would lead to a plague cure.

"I liked the script of *A Call to Arms* a lot," says *Babylon 5* star Bruce Boxleitner. "Since I knew I wasn't going to be continuing on to *Crusade*, it was my opportunity to enjoy and contribute to the new show. *A Call to Arms* did very well. It was TNT's highest rated movie. I thought it was great."

Since the *Victory* was destroyed in *A Call to*

Arms, the *Excalibur* became the vessel that streaked across the cosmos. Gideon assembled a team of specialists: Dureena Na'Feel, an alien thief who could break into anything; Max Eilerson, an alien cultures archaeologist, and Dr. Sarah Chambers, whose task was to find the cure. Along for the ride were Gideon's first officer, John Matheson and, appearing whenever it suited him, Galen, the Technomage. The commander of *Babylon 5*, Captain Elizabeth Lochley, also figured prominently.

Announced in April 1997 by the network, *Crusade* began filming on August 3 with its first episode, "The Needs of Earth."

"There was also a new kind of excitement I felt working on these sets and, of course, working with a new set of principal actors," recalls Trevino, who directed "Rules of the Game." "There was a certain sense of expectation. We knew we were on a new journey but we didn't exactly know where that journey would lead us.

"When I read the script of my episode, I must admit I was a bit disappointed. Part of this came from having just finished *B5* with the culmination of its five-year arc. There was so much going on at the end, the Psi-Corps, the Mars colony, the Narns, the Centauri, the Minibari — heck, it was a hard act for any series to follow. I expected more stakes to be evident."

However, Trevino considered *Crusade*'s basic premise intriguing enough to attract both a new audience and satisfy the loyal *B5* fans. "We knew that Earth was threatened by a plague that would soon wipe out all humanity unless a cure was found," he says. "So I think this was a pretty good premise to launch us onto a new saga.

"It was kind of spooky working on the same three soundstages that I had worked on for four years doing *B5* and finding new sets, a new ship and, of course, a new set of principal characters. And, of course, the journey was cut short. "

Actress Marjean Holden had it better than the rest of the *Crusade* cast: She appeared in the series as two different characters. She appeared in *A Call to Arms* as an Earthforce navigator, then was eager to audition for *Crusade*. "I went in and did *A Call to Arms*, and then a couple of weeks later auditioned for *Crusade*," recalls Holden. "I went through the entire auditioning process for that. Usually, if you take hold of a character on a show that actually continues on, that's it. Joe Straczynski said, 'No worries. We've done that before, so it's no big deal!' They were very open and it worked very well for us. I'm very appreciative of that."

Producers were so impressed with Holden, that they gave her the pivotal role of Dr. Sarah Chambers, the *Excalibur*'s resident medical officer. It was her job to work with Captain Gideon in finding a cure for the Drakh plague that was hanging over Earth residents like the sword of Damocles. Holden looks back at the experience as great fun but she was disappointed and frustrated that the series was so truncated. Her character was just beginning on a journey. "I didn't get to explore too much of it," she says. "*Crusade* ended just as it was getting good towards the end of the first season. That's when the development of my character was getting in. We were finding more possibilities for a cure. I wanted more interaction with some of the other characters but we didn't get that far."

Holden has very fond memories of her castmates. "We had a blast on everything we did. The most fun was that we were an ensemble cast. Gary Cole was great. I don't think Gary ever expected to do a science fiction show. He had such a dry sense of humor that I really enjoyed working with him. Peter Woodward is a very eclectic person. He got to let loose his personality in that role. He was perfect. Carrie Dobro was an alien before [on TV's *Hypernauts*] so she was quite used to that. We were the only two girls who were ever around, which was nice."

And then there was David Allen Brooks and Daniel Dae Kim. "David was so funny," Holden continues. "His character [Max] was always looking for neat little gadgets that he could play with. Struggling between being a good guy and a corporate guy, and finding his humanity, and that was just so much fun. Daniel and I never really had a whole lot to do together. We were meant to start communicating a little bit more in the later episodes. The one episode [in which we were] supposed to speak to each other, we didn't shoot."

Throughout the series' 13 episodes, the *Excalibur* crew had many adventures. They ran into other Technomages and encountered a non–humanoid alien who made crew members relive pivotal moments in their lives. The characters also explored dead worlds, gained better scientific knowledge of the Drakh plague with a symposium on Mars, and received help from *Babylon 5*'s Dr. Richard Franklin. They also hunted down an alien with valuable data crystals and met two aliens who had been trying to prove the existence of life in the universe other than their own.

Just a month into filming, news of behind-the-scenes drama began leaking. On September 8,

1998, on the film geek website Ain't It Cool News, it was revealed that an internal TNT memo had been written, proposing changes to the series. It asked for fistfights and more sexual content (suggesting that "horny aliens" come on board the ship and have sex with various characters). They wanted at least one of the characters to be a "sexual explorer."

This was a document that Joe Straczynski wasn't supposed to see. He did later acknowledge that the memo existed but it had been "withdrawn."

To understand how *Crusade* came to a screeching halt, we pick up the show production after five episodes. There was a two-week shooting hiatus in mid–September and in this time two things were done: An upgrade of the various sets and a costume change.

At the end of the hiatus period, on October 19, the show's chronology was shifted. The episode that was to have been the series opener, "Racing the Night," an "adventure in progress" introduction to the characters, was shoved aside in favor of a story titled "War Zone" which was a true origin story revealing how Captain Gideon was recruited for the mission and how his team joined the cause.

Because of the change in costumes, the order in which the episodes were broadcast was also affected. The first five episodes, in which the characters were in blue uniforms, suddenly became the final five episodes. These episodes were "The Needs of Earth," "The Memory of War," "Racing the Night," "Visitors from Down the Street," and "Each Night I Dream of Home."

All episodes filmed after the hiatus break, where everyone wore gray-and-red uniforms, became the *first* eight episodes to air. In the final episode filmed (but aired as eighth), "Appearances and Other Deceits," a fashion designer came aboard the *Excalibur*, prompting the costumes change. Then further filming was suspended.

Straczynski described *Crusade*'s woes as being the result of a political dispute between the Los Angeles and Atlanta offices of the network. The L.A. office was satisfied with the show's progress but the business affairs office in Atlanta wanted to exercise greater creative control. They had written copious notes and had asked for more sex and violence. There were 20 pages of notes concerning the show's content and Babylonian Productions were appalled at what they were being asked to do.

On February 26, 1999, Straczynski announced the show would not continue. He never received a specific reason why the show was being canceled. "It was quite a shock when they pulled the plug," says Holden. "Joe wasn't going to compromise his integrity to make a show that he didn't want to make, which I totally respect."

At this point, the show was not scheduled to air on the network until June, so immediately negotiations were initiated with other networks.

The Sci-Fi Channel wanted the show very badly, and engaged in heavy numbers crunching, but their budget for that year had already been allocated to other acquisitions such as Steven Spielberg's *Taken* miniseries, Frank Herbert's *Dune* miniseries, *The Invisible Man*, *Farscape*, *First Wave*, *Sliders* and *Poltergeist: The Legacy*.

Sci-Fi Channel also wanted as part of the package *Babylon 5* reruns, which were held at the time by TNT. But the Turner network made it difficult for anyone else to purchase the television series that they launched. Leery about selling Sci-Fi Channel two TV series, and then perhaps watching them become successful there, TNT attached an exorbitant price tag to the properties.

"I don't understand, and I never have, the whole studio fear," says Holden. "What it is that makes them so fearful of the possibility that if they find [a promising TV property], if they're not going to follow through themselves, that someone else can take it and make it a hit. Let the show go where it's meant to be. Because then, that way, the material gets out there. It's like, 'Hey, if it doesn't work here, then it'll work there.'"

Warner Bros., the production company that financed the show, decided to "fold and hold" the sets, and allow the show to air in June with the hopes that strong ratings would prompt a second season. But additional complications such as actors contracts and studio space rentals made a rebirth too difficult and expensive.

In 1999, Scot Safon, TNT's vice-president of marketing, talked with Rob Owen, a reporter with the *Post-Gazette*. Safon told Owen that the network's expectations for *Crusade* didn't synch with what was delivered. "The scripts were very intelligent and well-rendered but extremely heavy on the talk and light on action," Safon said. "Joe was providing an adventure of the mind, and the network expectation was that it would be more visceral. That kind of back-and-forth between a network and a creator is part and parcel of what happens every day in Hollywood.

"I don't think it was the nature of Joe's deal with us that he would consider all input and agree to none of it," Safon said. "The actual execution was the flash point here. The creator and the network had fundamentally different expectations in not only what the end product would be, but what the process would be."

Fans were well aware, even before the first episode aired, that the show had been stalled by production problems. They hoped that strong ratings would be racked up, thus encouraging the network to reconsider its decision. A lot of eyes were on the ratings reports. When *Crusade* did begin airing on June 9, 1999, the network advertised it as a "limited series," which sounded foreboding.

Had the show continued, there was at least four new scripts ready to be filmed.

In "Value Judgments," written by *Crusade*'s reference editor, Fiona Avery, the *Excalibur* crew attempted to break into a vault on a planet and discovered that it was actually held shut by a "telepathic lock" requiring a telepath with a P10 telepathic rating. And since Matheson's rating was only a P6, they looked to another telepath named Al to help them break it open. Arriving at the residence, Gideon and his team were shocked to discover that Al was Psi-Cop fugitive Alfred Bester (to have been played by guest star Walter Koenig who originated the character in *Babylon 5*). On the run since the Telepath War and the dismantling of the Psi-Corps organization, Bester had been "laying low." In exchange for his liberty, Bester agreed to attempt opening the lock. Once unlocked, Dr. Chambers discovered water with unusual properties that would be valuable in medical treatment. Meanwhile, as requested, Bester was ejected into hyperspace in a shuttle and later picked up by a rogue Psi-Corps vessel.

The next script written for the show, slated to be the 21st episode of the season, was titled "Ends of the Earth" by J. Michael Straczynski. Gideon learned that an alien ship, quite possibly the same one that destroyed his earlier vessel, the *Cerberus*, was in the vicinity of the *Excalibur*. Almost recklessly, he pursued the enemy hoping to avenge those who died aboard the *Cerberus*. The *Excalibur* pursued the enemy ship into Hyperspace and into an asteroid field.

In a script intended to be the season finale, "End of the Line," writer Straczynski resurrected a link to the main villains in *Babylon 5*—the Shadows. Resembling large spiders, the Shadows (a malevolent race from 1,000 years ago) fought their nemesis, the Vorlons. Both races entered dormancy at the end of that conflict. The Shadows

and the Vorlons were defeated by Captain Sheridan's massive coalition, the Army of Light, and the two long-time enemies agreed to leave the galaxy in peace.

In this story, Gideon and the *Excalibur* traced an alien signal related to the destruction of the *Cereberus* to an obscure asteroid. There, they were surprised to discover an Earthforce base. They're warned away, but Gideon covertly returned to the base with Galen's help. Skulking around inside the base, Gideon made a startling discovery. Earthforce personnel have secretly collected Shadow tech left behind to exploit, for their own nefarious purposes. The base commander offered Gideon an opportunity to join his team. But that's when Galen blasted his way into the area, and pulled Gideon out of harm's way. With Galen's help, Gideon returned to the *Excalibur*. Armed with this newfound knowledge, Gideon swore that he would do everything possible to expose the operation. Gideon ordered *Excalibur* to Mars. There, just as he was about to convene an important meeting with the Mars government, a hidden assassin set his gun sight on Gideon ... and fired.

This was the cliffhanger that would have ended *Crusade*'s first season.

On December 7, 2004, Warner Bros. Home Video released a *Crusade* DVD box set containing all 13 episodes. When the behind-the-scenes extras were being assembled, and Straczynski was asked to provide commentary on episodes, he was quite happy to do so. The *Babylon 5* DVDs were selling extremely well and it was hoped that *Crusade* would sell just as well. However, he laid down the provision that he would do so if he could tell "the real story" behind the making of the show and how he felt TNT had shot themselves in the foot.

They videotaped his comments, recorded his audio commentary on two episodes and continued with the DVD production. When the DVDs were released, news quickly reached fans that in the first pressing, Straczynski's "The Truth" commentary was not used. Another interview, filmed earlier, had been substituted. Straczynski was upset and demanded that, in the second pressing, they remove his episode commentaries as he felt their failure to use his "Truth" commentary was a breach of contract. All future editions of the *Crusade* DVDs will have no audio commentaries.

One unusual aspect of the show was the way in which the producers approached the depiction of "virtual alien worlds." Rather than make their own decisions about the environment's look, producers Netter and Copeland decided to go outside of the moviemaking industry for consultations. For every story in which the *Excalibur* would visit, say, an alien dead world (as seen in "Racing the Night" and "The Memory of War"), a copy of the script was sent to scientists at NASA's Jet Propulsion Laboratory (JPL) with detailed questions from the filmmakers who wanted advice on how best to depict planetary and environmental situations.

John Copeland felt strongly that basing their fiction on scientific reality would be more inspiring and visually interesting than creating their own fiction.

A formalized relationship was hatched between Babylonian Productions and JPL's Technology Affiliates Program. This meant that whenever the production submitted scientific questions, JPL's then–TAP Business Alliances Manager, Joan Horvath, would route the query to the best qualified resource person who would reply with detailed notes. The various departments on the show (visual effects, costumes, production design) would then adjust their creative work. This meant that when we saw Mars in the premier episode, JPL's fingerprints were present.

Beyond just helping in visualizing alien worlds and environments, JPL's advice influenced production designer John Iacovelli's concept and execution of the starship *Excalibur*.

Asked to describe JPL's relationship with *Crusade*, Horvath replies, "Any science fiction show has to balance entertainment, suspension of disbelief, and a desire to have as accurate an extrapolation of science as possible. A lot of times moving the story ahead (to travel faster than light, for example) has to trump science accuracy. But I think where we were the most useful for the production staff was in helping them brainstorm. For example, we'd find them pictures of planets, rocks and so on — and the art department could run with things they might never have found on their own but were more interesting-looking than random creations would have been."

Horvath later became the CEO of Takeoff Technologies, a consulting firm that specialized in bridging the gap between Hollywood and technologists.

"I remember one of the first questions we got was, 'Will there be floor lamps in *Crusade*'s time?' says Horvath. "This sounds like a ridiculous question, but it has implications for how power is transmitted, how people operate. I actually use that question as an icebreaker in a graduate class I teach about innovation. So I think the bottom line was: Both sides helped the other brainstorm a bit, and certainly I liked the result. I just wish there had been more episodes!"

Director Tony Dow, who helmed two episodes, actually has a visual effects background, having worked in the made-for-television movies *The Adventures of Captain Zoom* and *Doctor Who* in a visual effects capacity.

"I'm not sure how helpful [their advice] really was, although it sounded great, because the JPL guys didn't understand the filmmaking process," admits Dow. "I read the notes each week hoping to find some little thing I could incorporate. As I recall, the only thing I used was a note that said the most useful item on the space capsules is gaffer's tape, which I thought was a kick, so I went around the command center on the ship sticking gaffer's tape on the walls, holding up wires or whatever. The crew thought I was nuts and I'm sure nobody ever noticed the makeshift repair work. As for the virtual sets, I don't recall them having much impact on the filming. In my shows, I think paintings were used to extend and/or expand an environment, which meant we were working on a constructed set with blue screen in the background or out a window."

Marjean Holden remarks, "We did such great work for the time frame we were given and what we were given. We did our absolute best and had fun. And had we continued, it would have been like *Babylon 5* which would have been absolutely fantastic. It's a shame because the *Babylon 5* universe was never explored and tapped into. From what Joe was saying, and what they told us about the story, there were such possibilities. It was going to be amazing."

CAST NOTES

Gary Cole (Capt. Matthew Gideon): Cole began his acting career on stage in Chicago and has Off-Broadway credits in New York. He began acting as Snoopy in a high school production of *You're a Good Man, Charlie Brown*. His diverse range of film and television roles include the evil sheriff in *American Gothic* (1995) and Mike Brady in *The Brady Bunch Movie* (1995) and its sequel *A Very Brady Sequel* (1996). He was astronaut Edgar Mitchell in HBO's award-winning mini-series *From the Earth to the Moon* and played the U.S. vice-president on *The West Wing*.

Tracy Scoggins (Capt. Elizabeth Lochley): See the *Babylon 5* chapter Cast Notes.

Daniel Dae Kim (John Matheson): Born in South Korea, Kim has been seen on *NYPD Blue*, and *Seinfeld*. After *Crusade* he landed roles in *24* and hit it big in the role of Jin on ABC's monster hit *Lost*. In 2005, *People* magazine named him as one of the Sexiest Men Alive.

David Allen Brooks (Max Eilerson): Brooks' first professional role was on *The Edge of Night* in 1981. He's made TV series guest star appearances on *Quantum Leap*, *The Sentinel*, *JAG*, and *Walker, Texas Ranger*. His feature credits includes *Jack Frost 2: Revenge of the Mutant Killer Snowman* (2000), *Castaway* (2000) and *Dodgeball* (2001).

Carrie Dobro (Dureena Nafeal): Originally from New York, Dobro's first role in science fiction television was Kulai in the ABC SF series *Hypernauts*, produced by John Copeland. She's appeared in *Beverly Hills 90210*, *Silk Stalkings* and *The Young and the Restless*. A two-time Dramalogue winner, Carrie has appeared in over 50 stage productions Off-Broadway and in regional theaters. She's appeared in every genre from Shakespeare to farce. She also does standup comedy.

Peter Woodward (Galen): Woodward was born into a family of actors: His father is Edward Woodward (*The Equalizer*), who guest-starred on *Crusade* as a fellow Technomage in "The Long Road." His brother and sister are also actors. A graduate of the Royal Academy of Dramatic Arts, Peter joined the Royal Shakespeare Company and appeared in productions such as *A Midsummer Night's Dream*. He's also a fight arranger, writer and producer. His interest in weapons and history led him to producing and hosting the History Channel's documentary *Conquest* (2002–2005). He wrote a feature, *Closing the Ring* (2007), directed by Richard Attenborough. He's also guest-starred on *Stargate Atlantis* ("The Tower"). Woodward reprised his role as Galen in the direct-to-DVD movie *Babylon 5: The Lost Tales* (2007).

Marjean Holden (Dr. Sarah Chambers): Holden spent 20 years in front of the camera as an actress and stuntwoman. She was a master vampire in John Carpenter's *Vampires* (1998), a four-armed fighting machine in *Mortal Kombat: Annihilation* (1997), and a bad girl in *George of the Jungle 2* (2003) and *Hostage* (2005). She got her start in *Bill and Ted's Excellent Adventure* (1989) and co-starred with Daniel Goddard in *Beastmaster: The Legend Continues*. TV guest star roles included *Star Trek: DS9*, *Tales from the Crypt* and *JAG*. Recently, she left the acting world and has focused her energies on being a producer and a motivational speaker.

SOURCES

Garcia, Frank. "*Babylon 5: Crusade:* The Doomed Series— The Sequel to *Babylon 5*—premieres on TNT." *Cinefantastique* 31:7, August, 1999.

Owen, Rob. "TNT Cancels 'Crusade' Before Its Launch Date, but Not Before Giving a Novice Actor His Big Break." *Post-Gazette*, June 6, 1999.

Dark Angel

(2000–2002)

In the year 2019, Max, a genetically enhanced female super-soldier, has escaped from a secret government institution. Living in Seattle, Washington, under an assumed identity, Max tries to lead a normal life while searching for her genetic brothers and sisters who are also loose in the world.

Cast: Jessica Alba (Max, X5–452), Michael Weatherly (Logan Cale/"Eyes Only"), Kevin Durand (Joshua) *Year 2*, Jensen Ackles (Alec) *Year 2*, Alimi Ballard ("Herbal Thought"), Richard Gunn ("Sketchy"), J.C. Mackenzie (Reagan "Normal" Ronald), Valerie Rae Miller ("Original Cindy"), Jennifer Blanc (Kendra Maibaum) *Year 1*, John Savage (Don Lydecker) *Year 1*, Ashley Scott (Asha) *Year 2*, Martin Cummins (Ames White) *Year 2*

Created by: James Cameron, Charles Eglee; **Executive Producers:** James Cameron, Charles H.

Eglee, Rene Echevarria *Year 2*; ***Co-Executive Pro-ducers:*** Rene Echevarria, Joe Ann Fogle *Year 1*, Rae Sanchini, Marjorie David, Kenneth Biller *Year 2*; ***Supervising Producers:*** Steve Beers *Year 1*, Patrick Harbinson; ***Producers:*** Stephen Sassen, Janace Tashjian, Rae Sanchini *Year 1*, Michael Angeli *Year 2*; ***Co-Producers:*** Janace Tashjian, Doris Egan, Ron French *Year 1*, George Grieve, Gina Lamar, Moira Kirland Dekker *Year 2*; ***Associate Producer:*** Gina Lamar *Year 1*; Consulting ***Producers:*** Ira Steven Behr, David Simkins *Year 1*, Chip Johannessen; ***Writers included:*** Charles Eglee, Rene Echevarria, Doris Egan, Jose Molina, David Zabel, Moira Dekker, Michael Angeli, Ira Steven Behr; ***Directors included:*** David Nutter, Michael Katleman, Paul Shapiro, Jeff Woolnough, John T. Kretchmer, Thomas J. Wright, James Whitmore Jr., Allan Kroeker, Bryan Spicer, Kenneth Biller, James Cameron; ***Director of Photography:*** David Geddes; ***Production Designer:*** Jerry Waneck; ***Guest Stars included:*** Peter Bryant (Bling), Byron Mann (Det. Sung), Fulvio Cecere (Manticore Agent Peter Sandoval), William Gregory Lee (Zack), Nicole Bilderback (Brin), Robert Gossett (Col. McGinnis), Brian Markinson (Dr. Sam Carr), Jake C. Bell (Sebastian), Rehka Sharma (Dr. Shankar), Lisa Ann Cabasa (Tinga), Nana Visitor (Manticore Director Renfro), Craig Veroni (Otto)

20th Century–Fox Television/Cameron-Eglee Productions/Fox Television; 2000–2002; 60 minutes; 42 episodes; DVD status: Complete series

On the evening of March 23, 1998, standing in front of a television audience of about 57 million people, producer-writer-director James Cameron held two Academy Awards in his hands and declared "I'm the king of the world!" He had just won the Best Picture and Best Director awards for his film *Titanic* which, by the end of the evening, was given 11 Oscar statuettes. It was a film with a shooting budget of over $200 million that, incredibly, grossed approximately $1.8 billion worldwide, making it the highest grossing film of all time (not adjusted for inflation).

The question on everyone's mind was "What will James Cameron do next?" For that answer, flash forward to the evening of October 3, 2000. Fox Television network premiered a two-hour film titled *Dark Angel,* starring a relatively unknown teenage actress named Jessica Alba. It was the debut of an action-adventure science fiction series created by Cameron and his partner Charles Eglee.

The time: the year 2019. The place: Seattle. A lithe young woman, Max Guevera, by day appeared to be an ordinary bike courier for Jam Pony Express. She lived in a condemned building, rode a sleek black motorcycle, and had a circle of close friends at the workplace. But Max's deep secret was her upbringing: She was a genetically enhanced super-soldier who had escaped, ten years earlier, from Manticore, a secret government facility where children were bred to be soldiers and assassins. Code-named "X5," this particular batch of soldiers had special and very deadly abilities. Their vision was like telescopic lens. They could zoom in on objects very far away. Their physical strength was exceptional. Their hearing was also heightened. They could dodge bullets with their super-speed. X5 soldiers were also capable of leaping up or down great heights with ease. As seen in the opening two-hour film, Max even had the remarkable skill of listening to the speed dial tones of a telephone and identifying the numbers being used. Over the course of the series, other abilities (such as the ability to breathe underwater for long periods of time) were revealed.

One evening in 2009, in Gillette, Wyoming, the Manticore children (including Max) burst out and scrambled into the snowy forest. Their specialized training helped them elude their masters and, despite being pursued by security teams on snowmobiles, the "Transgenics" slipped into the night and scattered into the world. Donald Lydecker, one of Manticore's senior officials, made it his personal mission to hunt down and retrieve every one of the soldiers who had escaped. An identifying mark that would help him find the fugitives, unique to all of the escapees: a tattoo on the backs of their necks—a bar code signifying their designation. At Manticore, Max was known as code name X5–452.

In the ten years since the escape, Max made her way into the world and settled down in Seattle. In the series opener, she encountered Logan Cale while attempting to snatch an Egyptian statue from his apartment. Interrupted before she could succeed, she smashed her way out. Impressed with her abilities, Logan used his skills and resources as the secretive, underground cyberjournalist "Eyes Only," and confronted her at her workplace, the courier company Jam Pony Express. Logan tried to convince Max to use her abilities to help people, but she was more interested in staying buried and looking for her genetic "brothers and sisters."

Later, while protecting a woman, Lauren, who was ready to testify against a mobster, Logan got injured in a spectacular gunfight. Max visited him at the hospital and her emotions were stirred. Her compassion for Lauren's child, Sophy, who had been snatched by the mobsters, pushed her forward. She went directly to the home of the mobster, Edgar Sonrisa, and convinced him that she could deliver Lauren to him. Using her abilities as an X5 soldier, Max learned where Sophy was being held and managed to retrieve her, from under the nose of her own pursuer, Lydecker, and returned the child to her mother.

Months later, Logan was continuing to recover from his injuries, and now used a wheelchair. Max and Logan came to an agreement: Max would help Logan save the world in exchange for his investigations into her past and Manticore's nefarious deeds.

"Chick and I set for ourselves a goal of creating a kick-ass one-hour TV series together," says James Cameron, series executive producer and co-creator with Charles "Chick" Eglee, an old friend from the days when they worked on Roger Corman film projects, notably *Piranha II: The Spawning* (1983). The duo formed a production company and got Fox Television interested in a series.

"We didn't want to do a comedy," says Cameron. "Both of our strengths were in drama. He was less tuned into science fiction than I was. We talked about a number of different ideas. Some were straight dramas. One of them was a family drama. A couple of others were science fiction. We narrowed it down to four or five contenders. The original title between the two of us for *Dark Angel* was 'Experimental Girl.'"

One of the predominant themes in Cameron's films has been strong female action heroes. The film characters Sarah Conner from the *Terminator* films, Lindsay Brigman from *The Abyss* and Helen Tasker from *True Lies* are all prototypes of the modern-day big-screen action heroine. (Granted, Cameron inherited Ellen Ripley from Ridley Scott's *Alien* when he filmed *Aliens*, but he made her even more powerful by having her lead an assault team to a planetary surface filled with deadly aliens.) With the decision to turn his talents to a television series, Cameron retained his attraction to, and fascination with, this archetypical character.

"We started with the idea that she was a genetic construct," continues Cameron. "She looked normal on the outside but was different on the cellu-lar, genetic level. We explored what that could mean. Do her eyes look different? Were there things that manifested themselves? Were there negatives to it? We wanted her to have flaws, things that were built in — like Kryptonite."

Cameron refers to the fact that Max and the other X5s had one major chink in their biological armor: a neurological flaw that sends her into an epileptic-like seizure without a drug called Tryptophan (a simple food additive, an ingredient in milk) which was needed to raise the levels of Serotonin in her brain. "That actually went away as the series progressed," he says. "But in the pilot and in some early episodes she had a deficiency."

Beyond the character sketch of a genetically enhanced heroine, Cameron and Eglee added another layer, detailing the sociopolitical landscape of this future world. Max lived in a post-disaster environment where, a few months after the X5s escaped in 2009, an electromagnetic pulse exploded over the U.S., wreaking havoc with world economy and all electronics. The country was sent into a tailspin and even now ten years later, it was still trying to recover. "We were intrigued by the idea of a future that was in some ways post-apocalyptic or post–social collapse," says Cameron. "The more we talked about it, the more we got excited about it. So I would say it was a good hybrid of my interests and his interests."

With a series outline and characters sketched out, Cameron and Eglee began casting the series and their most important task was to find a young, unknown actress to play their super-heroine. The requirements were daunting: She would have to be a very physical, and yet attractive woman who could handle strong dramatic scenes and engage in incredible action (hand-to-hand martial arts, extensive wire work, fast motorcycle driving, etc.). Casting the lead so early in the process was important because physical training for the specifics of the role would be required. The regimen included weight training five days a week, with gymnastics three times a week.

According to an Eglee interview in *Starlog* magazine, 1,000 girls from Los Angeles, New York, Vancouver and Toronto were considered. Cameron says that when the audition videotapes were whittled down to about 20 or 30, he started looking at them. "We were going through them so fast, I didn't even register names. I think we were kind of numb, you know?" says Cameron. "I looked at everybody." When he got to Jessica Alba's tape, he noticed that she wasn't that impressive. It was a scene where Max visited Logan at the hospital after his near-fatal encounter with the bad guys. "She had her head down, she was reading out of the script, her hair didn't look that great," recalls Cameron. "She wasn't really in shape. I don't think she ever really worked out very much. Everybody thinks, 'Ohh, it's a no-brainer, she's so gorgeous, she's so beautiful!' But she was 17 years old. She wasn't particularly well represented at the time. She didn't present herself all that well. But there was something about the way she read the scene that copped an attitude that I liked. I thought, 'This girl needs to be defiant. She needs to have such great confidence in herself. [The character] has been a loner. She survived on her own. She's unique in the world. [Jessica] has to express that. She had some major attitude — I liked that.'"

As he made his way through the various tapes, Cameron found himself returning to Alba's tape, and then said, "I want to see her!"

"We wound up seeing [another] girl too and reading her but there was definitely a spark there with Jessica. When she came in to read, it was instantaneous. Chick was in the room for the reading. I worked with her for a while. It wasn't quite a full-on screen test, [but] it was more than just a cold reading in the office. We started seeing her bone structure, her eyes— what kind of an actor she was. She was quick on her feet. She had a very alive mind. I look for that in an actor. There's so much thrown at them so quickly. They have to be very mentally agile. She just seemed like she was going to be able to pull it off. If you think about it, it was going to be a very scary thing. There's a lot of pressure and scrutiny."

With the cast and script finalized, the company set up shop in Vancouver, Canada. Directing the two-hour pilot was veteran genre director David Nutter, who had successfully launched *Millennium*, *Space: Above and Beyond* and *Roswell*. Nutter recalls how sharply drawn the pilot script was. "Everything was so visually detailed and clear what to do," he says. "It was really written for a director to come in and do this how they wanted it. It's quite awe-inspiring to sit down with Jim Cameron and say, 'What do you want?' I did three days of meetings with Jim where we went through the script scene by scene. And he gave me thoughts and what the intent of scenes would be, and then said, 'Go make it!'"

By this time, almost all of the cast had been finalized, except for the actor to play antagonist Don Lydecker. Nutter says he was in on that casting and helped give the job to John Savage.

One of Nutter's favorite pilot memories was spending a Sunday afternoon with 40 Manticore kids as they received very radical haircuts, more than a buzz cut, as required by the script. "Jim Cameron was very big into making sure all of the kids' haircuts were, as he would say, 'high and tight,'" chuckles Nutter. "Some of these kids had long, long hair. And a lot of parents [of the kids] were taking lots of pictures. It was quite an experience!"

For Nutter, three sequences were especially effective, starting with the Manticore children breaking out of the high-security facility and scattering in the snow in their bare feet. Another sequence was a major stunt moment when Max jumps from a major metropolitan building and onto the roof of the next building. "We had a stuntwoman, Melissa Stubbs; she flew from the 40th floor of one tower to the 40th floor of another tower," says Nutter. With five cameras strategically placed all around the area, it was actually done live with Stubbs, and then later on a blue-screen stage with Alba for realism. The whole sequence only required two takes. "We did two sequences. One was a freefall from the side of a building and the other was a swing from one side to the other. It was a very tense evening."

The third aspect of the pilot that Nutter looks back on is the birth and growth of the dramatic relationship between Logan and Max. "The personal stuff between the two of them was really important and strong," he says. "One of my favorite parts is a scene that was actually reshot, that I wasn't involved in. That was the very ending, when Jessica goes to see Michael in his wheelchair. When I shot the scene, she was a little more emotionally afraid and felt more emotion about what had happened to Michael and not quite as tough. But the thought was she was too emotional, too much, too quick. They wanted [that emotion] held for the end of the scene, when she saw the picture of her friend, who was still an escapee.

"I liked it because you saw the other side of Jessica's character. That she had feelings for Michael's character. That she felt bad about what happened to him."

During the pilot, Cameron spent his time in Los Angeles supervising the scriptwriting, casting and some makeup designs. "David looked like he had it pretty well in hand," he says. "Chick and I were writing the script right up to the last second. Chick was more involved on a day-to-day basis with the pilot. I reviewed the dailies, making comments, was involved in the editing primarily. There were a couple of stunt gigs that I helped choreograph, from afar, like some of the wire stuff when she jumps off the roof and transfers to the other building."

Initial critical reaction to *Dark Angel* was strongly positive with a few corners of dissension. Howard Rosenberg of the *Los Angeles Times* (October 2000) noted, "If pouty faces and sexy walks could destroy, the highly arresting Max would be wiping out the entire planet. It's actually quite moving. And she looks great on her bike."

Rolling Stone magazine remarked, "Instantly addictive! Superfine babes with bar codes!"

Time magazine gave the series its "Biggest Buzz" note and also said, "[Alba] has the grace and moves needed for all that running, rappelling and cat burgling, but with an emotional range unusual among action babes."

The *Orlando Sentinel* declared: "Television's newest warrior woman possesses skills worthy of Catwoman, Xena, Emma Peel and Wonder Woman."

But not all voices were singing the praises of the show. In a *Sci-Fi Weekly* review, Cindy White noted, "The main problem is that Alba doesn't breathe any life into the character of Max. She's too cool, too perfect. Her range of delivery extends from flat to monotone. It doesn't help that she's given dialogue that's supposed to sound like hip future-speak (try counting the number of times she uses the word *whack*) but that just comes off awkward."

Joyce Millman of Salon.com, an online magazine, remarked, "Cameron and Eglee give us very little incentive to care about Max as a *person,* the way we care about Buffy or Faith. And that's because Max is little more than lips and ass and a premise reminiscent of other, better shows. *Dark Angel* is a wish-fulfillment show for every guy who's had all he can *stand* of mature heroines with mommy power and big muscles. Lousy with jailbait fetishism, *Dark Angel* is the most expensive Britney Spears video ever made."

In the first season, Max juggled "Eyes Only" missions (helping other people by using her abilities) and continued to search for her Manticore brothers and sisters. She also managed Jam Pony life which often intruded with the other activities. In "Prodigy" she even had an encounter with her pursuer Lydecker when they were both involved in a hostage situation. Eventually, Max's Manticore brothers Zack and Ben did catch up with her in Seattle as did her sister, Tinga. But lurking in the shadows were always Lydecker and his Manticore minions. Max also had to contend with the fact that her closest friend, Original Cindy, eventually learned of her true identity as a superhuman X5 and her alliance with Logan Cale.

In the season finale, Lydecker's position at Manticore was usurped by Madame X (a.k.a. Dr. Elizabeth Renfro) and he did the unthinkable: He

Jessica Alba as Max Guevera in *Dark Angel* (© Fox Television).

collaborated with the escaped X5s in an attempt to take down Manticore. Although the DNA lab was destroyed, the season ended with Max apparently dead and in the hands of the Manticore handlers.

"The first season had some great stuff in it," notes Cameron. "I thought it ended strongly. Max gets shot and needs a heart transplant. I thought there were a couple of episodes that were a little goofy and there was some makeup stuff I didn't like."

In year two, Max was brought back to life when Zack sacrificed himself so that she would live. His heart was transplanted into her. Still held prisoner inside Manticore for "retraining and indoctrination," a euphemism for more brainwashing, Max yearned to escape. While there, she discovered hidden labyrinths in the facility sewers that held more insidious scientific experiments. The "transgenic" beings imprisoned there were visibly non-human, the results of early attempts to experiment and commingle human and non-human DNA. Their genetic code were spliced and scrambled, making them spent and forgotten *Island of Dr. Moreau* refugees. One in particular, Joshua, who had a "dog-face" because he was spliced with canine DNA, became friends with Max. Joshua claimed he was the first "transgenic" of the experiments created by a scientist named "Sandeman." In spite of heavy prosthetics makeup, actor Kevin Durand was able to take the character and make him sympathetic and also convey a personality.

Meanwhile, Logan exposed Manticore in an "Eyes Only" streaming video bulletin, finally alerting the general public. But he didn't have Manticore's location. To silence "Eyes Only," Renfro extracted the information from Max. Alec and Joshua helped Max break out of the facility and she rushed to his apartment to save Logan, but their kiss became deadly to him. She was infected with a deadly "genetically targeted retro-virus" designed to kill Logan through physical contact. To get the antidote, Max returned to Manticore, but found it in flames. She freed the remaining X5s and "transgenics" and was able to confront Dr. Renfro and demand the antidote. A guard's bullet struck Renfro. Before she died, Renfro croaked, "Find Sandeman!" Max escaped with the antigen needed to save Logan.

All the "inmates" had now escaped into the world. With Joshua in tow, Max returned to Seattle where, with Logan's help, she found an abandoned and unused house where Joshua could stay.

"There were some cool, interesting characters that were created through makeup," says Cameron. "I actually did the design sketches for Joshua's makeup. I didn't sculpt it but I designed the look of the character, which was fun."

Over the course of the second season, Max dealt with new adversaries who were well aware of what she looked like and that she was living in Seattle. It made life more difficult. However, this time she had more help. There was Joshua who was around to be a friend and advise when he could. Alec, a fellow X5 who escaped with her from Manticore, joined her in the employ of Jam Pony. Alec was played by Jensen Ackles, who had already played Ben, Alec's twin, in the first season. The introduction of both Joshua and Alec served to bring a more lighthearted feel to the series. But life for the trio continued to be dangerous.

The new adversaries were Ames White, a Manticore agent charged with the challenging task of retrieving the escaped transgenics and X5s. And with so many transgenics and X5s loose, Max, Alec and Joshua constantly had their hands full making sure they weren't caught by enemies, without having themselves exposed in the process.

In addition to all this, Ames White was a member of a secret breeding cult, a formidable force even stronger than the Manticore X5s. There was also Sandeman, the scientist who engaged in the secret Manticore experiments that spawned the transgenics and the X5s, and a renegade member of the cult.

Max and Logan's relationship, which reached a romantic plateau in season one, was now even more complicated because of the Manticore retrovirus. Consequently, romantic overtures were not possible until an antidote to the virus could be found.

Behind the cameras, Jessica Alba and Michael Weatherly became romantically intertwined and were actually engaged for a period of just over two years, ending in August 2003. Director John Kretchmer, who directed Alba in "Female Trouble," noticed the relationship. "I don't think that being involved with each other necessarily helps with chemistry," Kretchmer says. "Often that gets in the way. Frankly, I think it is generally better to deal with actors who are not involved. They don't bring their issues from home, and they can't gang up on me as easily. There are, of course, several famous exceptions: The Lunts, Paul Newman and Joanne Woodward, Jessica Tandy and Hume Cronyn — all had tremendously successful marriages and professional partnerships. But my experience has taught me otherwise."

"I liked the direction we took in the second season," says Cameron. "We were going somewhere with it. We had a real payoff in mind and were laying in those seeds towards the last third of the second season.... Chick and I worked closely with a really good writing team that really hit their stride."

But unfortunately, as history showed, Fox Television didn't agree and the series came to a screeching halt at the end of the second season. It was because of Cameron's strong personality and passion that the show ended not with a whimper but with a bang.

"We wanted to culminate with the season finale ["Freak Nation"] which I directed, opening the door to a new version of *Dark Angel* in the third season where they were much more out in the street, and they weren't quite as undercover," says Cameron. "It was about true humans, or non-genetically altered ones, having to adapt to living with these people in their midst. It was a lot like [the Marvel Comics superhero group] X-Men."

The finale, which was not intended to end the series, became in effect a cliffhanger without resolution (except in novelizations authored by Max Allan Collins subsequently published by Del Rey Books; two books directly followed the end of the series).

In "Freak Nation," the world is aware of the existence of "transgenics" inside a 20-block region known as Terminal City. Many of them (including the series X5, X6 and X7s) were barricading themselves in for safety. But on the outside, Ames White prepared an assault team with orders to kill Max. Life became complicated when Joshua and a pregnant X5 were pursued by the authorities and they ended up in a hostage situation at Jam Pony Express where Max and Alec's identity as X5 refugees were exposed. Logan witnessed the tense situation via TV's live coverage and he prepared to help. An attempt to escape Jam Pony for Terminal City failed when rooftop sharpshooters killed one of the non-human transgenics. Ames White, now in charge of the incident, ordered his team to mount an assault, while inside everyone prepared for the invasion.

As White's men entered the second floor of the building with all their weaponry drawn, the X5s ambushed them, dropping down from the ceiling. Hand-to-hand combat and gunfire broke out among the combatants. When the X5s succeeded

in putting down the invaders, they developed an ingenious plan to exit: Dressed as soldiers to give the illusion that White's men had succeeded in the mission to capture their prey, Alec escorted Max and the non-human transgenics to the waiting van, and quickly departed for Terminal City. When the police negotiator found White and his men inside, a car chase ensued all the way to Terminal City. Safely arriving at their destination, Max and Alec averted a bloody confrontation with the police when Terminal City's non-human residents surrounded them.

Three days later, the siege continued. On the roof of their camp, Joshua raised his homemade flag and they pledged allegiance to their solidarity.

When a director for the season finale "fell out" of the schedule, James Cameron decided it would be fun to direct the segment. "I remember everyone was tired. We were coming into the end of the season. The last thing they wanted to do was deal with the hardest episode ever. But when I stepped in and directed, we got everybody together and said, 'Look, I'm not going to anything that's outside the bounds of what's possible. You have to tell me what you can and can't do.' I think everyone just wanted to do the maximum."

Like his feature filmmaking, Cameron took the energy and pacing that was his trademark, and applied it here. Filled with action, it was ratcheting up the excitement for a potent finale. "It was pretty insane," says Cameron. "There was a three-day stretch where we were shooting a big fight scene.

We did 95 [camera] setups in one day. We did 115 setups in the following day. And I think something in the high 80s in the third day. We just went gonzo! The 'A' operator and the 'B' operator and myself, sometimes we'd all be in on the setup. We didn't use dollies. We didn't use sticks [tripods]. It was all hand-held. I was hand-holding on the shoulder, on the knee, down low, kind of shotgunning from under the arm in kind of a football position and we were just hauling ass.

"I had a great time. It was physically and mentally exhausting but we really pushed the envelope with a small, well-trained crew."

But the shoot did not go well for everyone. WWE wrestler Amy Dumas, best known as Lita, endured an injury during the major fight scene with Jessica Alba's stunt double. As she described in her 2003 Simon & Schuster autobiography, *Lita — A Less Traveled R.O.A.D. — The Reality of Amy Dumas* (pages 291–299), she was hired to guest star as one of White's assault squad. The scene had Lita engaging in one of her signature wrestling moves, the "hurricanrana," which is jumping on a person's shoulder and using your body to "throw" the opponent over yourself. As she describes it in her book, "I jumped off a desk, up onto her shoulders and as I was swinging through, she lost her balance and buckled at the knees. As her legs collapsed under her, she dropped me and I landed square on my head and shoulders." After the stunt, Dumas realized she couldn't get up and needed help. In the following days she began noticing how badly she was feeling and it was eventually determined that what appeared to have been a "stinger" injury was actually three cracks in her C5 and C6 vertebrae. In other words, she broke her neck. Surgery and 15 months of physical recovery followed.

Recalling the incident a little differently, James Cameron says, "Our contention is that we were not even shooting. She went into rehearsal. It was an old injury. It was something that she had gotten from the WWE days. But she was still in the WWE at that point. She definitely had an injury that manifested itself. But it wasn't from anything the stunt team did. She was showing them her move on a workout mat. And she hurt herself."

"Freak Nation" was Cameron's first opportunity to actually direct Alba in an episode. "She's such a pro," notes Cameron. "She was so 'there' for me. I think she was kind of hungry for real, honest-to-god character direction. Unfortunately, TV directors ... they're all about making the day one or two takes. I don't think I did anything more than three takes. But I was trying to give her the kind of input that would pull something out of her. She was pretty good in that episode. I mean, she was good in all the episodes. She generates from the inside — she doesn't need a lot of strong direction."

The finale's story was so dense that the final running time went beyond the standard 42 minutes and stretched to 50 minutes; it aired as a 90-minute special on Friday night, May 3, 2002.

Cameron reports that Fox TV wasn't very keen on the series and that worried him. "The reason I went into directing the finale was because I wanted [the network] to see what the potential for the next season would be," says Cameron. "In the final episode we put in all the seeds of the elements that would come into fruition. [Max] would go into the next level of her abilities."

Cameron wouldn't discuss the nature of the unmade third season's content, but the Second Season DVD release sheds light into the hidden backstory to the whole series. Co-creator Eglee revealed in the "Freak Nation" audio commentary that thousands of years ago, a comet had wiped out 90 percent of the human race but a few survived because of their unique genetic materials. This "antibody" was protected and preserved throughout the ages via a blood cult and survived into the modern age. The Manticore scientist, "Sandeman," broke away from the blood cult with the goal of spreading the antibody into the general public so that in "the next coming" of the comet, Earth's residents would not perish. Manticore was a military project, a splinter from this cult group, and Max was "The One"— the genetic model that was needed to distribute the cure to save humanity. "Max was going to be the savior of the human race! And that was why everybody was after her for so long," on the DVD commentary noted Eglee. "We were going to do some sort of an airburst, where she would spread this antibody through some sort of a cold or a flu ... to be dispersed through the human race and just have saved everyone. These people [transgenics} who are hated and are persecuted are going to hold the key to the survival of the human race.

"We were tacking towards something that was perhaps a little bit bigger in scope and it was going to involve the siege of Terminal City and have a cast of thousands and [was] probably going to be un-produceable."

At one point, the producers actually believed a green light was given for a third season. "They called us on Saturday and told us we were on the schedule and we'd been picked up," says Cameron. "We got together Saturday night and celebrated. Sunday goes by, and Monday morning we get a call saying, 'No, you're not on the schedule! It's been changed.' I've never heard of that happening. But then, I'd never been around television. In television, anything can happen!

"We were supposed to be on a plane on Monday to go to the [network] upfronts in New York on Tuesday. They called us that day and told us not to go! I was pissed! I won't make any bones about it. I would never make another series for Fox Television. I mean, I like the Fox guys on the feature side. All the network people at Fox are different now anyways, so maybe I shouldn't say never."

The reason for the cancellation, as Cameron understood it, was typical of television-making— the hard, cold numbers of corporate economics. "They were in this kind of freaked-out panic state about the ad revenues being slashed down," says Cameron. "Their entire annual revenues were cut down two-thirds of what it had been. They didn't know how to cope. It's not like they took us off and put a cheaper show in our place. It was just a knee-jerk, 'Try anything!' It was just like 'The ship is sinking, the plane is going down — try anything!' And that was the basis of the decision, I really believe."

Is this really the end of *Dark Angel*? Since other SFTV shows such as *Alien Nation, Farscape*, the Bionic shows, *Firefly* and of course *Star Trek* and *The X-Files* were able to reassemble their original casts for a film or mini-series, dead is not always dead. In other genres— drama and comedy — we have witnessed similar resurrections. Nostalgia continues to be a powerful enticement for producing such reunions and Cameron knows it. "There might be a *Dark Angel* movie some day," he says. "We've talked about it."

In the end Cameron, a renowned filmmaker with an extensive history in fantastic filmmaking on the big screen, says that he learned as much from this, his first foray into dramatic television production, as he does when he's doing big-budgeted feature films. Each medium, he says, has something to offer. "Even though I was able to use a lot of what I learned as a filmmaker, you're telling a story over such a long period of time," says Cameron. "The characters, themes and plots evolve very slowly. It's a completely different art form. How do you create a riveting hour and at the same time have it be a part of a much greater story arc that moves at such a glacial pace?

"You're keeping the long game in mind and you're working very rapidly with a team of writers, trying to create a great, punchy hour. And every hour, you sort of live or die by that hour. That's the nature of it, because of the way the ratings work. You're fighting a new battle every week. I didn't find the biggest challenge to be the budget aspects of it because people in television are used to working fast. The crews are used to that. You have to be inventive. You can't do the big makeup gig and you can't just throw visual effects at it. It forces you, in many ways, to be a better writer. I think the best writers are in television."

By contrast, Cameron feels that feature film screenwriters are a different breed with a different set of problems to overcome. "There is ... I don't want to say a laziness, but there is a lack of discipline because they can just write anything," he says. "But in television, you have to do it

through character. It's much trickier, especially when you're dealing with big themes and a big story arc. We were trying to do science fiction on a TV budget, which is always difficult.

"Dealing with science fiction sometimes it takes you down a path. As a filmmaker, I might be frustrated with a piece of makeup here and there, or something I considered to have weakened an episode, but overall I'm really proud of the series. I'm proud of what the writers created. I'm proud of what Jessica and the other actors were able to do."

CAST NOTES

Jessica Alba (Max Guevera): Alba was just 12 when she took her first acting class. Early television work included appearances on the medical drama series *Chicago Hope*; her feature film debut was in 1993's *Camp Nowhere*. She had a recurring role in Nickelodeon's 1994 comedy series *The Secret World of Alex Mack*. That same year she filmed the Australian-based TV series *Flipper* and became a PADI-certified scuba diver. Other TV series soon followed: *Brooklyn South, Beverly Hills 90210,* and *The Love Boat: The Next Wave.*

Alba's career soared to greater heights after *Dark Angel*'s cancellation in 2002. She vaulted into lead roles in major feature film releases such as *Honey, Sin City, Fantastic Four* and its sequel, *Fantastic Four: The Rise of the Silver Surfer.*

In their March 2006 issue, *Playboy* named her one of the 25 sexiest celebrities and the Sex Star of the Year. Alba objected to *Playboy* using a photo of her on their cover, implying she had a photo layout inside the magazine. (The photo was a promotional image from her 2005 feature *Into the Blue*.)

In their July 7, 2006, issue, *Entertainment Weekly* named Alba their "Must Girl of Summer."

Michael Weatherly (Logan Cale): Born in New York, Weatherly began his career on television with guest appearances on *The Cosby Show, Charmed*, and *The Crow: Stairway to Heaven*. Since *Dark Angel*, Weatherly has appeared in the series *JAG* and most recently in *Navy NCIS*.

Alimi Ballard (Herbal Thought): Ballard began acting in the early '80s in the daytime drama *Loving*. He guest-starred on a number of television series and appeared in the movie *Deep Impact* (1998). Aside from a semi-regular role on *Sabrina, the Teenage Witch*, most of Ballard's roles were guest appearances on such shows as *Nash Bridges* and *NYPD Blue*. Since *Dark Angel* he has been seen in *CSI* and in a semi-regular role in the series *NUMB3RS*.

Richard Gunn (Sketchy): Gunn graduated with honors from the University of California, Santa Cruz, then moved to Los Angeles to pursue an acting career. For four seasons he had supporting roles with Shakespeare Santa Cruz. He is best known for his role in *Dark Angel*.

J.C. MacKenzie (Normal): MacKenzie was born in Ontario, Canada. He was a 21-year-old student at Concordia University when he saw his first play. Within two years, he was accepted at the London Academy of Music and Dramatic Art. His first television appearance was in an episode of *Alfred Hitchcock Presents* in 1988. After that he appeared in many shows including *Baywatch*, *Law and Order*, and *Poltergeist: The Legacy*, He joined the cast of the short-lived series *Murder One* and appeared in several episodes of *The Practice*. He appeared in *Total Recall: 2070* and in *Earth: Final Conflict*. Since *Dark Angel*, Mackenzie has appeared in episodes of *Monk*, *CSI Miami*, *Law and Order: Special Victims Unit*, *CSI*, *Navy NCIS* and *24*.

Valerie Rae Miller ("Original Cindy"): Miller was born in Lafayette, Louisiana. She began her career as a stand-up comic. After landing her role in *Dark Angel*, Miller served as the host for the game shows *Gladiators 2000* and *Peer Pressure*. She was also the host of the short-lived *One Saturday Morning* on ABC.

Jennifer Blanc (Kendra Maibaum): Blanc was born in New York and attended that city's Professional Children's School. Her first television appearance was in a series called *Old Enough*. After that she appeared in *Beverly Hills 90210*, several episodes of *Hull High*, *Married with Children*, and *Saved by the Bell* and had a small role in *The Brady Bunch Movie* (1995). She was a semi-regular on *Party of Five* and made guest appearances on *Grace Under Fire*, *Touched by an Angel*, and *Providence*. Since *Dark Angel*, Blanc has appeared in *CSI* and *Veronica Mars*. She is the owner of a clothing store in Hollywood

John Savage (Lydecker): Savage was born in New York. His first major role was in Michael Cimino's breakthrough Vietnam movie *The Deer Hunter* in 1978. He was featured in the movie version of the musical *Hair* (1979) and later had a brief but powerful role in *The Thin Red Line*. He has also played many roles on the small screen including a notable guest appearance on *Star Trek: Voyager*'s two-part "Equinox." He had a recurring role on HBO's *Carnivale* and has

also been seen in *Law & Order: Special Victims Unit*.

Ashley Scott (Asha): Scott was born in Louisiana. After a career in New York as a fashion model, Scott moved to L.A. to pursue acting. She played a very small role in Steven Spielberg's *A.I.* before landing her role in *Dark Angel*. Afterwards she played Batman's daughter, Helena Kyle, in the short-lived superhero series *Birds of Prey* and acted in such films as *S.W.A.T.*, *Trespassing*, *Walking Tall*, and *Into the Blue*. Scott starred as Emily Sullivan on the CBS post-apocalyptic drama *Jericho* (2006).

Martin Cummins (Ames White): Cummins was born in North Delta in British Columbia, Canada. Following his first television appearance in the Canadian series *Danger Bay*, he appeared in *My Secret Identity*, *21 Jump Street*, *Omen IV: The Awakening* (1991), *The Commish*, several episodes of *Neon Rider*, *Highlander*, several episodes of *M.A.N.T.I.S.*, *Poltergeist: The Legacy* and two episodes of *The Outer Limits*. Since *Dark Angel* he has appeared in *Stargate SG-1*, *Andromeda* and several episodes of *Smallville*. He has also been seen in *Painkiller Jane*, *Kyle XY* and *The 4400*.

Kevin Durand (Joshua): Durand was born in Thunder Bay, Ontario, Canada. His first appearance was in an episode the series *Exhibit A: The Secrets of Forensic Science*. He had a small role in *Austin Powers: The Spy Who Shagged Me* (1999) and was seen in episodes of *The Outer Limits*, *E.R.*, and *Stargate SG-1*. Since *Dark Angel* Durand has appeared in the mini-series *Taken* and the pilot episode of the WB's *Tarzan*. He had roles in the movie *The Butterfly Effect* (2004), the television series *Touching Evil*, episodes of *Andromeda*, *CSI*, *The Dead Zone*, *Without a Trace* and the movie *Wild Hogs* (2007).

SOURCES

Boedeker, Hal. "Dazzling 'Dark Angel' Actress Takes Wing as a Futuristic Superheroine." *Orlando Sentinel*, October 3, 2000.

Dana, Will. *Dark Angel* Review. *Rolling Stone*, no. 851, October 12, 2000.

Dumas, Amy. *Lita: A Less Traveled R.O.A.D.: The Reality of Amy Dumas*. New York: Pocket, 2003.

Millman, Joyce. "Be Afraid, Be Very Afraid ... James Cameron's 'Dark Angel,' Full of Jailbait Fetishism, is Genetically Engineered T&A." Salon.com, October 3, 2000.

Poniewozik, James. "2020 Vision." Time 156:14, October 2, 2000.

Rosenberg, Howard. "New With a Twist: Foxy

Android and Dot.Com Detective." *Los Angeles Times*, October 3, 2000.

Spelling, Ian. "Dark Genesis—Thanks to Charles Eglee, Dark Angel will soon descend to TV." *Starlog* no. 279, October 2000.

White, Cindy. "Dark Angel James Cameron Brings a Cyber-sexy Anti-heroine to Television." *Sci-Fi Weekly*, October 2, 2000.

Dark Skies

(1996–1997)

A series about the secret war between hostile extraterrestrial aliens and a secret government agency, Majestic-12, against the backdrop of historical events in the United States during the 1960s.

Cast: Eric Close (John Loengard), Megan Ward (Kimberly Sayers), J.T. Walsh (Capt. Frank Bach) **Created by:** Bryce Zabel, Brent V. Friedman; **Executive Producers:** Joseph Stern (pilot), Bryce Zabel, James D. Parriott; **Supervising Producer:** Brent V. Friedman; **Producers:** Bruce Kerner (pilot), Brad Markowitz, Steve Beers; **Co-Producers:** Mark R. Schliz, Bernie Laramie; **Associate Producer:** Robert Parigi; **Writers included:** Bryce Zabel, Brent V. Friedman, Brad Markowitz, James D. Parriott, David Black; **Directors included:** Tobe Hooper, Lou Antonio, Winrich Kolbe, Thomas J. Wright, Steve Beers; **Directors of Photography:** Steve Yaconelli, Bill Butler; **Production Designer:** Gregory Melton; **Costumes:** Darryl Levine; **Special Effects Makeup:** Derik Wingo; **Music Theme:** Michael Hoenig; **Guest Stars included:** Jack Lindine, Richard Gillilland, Joe Urla, Don Moss, Wayne Tippit, Jeri Lynn Ryan (as Juliet Stewart), Conor O'Farrell (as Phil Albano), Tim Kelleher (as Steele), Charley Lang (as Dr. Charley Halligan)

NBC/Paramount; September 1996-May 1997; 60 minutes; 19 episodes

Our secret war with extraterrestrial aliens has been exposed. But there has been no uproar, no controversy or mass hysteria in the world. Why? Because everything was revealed in the *fictional* television series *Dark Skies,* which ran for 19 episodes in 1996 as a prime-time drama on NBC. If you examine the series episode by episode, you'll be stunned to see that President Truman, President Kennedy and The Beatles all had their private encounters with the extraterrestrials.

Dark Skies came about when two of Holly-

wood's most experienced producers met for the first time and sat down, ruminating about their next project. The discussion turned to the UFO phenomenon and that's when the creative electricity in the air became a neon sign. "It just came to us—what if we fused the two greatest conspiracies of all time together?" says executive producer and co-creator Bryce Zabel. "We came up with the Unified Field Theory of conspiracy—who killed JFK and why, and whether Roswell was a real event or not. The essence of the series is that John Kennedy was assassinated because he was going to tell the truth about UFOs in his second term."

"I told Bryce about a very credible Washington insider I knew who had told me there was intelligent, extraterrestrial life here on Earth," says supervising producer and co-creator Brent Friedman. "That sparked some conversations about Roswell and the possibility it really occurred. And if it did, how could events like JFK's assassination, Watergate, Vietnam, etc.— how could those events have any meaning historically unless they were somehow tied to the alien truth?"

With the basis of the series forming their imaginations, Zabel and Friedman went to work. The first task was to shape the "series pitch" proposal into an unconventional form to generate interest, and provoke the network executives receiving it, to immediately pick up their phones and say the words, "We're interested!"

"We started creating an ultra-classified briefing book that was meant for high-level top secret people that basically told them about the UFO cover-up and how it all happened and made the case that, in 1994 and 1995, the government was going to have to come clean and tell people what was going on," explains Zabel. "And the best way to get the public prepared for it was to do a television series about the truth, so that they could see it as fiction at the beginning and later come to understand the truth. So we were already mixing reality and non-reality in a way that I think was pretty fascinating. We did this whole briefing book before we showed it to anybody."

According to Friedman, the briefing book took a month to develop. "We were inventing the world of our series through faux classified documents, internal memos, and re-interpreted historical records," recalls Friedman. "And, best of all, there was no one involved at that point to tell us we were crazy. We believed we were onto something highly entertaining and, as it turned out, we were."

Using their industry contacts, Zabel and Friedman managed to get their "top-secret" document into the hands of Jeff Sagansky, president of CBS, who had just left the Black Rock network and was preparing to become an independent producer. He went through the material and loved it and managed to get the two creators a deal at Columbia Television. With a studio on board, the next step was to get one of the "big three" networks interested. For maximum penetration, copies of the "classified" briefing book was sent to ABC, NBC and CBS on the same day. Zabel describes the briefing book as a black notebook with a gold foil seal. To accentuate the material, written on the notebook was a warning: "By breaking this seal you accept the responsibility for this knowledge and if you betray it, you're up for treason charges." And to top it off, a brown paper bag with twine string was used to package the notebook with a bold declaration: "Top Secret — Confidential!" Apparently the executives were not intimidated because to actually read the notebook, they had to take a pair of scissors and cut the twine. Had there been intimidation, the plan would have backfired, and there would have been no sale!

After making their presentations, Zabel and Friedman sat back and waited by the phone to see who would pounce. Their pitch was successful as the phone did ring ... two times. Both CBS and NBC wanted the show. A bidding war between the networks was forestalled because Sagansky had decided that the show would be sold to the very first interested party. After a series of meetings at NBC, the network commissioned a pilot script. The actual filming of the two-hour pilot

presentation was in November 1995. "They liked it a lot and ordered six backup scripts but didn't order it to series until May 1996," says Zabel. "That was unusual. I felt like I had been working on Dark Skies a long, long time before it even had got ordered."

Zabel was an appropriate person to develop Dark Skies because he had a long fascination with UFO-ology, and had written a 1993 Sci-Fi Channel movie titled Official Denial, which was about the Roswell UFO incident. Plus, he was someone who had grown up during the 1960s, when John F. Kennedy was president.

Zabel and Friedman used the resources at their disposal and crafted an intricate timeline to help them map out the series' storylines. In this timeline, four columns were set up. The first column were the dates. The second column were historical United States events as revealed by their collection of Time and Newsweek magazines, complete from the 1960s to the present. "We pulled out the big and little events from them," says Zabel.

The third column was a detailed historical account of all the known UFO incidents and reports. The fourth column was their interpretation of the events that linked the historical U.S. events and the UFO incidents. Says Zabel, "For instance, the 1965 power blackout in New York was at the same time as when Dorothy Kilgallen died, which was at the same time as a major UFO event in New Hampshire and so that became an episode, 'To Pray in Darkness,' where we tied together Dorothy's murder, the UFO event and the power blackout. We assembled this massive timeline and went back and reinterpreted history for the best possible, most paranoid scenario that we could come up with. It was an incredibly difficult process but also incredibly fun. We just kept laughing. We said, 'I can't believe we're getting paid to do this!'"

And just how elaborate was this connect-the-dots of UFO-ology and U.S. history? It stretched from 65 B.C. to the year 2010. If the show had succeeded and remained in production for several years, the timeline of events would have caught up to real time by the 1999–2000 television season. "Dark Skies was meant to be a big millennium show," admits Zabel.

What made this show stand out was that the producers insisted they actually had "inside knowledge" given to them by a real UFO expert whom Zabel christened "John Loengard." And this man claimed he experienced it all and gave the producers the data they needed to tell his story.

Zabel posted on his personal website a letter written by "Loengard" asking that his real-life story be told under the guise of fiction.

In part, that letter reads, "The truth must be told. You have been chosen as the instruments to achieve this objective. The truth, however, must not be represented as truth. Too many people who are needed in the struggle will die. The cover of fiction must be used to present the truth.... Do not be afraid. The fight for humanity demands your courage."

Says Zabel, "A lot of the fans were going, 'Wait a minute ... what the hell are you saying? Are you saying there's a real John Loengard?' And Brent and I would always say, 'That's our story.' You can imagine what the fans thought, knowing this letter existed."

Says Friedman, "The 'real' John Loengard was a key source of information. Some of which we used almost verbatim, other stuff we took much greater creative license with. Many aspects of Majestic-12 were apparently quite accurate. Their methods, their political, military, scientific make-up [was depicted in the series]. So I guess the verbatim part refers primarily to the cover-up."

The one aspect of the show that just blew Zabel and Friedman's minds was the fact that a major communications conglomerate, NBC, was allowing two creative Hollywood producers to spend about $45 million to create 20 hours of television and declaring "that John Kennedy was killed because he was going to tell the world about UFOs! We just thought this is the craziest thing — only in America!" grins Zabel.

In the series pilot directed by horror-meister filmmaker Tobe Hooper, young John Loengard and his fiancée, Kim Sayers, arrive in Washington D.C. in 1963, preparing for their new jobs as government staffers, John working as an assistant to a Congressman, Kim employed inside the White House. When the Congressman assigns Loengard to investigate Project Blue Book, the U.S. Air Force's probe of the UFO phenomenon, his "nosing around" attracts the attention of Capt. Frank Bach, leader of the top secret agency Majestic-12. They are in a secret war with extraterrestrials who made first contact with U.S. government officials during the 1947 Roswell incident. After Loengard is warned off, he just digs deeper and discovers Bach's identity. As a result, Bach recruits Loengard into the agency as a field agent.

At Majestic-12, Loengard learns about the alien Hive, who have the ability to infect human bodies, spreading ganglion inside the bodies to gain control. The Hive are telepathic in nature and communicate with each other in a "hive consciousness." They were, effectively, body snatchers.

After learning Majestic-12's secret agendas and brutal methods, Loengard becomes disillusioned and is determined to give the world the knowledge of the existence of aliens. But, of course, Bach disagrees. Loengard steals a shard of an alien artifact from Bach and gives it to Robert Kennedy, who fills in the President. When Bach learns of Loengard's secret meetings with the attorney general, he takes rash steps to protect Majestic-12's secrecy. Loengard and Sayers go on the run. Later, Kim is abducted by the aliens herself, and the residual psychic trauma gives her clues to their activities on Earth.

As the series progressed, Loengard and Sayers essentially became a thorn on Majestic-12's hide, and Bach sparred with them every step of the way. On one side Loengard constantly looked for means of exposing the existence of the aliens and of Majestic-12's covert activities, while on the other, Bach and his team did everything they could to stop Loengard. But occasionally, they joined forces to stop the aliens from further infiltrating or harming the human race.

In subsequent episodes, after Kennedy's assassination, Loengard learned the truth regarding the Roswell incident, thwarted an alien plot to transmit signals along with The Beatles' appearance on *The Ed Sullivan Show*, and participated in the birth of the U.S. government's secret Area 51 base in the Nevada desert. Also figuring in the alien Hive plots were strange animal mutilations, and manipulation of the racial strife in Mississippi with the deaths of civil rights workers. Loengard and Bach also sparred as the Warren Commission convened to study the Kennedy assassination. The result of this match had Loengard and Sayers being folded back into Majestic-12 and with a new ally: Juliet Stewart, representing the Russian equivalent of Majestic-12. Other skirmishes with Hive operatives included encounters at Vietnam, during the Watts riots, and at anti-war demonstrations.

To put the faces of these characters on the small screen, the producers launched into a grueling casting process. "NBC told us they had a holding deal with Eric Close and that they would look very fondly on any series that actually used him," recalls Zabel. "Our attitude was, unless we hate him, we better use him, because we want to get on the air.

"So Brent and I met with Eric and thought that

Jackie Zabel, Eric Close and Bryce Zabel attend a launch party on September 26, 1996, the night of the series' premiere (courtesy Jackie Zabel).

he had exactly the quality we were looking for. He could play that John Loengard who shows up in Washington D.C. and is very naive and fresh-faced, and then his fall from grace would be more fun to watch. So we said, 'Great! We'll go with Eric,' and at that point NBC said, 'Wait a minute, we're not sure you should, we're looking at other people and we need to do a screen test of Eric!' So after making us sort of hire him, then they said, 'Well, we'll have to think about it....' Which only made Brent and me like Eric even more." The first runner-up for the role was Josh Brolin, actor James Brolin's son.

For the role of Kim Sayers, Loengard's fiancée, Zabel recalls that "Megan was among a number of actresses considered and there was a full casting process. With every callback, Megan was always there and eventually she was at the top of all our lists and we got her." Although the network wanted another actress, the producers were allowed to make the final decision.

For the series' protagonist, Capt. Frank Bach, the leader of Majestic-12, Zabel says that from the start, he and Friedman wanted J.T. Walsh. The task was convincing the actor, who was having a fine feature film career, to commit to a prime-time TV series. "We made him an offer and he took it," recalls Zabel. "And this was the last thing he ever did. He died the summer after Dark Skies was canceled. We killed him in the final episode anyway. He gets shot eight times, so he died in the series and then died in real life."

Late into the series, Jeri Lyn Ryan joined the show as Juliet Stewart, a Russian "Aura-Z" agent. She subsequently played Seven of Nine on Star Trek: Voyager.

The next step was flipping the pages back to a different era — the 1960s. To a degree, this is fairly simple to do in Hollywood when resources allow producers to find vintage car clubs for vehicles from that period, and to dig into the warehouses of clothing from the era. One challenge was finding suitable locations for specific script requirements. No modern buildings could be seen, nor modern-day street level facades. "I'm very good at research. I was very confident that we had the details of history accurate," says Zabel. "We wanted everything to be accurate. When we used a song, the song came from the top 10 list or something like it, from the actual month that the episode took place. That sense of mission and purpose that we brought to the endeavor translated to all of the department heads. For example, the music people knew it was not okay to use a song from 1968 in the year 1964. I've seen movies do that and it just drives me crazy. We felt that was critical because we knew the concept was zany and insane — JFK and UFOs. We wanted everything else to feel authentic. That was the only way to make the experience and the ride the most fun possible."

"I think my favorite 're-creation' moment was actually cut from the pilot," notes Friedman. "It involved doing a 'Forrest Gump' with Loengard in the White House during Jackie [Kennedy's] famous TV tour. We actually had a scene where John came to the White House to speak with Kim Sayers and accidentally walked into the live TV tour, all of which required we recreate a room in the White House and then seamlessly integrate Loengard into the existing footage. How painful it was to cut that from the finished film."

Another scene cut from the pilot was a recreation of Martin Luther King's "I have a dream" speech (held at Washington D.C. on August 28, 1963, with 200,000 supporters attending). "We began the production with three days in Washington D.C., around Thanksgiving time, when it was colder than hell," recalls Zabel. "But many of our scenes were supposedly summer, so there's the scene of Eric Close and Megan Ward arriving in D.C., in the pilot and it was very cold but they're in their shirt sleeves. That speech had taken place in August 1963, and we had to have our people pretend it was a hot August day when, in reality, it was 20 degrees. So we would take our shots while the actors had their jackets at their feet and they'd be in their shirt sleeves, cheering and singing, and then when we yelled cut, everyone would throw their jackets back on, because it was so bitterly cold."

Brent Friedman says that his favorite memory of the shooting of the pilot was the location where a giant crop circle was created in a wheat field in Grapevine, California. "Walking around in that field, inside that design, was exhilarating," he says. "The sheer scale of it was exactly as I'd imagined it when we wrote the scene." Only a handful of guys were needed to make the crop circle. "It had to be re-made the day of shooting because

the bent-down stalks started springing back up!" chuckles Friedman. "Which raises questions about the apparent hoaxes and why those stalks stay down for weeks or months on end. And I always loved the detail of having the barbed wire fence melted. That was Tobe Hooper's idea, I seem to recall."

In another scene, which takes place inside the Majestic headquarters, a "test monkey" was taken over by the alien hive. The filmmakers used both a real monkey and a small person inside a monkey suit. "We hired the guy who plays 'Mini-Me' [from the Austin Powers films], Verne Troyer, who actually put on a monkey suit," says Zabel.

The fictional characters, Loengard and Sayers, interacted with assorted real-life historical characters (played by actors) who inhabited that time and location. Quantum Leap had a similar approach which was called "kisses with history": Time traveler Sam Beckett would "leap" into different time periods and, say, encounter a very young Michael Jackson or Buddy Holly. In Dark Skies' case, political figures were prominent in the series pilot, portrayed by look-alike actors: President Truman, Nelson Rockefeller, Attorney General Robert F. Kennedy and his brother President John F. Kennedy. Real-life UFO abductee Betty and Barney Hill were also portrayed in the episode. In later episodes, we saw millionaire Howard Hughes, UFO expert J. Allen Hynek, FBI director J. Edgar Hoover, actress Marilyn Monroe, astronomer Dr. Carl Sagan, and even The Beatles (seen making their American debut on The Ed Sullivan Show). Brent Friedman says there were specific guidelines in how they could incorporate a real-life person into the series without permission. "I believe the main issue was whether they were dead — in which case, we had carte blanche to use them as we saw fit," he says. "But if they weren't, they had to be considered public figures, which most were. I think the biggest liberty we took was in the final episode where Loengard takes the place of then- governor [of California] Ronald Reagan, whom we learn is scheduled to be abducted. Loengard then goes on to get himself taken."

When the series began to air in the fall of 1996, viewer feedback was mixed, says Zabel, because of a perceived competition with another genre show: Chris Carter's The X-Files. "There were a lot of X-Files fans who thought Dark Skies was trying to play in its field, and they were very protective of X-Files," says Zabel. "But they weren't very similar at all. X-Files was about all kinds of

Dark Skies executive producer and co-creator Bryce Zabel, left, on location in Washington, D.C., during the shoot of the two-hour pilot. He is with supervising producer and co-creator Brent V. Friedman. They are re-creating a historical scene with Dr. Martin Luther King, later cut from the pilot (courtesy Jackie Zabel).

Young Jonathan Zabel is coached by his father, executive producer Bryce Zabel, during *Dark Skies'* final episode, where Jonathan played John Loengard's son (courtesy Jackie Zabel).

different things. We were only about UFOs, we took place in the 1960s and there was no mystery. We said UFOs are here. We were a completely different show but there were a lot of *X-Files* fans before they had even seen the show, who were up in arms about it.

"So, the very audience that should have been our audience at the time, was split. It was a bumper year for conspiracy theorists and alien enthusiasts. But I never thought *The X-Files* comparison was a fair rap in any way and I think time has proven me right about that."

Ken Tucker, writing for *Entertainment Weekly* (September 1996), gave *Dark Skies* a C- rating and he declared, "*Dark Skies* will be highly entertaining for fans of *The X-Files*, since *Skies* rips off *X-Files* with amazing gall…. [T]he truth is, this is a damn silly show."

"We actually had a bomb scare once at our production office," Friedman says. "Some character in shades and hoodie, who looked like the Unabomber, dropped off an unmarked box wrapped up in a brown bag, and then fled before anyone

could get his name. Security was alerted and the entire production office was evacuated until a bomb squad could determine the contents were not a bomb at all, but rather a spec script for the show."

The irony of the incident, says Friedman, was that the script wasn't even a very good one. "The guy wasn't trying to terrorize us, he was just submitting his writing in the spirit of the show which, unfortunately, we were *way* too caught up in," he says, irked at having lost half a day of production. "The reaction at first was suspicion, fear, panic, then anger when it was just a hoax. Eventually, a day or so later, we were able to laugh about it."

Friedman says doesn't recall if there was contact information attached to the script in the event the producers wanted to purchase it. "We liked to fantasize that someone might want to silence us because we were too close to the truth, but aside from that 'bomb scare' we never had any real trouble from the lunatic fringe … at least nothing I can talk about on the record!"

Despite the fact that the show was a one-season

wonder over a decade ago, Friedman reports that he continues to receive fan feedback. "I still get emails from diehard fans, as well as people who want to see the show for the first time, and the show is usually referred to as 'an undiscovered gem.' There've been a number of good fan sites over the years, but reading recaps and reviews really doesn't do the show justice. Just being able to sit down and watch all 20 hours over the course of a couple nights or a long weekend, that is an experience I personally cannot wait to have because I honestly haven't watched the show since it aired on NBC."

Dark Skies ended up as a victim of corporate financial practices and policies, as Zabel explains. "We were part of what NBC called a 'Thrill-ogy Night.' *Dark Skies* was on at [Saturday night] 8 o'clock, *The Pretender* was on at 9 o'clock and *The Profiler* was on at 10 o'clock. *Profiler* was 100 percent owned by NBC. *Pretender* was 50 percent and *Dark Skies* was zero percent owned by NBC. And they canceled them exactly in this order: *Dark Skies*, *Pretender* and finally *Profiler*. We were one of the first casualties of the financial syndication rule changes, where networks could start to own the programs they were airing."

In the end, *Dark Skies* won a 1997 Emmy award for Best Main Title design and was nominated for Best Main Title music theme (composed by Michael Hoenig). (The series soundtrack was released in 2006 and is available from Perseverance Records.) That same year, the Academy of Science Fiction, Fantasy & Horror Films nominated *Dark Skies* for three Saturn Awards: Best TV Series, Best Actor (Eric Close) and Actress (Megan Ward).

On the flipside, *Entertainment Weekly* magazine made the series #3 in its list of the five worst shows of the season.

"I look back on it as the most satisfactory creative experience of my career," says Zabel. "If I look at the pilot it is about 90 percent of the way I saw it in my head. So I feel very positive and very good about it.

"Because we set it in period and because we paid such meticulous attention to detail about that period, it's not aging, it's not going to become outdated and embarrassing. It'll never be like a *Starsky & Hutch* episode, like 'Oh my god, that looks so bad!' It's always going to be worth watching. I would imagine 25 years from now people will be able to enjoy *Dark Skies* because it's going to be a high quality, excellent high production expression of this crazy idea, that it is so

well realized, that's why it has these passionate fans."

Zabel says he hopes one day he will have the opportunity to complete the storytelling if a DVD box set of the series is ever released. Because of financial difficulties in obtaining clearances for the period music rights, two companies backed out of plans for a DVD release. Although Zabel says he's disappointed, he still has dreams. "I would hope a DVD set will be popular enough that it will make somebody say, 'Let's do a movie where we can answer some of the questions,'" says Zabel. "I would love to do that. To do a *Dark Skies* movie, it would call for someone to say, 'The show's off the air for ten years, but we're going to do a reunion show.' I wish they would. The Sci-Fi Channel could create quite a business model for themselves by giving orders for series of the past. But they don't seem to do that."

CAST NOTES

Eric Close (John Loengard): Close was born in Staten Island, New York. He began his acting career in the early '90s with roles in such shows as *MacGyver* and *Santa Barbara*. He appeared in *Hercules and the Lost Kingdom* (1994 TV movie) and then later in the series *Hercules: The Legendary Journeys*. After *Dark Skies*, Close was featured in the short-lived series *Now and Again* and *The Magnificent Seven* and in the mini-series *Taken*. He is currently starring in the television series *Without a Trace*. Close is a serious family man and a devout Christian.

Megan Ward (Kimberly Sayers): Ward was born in Los Angeles, California. She began her acting career in the early '90s in direct-to-video features such as *Crash and Burn* (1990) and *Goodbye Paradise* (1991) She appeared in the movies *Trancers II* (1991), *Encino Man* (1992) and *Trancers III* (1992) before joining the cast of *Class of '96*. She appeared in *Freaked* (1993) and *The Brady Bunch Movie* (1995) and in several episodes of *Party of Five*. After *Dark Skies* she was a semiregular on *Melrose Place* and made appearances on the new *Fantasy Island*, *Friends*, *CSI*, *Navy NCIS*, *Boston Legal*, *7th Heaven* and *Sleeper Cell*. Most recently she has had a recurring role on the daytime drama *General Hospital*.

J.T. Walsh (Capt. Frank Bach): Walsh was born in San Francisco. He acted in off-Broadway productions in the mid-'70s and throughout the '80s before getting his big break in the Broadway play *Glengarry Glen Ross*. He appeared in the films

Eddie Macon's Run (1983), *Power* (1986), *Hannah and Her Sisters* (1986), *The Russia House* (1990), *Backdraft* (1991), *A Few Good Men* (1992), *Needful Things* (1993), and *The Client* (1994). On television he appeared in *Lois and Clark: The New Adventures of Superman* and *The X-Files* before joining the cast of *Dark Skies*. After that he had a small number of roles until his last film, *Pleasantville*, in 1998. Walsh died of a heart attack shortly after.

SOURCES

"1996 Best/Worst TV." *Entertainment Weekly* no. 359–360, December 27, 1996.
Tucker, Ken. "The X-tra Files: Hoping Saturday Night's All Right for Frightening, NBC's 'X-Files'-Inspired Trio, 'Dark Skies,' 'The Pretender,' and 'Profiler,' Proves That Imitation Isn't Always Flattering." *Entertainment Weekly*, September 20, 1996.

The Dead Zone

(2002–2007)

Six years after going into a coma, Johnny Smith awakens and discovers that he now possesses the psychic ability to see the past and future of anyone or anything that he touches. His fiancée, Sarah, has married Walt, the town sheriff. Johnny's psychic ability gives him many positive and negative experiences, altering the lives of many others and his own.

Cast: Anthony Michael Hall (Johnny Smith), Nicole DeBoer (Sarah Bannerman), Chris Bruno (Sheriff Walt Bannerman), John L. Adams (Bruce Lewis)

Based on characters created by Stephen King; Created for television by Michael Piller and Shawn Piller; **Executive Producers:** Michael Piller, Lloyd Segan, Robert Lieberman *Year 1*, Karl Schaefer *Year 3*, Tommy Thompson *Year 4–5*, Scott Shepherd *Year 6*, Shawn Piller *Year 6*; **Co-Executive Producers:** Karl Schaefer *Year 2–3*, Michael R. Perry *Year 3*, Shawn Piller *Year 4–5*, Anthony Michael Hall *Year 6*; **Producers:** Shawn Piller, Robert Petrovicz *Year 1–3*, Michael Taylor *Year 2–3*, Moira Kirland *Year 3*, Anthony Michael Hall *Year 4–5*, Stefani Deoul, Madeleine Henrie *Year 6*; **Supervising Producers:** Shawn Piller *Year 3*, Michael Taylor, Loren Segan, Christina Lynch *Year 4–5*, Craig Silverstein *Year 2*, Matt McGuinness *Year 6*; **Co-Producers:** Anthony Michael Hall *Year 1–3*, Kira Domaschuk, Michael Taylor *Year 1*, Drew Matich *Year 6*; **Associate Producers:** Eric A. Stillwell, Amber Woodward *Year 3–5*; **Consulting Producers:** Harold Tichenor *Year 3*, Juan Carlos Coto *Year 4–5*, Ann Lewis Hamilton, Richard Hatem *Year 6*; **Writers included:** Joe Menosky, Michael Cassutt, Michael Taylor, David Benz, Jill Blotevogel, Laura J. Burns, Melinda Metz; **Directors included:** Mike Rohl, Michael Robison, James Head, Mike Vejar; **Director of Photography:** Stephen McNutt; **Production Designer:** Lance King; **Visual Effects:** Stargate Digital Canada; Music Theme "New Year's Prayer" by Jeff Buckley *Year 1–3*, "Dead Zone Epic" by Blues Saraceno *Year 4–6*; **Guest Stars included:** Ally Sheedy, Robert Culp, Richard Lewis, David Ogden-Stiers (as Reverend Gene Purdy), Kristen Dalton (as Dana Bright) *Year 1–3*, Sean Patrick Flanery (as Greg Stillson), Garry Chalk (as James Stillson) *Year 3–4*, Spencer Achtymichuk (as J.J. Bannerman) *Year 1–5*, Connor Price (as J.J. Bannerman) *Year 6*, Sarah Wynter (as Rebecca Caldwell) *Year 3–4*, Sonja Bennett (as Sarah Caldwell) *Year 3–4*, Frank Whaley (as Christopher Wey) *Year 3–4*, Martin Donovan (as Malcolm Janus) *Year 6*, Laura Harris (as Miranda Ellis) *Year 5–6*, Cara Buono (as Sheriff Anna Turner) *Year 6*

USA Networks/Lion's Gate Television/Piller2/Lloyd Segan Company; 2002–2007; 60 minutes; 80 episodes; DVD status: Complete series

Based on Stephen King's best-selling novel, *The Dead Zone* was producer-writer Michael Piller's translation of the story to a television format. In the novel, John Smith was a boy who had injured himself while playing ice skating, damaging a crucial part of his brain. As an adult schoolteacher, he fell into a coma as a result of a car accident. When he woke up, he was astonished to discover that he'd gained psychic powers. A previously unused "dead zone" in his brain became active. Whenever he touched a person or object, he could "see" the past, present or future. Smith was also dismayed to find that, he'd lost his job and that his fiancée, Sarah, had remarried. John's psychic abilities came into play when he helped the local sheriff identify a violent serial killer. But with each vision, John grew weaker. The most startling of all visions occurred while meeting a political candidate, Greg Stillson, and being confronted with horrifying apocalyptic visions of a future in which Stillson became president of the United States. Smith's precognition also revealed his own death, in the process of assassinating Stillson. In 1983, the novel was adapted by filmmaker David Cronenberg for a film starring Christopher Walken as Johnny and Martin Sheen as Greg Stillson.

Michael Piller redeveloped the series so that Sarah had married the local sheriff, Walt Bannerman, and that the son they were raising was actually Johnny's biological son. Piller also surrounded Johnny with a unique social circle: Bruce Lewis hung around as his physical therapist, and Reverend Gene Purdy was his enigmatic legal guardian who had been the steward of the family home and finances. Dana Bright, a tabloid newspaper reporter, joined the circle as someone initially curious about Johnny's unusual abilities. Gradually, she became a friend and linked romantically, albeit briefly, with Johnny.

To maintain the premise as an ongoing format, Johnny's visions didn't result in a progressive weakening physical state. Johnny's physical recovery, however, was indicated by a walking cane that he would carry around with him. This would become, itself, an important plot arc device later in the series.

Writers of the show would thrust Johnny into situations where his psychic powers were pivotal in changing the course of people's lives or how events would play out, depending on what he would see (or not) in his vision.

In the series' writers guide, Piller instructed potential writers to understand the nature of Johnny's powers. Psychometry is a phenomenon where the psychic senses the history of a physical object by holding it. For example, if Johnny Smith were to place his hands on this book that you're holding right now, he would immediately be transported back in time, and learn the complete history of this particular copy, as it came out of the printing press, was placed in a cardboard box, got picked up by librarians and placed on the bookshelf. Quite likely, Johnny would also gain an encyclopedic knowledge of everyone that has picked up this copy of the book and thumbed through these pages.

Clairvoyance is having visions, sometimes foggy, of the past, present or future. Related phenomena are precognition, which is predicting future events, and retrocognition, discovering past events. Clairsentience is sensing what has happened in a room. (This is explored in detail in "The House" when Johnny learned what took place in the family mansion when his parents were younger.)

Piller urged writers to keep the "thriller" aspects of the storytelling but also to remember the humor, which author Stephen King delivered in all of his books. The writer's guide emphasizes reverence to King's original work.

Piller also warned writers that although Johnny could conjure up a vision by sheer will, he didn't have complete control over it. Often visions wouldn't come when desired, and sometimes they would when not desired. Plus, future visions are not set in stone. Johnny can sometimes alter the future with the given information.

With these flexible parameters, the potentials for a long-running series was set.

In the first two episodes, Johnny helped Sheriff Bannerman in his hunt for a serial killer, as mirrored in the novel. In fact, the opening episode was titled "The Wheel of Fortune," a chapter title in the original book.

Recalling his first reading of the series pilot script, star Anthony Michael Hall noted, "I thought it was very intense. I enjoyed the character development and it had a real emotional payoff. In the third act, everyone kind of takes a leap and takes a step forward in their lives. Johnny rehabilitates somewhat [from the accident injuries]. Sarah is happily involved with her family. And even the doctor is reunited with his mother in Vietnam. It's beautiful, it has a real impact emotionally." Hall reveals that he broke Johnny Smith down into distinct components: "It's actually three-fold, the way I approached the character — physical, mental and also spiritual."

Playing Johnny Smith was an important challenge because the series succeeded or failed on his performances. Hall found the character interesting and fun. "I enjoy playing the part so much," says Hall.

In his discussions with Piller, Hall discovered that the show owed a lot to Rod Serling's *Twilight Zone*. "That's exactly his intention," says Hall.

"He wants to do classic, breakthrough television. It's like being an athlete and being drafted to a top team on the first round. I'm so grateful to Michael Piller and USA Networks. Everyone's doing great work. The entire crew is really invested in making this show one of quality. There's a great energy on the set for that reason."

Hall reveals that he actually has two psychic friends and that they were supportive of him in this project. "I'm always asking questions and doing homework. When I got this, it was wonderful because I was suddenly able to interview them to a certain extent and also do a lot of reading on Edgar Cayce, for example, a renowned psychic. He's been a personal inspiration for me in the role. What he did was incredible. He used his enormous psychic talent that God gave him to really help people as a form of therapy. He would do past life regressions and readings for people and all kinds of constructive work. I'm taking that as a positive cue."

Becoming involved and changing people's lives becomes a great burden for Johnny Smith because it is so easy, on a daily basis, to get pulled in. Smith would have to become a hermit, to cut himself off from the outside world, to avoid having psychic visions, but he is not a social phobic. His decisions often became a pivotal factor in which way events turns. Will he do the right thing, or will there be a mistake? This premise made for great dramatic stories and puts the characters into uncommon situations and ethical dilemmas.

Being a psychic means the very act of touching some*one* or some*thing* can propel the storyline forward to the dark or the light. "The psychic visions are triggered by touch," says Hall. "It could be inadvertent. Someone bumps into him or I touch someone deliberately. That triggers a psychic vision and the audience goes subjectively into my point of view. And arrives into different scenes. It gets more intense in terms of the visuals, in jumping back and forth from linear live-action and vision time which can be past, present or future. It's really brilliant."

The psychic visions become very intense and surreal, thanks to innovative, *Matrix*-like visual effects and photography. These scenes were so finely executed that they became the series' instantly recognizable "signature" moments.

For example, in the first year episode "Netherworld," Johnny experiences a vision during a birthday party, and suddenly, flames appear. "People are surrounding the dining room table and all of a sudden Nicole walks in with a birthday cake," recalls Hall. "It's supposed to be my birthday party. I'm on the perimeter of this party and I'm looking in. No one sees me. And suddenly, the room catches fire. They created it with real live fire on the set and also digital enhancements. All of a sudden the room catches fire and I'm the only one who can see it. I'm kind of standing outside of it, even though I'm yelling at everyone to run for cover. But no one can hear me. It's very surreal. They had these pilots that flames would ignite from. They made sure we were all five or six feet away from the pilots in the filming of this scene, but once they went up, the flames were four or five feet tall around us. It was very just surreal because I had to go in and try and save the day, but yet, no one can hear me because we're in Dead Zone time. It's really been interesting."

Talking about his first screening of the series pilot, co-star David Ogden Stiers remarks, "I was mesmerized. I'm unused to this quality of writing in television." Stiers was surprised and delighted at the presentation. "I just got a script last night ... that is as exciting, challenging and as really smart as anything I've ever been reading for television. I'm constantly intrigued and admiring of the quality of writing. Every story I've read have been absolutely its own extension of the idea. They don't do the same plot over again."

Stiers, who played Reverend Purdy, was a latecomer to the cast. Michael Moriarty played the reverend in the pilot, which was reshot to include Stiers. In fact, another actress, Kendall Cross played Dana Bright before Kristen Dalton was hired.

Elaborating on what he found fascinating about the Johnny Smith phenomenon, Stiers says, "Johnny has moral, ethical problems on whether he will get involved with people. He's not fond of touching people because he then knows that requires him to act. If he doesn't want that responsibility, he's happy to live his own. He's happy to help when he can, but he's not in the psychic business. I love the fact that he's weary about insights into people's minds because he might have to act. And that action might require him to intervene in ways that he finds personally objectionable or inevasibly manipulative.

"Once he's done it, it's something that he's going to have to live with. I think the most astonishing thing about the integrity of this piece is that we're watching Johnny's learning curve in an anthology framework."

Stiers was equally impressed with star Anthony Michael Hall and his work ethic on the set. "He has an extremely difficult task to accomplish.

Michael is in every bloody scene. His work curve every week is way beyond anything I've ever done. He's prompt, prepared, courteous, helpful. He lets you know when he needs something from you without demanding it. This is not easy, in terms of time and emotional investment and in terms of what he has to play."

Producer and co-creator Shawn Piller says that he was very pleased with the casting of Nicole De-Boer as Sarah Bannerman. "Nicole is just this charming, radiantly beautiful and sweet girl next door and that's as an actress and as a person," he says. "I think she brings a lot to the show. Her character is such that you can't but help fall in love with her, even when she's torn and not necessarily doing the right thing. I think people can sympathize with her. They feel for her when she's not doing something right. Nicole is a really strong actor and has the experience in television and has the confidence within herself."

In his first year as a psychic, Johnny was a member of a jury and a hostage in a bank robbery, and was charged with witchcraft in a small town. He would also use his powers to help an old man find a lost love from World War II. On one occasion Johnny even found himself in psychic link with an Indian shaman from a different era, in a weird form of time-travel communication.

Although Johnny gained a public persona as "the town psychic," many people perceived him as a fraud. But he would prove prophetic each time.

Johnny's apocalyptic visions of Greg Stillson, from the novel, were also adapted here, introduced in the Year One finale episode, "Destiny," and starring Sean Patrick Flanery in the politician's role. "We set up Stillson to put the building block into place," says executive producer Michael Piller. "We expect that to go on for a long time," as an ongoing, slowly developed "mythology" thread to follow as the series progressed. Stillson's story often echoed what King wrote but, as with many other elements in the series, it was a story that evolved in its own fashion.

"A lot of people might have expected us to continue the Stillson story in the first episode [of the second year], and yet, I wanted that story to take a long time to tell," says Piller. "I really felt that we'd get a percentage of new viewers who had heard about the show and check it out for the first time and I didn't want them to feel left out by having a continuing storyline. We made references to all the issues that we'd left on the table at

the end of last year. And then we moved ahead with a new story that was really about Johnny's now-growing reputation and how it ultimately brings all kinds of unwanted attention.... I love exploring the dangers of fame and celebrity. I think its a very interesting subject."

In the second year, personal relationships were explored in greater depth. In the two-parter "Descent," and "Ascent," Walt and Johnny got trapped inside an old coal mine. To prevent an injured Walt from going into a coma, Johnny psychically connected with him in an effort to pull him out. In the process, Johnny was surprised to learn that Walt believed Sarah and Johnny's love was true and were meant to be together. However, upon returning from his coma, Walt did not remember anything.

Later in the year, when the father of Johnny's friend Bruce died, Johnny learned more about Bruce's family history and relationship with his preacher father. "'Zion' is essentially an opportunity for us to explore the life and motivations of Bruce," says Piller. "It's an alternate reality show that shows a path not taken if Bruce had not left home after arguing with his father as he did many years ago."

In other stand-alone stories, Johnny fenced with kidnappers, took on a giant corporation over potentially deadly defective products, encountered the mob, and prevented a SARs-like epidemic.

In April 2003, the series began a three-month hiatus, returning in July with six additional episodes on the USA Network. One of the most unusual of the six episodes was "The Hunt," which had the covert intelligence community asking Johnny for his help in finding Middle Eastern terrorists. This was Michael Piller's attempt to address "What would happen if the government asked Johnny Smith to help hunt down Osama Bin Laden?" Although initially the intent was to be explicit that the wanted man was in fact Bin Laden (the episode's original title was "The Hunt for Osama"), at the last minute the network pulled back and removed all references to the name of the terrorist.

One of the problems of writing a script of this nature was that the fictionalized story could not contradict real-life events. How could it be written that Johnny's visions helped in capturing or killing Bin Laden, if in real life he was still free? "We could take the ending, 'Yeah, Johnny does find Bin Laden...' and catch the guy but now that we've taken the name out, it erases the risk of that problem," says Michael Piller. "What would have been awkward is if we had been talking about Bin Laden and they had him in custody."

Ostensibly, the psychic unit portrayed in the episode was based on a real unit, the Remote Viewing program at the CIA. Piller co-wrote the story with Joe McMoneagle, who was involved with that unit. But the government won't confirm or deny the existence of such a program.

Ironically, the program was scheduled to air in the spring-summer of 2003, just as the Americans attacked Iraq in search of "weapons of mass destruction" that weren't found.

Piller explains that with *Dead Zone,* he was always looking for ways of addressing real-world issues and topics. "The Hunt" explored terrorism, "Plague" involved SARs-like epidemics, "The Outsider" discussed corporate responsibility and liability, "Scars" echoed the Vietnam War, and "Cycle of Violence" starkly portrayed a Columbine-like scenario at a high school.

The Greg Stillson "mythology episodes" ramped up significantly in the second year finale, "Visions," where Johnny gained more information and details. Someone living in that future, Christopher Wey, a man with a psychic connection to Johnny, was at first a mysterious man in visions. Soon Johnny understood that averting catastrophic events would require all of his energies.

At the end of the second year, Piller examined the public's reaction in contrast to the first year. "I read billboard comments on virtually every episode to see how they're playing around the country," he says. "The audience feedback, the response that I got back personally, was that this was a far better season than the first season. The feedback has been far more positive."

The third year began with "Finding Rachel," in which Johnny was accused of murdering one of Greg Stillson's campaign volunteers. Johnny met Rebecca Caldwell (Sarah Wynter), Rachel's sister, who would appear in five episodes in this year. Initially, she believed that Johnny was responsible for her sister's death, but because of Johnny's evolving psychic visions, Rebecca realized others were responsible. Johnny and Rebecca returned to Rachel's mystery in the Season Three finale, "Tipping Point," and unraveled the mystery in the fourth year's premiere, "Broken Circle."

In stand-alone third-year stories, Johnny encountered a radio "shock jock" who was hostile towards him, crossed swords with a pair of lawyer twins, determined the outcome of a friend's wedding, and confronted an angry student who brought a gun into a high school. In one vision, Johnny even saw himself murdering someone.

As noted by Michael Piller: "The question remains, 'What is Johnny?' Is he a prophet or is he just a guy trying to deal with a remarkable power? That unanswered question is always at the back of our minds. 'Is there more to Johnny than even he realizes?' I think there are a lot of things that even he doesn't know about!"

Because Piller was a producer on *Star Trek: The Next Generation* and the co-creator of *Star Trek: Deep Space Nine* and *Star Trek: Voyager,* for him the process of writing has never been about the science fiction aspects but about people and the human condition. With *The Dead Zone* he accentuated this philosophy. "I think the whole purpose of being a writer is to explore the world with everyone," he says. "I only try to do shows that give me the opportunity to do that. I think *TNG, DS9* and *Voyager* all had that potential on a weekly basis to give us some kind of a metaphor for the life we live in. Johnny is about as metaphorical, but ultimately, he can take us, as a character, into almost any kind of story. That's the great fun of writing this show."

The *Dead Zone* series had a 13-episode first year, but ballooned to 19 episodes for the second year, and back down to 12 in its third year, totaling 44 episodes. The USA Network ordered up the fourth and fifth years as a total of 23 episodes, which were shot back-to-back in 2005. Episodes were broadcast as "summer" programming with 12 shows in 2005 and 11 in 2006.

The first episode of the fifth year, titled "Forbidden Fruit" (June 16, 2006), was directed by Shawn Piller and dedicated to his father Michael, who passed away after a long bout with cancer on November 2, 2005.

Recalling her relationship with the veteran writer-producer Piller, director Rachel Talalay remarks, "He is the man. He is absolutely remarkable. A man of few words. He doesn't give you a lot, but when he talks, you listen. He was so experienced. I learned a ton even in that short period of time that I worked with him. His experience was phenomenal. You just quietly listened and absorbed. He was a master at this stuff. It was interesting to see him make a change. Again, character, character, character. And then enjoy the thrilling twists of science fiction."

Two members of the show's cast, John L. Adams and Chris Bruno, stepped behind the camera, directing the episodes "Revelations" and "Independence Day," respectively.

Regarding the fifth-year episode "Symmetry," Talalay says she was initially handed a script that the network didn't like because it was "too confusing," but she found it to be "brilliant! One of the best pieces of writing I've read in a long time."

However, the story endured many rewrites before reaching its final form, just the night before shooting was to begin. "I got a whole new script which was really just a more simplified homage to the original script," she says. "It went back to all the things that were original and clever in the original script. It took out about 30 percent of the stuff to just make it more straightforward. And it's not a straightforward episode at all!"

In this story (which was originally titled "Johnny's Ladder," a homage to the 1990 cult horror film *Jacob's Ladder*), Johnny has visions from three different points of view. He comes to realize he's reliving the same day over and over from three different people, one of whom is himself. Like many other *Dead Zone* tales, this was a story that truly challenged a viewer to listen and watch closely because of the shifting POVs and events.

"There were a lot of conversations about 'At what point do you want the viewer to know what's going on?' At what point does confusion turn you off or intrigue you onward?" Talalay explains. "The majority of the conversation was about how to simplify so that the viewer is not so confused, thinks it's cool and wants to get to the end of the puzzle. There's no stock answer for that.

"When we edited the film, we changed it quite a bit to be clearer earlier on, even though I'm under the impression that it's not that clear, ever! I think it's a gutsy decision to make an episode 'out there.' I really like it because it's smart and it's challenging. My mind works with the puzzle. I found the whole experience fascinating.

"With Michael Hall, there were times I had to say, 'Okay, you're not Johnny now, you're this character at this moment.' We jumped back and forth so much."

The fifth years' ratings were good enough that on September 18, 2006, the network ordered up yet another 13 episodes for the series' sixth year (aired in the summer of 2007). With a desire to return to the character-driven stories of the early seasons, for more stand-alone Johnny-centric stories, the company moved from its base in Vancouver, B.C., to Montreal, Quebec. Along with that move, new producers, writers, directors and a new cinematographer were brought in to inject some freshness into the show. Scott Shepherd, a veteran writer-producer whose credits includes

the new *Outer Limits* and *Tru Calling*, joined the production as executive producer. In the sixth season's premiere episode "Heritage," major events occurred, shifting the show's direction. Sheriff Bannerman was killed in a fire. Connor Price took over the role of J.J. from Spencer Achtymichuk (another child actor, Dominic Louis, originated the role in the early episodes of the first year). The series' focus and direction also shifted: Reverend Purdy disappeared after his church burned down and Bruce landed a job elsewhere.

Essentially the show's focus became Johnny and Sarah's relationship, and supporting players that helped carry the series for five years were set aside. A new sheriff entered the picture, Anna Turner (Cara Buono), a by-the-book procedural officer who didn't trust Johnny.

The show's primary "mythology story," the Greg Stillson saga, also appeared to come to a close. Now vice-president of the United States, Stillson's "evil henchman" Malcolm Janus, who had been "leaning on" Reverend Purdy, died in the altercation inside Purdy's church, that resulted in Walt's death and the church fire. Now, when Johnny shook Greg Stillson's hand, he no longer had a vision of Washington D.C. in flames, suggesting that the future Armageddon has been averted.

In the sixth year finale, "Denouement," Johnny was startled to discover that his father was still alive. And Greg Stillson was responsible for keeping that secret. This was the investigation that Walt Bannerman was working on just prior to his death. He had learned the details and Stillson was responsible for Walt's death. In a further dramatic twist, Johnny learned that both his father and his son had the "dead zone" psychic ability. In a direct link to the 1983 Cronenberg feature, Tom Skerritt appeared as Johnny's father.

On December 19, 2007, the USA Network cancelled *The Dead Zone* along with *The 4400*, as first announced by *TV Guide* columnist Michael Ausiello in his Internet blog.

The next day, the USA Network's vice-president of Original Programming, Jeff Wachtel, told *The Hollywood Reporter*, "We wish we could keep all our great shows alive forever. But we feel we need to give some of our new shows a platform to grow, and it's with great sadness that we say goodbye to two shows that had a great run and helped create the resurgence of original programming on our network and on all of cable."

Rarely has a popular literary property been adapted for television without the participation of its author, and become so successful. When the series pilot, "The Wheel of Fortune," aired on June 16, 2002, it garnered an exceptional 4.7 rating, representing 6.4 million viewers, according to a Nielsen cable ratings report. By the time the sixth season premiere, "Heritage" aired, just 2.12 million viewers tuned in.

That *The Dead Zone* reached six seasons as a hit cable TV series, in an arena with a viewership much smaller than the "big four" networks, is a tribute the creative artists in front of, and behind, the cameras.

CAST NOTES

Anthony Michael Hall (Johnny Smith): Michael became famous as a teenage actor appearing in a string of successful comedies. *National Lampoon's Vacation* (1983) with Chevy Chase led to a pair of John Hughes–directed comedies, *Sixteen Candles* (1984) and *The Breakfast Club* (1985). He also starred in *Weird Science* (1985) and became the youngest cast member of *Saturday Night Live* in the 1985–86 year. In the 1990s he starred in Tim Burton's cult comedy *Edward Scissorhands* (1990), and starred with Will Smith in *Six Degrees of Separation* (1993). In 1999 he played Microsoft co-founder Bill Gates in the TNT movie *The Pirates of Silicon Valley* with Noah Wyle. He made his directorial debut with *The Dead Zone*'s third year episode, "The Cold Hard Truth," guest-starring comedian Richard Lewis.

Nicole DeBoer (Sarah Bannerman): See the Cast Notes for *Beyond Reality*.

Chris Bruno (Sheriff Walt Bannerman): Born in Connecticut, Chris was an avid skier but an injury sidelined him. He auditioned for a play and was cast in the lead of *The Mandrake*. Later, at the State University of New York, he played college baseball while performing in plays. He joined the cast of NBC's *Another World* (1991) and ABC's *All My Children* (1995). Performing standup at The Improv and L.A. Cabaret led to guest appearances on *The Nanny* (1998), and *JAG* (1998). He made his directorial debut with *The Dead Zone*'s fifth year episode "Independence Day."

John L. Adams (Bruce Lewis): Moving to Los Angeles from North Carolina, John began a career as a stand-up comedian performing at The Improv, The Laugh Factory and The Comedy Store as well as the Riviera Casino in Las Vegas. In 2001 he became a regular on *Just Luck*, a short-lived series. He guest-starred in the *Dharma & Greg* pilot and on *The Parenthood* and *Pacific Blue*. On stage, he's played the Scarecrow in a production of *The Wiz*. He made his directorial debut with *The Dead Zone*'s fifth year episode "Revelations."

SOURCES

Ausiello, Michael. "Updated: USA Expresses 'Deep Sadness' Over Dual Cancellations." TV Guide Online, December 19, 2007

Earth: Final Conflict

(1997–2002)

In the early 21st century, the Taelons arrive on Earth and offer humans access to their advanced alien technology. But a secret Liberation force learns that the truth behind the Taelons' presence and their secret agendas may imperil the entire human race.

Cast: Kevin Kilner (Capt. William Boone) *Year 1*, Robert Leeshock (Liam Kincaid) *Year 2–4*, Jayne Heitmeyer (Renee Palmer) *Year 2–5*, Lisa Howard (Capt. Lili Marquette) *Year 1–2*, Von Flores (Sandoval), David Hemblen (Jonathan Doors) *Year 1–3*, Richard Chevolleau (Augur) *Year 1–3*, Leni Parker (Da'an) *Year 1–4*, Anita La Selva (Zo'or) *Year 1–4*, Melinda Deines (Juliet Street) *Year 4–5*, Alan Van Sprang (Howlyn) *Year 5*, Guylaine St. Onge (Juda) *Year 5*

Recurring Cast: Majel Barrett Roddenberry (Dr. Julianne Belman), William deVrey (Joshua Doors), Kari Matchett (Siobhan Beckett), Barry Flatman (President Thompson), Janet-Laine Green (Dr. Melissa Park), Montse Vlader (Maiya); ***Created by:*** Gene Roddenberry; ***Executive Pro-***

ducers: David Kirschner, Majel Roddenberry, Richard C. Okie *Year 1*, Seaton McLean *Year 1–2*, Carleton Eastlake *Year 2*, Paul Gertz *Year 2–5*; **Co-Executive Producer:** Paul Gertz *Year 1*; **Producers:** Stephen Roloff, John Calvert; **Line Producers:** Sherri Saito *Year 1*, Emanuele M. Danelon *Year 2*; **Associate Producer:** Angela Mastronardi *Year 3–5*; **Writers included:** John Whelpley, Howard Chaykin, Robin Bernheim, Ethlie Ann Vare, Lisa Klink, Raymond Hartung, Jonas McCord, George Geiger, Cory Tynan, Daniel Cerone; **Directors included:** Ross Clyde, Brenton Spencer, James Head, Martin Wood, Allan Kroeker, Allan Eastman, Jeff Woolnough, Andrew Potter; **Directors of Photography:** Michael McMurray, Thomas Durnan; **Production Designer:** Stephen Roloff; **Costumes:** Madeleine Stewart; **Visual Special Effects:** Neil Williamson, Anthony Paterson, Calibre Digital Pictures, Nerve FX Inc., C.O.R.E. Digital Pictures; **Music Theme:** Micky Erbe, Maribeth Solomon; **Guest Stars included:** Lisa Ryder, Maurice Dean Wint, Margot Kidder, Andrew Jackson, Anne Marie Loder, Christina Cox, Marina Sirtis

Syndicated/Tribune Entertainment/Roddenberry-Kirschner Productions/Alliance-Atlantis/Baton Broadcasting Corp./Tele-München/Polygram Television International/CTV Television Network/CHUM Network; October 1997-May 2002; 60 minutes; 110 episodes; DVD status: Seasons 3–5

Gene Roddenberry was a more prolific writer-producer than the general public gives him credit. Recognized throughout the world as the creator of *Star Trek*, Roddenberry was actually more imaginative because of several lesser-known projects and a few that didn't even make it to the soundstages. In the 1970s he created and produced four made-for-TV movies that were exciting and provocative pilots for proposed TV series: *Genesis II* (1973), *Planet Earth* (1974) (about the rebirth of civilization in a post-disaster scenario), *The Questor Tapes* (1974) (about the construction of an intelligent android in search of his creator), and *Spectre* (1977) (a Sherlock Holmes–type adventure into the supernatural). For various reasons, none of these movies became a series.

Another of Roddenberry's unproduced television series concepts, originally developed for CBS, was the bold *Battleground: Earth*, written for 20th Century–Fox. It would take 20 years for the idea to become a reality as *Gene Roddenberry's Earth: Final Conflict.*

Battleground: Earth, a second draft script written by Brian MacKay, with a story by Roddenberry, dated July 1978, was very similar to what finally did get aired as the series' premiere episode. It was, to say obliquely, a "simplified edition" of the filmed 1997 pilot. It was about William Boone, a Nebraska chief of police who saves a Taelon from an assassination attempt by a resistance group which included one of Boone's close friends. The Taelon (no personal name is used) is so impressed with Boone's protection, they want to recruit him to become an "inspector" and work for the Companions. But there's a catch: Boone must be "implanted" which "coerces" him to do their bidding. The implant here is a scar between the eyebrows. Unlike the final version, Boone is pushed and shoved to the Companion-controlled Washington D.C. for a "debriefing" which is really a secret attempt to "implant" him. Lili Marquette, of the Resistance, warns Boone and encourages him to take the job because the doctor who will be performing the implant is one of them, and has "weakened" the implant's abilities so that he can retain his free will. Boone agrees and embarks on his double-life as both a Companion "inspector" and a Resistance mole.

What's not in the original script is the billionaire Jonathan Doors, the Taelon holographic technology and shuttles, the "Skrills," Sandoval and the killing of his wife. Those were all details laid in for series progression. The futuristic weapon seen here is a "Zator" which is a simple hand-held device that fires a powerful laser beam.

Curiously, the physical description of the Taelons is very different in this script than in final form. On page seven, the alien is described as "an upright bi-ped with two 'arm' appendages. Its skin purplish colored and is taller than a human and its head is larger. It has no nose and only a slit for a mouth. In places of ears there were two small flaps. Its clothing is of unusually fine metal mesh with iridescent hues. In the center of the chest is a 'survival pack' which converts oxygen into carbon dioxide. There is a faint glow and [it] produces a low humming noise when in use. When the Taelon speaks the voice is highly-pitched, almost female or childlike."

According to author David Alexander, who wrote Roddenberry's authorized biography, producer Cy Chermak was mounting the series for CBS. He got as far as putting out a call for ten scripts with costumes being designed when it was abruptly shut down by the CBS brass. Apparently, it was "too realistic, too frightening" for presentation on television. One actor who had been considered for a lead role, presumably that of Chief William Boone, was a handsome young up-and-comer who had spent a lot of time auditioning and filming pilots. It wasn't until 1980 that he struck gold with his very own prime-time detective drama series, *Magnum P.I.* That actor was Tom Selleck.

Roddenberry was, at the time, in England producing his television movie *Spectre*. He subsequently reopened an office at Paramount, attempting to revive *Star Trek* for the big screen.

Credit for reviving *Battleground: Earth*'s script goes to Roddenberry's wife, Majel Barrett Roddenberry. After his death in 1991, Majel sorted Gene's papers and came across the material. She decided that it was time the concepts were brought to life and shopped it around Hollywood. Answering the call was David Kirschner. A veteran film and television producer, Kirschner had produced horror films (*Child's Play*), animated feature films (*The Pirates of Dark Water, The Pagemaster, Cats Don't Dance, Titan A.E.*), and comedies (*The Flintstones*). Working with him at David Kirschner Productions was Paul Gertz, who had co-produced *The Pagemaster* and *Titan A.E.*

"I had been a huge *Star Trek* fan of the original series for years and that served me well," recalls Gertz. "She responded to that. We took Gene's creation and developed the show. The original script was really 'big,' I remember. It was really violent. It wasn't that we had to update it. We changed it quite a bit. The essential concept was there — the implant, the Taelons, all that was still there."

The scenes depicting the attempted assassination of the Taelon, Gertz felt, were "too big" for television and required modifications. Plus, the producers felt there ought to be more elements integrated into the first story that would help mount an ongoing series format. This accounted for the installation of the FBI agent Sandoval and the billionaire Jonathan Doors, as well as others like Dr. Julianne Belman, a member of the Resistance. "There were broadcasters involved and different people had notes and we had to [make the show affordable]. Plus, it took us a while to figure out where we wanted to take the show. So that's another reason, we wanted to take it into a certain direction and we had to set that up in the pilot. Some of that wasn't [in the original script]. Majel felt, in the years he had written that piece, [she] had become much more interested in a universal peaceful message even though we were doing an action show."

Kirschner and Gertz were given enough information to build a full-blown TV series. "We didn't have to struggle too much about staying with his vision because it wasn't as if he had an entire series arc mapped out for the show or even what the ultimate mystery was. We had a pilot script and a couple of premises. But we didn't have an entire series mythology mapped out. We just took what he created initially and built on that. We weren't sitting around in the beginning, thinking, 'Gee, what would Gene have wanted?'"

In the revised version of the pilot, adapted by producer-writer Gertz (but still credited to Roddenberry), now titled "Decision," the *Battleground: Earth* universe was updated and customized for a full-fledged year with new characters and situations.

In the opening episode, Captain William Boone, assigned to arrange for security of the alien Taelon Da'an at a public gathering, saw billionaire Jonathan Doors shot down by an assassin. In the rush to find the shooter, Boone was amazed to witness the killer rapidly descend by wire from the building and he recognized the man as a close friend, Ed, the best man at his wedding. As Ed escaped, Doors was declared dead by Dr. Belman. Boone began his own private investigation. Later, Da'an invited Boone to become a Companion Protector, a job he declined. He was planning to retire and start a family with his wife Katie. When Katie was forced off the road by a mysterious man and died, Boone was devastated.

Led to a local nightclub by Companion shuttle pilot Capt. Lili Marquette, Boone was surprised to meet Ed and even more surprised to learn that Jonathan Doors was alive, having faked his death. Doors explained that he wanted to "go underground" and secretly investigate the Taelons. They (and Dr. Belman who helped with creating the illusion) were members of a Resistance group, determined to learn the Taelons' true agenda on Earth. They encouraged Boone to take the Companion Protector job to have someone "on the inside" learn of the Taelons' true motives and activities on Earth. When Boone accepted the job, he allowed the aliens to inject into his body a CVI (Cyber-Viral Implant), which granted him enhanced mental powers and total recall. The CVI also injected a strong "motivational imperative" to serve the Taelon interests. Unknown to the Taelons, however, Dr. Belman had secretly modified the CVI without the "imperative" so that Boone's mind was still his own.

He was also given a Taelon "Skrill" creature

(embedded into his right forearm), a powerful Taelon weapon that fired energy bolts upon mental command. The Skrill was, in fact, a self-aware sentient entity. With a new job and alien technology given to him, Boone was ready to search for his wife's killer and embarked on the most dangerous mission of his life — straddling a covert and overt role, either one of which could cost him his life.

"The scene in the square in Toronto, where it was filled with people, when Da'an arrives on a shuttle, was a very expensive and big gigantic shot to get," says Gertz. "It was almost a metaphor for the entire series. We were landing on the television landscape where Da'an was landing in front of all these people in the square. Watching the entire crew there, it was just an amazing feeling. David Kirschner used to always say to me, 'The greatest thrill is always to walk on the set and see 200 people working and you realize it's straight from your imagination. You think of something and 200 people build it, light it, act it, and shoot it. That's an incredible feeling.'"

After the events of the first episode, the first year played out broadly as a science fiction adventure drama in the near-future with a backdrop of a world three years into a relationship with an alien race that arrived on Earth, bringing gifts and alien technology.

The Taelons who arrived on Earth were tall, slender and humanoid beings with pale skin. The Taelon ambassador for North America was Da'an, who appeared to be compassionate towards the humans. Because of their asexual appearance, for convenience Da'an was referred as a "he." Says actor Robert Leeshock, "When I saw the Taelons for the first time, I was very intrigued by them. That whole thing, 'Are they men or women?' It's hard to try and figure that out!" In fact, the producers hired only women to play Taelons, electronically modulating the voices to be deeper to accentuate the androgynous illusion. This technique was not new. In 1966, in Star Trek's first pilot, "The Cage" (a.k.a. "The Menagerie"), three women were put under elaborate prosthetics to play the alien Talosians and male voices delivered the dialogue.

Another Taelon, Zo'or, who often sparred with Da'an when they congregated during sessions of the Taelon Synod (the Taelon leadership, 13 of the leading figures who set policies and made decisions), was a more aggressive and militant figure. Zo'or was the agitator of the group, always thinking of their race first and the humans second.

The Taelons' highly advanced technology was organic in nature. One of their contributions was "interdimensional travel." The Taelon shuttle that Capt. Marquette piloted, using holographic controls, jumped from one destination to another by traveling through "interdimensional space." This technology revolutionized the Earth's transportation industry when it was introduced in "Through the Looking Glass." The public could now use "Interdimensional Portals" (they could step into an ID "grid" and instantly be transported from one location to another). The vast distances on Earth were rendered meaningless.

Other players in this web of drama was FBI Agent Sandoval, who had a real "Imperative Implant" which pushed his motivation to serve the Taelons, making him a formidable enemy to the Liberation. Helping Boone and Marquette on the technical level was Augur, an electronics wizard.

Casting the series, says Gertz, was an intensive process because of the many different "production entities" that participated in its financial and creative aspects. "We had Tribune Entertainment and they were a major player and this was their first foray into first-run syndication," says Gertz. "We also had Atlantis Films here in Canada. It was the biggest show they'd ever done. And then we had a big broadcaster in Canada and we had the Roddenberrys. There were a lot of voices, and of course ours [as producers] as well, who wanted to weigh in on the casting."

Because the series was going to be filmed in Toronto, Canada, many of the actors were cast locally. With exception of Kevin Kilner, who was an American, just about all the supporting players were Canadian. Lisa Howard, familiar to genre audiences from her role in Highlander, was cast as Capt. Lili Marquette. Von Flores, who had appeared in William Shatner's TekWar, was cast as FBI Agent Sandoval. One challenge was casting the Taelons; the goal was to present an asexual appearance with alien-like mannerisms and vocal inflections. Canadian actress Leni Parker became Da'an. "She had the right look," says Gertz. "She really had a lot to do with what the Taelons ultimately became. She really did a great job."

In the first year, Boone and Marquette discovered that aliens had landed by an Amish village and were killing its residents in the form of miniature butterflies. Boone had to use his Skrill to destroy them. In another episode, Boone was shocked to discover that a Taelon named Ma'el had arrived on Earth centuries ago and prophesied that humans would become equal to the

Taelons. At the year's end, an ancient Taelon enemy was revived on Earth: Ha'gel, a Kimera who was an ancestor of the Taelon race. He had the ability to shape-shift and take on human form. He assumed the identity of agent Sandoval and impregnated another Companion Protector, Capt. Siobhan Beckett. Boone confronted the alien, and was severely wounded. Simultaneously, the alien disintegrated as a result of Boone's Skrill energy blast. Meanwhile, the Liberation realized that Beckett was impregnated during her encounter with Ha'gel. In the final images of the episode, we saw a scarred and presumably dead Boone floating in a blue tank and Zo'or vaporized him with blue Taelon light. This episode, "The Joining," was effectively Kevin Kilner's final episode as a regular on *E:FC.*

The critical reaction was encouraging. Kathie Huddleston, writing for *Sci-Fi Weekly*, an online newsmagazine produced by the Sci-Fi Channel, said prophetically, "While it's doubtful *Earth: Final Conflict* will have the longevity of *Star Trek*, it could have a healthy future if the show's creators are true to Gene Roddenberry's vision."

When the series pilot aired, it finished at the top 10 of all syndicated programs.

The filmmakers decided that for the second year, a new lead star was needed. According to Gertz, "The broadcasters felt we could reach a different audience by replacing the lead so we did that. Kevin Kilner did a great job but it was believed we could reach a larger audience with a slightly different kind of casting. So we changed the lead character and brought in Robert Leeshock."

Any time the star of a series departs, either by choice or "for dramatic reasons," the audience may or may not continue watching. The fan audience had grown to like Boone, although some felt he was not as emotive as he could have been.

Another factor that may have prompted a change was Kilner's behavior on the set. A stickler for logic and continuity, Kilner would sometimes stop filming and blurt out, "Logic bomb! Why does this happen? It doesn't make sense!" and complain about plot points. Sometimes his complaints were justified, but others not. The producers also felt the character chemistry was not working. And so for these and, perhaps, other reasons, the pink slip was presented.

Stepping in was a relatively unknown stage and television actor, 31-year-old Robert Leeshock. He essayed a new human-alien hybrid character, Liam Kincaid.

"I didn't want to see too much prosthetics!" chuckles Leeshock. Remembering his audition, Leeshock says, "I walked into the second casting session in New York. [Producer] Jonas McCord was in there. There was something about Jonas, the way he sat there, where I had this strange, very good hunch. I said, 'This guy just gets me!' For some reason he was very cool and laid back. I got

Robert Leeshock as *Earth: Final Conflict*'s Liam Kincaid, a Liberation leader fighting against the Taelons (© Alliance-Atlantis Communications).

this audition material. I took the direction and it made my performance better. I left the audition and just let out a feral kind of scream. I couldn't do a better job! It felt so liberating because it was very challenging material. They gave me material that really explored the dark side of the character. There was a dark side and a very bright, hopeful side. So, as an actor it was very challenging."

While in the hands of the Liberation, a revived Beckett gave birth to a baby boy which grew incredibly fast, and became the adult Liam Kincaid, in a very short time. Kincaid was kept from Beckett as she was returned to the Taelons. Because of his unique heritage, which was half–Kimera and half human, he possessed strange alien powers, known as the *Shaqarava*. A blinding energy from the palms of his hands was a weapon and a personal force field, and was also used to heal injuries. After saving Da'an from an attack by a Jaridian probe, Kincaid became the Companion Protector and, secretly, the new leader of the Liberation, picking up where Boone left off.

"They had a real interesting take on the character," says Leeshock. "But then I think they started to listen to chats on the Internet. There wasn't much sympathy for a character with his attributes, a guy who comes into a room who is 'invulnerable.' The character described to me was interesting only as long as the character wasn't sure from where these powers originated, as if the discovery of these powers could have been shared by the character as well as the audience. Some of the audience didn't see it that way. And I think the writer's explanation of the loss of these powers was lame. They didn't stick to their own mythology, which evidently was built on quicksand. It was a well-designed character, but with no follow-through.

"Where is the courage in that? In a matter of only one episode, they took away Kincaid's powers, this energy that came out of his palms. 'Well, one day I had them, and then the next day I didn't,' about as thought-out as a herpes sore on your lip that just disappears [*laughs*]! That was the best they could explain it? They determined that a hero can't have a power that makes him invincible. Okay, Superman had Kryptonite. The need to take the power away can be justified. Taking the powers away made the character more vulnerable, which it may have needed to be. The purpose was served but the execution of that purpose wasn't thought-out very well."

In the second year, Zo'or attained the position of leader of the Taelon Synod with Sandoval has his protector. Adding to the tensions with Earth, Zo'or believed that the humans should serve the Taelons while Da'an wanted to treat them as equals. One of the Taelons' darkest secrets was that they were at war with another alien race, the Jaridians. And when the Jaridians arrived on Earth, they believed the humans had sided with the Taelons. Over the course of the year, Kincaid eventually revealed his true identity to Beckett, just as she died. In the finale cliffhanger, an assassination attempt was made on President Thompson and all evidence pointed to the Liberation. As a result, Thompson declared martial law and ordered the arrest of Liberation members. Meanwhile, Lili had gained access to the mothership's self-destruct controls and contemplated triggering it, to get rid of the Taelons once and for all.

"Any TV series takes on a life of its own and this one definitely took a life of its own," says Gertz. "The second season wasn't as much fun as the first season. There was a lot more scrutiny.... Broadcasters wanted to retool the show. There was a debate among the different broadcasting entities where to take the show and we lost our way a little bit that year.... I think there were some moments that season where it really shined. But for the most part on season one we hit our stride pretty frequently. In season two with a new lead, it was kind of a new concept that was also starting over again so I don't think we hit it as well in the second season as we did in the first season although we did have some good shows but not as many as we did in the first season. The series concept was difficult to service. People really loved to see the aliens but by nature the Taelons were somewhat passive. That was their mythology. So we brought in their alter egos which was the Jaridians, and there was more to explore."

In the opening of the third year, the faces changed once again. Lisa Howard, no longer a regular character, appeared in only four episodes in the year. (The reason was that Howard was having a baby and wanted to spend time with her family.) Arriving as a new cast member was Jayne Heitmeyer as Doors International CEO Renee Palmer who, together with Liam Kincaid, was at the forefront of the Liberation against the alien races.

The plotting was fragmented in the third year. The chessboard, as it were, was active with many different figures moving about. Lili Marquette was captured by Sandoval aboard the Mothership. Her DNA was altered and she was sent off into deep space to an unknown destination. Liam and Augur believed her to be dead. Renee Palmer, working separately for Doors, occasionally teamed up with Kincaid and the Liberation on various missions. The Taelons' agenda primarily was to find ways, technological or biological, to make use of humans in their battles against the Jaridians. Jonathan Doors died while in the hands of his son Joshua. In an episode late into the year, Liam and Zo'or discovered an artifact from Ma'el's work on Earth, revealing that humanity is the missing link between Taelon and Jaridian, and without humanity, both species would perish.

Marquette later appeared when she accidentally gave Interdimensional Portal access to the Jaridians. In the finale, she returned to Earth pregnant with a Jaridian child, from her union with Vorjack. But in order for the child to live, a Taelon must die.

"Season three was really the most fun for me," recalls Gertz. "Season one, we had a staff of writers who, for the most part, didn't stick around for most of the season. So the first season for the most part I was on my own. Season two I did have a writing partner, and shared for most of it, and he left halfway through. And then another group of people was brought in and that was a bit of a mishmash. Season three was the first time I was able to bring in my own crew. And I had a wonderful year. Being in the writer's room with others is just the best feeling because writing by nature is a solitary endeavor. You spend a lot of time alone. But to be able to sit in a room with a group of writers and map out a season and throw ideas on the wall [was fun]."

Before the start of the fourth year, there was more cast upheaval. Richard Chevolleau, who played Augur, a key ally in the Liberation's activities, exited the series. His replacement, Juliet Street (Melinda Deines), was an intelligent, exuberant, crackerjack hacker.

Beginning in April 2000, at the start of the series' fourth year, a new technological component was added to the series' filmmaking process: Sony provided one of their first production models of their CineAlta digital production system for *Earth: Final Conflict.* The Digital High Definition Camcorder (HDW-F900) was a first for episodic television. Today, the use of digital camcorders is quite common.

In the fourth year premiere, Marquette gave birth to her half–Jaridian and half-human child and escaped on a shuttle to safety. (Never to be heard from again. This was a plot that was considered for follow-up in subsequent episodes, but abandoned.) In the later half of the year, it was discovered that the Taelons were dying. Their "core energy" was fading and so many of them entered "stasis" to conserve their energies. The Taelons and the Jaridians were once the same race, called the Atavus, but an evolutionary split had occurred.

In the events depicted in the fourth year finale, "Point of No Return," Ma'el's secret regeneration chamber was discovered by Liam, Juliet and Renee. To survive, both the Taelons and the Jaridians must put aside their hostilities and engage in a "joining" at a regeneration chamber planted on Earth underneath a volcano by the Taelon scout Ma'el, who had arrived centuries ago.

In the final scenes, the remaining members of Jaridia and Taelon, with Liam Kincaid in the center, coalesced in a blinding white light as the volcano violently erupted. Renee, Augur and Juliet escaped just before it blew up.

Because of his unique heritage as a human–Kimera hybrid, Kincaid had his own role to play in the process. Leeshock is very candid when he expresses some confusion, even to this day, as to the purpose of his character. "I always thought my character was a connection to all species," notes Leeshock. "My character was the key to unlock the miscommunication between the Taelons and the human beings. That's what I assumed the arc was. The more my awareness grew as a character, the more I would be able to shed light on both the Taelons and the humans. So that somehow through the inner struggle within my character, [there] would be some revelations for the rest of humanity as well as the Taelons. And also the combination of me uniting the Taelons with the human beings would then serve to ward off any threat from any other alien races out there.

"In that episode I don't see that arc being addressed or completed. Maybe that was my own ignorance to assume that was my purpose as that character. I was left confused as to what was the purpose of the character. Maybe the character served that purpose to facilitate that union. That could make sense to me."

Summing up his fantastic journey on the series, Leeshock remarks, "The whole experience was a pretty life-changing event. In the beginning it was very exciting and challenging. It was a little sobering when you understand all the politics that go with business and creating television. And then you get a little discouraged when you realize there are many egos involved. And then it's disappointing when you realize that, maybe, you're just a pawn in someone else's economic game. It ends kind of soberly when you realize you're just an economic casualty. When it comes down to it, it's just a business. It was an evolving process. But in a lot of ways it was meeting kind, friendly people who are very creative. And you sort of have to wean out the creative, interesting people from the ones who are just there to get a paycheck."

Fortunately, Leeshock didn't leave the series feeling completely cynical. He made many friends, felt welcomed and learned a lot as an actor. "Meeting Eugene Roddenberry, and his mother Majel, I got a glimpse into what an incredibly principled and ideological world that Eugene's father had created," says Leeshock. "I felt a responsibility to uphold that legacy that was created by him. To become friends, and to hold on to that friendship with Eugene makes me understand who his father was. And what an honor it was to serve as a character in this man's universe.

"The true friendships remain. The fact that Eugene and I are still friends to this day makes me understand the seed of what the Roddenberry legacy is all about. To retain that friendship, and that of another guy [producer-writer] Jonas McCord, who was basically responsible for hiring me. Those lasting friendships are the ones that stay with me and remind me of this very humanitarian experience I've had."

Gertz says that it wasn't guaranteed that the show would see a fifth year, despite the mandate to reach that far so the show could be sold into syndication as a five-year package capable of being "stripped" weekly by local stations. "I don't think season four was a particularly satisfying year for people. [It was decided] to bring in a new premise and a new take on the aliens to give the show some spice and a reason for people to come back."

In the premiere of the fifth year, viewers were greeted with an *E:FC* that was essentially a "reboot" of the series premise. With the demise of both the Taelons and the Jaridians, the aliens now were the original species: the Atavus. And they were evil. And Renee Palmer was now the heroic figure of the series with Juliet Street.

The leader of the Atavus, Howlyn, declared that their race visited Earth centuries ago, but were driven into hibernation. They fed on humans to survive and now were determined to conquer Earth. Sandoval rescued the aliens and beamed them aboard the Taelon Mothership, creating a new threat to humanity.

For the bulk of the fifth year, with Sandoval's help the Atavus keep their existence hidden from humanity using the Mothership as their base, and Renee spent her time trying to convince the U.S. government and the world that the Atavus exist and they were humanity's greatest threat.

"The last season of *Earth* was becoming more of a horror show, which was fun," says director David Winning. "It became a vampire show like *Night Stalker*. I really liked what Alan Van Sprang brought to Howlyn. He's a good actor."

"The producers wanted a sexy reptilian vampire!" says Van Sprang. "There had been Atavus before in the show, that looked nothing like we did. But I assumed they wanted something new, something fresh and exciting, and to them sexy reptilian vampires was on the menu."

To accentuate this character's aura, Van Sprang was given elaborate prosthetics makeup and a costume that transformed him from human to an ancient alien resurrected in the 21st century with a sinister visage, long smooth hair and very, very long fingernails.

Van Sprang says the producers wanted a purely evil character in Howlyn. "It was a total domination of Earth and farming humanity as a food source for me, and herding them around with total manipulation and domination. After the first few episodes of saying, 'Okay, he's a bad guy,' I said to myself, 'There has to be something more to this.' I tried to make him a little more realistic, more fallible. That's what I was attempting to do in the latter part of the season. I found doing that a little more interesting. We had some directors who would come in and say, 'We need you to really get angry here and shout,' and I'd say, 'No, I'm not going to do it. I've done that a million times up to this point. If you want me to shout, you've got one or two words I'll scream out but I'm not interested in making him a young, screaming guy anymore because I'm trying to make this arc.'"

Filming was grueling but rewarding for Van Sprang, who says he made many friends during the process. "The 22 episodes seemed to go by so fast. Jayne was fantastic. Melinda and I spent a lot of time on the set, and Von and I became good friends. It was one of the best experiences I've ever had in terms of the cast and crew and producers."

One of the highlights of the fifth year was the return of William Boone (and actor Kevin Kilner). When we last saw him, he appeared frozen inside a blue-gel water tank, scarred and presumably dead. In two episodes written by Gertz,

"Boone's Awakening" and "Boone's Assassin," his return to life four years later illustrated how he became, literally, a man out of time.

"We always felt that the Boone storyline needed some closure," says Gertz. "We had a lot of fans never forgive us for losing Boone to begin with. I felt strongly, and everyone agreed, that we had a lot of Boone fans. We had a lot of Internet dialogue [with fans]. You want to give viewers what they want."

In "Boone's Awakening," Sandoval baited Renee Palmer by reviving Boone in order to get her into the hands of the Atavus. The story ended with Renee killing Boone's sister Sarah to save his life as she was used as a pawn, having become a "hybrid."

In the follow-up episode, "Boone's Assassin," Boone and Palmer used an Atavus crystal to locate all the Atavus hives on Earth and they were ambushed while attempting to destroy a hive. Zo'or was revived and became a female Atavan.

"We pretty much shot [the episode] 'Final Conflict' in sequence," says Van Sprang. "When I died, that was it, my last moment on *Earth: Final Conflict.* I remember sticking around the studio so they could wrap up with Von and Jayne. I remember feeling really sad for Von and Jayne because I knew, especially for Von, he had been there for all five seasons. I was more concerned for how Von was going to take the ending of the series than I was for myself."

Sci-Fi Weekly's Kathie Huddleston wrote of the fifth season, "For a series with a revolving door of cast members, uneven story lines and questionable heroes, *Earth: Final Conflict* has always remained interesting. While the writing has been inconsistent, the casting, the production and the special effects have continually come through and made the series watchable. And when it's good, this series can be very good."

Director David Winning says, "There were so many original *E:FC* fans who just turned their back on the show when Kevin went, because it went in a completely different direction. When *E:FC* started, it was a little bit *X-Files*–like. It could have been that kind of strange, iconic show that *X-Files* turned into but I think they lost the focus of it. You lose audience when you lose characters and things change. There's a lot of people that didn't like the fifth year because of the Atavus."

Stephen Roloff, the series' producer and production designer, reflects on his five-year journey on the series, "There were some things that were enormously fascinating and some things that were disappointing. The show was always at the mercy of somewhat conflicting interests. It was a very strange show because, in five years, it never found that 'center.' There was Majel Roddenberry at one side who represented the Roddenberry legacy, which to me as well as other people, represents the hope of science fiction. We're now in the future and we're now evolved. On the other side was Tribune, which was a very popular syndication company, who were interested in action-adventure. They wanted all the sizzle and pomp that comes along with that, which is a very different kettle of fish from the core Roddenberry ideology. We found ourselves in the middle of that as producers and writers. As a result the show had difficulty finding its gravitational center. There were a number of different 'takes' on what the show was. There really wasn't consensus. It went through a number of executive producers and a number of show leads. We had three different leads over the course of five years. That discontinuity was the [series'] Achilles' heel.... It really changed from season to season."

This became a double-edged sword for the show. Fresh and new ideas were introduced, but then character directions and continuity became increasingly erratic. Leeshock says of his dismissal, "It was just driven by economic reasons. They explained to me that [dropping the character] was more a business decision on their part. They wanted to minimize the production costs. That was the driving force to creating the fifth season."

The series' developmental structure ended up being in three phases: Phase 1 was the first year, a representation of Roddenberry's vision of the series. Phase 2 was a further expansion of that premise during years two and four but with original ideas and different characters thrown into that mix, notably Kincaid, Palmer and the Resistance people. Many new details were added such as the war with the Jaridians, the existence of the Atavus, and the Taelon "Volunteers." And phase three was the fifth year, which was a deliberate reinvention of the series' premise. The original aliens were merged with their enemies and from that sprang the new species the Atavus. The show's creators could have made a better series had there been a more consistent approach to the plot and characters.

CAST NOTES

Kevin Kilner (Capt. William Boone): While attending Johns Hopkins University in his native Baltimore, Kevin was a member of the National Championship Lacrosse Team. Kevin began his acting career with a role in the movie *Home Alone 3* (1997). After *Earth: Final Conflict* he appeared in a number of films including *The Brainiacs.com* (2000), *American Pie 2* (2001), and *A Cinderella Story* (2004).

Robert Leeshock (Maj. Liam Kincaid): Leeshock, a native of New Jersey, graduated from Cornell University with a degree in Engineering in 1989. He enrolled in acting classes in New York, while waiting tables, doing commercials and performing in theater productions. His first acting role was in the daytime drama *Loving*. Eventually Leeshock appeared in over 30 commercials and starred in the soap operas, *All My Children, Guiding Light,* and *Another World*. He also appeared in the prime-time *Beverly Hills 90210*. After *Earth*, Leeshock starred in *As the World Turns* and *One Life to Live*.

Jayne Heitmeyer (Renee Palmer): Born in Montreal, Canada, she has appeared in many science fiction and horror TV series and films. Her first film was 1992's *Coyote*. She made appearances in the TV series *Sirens, Sci-Fighters* (1996), *Twists of Terror, The Lost World* (1998), and *Night Man*. Since *Earth: Final Conflict* she has been seen in the movies *Xchange* (2000), *Stardom* (2000) and on many TV series and movies for TV including *The Snake King, A Killer Upstairs,* and *Canadian Case Files*.

Lisa Howard (Capt. Lili Marquette): Howard was born in London, Ontario. Aside from *Earth: Final Conflict* she is best known for her role as *Dr. Anne Lindsey* in *Highlander: The Series*. She also made guest appearances on the series *Perry Mason, Days of Our Lives, Wings, Forever Knight, RoboCop: The Series, The Pretender* and *Suddenly Susan*. Howard is married to producer-writer Daniel Cerone, who worked on episodes of *Earth: Final Conflict* and *First Wave*.

Von Flores (Sandoval): *Filipino-American* actor Flores has enjoyed leading roles in a number of television productions, including the series *FX: The Series* and *Kung Fu: The Legend Continues*, and the TV movies *TekWar, TekJustice* and *TekLords*. He has guest starred on *The Adventures of Sinbad, Lonesome Dove, E.N.G., Street Legal* and *Night Heat*. Flores has also appeared in feature films, most notably in the critically acclaimed *I Love a Man in Uniform* (1993) and *Eclipse* (1995).

David Hemblen (Jonathan Doors): Born in London, England, Hemblen has had a healthy career in theater, film and television as both an actor and director. He has appeared in more than 20 series and 30 films, and his stage career includes more than 70 productions as actor-director at major Canadian theaters. He is probably best known for his portrayal of Lord Dread in *Captain Power and the Soldiers of the Future* (1987–88). He has also been in *The Twilight Zone, Short Circuit 2* (1988), *TekWar, Robocop, Forever Knight, Witchblade* and *Nero Wolfe*.

Richard Chevolleau (Augur): Chevolleau, born in Kingston, Jamaica, soon emigrated to Toronto, where he was raised. Aside from his role on *Earth: Final Conflict*, Chevolleau has made numerous guest appearances on Canadian TV series. He won a Gemini award in 2004 for his appearance on the television show *The Eleventh Hour*. He currently lives in Toronto with his two daughters.

Leni Parker (Da'an): Parker was born in New Brunswick, Nova Scotia. She began her film career in 1990 with a role in the film *You're Driving Me Crazy*. She went on to play minor roles in such series as *Are You Afraid of the Dark* and *Sirens* and in the TV movie *Hiroshima* (1995). She played Corp. McDonald in 1994's *Screamers* and had a recurring role in the Canadian TV series *Emily of New Moon*. She also played a role in 2000's TV version of *Hound of the Baskervilles*. Since *Earth: Final Conflict* she has been seen in a number of TV series including *Mambo Italiano* and *Moose TV*.

Anita La Selva (Zo'or): La Selva began her career with the 1987 TV movie *A Conspiracy of Love*. She continued on with guest spots on television series such as *Forever Knight, Secret Service, Million Dollar Babies,* and *TekWar*. Since *Earth: Final Conflict* she has appeared in the 2004 film *Dead End Road* and in the TV movie *Trudeau 2: Maverick in the Making* (2005).

Melinda Deines (Juliet Street): Deines was born in Alberta, Canada. She learned acting at Ryerson Theater School in Toronto. She has been seen in the short-lived *Nancy Drew* series in 1995. Since *Earth: Final Conflict* she has guest starred in such series as *Mutant X* and *Sue Thomas: F.B.Eye*.

Alan Van Sprang (Howlyn): Van Sprang's extensive list of television credits includes *Stolen Miracle, Soul Food, Drop the Beat, D.C., Traders,*

The City, PSI Factor: Chronicles of the Paranormal, Code Name: Eternity, Le Femme Nikita, Made in Canada, The Raven, Viper and *Dangerous Intentions.* He also appeared in several feature films, including *NARC, Steal this Movie, The Uncles, Masterminds* and *Resident Evil: Apocalypse.*

Guylaine St. Onge (Juda): St. Onge was born in Quebec. After working as a model and a dancer she appeared in the Canadian television series *Mount Royal.* Since then, St. Onge was a regular on many shows including *Lonesome Dove* and *Fast Track.* She guest starred in *The Newsroom* and *Foolish Heart,* and also made guest appearances on *Le Femme Nikita, The Outer Limits* and *Largo Winch.* She had roles in the movies *One Way Out* and in *Angel Eyes.* She died of cervical cancer in 2005.

SOURCES

Alexander, David. *Star Trek Creator: The Authorized Biography of Gene Roddenberry.* New York: Roc, 1994.

"Alliance Atlantis' Sci-Fi Action Drama Series Gene Roddenberry's Earth: Final Conflict Becomes First Episodic Television Production in the World to Film in Sony CineAlta 24P." Press release, Alliance-Atlantis, June 2000.

"Battleground: Earth." Screenplay by Brian McKay, story by Gene Roddenberry. Second draft, January 3, 1977.

Huddleston, Kathie. "Gene Roddenberry's Earth: Final Conflict: Gene Roddenberry Offers Another Compelling Future." *Sci-Fi Weekly,* October 1997.

Earth 2
(1994–1995)

In the year 2192, most humans live on space stations because Earth is essentially dead. A group of explorers decide to colonize an alien planet rich in natural resources and begin their trek to a western seapoint called New Pacifica.

Cast: Debrah Farentino (Devon Adair), Clancy Brown (John Danziger), Jessica Steen (Dr. Julia Heller), Rebecca Gayheart (Bess Martin), John Gegenhuber (Morgan Martin), J. Madison Wright (True Danziger), Sullivan Walker (Yale), Antonio Sabato Jr. (Alonzo Solace), Joey Zimmerman (Ulysses Adair)

Created by: Billy Ray and Michael Duggan & Carol Flint & Mark Levin; **Executive Producers:** Michael Duggan, Carol Flint, Mark Levin; **Supervising Producer:** Cleve Landsberg; **Producer:** Tony To; **Co-Producer:** P. K. Simonds; **Associate Producers:** Chip Masamitsu, Janace Tashjian; **Coordinating Producer:** John P. Melfi; **Consulting Producer:** Christian Williams; **Writers included:** Billy Ray, Jennifer Flackett, David Solmonson, Michael Duggan, Carol Flint, Mark Levin, Eric Estrin, Michael Berlin, Carl Cramer, Arthur Sellers, Heather MacGillvray, Linda Mathious; **Directors included:** Scott Winant, Joe Napolitano, Felix Enrique Alcala, John Harrison, Daniel Sackheim, Janet Davidson, Deborah Reinisch, Michael Grossman, Jim Charleston, James Frawley; **Guest Stars included:** Lisa Ebyer, Julius Carry, John David Garfield, Kevin Wiggins, David Elliot, Lilyan Chauvin, Roy Dotrice, Christopher Neame, Erin Murphy, Tim Ransom, Francia DiMase, Richard Bradford (as Cmdr. O'Neill), Marcia Magus (as Magus), Terry O'Quinn (as Reilly), Tim Curry (as Gaal); **Directors of Photography:** Felix Enriquez Alcala, Stephen Lighthill; **Music:** David Bergeaud; **Special Creature and Makeup Effects Created by:** Greg Cannom; **Visual Effects:** Dream Quest Images

November 1994-May 1995; NBC/Universal/Amblin Entertainment, Inc.; 60 minutes; 22 episodes; DVD status: Complete series

"This is a land where magic happens!" Those are the words of a ten-year-old girl who sees this alien planet with wonder. The ratings were magic too, as *Earth 2* premiered in the top ten. But by the following January, viewership had spun into oblivion.

Rather than a hard-edged action-adventure series, *Earth 2* was more of an ecologically minded, character-driven show. Devon Adair was a single mother, born and raised on a space station. Her son had been born with "The Syndrome," a disease caused by living in the sterile space station environment. Returning to Earth was not an option; it was now a trash heap, overrun with rats, with its resources depleted by over-population, atomic wars and a thinning ozone layer.

Devon believes the natural environment of a new, pristine planet (G-889) can cure her son. She and two dozen colonists go into suspended animation for a 22-year journey to this world. Two hundred forty-eight other families, on other space stations, will follow later. But sabotage by government operatives (who want this rich planet for their own purposes) causes Devon's space station to spin out of control as it approaches the planet. Everyone awakens in time to use their escape pods, which land on the alien planet.

Their new surroundings are picturesque, with streams, trees, and blue skies, but as they undertake a trip to New Pacifica (near an ocean thousands of miles away) the forests are replaced by harsh terrain of rocky hills and valleys. Devon pushes the pioneers hard, determined to make New Pacifica operational by the time the other families arrive in 26 months.

Steven Spielberg's Amblin Television brought in writers Mark Levin, Carol Flint and Michael Duggan to create Earth 2's premise. "Carol and Mark and I were given the sentence 'Wagon Train in space' or sometimes 'Wagon Train on another planet,'" says Michael Duggan. "A writer named Billy Ray had already done a presentation document for Amblin. He had done a good job starting off the concept, but Universal and Amblin wanted more experience behind it, not that we had much. It was late in the selling season, and initially we turned it down, or at least I did. I felt it was too late to get it up and running, should we actually sell it. Universal was relentless, as they knew they had a hungry buyer in NBC. I thought that if Mark, Carol and I all jumped on it, we might have a chance to write it fast and mount the production in time to get on the air. Though none of us had ever done sci-fi per se, Mark and Carol were very good and experienced writers as well as producers. Universal and Amblin asked us not to contact Billy Ray, probably for legal reasons. If I had to do it over again, I would definitely contact him. He had done a hell of a lot of work on it, but given that the three of us were in a sprint to finish the work, we really never gave it much thought."

As for Spielberg, "Steven kept a fair distance, more out of respect for our process, and due to the fact that he was knee-deep in a couple of movies," says Duggan. "He did send us a very complimentary note after screening the pilot. He was available if needed, but the pace of that first season barely gave us enough time to breathe." The original idea was that the colonists' trek would take several years, with character conflicts, alien encounters and natural disasters making good grist for stories. Spielberg watched all of the show's dailies, read the scripts and offered suggestions but it was up to the three writers to actually produce the show.

One important contributor to the pilot film was Hugo Award–winning SF writer Greg Bear. "Carol Flint contacted my friend, Alan Brennert, for assistance with Earth 2's science fiction background," he recalls. "Alan referred Carol to me, and I agreed to serve as an advisor. I worked with Carol and the design and production department, and looked over the pilot script, making suggestions as to how to focus and improve the story's technical details and increase scientific credibility. After the pilot, the producers decided they did not need my services any more." Of his brief association, Bear says, "One of the most enjoyable aspects of advising on the show was working with Carol Flint, a true professional. The most fun part was consulting with the design department. I've always wanted to be a special effects artist! They were a terrific group, wide open to suggestions. We talked for hours about aspects of the show's design. Even after my contract was not renewed, I took calls from the design department but to my chagrin, could no longer play in that wonderful sandbox."

Character-wise, in addition to Devon and her son Ulysses, there was John Danziger, a mechanic who has a hard time accepting Devon as their leader. "You're crazier than I heard," he snarls when she sets up a punishing work schedule. However, Danziger, a widower, begins to respect Devon and they become friends. His daughter, True, has extraordinary curiosity about this world and often goes off alone exploring. And there's Yale, who tutored Devon when she was a child. Part cyborg, he can access information via a computer chip in his brain.

Morgan Martin is the cowardly bureaucrat who was supposed to spy on these travelers but is now marooned with them. Obsessed with his own self-preservation, he trembles with terror at the slightest hint of danger. His beautiful wife Bess is a calming influence on him but even she gets annoyed by his frantic antics.

Dr. Julia Heller is torn between her loyalty to her government (to whom she makes secret virtual reality reports) and her concern for the castaways. Nearly lost in the shuffle is Alonzo, a young pilot. He develops a psychic bond with bipedal subterranean warriors called Terrians, who are fiercely protective of their world and stalk the human interlopers. There are also the Ewok-like creatures known as Grendlers, who make comical noises, with ooze dribbling from their huge mouths. They are nuisant scavengers and steal food from the colonists.

The show's writers strived to make the human element a priority. "We wanted it to be character-oriented," says Duggan. After *Earth 2*'s pilot was greenlighted, several locales were investigated for location filming, including Australia, Hawaii, North Carolina, Vancouver and Calgary. Instead, it was decided that the rocky area just outside Sante Fe, New Mexico, would suffice. Some fans thought the New Mexican desert looked too familiar.*

Once filming got underway, the cast and crew experienced onslaughts from nature: heavy rainstorms that delayed filming; lightning storms that sent everyone scrambling for cover; cold and hot spells that gave cast and crew members colds; and wild bears that stole food and supplies. But like hardy pioneers of the west, the *Earth 2* personnel persevered.

"I was the first assistant director for half of the shows, so I have many, many weather stories," says director Janet Davidson. "One day I looked around and there wasn't a cloud in the sky. Within 15 minutes, we were in the middle of a horrible storm. Our camera assistant's hair went straight up, meaning she had become a target for lightning. As she tried to run for cover, someone knocked her down to safety. We had complete sets washed away by rain, rattlesnakes at our feet, and freezing temperatures. It still remains one of my career highlights. But because of the difficulties in shooting, no one director could ever finish their episode. Assistant directors had the job of doing a lot of second unit filming to finish a show."

The *Earth 2* characters drove a powerful Trans Rover, which was activated by voice commands. There was also a yellow metallic robot called Zero (played by stunt coordinator Tierre Turner) who did little but stomp around in the background. The robot occasionally yelled, "Warning! I read an approaching projectile!" or "I have a wide variety of retractors available." Danziger had disdain for the lumbering bucket of bolts and the robot became less visible as the series progressed.

In the early episodes, the settlers encountered a stranded astronaut named Gaal, played by a grinning, straggly-haired Tim Curry. No one trusts Gaal and for good reason; he has his own devious plans. But when a perceptive Yale suggests leaving the sinister man behind, Devon rebuffs him with, "He's a human being! We can't leave him behind." So Gaal is allowed to accompany them. This gives Gaal a chance to trick young True into believing his tall stories and getting her to lie and steal for him. All the while he's making deals with the Terrians. When True realizes Gaal is using her, she snatches the villain's protective necklace. He's pulled underground by the Terrians, screaming, and is never seen again.

J. Madison Wright was a wonderfully expressive actress as True but her early escapades, such as sneaking off from camp, stealing the Trans Rover, eavesdropping on untrustworthy adults, mingling with aliens and giving piercing cries of terror whenever she encountered danger, tended to detract from the planet's ominous atmosphere. Her role was cut back to give the adults more room to maneuver

But *Earth 2* couldn't escape its derivative, Western-type roots. Novelist Arthur C. Clarke (*2001: A Space Odyssey*) called it "the Donner party in space" (referencing the 19th century pioneers who turned to cannibalism when trapped in a snowy valley) while *The Houston Chronicle* said, "Circle the wagons—The Terrians are coming!"

But even the ill-fated Donners couldn't do what Dr. Julia Heller could do—use her incubator machine to turn an embryo into a fully matured horse! "Horses magically popping out of cans!" the cowardly Morgan shrieks. "No decent food! No toilets! I want to get out of here!" The frightened bureaucrat never fathomed this weird world of science and mysticism.

As the series progressed, some characters evolved. Julia learns her holographic government boss is a liar and she forever disconnects her communications with him. Danziger, the most grounded male character, falls prey to human foibles when he shoots and kills one of the grunting Grendlen animals. After a variety of excuses,

A more eerie setting may have been the Trona Pinnacles in California, a dry lake basin with the strangest-looking geological features in North America. This was where TVs Lost in Space (in 1965) had done all of its second unit work. Tim Burton later filmed his Planet of the Apes (2001) in the rugged location.

he tearfully confesses that he really shot the creature in a moment of fear. In "Grendlers in the Myst" we learn more about True's loneliness and how she misses her deceased mother. "That was actually from my experience with my own mother's death," recalls its director, Janet Davidson. "A young girl in a strange place without a mother is a universal theme, one that is not explored much."

Morgan, on the other hand, continued his terrified rants about living on this world. He shoots at unarmed Terrians, uses a ground-freezing machine that nearly kills the other colonists, unwittingly causes the Trans Rover to topple over and injure Danziger, conspires to steal precious minerals from the planet, sneaks food when no one is looking, and whines that he's afraid of dark caves. Morgan is such a wuss that even Julia knocks him out with a good smack when he refuses to obey her orders. Devon gets exasperated by Morgan's childish behavior. "He's an adult," she chides to Bess as the wife coddles her shivering husband. "Why don't you treat him as one?"

None of the male characters could escape the estrogen-driven orbit of the series. The women ruled. Devon Adair (played with strength and compassion by Debrah Farentino) was the leader. Julia Heller, as the doctor, had life-and-death power over everyone else. And Morgan was led by the nose by his wife, Bess. Young True not only helped destroy the male villain (Gaal) but frequently disobeyed her father's orders. Meanwhile, Alonzo blamed himself for crashing the ship and was now a powerless, grounded pilot, while Yale stood obediently by the side of Devon. The male characters were essentially rendered inert in contrast to the well-delineated female characters and the charismatic actresses who portrayed them.

"The cast was really quite wonderful but Debrah was always underrated," says Davidson. "I think it was during Earth 2 that she found her love. I looked into her eyes one day and I just knew she was pregnant. Turns out she was, and she didn't even know it yet." Farentino also kept in touch with the outside world during location shots. "Debrah had a knack for cell phone reception," says Davidson. "No one else could get a call out. She would be sitting in the middle of a field, talking to someone. She even had a pouch made on her costume for her cell phone. During a scene with Clancy, she forgot to turn her cell phone off. It rang and we all just stood there. Finally she answered it and the director cut. From then on, we always had a prank regarding cell phones and Debrah."

Media reviews of Earth 2 were encouraging. "The pilot is uneven but there's no denying the series' potential," said Joyce Millman of San Francisco's Free Press. "The scenery is gorgeous, the writing is often evocative and Farentino gives a beautifully detailed performance." On the other hand, Millman didn't care for "[t]he chatty robot and a weaselly bad guy straight out of Lost in Space." The Houston Chronicle drew parallels with old sagebrush sagas and added, "It's Lost in Space, light years updated, sci-fi family style. But it could be a big winner."

It was also a lot of work. Director Joe Napolitano recalls his first episode: "I was driving around with the location manager, looking for locations. We keep driving and driving for hours on this dirt road and we took a walk into the rolling hills and the rocks. I said, 'Wow, this is fantastic! But how are we going to shoot here?' The location manager said, 'Why not?' I replied, 'How are you going to get everything out here? We're on a dirt road, in the middle of nowhere.' Since the show was set on another planet, you couldn't allow viewers to see any wires or totem poles, or streets or signs. You had to film out in the middle of nowhere. Being budget-conscious, I said to him, 'How do we shoot out here? It'll kill my day!' He replied, 'We do this all the time!' They had the most elaborate transportation departments I've ever seen. Every department had its own all-terrain vehicle set up. They would load things up and they would just do it." Despite that efficiency, he points out, "It was a very expensive show to do. That's probably what ultimately broke it. It's very difficult to do it for a price, especially on a first season. You have to try and keep the money down."

The special effects of Earth 2 were a mixed bag, but they were enhanced by the series' superb cinematography and the repeated shots of two moons bobbing over the craggy landscape. The show's weekly title sequence conveyed the mystery of this world, and David Bergeaud's music was beautiful and rousing. Earth 2 had an extremely loyal base of fans in its 8 P.M. Sunday time slot, and in its first few months, the show retained a top 40 standing. By January 1995, the viewership fell dramatically. Some of this was due to frequent pre-emptions for basketball games and movies. Another factor was that the show's format of exploration was constricted by its complex, often mystical tapestry. There were confusing subplots involving the Terrians (Ulysses' illness is cured by his simpatico with the Terrians), fuzzy encounters with other humans, shadowy government conspiracies, flashbacks, time travel, and politically correct environmental themes. When interspersed with the already rich conflicts of the protagonists, it made for a thick mixture that the mainstream audience may have found too hard to fathom or believe.

Occasionally, there were moments of uncluttered discovery, such as when Devon and Danziger explore a mountain cliff and spot an emerald-colored lake in the distance. Danziger climbs down the cliffside, and discovers the lake is made of acid. There were no overly complicated scenarios here, no messages or supernatural overtones, just a potent reminder of the deadly differences that could await human beings on an alien world.

"*Earth 2* would be considered a hit today," says Janet Davidson. "Our numbers were weak in those days, but would be strong today. With the ease of current CGI, we could have done much more interesting things. I was always, along with the crew, trying to get more thought placed into the show about *our* planet Earth, our own wonderful environment, and how we need to care for it. Today, *Earth 2* could be a lesson in green living."

In the last aired episode, "Flower Child," flower vapors take over Bess and Morgan and direct them to a bottomless pit, where the pair expel spore vapor from their mouths and a fiery explosion erupts from the pit. It releases gas into the atmosphere and the season of spring begins over the planet. This episode made it clear that humans were needed to complete this climate cycle and they will now be an integral part of this alien world.

Earth 2's stay on NBC was over. Fans donated $3,500 to place an ad in *Daily Variety*, pleading for another year. Even Steven Spielberg was impressed by the fans' attention. But the ratings had spoken. "We were aware of the fan base," notes Duggan. "Shows like this tend to pull in a certain type of loyal base — always imaginative and well read, and incredibly willing to offer feedback. Because we were always so rushed, we rarely had time to catch up with the email or letters." Looking back, he says, "The strengths of the show were good characters, a good world and backstory, etc. But we were flying by the seat of our pants. We had inconsistent stories and tonality at times. A second season would have ironed all of that out. The outlines for the first group of shows for the next season were very strong."

"The pilot show had real promise, and was enjoyable to watch," says Greg Bear. "The series could have developed into something special, had it been given time, perhaps on a par with *Farscape* or *Battlestar Galactica*."

At a 1997 convention, an original *Earth 2* script sold for $400 and fans on the Internet continued to express hopes of a reunion movie. Jessica Steen later cornered a Universal TV executive and asked why the show had been canceled. She was told that it came down to money. The mediocre ratings didn't justify the expensive location work.

"It was really Universal's reticence to step up to what the show would cost," explains Duggan. "NBC was very supportive. They showed up with more money when they realized the studio wouldn't. The location shoot in Santa Fe was one factor in its cancellation, but truthfully, not enough to hang it on. The deals we had cut with locals and a large deal we had cut with New Mexico made it very affordable. And our line/creative producer Tony To put together a crew in Santa Fe that pulled off incredible stuff for our budgets. The budgets could have been overcome but there were many studio politics involved in the demise of the show."

Duggan confirms the network was interested in another season. "NBC had a tentative offer on the table for an initial order for a second season," he says. "Debrah Farentino was pregnant at the end of the first season and she was just starting to show. Had we started shooting a second season, she would have been in the last stage of pregnancy. We pitched NBC story ideas for season two, which dealt with Farentino's real-life pregnancy by putting her character in cryo-sleep. We suggested we shoot those scenes right away, before going on hiatus. NBC liked the idea and gave us the tentative go-ahead. That's when Universal balked. They wanted to change the creative direction in order to cut costs. The studio's idea was that the group had now reached New Pacifica and thus the studio could pull the show back to L.A. and shoot on the lot. As producers, we felt it was creatively wrong, and not much of a cost saver. Universal went ahead and pitched a new, cut-down version of the show, with new producers. NBC passed. Shortly after, I ran into Steven Spielberg at a benefit. He asked why we hadn't reached out for help when we needed it most with this political fight we had with Universal. In retrospect, I wish we had. Surely, he would have had an impact."

When the series was released on DVD in 2005, Justin Rude of *The Washington Post* noted with nostalgia, "While not groundbreaking, *Earth 2*'s ideas were fresh considering the scope of sci-fi presented on network television. It was another decent show lost to impatient network expectations."

CAST NOTES

Debrah Farentino (Devon): As a child, she excitedly watched the *Apollo 11* astronauts walk on the moon in 1969. She immediately began saving up her money, hoping she could one day buy a trip to the moon. The actress also admitted she loved *Lost in Space* as a kid but when she was offered *Earth 2*, she refused to read the pilot script, thinking it would be juvenile SF. Once she read it, she realized it would be a real human adventure. Farentino, who originally studied to be a biologist, is the ex-wife of actor James Farentino. In 1995, as *Earth 2* was coming to an end, she was named as one of the 50 Most Beautiful People in the world by *People* magazine. One of her earliest TV credits was William Shatner's cop show *TJ Hooker* in 1984 (where she was billed as Debra Mullowney). Her post–*Earth 2* credits included *Outer Limits*, *NYPD Blue* and the starring role in the TV series *Eureka* (2006).

Clancy Brown (Danziger): He graduated from St. Albans Prep School in Washington D.C. and then went on to Northwestern University's theater program in Illinois. As a boy he grew interested in acting after discovering the world of William Shakespeare. One of his first TV appearances was on *The Dukes of Hazzard* (1983). He later did films such as *The Bride* (1985), *Highlander* (1986), *Pet Sematary 2* (1992) and *Shawshank Redemption* (1994). He later appeared in *Starship Troopers* (1997). He's also an in-demand voice artist and has provided character voices for many cartoon series since the 1990s (*Gargoyles*, *The Batman*, *Superman*, *SpongeBob Squarepants* and *Justice League*). He was also a regular on the supernatural series *Carnivale* (2003–2005).

Jessica Steen (Julia): Born in Toronto, Canada, she started as an extra on Canada's *SCTV* series and appeared on the homegrown Canadian shows *The Littlest Hobo* and *The Edison Twins* in the early 1980s. In 1987 and '88 she starred as pilot Jennifer Chase in *Captain Power and the Soldiers of the Future*. Steen dismissed *Captain Power* at the time, thinking it was just a kids show, but was surprised by letters from young women who were inspired by Jennifer's strong, resilient nature. Her next series was the critically acclaimed *Homefront*

(1991–1993), a show set in Ohio just after World War II. She also appeared in the blockbuster film *Armageddon* (1998) and had TV guest roles on *Navy NCIS*, *Outer Limits* and *Touched By an Angel*. She originated the role of Dr. Elizabeth Weir on *Stargate SGI* (in a two-parter called "Lost City," designed as a spin-off episode for *Stargate Atlantis*) in March 2004 but, much to the disappointment of her fans, she was replaced for the subsequent series by Torri Higginson.

John Gegenhuber (Morgan): The description of Morgan in the *Earth 2* story bible was that he had gone to the "Dr. Smith school of space travel." Gegenhuber was thrilled, *Lost in Space* had been one of his favorite shows growing up. After *Earth 2*, he appeared in *Seven Days*, *Star Trek: Voyager* and *The Pretender*. He's also a writer and professional puppeteer.

Rebecca Gayheart (Bess): The Kentucky-born actress originally read for the role of Dr. Julia Heller but the producers felt her quiet strength was perfect for Bess, who counterbalanced her husband's panic attacks. Gayheart started out as a model and was well-known for her Noxzema facial cream advertisements. Since *Earth 2*, she has appeared on *Beverly Hills 90201*, *Nip/Tuck*, *MAD TV*, *Ugly Betty*, *Hercules* and the film *Scream 2* (1997). *Earth 2* remains a positive memory for her and she felt the series was improving as it went along.

J Madison Wright (True): This former child actress began modeling at the age of five and made her acting debut in an episode of TV's *Grace Under Fire* in 1993. She was ten when she was cast in *Earth 2*. Her later credits included *ER* and the unsold pilot, *The Warlords: Battle for the Galaxy* (1998). Shortly after retiring from acting, she was diagnosed with a degenerative heart condition and received a life-saving heart transplant in March 2000. Clancy Brown, who played her father on *Earth 2*, helped raise money to cover her medical expenses. She recovered but sadly, just after her honeymoon in July 2006, she passed away from heart failure. At the time of her death, she was planning to teach English in high school.

Sullivan Walker (Yale): He taught education classes in his native Trinidad before moving to New York to study acting. It was his featured role in Paul Hogan's *Crocodile Dundee* in 1986 that set his career rolling. Roy Dotrice was one of the actors considered for the role of Yale but Walker won it. After the series, he did episodes of *Law and Order*, *The Sentinel* and *The Pretender*.

Antonio Sabato Jr. (Alonzo): Born in Italy, his

father was a western cowboy star. He came to the U.S. at age 12 and later played Jagger on *General Hospital* (1992–1994). His other appearances included *Outer Limits*, *Melrose Place* and *Lois and Clark: The New Adventures of Superman*. In 2005 he joined the cast of the soap opera *The Bold and the Beautiful*. Sabato has reportedly said that he considered *Earth 2* "a dreadful show."

Joey Zimmerman (Ulysses Adair): He made his acting debut in the TV film *Jack Reed: Badge of Honor* (1993) and appeared in the film *Mother's Boys* (1994). More recently he's starred in the TV film *Halloweentown III* (2004).

SOURCES

Chrissinger, Craig W. "Brave New World—The People of Earth Get a Second Chance on a New TV Frontier Off on Another Planet." *Starlog* no. 209, December 1994.

_____. "Company Man—Exploring Earth 2 as Government Liaison John Gegenhuber Lives Out His Childhood Fantasy." *Starlog* no. 212, March 1995.

_____. "Wilderness Leader—Debrah Farentino Realizes a Childhood Dream of Space Travel, Exploring Earth 2." I no. 211, February 1995.

Hicks, Chris. *Earth 2* Review. *Deseret Morning News*, 1994.

Hodges, Ann. *Earth 2* Review. "'Earth 2' Soars to New Sci-fi Heights." *Houston Chronicle*, November 5, 1994.

Letters page. *Starlog* no. 223, February 1996.

Millman, Joyce. *Earth 2* Review. "'Earth 2': A Planet of One's Own—New Sci-fi Series is Lost in Space but Found on the Ground." *San Francisco Free Press*, November 11, 1994.

Farscape

(1999–2003)

Astronaut John Crichton, piloting an experimental craft around Earth, gets drawn into a wormhole and thrown out on the other side of the universe. Suddenly in the middle of a space battle, he finds himself aboard a living ship with a group of escaping prisoners. Chased by Peacekeepers, they flee farther into the Uncharted Territories, looking for safety and a way home.

Cast: Ben Browder (John Crichton), Claudia Black (Officer Aeryn Sun), Anthony Simcoe (Ka D'Argo), Virginia Hey (Pa'u Zotoh Zhaan) *Year 1–3*, Jonathan Hardy, (Voice of Dominar Rygel XVI), Lani John Tupu (Voice of Pilot), Lani John Tupu (Crais) *Year 3*, Wayne Pygram (Scorpius) *Year 3–4*, Gigi Edgley (Chiana) *Year 2–4*, Paul Goddard (Stark) *Year 3*

Recurring Cast: Tammy MacIntosh (Jool), Kent McCord (Jack Crichton/Ancient), David Franklin (Braca), Melissa Jaffer (Old Woman Noranti), Raelee Hill (Sikozu), Rebecca Riggs (Meleon Grayza); **Created by:** Rockne S. O'Bannon; **Executive Producers:** Rockne S. O'Bannon *Year 1*, Brian Henson, David Kemper *from episode 7*, Robert Halmi, Jr., Kris Noble *Year 1*, Rod Perth *Year 2*, Juliet Blake *Year 3–4*, Richard Manning *episodes 22 to 34*; **Co-Executive Producers:** David Kemper *until episode 7*, Naren Shankar *episodes 22 to 34*, Richard Manning *episodes 22 to 34*, Justin Monjo *episode 57 onward*; **Supervising Producers:** Justin Monjo *episodes 45 to 56*, Mark Saraceni *Year 4*; **Co-Producer:** Andrew Prowse *Year 3*; **Producers:** Matt Carroll *Year 1*, Sue Milliken *Year 2 & Year 4*, Anthony Winley *Year 3*, Andrew Prowse *Year 4*; **Line Producers:** Richard Clendinnen *Year 1*, Anthony Winley *Year 2*, Lesley Parker *Year 3*, Anne Bruning *Year 4*; **Associate Producers:** Andrew Prowse *Year 2*, Lily Taylor *Year 4*; **Consulting Producers:** David Wilks *episodes 2 to 6*, Richard Manning *episodes 7 to 22*, Doug Heyes, Jr. *episodes 18 to 22*, Sue Milliken *Year 3*; **Executive Consultants:** Rockne S. O'Bannon *Year 2–4*, Richard Manning *episodes 1 to 7*, Ro Hume *Year 1*, Carleton Eastlake *episodes 55 to 62*, Emily Skopov *Year 4*; **Creative Consultants:** Sally Lapiduss, Justin Monjo *Year 1*; **Writers included:** Rockne S. O'Bannon, Carleton Eastlake, Richard Manning, Doug Heyes, Jr., David Kemper, Naren Shankar, Michael Cassutt, Ben Browder; **Directors:** Andrew Prowse, Brian Henson, Pino Amenta, Brendan Maher, Tony Tilse, Rowan Woods, Ian Watson, Peter Andrikidis, Catherine Millar, Michael Pattinson, Ian Barry, Kate Woods, Karl Zwicky,

Geoff Bennett; **Directors of Photography:** Craig Barden *Year 1*, Russell Bacon *Year 2–4*; **Production Designers:** Ricky Eyres *Year 1–2*, Tim Ferrier *Year 2–4*; **Visual Effects:** Garner McClellan Design *Year 1*, Animal Logic *Year 2–4*; **Guest Stars:** Natasha Beaumont, Chris Haywood, Francesca Buller, Felix Williamson, Claudia Karvan

Sci-Fi Channel/The Jim Henson Company/ Hallmark Entertainment/Nine Network Australia *Year 1*; March 1999–March 2003; 60 minutes; 88 episodes; DVD status: Complete series

The first-year title sequence of *Farscape* tells viewers the premise, with narration provided by Ben Browder's John Crichton. As startling images of aliens and space flash by, Browder says, "My name is John Crichton, an astronaut.... A radiation wave hit and I got shot through a wormhole.... I'm lost in a distant part of the universe on a ship, a living ship, full of strange alien life forms.... Help me, help me. Is there anybody out there who can hear me? I'm being hunted by an insane military commander.... Doing everything I can, I'm just looking for a way home."

This seemingly simple idea, of a contemporary human thrust into the midst of a very alien society, sprung from the mind of series creator Rockne S. O'Bannon.

O'Bannon, who wrote the screenplay for *Alien Nation* and created NBC's *seaQuest DSV*, started working on what would become *Farscape* after meeting Brian Henson. Henson had taken the helm of the Jim Henson Company after his father's death, and was interested in making a more adult television program which could use sophisticated animatronic puppets. O'Bannon worked on developing the series, then called *Space Chase*, and he and Henson looked for an interested network.

When the Fox network ordered four scripts in 1997, O'Bannon brought in David Kemper, who had worked with him on *seaQuest DSV*. Ultimately Fox as well as the other regular networks passed on the series. A few years passed by with no takers. Henson, O'Bannon and Kemper all moved on to other projects but stayed in touch. The strong potential of *Space Chase* was too good to give up. Finally the Sci-Fi Channel got wind of the project which by this time had been floating in Hollywood for a couple of years, and decided to give *Farscape* a chance.

"When we sold *Farscape* to the Sci-Fi Channel, the network had been around for a few years, but had subsisted almost entirely on reruns of old SF series," recalls O'Bannon. "They had just begun producing new episodes of *Sliders*, which they'd picked up off the Fox network. But Rod Perth, then-president of Sci-Fi, was looking for a completely original series that could serve as the flagship of the nascent network. He read a couple of the *Farscape* scripts we'd written when we were in development for Fox, and called in Brian Henson and me. We talked about our vision for the series, and Rod signed on for a year's worth."

And so, *Farscape* was launched. "It was the perfect fit," continues O'Bannon. "Because the network didn't want a conventional, outer space 'ship' show, the Henson Company was known for producing distinctive and highly creative projects, and I was at a place in my creative career where I was ready to really step out from what I'd been seeing on television all my life. So from the very beginning, all three entities— network, production company, and I — were making the same show."

However, there was one marketing problem to consider. The Jim Henson Company was most famous for their Muppets and family feature fare such as *The Dark Crystal* and *Labyrinth*, while *Farscape* was intended to be adult science fiction. "Whenever you're trying to sell something that can't be easily categorized, the job becomes tougher," says O'Bannon. "The network had the unique show they wanted, but the question was, 'How do you make the audience understand that just because it's the Henson Company and it has animatronic characters in it, this isn't a show for kids, or a cousin to the Muppets?' That was always difficult, because any marketing artwork that included our characters and said 'From the Jim Henson Company' couldn't help but suggest a younger tone. It wasn't until the show began to air and viewers began to discover it for themselves, that the show's uniqueness started to become apparent to viewers and potential viewers."

Ben Browder, probably best known as Sam in *Party of Five*, was cast as the lead, John Crichton, a sort of Everyman thrust into an alien environment. The show would be made in Australia, for both creative and financial reasons.

"Once we were there and began to experience the incredible talent pool available there, we found it was the place to be," says O'Bannon. "It's not overstating it to say that *Farscape* would not have been the show we've all come to love if we'd shot anywhere other than Australia."

According to Carleton Eastlake, a writer and executive consultant on the series, "The show was

Claudia Black as Aeryn Sun and Ben Browder as John Crichton in *Farscape* (© USA Networks/Sci-Fi Channel).

scattered around the globe with the production headquartered in Sydney, Australia, the American network [Sci-Fi Channel] split between New York and Los Angeles, and the lead production company [Jim Henson Company] spread across Los Angeles and London. But even in Sydney, the show was all over the place. The stages were in suburban Sydney, the effects house was on the Fox lot in downtown Sydney, and the locations were often out in the wilderness."

Cast in supporting roles were Australian actors. Virginia Hey (*Mad Max 2: The Road Warrior*) was selected to play the serene priestess Zhaan. Anthony Simcoe was cast as the Luxan warrior, Ka D'Argo. Two other aliens, the deposed Hynerian monarch Rygel, and Pilot, fused with the living ship *Moya*, were animatronic puppets, the first voiced by Jonathan Hardy, the second by Lani Tupu. Claudia Black (*Pitch Black*) was chosen for the role of Aeryn Sun, an alien who appeared human, but was a Sebacean Peacekeeper.

As production got underway in Australia, O'Bannon and Kemper found a wealth of Australian talent ready to help create a new science fiction environment. The fact that only Browder was American, while just about everyone else in front of and behind the camera was Australian, helped create the very exotic and alien environment. *Farscape* looked like no other television show and had a fresh, new premise.

One of the challenges of the series was to find writers besides O'Bannon and Kemper who would not think about a military command structure or a *Star Trek* episode as they worked. "We writers simply wrote what would engage us as viewers," explains O'Bannon. "Among television, films, books, we've all heard so many thousands of stories in our lifetimes. It takes a great deal to truly surprise and engage an audience in a way that they perhaps haven't experienced before. That's what we were trying to do with *Farscape* as often as we could."

In the first episode, three prisoners (D'Argo, Zhaan and Rygel) are trying to free themselves and the living ship *Moya* from Peacekeeper control. Crichton's module pops out of a wormhole in the middle of their battle. The prisoners bring Crichton on board. When *Moya* speeds away from the battle, Officer Aeryn Sun also gets dragged along. She doesn't know that Captain Crais wants revenge on Crichton, who he believes killed his brother. When she tries to return to the Peacekeepers with Crichton, Aeryn is declared

contaminated. She and Crichton escape back to *Moya*. They have no choice but to join *Moya*'s passengers and flee from the pursuing Peacekeepers.

Crichton could be anyone in the audience. He has no idea where he is, how he got there, or how to get home. He is injected with translator microbes so he can understand much of the alien languages, but he does not know anything about his new companions. Everything about them is alien. He spends most of the first year just trying to stay alive.

Humor becomes one of Crichton's defenses as time goes on. His contemporary pop cultural references became one of his trademarks. These were both scripted and ad-libbed.

Much like Buck Rogers (particularly producer Glen Larson's 1979 TV series incarnation of the pulp character), Crichton is a fish out of water. These were two characters transported into space inside their spaceship and their first encounter upon arrival at a point in space is with aliens. Both characters hang on to all that they know from Earth's cultural history as a lifeline to their sanity. The effect, naturally, was that no one around them understood what they jabbered about.

Toward the end of the first year, a lithe runaway Nebari named Chiana (Gigi Edgley) joined the group aboard *Moya*. Fans just starting to get comfortable with the very alien and bizarre *Farscape* characters were initially nervous and upset: The writers were giving a clear signal that *Farscape* was not going to follow any formula. In fact, the writers often tried to make viewers uncomfortable. Throughout the series, new regular and recurring characters were introduced, and characters died, even popular ones. It wasn't unusual to have actors play various roles in and out of makeup. "One of the advantages of so many guest characters being in heavy makeup was that when you found an actor who was a terrific talent, you didn't have to mark them as 'used goods,'" says O'Bannon. "You could use them over and over, either in makeup as another character, or without makeup. Fans certainly seemed receptive to the evolving cast changes. It created a sort of ensemble feeling to the production."

In year one, Crichton achieved some level of understanding and comfort in the midst of his new surroundings. But things got turned upside down at the end of the first year with the appearance of the half–Scarran, half–Sebacean Scorpius (Wayne Pygram). Scorpius, initially envisioned

A montage of *Farscape* characters. Front row, from left, Anthony Simcoe, Ben Browder, Claudia Black, Lani John Tupu, Virginia Hey. Back row, from left: David Franklin, Rebecca Riggs, Francesca Buller, and Wayne Pygram (© 2005 The Jim Henson Company).

as an evil Mr. Spock, has amazing strength and mind control abilities, and wants Crichton's understanding of wormholes to make the most powerful weapon in the galaxy. He tortured Crichton in the Aurora Chair ("Nerve"), which convinced him that Crichton knew more than he was telling. Scorpius would never stop chasing Crichton until he possessed the wormhole secrets. And Crichton wants to stop Scorpius. The last episode of year one featured an amazing visual cliffhanger, as D'Argo and Crichton float free in space above Scorpius' military base, on fire as a result of their actions. Crais has been disgraced, and has run off with *Moya*'s offspring, *Talyn* (a baby living ship).

By this time, the small army of people making *Farscape* hit their stride. The show found its audience, becoming the Sci-Fi Channel's most-watched program. It also became a hit in the other countries where it aired, including England and Canada. The fans, called "Scapers," flocked to the Internet, where they could post messages on the official bulletin board, or create sites of their own. Since *Farscape* had not yet aired in Australia, the Internet provided the only link between the people making *Farscape* and the fans watching it. The actors and writers frequently visited *Farscape* sites, both reading, posting, and chatting. There were unofficial meetings and conventions. It wasn't long before the announcement of *Farscape*'s first official convention, something that would become an annual event in California. *Farscape* also captured the attention of the media. Matt Roush of *TV Guide* gave the show a "Rave" and called it the best science fiction on television.

Ratings looked good, and a second year started production. Most, but not all of the creative team stayed intact. O'Bannon stepped back in the second year, becoming executive consultant. David Kemper, running the show in Australia and back and forth between there and Los Angeles, created an atmosphere where creativity flourished and everyone working anywhere on the show had input. There was a spirit of invention and discovery. Unlike some other SF epics, this was not a universe where all the events were pre-planned from the get-go. The filmmakers reveled in their freedom to "make up the universe" as they went along.

Key writer-producers, like Richard Manning, well known to *Star Trek* fans, and Justin Monjo, new to science fiction television, put their own spin on the *Farscape* universe. A core group of Australian directors continued to make every episode look like a feature film. Animal Logic (a company that had worked on *The Matrix*) took over the visual effects.

At this point, all the key elements of the series were in place. Episodes would vary wildly in tone and content through every year. There were wacky comedies, bizarre episodes involving mind-altering drugs, aliens and space, big battles, huge heroics, love stories, visits to Earth or what looked like Earth. The characters formed bonds with each other. Many would say that *Farscape* was a character-driven show. Aeryn and Crichton turned out to be soul-mates, developing a very serious, but not simple, relationship. Scorpius, with his own agenda, also introduced the two species battling for control of space, the Sebacean Peacekeepers and the Scarrans. All wanted wormhole weapons. For this they needed to get Crichton, who continued to learn more about wormholes, with some involvement by a race called the Ancients.

Whereas in year one, Crichton achieved some sense of comfort and control in his new surroundings, in year two, he literally descended into madness. In "Crackers Don't Matter," Crichton saw hallucinations of Scorpius. Over time, the audience learned that Scorpius had put a copy of himself on a chip into Crichton's brain, trying to get the wormhole information directly. By the end of the second year, Crichton's insanity forced the others to try and get the chip out. He was left on a doctor's table with his head open, Scorpius in possession of the chip, and Aeryn dead.

Year three's theme was summed up by the title of the first episode "Season of Death." Eventually Zhaan died as a consequence of reviving Aeryn. Crais, who joined Crichton and Aeryn to help stop Scorpius from acquiring wormhole weapons, sacrificed himself at the end of the year. Crichton gained some control over the Scorpius clone, which didn't leave with the chip. In between, a perfect copy of Crichton died, trying to keep wormhole knowledge away from both the Peacekeepers and the Scarrans.

The doubling of John Crichton during year three provides a good example of the "*Farscape* spin" on science fiction. The *Farscape* writers, having penned episodes of various *Star Trek* incarnations as well as many other genre shows, were determined to do science fiction plots in new ways. Rather than making a clone of Crichton in the episode "Eat Me," they doubled him, making two identical, real Crichtons. One stayed on board *Moya* and had wacky adventures. The other John, henceforth dubbed "Talyn John," joined Crais and Aeryn on Talyn. From then on, their experiences diverged. Talyn John fought to keep wormhole knowledge away from the Scarrans. He also embarked on a glorious love affair with Aeryn.

When Carleton Eastlake was brought in to help with the scripts over a ten-episode stretch, he was surprised by the frenetic pacing of the production as its creators struggled to pull together a weekly TV series while straddling production offices in three continents. Story meetings with producers, story editors and other writers were not typical Hollywood affairs, he says. Most of the meetings were held on the go in Sydney, Australia. "On most Hollywood shows, you go into some sort of office-like place and then spend endless hours in an air-conditioned conference room breaking stories," says Eastlake. "*Farscape* was a little different." A typical story conference would be attended primarily by producers David Kemper and Richard Manning, writers Justin Monjo and Lily Taylor, and Holly, a USC film intern. What was unusual about these conferences was that they would take place in Kemper's BMW automobile, "driving on the wrong side of the road at warp speed, racing between the effects house and the new theme music composer's studio and then the stages, and so forth," chuckles Eastlake. "David, who is an incredible multi-tasker, worked two different cell phones ringing from London, New York and L.A., while we all tossed ideas around along with our lunches. In short, there was an amazing similarity between our story meetings and, say, a typical war council among the *Farscape* characters on screen with David in sort of the Crichton role.

"One reason we spent as much time in the car as possible was that the Bimmer's air conditioning worked, unlike the swamp cooler in the writers' vast loft at the sound stages, which made a lot of noise, raised the humidity level to unbearable heights, didn't cool anything, and was finally hauled away by an air-conditioning technician who warned us that the thing was probably breeding Legionnaire's bacterium.

"There's a reason the *Farscape* characters were always in motion bouncing through wormholes around the galaxy but only occasionally visiting home or a simulation of home — it was autobiographical."

Eastlake was brought in because Kemper felt it was time for John Crichton to die. That is, the "doubled" Crichton who was living aboard the *Talyn* with Aeryn and Crais. As detailed in the two-part episode "Infinite Possibilities," John and the Ancient (who has taken the form of his father Jack, as played by Kent McCord) make their way to a planet to find Furlow, who gained access to John's knowledge of wormhole technology, and to prevent her from making that knowledge available to the Scarrans. When they meet Furlow, they realize that a Scarran dreadnaught is on the way and Jack devises a weapon to destroy the dreadnaught while John battles with Scorpius' neural clone.

When Furlow secretly betrays John and Aeryn by killing the Ancient, John completes the weapon himself and attempts to launch it against the dreadnaught. But a malfunction gives John a strong dose of radiation. He succeeds in launching the weapon and destroying the dreadnaught in a spectacular fashion and returns to *Talyn*. There, he dies in Aeryn's arms. (Aeryn subsequently wanted nothing to do with the other John.)

"My chief — and only — contribution to the mythology of the show was how wormholes could be a weapon," recalls Eastlake. "There had been ominous references to this throughout the series, but no one had had time to sit down and figure out the particulars. So I thought about it and pitched the idea that control over wormholes meant that aside from the obvious value in being able to jump behind enemy lines, they could also be used as the ultimate world-destroying solar-plasma weapon. That was an easy idea to sell!"

While devising a means of doing away with John Crichton, Eastlake recalled his world history and talked with Kemper. "I still remembered reading with horror about the death in the early days of the Manhattan Project of the first human to see the 'blue flash' of Cherenkov radiation from a fission reaction with his bare eyes," says Eastlake. "He, of course, died a horrible death from radiation sickness. Once David told me Crichton

had to die, I told him the story of the blue flash. He found it very moving, so the concept of Crichton seeing the blue flash but denying it and getting on with the business of saving his friends became the theme the two hours steered towards."

The scriptwriting task was pushed back until just two days prior to his return to Los Angeles from Australia, so Eastlake talked his way into a two-parter episode. "I might as well just write a DVD-friendly two-hour script which would basically free up three writing weeks all at once," grins Eastlake. "That was also an easy idea to sell!"

Kemper was amenable because the very next episode was the difficult and expensive "Revenging Angel." That episode, a loving homage to Warner Bros.' "Looney Tunes" cartoons, had Crichton in a deep coma and battling it out with both Scorpius and a "Toon'ed" D'Argo inside his head. And because it was inside his head, it was easy to conjure up animated analogs of the various characters. "Revenging Angel" was one of the series' most audacious episodes. Could the show really retain credibility afterwards? It was David Kemper who developed the idea and wrote out the animated segments first, so that an Australian animator could get started, and then fit it to the "live-action" sequences afterwards.

"Seeing David work on the episode was quite entertaining, because it meant that we got to watch a great many classic cartoons and break down how their gags worked, and it was all pretty stress-free for us because David was so deeply into doing that one himself, we weren't doing the usual group story work on it," says Eastlake. "When I saw it, I thought David had captured the spirit of the golden era of these cartoons perfectly, and the reputation of *Farscape* for going where no show had gone before was further confirmed."

Once Eastlake worked up his script in Los Angeles, location and budget problems surfaced. The problems were two-fold: Although the locations were terrific visually, it was also incredibly big which meant it wasn't credible that our little band of heroes could protect the area. This was solved with artificial intelligence cannons and Rygel manning one malfunctioning cannon. A space battle to recover the stolen wormhole generator was too expensive so someone suggested "Rewrite it as a dune buggy chase!" which provided for exciting location battles.

Says Eastlake, "David and Ricky turned out many, many rounds of change pages, as they always did, in part because David would never run out of new ideas about an episode and kept feeding them into the script until it was in post! In the end, the two hours looked fabulously rich visually, tested Rygel's and Crichton's conflicting moral values to the core, and gave the supernumerary Crichton a big sendoff while leaving the remaining Crichton with the certainty that he had potential access to enormously destructive technology which meant that he had crushing moral responsibilities. So I was happy."

"Each season I grew a little farther from the hands-on role I had in getting the series up and running," says O'Bannon. "I did a great deal of rewriting of scripts in seasons one and two, but by season three, I hand-picked three 'signpost' scripts that I wanted to write: Aeryn meeting her mother, the reunion of the surviving John with Aeryn, and the death of Crais and the destruction of the Scorpius's wormhole experiment."

In year four, the large political landscape of Scarrans against Peacekeepers continued, as Crichton and the others tried to stop the escalating tension. John returned through a wormhole to Earth, which became a potential target of attack. Aeryn realized that she was pregnant with Crichton's child. The year offered a mix of stand-alone adventures, while leading to further confrontations between Crichton, the Peacekeepers, and the Scarrans and Scorpius, who wound up aboard *Moya*. When the year ended, relative peace seemed at hand after John closed the wormhole to Earth. John, with Aeryn, in a boat floating near *Moya*, proposed to Aeryn. At that minute a ship appeared and a weapon disintegrated both of them — "To Be Continued."

Although the Sci-Fi Channel, at third year had ordered both a fourth and fifth year, O'Bannon said that they did have an "out" for changing their minds on fifth year and they ended up exercising that.

Despite continued critical success, multiple Saturn awards, and even an Emmy nomination for costumer Terry Ryan, the show ended abruptly. Ratings had flattened, and even declined. *Stargate SG-1*, now on the Sci-Fi Channel, drew more viewers. Plus, *Farscape* cost a lot of money to produce. The fourth year ended with a cliffhanger which aired in March of 2003.

"Unfortunately, the expense of the show reared its head, the network tried some hardball tactics, and it backfired on all of us," O'Bannon says. The "tactics" involved offering the production company a shortened year of about ten episodes. The producer's reply: "No!" "From what I understand, the network was as shocked and upset as anyone

that their tactic had resulted in no fifth year," says O'Bannon.

Outraged fans jumped into action. They first heard about the cancellation from David Kemper in a September 6, 2002, chat on the Sci-Fi Channel website. Kemper wrote, in part, "We are two days away from shooting our last scenes of year four. As you know, Sci-Fi has picked us up for fourth and fifth year. But as with everything done on the corporate level, there was an out clause built into Sci-Fi's pickup schedule. As of yesterday, we were informed, after massive efforts by everyone at Henson and working on the show ... that Sci-Fi was not going to exercise its option to pick up the fifth year.... Tuesday will be the last time Ben dons the uniform of Commander John Crichton. We are all hugely sad. I am shaking as I write this. Yesterday, we all cried on the set."

The Internet lit up with Scapers looking for a way to keep *Farscape* going. They raised money, wrote letters, and placed ads in trade magazines. CNN did a story on the fan campaign and interviewed Browder.

No one gave up, not the fans, nor the people making *Farscape*. Apparently impressed by the fans' dedication to the show, a financial backer made it possible for the Jim Henson Company to finish the story. Eighteen months after the series was shut down, production on *The Peacekeeper Wars*, a four-hour mini-series with a budget of $20 million, was greenlighted. The mini-series aired in October 2004 on Sci-Fi Channel. Ratings were strong, about six million aggregate viewers, but not any higher than the show's ratings for the fourth year. It appears that the mini-series did not attract any new viewers to the saga.

"Because of the incredible fan outpouring of support, Brian Henson was able to find funding to produce the four-hour *Peacekeeper Wars* entirely independently," says O'Bannon. "It was a testament to the passion everyone felt for the series that all the cast we wanted back, as well as the key creative personnel behind the scenes, all returned. The story that David Kemper and I used for *Peacekeeper Wars* was part ideas that David had for a fifth year, and part new invention."

Eastlake says he recalls helping Kemper "break" the Peacekeeper Wars story arc at his house when it was a year four and five bridge, and so when the mini-series finally aired, "I wasn't able to just sit back and enjoy it," he says. "Instead I saw it in very analytical pieces, recalling what had survived from the intended arc, and how it was in a certain sense autobiographical about the ending of the show and so forth."

All the main regular and recurring cast returned, as did some guest stars from past episodes. Although the end of the series made it appear that Aeryn and John were vaporized, they were rescued by Rygel who swam under the ocean and retrieved all of their vaporized bits and, using alien technology, reconstituted them back to life. Aeryn and John immediately got caught up in the galaxy-wide Scarran-Peacekeeper War.

Eventually, and at great cost, the warring sides were brought to the peace table. D'Argo lost his life in battle, and Jool died, as did many others. Crichton used his wormhole knowledge to force the peace, barely surviving himself. He and Aeryn married in between battles, and their son, named D'Argo, was born during a fire fight. In the end, Crichton survived, ready to embrace the peace with Aeryn and their child. Although Crichton cannot return to Earth, he has made a new home.

"*The Peacekeeper Wars* was terrifically satisfying," says O'Bannon. "Even though the production had been dark for over a year, everyone picked up as if no time had passed. Actors, crew, etc., just leaped right back in as if only a weekend had passed. The way *Peacekeeper Wars* ends, it can either be a satisfying conclusion to John Crichton's adventures, or the closing of a chapter, with new chapters yet to come."

On July 16, 2007, Sci-Fi Channel announced the resurrection of *Farscape* as a ten-episode series not for television, but for the Internet, as "webisodes." The same network's *Battlestar Galactica* had experimented with the form in the fall of 2006, when they unveiled ten "web-isodes," or "mini-episodes," titled "The Resistance." Two to three and a half minutes in length, they could be viewed on their website.

"Sci-Fi Channel is anxious to get into web-based broadcasting in a big way, and I think they liked the idea of creating original programming that already has a built-in recognition factor and passionate fan base. They approached us, and Brian and I said, 'Frell yeah!'" exhorts O'Bannon, who uses the invented Sebacean swear word, an analogue of Earth's raw word for sexual intercourse.

On July 25, 2008, announced during the 2008 San Diego Comic-Con, Boom! Comics unveiled the commission of a four-issue mini-series comic book based on *Farscape*. And the good news was that Rockne O'Bannon would write the series. "It's all canon," he said at the convention. "This is a dream opportunity for me. The comic book series starts off directly where the *Peacekeeper Wars* mini-series left us. It's like we're finally getting to experience Season Five. The stories in the ongoing comic series will completely tie into the upcoming *Farscape* webisodes. *Farscape* lives!"

"For me, the *Farscape* experience couldn't have been better," says O'Bannon. "Working with fantastically talented people creating something that audiences really appreciated. Doesn't get better than that. There's talk of a feature film version, also anime. I'd like to think that everyone who worked on the series had a good enough time, and felt the experience was creatively fulfilling enough, that they'd all love to be part of it again, when and if the time comes."

CAST NOTES

Ben Browder (John Crichton): Browder graduated from the Central School of Speech and Drama in London, England. He's a veteran of Shakespearean stage productions, and roles in the films *Memphis Belle* (1990) and *A Kiss Before Dying* (1991). Before *Farscape*, he had a recurring role in TV's *Party of Five* (1996–97). After *Farscape* he played actor Lee Majors in a docudrama, *Behind the Camera: The Unauthorized Story of Charlie's Angels* (2004). In 2005 he joined *Stargate SG-1* as Col. Cameron Mitchell when Richard Dean Anderson stepped away from the series.

Claudia Black (Aeryn): Prior to *Farscape*, this Australian-born actress became familiar to North American audiences via her appearances in the TV mini-series *Seven Deadly Sins* (1993) and *Hercules: The Legendary Journeys* (1997). Later, she appeared in the feature films *Queen of the Damned* (2002) and *Pitch Black* (2000), and acted on TV's *Xena: Warrior Princess* and *Beastmaster*. In 2005, what started out for Black as just a guest-star appearance on *Stargate-SG-1*, evolved into a regular role in the series' tenth year.

Virginia Hey (Zhaan): Hey began her career as a model, and was spotted by casting directors who placed her in Mel Gibson's *Mad Max 2: The Road Warrior* (1981) as the Warrior Woman. The Australian actress later appeared with George C. Scott in *Mussolini: The Untold Story* (1985), with Timothy Dalton in the James Bond thriller *The Living Daylights* (1987) (as Rubavich) and with Christopher Atkins in *Signal One* (1994). As a result of her performance in *Farscape*, in 2000, she was nominated for a Best Supporting Actress Saturn Award. Now based in Los Angeles, Virginia teaches meditation and has established herself as a professional (drawing) artist. She's also worked as a fashion stylist and as a fashion editor in Australian magazines.

Anthony Simcoe (D'Argo): A graduate of the National Dramatic Arts in Sydney, Australia, Simcoe holds a Master of Fine Arts degree in drama, and specializes in actor training. He works as a teacher and a director. He's directed short films and TV pilots. Before *Farscape*, Anthony made TV appearances in *Arthur Conan Doyle's The Lost World* and *Beastmaster*. Anthony also sings with a band called "Signal Room" (a.k.a. "Number 96") along with *Farscape* actor Wayne Pygram. In 2002 he was nominated for a Best Supporting Actor Saturn Award for *Farscape*.

Jonathan Hardy (Rygel's voice): Born in New Zealand, Hardy is an actor, writer and director. He wrote the screenplay for the 1980 Oscar-nominated film *Breaker Morant*. As an actor, he's appeared in *Mad Max* (1978), with TV appearances on *Mission: Impossible* and *The Thorn Birds: The Missing Years*.

Gigi Edgley (Chiana): An Australian actress, Edgley has a B.A. in theater from Queensland University of Technology. She's talented in jazz, ballet and character dance plus martial arts. On television she's appeared in *Arthur Conan Doyle's The Lost World* and *Beastmaster*. One of her most recent acting credits is a feature, *Last Train to Freo* (2006).

Wayne Pygram (Scorpius): Pygram began his acting career in the theater. He's appeared in *Farewell to the King* (1989) and *Return to the Blue Lagoon* (1991) and on television he guest-starred in *Time Trax*, *Arthur Conan Doyle's The Lost World*, and *Lost* (as Isaac). The Australian actor was a young "Grand Moff Tarkin" in *Star Wars Episode 3: Revenge of the Sith* (2005).

Lani Tupu (Crais/Pilot's voice): An award-winning New Zealand–born actor and director, Tupu is a graduate of the New Zealand Drama School. He helped found an Australian theater group called "The Walkers and the Talkers." One of Lani's earliest film roles (billed as Larney Tupu) was in Dolph Lundgren's *The Punisher* (1989). He's made TV guest appearances on *Mission: Impossible*, *Time Trax* and *Arthur Conan Doyle's The Lost World*. Lani originally auditioned for the role of D'Argo.

Paul Goddard (Stark): A British actor, Goddard has a theater background, often working for the Sydney Theater Company. His film appearances included *Mighty Morphin Power Rangers: The Movie* (1995) and he was Agent Brown in *The Matrix* (1999). He was also in Jane Campion's *Holy Smoke* (1999). His TV guest appearances include a *Hart to Hart* MOW titled *Harts in High Season* (1996) and *Arthur Conan Doyle's The Lost World*. Paul originally auditioned for Scorpius.

Firefly

(2002)

Malcolm Reynolds is the captain of Serenity, a small cargo spaceship more than 500 years (A.D. 2517) in the future. He and his crew make a dangerous living in the frontier regions of space as they salvage, transport and cut deals.

Cast: Nathan Fillion (Capt. Malcolm Reynolds), Gina Torres (Zoe), Adam Baldwin (Jayne Cobb), Ron Glass (Shepherd Brook), Morena Baccarin (Inara Serra), Alan Tudyk (Hoban "Wash" Washburn), Sean Maher (Dr. Simon Tam), Jewel Staite (Kaylee Frye), Summer Glau (River Tam) **Created by:** Joss Whedon; **Executive Producers:** Joss Whedon, Tim Minear; **Producers:** Gareth Davies, Ben Edlund; **Associate Producers:** Lisa Lassek, Brian Wankum; **Writers included:** Cheryl Cain, Drew Z. Greenberg, Josh Whedon, Tim Minear, Jose Molina, Brett Matthews, Jane Espenson; **Directors included:** Tim Minear, Michael Grossman, Vern Gillum, Vondie Curtis-Hall, Marita Grabiak, James A. Contner, David Solomon, Allan Kroeker, Tom Wright; **Guest Stars included:** Gregg Henry, Melinda Clarke, Larry Drake, Michael Fairman, Michelle Ferrara, Branden Morgan, Doug Savant, Jason Gray, Christina Hendricks, Blake Robbins, Gregory Itzin, Mark

Sheppard, Edward Atterton, Richard Brooks, Bonnie Bartlett, Craig Vincent, Larry Pennell, Sandy Mulvihill; *Firefly Theme:* Words and Music by Joss Whedon. Performed by Sonny Rhodes

Fox Television/20th Century–Fox; September–December 2002; 60 minutes; 14 episodes; DVD status: Complete series

Cancelled by Fox in 2002 after only 11 aired episodes, *Firefly* returned as a feature film in the fall of 2005. The series had done so well in DVD sales, Universal Pictures took a gamble on reviving it as a feature film. The movie *Serenity* picked up where the short-lived series left off, reuniting all of its cast members.

After his success with the fantasies *Buffy the Vampire Slayer* (1997–2003) and its spin-off, *Angel* (1999–2004), writer-creator Joss Whedon created a western set 500-plus years in the future. The world was picking itself up after a civil war; things were futuristically retro (the taverns looked 19th century but had holograms). Earth's resources had been depleted, so terraforming was used to give other planets and moons habitable atmospheres. The Alliance government (an amalgamation of America and China) ruled most of the galaxy, while at the other end of the spectrum were The Reavers, mutant zombies who ate human flesh and preyed on defenseless ships and settlements.

Caught in this interstellar clutter was a former resistance fighter, Captain Malcolm Reynolds. He was opposed to the Alliance unification of planets and bristled at its fascist laws but he was not keen on thieves and rogues either. To eke out a living, his ship transported animals, supplies, and whatever other cargo, legal or illegal, he could find.

When Whedon pitched the series to Fox, the executives' ears perked up in disbelief when he described it as *Stagecoach in Space*. Fox accepted the series, but more on Whedon's track record rather than a passion for the material. Whedon's inspiration came from reading the Pulitzer Prize-winning book, *The Killer Angels* (by Michael Shaara), about the 1863 battle of Gettysburg. The heroism and the struggles of 19th century characters fascinated him. Captain Reynolds never encounter aliens, time warps or other SF staples but instead bartered for fuel or tried to make payments for ship repairs. Mining, raising livestock, transporting food and hunting criminals was the chief means of making a living for ordinary citizens.

Mal Reynolds' crew had their own dysfunctional backstories: Zoe, the tough first mate of *Serenity*, served with Reynolds during the civil war. Her husband, Wash, is the fun-loving pilot of *Serenity* and leaves the violent derring-do to his wife. Kaylee is the ship's sweet, young mechanic and Book is a priest who has dedicated his life to a higher power. Inara is a courtesan, a space-age hooker who has strong feelings for Mal. Jayne Cobb is the resident bully-boy, a mercenary who is always saying politically incorrect things. Dr. Simon Tam began as a passenger when he smuggled his sister, River, aboard to escape government agents. River had been kidnapped by the Feds, who traumatized her mind with experiments. River's presence makes *Serenity* a target of the government, but Mal allows Simon to stay aboard because he's an expert doctor. But as he tells Simon, "You can stay as long as you keep your sister from doing anything crazy." River is definitely the weird duck of the show. Mute at first, with odd behavior, psychic powers and a robust temper, she unsettles those around her. Jayne thinks she's a witch and Mal just wishes she would knock off the weirdo act and mend herself.

Originally, Whedon had only five characters in his series' outline but upped it to nine. Casting went smoothly, except when it was decided that Rebecca Gayheart (initially cast as Inara) wasn't quite right for the role and Morena Baccarin stepped in.

Meanwhile, some of Whedon's most devoted fans were asking themselves why he was doing a "space western." Even *Firefly* writer Jane Espenson was initially dubious: "I've always thought of westerns as brown dusty films with no women in them. All plot and no love. But the mixture of the two genres is actually a classic one. What does 'final frontier' refer to, after all? Besides, when Joss has a vision for a project in his head, you don't think, 'I wonder *if* he'll make that work.' You think, 'I wonder *how* he'll make that work.'"

According to director Marita Grabiak, "Whoever said a space western is not a good idea must be part of the dumbing down of America. Hasn't the western, a purely American art form, always been a staple of entertainment whose job it is to directly reflect the cultural and political climate of its time? It's an arrogant cultural elitism to say 'a space western is not a good idea.' It's an illusion to believe there is such a thing as 'not a good idea.' Genres don't contribute much to the success or failure of a show. There is only good writing and bad writing."

It was in 1999, during the third year of *Buffy*, that Whedon's writing team first heard of *Firefly*. "We knew what kind of people Mal, Kaylee, Zoe, Wash, Inara and the rest were, before any actors came in to read for their parts, because Joss was talking to the *Buffy* staff about the *Firefly* characters long before he wrote anything," says Espenson, a staff writer-producer on *Buffy*. But when Fox screened the pilot, they felt it was *too* western and wanted space aliens added. Whedon refused but he did placate them by adding more action and humor to later episodes. It was an unglamorous world outside the *Serenity*. Not only were peoples' clothes grubby, but so were their morals, compromised by the harsh life they led. Malcolm Reynolds struggled with his conscience, just as all the others battled *their* own demons. But generally, these were good people.

Whedon was particularly fascinated by the strengths of women and in the flaws of men. This explains some of the traits seen in his *Firefly* characters. Many of the show's fans could identify with the *Serenity* crew, a group of outsiders and free thinkers who didn't fit into the rigid conformity of society. Whedon was happy with his cast's chemistry, but Fox pressured him to make Captain Mal Reynolds "more likable." But Mal remained the classic anti-hero. "You have a job, we can do it," he says. "We don't much care what it is." He also preferred flight rather than fight whenever danger arose.

Fox gave *Firefly* the 8 P.M. slot on Fridays, considered a death slot, but Whedon felt such low expectations meant that any ratings firepower *Firefly* could muster would impress Fox. But instead of airing the two-hour pilot, the network debuted with a later segment, "Train Job," where Mal and Zoe steal a shipment of Alliance goods from a train, only to find the boxes contain vital medicine for ill townspeople. Mal won't let people die, even if it means losing big bucks from the men who hired him to steal. He turns the shipment over to the ailing folks. Whedon felt "Train Job" confused first-time viewers. The debut episode ranked 63rd that week and the series' ratings remained poor during its 11 episode run. Ironically, the two-hour pilot would eventually air, as the *last Firefly* episode broadcast on Fox.

Throughout the episodes there was a country music pickin' soundtrack, hammering home that this was the frontier in space. Some characters used old-fashioned six-shooters, others used laser guns. Some people rode horses, others soared on hovercraft. Mal remained a contradiction. He could be profound ("Men of God make everyone feel guilty and judged") or simple ("A bad day is when someone's yellin' spooks the cattle."). River is eerie but sensitive. When the *Serenity* transports cows, River makes psychic contact with the mooing animals and Mal becomes concerned that River's mumbo-jumbo could upset the cows.

During dinner, when Jayne spits to clean his knife, he misses and the spittle goes into Simon's food bowl. River explodes in a rage and slices Jayne across his chest with a knife. Jayne demands the brother and sister be ejected from the ship but Mal refuses, even though River mystifies him as well.

But Mal is no altruist. In "Ariel," Simon wants to sneak into an Alliance hospital to learn what they did to River's mind, so that he can cure her. Mal agrees to help but only when he's promised payment. Simon learns that River was subjected to lobotomies, which cause her nightmares and outbursts. Meanwhile, Jayne makes a secret deal with the Feds to capture Simon and River. But that plan fails and once everyone is safely back on *Serenity*, Mal hits Jayne with a wrench and threatens to kick him out of an airlock. "I didn't think you would ever do such a thing," the captain rages over Jayne's betrayal. "The money was too good!" Jayne whimpers. His life is spared but it's clear Mal is offering him a one-time pass.

But Jayne can also be unintentionally funny. When they land on a sun-baked planet, Jayne is afraid his former partner-in-crime might recognize him, so he steps out of the ship wearing big black biker goggles, a hood and a heavy coat. "Aren't you being a little over-cautious?" asks Mal wryly. That episode, "Jaynestown," is set on a planet where mud is manufactured and cheap labor is at a premium. When the crew finds a clay statue of Jayne in the town square, Jayne gets the shivers. "That's an eerie-ass piece of work," he remarks. The townspeople consider him a hero because he once stole money from a magistrate but in Jayne's haste to fly away, he dumped the payroll overboard. The money floated down to the poverty-ridden townspeople and they've hailed him as a space-age Robin Hood ever since.

But Jayne's bitter ex-partner Stitch was imprisoned for the robbery and it leads to a showdown between Jayne and Stitch. When a townsperson jumps in front of Jayne to take a bullet, Jayne angrily kills Stitch with a knife and, in a pique of conscience, he smashes his own statue, telling the people he's no hero. "It was a good script by Ben

Edlund, a location that fit well, and beautiful photography that was fast and efficient, allowing me to gather what was needed to tell the story," says director Marita Grabiak. She also praises "a great art department, and fantastic visual effects. The actors were so on the ball: energetic, prepared, creative and professional. I have worked with Nathan, Adam, and Gina on other shows, but *Firefly* was magic. It was the most outstanding experience in all my career as an episodic director." Her good friend Tim Minear, the series' executive producer, recommended Grabiak to Joss Whedon. "Joss is a producer who lets you do your job," she says. "He lets you do your best by allowing you to direct. He gives you the tools and the support, and then threatens you with bodily harm to make it good, in his kindly joking way. I would work for him any time, any place." But she recalls her episode was tough going, filming "under the scorching September sun of California Canyon country the day we did the big fight. It was a monster day of scheduling, and a challenge in terms of what we needed to accomplish: landing on the planet, leaving the planet, tramping through town and driving on carts. After lunch, we staged the big stunt fight, with 100 extras, a gun blast to the chest, and a big knife stick gag. Then we had a statue to topple. The sun wreaked its savage brutality on cast and crew alike. The actor who played Stitch [Kevin Gage] had heavy makeup, including prosthetic scars [and] a heavy wig and he was melting like cheese. We put him under an umbrella as much as possible with a mini-fan. I'm sure he was miserable. I felt sorry for him. The director of photography David Boyd and his operators were amazing. We did an astonishing 82 camera setups that day. The norm is between 20 to 30."

The other challenge was creating a unique-looking mud planet. "That was a major concern for me," she recalls. "The producers wanted a departure from the traditional western town. We found a ranch in L.A.'s canyon country that was used for *The Time Machine* [the 2002 version]. That movie's Morlock bamboo was still up in one area. Production designer Carey Meyer and his staff were amazing: They enhanced the bamboo and built a main street of a bustling mud village, with lots of personality. Since I needed a mud-works, I asked if a large pit we found could be filled with water, with all kinds of mysterious, junky machinery cluttering up the place as décor. That was a lot to ask for, especially at a location where they had to build mud house exteriors and dress it to look like a bustling community. But it all turned out wonderfully."

Grabiak recalls filming the climactic scene in the town square, where Jayne refutes his "God status." "When Jayne hovers over the body and then rises to chastise the crowd with a reference to false hero worship, 'There ain't no people like that, only people like me,' that scene gave me chills. Emotional scenes like that, which connect with the actor and are well written, usually give me tears in my eyes while I am directing, in the midst of watching the camerawork, the lighting, checking framing, actor performance and dialogue. It startles you and it's a real event to know you have captured that emotion on film."

That scene was special for another reason. "My son, Kristian Kolodziej, 11 years old at the time, played the non-speaking role of the kid who recognizes Jayne in the bar and informs the town. Producers usually shy away from hiring relatives, so my son had to pass the photo inspection test. We were looking for an Oliver Twist type. I thought my son had a good look for the part, so I submitted him. He had a great time and liked hanging out with the actors who were so cool and funny. They were attentive, especially Nathan, who is really charming and engaging. When we did the scene where the boy was supposed to pull the big knife out of Stitch and hand it to Jayne, the sun was really blinding my son's eyes badly. He could barely open them, let alone see where the knife was. We didn't have time to set up an overhead shade maker, so I told him on my cue to force his eyes open and reach in this direction and I could edit before he removed the knife. It worked."

During the series' brief life, other characters had their moments too. When Zoe and her husband Wash talk about River's paranormal powers, Wash says in amazement, "Psychic powers? That sounds like something out of science fiction." Zoe replies, "We live in a spaceship, dear."

"The *Firefly* characters were so clearly drawn, and the language so well-crafted, and the stories so tight, it made it all easier," says Espenson. "Each character was so different from all the others. If you wanted to change who spoke a particular line, you had to do major surgery just to make the line sound like them." Yet there was a theory that the quirky characters were preventing mainstream audiences from embracing *Firefly*. Many of the guest characters, traders, outlaw Feds and other double-dealers were equally eccentric. But Espenson preferred writing for a bright cult audience who relished offbeat story-telling. "Writing for a sophisticated audience is better, you can reward them with a more complete world, with complex characters. Sure, some viewers are hypercritical, but that's just the flipside. If you create a very real world, people are going to judge it against higher standards."

Espenson wrote one of the most popular episodes, "Shindig," where the crew lands on the planet Persephone and Mal attends a high-class party with his date, the dolled-up Kaylee. It's part of a plan to secure a lucrative transport job, but the local crimelord, Atherton Wing (Edward Atterton), makes a pass at Inara and Mal gets jealous. A sword duel between the men is called for, which is unfortunate, since Mal has little proficiency for swordplay. Inara tries to instruct him before the duel and Mal barely wins the contest, shaming the stuffy Atherton.

"It was not an idea that I pitched," Espenson recalls. "I'm sure the idea behind 'Shindig' was Joss. And after any episode was written, Joss would take a pass at it. He could fix any problems with how a character was written."

"Shindig" allowed fans to see Mal's insecurities as he tries to mask his jealousy, Kaylee's vulnerability as she's shunned by snobby women and Inara's deep caring for Mal. Espenson says the *Firefly* team did everything they could to bring her script to life. "I loved how the episode turned out," she says. "I wrote a card game, and they gave me metal Chinese playing cards. I wrote a sword-fight at a grassy pond at dawn and that's what I got. I wrote a floating chandelier, for heck's sake, and I got a floating chandelier. The costumes, props, set decoration and the sword-fighting and the direction and the beautiful performances were incredible. Mal was honest and Kaylee was touching and Inara was deep. The attention to detail was more like a feature film than a TV show."

She recalls some dealings with Whedon as fun and quirky. "Joss would interact with the furniture in the writers' room," she recalls. "He'd lift up a big armchair and walk around with it over his head, or climb up on top of the chair or tip it over or stand on the armrests. And all the time he'd be talking about some problem in the show. It was a very charming combination of physical quirk and mental brawn. Maybe breaking out of conventional ways of interacting with a chair was a way to break his mind out of conventional ways of interacting with a story." Espenson would later edit the book *Finding Serenity: Anti-Heroes, Lost Shepherds and Space Hookers in Joss Whedon's* Firefly

(2005), a collection of non-fiction essays on the show.

Marita Grabiak also saw genius at work on *Firefly*. "If you are Joss Whedon or Tim Minear, then you are a brilliant creator of story plots. You create interesting characters who interplay in fascinating ways and situations with realistic and brilliant dialogue. You intellectually challenge your audience, who hunger for more."

Another good show, "Heart of Gold," written by Brett Matthews, has Inara ask Mal for help. Her friend Nandi runs a bordello on another planet and her ladies are being threatened by a violent aristocratic man named Rance. He takes the baby of one of the young women, claiming it's his son. Mal and his crew help the women secure their bordello and in the process, the captain falls in love with Nandi (fetchingly played by Melinda Clarke). It's his first serious relationship in years. "You gonna remember where everything goes?" Nandi asks as they prepare to make love. "Let's just say I plan to take it real slow," he says. In a climactic gun battle, the good guys barely win, the baby is recovered, but Nandi is shot down by Rance. An angry Mal turns Rance over to the women, and he is shot dead by the baby's mother.

The series began to amass thousands of fans, who called themselves Browncoats, and critics were generally excited. Ken Tucker of *Entertainment Weekly* called the series "[d]aring...*Firefly* benefits enormously from Whedon's ability to take clichés of any genre and give them a good hard yank." Science fiction author Orson Scott Card, who had resisted watching the series at first, later called *Firefly*, "the greatest science fiction television series ever created."

Whedon's dream that *Firefly* would last seven years ended after only 11 aired shows. The Friday night death slot had lived up to its name. Several pre-emptions for baseball playoffs had also ruined its momentum. It finished with a seasonal ranking of 129th out of 159 shows for the 2002–2003 season. Whedon called the cancellation "a gut punch" and announced the show's cancellation to the cast during filming. In the last episode, "The Message," there is a scene where Mal, Zoe and Inara sit around a dining table, exchanging festive stories. That scene was filmed the day after the cancellation was announced. The actors were stunned and depressed over the bad news.

Three episodes of *Firefly* were never aired on Fox: "Trash," "Heart of Gold" and "The Message." But Whedon was determined to fight cancellation. "Don't think for a moment that I've given up on this show," he stated. He went to ABC, CBS, NBC, UPN and The Sci-Fi Channel, but they all turned down the chance to resurrect *Firefly* in any form, despite a online campaign called "Firefly: Immediate Assistance," which mobilized thousands of fans to support the show. Whedon kept trying, but his cast began to lose faith and they moved onto other projects.

"*Firefly*'s cancellation makes you despair that material as fresh and uplifting as this can fail to find an audience," *TV Zone* magazine said, "especially when the likes of *Star Trek: Enterprise* and *Stargate SG-1* thunder on." But Whedon wasn't content with posthumous acclaim, he was determined to bring the show back. Over 500,000 *Firefly* DVD sales got the attention of Mary Parent, vice-chairman of Universal Pictures (and a fan of Whedon's work). She was instrumental in seeing that Whedon was permitted to do a feature version. "We've been huge fans of Joss for some time," said Parent at the time. "He's a great storyteller with a knack for creating interesting worlds."

Fans hoped the film would lead to more films or a revived series but Whedon played it cool. "My first hope is to make a good movie. Anything beyond that would be arrogant."

Shooting started in July 2004 and the film, written and directed by Whedon, was released in September 2005. All of the original cast was back as the *Alliance* continued its violent efforts to steal River away from the *Serenity* crew. To the dismay of many fans, Wash and Book are both killed in the film.

There was hope that the $40 million film would be a modest blockbuster. Universal had early screenings to generate strong word of mouth from fans but after a month's release, it had a unspectacular gross of $25 million. It was mainly just the fans who showed up. By August 2006, it still lagged, with a worldwide total of $38 million. But like the TV series, the DVD sales later proved excellent. And the cast felt they had beaten the odds by having a feature film produced in the first place. "When *Firefly* was cancelled, I was heartbroken," Nathan Filion told *Sci-Fi Wire*. "I wanted another crack at it. For me, the movie was sweet, sweet revenge, served cold." (Up to this time, *Police Squad*, a 1982 cop comedy starring Leslie Nielsen, had been the only failed TV series to return as a feature film — in this case, a series of *Naked Gun* films.)

Critics gave the film generally high marks. "The finished product is a triumph," said Peter Hartlaub of *The San Francisco Chronicle*. "[Although] clearly written by someone who grew up worshipping at the altar of Han Solo, this genre picture is still a thrillingly original SF creation.... [T]he comic book convention crowd will still be hailing this film 30 years from now."

Robert K. Elder of *The Chicago Tribune* noted, "It's a brash, funny, action-packed bit of sci-fi ecstasy ... and a giant raspberry to the execs who let *Firefly* fall out of the sky!" *The Dallas Observer*'s Robert Wilonsky gave it a back-handed compliment: "It's but a witty, engaging hodgepodge of archetypes and clichés. It retreads not only the TV show's storylines but also those of every *Star Trek* and *Gunsmoke* episode."

But the film concentrated on the heart of the characters. *Variety*'s Derek Elley remarked, "What makes *Serenity* refreshing is its avoidance of CGI, which gives the picture a much more human dimension."

There were also the dissenters. Vancouver film critic Katherine Monk lamented, "It doesn't offer much in the way of entertainment or substance for the non-aficionado.... [I]t feels like a cheap version of any off-the-rack *Star Trek* franchise."

"It's a good flick for Zen-action types," Chris Hewitt of Knight Ridder said, giving it a C+ and noting, "The characters are richer than the stereotypes we usually get in this sort of movie."

Jane Espenson felt *Firefly*'s leap to the big screen was a success. "I loved *Serenity*. It was fascinating seeing those characters on the big screen. I loved that Joss told a story about a great power that created its own enemies. It was very powerful."

Marita Grabiak was also impressed. "I loved the movie, and seeing those actors filling the big screen. I was so happy for them." Like the TV series, *Serenity* did well in DVD sales. Whedon and Brett Matthews also wrote a comic book miniseries titled *Serenity: Those Left Behind*, published by Dark Horse Comics in 2005.

What trails *Firefly* blazes next remains to be determined but already, it will go down in history as a show that beat the odds.

CAST NOTES

Nathan Filion (Capt. Reynolds): Born in Edmonton, Alberta, Filion at first planned to be a high school English teacher. He was attending the University of Alberta when he made his TV debut in the film *Ordeal in the Arctic* (1993). He was then a regular on *One Life to Live* for three years. His film credits include *Saving Private Ryan* (1998), *Dracula 2000* (2000) and *Waitress (2007)*. He also played the villainous Caleb in the last few episodes of *Buffy the Vampire Slayer*.

Gina Torres (Zoe): Having just battled flying mechanical monsters as the lead heroine in *Cleopatra 2525*, Torres wasn't interested in reading the outline of *Firefly*, concerned she would be typecast in SF adventure. Her agent asked her to read it and she was hooked. The New York City-born actress, whose parents came from Cuba, made her TV debut on daytime's *One Life to Live* and later had recurring roles as Nebula on *Hercules: The Legendary Adventures* (1997–1999) and *24* (2004). Her films include *Matrix Reloaded* and *Matrix Revolutions* (both 2003).

Adam Baldwin (Jayne): The Chicago-born actor hit it big with two major films early in his career, Robert Redford's Oscar-winning *Ordinary People* (1980) and *My Bodyguard* (1980), as the sullen teen who protects a scrawny schoolmate. His other credits include *Full Metal Jacket* (1987), the TV mini-series *From the Earth to the Moon* (1998) and the TV remake of *The Poseidon Adventure* (2005). He also had recurring roles in *The Visitor*, *The-X Files* and *Daybreak* (in 2006).

Ron Glass (Shepherd Book): Best known as Detective Ron Harris on TV's *Barney Miller* (1975–1982), he moved to Los Angeles in 1972 to pursue acting and appeared on *Hawaii Five-0*, *All in the Family* and *Hart to Hart*. He went on to do episodes of *Friends* and *Star Trek: Voyager*.

Morena Baccarin (Inara): Born in Brazil, she grew up in New York City, appeared in the improvisational film *Perfume* (2001), and won acclaim for her theater role in *Way-Off Broadway*. Her other credits include *Roger Dodger* (2002) and episodes of *Stargate SG-I* and *Heartland*.

Alan Tudyk ("Wash"): From El Paso, Texas, Tudyk did a lot of stage and theater work and founded the Court Jesters Improv Theater group. His feature films include *35 Miles from Normal* (1997), *I, Robot* (2004) and *Knocked Up* (2007).

Jewel Staite (Kaylee): Born in White Rock, B.C., Canada, she started working as a model and did TV commercials at age six. At 14 she appeared in an episode of *The X-Files* and also did shots on TV's *Honey I Shrunk the Kids* and *Seven Days*. She played Catalina on Nickelodeon's *Space Cases* (1996) and joined the cast of *Stargate: Atlantis* in its fourth season (2007), as Dr. Jennifer Keller.

Sean Maher (Simon): Maher was born in Westchester, New York. It was a summer camp play that got him interested in acting as a child. He at-tended New York University's Tisch School of Arts and did much theater before moving out to California. His TV credits include *Party of Five*, *CSI Miami* and the telemovie *Wedding Wars* (2006).

Summer Glau (River): A lifelong ballerina, born in San Antonio, Texas, she made her acting debut in Joss Whedon's *Angel*, and did many TV commercials. At first her acting inexperience made her nervous and uneasy playing River but she prevailed and brought one of *Firefly*'s most intriguing characters to life. Her TV work encompasses *The 4400*, *Cold Case* and *CSI*. She signed up as a regular on TV's *The Unit* in 2006. Later, she co-starred in *Terminator: The Sarah Connor Chronicles* (2008).

POSTSCRIPT

Firefly's dogged determination to beat the odds—from short-lived TV series to successful DVD sales to the production and release of a major motion picture — is attributable to its fans. Perceptive and articulate, these dedicated viewers brought the show back from the brink of oblivion with their support. Michael Bailey, a radio personality and writer in Portland, Oregon, is one such a fan and he offers some insight into why *Firefly* has attracted such loyalty:

> When Joss Whedon's outer space western *Firefly* landed Friday nights on Fox, many of us who discovered it became instant fans. We're called "Browncoats" after the uniforms worn by main characters Mal and Zoe, Independents on the losing end of a war against the authoritarian Alliance.
>
> What grabbed me from the start was the show's energy, not to mention its tight ensemble cast and perfectly placed special effects that establish a universe beyond each episode's immediate framework. Then there's the writing — dialogue so rich and shiny it stands on its own in peaks, like icing on a layer cake.
>
> I was bowled over by what my daughter Cassie has christened "Mal Moments." These sudden, decisive blows for frontier justice raise the bar for the rest of the show's action. In the episode "The Train Job," for example, Mal, having escaped the clutches of the villainous Niska, stands alongside his ship, *Serenity*, and addresses one of the defeated heavies: "Now this is all the money Niska gave us in advance. You bring it back to him, tell him the job didn't work out. We're not thieves. But we are thieves. Point is, we're not taking what's his. Now, we'll stay out of his way as best we can from here on in. You explain that's best for everyone, okay?"
>
> The brute rises, towers over Mal, his face a slash of hatred: "Keep the money. Use it to buy a funeral. It doesn't matter where you go or how far

you fly — I will hunt you down and the last thing you see will be my blade."

At that, Mal kicks the thug hard, pushing him backwards, where he's sucked into one of *Serenity*'s engine intakes and vaporized into a zillion atoms. Problem solved. That was my first "Mal Moment." I was stunned. It was brilliant. Here was a science-fiction television hero acting in a flawed, but rational — namely, fully human — manner. It was gritty, realistic, edgy.

Mal's name says it all. As psychic passenger River Tam notes, "Mal. Bad. In the Latin." And that's good. This SF hero is a complete, thinking human being, capable of both brave and selfish acts, humor and, when necessary, drastic measures, all governed by a strict sense of fair play and common decency. In "The Train Job," for instance, Mal relinquishes the cargo he's just stolen (from the all-powerful Alliance, so it's okay) once he discovers the contraband is medicine needed to treat hundreds of sick and dying miners. He does so despite his own desperate need of the heist's payoff to keep *Serenity* flying (they live on "the raggedy edge," you see) and knowing full well that going back on the deal means trouble for himself and his crew.

And what a crew! This is a diverse, fully drawn, morally centered group (with the exception of a man called Jayne, who really *is* bad, and once again, that's good). They speak an eclectic, cowboy-style English that includes some Chinese swear words and lots of down-home phrasing.

One of my favorite characters is *Serenity*'s mechanic, the sweet, oversexed tomboy Kaylee, who has a knack for mending broken engines— and speaking plainly. When Mal first asks how she fixes things, Kaylee explains, "Just do it, that's all. My daddy says I got a natural talent." When *Serenity*'s engines go dead in the episode "Out of Gas," Kaylee apologizes: "I'm sorry, captain...I'm real sorry. Shoulda kept better care of her." A basically intuitive mechanic, Kaylee is incapable of technobabble. And on those rare occasions when her explanations verge on the esoteric, Mal soon sets things straight: "I need that in Captain Dummy talk," he says.

Joss Whedon is too interested in his characters and their interactions to dwell on mock science. *Firefly* posits a future where the technology has come a ways, but those dealing with it are human beings with the same strengths and weaknesses humans have always had. Aliens might be out there somewhere, but for now, Mal, his crew, and those who populate the Alliance worlds have enough on their plates— no need for bug-eyed monsters stir-

ring things up. The Reavers (humans gone seriously south) are spooky enough, and the struggle of Mal and company versus the Alliance more than sufficient to propel *Firefly*'s stories.

I'm lucky enough to live in Portland, Oregon, a major hub of Browncoat activity. Polled on what makes the show special, pdxbrowncoats.com members voiced general agreement, as summarized by Browncoat Lynn Siprelle: "*Firefly* is about the tension between justice, law and survival, spelled out in the life of one man. Mal is on the losing side in a civil war, but he knows it weren't the wrong side. He's driven to common thievery to survive, but he won't steal from poor folks. He constantly strikes subversive blows against the Alliance that, while usually illegal, are usually just. Mostly these blows are small, tiny, even minuscule things no one else would even notice but that keep his soul alive."

I second that.

If you've never breathed the heady atmo of *Serenity* and her crew, step aboard next opportunity. My guess is you'll enjoy the ride.

SOURCES

Bianco, Robert. *Firefly* Review. "Be Sure to Catch This 'Firefly.'" *USA Today*, September 18, 2002.

Elder, Robert K. *Serenity* Review. *Chicago Tribune*, August 24, 2007.

Elley, Derek. *Serenity* Review. *Variety*, August 22, 2005.

Gillatt, Gary. *TV Zone* no. 159, 2002.

Goodman, Tim. *Firefly* Review. "Sci-fi 'Firefly' is a Bonanza of Miscues from 'Buffy' Creator." *San Francisco Chronicle*, September 20, 2002.

Hartlaub, Peter. *Serenity* Review. "'Serenity' Earns Director Whedon Spot On Sci-fi's Mount Rushmore." *San Francisco Chronicle*, September 30, 2005.

Hewitt, Chris. Knight Ridder, 2005.

Monk, Katherine. *Serenity* Review. *Vancouver Sun*, October 3, 2005.

Nazzaro, Joe. Interview with Joss Whedon. *Starlog* no. 303, October 2002.

_____. Interview with Joss Whedon. *Starlog* no. 318, January 2004.

Tucker, Ken. *Firefly* Review. *Entertainment Weekly*, October 4, 2002.

Wilonsky, Robert. "Have Gun, Will Space Travel — Serenity Spins a Classic Tale Way Out West." *Dallas Observer*, September 29, 2005.

First Wave
(1998–2001)

*Aliens in human form are plotting to take over the Earth. Cade Foster, a former thief,
tries to expose the invasion to a disbelieving world.*

Cast: Sebastian Spence (Cade Foster), Rob La-
Belle ("Crazy" Eddie Nambulous), Roger R. Cross
(Joshua) and Traci Elizabeth Lords (Jordan Rad-
cliffe) *Year 3*
Created by: Chris Brancato; **Executive Produc-
ers:** Larry Sugar, Francis Ford Coppola, Chris
Brancato; **Producers:** Matthew Loze, Tara Mc-
Cann; **Co-Producer:** Randy Cheveldave *Year 1–2*;
Associate Producers: Ian Hay, John Barbisan *Year
3*; **Coordinating Producer:** David DeWar; **Writ-
ers included:** Daniel Cerone, Chris Brancato,
Michael Thoma, Paul Eckstein, Albert J. Salke,
Bill Conway, David Wilcox, Theresa Rebeck; **Di-
rectors included:** Brenton Spencer, Michael Ro-
bison, Brad Turner, Larry Sugar, Rob LaBelle,
Mike Rohl, William Corcoran, George Mendeluk,
Randy Cheveldave, Jorge Montesi, Shawn Levy,
Rene Bonniere, Holly Dale; **Guest Stars included:**
Christina Cox, Michael Hogan, Sable, A.J. Cook,
William B. Davis, Christopher Judge, Lorena
Gale, Ellen Dubin, Gillian Barber, Jim Byrnes, In-
grid Kavelaars, Coco Yares, Lisa Howard, Dana
Brooks (as Col. Grace), Alison Matthews (as
Maya) and Stacy Grant (as Hannah Foster)
The Sci-Fi Channel/American Zoetrope and
Pearson International; 1998–2001; 60 minutes; 66
episodes

One critic griped that Sebastian Spence played
the role of alien hunter Cade Foster too humor-
lessly, but give the guy a break. If you were Cade
Foster and your life as a security salesman had
been torn apart by aliens, you wouldn't be a bar-
rel of laughs either.

Foster's nightmare begins while giving a sales
presentation in an executive boardroom. In the
middle of his talk, he sees a ghastly, severed head
staring up at him from his briefcase. This leads
to his credit card and bank funds being mysteriously wiped out. An anonymous email is sent to
Foster's boss, detailing his past life as a criminal.
"Thirty-two thefts, 3 bank holdups, an expert
forger, a master of disguises, uses no weapons but
is considered dangerous," it reads. Foster is fired
immediately.

When a deflated Foster comes home, he finds

his house vandalized and his terrified wife cow-
ering in a bathtub. They both learn that Foster is
being targeted by extraterrestrials (the Gua) in
their bid to take over the world. Foster finds a lost
book of prophecies, written by the celebrated
physician and occultist Nostradamus in 1564, that
predicts, in a series of puzzling quatrains, that
Earth will be destroyed by three waves—secret
invasion (which is happening now), followed by
an outright attack from the skies, and finally Armageddon. Nostradamus points to Foster as "The
Twice-Blessed Man," the savior who is destined
to stop the invasion. The horror continues when
Foster, in the middle of making love to his wife,
sees her turn into a squid-like creature that tries
choking him with a slimy tentacle. He barely escapes and learns that the real Hannah has been
murdered. Framed for the killing, Foster must flee
police as he hunts for the aliens.

Francis Ford Coppola and his company American Zoetrope was interested in doing an action
TV series and they tapped writer Chris Brancato.
Brancato began his career as a production assistant on the 1980s horror anthology *Tales from the
Darkside* and wrote the sensual alien-invasion adventure, *Species II* (1998). He admits *First Wave*
was inspired by the 1960s classics *The Fugitive* and
Rod Serling's *Twilight Zone*.

"When *First Wave* aired, some SF fans said, 'Oh
no, not another alien invasion series! How many
more of those do we need?'" says Brancato. "But
that turned to, 'This is better than I thought it
would be!' That was gratifying. A lot of that has
to do with our characters. We layered Cade Foster with reluctance, frustration and anger." The
aliens want Earth's natural resources and if their
reconnaissance determines humans are a weak
species, an all-out invasion will be launched.

Brancato didn't want comparisons made with
the TV show *The Invaders* (1966–68). *The Invaders'* hero, David Vincent (played by Roy
Thinnes), lost his girlfriend, watched his business
partner murdered and had his career reduced to
rubble by the evil ETs. Criss-crossing the country,
he tried to hunt down the aliens and prove that
they existed. As in *First Wave*, the aliens glowed

and vanished when killed. In both cases, the heroes were assisted by their best friend, both computer experts. (In *The Invaders*, Ed Scoville was played by Kent Smith.)

Although *The Invaders* had been a top 30 hit on ABC its first year and *TV Guide* later proclaimed David Vincent as one of TVs all-time legendary heroes, Brancato dismissed *The Invaders* as a forgotten show. Besides, *First Wave* was too busy trying to carve out its own identity. Sebastian Spence, who reminded Brancato of a cross between James Dean and Clint Eastwood, was a good-looking hero, although he was considered too young for the role at first. Three older actors were front-runners.

"Months went by after I auditioned," says Spence. "I said, 'Okay, I don't have a chance for this one,' and I moved on. I understood their reasoning. They wanted someone older, a character that would have more at stake as his life was absorbed by these aliens. A younger guy would probably not have as much to lose and it would be less dramatic. But I don't think they were that excited by the older choices they had, so they considered me as a younger choice. When I did the audition, it was a five-page monologue and I was nervous as hell. Frankly, I blew it. But they still saw some quality in me that they liked. When I finally got the call, months later, I was surprised." Brancato felt Spence projected genuine emotion that audiences could relate to.

Foster's sidekick, Eddie, was a loner who lived in a trailer and published a popular anti-government e-zine called *The Paranoid Times*. Eddie is slow to trust Cade, and prefers his addicted lifestyle of Diet Pepsi, fries and tacos. Rob LaBelle, with his unkempt appearance and whiny, terrified voice, was perfect as Eddie. Unlike Cade, who faced the aliens head-on, Eddie reacted like most real people: The aliens scared the hell out of him. He grew braver as the series went on. "He may not know how to button his shirt straight but you see he's a genius at telecommunication and computers," says LaBelle. "But it wasn't until the second year that he got into the action."

Eddie has been burned by three disastrous marriages and a feeling that "people want to screw with his mind," says LaBelle. "He has retreated to cyberspace but he's basically a good man who wants to right wrongs." Eddie has enormous respect for Cade, who he feels will save the world. "His association with Foster gives him something to live for but they still [butt] heads and bicker. Cade is headstrong, like, 'I'm gonna do this now!' while Eddie is, 'Hey man, that's wrong!' But they have a strong bond. They have to trust each other or else they're screwed." That friendship extended to the two actors. "There's a real sense of trust between me and Sebastian," said LaBelle. "He's got

Sebastian Spence as *First Wave* alien resistance fighter Cade Foster (© USA Networks/Sci-Fi Channel).

the hardest job — he works 16 hours a day and he's in every scene. But he's a great sport, with an incredible heart. He's a wonderfully down-to-earth man."

First Wave was almost predatory in its efforts to capture the coveted 18–34 demographics. Brancato called the series "sexy sci-fi," and most episodes had scantily clad women. The idea was that since attractive people are more successful, influential and better able to manipulate, Foster's female adversaries would often resemble *Playboy* centerfolds. A cynic might cringe at such premeditation, but *TV Guide* thought the show was dynamite: "It has something for everyone. Fans will love *First Wave*."

Brancato tried to hit all of the marketing bases, and regularly chatted with fans on Internet bulletin boards. "As the series went on, we asked ourselves, 'Are we showing enough from the aliens' perspective? Is there enough sexuality in the show? Is there too much talking head stuff and not enough action?' But the fans' reaction was strong and positive. Yes, there were some things we wanted to do but couldn't. We considered a show set in England but for budget and story reasons, that wasn't done."

Fans didn't relate to Colonel Grace (the middle-aged woman assigned to hunt down Cade), so the character was abruptly dropped during year one.

Foster quickly learned that he had been secretly experimented on by the aliens. 117 human subjects were tested, to determine their mental and physical strengths. All died except one: Cade Foster. He was returned to society by the aliens, without any memories of what had happened. This was why he had been targeted by the invaders: They knew he was strong enough to stop their invasion.

The early publicity characterized Foster as part Bruce Willis of *Moonlighting*, and part Robert Redford from *The Sting*. But the war took a toll on Foster's easy-going manner and that suited Spence fine. "Foster exacts revenge on the specific alien who killed his wife but that doesn't eliminate his fight. He's still angry that these aliens have screwed up his life and now threaten to wipe out the human race. He's totally focused on driving back these creatures."

In that first year, Foster discovered humanoid fish creatures that were being bred on a farm, a doorway that opened into another dimension, superhumans created by DNA mutations, and even a rock band whose music inspired violence. Evidence of the alien invasion conveniently disappeared. In "Elixir," it's hard to forget the image of Foster vainly (and lamely) lunging forward to save vials of a rejuvenation chemical from flames. But he did learn more about his adversaries, including that the Gua came from a cluster of galaxies called Abell 2029, one billion light years from Earth. In the aliens' true form, they resembled a cross between a squid and an alligator.

Foster also encountered Joshua, an alien disguised as an African-American man, who opposed the Gua's invasion plans. "The idea that Joshua was against his race sliming humanity was an interesting twist," says Spence. "Foster and Joshua had this mutual respect but there was a lack of trust. But it gave Foster hope that if one alien is against the invasion, maybe there are others."

Joshua remained inscrutable in that first year. "He began as a very rigid character," notes actor Roger Cross. "But soon a true friendship developed between him and Foster." All of the lead actors developed a camaraderie that translated to the screen. "We all connected," says Cross. "I did my thing, they did their thing and it worked. Our show didn't rely on a lot of special effects or prosthetics. It was a drama first, so we were able to really perform as actors."

In the last episode of year one, Joshua argues against an attack on Earth but Maya (the striking female Gua leader) presses her case to launch a full-scale invasion. Joshua uses flashbacks to convince his race that Earthlings are worthy of respect. The cliffhanger ends with the Gua preparing to vote.

Reviews for the series were mixed. Joyce Millman of *Salon* called it "too cheesy" for sophisticated SF fans and at the same time "utterly humorless." Nevertheless, she appreciated its "almost quaintly straightforward" approach and concluded, "[I]t's a diverting enough sci-fi chase show but not in *The X-Files* league." SCI-FI.com's Patrick Lee noted the show's peculiar lack of energy. "*First Wave* fails to generate much more than a passing interest," he said. "The main shortcoming is the central character, Cade Foster. He's surprisingly colorless. Though the producers have tried to dress up his character with noirish voiceovers, they come off sounding labored and artificial."

As the first year wrapped up, Britain's *TV Zone* magazine noted, "Despite several truly appalling and derivative stories, the series shows potential."

The first year was a solid if unspectacular success on The Sci-Fi Channel and the show was given a two-year extension. Joshua successfully prevented a Second Wave invasion as year two began, and Foster continued his cross-country odyssey but he was growing increasingly bitter. "Cade was now losing a part of his humanity," stated Spence, who pushed writers to make Foster more hostile.

In year two adventures, Foster was pitted against an alien woman on a desolate island, teamed up with a Washington D.C. reporter to expose the aliens, found himself worshipped by rogue bikers who have been fighting against the aliens, and discovered a football team under the control of an alien beauty.

"We got away from Cade traveling around, shaking people and yelling, 'Listen to me, you idiot—the aliens are here!'" laughs Spence. "He became more militant as he tried to root these bastards out. He was subjected to the tremendous weight of battling this invasion and he grew darker. We saw that he was willing to destroy himself to destroy them. That intensity challenged me as an actor."

Spence got quite a workout as the first year wound down. "The physicality of the show took a toll," he admits. "When you play a chap who does a lot of running, a lot of fighting and is being beat up by aliens who are supposedly three times stronger than you every week, it's rough." The work aggravated his old back injury; as Spence recovered from surgery, Internet rumors were rampant that Spence wouldn't be back for year two, especially when a casting call went out for a new character. But it turned out that the casting call was strictly for insurance purposes, in case the actor didn't recover for another year.

In the episode "The Believers" that wrapped up year two, Foster and Eddie commandeer a TV station to alert 200 million viewers to the aliens' existence. "I'm doing this because I have no other options," Foster states, but Crazy Eddie is scared. "I feel it in my bones, Cade—this is the day we die." He's half-right. The cliffhanger has Foster shot to death on live television by a sniper. The camera pulls back from Cade's body, his open eyes looking upward as a pool of blood seeps behind his head. We see the sniper putting away his gun. It's Eddie.

"I pulled the trigger," Eddie later deadpans in "Mabus," the year three opener. "Now let me explain why." It was a clone of Foster that really died, created by the aliens to house their alien leader, Mabus. But Cade and Eddie steal the copy and set the clone up to be shot on TV, to create a martyr profile for Cade and to fool the police into thinking Foster is dead. Although we see a blank-looking Eddie packing away the murder weapon, he later tells Cade, "Man, shooting you was the toughest thing I've ever done!"

Those kind of plot twists impressed LaBelle. "Not only were our scripts good but it was a great show to work on, with 95 percent of the crews returning every year. It may not have been a big-budget show but it was a terrific place to work. Even guest stars would say, 'Man, this is a fun place to work,' and that's true, it was a gas!"

Frequent *First Wave* director Holly Dale agrees. Dale is one of Canada's most accomplished film and television directors, including the award-winning documentary *P4W: Prison for Women* (1981), about the lives of five women in prison. With her partner, Janis Cole, she made several more hard-hitting documentaries, as well as the fictional feature film, *Blood and Donuts* (1995), a quirky vampire tale. For such a respected and acclaimed documentary filmmaker to be directing TV aliens seemed bizarre but Dale wanted to break out into drama and *First Wave* was a natural fit. "I love science fiction and I thought *First Wave*'s concept was fabulous," she says. "And I proved to have as much muscle in directing segments as any guy. It's funny, in Toronto, I'm primarily known as a director of dramatic series and in Vancouver I'm known as a science fiction director [*Stargate, Jeremiah*]."

Despite the enthusiasm of its cast and crew, high ratings and media attention stubbornly eluded the show. In an effort to change that, the character of Jordan Radcliffe (played by former porn star Traci Elizabeth Lords) was added in the third year. Lords won the role over 90 other actresses. Jordan becomes Foster's ally and leads a underground militia, The Raven Nation. She's out for blood—the aliens were responsible for the deaths of her parents and brother.

Jordan's soldiers consider Cade a hero but he and Jordan clash. When she kills a Gua prisoner in cold blood, Cade protests and she snaps, "Love thy enemy? Screw that!" Her Raven Nation forces are later wiped out by the aliens, leaving only Cade, Eddie, Jordan and Joshua to continue the war. The sexual tension between Cade and Jordan is toyed with but never consummated. Mabus takes over Jordan's body in "The Vessel," and it takes several episodes for Cade to purge the spirit of Mabus from Jordan's body.

Holly Dale directed Jordan's debut in "Raven Nation," but feels the addition of Traci Lords was an ill-conceived marketing move. "They were trying to attract a different kind of audience, so they brought in an ex-porno star, and frankly, it was a mistake," she says. "Nothing against Traci but Sebastian had great chops. He's incredibly talented and the fan base was attracted to him and Rob. When Traci got cast, the excitement wasn't about the storylines going in a more exciting direction, it was more like, 'Wow, we have an ex-porno star.'"

Meanwhile, the cast of *First Wave* found recognition in the most unlikely places. A small child once pointed to Roger Cross in a church and whispered "Joshua!" "A teacher told me that he often discussed *First Wave* in class with his students," says Cross. "That fascinated me. *First Wave* ... in a classroom?"

As the series progressed, it featured more sophisticated photography, editing and wilder storylines, including time travel to the future. "When a show reaches its third season, viewers will often go, 'Okay, they ran through their mill of stories and now they're just repeating themselves,'" says Brancato. "Well, that's bad! That's tired television, but often you see a show's quality diminish as it continues. A good television series evolves and we really strived to make *First Wave* better."

An example was "Terminal City," where Cade travels to the year 2009 (economically presented as a warehouse district — rusted cars, old buildings and lots of Canadian shrubbery) and meets himself in the future, a long-haired, burned-out cynic who blames himself not only for killing Jordan years ago but failing to stop the Second Wave. Present-day Cade manages to change history and returns to his own time, determined not to let this dismal future play itself out.

Brancato hoped that a fourth year would have an all-out war with the Gua but the show was canceled. In the last episode, "Twice Bless'd," the four heroes are held captive in an asylum, each one nearing derangement until Cade realizes they're being manipulated by Mabus. Breaking free of his mental fog, Cade sees millions of Gua husks in suspended animation, about to be awakened for the Second Wave. Mabus, now in human form, and holding a powerful Gua hammer, taunts Cade with news that Foster has been a Gua agent all this time. Foster, pretending to believe this, shoots down his three friends as proof of his loyalty to Mabus. Mabus lets his guard down and Foster destroys the alien leader and uses the hammer to revive his three friends. The alien husks are destroyed and Eddie exclaims, "We did it — we've stopped the second wave!"

The last scene shows the four driving off in a convertible, with Cade and Jordan laughing and Eddie and Joshua exchanging hearty high-fives. "We literally got the word of *First Wave*'s cancellation while shooting on the set," says William Corcoran, the director of this last episode. "It was cold and brutal and it left us all feeling gutted. I tried to rally the troops and end the show on a positive note. I felt the show's loyal fans deserved to see the show go out with a big bang." Corcoran enjoyed his time on the series and says, "I was proud of my episodes. Tracy was very committed to her work as was Sebastian and Rob. But like many series I have worked on, *First Wave* had run its course and its credibility."

Cast Notes

Sebastian Spence (Cade Foster): A native of St. John's Newfoundland, Spence began acting in local theater. His father was a playwright and his mother was an actress, and they inspired him to go into the arts. His first film was the award-winning Canadian film *The Boys of St. Vincent* (1993) where he played a young man haunted by memories of sexual and physical abuse. The actor, who points to *Blade Runner* as his favorite film, also had guest roles in *The X-Files*, *Sliders*, *Battlestar Galactica*, and *Outer Limits*. His TV films include *The Lone Ranger* (2003) and *Category 7: The End of the World* (2005).

Rob LaBelle (Crazy Eddie Nambulous): In tenth grade he starred as McMurphy, the lead character in a stage production of *One Flew Over the Cuckoo's Nest*. LaBelle was a friend of Chris Brancato since their Brown University days in Rhode Island in the early 1980s. Brancato felt LaBelle would be ideal as Eddie but the actor had to convince a couple of other people who didn't want him for the role. His other credits include *Quantum Leap*, *The X-Files*, *The 4400* and *Star Trek: Voyager*. *Deadly Skies* (2005) and *Eureka* (2006) are two of his TV movies. Some people still run up to LaBelle, mistaking him for the exuberant, Oscar-winning Italian director Roberto Benigni.

Roger R. Cross (Joshua): Born in Jamaica, he moved to Vancouver when he was eleven. Cross has a martial-arts background and, while working as a stuntman in *21 Jump Street*, he was encouraged to go into acting but remained undecided. Soon after, he fell into a raging river in China during a break in the filming of the film

International Rescue and had he not grabbed onto a last rock, he would have been swept to his death over the falls. He decided life was too short and he plunged into acting full-time, studying at Peter Breck's Acting Academy in Vancouver. After *First Wave*, he appeared in the feature *Chronicles of Riddick* (2004) and, starting in 2005, co-starred as agent Curtis Manning in *24*.

Traci Elizabeth Lords (Jordan Radcliffe): Born and raised in Ohio, her family later moved to Los Angeles. She began her career as a model but then got into porn films as a teenager. One of her first mainstream films was *Cry-Baby* (1990) with Johnny Depp. Although athletic, Lords had to learn Ninja moves and how to fire guns for *First Wave*. Her other TV credits include *MacGyver*, *Tales from the Darkside* and *Hercules*. She also did Stephen King's *The Tommyknockers* (ABC, 1993) and the motion pictures *Not of This Earth* (1988) and *Chump Change* (2004).

SOURCES

Lee, Patrick. *First Wave* review. Sci-Fi.com, March 1998.

Millman, Joyce. *First Wave* review. "The Xerox Files—Two New Sci-fi Series from Former X-Files Writers Copy the Original's Formula but Leave Out Main Ingredients." Salon.com, March 8, 1999.

Phillips, Mark. "Alien Notions—Sebastian Spence Sacrifices His Humanity to Stop the First Wave." *Starlog* no. 267, October 1999.

_____. "Conscientious Objector—As the Gua Joshua, Roger Cross Searches for Humanity on First Wave." *Starlog* no. 268, November 1999.

_____. Interview with Rob La Belle. *Starlog's Sci-Fi TV* no. 7, 1999.

_____. "The Invasion Continues—First Wave is Here and There are More Alien Thrills to Come." *Starlog* no. 271, February 2000.

Spragg, Paul. *TV Zone Special* no. 35, 1999.

Harsh Realm

(1999–2000)

Army Lt. Thomas Hobbes enters the virtual reality world "Harsh Realm" in search of a renegade general. He must do everything he can to accomplish his mission and stay alive.

Cast: Scott Bairstow (Lt. Thomas Hobbes), D.B. Sweeney (Mike Pinocchio), Terry O'Quinn (General Omar Santiago), Maximilian Martini (Major Max Waters), Rachel Hayward (Florence), Sarah-Jane Redmond (Inga Fossa), Samantha Mathis (Sophie Green)

Executive Producers: Chris Carter, Daniel Sackheim, Frank Spotnitz; **Co-Executive Producer:** Michelle McLaren; **Supervising Producer:** John Shiban; **Producer:** George A. Grieve; **Co-Producer:** Janace Tashjian; **Consulting Producers:** Tony To, Vince Gilligan; **Director of Photography:** Joel Ransom; **Music by** Mark Snow; **Writers included:** Frank Spotnitz, John Shiban, Chris Carter, Steve Maeda; **Directors included:** Daniel Sackheim, Cliff Bole, Kim Manners, Larry Shaw, Bryan Spicer, Tony To; **Guest Stars included:** Steve Makaj, Michael David Simms, Raymond Cruz, Lance Henriksen

Fox TV Network/20th Century–Fox Television/Ten Thirteen Productions; October 1999–April–May 2000; 60 minutes; 9 episodes; DVD status: Complete series

Contrary to what some viewers might assume, *Harsh Realm* was not a rip-off of the Wachowski brothers' famed movie series *The Matrix*, which blasted its way into cinemas in 1999. It's not *Tron* or *VR5* either. To understand *Harsh Realm* the TV series, we have to go back to the source material that inspired it: A 1992 comic book by writer James Hudnall, artists Andrew Paquette and inker John Ridgway. The concept and characters are markedly different from this television series created by Chris Carter. It was actually executive producer-director Daniel Sackheim who had found the comic book and saw it as a potential launching pad for a series so he gave it to Carter who also liked it, and decided to use the ideas from it to refashion his own *Harsh Realm*.

Hudnall recalls, "I wanted to do a science

fiction comic, and one night I had a vivid dream. I was in a strange land and I needed glasses to see well. I came across a pool shaped like an eye. There was a stone island in the center like an iris. A sign by the pool said it was the eye pool and would cure all vision. So I splashed the water on my eyes and I no longer needed glasses. Then I came across a walled city, like in medieval times. The gates of the city opened and an army poured out and then I woke up. In the shower that morning I tried to imagine how I could use this dream as a story and *Harsh Realm* came about. I set it in a 'pocket universe' based on role-playing games."

Hudnall's *Harsh Realm* was about a futuristic, technology-rich world where a private eye named Dexter Green is approached by parents who say their son has entered into a "pocket universe" created by a super-computer called Harsh Realm and has never returned. When Dexter goes on the hunt, he realizes he's entered a fantasy "theme" world where there is magic and medieval technology. There, Dexter discovers a woman who has also escaped from the real world and is practicing magic, and she helps him look for the son, Dan Crawford. They discover that Dan has become drunk with power and is a threat to all the Harsh Realm's inhabitants.

In Chris Carter's *Harsh Realm*, which premiered on Fox on October 8, 1999, the virtual world was not a mystical, magical land but a modern-day military scenario. Army Lt. Thomas Hobbes was sent into the Harsh Realm to take out a renegade general, Omar Santiago, who had absconded with the program and had recast the city under his rule. Previous assassination attempts against him had failed. The government in the real world wanted Santiago and their program back. Thrown into the digital recreation of this entire world without any information at all, Hobbes eventually hooks up with a fellow soldier, Michael Pinocchio. But their efforts to get at Santiago are frustrated by the general's number one man, Lt. Max Waters, who has orders to hunt down and bring in Hobbes and Pinocchio. Theirs is a complicated relationship: Hobbes had saved Waters' life in the real world a few years earlier. On the run, Hobbes and Pinocchio are also joined by Florence, a mute. Hobbes comes to realize this was not just a game but a complete environment where no rules apply.

Of the two of them, Hobbes was more naive about existence in the Realm. He had to learn the difference between those who were "hooked up" to the real world and others who were mere "virtual characters" representing those in the real world. He reacted emotionally and was sidetracked from his mission because of the "virtual" equivalent of his fiancée, Sophie (who did not recognize him). As it transpired in the pilot, the Realm Sophie was "digitized" (killed) by Lt. Waters, Later, Hobbes would also find the Realm edition of his dying mother. Pinocchio, by contrast was very jaded, but knowledgeable about the Realm's rules, and he often guided Hobbes through hidden gateways and "glitches" in the system that they could use to their advantage.

Meanwhile, in the real world, Hobbes' fiancée, Sophie has been privately told by Inga Fossa, a mysterious woman who is capable of freely traveling between the real world and the Harsh Realm, that Hobbes (whom Sophie thought had died) is still alive.

"Chris was concerned that this idea [of the series] would not be relatable, or scary, to the average viewer," explains executive producer-director Daniel Sackheim, who had developed a relationship with Chris Carter during *The X-Files*. "He felt the military game angle played to the general public's inherent distrust of government. In other words, the audience could at some level believe that the government could actually have something akin to a virtual war game depicted in our show. This was a theme that he exploited to much success in *The X-Files*.

"This approach seemed to make sense to me. I really liked how elements of it paid homage to [Francis Ford Coppola's 1979 film] *Apocalypse Now*, the search for Col. Kurtz, through a dangerous and surreal environment. I thought there was a lot of potential here and a lot of stories that we could tell."

The road from comic book to TV screen was long and winding for Hudnall and Paquette. At one point in the early 1990s, Hudnall had been in discussions with NBC about a series treatment. "I would have been involved, but it fell through," he says. Hudnall's manager made the comic book available to Sackheim, who gave it to *X-Files* producer and creator Carter as a potential property for a TV series. "I had a choice between Chris Carter and James Cameron at one point," says Hudnall. "Both were interested in the project. I chose Carter because I figured he would get it done, whereas Cameron sits on projects for years. And I was an *X-Files* fan."

But from there, Hudnall and Paquette's world

got a little bit harsher. Their publisher Harris Comics, Inc., who also publish Vampirella comic titles, didn't tell them that a Hollywood deal had been struck as late as when the pilot had begun filming. Meanwhile, Hudnall and Paquette were upset that Carter would be given a "Created by" credit at the beginning of the show (the acknowledgment of their comic book would be relegated to the end credits with an "Inspired by" card). Hudnall and Paquette were so unhappy with this arrangement that they sued Fox Television and Carter for better crediting and financial participation in the television series.

Carter, on the other hand, felt strongly that he had reworked the story and premise to a level where he had created an original work and that the comic book had only served as an "inspirational" source.

"Carter optioned the comic, used the title, the basic premise, lots of plot points," recalls Hudnall. "While he changed the setting and the characters, his characters served the same function in the story. The teenager became a power-mad general and the detective became a soldier hunting that general. The sidekick is a wacky fighter. In my story, the love interest was also a sidekick, he changed that for the most part. But he optioned my book, used it, yet changed it so he could claim he 'created it.' I don't dispute that he created the TV show. But to not even give us any credit at all (which was the case at first) was unbelievable. So I asked for, then demanded a credit. We had to sue to get one. I did not want to sue anyone, but they left me no choice."

In March 2000, Hon. Judge Martin of the 7th District Court in New York ruled in favor of Hudnall and Paquette. Fox Television had to place a card after the "Written by" credit that said, "Inspired by the comic series *Harsh Realm* created by James Hudnall and Andrew Paquette, Published by Harris Comics," to be run close to the credit "Created by Chris Carter."

In response to the judgment, Fox Television told the Hollywood industry trade newspaper, *Variety*, "We are pleased that the court vindicated our position that Chris Carter is the creator of the *Harsh Realm* television series and that the court adopted the 'inspired by' credit that Fox had already included in the show as a good-faith effort to resolve this matter."

Feedback from *Harsh Realm* fans was mostly sympathetic, says Hudnall. "Those who didn't understand my position, I tried to set straight. Some fans online thought I was trying to derail the show or was responsible for it being canceled, but nothing could be further from the truth. I wanted to see the show succeed, just with my credits intact."

Today, Hudnall continues to develop properties for Hollywood. "People sue each other all the time in Hollywood. They just treat it like business as usual. If anything, it kind of made us heroes in the eyes of other creative people who feel abused by the system. We stood up to some big players. I've had other deals since then including one with Universal for a feature. No one remembers the lawsuit except for *Harsh Realm* fans and media people.

"I look forward, so I'm not really concerned about what happened anymore. I think this issue was settled."

Filming *Harsh Realm* was done mostly outdoors, in the forested outskirts of Vancouver, British Columbia, a Canadian city with a robust filmmaking community. Many Hollywood films and television series are made here, including *The X-Files* and *Sliders*.

Because Hobbes, Pinocchio and Florence were constantly on the go, this meant there were very few permanent sets in use. And location shooting is arduous and expensive. Sackheim explains. "The average TV series, cop and lawyer show, etc., utilizes standing sets that they depend upon to minimize the number of days on location. This helps keep the budget down. There are additional costs incurred for transportation, location fees, equipment rentals and longer hours for the crew. As a consequence, the average network series shoots between four and six days on their standing sets. Given the conceit behind our show (two wandering fugitives), we had very few permanent sets though we routinely built a number of swing sets (temporary sets that relate to a specific episode) and we spent an average of six days on location. That made the show more difficult to execute, but there was the upside of a moodier tone and bigger production value.

"An additional challenge involved our need to make the world feel somewhat different from the real world. There were sets that needed to play to the post-apocalyptic quality of the city."

For example, in the second episode, "Leviathan," "we created a large scale refugee camp. This is a costly thing to do on a TV budget."

Sackheim reveals that although the network had an initial order of 12 episodes, "they canceled the show as we were completing the ninth episode, 'Camera Obscura.' My sense is that Doug

Harsh Realm's D.B. Sweeney, left, Scott Bairstow and Terry O'Quinn (© Fox Television).

Herzog, who was president of the network at the time, never really felt comfortable with the genre. So, while I can't blame everything on the network, I do believe that they never really embraced the show, and as a consequence did not put much effort behind trying to build an audience."

Fox TV had only aired three episodes when the cancellation was announced. The news was abrupt and stunned the show's cast and crew, who were all high on the work and material.

This was unfortunate because response from television critics was, initially, strong. Howard Rosenberg of *The Los Angeles Times* wrote that the series was not equal to *The X-Files*, "but shows promise.... Carter's latest venture is seductively mystifying from the moment its dark curtain descends gloomily on its protagonists, stranding them in a culture of high-density combat and danger.... The only disappointment here comes when, after building up Santiago to be some kind

of kinky renegade along the lines of Marlon Brando's insane, despotic Col. Kurtz in *Apocalypse Now*, he turns out to be the unmenacing O'Quinn, who has a commanding officer of his own. The horror. It's a small price to pay, though, for an otherwise intriguing hour...."

All nine episodes later (March 2000) were broadcast by the FX Network. It was here where the Hudnall-Paquette acknowledgment was added to the front credits by court judgment. The series is now available on DVD.

Speculating on why the show didn't "take hold" with an audience, or why the network was not as supportive of the series and its concept as they hoped for, Sackheim says, "Chris [Carter], Frank Spotnitz, and myself have pondered this question on more than one occasion. We all have different theories. I suspect the audience never really embraced the characters, and may have been turned off by the somewhat bleak tone of the show. Also, as you recall, *The Matrix* had just been released, and that was a pretty tough act to follow, given the limitations of a TV series."

Harsh Realm was unplugged, leaving many unanswered questions. "Will Hobbes and Pinocchio ever accomplish their mission and defeat Santiago?" "What was Inga Fossa's true motives? Whose side was she on? She had ease of access to Santiago in the Harsh Realm and to the real world, where she informed Hobbes' fiancée of his continued existence." "Various virtual characters had tabbed Hobbes as being 'The One.' Why?" "How could the government have had ease of access to the Realm and yet, be unable to find the mainframe and Santiago himself?"

Sackheim does reveal one tantalizing plot point concerning General Santiago's master plan. "The mythology was going in an interesting direction," he says. "One element we never got to play out involved General Santiago's plan to detonate a number of nuclear devices in the real world, leaving him the supreme ruler of the only habitable place on Earth. At least, I seem to remember Chris talking about that."

CAST NOTES

Scott Bairstow (Tom Hobbes): Bairstow was Ned Grayson on *Party of Five* (1998–2000) and was Newt Call in the *Lonesome Dove* (1994) TV series and a spin-off called *Lonesome Dove: The Outlaw Years* (1995). After *Harsh Realm,* he was cast in a Steven Spielberg–produced TV pilot, *Semper Fi* (2001), and a short-lived fantasy series, *Wolf Lake.* He also appeared in the *Twilight Zone* episode "Hunted."

D.B. Sweeney (Mike Pinocchio): When he graduated from university, Sweeney got cast in a Broadway stage production of *The Caine Mutiny Court Martial.* Television roles included *Spenser: For Hire,* the daytime soap *The Edge of Night, CSI: Miami* and a lead role in the short-lived fantasy series *Strange Luck* (1996). D.B. garnered attention in the baseball movie feature *Eight Men Out* (1988) playing Shoeless Joe Jackson. Other feature credits included *Memphis Belle* (1990), *Fire in the Sky* (1993), and *Hardball* (2001). Recent guest-star credits includes the post-apocalyptic drama *Jericho.*

Terry O'Quinn (Gen. Omar Santiago): One of Hollywood's busiest performers, O'Quinn began acting in the 1970s. He's appeared in *Space Camp* and *The Rocketeer* (as Howard Hughes). His genre TV credits includes *Earth 2, Star Trek: The Next Generation* and *The X-Files.* He co-starred with Lance Henriksen in Chris Carter's *Millennium* (1996–98). He's also appeared in *Alias* and *JAG,* and hit it big with ABC's monster hit series *Lost* as John Locke.

Rachel Hayward (Florence): Born and raised in Toronto, Hayward began her career as a model and acting in commercials. With a degree in Graphic Design and Fine Arts, Hayward divided her time between freelance designing and actress-

ing. She has extensive film and TV credits. Her feature credits include *Breaking all the Rules* (1985), *Time Runner* (1993), and *The Final Cut* (1995). Her TV credits include appearances in *Stargate SG-1*'s series pilot "Children of the Gods," *Millennium, The Dead Zone* and *Jake 2.0* (the recurring role of Executive Director Valerie Warner).

Samantha Mathis (Sophie Green): Mathis was in *Pump Up the Volume* (1990), *The American President* (1995), *American Psycho* (2000) and *The Punisher* (2004). She starred in the short-lived series *First Years* (2001) and *The Twilight Zone* ("Into the Light") and had a role in the TNT fantasy mini-series *The Mists of Avalon* (2001).

Sara-Jane Redmond (Inga Fossa): Redmond has an extensive background in dance and theater. She studied acting in Vancouver, Canada, at the William Davis Center. Her work on Chris Carter's *The X-Files* and *Millennium* encouraged her to continue with acting. Her TV guest star appearances includes *The Outer Limits, Smallville, Andromeda, Dark Angel* and Steven Spielberg's Sci-Fi Channel mini-series *Taken* (2002). She had a recurring lead role in the Canadian-made crime drama *DaVinci's Inquest* (1999–2005)

SOURCES

"'Harsh Realm' Ruling: A Federal Judge has Ruled that Any Future Airings of the Harsh Realm TV Series Must Include a Credit that the Concept was Inspired by the Original Comic Book's Creators." Cinescape Online, March 2, 2000.

Rosenberg, Howard. "Harsh Realm Makes Murkiness Quite Charming: The New Series from Chris Carter Isn't the Equal of 'The X-Files,' but it Shows Promise." *Los Angeles Times,* October 7, 1999.

The Invisible Man

(2000–2002)

A former burglar is given an experimental biosynthetic gland which allows him to become invisible. Darien Fawkes now works for a government agency on dangerous and often bizarre missions.

Cast: Vincent Ventresca (Darien Fawkes), Paul Ben-Victor (Bobby Hobbes), Shannon Kenny (The Keeper/Claire), Eddie Jones (The Official/ Charles Borden), Michael McCafferty (Albert

The Invisible Man

Eberts), Brandy Ledford (Agent Alex Monroe) *Year 2*; Based on the novel by H.G. Wells; **Created for Television by:** Matt Greenberg; **Executive Producers:** Matt Greenberg, Jonathan Glassner; **Co-Executive Producers:** Valerie Mayhew, Vivian Mayhew; **Supervising Producer:** Edward Ledding; **Producer:** Matt Greenberg; **Associate Producer:** Paul M. Leonard; **Consulting Producer:** Peter Hume; **Visual Effects Supervisor:** Greg Tsadilas; **On-Set Visual Effects Supervisor:** Gerard Black; **Writers included:** Gabrielle Stanton, Ashley Gable, Jonathan Glassner, Anne McGrail, Dean Orion, Steven D. Binder, Peter Hume, Mark Cullen, Craig Silverstein; **Directors included:** Greg Yaitanes, Adam Nimoy, Michael Grossman, Bill L. Norton, Ken Girotti, Jay Tobias, James Contner, Joshua Butler, Breck Eisner, David Levinson; **Guest Stars include:** Catherine Dent, Jack Banning, William H. Bassett, Dennis Lipscomb, Wil Wheaton, Paul Collins, Armin Shimerman, John Beck, Joe Spano, Priscilla Barnes, Nan Martin, Rebecca Chambers, Spencer Garrett (as Jarod Stark), Idalis DeLeon (as La Llorona) and Joel Bissonette (as Arnaud de Fehrn)

The Sci-Fi Channel/Distributed by USA Studios/Stu Segall Productions (San Diego); June 2000-February 2002; 60 minutes; 46 episodes; DVD status: Complete series

"Invisibility sucks." So said writer Leslie Stevens after launching two invisible men TV series in the 1970s: *The Invisible Man* (David McCallum as a scientist) and *The Gemini Man* (Ben Murphy as a secret agent). Both series flopped. Even the British *Invisible Man* series (1959–1960) didn't go more than a year.

Each featured bland, stereotypical heroes. While their special effects were good for their time, computer generated images (CGI) opened up a whole new universe by the 1990s. In April 1998, producer Dick Wolf (*Law and Order*) planned to star Kyle MacLachlan in an *Invisible Man* series for Fox. It was going to be set in modern-day New York City, and would reflect a "strong, complex realism" along the lines of *The X-Files*. That project didn't materialize.

When The Sci-Fi Channel contacted writer Matt Greenberg about doing their own invisible man series two years later, he was reluctant; how do you put a new spin on a very old premise? He decided on an adventure-satire angle, featuring a former thief who was quirky and selfish, yet ultimately a good guy.

Star Vincent Ventresca signed up to play Darien Fawkes because of the show's emphasis on characterization. "Invisibility was the least interesting part for me," Ventresca says today. "The show was really about the people and their relationships."

The pilot introduces Darien as he's scaling a high-rise building. When he's caught stealing by an old man, the elderly gentleman collapses from a heart attack. While trying to revive the man, Darien is arrested. His efforts to resuscitate the man are misconstrued by police and headlines scream, "Burgling Molester of the Elderly." Sent to jail, Darien starts picking the lock but he screams when a spider lands on him (his phobia) and he's sent to solitary confinement. By now it's clear this is an invisible man who straddles both satire and adventure.

His brother Kevin, a young scientist, promises Darien freedom if he'll participate in a risky experiment where a biosynthetic gland is surgically attached to his cerebral cortex. This will secrete a hormone called Quicksilver, which bends light, allowing Darien to become invisible.

Darien reluctantly agrees to risk surgery over life in prison but he gets into an argument with a Swiss doctor prepping him for surgery. The doctor insists the pop group ABBA is Swedish. Darien insists they are Swiss. The doctor reacts, 'Impossible! A Swiss man would never make lyrics like that.' Darien is also suspicious of one of the doctors, Arnaud de Fehrn.

After the surgery, Darien learns that adrenaline, fear and anger will trigger the gland, making him invisible. But he soon regrets his decision and his brother asks, "Then how was I supposed to get you out of jail?" Darien replies, "The old fashioned way — guns and explosives."

Darien agrees to try invisibility for a couple of weeks. However, unbeknownst to Darien and Kevin, the experimental gland has been mutated by Arnaud. If Darien remains invisible for more than 30 minutes, he will turn into a psychotic madman. An antidote, Counteragent, is created to prevent these attacks of rage. When Arnaud's terrorists invade the lab and steal the Quicksilver designs, Kevin is mortally wounded and Darien clutches his dying, blood-soaked brother.

Darien is now forced to work for The Official, a devious but patriotic government man, and is teamed up with a cynical former FBI agent, Bobby Hobbes. Surgical removal of the Quicksilver gland will kill Darien, so he hopes to find a cure for his condition. Meanwhile, in exchange for his Counteragent shots, he has to continue to work for the government agent. One bonus is working with the beautiful Keeper, a woman who keeps tabs on his health.

Darien fits in with this oddball group. Hobbes is a former Desert Storm soldier ("Underpaid, disgruntled and overworked" is how actor Paul Ben-Victor describes him). Hobbes keeps clashing with Darien on investigative procedures, while Claire (The Keeper) is cool and reserved, looking after Darien like a pet rather than a man. They all report to the rotund Official. Once a big man in government, The Official is now simply a big man, strumming the lower rungs of power as head of The Agency. It's an organization working under the auspices of the Department of Fish and Game.

It was the close relationship between Darien and Hobbes that grabbed viewers. Ventresca was cast first and he recalls, "They brought in five guys to read for Hobbes but when I read with Paul, I couldn't get through the scene without breaking up. We had this instant chemistry. He was perfect for the role."

Paul Ben-Victor, however, wasn't sure he wanted to do the show. "I had other things happening in my life," he says. "Vinnie came over to my house and said, 'You gotta do this!' I knew instinctually he was right. When I first met Vinnie at the audition, I was in his face and he was laughing at me. I'm this short bald guy, he's this tall skinny guy, and instantly, we had chemistry. It was a lot of fun working with him. Vinnie has a tremendously magnetic personality and we've been good friends ever since."

"In one show, the gland caused Darien to get a cold and he keeps sneezing," recalls Ventresca. "I said to Paul, 'I'm gonna really sneeze in your face,' and he's like, 'Yeah, right.' So I let out a big ol' wet sneeze, right all over his face. It was really funny! To be able to experiment like that, creatively, was great."

Many of the special effects for previous invisible men series were done through expensive blue screen. CG made this new invisible man much easier to create. Janet Hamilton Muswell, who had done visual effects for *VR5*, was supervisor of visual effects for the *Invisible Man*'s pilot. "The subsequent series was done by my team of CGI artists that I had set up for the pilot," she says. "Our CGI department was created just for *Invisible Man* and it was fun to put together such a crack team. We got the best possible results. The pilot had many challenges, mainly being the lack of money and the incredibly long hours on set.

We shot in Mexico and San Diego and I spent the whole shoot dreading a tarantula spider scene, where we used real spiders, not CGI! I hate spiders. I worked on the film *Snakes on a Plane* and I love snakes but I hate spiders!"

While the producers of the 1975 *Invisible Man* (with David McCallum) ruefully admitted they had to make their invisible man stumble around a lot, so that viewers could "see" him, Muswell didn't face that challenge. "Our invisible man wore clothes a lot, so you *could* see him," she says. "In the pilot we saw him through heat sensor glasses in one part of the show, so again, we could see the body of the man running. We never made him clumsy, as far as I can remember."

The Invisible Man's missions stretched from serious to humorous. (In year two, Bigfoot tries to mate with Darien. The shaggy beast is attracted to his Quicksilver gland.) Darien's humor always prevailed (his oft-repeated exclamation is "Aw, crap!") and there were many inside jokes. When Darien questions a man in a Mexican eatery, a poster of the 1933 Claude Rains film *The Invisible Man* is in the background. Gloria Stuart, who co-starred in that classic film, appeared as Darien's grandmother in "Father Figure."

"Our version was more of an irreverent comedy," says writer Jonathan Glassner. "Invisibility is a premise that's hard to take too seriously. The things Darien can do on a serious note are very limited. In story meetings the question was always raised, 'What can we have Darien do this week other than steal something or spy on someone?' It was much easier to come up with funny things. My favorite moment in the series is when Darien sees a street mime and decides to mess with him. He becomes 'the wall' that this mime keeps bumping into. As the mime fights with this invisible man, the crowd is watching and thinking this is an amazing mime. It's a very funny sequence."

The black humor of the show is on full display in "Catevari." After a mental patient named Charlie massacres a dozen doctors, a nurse on the scene apologizes to Darien and Hobbes. "You must please excuse the air of chaos and hopelessness," she says. "As you can see, we are very shortly staffed at the moment." The Official orders Darien to find Charlie. "Charlie can't kill who he can't see," he reassures a nervous Darien. Charlie is an old friend of The Official and injections of experimental poison allow him to kill with a single scratch, turning victims' brains into "mush." Just before authorities are forced to kill him, Charlie expresses regret for his killing spree.

Fans liked the interaction between Darien and Hobbes, which was no surprise to Ventresca. "The invisibility added a quirky element to the old-fashioned buddy genre. Hobbes and Darien really cared about each other. People stop me today and say, 'I really liked you and that other guy.' They don't say, 'Hey, the invisibility was really cool.'"

Not everyone appreciated the humor. "The story of an invisible man is a dish best served cold: dark and disturbing, yet the inspiration for this latest version seems closer to Chevy Chase's *Memoirs of an Invisible Man*," said *Entertainment Weekly*. "It's an inane plot that only makes our interest disappear."

In the second year, there was a last-minute attempt to attract more male viewers by adding tough-talking agent Alex Monroe, played by the attractive Brandy Ledford. Monroe wanted to find her missing young son but the character of Alex was resented by many female fans. Even Ledford had some regrets years later. "I don't know why I made her such a bitch," the actress candidly lamented to *TV Zone* magazine. "It didn't allow viewers to warm up to her."

"The first year in particular was magical," says Paul Ben-Victor. "It was chemistry of the cast, combined with the quirky storylines. Out of the 40-odd episodes we made, a third of them were pretty damn good. The producers let us do our thing and we knew fans were digging the show."

As the second year wound down, Ventresca felt the show would go on. "I thought the show was kind of a hit and assumed we would do another year." He learned of the show's cancellation when he read a *New York Times* article on the Sci-Fi Channel's new season and found no mention of *The Invisible Man*.

Cancellation was announced shortly thereafter. But the actor was familiar with the ratings game. "It had a lot of loyal fans but if a show doesn't grow, you can't ask them to do more than what we did, 46 episodes."

One of the shows' problems was that it was syndicated simultaneously to being aired on the Sci-Fi Channel, which diluted the cable's ratings numbers. Its numbers in general syndication were, according to Ventresca, "fantastic."

Faced with the possibility that the series was going to end, writer Craig Silverstein decided to provide some kind of resolution at the end of year two and cured Darien's need for counteragent

shots in the last episode (although he still retained the power of invisibility).

Fan efforts to get the series revived for a third year were unsuccessful but even today, some fans still hold out hope for a one-shot movie.

Cast Notes

Vincent Ventresca (Darien): Born in Indianapolis, he was the youngest of 11 children. He graduated from Indiana University with majors in theater and psychology. His TV credits include the role of Dr. Ed Tate in the series *Prey* (1998) and guest shots on *Twilight Zone* (2002), *Cold Case* and *Complete Savages*.

Paul Ben-Victor (Hobbes): The Brooklyn-born actor cringes whenever he admits that his first film was *Attack of the Killer Bimbos* (1988). His mother was a playwright and actress and although his first dream was to be a set designer and director, he ended up doing TV commercials, including a hugely successful Levis commercial in New York. This brought him to Hollywood, where he guested on shows like *The X-Files* and appeared as Moe Howard in the TV movie bio *The Three Stooges*. He also had a recurring role in HBO's series *The Wire* (2003–2006). "Paul and I instantly liked and respected each other," says Invisible Man co-star Vincent Ventresca. "We could be real and spontaneous on camera."

Shannon Kenny (Claire, the Keeper): The Australian-born actress admitted her knowledge of SF was pretty much limited to a single viewing of *Star Wars*. One of her hopes was for her character to become invisible on the *Invisible Man* series (in "Germ Theory," her character is infected with a bacteria that turns her *partially* invisible). Her other credits included the mini-series remake *The Invaders* (1995), episodes of *7th Heaven* and cartoon voices for animated series such as *Max Steel*, *Batman Beyond* and *Superman*.

Eddie Jones (The Official): He hitchhiked from Pennsylvania as a young man in hopes of pursuing his college dreams in California. A friend introduced him to acting in summer stock productions. He later co-starred as Pa Kent in the series *Lois and Clark* (1993–1997).

Brandy Ledford (Alex Monroe): Born in Denver, Colorado, her family moved all over the U.S. while she was growing up. Of her brief stint on *Invisible Man*, she said, "I played a smart, tough character and I got to be taken seriously as an actress." She later became a regular as the android Doyle on the last year of *Andromeda* (2004–2005).

Michael McCafferty (Eberts): He began his career in theater and music and appeared on TV shows like *ER* and *Six Feet Under*. The Minnesota-born actor kept in touch with *Invisible Man* fans by posting on Sci-Fi Channel's bulletin board during the series' run.

SOURCES

Eramo, Steven. "In the Pink—Invisible Man Co-star Brandy Ledford is Joining the Crew as New Android Doyle, and Tells Us Why She's So Much Happier in the Seefra System than Working with Project Quicksilver." *TV Zone* no 183, December 2004.

_____. "Silver Fawkes." *TV Zone* no. 142, September 2001.

Reviews of *The Invisible Man*. *Entertainment Weekly*, 2000 and 2002.

Shapiro, Marc. "On the Invisible Man Set." *Starlog* no. 277, August 2000.

Jake 2.0

(2003)

National Security Agency tech support flunky Jake Foley is accidentally bombarded with experimental nanotech "bots" who penetrate into his bloodstream. Now he's the NSA's "ultimate human upgrade" field agent.

Cast: Christopher Gorham (Jake Foley), Philip Anthony Rodriguez (Kyle Duarte), Judith Scott (NSA Deputy Director Louise Beckett), Keegan Connor Tracy (Diane Hughes), Marina Black (Sarah Heywood)

Recurring Cast: Miranda Frigon (Sarah), Rachel Hayward (Executive Director Valerie Warner), Grace Park (Fran Yoshida), Jesse Cadote (DuMont); *Created by:* Silvio Horta; *Executive Producers:* David Greenwalt, Silvio Horta, Robert Lieberman, Gina Matthews, Grant Scharbo; *Supervising Producer:* Javier Grillo-Marxuach; *Producers:* Bernard Bourret, Richard Davis, Jean Desormeaux, Mark Wilding; *Co-Producers:* Mark Wilding, Billy Redner; *Associate Producer:* Craig Yahata; *Writers included:* David Greenwalt, Javier Grillo-Marxuach, Silvio Horta, Gina Mathews; *Directors included:* Robert Lieberman, Allan Kroeker, Steve Miner, Jorge Montesi, David Straiton; *Directors of Photography:* Steve Danyluk, David Geddes; *Production Designers:* Peter Cosco, Graeme Murray; *Visual Effects:* Stargate Digital Canada; *Guest Stars included:* Lee Majors, Carly Pope, Brendan Fletcher, Jim Byrnes, Laura Harris, Kandyse McClure

UPN/Viacom Productions/David Greenwalt Productions/Matthew Scharbo Productions/Roundtable Entertainment/Silent H Productions; September-December 2003; 60 minutes; 16 episodes

NATIONAL SECURITY AGENCY INTERNAL AFFAIRS REPORT—CLASSIFICATION: TOP SECRET—For Your Eyes Only. Subject: Jake Foley. NSA Tech Support Specialist. One of our own has become the world's first "Nano-technology" enhanced human being as a result of a freak laboratory accident that injected experimental "Nanites" into his bloodstream. [Reference Appendix A21X for details. Requires valid password]. Results: Now possesses extraordinary superhuman-level powers including super-strength, super-speed, super-hearing, super-vision and has the ability to manipulate electronic equipment by sheer mental concentration. [Reference Appendix A22Xi for examples of Foley's abilities. Requires retina scan.]

Current Status: NSA field agent. Effective immediately. Trained by NSA field agent Kyle Duarte. He is under the orders of NSA Deputy Director Louise Beckett and under constant medical supervision by Doctor Diane Hughes. [Reference Appendix A23Xii for full medical report]. END FILE.

Silvio Horta created *Jake 2.0*, a pastiche of genre elements. In this stylistic SF-action-adventure series, Jake Foley was an ordinary guy who, under extraordinary circumstances, gained superhuman powers. That's a comic book premise but without the costume. Because he worked in the U.S. intelligence community, the National Security Agency's hi-tech headquarters echoed the 1960s spy series *The Man from U.N.C.L.E.* complete with the gadgets. When Jake leaped into action, because of the thousands of microscopic "nanites" streaming through his bloodstream, the scenes were very reminiscent of the "Bionic" shows from the 1970s (*The Six Million Dollar Man* and *The Bionic Woman*). These elements, combined with original characters fleshed out by the cast, made for an appealing 21st century SF action hero.

Javier Grillo-Marxuach, the series' supervising producer, first met Horta while they were working together on *The Chronicle*, a short-lived 2001-02 fantasy series, and he came to admire Horta's style of creating characters. "One of the things I love most about Silvio's writing is the way he portrays ordinary people responding to the extraordinary and absurd—and I don't mean this only in the context of science fictional situations," he says. "He has an ability to create these funny, quirky, interesting characters and put them in emotional places to which we can all relate, even when what's around them is completely unbelievable. That's what made *Jake 2.0* a cool show to me. It was about an extremely sympathetic point-of-entry character who often infuriated his co-workers because he just wasn't entirely in tune with their modus operandi. Frankly, there is a humanity and charm to Silvio's writing that's missing from most SFTV. It sets his work apart."

It was Horta's conscious decision that Jake Foley would have a distinctive personality—he was a tech support geek who carried a torch for a classmate, Sarah Carter, and longed for the glamour of becoming an NSA field agent before his nano-tech accident. In fact, he had applied twice for field agent training, and was turned down. Later, Foley worked closely with Dr. Diane Hughes, who took over the nano-tech project from her predecessor and served as Jake's "minder." To use a *Six Million Dollar Man* analogy, Diane was to Jake as Dr. Rudy Wells was to Steve Austin.

"They didn't have a really firm concept of Diane at first, but I always do back stories," says actress Keegan Connor Tracy, who was cast as Diane. "I knew that she had parents in the sciences who were really smart and that she had pushed herself through school before she was socially ready. She was a woman in a man's world so her 'goofiness' was rooted in a very real way."

Tracy actually began her audition reading for the role of Sarah Carter, "I was just so goofy and dorky with it, they switched me over to Diane. She wasn't really fleshed out at the time and that gave us all a direction to go in," says Tracy. "At first I was very skeptical. I really wanted a comedy that season and here I ended up on a one-hour sci-fi. But as soon as I saw what Chris was

doing, I knew it was working and then we all had such great chemistry. It convinced me that it wasn't such a bad genre after all!"

Grillo-Marxuach says that as the stories went forward, the producers tried hard to craft plots and situations that wouldn't brand *Jake 2.0* as a "standard" superhero show. "We were encouraged to come up with ways in which Jake could solve problems that exploited his 'nanite' abilities in ways outside of the realm of mere superhero powers," he says. "We tried to explore areas that aren't usually explored in the superhero genre: Could Jake have sex? How would he feel about killing people or even hitting them, when it's something he had never done before he got his superpowers? How could he realistically deal with having a nemesis? That was the heart of the show, exploring them without ever taking the utter strangeness of Jake's situation for granted."

As a further example of the series' style and tone, Grillo-Marxuach discusses the three produced scripts he wrote. The first, "The Good, The Bad, and the Geeky," was about Jake going undercover as the renegade computer whiz expert DuMont to meet four other electronics experts who had stolen funds from the Federal Reserve Bank. "In the original draft almost every line was some kind of sci-fi reference!" he chuckles. "It was fun to try and write an episode that made sense at a character level but also have a supporting cast that was entirely named after characters from [the 1982 SF feature film] *Tron*.

In the second story, "Whiskey-Tango-Foxtrot," a general told the NSA that a "mini-nuke" had been stolen. He believed that a traitor was lurking within a Special Forces unit. To find the culprit, Jake went undercover as a new team member. Although he had just been given a crash course in being a highly skilled soldier, the NSA team relied on Jake's unique "nanite" abilities to help present the illusion of his skills.

"'Whiskey-Tango-Foxtrot' was one of those episodes that just seemed to pour out of me as if I was channeling the mutant offspring of Lee Ermey [the actor who frequently plays military figures] and Aaron Sorkin [*The West Wing* creator-writer]!" says Grillo-Marxuach. "It was written at a time when the production was falling behind, so it was done very quickly and when I look back at some of the monologues and the content of that show, I am very happy that I could write a piece that had something to say about honor and duty without coming off as an anti-military Hollywood liberal."

In "Get Foley," the third Grillo-Marxuach script (an episode that did not air in the series' original run but later surfaced in the UK), Jake suffered from amnesia and made a living as a fighter inside a secret fight club. Naturally, Jake was deemed as a superstar fighter because of his superhuman abilities. But what made the episode stand out was that Diane located Jake before the NSA did and she tried to jog his memory of his true identity. In one scene, they became romantic in a motel room. "One of my favorite scenes was when Diane and Jake finally kissed," says Tracy. "It was so heartbreaking for her to get what she wanted and it was wrong on so many levels. It was sad."

"David Greenwalt instructed me to write it like a John Garfield boxing movie," says Grillo-Marxuach. "It was a small and very emotional story about the hearts of the characters, and it had a lot of moments that paid off relationships we developed over the season. Silvio gave me a huge amount of trust."

As with any television series, the show's appeal lives and dies by the actors who deliver the lines. Their personalities draw in the audience who wants to spend an hour with them each week. Grillo-Marxuach says that across the board, he was very pleased with the chosen actors. "We lucked out with that ensemble," he says. "Chris Gorham pretty much was Jake. He had to trust us because we wrote Jake as a really geeky character, and many actors would try to shy away from some of the more nerdy parts of a role in order to not look bad or be typecast. But Chris sold the character in a very honest way.

"Judith Scott [as Jake's boss] nailed everything we gave her and brought a huge amount of humanity to a character that could have been a one-dimensional superior. She was an absolute treat to watch because she always added something — a look, a piece of business, an emotional inflection that made you know that her character had a lot more going on behind the eyes than you would ever know.

"Philip Anthony Rodriguez [as agent Kyle Duarte] is a star. A total leading man and a true gentleman who took the sometimes thankless role of the stoic foil for Jake and turned it into something with a lot of soul and dignity."

The glue to the show, notes Grillo-Marxuach, was Jake's relationship with his doctor, Diane. "Keegan was absolutely of the essence. Her character's relationship with Jake was a cornerstone of the series and the fact that it worked so smoothly is a credit to her as well as Chris."

Since Jake was completely untrained as a spy in the field, it became Kyle Duarte's task to bring their "Nanite" agent up to speed. As the show progressed, Jake became more proficient with his unique abilities and yet still retained the goofy quality that labeled him as "a geek."

One of the highlights in this short-lived action series was a special guest star appearance by Steve Austin himself — actor Lee Majors. For the episode "Double Agent," Majors came aboard as Richard Foxx, a legendary retired NSA agent. When an elusive female Russian agent slips past the NSA agents in a stakeout, they're forced to recall one of their own for assistance. Jake is surprised at Foxx's eccentricity and when he's dragged along for the ride to locate their target, Jake feels like he's jumped into a roller coaster. Later, NSA is surprised when another Foxx shows up, dressed impeccably and with a different personality. Are there two Foxxes running around? In the end, Diane's DNA analysis of tissue samples from both Foxxes reveals a startling conclusion. And when Jake and Kyle confront Foxx at his residence, they're befuddled to see Foxx talking to an imaginary person ... apparently his other self. With a little prodding, Jake manages to help Foxx reintegrate his personality and force the "other Foxx" to disappear. His was a case of post-traumatic split personality.

"*Jake 2.0* was essentially a 1970s 'superpower' show updated with a modern sensibility and a quirky, Silvio-esque sense of character, so when the network suggested that we do a 'stunt cast,' we immediately thought of Lee Majors and Lindsay Wagner for the role of Jake's parents," says Grillo-Marxuach. When Wagner declined, the double agent role was customized for Majors. "It probably worked out for the best because it made the whole thing less of a 'stunt' and gave us the opportunity to create a really interesting and fun character in Richard/Dick Foxx," continues Grillo-Marxuach. "The breakthrough there was to make the character a split personality. When David Greenwalt came up with that, it broke the thing wide open and the episode became this really fun romp but with a dark core, that brought the hazards of the job back to Jake in a very real way."

Majors' arrival on the Vancouver set for this episode was something of a nostalgia trip for the production crew. They pulled out from storage their Bionic memorabilia and had him sign the merchandise. For Tracy, having the opportunity to meet and work with the former Bionic Man was "wild!" When I was a girl, I was going to marry Steve Austin," she chuckles. "I had the doll and everything and was crushed when he married the Bionic Woman. He was really sweet and it was funny because my mom was there that week and even though she's met many famous people with me, she was totally star-struck by Lee Majors. I guess because he was really someone from her generation. He was sweet and left a signed picture for all of us. It was like being seven years old and meeting Steve Austin. Getting my picture taken with a guy who was one of my childhood idols was just outstanding."

The Bionic influence extended beyond the stunt casting. Grillo-Marxuach admits that when the network asked for an expositional 30-second opening title, laying out the show's premise, he and Shawn Paper, their editor, looked at *The Six Million Dollar Man*'s main theme for inspiration. "When I wrote it, and we cut it together, we really tried to give it a similar feel," he notes.

Jake 2.0's short life was typically due to low ratings; despite the creative synergy by the cast and crew, UPN dropped the ax mid-season. "It's very easy to overanalyze these things," sighs Grillo-Marxuach. "UPN did their best to launch and support the show, but we were in competition with *Angel* and *Smallville* and God knows what else. *Angel* and *Smallville* were already established, so a lot of what could have been our fanbase was otherwise engaged! What can you do? As a writer, you show up, bring your game and hope for the best. In this case, we were a small show in a small network and we got lost. Sadly, most shows end this way; huge hits are the bigger rarity."

In fact, the cancellation wasn't just mid-season, but in fact mid-episode. The cast and the entire *Jake 2.0* staff were on location in the heart of the Vancouver business district when the word came down. "I had been talking about 20 minutes beforehand to one of the producers and then he called me as I was literally in the van on my way to work to tell me we were canceled," recalls Tracy. "Chris [Gorham] stood up and told everyone right off the bat. I couldn't stop crying. It was emotional on a lot of levels. We were all sad. It was pretty emotional because we really were very close and happy as a group. But we got the news on the first day of the last episode so that by the last day, we'd accepted it."

The last episode filmed was "Upgrade" (not aired in the U.S.) and in one night scene we witness an assassin scale the side of a well-known Vancouver landmark, the Hotel Vancouver. It was during the shooting of this portion of the episode that the cancellation notice came down. Says Tracy: "I do have tape from the DV camera of me yelling up to 'Chris,' 'Don't do it, Chris! You'll get another show!' It was a good effort at breaking the sad mood we were all in after having just been canceled.

"I spent the week filming everyone and made a little movie for myself of *Jake 2.0* that I still go back and watch once in a while. The last day on set was like being punch drunk. We were silly and goofy. The director kept saying that it felt like 're-arranging deck chairs on the *Titanic*.' We laughed, we all cried, it was sad. When we went to film the last scene Jake and Diane would ever have, it was still mid-week. That was when I really lost it. We went to do the rehearsal and I realized, 'These are the last words these characters will ever speak,' and it broke my heart. I started to bawl and had to leave the set for a minute to compose myself. I had a great affinity for Diane and Jake and I felt sad for them. When 'big' characters end, it's like a little death."

The immediate consequence of the cancellation was lopping off the series' finale which was to be written by Grillo-Marxuach.

"We knew that the jig was up about halfway through the season and deliberately went about creating an arc that would carry us to a satisfying endpoint," recalls Grillo-Marxuach. "Our order was 19 episodes, so our goal was to develop the villain DuMont as an ongoing threat to Jake. By the end of the season, DuMont was to escape from jail, steal the next generation of nanites from the NSA and develop his own superpowers, and give Jake a computer virus that could only be cured by painfully removing the nanites in a high-powered magnetic field. The idea was to strip Jake of his abilities and show that he did actually develop the skills to be a good agent without them. The series was to end with Jake finding and killing DuMont once and for all before joining the NSA as a regular agent and settling down with Diane (who was to leave the NSA for the private sector). This entire arc was outlined and approved, but UPN pulled the plug the show on the very same day I was to begin writing the series finale! It's sad, because we came to this place where we had a nice send-off planned for our characters... but it was just not to be. Still, we had a lot of fun, and we truly loved the show and the characters. In a situation like this, you just have to look at the bright side and say 'It's too bad we got canceled, but 16 episodes is better than none!'"

Tracy believes the reason the show didn't catch fire and was quickly canceled had to do simply with a failure to make audiences aware of the program. "Everything done on the set by everyone was A-1. We had great characters, interesting plots, fun shows, great sets and lighting, etc. The real mistakes were made much higher up, like advertising and promotions. Did anyone ever know what night we were on? Oh, and how about you pull us for six weeks, just as we get rolling? Oh, and God forbid you change our time to eight o'clock."

Jake Foley may have been a superhuman spy, but there was one villain he couldn't defeat: a boardroom of TV network executives who didn't support the mission.

Cast Notes

Christopher Gorham (Jake Foley): Before *Jake 2.0*, Chris appeared in *Party of Five* (1997-98) as Elliot, *Popular* (1999-2001), and *Felicity* as Trevor (2001-02). He also co-starred in *Odyssey 5* (2002). After *Jake 2.0*, he co-starred in *Medical Investigations* (2004-05), and had a recurring role in *Out of Practice* (2005-06).

Philip Anthony Rodriguez (Kyle Duarte): A theater veteran, Philip began acting at the age of 10, and has appeared in many Broadway and off–Broadway productions including *The Buddy Holly Story* (in the title role) that won him a Dramalogue award. He's a member of the Salsoul Comedy Troupe, a bilingual improv group in New York. On television he's appeared in *ThirdWatch*, *Star Trek: Enterprise* ("Horizon"), and *JAG*. He also does voice work for various videogames.

Judith Scott (Louise Beckett): An alumnus of Second City Theater, Judith has written and performed in Toronto and Chicago. Her theater credits includes *A Comedy of Errors* and *The Tempest*. On film she's appeared in *Doctor Doolittle*, *The Santa Clause* and *Opportunity Knocks*. On television she appeared in *RoboCop* (1994) ("What Money Can't Buy"), *CSI: Crime Scene Investigation* (2000), and *E.R.* (2006).

Keegan Connor Tracy (Diane Hughes): Born in Ontario, Canada, Keegan holds a B.A. in psychology and runs her own production company, writing film and TV scripts. Best known for her role in the critically acclaimed Showtime series *Beggars and Choosers* (1999), Keegan won many fans as the wacky Audrey Malone, the ditzy daughter of Rob Malone (Brian Kerwin), the head of struggling network LGT. Contrast this with her acclaimed role as an ex-junkie on *DaVinci's Inquest* for which she won the 2002 Leo and a nomination for Canada's Gemini Awards. In features she's co-starred in *Duets* (2000), *40 Days and 40 Nights* (2002), and *Final Destination 2* (2003). On television she's guest starred on *Dark Angel*, *Millennium*, *First Wave*, *Seven Days*, *The 4400*, *Stargate SG-1*, and *Supernatural*.

Marina Black (Sarah Heywood): A Los Angeles actress, Marina appeared in seven of 16 *Jake 2.0* episodes. She is well known to TV audiences as the best friend Parker in *Six Feet Under* (2001-02). She co-starred with Jason Behr (Roswell) in the independent feature *Happily Ever After* (2004). Other film credits include *Swordfish* (2001) and *Ted Bundy* (2002). More recently she appeared in *CSI: Crime Scene Investigation* and *CSI: New York*.

Jeremiah

(2002–2004)

In a 21st century futureworld, 15 years after "the Big Death" where adults perished in a biological virus attack, all those who were under 13 have survived and grown up to reclaim the world. Two wanderers, Jeremiah and Kurdy, meet up and join forces with those ensconced inside "Thunder Mountain" and help rebuild civilization. Meanwhile, Jeremiah is searching for the cryptic "Valhalla Sector" where his father may still be alive.

Stars: Luke Perry (Jeremiah), Malcolm Jamal-Warner (Kurdy), Sean Astin (Mister Smith) *Year 2*, Joanne Kelly (Libby) *Year 2*

Recurring Cast: Peter Stebbings (Markus Alexander), Ingrid Kavelaars (Erin), Byron Lawson (Lee Chen), Enid-Raye Adams (Gina), Robert

Wisden (Devon), John Pyper-Ferguson (Sims), Alex Zahara (Ezekiel); Based on the graphic novels by Hermann Huppen; Created by J. Michael Straczynski; *Executive Producers:* J. Michael Straczynski, Sam Egan *Year 1*, Luke Perry Joe Dante, Michael Finnell, Scott Mitchell Rosenberg, Ervin Rustemagic; *Co-Executive Producer:* Grant Rosenberg *Year 2*; *Producer:* George Horie; *Co-Producers:* Steve Geaghan, Stephanie Germain, Ben Brafman, Gregory Noveck, Sara Barnes *Year 2*; *Associate Producer:* Sara Barnes *Year 1*; *Consulting Producer:* Peter DeLuise *Year 1*; *Writers included:* J. Michael Straczynski, Sam Egan, Sara Barnes; *Directors:* Russell Mulcahy (Pilot), Mario Azzopardi, Sean Astin, Ken Girotti, Michael Robison, Brad Turner, Peter DeLuise, Martin Wood; *Directors of Photography:* Henry Chan, Michael C. Blundell; *Production Designer:* Steve Geaghan; *Visual Effects:* Gajdecki Visual Effects, Rainmaker Digital Pictures; *Music by:* Tim Truman; "Looking at Forever" theme sung by Paul Van *Year 2*; *Guest Stars:* Robert Foxworth, Kimberly Hawthorne, Kandyse McClure, David McCallum

Showtime/MGM-TV/Lion's Gate Television/ Platinum Studios/Jeremiah Productions Ltd., 2002–2003; September 2004 (final eight episodes); 60 minutes; 35 episodes; DVD status: Season 1

The inspiration for this post-disaster series came from a surprising source: a series of European graphic novels by Belgian artist Hermann Huppen, first published in 1977, which gained a worldwide following and was translated into 26 languages.

Scott Mitchell Rosenberg, CEO of Platinum Studios, a company that specializes in comics-to-film properties translations, recognized the books for their potential as a television series.

"*Jeremiah* predated *Mad Max*," says Rosenberg. "I was first introduced to *Jeremiah* a long time ago, and published it when I had Malibu Comics, right at the time when we were publishing *Men in Black*. I thought it had a cool world, and I liked the relationship between Jeremiah and Kurdy. They lived in a futureworld that wasn't futuristic in the usual sci-fi sense.

"Ervin Rustemagic, my friend and producing partner, had been producing the comic and translating it into various languages through his company, SAF, since its inception in the '70s, and he also managed the creator, Hermann Huppen," continues Rosenberg. "The problem I had was that it was a European graphic album in full,

beautiful color, and that kind of format didn't work in the U.S. comic world in the '90s. So I published it as a black-and-white independent to build up a cult audience here.

"I then acquired the media rights and started figuring out with my staff at Platinum how to position it for TV," he recalls. "*Jeremiah* was a particular challenge because Jeremiah and Kurdy are going to new locales on a regular basis, so it's not an inexpensive show to make, but their journey is really a significant portion of the show."

Huppen's scenario focused on racial wars. Those shepherding the property were worried about changing elements in the book. Rosenberg approached J. Michael Straczynski, who had created and produced the much lauded space epic *Babylon 5*, and asked him to consider the project.

Straczynski looked at the premise and developed an approach that he felt would be good for television. Primarily, he changed the theme to rebuilding the world. The series wouldn't explore the very bottom of a crumbled society, but catch it in the upswing of reconstruction. Straczynski cast it somewhat as a "road show" with Jeremiah and Kurdy traveling around the country in a military Jeep. Also, the characters would be much older than seen in the print edition.

Rosenberg went for Straczynski because of his unique ability to shape a universe. "And *Jeremiah* is no less than a whole universe," says Rosenberg. "Fifteen years earlier, a catastrophe killed every adult in the world, and only the children remained. It raises a lot of questions. Which technology gets wiped out, and what little bits remain in different places? What happens when someone with a generator gets an old computer to work for brief periods of time? Are there still communications satellites up there, or have they all fallen out of orbit? Kids may know how to use technology, but they don't know how to build it or repair it. As Joe pointed out, if something broke inside a calculator, nobody in this world would have the ability to fix it."

Once Straczynski tendered his pilot script, which was very well received, the project suddenly got a green light. Shooting commenced in Vancouver, Canada in the fall of 2001. Actors Luke Perry, from *Beverly Hills 90210*, and Malcolm Jamal-Warner, from *The Cosby Show*, were cast in the leads. They liked each other, and had strong on-camera chemistry.

"It's a show about Jeremiah and Kurdy's relationship," says Perry. "As long as you have those two things, everything else is gravy. It's good to

Luke Perry and Enid-Raye Adams (courtesy Enid-Raye Adams).

have a basic bond to the show. That relationship and seeing these two people be together and how they figure this world out. What they learn from each other. What they do to affect each other. What it takes to survive. How they can help other people. The fact that people can still help other people and are trying to do so. Those are interesting dramatic elements we get to explore and we can take it to different directions."

"We have had a really nice on-screen dynamic," agrees co-star Jamal-Warner. "A lot of that has to do with the fact that we got on very well with each other in life; a lot of that did translate to the camera, and I'm definitely most proud of that, given whatever strengths or weaknesses the particular episodes had here or there, the one constant was the dynamic between Jeremiah and Kurdy."

In addition to being the star of the show, Perry was also the executive producer. Looking back at the series' first season, he says, "A lot of it worked, some of it didn't. Joe [Straczynski] has a theory that you push something until it breaks, and that's how you know how far you can go with it. We pushed a lot of types of stories so far in certain directions, and they didn't work. But we know now

that's the limitations of going so far in that way. In the first season of a television show, that's a very important part of the process, determining the parameters. What works and what doesn't. The great thing about being in business with Showtime is they give you time to find the voice of the show. That's often hard to do, when you have a complex premise like we do; it's hard to get involved in the pilot. It takes a few episodes to get it up and going."

Because of Straczynski's participation, it was natural to assume a *Babylon 5* audience would gravitate towards the program, but *Jeremiah* was the opposite of what *B5* had to offer. "People have some expectations of a show like this because it's a science fiction program and written by a person like Joe, who is known primarily for writing science fiction," explains Perry. "And yet, on a weekly basis, we don't have that much science fiction in the premise. We haven't seen any aliens yet. Ours is not that type of science fiction.

"One of my favorite science fiction movies is a Kurt Russell movie, *Soldier* [1998]. Kurt had only, like, 20 lines of dialogue in the picture. There's special effects, but the story is basically simple.

Malcolm Jamal Warner, left, Enid-Raye Adams, Luke Perry and Sean Astin (courtesy Enid-Raye Adams).

People want to see simple stories told well. People watch television because they want to see actors connecting with each other and having real good human lives."

In the series pilot, "The Long Road," Jeremiah and Kurdy are led to "Thunder Mountain," a NORAD military installation whose top man, Markus Alexander, had survived the "Big Death." Jeremiah convinces Markus that he can't stay inside forever, that it is time to start reopening the doors and contributing to reconstructing the world. First-season stories focused primarily on Jeremiah and Kurdy's "recon missions" to make connections and, on the side, finding "Valhalla Sector," a region Jeremiah's father told him about.

When *Jeremiah* began filming its first episode on September 6, 2001, everyone involved understood that the series explored a post-disaster futureworld scenario. However, as Perry explains, five days later in New York City, the real world changed drastically: Terrorists attacked the World Trade Center and the Pentagon.

"I wish the show wasn't as pertinent as it seems to be now," admits Perry. "We had no idea how this material would be reflected upon. There was a lot of trepidation. Everyone was worried about it. We didn't know how to go ahead. Every day I woke up and the first thing I did was watch CNN to see how close this was going to be to what's going on the show. I was less than comfortable with the similarities. The concept of this show was that biological warfare got out of control. It was *supposed* to be fantasy and science fiction. We weren't supposed to be reality television. CNN's giving the market here. It scared the shit out of me.

"You can turn on CNN and see the technology that exists today. We've taken quantum leaps. I don't see it doing mankind a service. It has taken us farther away from being the basic human beings that we are. That's why we have the fascination for shows like *Survivor* when we see all this stuff stripped away; *Fear Factor*, where people just want to see basic things like fear being experienced.

"Exploring the nature of power struggles and that sort of thing. Sometimes we need a little lack of technology. I wanted to explore the premise of how the absence of technology would help create man on a day-to-day level. "

At the end of the first season, Jeremiah did find "Valhalla Sector" and his father, but was caught up in a military power struggle. A corrupt U.S. president used his father's scientific knowledge to recreate the biological virus that had caused "The Big Death" and wanted to use that as a means of regaining power. Once he was vanquished, Jeremiah and Kurdy, along with denizens of Thunder Mountain, continued in their efforts to collect allies and organize society.

Actor Sean Astin arrived in the second season as the mysterious Mister Smith, a man who fervently believes that he receives messages from God. "Sean brings a great energy to the show, just as a person," says Jamal-Warner. "There's almost an infectious enthusiasm that Sean brings to a room, so that energy helped with the show, and definitely gives Kurdy and Mister Smith a nice dynamic, more on the 'get away kid, you bother me' vibe!"

A major new story arc was the emerging threat from Daniel, an unseen overlord of various regions. To protect their allies, Thunder Mountain recruited and assembled an army to defend against Daniel's men.

"There's been a lot of characters pushing a lot of plot," notes Perry. "Character development was the issue on the second year. I hoped to make the show more personal. The producers felt they needed to make some kind of a splash with a lot of explosions."

Personifying the army recruitment, actress Enid-Raye Adams was introduced in the second season's "The Question" as Gina, Jeremiah's aide and liaison at Milhaven, a town where he was appointed administrator. "I was trying to get on this show since it started," recalls Adams. "I'd read for several roles but it wasn't until I went in this time that it went my way. Oddly enough, I wasn't even supposed to read for Gina. I was reading for another role. They asked me if I would audition for her at the last minute. I had nothing prepared, just a couple of minutes to look over the [script] sides. What intrigues me is that Gina isn't actually a military type of person, despite the fact that she

is now in an army. She's someone who has had to do what she's had to do to survive. And now that takes her down a military path, which means we essentially see someone who's rather green being thrust into a combative training environment. We found ourselves out in the woods in full military gear including huge weapons. The first time I held my gun, I was overwhelmed by a somber sense of gravity. Your demeanor instantly changes when you hold a rifle. Although it's a prop, it represents something that can take human life. That wasn't lost on me."

In the final two-part episode, "Interregnum," Thunder Mountain prepared for an onslaught by Daniel's army. But when the attacking forces discovered, to their surprise, that Daniel was not a real person, only a faceless voice that ordered them about, an all-out war was averted.

Somewhat anticlimactically, the series ended at the end of a chapter.

Asked if being in the decadent *Jeremiah* universe changed the way that he looks at the real world, Jamal-Warner replies, "I was not sitting home watching the Vietnam War happening on TV, so there's this generation of us who don't know, really, what it's like for us to be in a serious war, let alone a possible nuclear war. There's a lot my generation inevitably takes for granted. At least for me, being in this show has made me kind of appreciate life a little bit more."

Summing up her view of the series' themes, Adams notes, "Given that our world is one that seems to be in perpetual conflict, it's comforting to know that no matter what atrocity a person faces, there is always hope. This is what resonates with me in the show the most. My feeling is that people are motivated by fear or love. And the wildest possible dream they could have is to be happy. This rings true for me in Kurdy's most disheartening moments and in the most determined moments for Jeremiah. Both of these men face unspeakable loss and devastation, but the simple act of writing a letter to a dead father says, to me, that they have the courage to believe in something better. And that's why I am so proud to be a part of this show."

Although Straczynski had prepared a five-year saga, *Jeremiah* wasn't renewed because Showtime, the series' broadcaster, decided to get out of producing science fiction programming. As it happens all too often in Hollywood, a change in personnel in the upper management changed the network's priorities. They had, in previous years, launched the successful *Stargate SG-1*, *The Outer*

Malcolm Jamal Warner and Enid-Raye Adams (courtesy Enid-Raye Adams).

Limits and the fantasy-suspense *Poltergeist: The Legacy.* Each of those programs were eventually canceled by Showtime but migrated, and had an extended life, at the Sci-Fi Channel.

When the network decided to cancel *Jeremiah*, it was actually before the second season had its debut in November 2003. Showtime aired the first seven episodes from October to November 2003, and aired the remaining eight episodes ten months later, in September 2004, as two-hour specials in a four-week marathon. The last eight episodes had their world premiere on a pay cable network in Canada in December 2003 and January 2004, so "the word was out" over the Internet of the episodes' content and the details about "Interregnum," the series' final two-parter episodes.

Loyal viewers were alarmed when, in November 2003, showtime announced the broadcast of the first seven episodes and called them the show's "second season." There was no reference to the other eight season-two episodes. Concerned fans networked with each other on the Internet and got busy. They wrote, faxed and phoned executives at Showtime, MGM and Platinum Studios in an organized effort to make their voices heard.

Rosenberg says that the show's cancellation wasn't official, so there was still hope. (And because it wasn't official, no one could proceed to "shop around" the show to other networks.) All that could be done was to demonstrate there was an audience who appreciated the series and, via good ratings, that the show deserved a third season. "This is the first time I was on the inside of a write-in campaign. I saw, daily, the impact it was having at the studio," Rosenberg says. "The campaign almost worked." In fact, as the seven episodes aired, each week the ratings went *up* for every single episode (except the last one) with no advertising or promotion from the network. It was the networks' number two series. "The only people promoting the show were Platinum Studios—without reimbursement from the network—and the fans," he says. "We printed out everything we found on the web, put it in binders and delivered it regularly to Showtime and MGM. We were 95 percent of the way there. The fans truly almost saved it. And if the administration hadn't changed at the network, the fan effort would have worked.

"Fortunately, all 35 episodes got aired, and told

a complete story. We call it a 35-hour maxi-series."

In a press release issued by Platinum Studios on November 8, 2003, Sean Astin remarked on the fans' dedication: "I am tickled that the fans took it upon themselves to influence the future of the show. I'm amazed at how quickly they were able to organize and synchronize their efforts. It shows they believe in what we're doing, just like I do."

Joining the *Jeremiah* team after his epic *Lord of the Rings* adventure was a positive experience for Astin. He responded to the show's material, and the character that was written for him, and he had a vested interest in its longevity: He had directed "The Face in the Mirror," the show's 13th episode, which was among the "lost eight episodes."

Joe Straczynski had such a difficult time with the MGM-TV executives that he publicly declared that he wouldn't return for a third season, as long as that administration was in place. Had *Jeremiah* been renewed for a third season, other show runners would have come in to fill the void. Grant Rosenberg, the second season's co-executive producer, was another person eager to see more adventures. Everyone on cast and crew were willing to have continued.

It may have seemed to be a failure, but there was a silver lining in the end, says Scott Rosenberg. "I'll tell you where it *did* work. It's gotten the development on a prequel feature film going!" He insists that *Jeremiah* still has much to offer. Platinum Studios has developed an elaborate multimedia program to further explore the *Jeremiah* universe. An electronic and print comic book based in Straczynski's universe was drawn up, a prequel feature film exploring "The Big Death" was under development, and the company also hoped to create other series or mini-series based on the property.

CAST NOTES

Luke Perry (Jeremiah): Perry starred in the long-running Fox TV series *Beverly Hills 90210* (1990–2000) as Dylan McKay. For 10 episodes he played a new inmate in the gritty prison drama *Oz* (2001). In his feature film debut, *8 Seconds* (1994), a film he co-produced with director John Avild-

sen, Luke portrayed a champion bullrider. Later, he also made appearances in major features such as Luc Besson's *The Fifth Element* (1997), *The Florentine* (1999) and *American Strays (1996)*. After *Jeremiah* he appeared in a mini-series, *Supernova* (2005), and the NBC-TV series *Windfall* (2006).

Says director Holly Dale: "He was really quite brilliant as an actor-slash-executive producer. Luke is a very smart, talented guy and he would bring his own ideas to the show. He also wouldn't get in the way of other people bringing what they could to the show."

Malcolm Jamal-Warner (Kurdy): Starting out as a child actor, Jamal-Warner appeared on *The Cosby Show* for eight years (1984–92) (and was nominated for an Emmy in 1986). The multi-talented artist has branched out into music with a jazz/funk band named Miles Long, performing poetry readings and directing comedy, documentary and music videos. He's done voice work for the children's show *The Magic Bus* and landed his own sitcom, UPN's *Malcolm and Eddie* (1996), which ran for four years. His stage work includes *A Midsummer's Night Dream* at the La Jolla Playhouse.

Sean Astin (Mister Smith): Sean made his acting debut opposite his mother Patty Duke on the *ABC Afterschool Special* "Please Don't Hit Me Mom" (1981). He was one of *The Goonies* (1985) and played the title character in *Rudy* (1993), but it was his Sam Gamgee role in *The Lord of the Rings* trilogy (2001, 2002, 2003) that catapulted Sean to even greater heights. In addition to acting, Sean has developed his skills in screenwriting and directing. He received an Oscar nomination for directing the short film *Kangaroo Court* and directed episodes of *Perversions of Science, Angel* and *Jeremiah*. His short film *The Long and Short of It*, which he wrote and directed, was filmed in New Zealand during the production of *The Lord of the Rings*, and is included on the *Lord of the Rings — The Two Towers* DVD.

Joanne Kelly (Libby): This Newfoundland actress has appeared in *Love and Sorrows* (2002), *The Bay of Love* and *Going the Distance* (2004). She's guest starred in *Mutant X* and *Tracker*, both in 2002. She's had recent roles in *Slings and Arrows* (2005), *Vanished* (2006) and the Sci-Fi Channel series *The Dresden Files* (2007).

Lexx: The Dark Zone
(1997–2002)

A giant, dragonfly-shaped spaceship carries an odd group of space explorers through a wacky and bizarre universe.

Cast: Brian Downey (Stanley Tweedle), Eva Habermann (Zev) *Year 1*, Michael MacManus (Kai), Xenia Seeberg (Xev) *Year 2–4*, Jeffrey Hirschfield (voice of Robot 7–90), Tom Gallant (voice of Lexx), Nigel Bennett (The Prince) *Year 3–4*
Created by: Paul Donovan; **Executive Producers:** Paul Donovan, Wolfram Tichy; **Producers:** Norman Denver, Stephen J. Turnbull, Wolfram Tichy; **Line Producers:** Andrea Raffaghella, Stephen Turnbull; **Co-Producers:** Bill Fleming, David Marlow; **Consulting Producer:** Willie Stevenson; **Writers included:** Lex Gigeroff, Paul Donovan, Jeffrey Hirschfield; **Directors included:** Paul Donovan, Srinivas Krishna, Chris Bould, David McLeod, Christopher Schrewe, Bill Fleming, Colin Bucksey; **Guest Stars included:** Stephen McHattie, Rutger Hauer, Malcolm McDowell, Tim Curry, Barry Bostwick, Britt Ekland, Louis De Grande, Tony Anholt, Michael J. Reynolds, Kate Rose, Janet Wright, Louise Wischermann, Anna Kathrin Bleuler, Patricia Zanetelli, Lionel Jeffries and Ellen Dubin (as Giggerota); **Directors of Photography included:** Les Krizsan; **Special Visual Effects:** Bob Munroe (C.O.R.E. Digital Pictures), Darryl Purdy, Steve Cooke; **Visual Effects Supervisor:** Tony Kenny; **Lexx ships Designer:** David Albiston
Sci-Fi Channel/Salter Street Films and TiMe Film and TV Produktion; Years: 1997–2002; Four TV movies and 57 hour-long episodes; DVD status: Complete series

Warning: If you've just eaten, keep your eyeballs and stomach away from *Lexx*. Where else but in this quirky Paul Donovan show does food squirt out of intestinal orifices and hot, frothy showers erupt from caterpillar-like nipples? That's life inside the Lexx, a giant, bio-chemically engineered creature the size of Manhattan, shaped like a dragonfly. It was organically grown to serve as a destructive weapon, destroying and feeding on entire planets.

Its pulsating innards are an entomologist's gastrointestinal dream: slippery stomach slopes of slime, pulsating membranes coated with sludge and messy plants that eat human flesh. This Canadian-German production may be the most unappetizing TV show ever made — not that there's anything wrong with that.

Boiled and mashed sweet potatoes (dyed orange) were used when Lexx's innards spray characters with goo. "Listen, stay away from sweet potatoes," warns *Lexx* star Brian Downey. "They taste as bad as they look." Rice pudding poured from intestines. Yummy!

Lexx began filming in the fall of 1995, in the Canadian province of Nova Scotia. The studio was a former warehouse for the Volvo automotive company. Creating a science fiction series in a bitterly cold Canadian warehouse was a nightmare. Nearly 60 percent of the series' background and special effects were computer generated images (CGI).

"This show is so ambitious we shouldn't be able to do it," co-producer Bill Fleming said during production. Additional scenes were filmed in Babelsberg, Germany — the city that spawned the silent film classics *Nosferatu* and *Metropolis*.

The creator, Paul Donovan, hated heroic, flawless SF heroes who saved the universe every week. Here, he created characters laden with insecurities, people whose primary drives in life were to nourish their own selfish sexual drives at whatever cost. "Paul is brilliant — as well as being a very thoughtful, honest producer in a world that breeds dishonest producers," noted Downey.

The *Lexx* characters live on The Cluster, a capital league of 20,000 planets. It's a dictatorship where human citizens utter a compliant, "I worship the shadow." The leaders are vindictive little brains in glass jars who decide to execute all humans on the planet. Prisoners are crushed under concrete slabs, and their brains and guts slurp out into the planet's protein bank. A security guard, Stanley Tweedle, manages to escape this horror with his beautiful sidekick, Zev, by blasting off in the *Lexx* spaceship.

Donovan loved the cowardly Dr. Smith character from the 1960s TV series *Lost in Space*, and made Stanley a combination of Dr. Smith and Charlie Chaplin. The spineless, middle-aged security guard finds personal power for the first time in his life as unofficial captain of the *Lexx*. But he's shackled by nerdhood. Women will have nothing to do with him and aliens exploit his neurosis.

Zev grew up sequestered in a sheltered environment as a child and developed into a bloated, middle-aged woman who was humiliated by her husband. She was sent off to become an obedient wife-slave but instead, her DNA was fused with a cluster lizard and she transformed into a youthful, sexually aggressive woman on the prowl. She kindly rebuffs Stanley's amorous advances as she is in search of a real man.

The third major character is the former assassin, Kai. He died 2,000 years ago but was reanimated by the ruthless Divine Shadow forces. He breaks away from them and suppresses his instinct for killing. During the *Lexx*'s voyages, he's kept frozen in cryostatis. Zev and Stanley thaw him out periodically when they get themselves into a mess. Kai slowly learns compassion and becomes friends with these two outcasts. When Zev nearly gets Kai killed during her pursuit of men, she apologizes to him. He says, forgivingly, "You were only looking after your needs."

Shortly after takeoff, the *Lexx* is sucked into a wormhole, which propels them into the Dark Zone, a universe of evil and chaos. From then on, this trio of misfits (along with their mechanical aide, a wisecracking robot head called 7-90) search for a new home, as well as proto blood that will allow Kai to live a normal life.

Lexx began life as four TV movies and recruited some impressive guest stars— Tim Curry, Barry Bostwick and *A Clockwork Orange*'s Malcolm McDowell, who, upon reading the script, exclaimed, "What the hell is this?"

Paul Donovan, an ex-physicist with a superb science background, admitted that *Alien*, *Get Smart*, *The Beverly Hillbillies*, Monty Python and the 1960s *Star Trek* (the only version of *Trek* that he liked) were rich veins of inspiration for *Lexx*. He was also a fan of *Dark Star* (1974), a low-budget, dark-humored SF film. He first created *Lexx* as a short film made up of computer effects in 1993. That intrigued investors and led to the $13 million that begat the four TV movies.

The *Lexx* ship has only a limited, rudimentary intelligence and speaks in the same dulcet tones as Hal 9000, the computer in *2001: A Space Odyssey*. Donovan patterned the skimpy Go-Go costumes from the fashions of classic *Star Trek*. Some of the sets were inspired by the gothic look of *Metropolis* (1927).

The characters in *Lexx* are unique. Robot 7-90 provides scientific analysis but prefers to spew venom towards Stanley, calling him "a pimple on the abyss of life" and "a decaying sack of carbon." Another time he recites a poem that mocks Stanley's life and punctuates it with a fart. The robot head is obsessed with sex, getting his mechanical jollies watching a porno film. He desires Zev's body but his memory banks are bitterly aware that since he's all robot head, his sexual options are extremely limited.

On the other hand, Stanley respects Kai, loves Zev and even tries to reason with 7-90 but can never get past the robot's sarcasm. And Zev, in her quest for a virile man, is often lured into alien sadomasochistic adventures, such as a steel blade swinging toward her crotch and hungry vines snuggling her body.

In one show, Stanley is lured into a spaceship by a beautiful woman, only to find she's a big slovenly man in disguise; the man forces Stanley to strip naked and squeal like a pig, *à la Deliverance*. Robot 7-90, listening to Stanley's fearful oinks, snickers, "So there is justice in the world!"

Stanley gets respect from no one. "What kind of loser flies around in a bug?" asks a lowly space technician. Yet Stanley is a hormone-driven pig. He coldly turns down a nice brunette woman because she's flat-chested and he goes lusting after a mega-mammaried bimbo.

Brian Downey remains fiercely protective of his character. "All Stanley wants is to avoid trouble," he says. "To be respected, be desired by the opposite sex, sleep in comfort and experience no pain. But he is brave when necessary and will never desert his friends."

Despite the first four TV films, Donovan wasn't sure whether the eccentric project would take off. One person who expressed absolute confidence was Downey. "I never had any doubt it would run its complete course," he says today. He relishes the memory of Donovan coming up to him as year two began and thanking him for his belief in the project. "That was the greatest compliment ever," says Downey. "I never regretted doing *Lexx*. Man, what a ride we had!"

One of the strangest characters encountered on their journeys is Giggerota, a man-eating (literally) woman, dressed up in the hides of men she has devoured. The lovely Ellen Dubin was cast as this loony creature. "When I first heard of the *Lexx* concept, I laughed my head off," she says. "I thought, 'This is the most unusual, strangest show that I've ever heard of!'" She was one of several actors and actresses brought in to read for the role. "Each of us had to read a one-page monologue that would eventually be read by the male lead, Stanley Tweedle. The monologue was about going to a planet and looking at these beautiful babes. They told us to do something unusual. I thought, 'Okay, it's a man's part but since I'm a girl, I'll be very sensual and fantasize about women. I remember thinking, 'This material is so weird and quirky.' So I laid down on the floor in the audition room and threw off my shoes very sensually and I saw the casting director's face wake up. Believe me, no one had thought of doing that! And I went for it, and got the part because they said I took a risk. So, the start of Lexx for me was wacky."

Dubin went on to create other characters for the series. "After Giggerota, I came back and played the Queen and the Pope." That episode, year four's "ApocaLexx Now," was set in modern-day Vietnam and showed how SF could sidestep some potent controversy. "I was the first female Pope in sci-fi history," she says of her role of a Miami real estate agent chosen to be the pope. "We knew audiences weren't ready for a spoof of religion, but in the episode, there is actually no reference to religion. Instead, golf was the new Catholicism! I worshipped the golf ball and the golf club. It was wacky, but that's how we got out of any trouble. I'm a very open-minded person and it's wonderful that women have been ordained in real life but we're a long way off from a female Pope. There's still a very big backlash against women and their place in the church."

In "Lafftrack," the Lexx orbits a planet called TV World, where Zev and Stanley participate in cut-rate TV shows with tacky sets. Stanley stars in a version of Three's Company while Zev hosts a reality show, teaching high school boys about sex. But the stomach-churning realm of wacky TV hosts, canned music and flashing lights masks a sinister world where Zev is slated for on-air decapitation until Stanley thrusts an electric rod through a Nazi-like officer's chest. The dying officer gasps, "Now that's entertainment."

The episode "White Trash" featured stereotypes who represented the lowest in morals and intelligence. A family of hillbillies board the Lexx: an overweight, mean-spirited father, a giggling teen son and a cute but vapid daughter. The father is immediately smitten with Zev, prompting incestuous jealousy from his daughter. "Pa, why do you always go for the gals with blubber on their

Ellen Dubin as Giggerota, the only character that recurred from the very first movie of the week to the end of the fourth season. "She'll eat everything in sight! Men, women, children, that's what makes her happy," laughs Dubin. "She didn't discriminate! She had a huge appetite and a zest for life" (courtesy Ellen Dubin).

bums?" To get even, the daughter turns her attentions to Stanley. When Pa learns that Stan slept with his daughter, he yells, "You diddled my little girl!" and in the ensuing chaos, the father chases Stanley with a giant bone. When the daughter reveals that her mother never loved him, her father pushes his own daughter down a shaft. He's later enticed by a woman who pops out of a giant plant and she devours him.

Other episodes have the same nasty, surrealistic images. In one show, a farmer tends to the thousands of living human heads that poke up above the soil. In "Love Grows," two cowboys slosh their way out of *Lexx*'s slippery stomach membranes and engage in sexual fantasies until they find a man-made virus has turned their private parts into female genitalia. Zev finds herself changing into a man, much to Robot 7-90's horror, until the *Lexx* spray-dusts her with an antidote. "It's violent and gory," Claire Bickley of *The Toronto Sun* opined of the series. "There are so many gross scenes of human vivisection, decapitation and severed limbs, that you begin to wonder if this entertainment is for people who pull wings off bugs."

But Paul Donovan had no worries. He said during production, "When we show *Lexx* to people, my favorite reaction is, 'This is horrible, why am I laughing?'" He described the series as *Dark Star* meets *Alien* meets *Beavis and Butthead*. He fully expected the audience to be adolescent males and was surprised when research showed the series had a strong female audience.

"*Lexx* may not be everybody's cup of tea," admitted Dubin. "Humor is a very funny thing. If you showed [a Laurel and Hardy comedy], some people may laugh and other people won't get it. Paul Donovan is an extremely brilliant, witty man. On the surface, it's like, 'Oh, these are crazy, wacky people!' but there are incredible innuendoes and double entendres, and intelligent references to old TV shows. It's very multi-layered. People may not get it at first, but once they see it, it's unforgettable."

Dubin's most memorable production story related to her role as Giggerota. "*Lexx* was one of the most physically demanding shows for me," she says. "The costume I wore in season one was made of rubber latex, and it was extremely heavy and smelly. When I was at lunch, no one would eat with me. At the back of Giggerota's costume was the head of the dead man she had skinned and eaten. The costume was based on an autopsy report. A wardrobe person told me she went and

looked at cadavers. And the stitch marks on the costume were gruesome, they were based on stitch marks that they put into people's dead bodies.

"After Giggerota died, I played four other characters on the series and one was the queen in 'Girltown.' I was a bobbing head in a bathtub, which we shot in a hot tub in an old war bunker in Germany. The challenge was wearing this huge black, tight wig and wearing a scuba outfit with weights to keep me in the water. I was just a head talking and it was very hot and sweaty inside the tub but extremely cold outside. I was uncomfortable but I used that to aid in my performance. I was getting tired and loopy from the hot water, so I ad-libbed some singing and made her wacky and off-center."

The aesthetics of the show could be questionable but no one could argue with its success. Its Sci-Fi Channel ratings were strong and the series was sold to 100 countries around the world. Alas, Donovan was unable to get two of his favorite actors to appear in the series, Lee Majors and Christopher Walken.

"It's dark, dangerous, funny and quite possibly the most magnificently sick TV sci-fi series ever," raved *TV Zone* magazine. "It's morally ambiguous storytelling, carried off with verve and style ... the special effects are superb." *The New York Daily News* called it "the most imaginative sci-fi since *The Hitchhiker's Guide to the Galaxy*."

Actress Eva Habermann was perfectly cast as Zev, her delicate features giving her a wide-eyed look of wonder and innocence and she made some of the ghastlier storylines palatable. But she had work commitments in Germany after the first four TV movies and had to leave *Lexx*. She returned for two guest shots in year two, to play her death scene.

In Habermann's last episode, "The Terminal," Zev turns into a pool of golden glop, gasping, "I had a good life for a girl who grew up in a box," as she dissolves. The show ends with Robot 7-90 weeping over her liquefied remains. But the glop is genetically engineered to create Xev, a different, harsher looking woman who has part of Zev's DNA. Xenia Seeberg was cast in this role after the producers auditioned over 400 gorgeous women.

Despite gooey gothic alien worlds and deviant guest characters, Donovan felt the cast was the key to the show's success. Certainly their characters were different for TV, people who made decisions not based on the greater good or even a moral compass but simply sniffed out adventures based on their own dysfunctional libidos and pervasive greed.

And as the series progressed, there was "Nook," where a planet of sexless monks who have never seen women get some lessons, and "Twilight," a *Night of the Living Dead* homage, where corpses rise to devour the living.

"If anything, *Lexx* was a bit overambitious, layered with literate allusions, great ironies, and raised the bar for CGI on television," observes Downey. "Show me another sci-fi show that has 20–30 CGI shots per episode and I will kiss their ass!" The actor also disliked SF series that were structured in a "neo–Fascist" way, where good guys won by brute force. "That is boring television," he says.

There is nothing boring about *Lexx*'s fans. "I was at a grocery store in Los Angeles, buying cantaloupes, and this woman went, 'Giggerota eats cantaloupes?!'" recalls Ellen Dubin. "I turned to her and started laughing. I said, 'Actually, Ellen eats cantaloupes, Giggerota eats people!' This woman had recognized my eyes. She said I looked skinnier in person. That's because of that fat, rubber latex suit I wore."

Downey recalls being terrified by a woman near the Thames in London. Upon seeing him, the woman began to tremble and pointed her finger at him. "It's you ... you're the one!" she screamed at him. "She was getting hysterical," recalls Downey. "I thought she was mistaking me for her abusive husband. I told her, 'No, whoever it is, it's not me!' Finally, after nearly exhausting herself, she finally gasped, 'You're ... you're Stanley Tweedle!' Jesus Christ! Talk about bizarre!" Downey gave her an autograph and sent her on her way.

The series' third year became more serialized, as the *Lexx* circled two dangerous planets, Fire and Water, for the entire season. British actor Nigel Bennett had a recurring role as a nasty prince on Fire, a planet where bad people end up. It's no surprise that when Stanley lands there, the prince thinks he is exactly where he belongs. The prince wants to use the *Lexx* to attack the good Water planet.

"They have no end of water—and we die of thirst," the prince rasps after torturing Stanley. "Is that fair?" And the water planet, superbly illustrated with CGI vistas of endless blue seas, is where Kai ends up. In the season finale, Kai enters the core of the Fire planet to save Stanley while computer 7-90 convinces Xev that the two planets must be destroyed.

In the fourth year, after both planets are blown

to bits, the satanic prince moves to Earth, to punish its evil inhabitants. When Stanley, Kai and Xev land on Earth, they experience all kinds of kooky adventure, from a Dracula-type count in Transylvania, hostile townsfolk in Newfoundland, UFO-obsessive people, FBI agents, a porn star, American freedom rangers, Las Vegas mobsters and female wrestlers.

Donovan decided to end the series after four years and the finale episode carried on in the bleak *Lexx* tradition. The Earth was blown up, Kai died for real and the *Lexx* succumbed to old age, forcing Stanley and Xev to jump aboard a baby *Lexx* spaceship and continue their space voyages. "The series made a big impact at the time but it is half-forgotten today," *TV Zone* grimly noted in 2007. But neither *Lexx*'s characters nor producers could complain. The life cycle of an insect is a brief one indeed and the *Lexx* had a very long life.

CAST NOTES

Brian Downey (Stanley Tweedle): Paul Donovan knew of Downey from a 1985 Canadian film, *The Adventure of Faustus Bidgood*. He cast him in the 1986 film *Norman's Awesome Experience* and then hired him for *Lexx*. A man of many talents, Downey loves to play the blues and is a guitarist, bassist and harmonica player. He appeared in the docu-drama TV film, *Shattered City: The Halifax Explosion* (2003).

Eva Habermann (Zev): Born in Hamburg, Germany, she was just a teenager when she began filming the *Lexx* TV films. On a 2003 list of Germany's 100 sexiest women, she was #17. She has had a busy career in TV and film, including the film *Der Clown* (2005) and the mini-series *Papa und Mama* (2006).

Michael MacManus (Kai): This Toronto native, who is a nephew of actress Helen Shaver, won a Genie Award for his role in the film *Speaking Parts* (1989). Paul Donovan credited MacManus with attracting a large female audience to *Lexx*. "A lot of women love him to death," Donovan told the *LA Times*. "Michael can go to any hotel in most of the world and people will be camped outside his door. It's intense."

Xenia Seeberg (Xev): She was filming a project in the Canary Islands when she got word that *Lexx* needed a replacement for Eva Habermann. She sent in a demo tape and Paul Donovan loved her dark humor and hired her. The German-born actress-classically trained dancer studied at Lee Strasberg's acting school in New York.

Ellen Dubin (Giggerota the Wicked, Queen and Pope): Dubin's Giggerota was the only *Lexx* character that recurred from the first movie of the week to the very end of the fourth season. "She'll eat everything in sight! Men, women, children, that's what makes her happy," laughs Dubin. "She didn't discriminate! She had a huge appetite and a zest for life." The actress was a series regular on *The Collector* (she was nominated for a Gemini award) and has guest starred on *The Dead Zone*, *Blood Ties* and *Mutant X*. The legacy of *Lexx* endures for her. "I get a lot of fan mail from women — they love the strong aggressive character!" she says. "Giggerota was a no-holds-barred character. Usually, even when women are strong in science fiction, very rarely are they that overt. But I'm very grateful to Paul Donovan, he gave me free rein to do anything. I called myself the sexual comic relief of *Lexx*. What a great ride! We continue to gain new fans worldwide."

SOURCES

Bickley, Claire. *Lexx* Review. "In Gory Lexx, Special Effects Rule — Lots of Brains, but No Thought." *Toronto Sun*, April 17, 1997.
Bloch-Hansen, Peter. Interviews with Cast of Lexx: "Alien Desires." *Starlog's Sci-Fi TV*, no. 7, October 1999.
Kenter, Peter. *TV North: Everything You Wanted to Know about Canadian Television.* Vancouver/ Toronto: Whitecap, 2001.
King, Susan. "Star Gazing." *Los Angeles Times*, July 29, 2001.
Nazzaro, Joe. "Lexx is More." *TV Zone* no. 142, September 2001.
Spelling, Ian. "The Stanley Tweedle Show." *Starlog* no. 286, May 2001.
Wright, Jonathan. *TV Zone* no. 112, March 1999.

Mann & Machine

(1992)

The personal life and cases of Police Detective Bobby Mann, who is partnered with a beautiful female android partner as they solve crimes in the near-future Los Angeles.

Cast: David Andrews (Sgt. Bobby Mann), Yancy Butler (Eve Edison), S. Epatha Merkerson (Capt. Margaret Claghorn)
Created by: Robert DeLaurentis, Dick Wolf; **Executive Producers:** Dick Wolf, Robert DeLaurentis; **Supervising Producer:** Michael Wagner; **Producers:** Brooke Kennedy, Kevin Donnelly, Glenn Davis, William Laurin; **Associate Producer:** Monica Wyatt; **Writers included:** Neil Cohen, Nancy Bond, William Laurin, Glenn Davis, Morgan Gendel, Nancy Ann Miller; **Directors included:** Vern Gillum, Bill Corcoran, Allan Arkush, Jim Contner, James Quinn; **Director of Photography:** Roy H. Wagner; **Production Designer:** Hilda Stark; **Costumes:** Catherine Adair; **Music Theme:** Mark Mothersbaugh; **Guest Stars included:** Christina Belford, Richard Burgi, Mitchell Ryan, Melora Hardin, Beth Toussaint, William Sanderson, Lisa Jane Persky, Samantha Eggar (Dr. Anna Kepler)
NBC/Universal Studios/Wolf Films; April–July 1992; 60 minutes; 9 episodes

Future Cop tried it for dramatic effect. *Holmes & Yoyo* tried it for comedic effect. This series tried it for eye-candy effect. It's a science fiction variation of the standard buddy cop theme: two homicide detectives working out of a police station precinct, solving crimes of the day. The twist? The lead detective is paired up with an unusual partner: an android. In the first two series, the leads were male. In *Mann & Machine*, the female partner was the very attractive, lithe Yancy Butler as Sgt. Eve Edison.

In the fall of 1991, NBC was looking for an action series featuring a sexy female lead. The discussions between NBC's then-president Warren Littlefield and veteran TV series producers Robert DeLaurentis and Dick Wolf ultimately led to the birth of *Mann & Machine*.

Wolf, a successful and respected producer-writer, had executive-produced the hit 1980s crime drama *Miami Vice* and had already created the original *Law & Order* series in 1990. So when NBC ruminated about an action series with a female lead, Wolf already was percolating series ideas with his friend DeLaurentis. They had first met when Wolf was looking for someone to replace him on *Miami Vice*, and while it didn't work out, the two separated with hopes that one day they would collaborate on a project. It was just a few years later at Universal Studios when both sat down and fantasized about what shows to invent.

"We were both big action fans, and while neither of us had ever done anything in the sci-fi realm before, it was something we were definitely attracted to," recalls DeLaurentis. "Universal had offered Dick the opportunity to turn the feature film *Darkman* into a series, and wanted to know if I'd be interested. I was and we began talking..."

The seeds for *Mann* were planted when James Cameron unveiled his ground-breaking blockbuster film *Terminator 2: Judgment Day* in the summer of 1991. "I told Dick about a rough notion I had for the pairing of a cyborg and a human, but something that would take advantage of the character delineation available in a long-form TV series," says DeLaurentis, who also supplied the story for the second "Bionic" reunion movie, *The Bionic Showdown: The Return of the Six Million Dollar Man and the Bionic Woman* in 1989, reuniting Lee Majors and Lindsay Wagner in their original roles. Another influence was a 1989 episode of the *Alfred Hitchcock Presents* remake series. DeLaurentis had written a script titled "Romance Machine," which was about a brilliant scientist who was not good with women, so he created a female android to do the romancing for him. "The notion of artificial intelligence was on my mind, particularly in terms of a female character."

Yet another inspiration was *Society of Mind* (1988), a book on artificial intelligence by Marvin Minsky, one of the world's leading experts on robotics and A.I. Minsky is also the co-founder of the A.I. laboratory at the Massachusetts Institute of Technology.

"The idea was very simple," DeLaurentis continues. "Take a female cyborg, someone who was created as 'artificial intelligence,' but also had some component of humanity, and pair her with a guy's guy, a regular cop. During the course of the partnership, she would learn what it meant to be a human, and subsequently a woman, from this not particularly sophisticated man.

"The TV version would be something akin to *Moonlighting* meets *T2*. We both immediately saw the possibilities, and became very excited. But as *Darkman* took precedence, we put it on the side burner."

Months later, when the *Darkman* development didn't pan out, Wolf and DeLaurentis found themselves at a boardroom at Wolf Productions, Dick's production company, with Littlefield and other creative executives from the network. "Warren pulled a folded page from a magazine out of his pocket, and it was an ad of a hot woman on a motorcycle, a poster for sex and danger and adventure. That's what he was looking for. A series that could capture some of those elements. It was at that moment that Dick and I exchanged a look, recalling our conversation about a sexy young female cyborg cop, and told him we might have something for him."

A few weeks later, in November 1991, after "fleshing out" the series concept, Wolf and DeLaurentis went into Universal and pitched the concept. "We naturally assumed it would be something for the following season, but NBC was wildly enthusiastic. Not only did they buy it in the room, but they asked us if we could have it on the air by mid-season."

The industry term "buy in the room" means that their verbal pitch was successful. This meant that the show development activity would go on overdrive for a potential broadcast in the spring of 1992. The first order of business was to write the pilot script, which took several weeks. "We handed it in before Christmas, and we got an immediate order for 13 episodes," sighs DeLaurentis. "Needless to say, we worked furiously to get it on the air in time. The thing I most remember was that it was the only time in my career that I worked on Christmas Day. That's how much of a time crunch we were under. Not only did we have to build futuristic sets and conceptualize futuristic wardrobe, but each story also had to have a 'futuristic' twist."

In the series' pilot, "Prototype," Detective Bobby Mann is incensed that his male android partner jeopardized his life in a confrontation with a villain. Captain Margaret Claghorn assigns him a new partner, Sgt. Eve Edison, who announces that she's an information retrieval expert. Just as they meet, they are assigned by Internal Affairs to investigate the possibility of dirty cops involved with a string of murders. When mysterious men attempt an assassination at Mann's house, Eve jumps through a window and manages to bring down one of the killers. Mann is startled to discover that his new, beautiful partner is an android.

Eve finds evidence that the killers are linked to Cody Shannon, one of the most honest cops on the force, but Mann is reluctant to accept the notion. Further evidence reveals that all the victims are connected to the same steel manufacturing company. After breaking into a safe belonging to the company CFO, Mann is shocked to see a cashier's check written out to Shannon. Later, when Shannon himself is shot, the evidence mounts and Eve discovers that the deceased victims were dealing with steel parts that could be assembled into a linear accelerator cannon, capable of launching warheads. A clue left at a victim's residence sends the team to a freighter where they locate the accelerator tubes and the dirty cops, who are apprehended. Mann comes to respect Eve for her abilities and becomes her mentor in all things human.

"The concept of a stylish crime drama was exciting and always a visual feast," says associate producer Monica Wyatt. "The feel was cool blues, high contrast and sleek. What was most charming about Eve's character was her childlike innocence and nerves of steel and fearlessness. The trick in dramas is to always create conflict or chemistry, which I think our characters had. We tried to show the evolution and growth of Eve, which was rather difficult since an android isn't capable of true human behavior. It was interesting exploring what we thought the android behavior might be; however, at times, you wished that she had a greater facility to feel. Eve was basically like a child in contrast to Mann's surly, edgy, been-there-done-that kind of character."

It was not easy finding actors to play Bobby and Eve. "Every once in a while, you find yourself in a TV cycle where there aren't a lot of good leading men available," says DeLaurentis. "Mostly due to the fact that in those critical late 20-early 30s years, they're trying to keep themselves available for movie careers. But we finally found David Andrews, and he was a really interesting actor willing to take chances." Ironically, Andrews had done a SF film a few years earlier also dealing with a robotic female, called *Cherry 2000*.

For Eve, DeLaurentis recalls an even more difficult process. "Dick and I had seen all the available actresses in L.A. and not found the right fit. We went to New York for several casting sessions, during which we opened the process up to actresses with little or no experience. I remember seeing a young woman who was very impressive. Her name was Julianna Margulies."

Margulies, then beginning her acting career,

was seriously considered but life took a different turn and she landed on Michael Crichton's long-running medical drama *E.R.* "And then we met Yancy Butler, straight out of Sarah Lawrence College, and we immediately knew we had our Eve," says DeLaurentis. "She instinctively understood the critical balance of playing a woman with an advanced 'artificial' intelligence, but with the humanity of a young, even childlike, woman. The main direction we gave her was to keep alive the spark of humanity, the childlike wonder of suddenly being thrust into a human world, a kind of strange innocence. And I must say she did it perfectly. She was truly amazing.

"Off-camera, Yancy certainly seemed mature for her age, not at all like a young woman who'd recently graduated from college," DeLaurentis says of the then-22-year-old actress. "She seemed like she was more in her mid-to-late twenties. Very self-possessed, very sure of herself. She was also sweet and funny and normal in every other respect. The most difficult thing by far was the shock to the system of the working hours. To have your first TV series be an action show is very difficult on anyone. We had to be careful not to burn her out."

Cast in the role of Captain Margaret Claghorn, Eve and Bobby's boss, was veteran actress S. Epatha Merkerson. Interestingly, Merkerson was in *Terminator 2* as Tarissa Dyson, the wife of the man who invented the technology making the apocalyptic future seen in the movie series a reality.

Every episode of *Mann & Machine* opened up with a teaser that revealed to the viewer Eve's POV video, examining the crime scene, taking photos of various objects and key "scene evidence" that would become crucial in the ensuing investigation. It was an introduction to Eve's perception and it was a quick introduction to that episode's crime file. The plots were almost standard crime drama fare, but spiced with a "futuristic component." The team had to deal with a serial killer using a dating agency for victims; black market dealers engaging in organlegging; and genetically unique babies. Other stories dealt with a mad bomber who blows up Bobby's house and a woman who is testifying against her husband's mobster employers.

Once the android was introduced, the producers were careful not to load the series with a raft of additional SF elements. The focus was on the crime drama, Eve's emotional growth, her developing relationship with her partner and the world around her.

Eve was a very physical person, capable of gymnastics and leaping from great heights and was a "dead shot" of a gun shooter. Possessed with a "neural net," she was designed to learn by experience. She had a supply of six artificial "eyes" used for specialized purposes. In one episode Eve detached her eye and stuck it on a wall, as a surveillance device on a suspect. In another episode, her laser eye opened up a wall safe. She also interfaced, literally, with the police's mainframe computer to engage in database searches and information retrieval.

With an emotional age of a seven-year-old, Eve viewed the world with a clean slate. Despite her fantastic physical and technical capabilities, she was quite naive. To accentuate this, Yancy Butler played her, very literally, as a wide-eyed young girl. Eve didn't blink and sometimes she had that "deer in the headlights" facial expression as a demonstration of this naiveté.

But this begs the question, how risky is it sending an android with such a young emotional age into the dangerous field of police work where lives are often at stake? Was Eve released from the factory too soon? Couldn't she have been released with a more mature emotional outlook? "The philosophical idea behind the concept was the notion that for police work you needed a high degree of sophisticated analytical intelligence, combined with great physical gifts, i.e., speed, strength, etc.," explains DeLaurentis. "And that you don't necessarily need a high emotional IQ to track down and apprehend bad guys. Now, that may be a specious notion, but it was the logic we were working off at the time." DeLaurentis goes on to say that actual field experience was needed to build that emotional experience and he was backed by Minsky's writings.

She would also be puzzled by idiomatic English slang (that was one database missing from her programming). But humor was very much a part of the character and Butler did a wonderful job of balancing the character with her personality, but also adding a stiffness to the performance, to denote the robotic component. Andrews' personality was the perfect foil for her. This is one of those rare moments when two distinct actors come together and create that elusive and sought-after "on-screen chemistry."

As examples of Eve's emotional journey, she experienced her "first friend" (in "Torch Song") and her "first lie" (in "Billion Dollar Baby"). In an effort to help a stressed-out and sleep-deprived Bobby Mann, she offered him an opportunity to

have sex (in "Mann's Fate") for "therapeutic" purposes.

DeLaurentis says that the filming of the series flashed by in a blur. "David and Yancy were very dedicated to their roles," he says. "I remember having endless conversations about the nature of intelligence and emotion, how they might interact if the relationship were real. They were both very smart, very responsive, and for the most part, they enjoyed themselves."

Regarding the series' action sequences, "There was a scene in the pilot where Eve casually jumps through a plate glass window," DeLaurentis says. (That moment was repeated every week on the show's kinetic and graphics-heavy main titles.) "There was also a great sequence filmed at the Griffith Observatory, where the team has tracked down some villains who've stolen an infant. At one point the baby is literally tossed over the side of a cliff, and Bobby has to leap to make the catch," says DeLaurentis.

The biggest leap, however, was for the episode "Mann's Fate." An over-the-top mad bomber, Lomax (chillingly performed by character actor Tom Towles), takes revenge on Mann for having him incarcerated in a sanitarium. In the story's climax, Lomax engineers his final confrontation with his nemesis on the top of an office tower that is set to explode. To save Mann, who is poison dart-drugged, Eve jumps from a helicopter and parachutes down to the rooftop. DeLaurentis recounted the day of that shoot: "I remember standing on the street below watching the stuntwoman do the scene, and her missing the roof on the first attempt and landing on the street below, which was fortunately blocked off from traffic. On her second attempt she succeeded, and the sequence had the look and size of a feature film."

Stylistically, the show wasn't set so far in the future that the company could not use existing Los Angeles locations or buildings. The show's look and feel were enhanced by interior "futuristic" set decorations and fashions by designer Catherine Adair. "Catherine was *brilliant* and she could do no wrong!" exclaims Wyatt. "She knew how to push the envelope with creative ingenuity. [It] makes me wish that we could wear such extraordinary fashions today. Yancy Butler also looked gorgeous in everything, which didn't hurt!" In "Torch Song," Eve has a new experience, trying out a series of wildly different and exotic dresses to wear at an upcoming concert. In a montage sequence, we see in quick succession a

David Andrews and Yancy Butler in *Mann & Machine* (© NBC).

splatter of colors, designs and fashion concepts, illustrating Adair's imagination.

The police station precinct featured a mainframe computer crime center, frequently used by Eve as she "hooked up" for database research and crime files access. Show stylization was prominent in flashy cinematography by director of photography Roy Wagner and the rock-jazz-funk score supplied by composer Mark Mothers-

baugh. One of today's busiest film and television composers, Mothersbaugh was one of the founding members of Devo, the 1980s New Wave band.

"We were constantly trying to push the 'cool' barometer in terms of the look and sound," says Wyatt. "The action sequences were a good example of this combination."

This "coolness" was demonstrated when, in action scenes, screen movement was kinetic but in slow-motion, saturated with a heavy rock music beat. Eve was always jumping and cartwheeling, full of gymnastics. "Mark Mothersbaugh was phenomenal!" continues Wyatt. "This was the first one-hour drama he had done up to that point and he elevated every scene that he scored! The show was very music-heavy and I know that Mark pulled countless all-nighters on our behalf. What a treat to have worked with him! His music segued beautifully from percussive action to funky comedy to tender, childlike musical underscore."

Although the initial series order was for 13 episodes, *Mann* ultimately ended its run with just nine episodes. DeLaurentis explains: "The show was originally designed to fill a specific time slot — Friday night if memory serves. But at the last minute the slot was switched to Sunday, up against one of the biggest hits on television at the time — [the CBS series] *Murder She Wrote*. Many shows had already failed opposite it, and I remember that Dick was furious at the network decision, but to no avail. In fact, when *Variety* reviewed the pilot, [reviewer] Brian Lowry said that while he liked the show, and it might be the thing to finally compete with *Murder*, he thought it more likely that it too would succumb to the competition. And he was right.

"The show had respectable ratings — the kind that would certainly keep it on the air in the current landscape — but at the time, it simply wasn't enough."

In an April 1992 review, *Entertainment Weekly* magazine graded the series a C minus. "*Mann & Machine* is basically nothing more than [Fred Dryer's 1984 crime drama series] *Hunter* with an android, and it carries a creepy, sexist subtext. We are told that Eve has 'the emotional development' of 'a 7-year-old child.' In practice, this means that Eve comes off as a dumb beauty led around by a man. When Bobby says, 'I have to take a shower,' Eve, who was programmed to observe human behavior, says innocently, 'Oh, can I watch?' Viewers are supposed to chuckle and be turned on at the same time, but sneers and turn-offs might be the real result. The fundamental trouble with *Mann & Machine* is that its robot is, by default, the sensitive one; the show's flesh-and-blood hero is just your basic macho jerk."

But strangely, the *Mann & Machine* story doesn't end with the series' cancellation. The network asked the producers for a presentation reel, to "sell the show" again. With help from director

Allan Arkush, highlights were cobbled together with some original footage and then screened by the network. "At that point, the network felt strongly that the show might work better as a strict female lead, as opposed to the 'team' concept," says DeLaurentis. "But the team concept seemed to be the essence of the show, at least to us. We all agreed — NBC included — that if we were to pare it back to a single-female-lead action show, we should re-conceive the concept. So they took the highly unusual step of giving us a pick-up, but for a new series. That series, also with Yancy Butler in the lead, was called *South Beach* and premiered the following summer."

David Andrews was out of a job, but Yancy moved ahead. Airing in the summer of 1993, *South Beach* was a crime drama series set in South Beach, Florida. Butler played a thief working for the government. It was a similar premise to Robert Wagner's 1960s–'70s action drama *It Takes a Thief*. "It also had respectable ratings but, without the futuristic spin of *Mann & Machine*, was ultimately canceled," says DeLaurentis.

Summing up, DeLaurentis says, "It was always intended, and in fact pitched, that the professional partnership between Bobby and Eve would become personal, and ultimately romantic. This was the heart of the show, we thought. We loved the notion that a human being, a flesh-and-blood man, could ultimately fall in love with a woman who was in large part 'artificial.' That would have been fun to write, not to mention groundbreaking, potentially giving new meaning to 'the war of the sexes.' Unfortunately, like many things in television, it wasn't to be. But we were grateful for the chance to try."

Butler told *Starlog* magazine that she remembers everything about the series: "Talk about getting shot out of a cannon. I had no place to go but down from there. It was wild. The options that are available now — FX-wise, musically and in terms of editing — are so far superior to what they were. And it was still an amazing show."

If *Mann* was remade today in the 21st century, says DeLaurentis, he would take the following approach: "Her powers would no doubt be updated and expanded, and that would no doubt lead one into a subsequent evaluation of her place in the human community, *à la The X-Men*. Is she lonely, for instance, or has she found the company of other cyborgs like herself?

"My first instinct would of course be that she's fallen in love with a human, but that love would be unrequited given the nature of her being. The resolution of that element alone (and it's parallel in the real world) would make for an interesting movie."

CAST NOTES

David Andrews (Sgt. Bobby Mann): Andrews was born in Baton Rouge. His first screen role was in 1984's *A Nightmare on Elm Street*. After that, he played several small roles on television before appearing in Stephen King's *Graveyard Shift*. Since *Mann & Machine* he has appeared as astronaut Pete Conrad in *Apollo 13*. That was followed by roles in a number of TV movies including a role as another astronaut, Frank Borman, in the miniseries *From the Earth to the Moon*. He has appeared in the movies *Fight Club* (1999), *Hannibal* (1999), *A Walk to Remember* (2002) and *Terminator 3: Rise of the Machines* (2003) and joined the cast of TV's *JAG* in its final season.

Yancy Butler (Eve Edison): Butler is the daughter of Joe Butler, the drummer for the 1960 rock group The Lovin' Spoonful. Butler began acting shortly after graduating from college. *Mann & Machine* was her first major role. Since then she starred in the series *South Beach* and *Brooklyn South*. Her most famous role was as the lead character in the comic book-based TV series *Witchblade*. She was in the 2006 Sci-Fi Channel film *Basilik: The Serpent King* and *Striking Range*. In 2007 she joined the daytime soap *As the World Turns*. More recently, she garnered a role in the 2008 political comedy feature *Vote and Die: Liszt for President*. The film won an Award of Excellence at the Accolade Film Awards.

S. Epatha Merkerson (Capt. Cloghorn): Merkerson was born in Michigan. She is a Tony Award–nominated and Emmy Award–winning American actress, known for her roles as Reba the Mail Lady on *Pee Wee's Playhouse* in the 1980s and as the no-nonsense supervisor, Lieutenant Anita Van Buren (1993-present), on the long-running crime drama *Law & Order* in the 1990s. At present she has been on the show longer than any other cast member. As of the 366th episode in the sixteenth season, she is the first actress to appear in 300 episodes.

SOURCES

Spelling, Ian. "Mark of the Witch: Yancy Butler Wears Sword & Sorcery Well in Witchblade." *Starlog* no. 279, October 2000.

Tucker, Ken. "Saint and Cyborg: In the Human Factor, the Doctor is a Heroic Guy Who Inspires His Medical Students. In Mann & Machine, the Robot is a Futuristic Gal Who Fights Crime." *Entertainment Weekly*, April 10, 1992.

Mercy Point

(1998–1999)

The adventures of the medical staff of the space station Mercy Point as they diagnose and treat humans and aliens in the year 2249.

Cast: Joe Morton (Dr. Grote Maxwell), Maria Del Mar (Dr. Haylen Breslauer), Alexandra Wilson (Dr. Dru Breslauer), Jordan Lund (Dr. Batung), Julia Pennington (ANI), Gay Thomas (Dr. Rema Cook), Brian McNamara (Dr. Caleb ["C.J."] Jurado)

Created by: Trey Callaway, David Simkins, Milo Frank; *Executive Producers:* Trey Callaway, Michael Katleman, Lee David Zlotoff, Joe Voci, Scott Sanders; *Co-Executive Producer:* Vahan Moosekian; *Supervising Producer:* Brent V. Friedman; *Producer:* Deborah Starr Seibel; *Associate Producer:* William Redner; *Writers included:* Gary Glasberg, David Simkins, Trey Callaway, Deborah Starr Siebel; *Directors included:* Lee Bonner, Joe Napolitano, Michael Katleman; *Director of Photography:* Joel Ransom; *Production Designers:* Greg Loewen, Graeme Murray; *Costumes:* Heidi Kaczenski, Terri Bardon; *Special Effects Makeup:* Stan Edmonds, Northwestern Effects Groups, Ltd.; *Visual Special Effects:* Rainmaker Digital Pictures, Toy Box West; *Music Theme:* Jon Ehrlich; *Guest Stars included:* Paul McGillion, Kirsten Robek, Fay Masterson, Zachery Ansley, Harry Groener, Glenn Morshower, Salli Richardson (Kim Salisaw), Joe

Spano (Dr. DeMilla), Trey Callaway (Hippocrates' voice)

UPN/Mandalay Television/Columbia Tri-Star Television; October 1998 and July 1999; 60 minutes; 7 episodes

The year is 2249. Mankind has ventured into the far reaches of deep space. Earth has become "beachfront property" for the elite. In the frontier outpost region known as Jericho, 50,000 humans and aliens live together in a series of scattered independent space stations, on the edge of an unexplored Sahartic Divide. An inter-species alliance has formed between the humans and non-humans and they govern under the auspices of the Inter-Species Council (ISC). *Mercy Point*, a self-contained state-of-the-art emergency hospital space station, is Jericho's port of call for the sick and injured. It serves all species, and is staffed by the galaxy's finest physicians.

That's the premise of this series, the brainchild of producer-writer Trey Callaway, who first envisioned a medical drama not as a television series but as a big-budget feature film. Inspired by the ideas of producer Milo Frank, in early 1997 Callaway developed and wrote a script titled "Nightingale One" and pitched it to all of the major studios in Hollywood but didn't get a lot of attention. But finally, at Peter Guber's production company Mandalay Entertainment, *Mercy Point* was born.

"Nightingale One," a story about a space station hospital 25 years in the future, dealt with the first alien contact with humans. "It had to do with the future of medicine," recalls Callaway. "I remember at the time, somewhat naively, saying at the end of my full-tilt picture pitch, in a room of movie executives, 'Oh by the way, this would make a great TV series!'"

The pitch was successful and the movie was bought. Callaway rendered three or four drafts and the studio was happy. But then something happened in the real world that sent "Nightingale One" falling into Earth orbit and burning up in re-entry. Paul Verhoeven's mega-blockbuster adaptation of Robert A. Heinlein's *Starship Troopers* was released. Although eventually the picture would do $121 million at the box office worldwide, it wasn't good business for the studio considering the production budget was about $100 million.

"[Sony] lost their appetite at that moment for any big-budgeted science fiction," sighed Callaway. And his script went on a shelf. Resuscitation came when someone at Guber's production company, who attended that meeting, remembered Callaway's last comment and gave him a call. Mandalay's TV division sold the UPN Television network on the concept. "It's always said this is a collaborative medium," notes Callaway. "Sometimes, in the best and worst cases, it is that. And this is one of the better cases."

However, the network asked for two key changes that altered the nature of the script: Set it 300 years in the future and in a universe where humans and aliens freely intermingle. "Behind those notes, from the beginning, I think was the intention that the show would become a companion piece to *Star Trek Voyager*," says Callaway. "They wanted to keep that audience.

"In terms of the adaptation, it was kind of liberating because I was able to borrow a lot of my character prototypes, but I really started over again and reconceived it completely as a series from the ground up."

In its next stage, the script (now titled *Mercy Point*) became a low-budgeted 30-minute "pilot presentation" which is a rough estimation of what the television series would look like. This is a tool frequently employed in Hollywood to help executives determine if a series is viable. Often, these "presentations" are for internal use and not meant for broadcast. If the project is greenlighted and doesn't evolve considerably, footage and scenes from this presentation can be folded into the actual aired series.

John DeLancie, *Star Trek: The Next Generation*'s "Q," essayed the role of Dr. DeMilla in the pilot presentation. Special effects wizard Steve Johnson and his XFX. Inc. company, which has a long list of SF film and television genre credits such as *The Abyss*, *Spider-Man 2* and *The Outer Limits*, realized the non-humanoid creature designs. "I think he was instrumental in helping us sell the show," notes Callaway. "His creatures were so utterly convincing.

"The presentation was shot here in Los Angeles with completely different sets. It was low-budget furnishings of what became our actual sets." In the transition from presentation to the series, three non-human characters were added to the cast, including an alien doctor and an android nurse.

Because Callaway had never done a pilot presentation, a writer named David Simkins helped out. Although Simkins didn't continue with the series, the credit garnered him a series co-creator credit with Callaway and Milo Frank.

The presentation was screened by the network and for the network affiliates across the country who would actually broadcast the program. UPN greenlighted 13 episodes, a half-season's worth.

When it came to casting, Callaway was not choosy who would portray his characters. He just wanted good actors. "I was very lucky," he says. "We had fantastic performers in Joe Morton and Maria Del Mar, who was extremely convincing as his female counterpart. The supporting players—there were a lot of up-and-coming [actors] who had mastered their craft. I think we were able to elevate it above being just another blue-screen effects show. I did a lot toward making it a compelling drama. To me, it's always being a matter of being a character-driven plot instead of being the other way around. As great as science fiction is with visual effects, it has to take a backseat to what is going on with people's hearts and minds. I had a cast in *Mercy Point* that was definitely up to the task."

Populating the space station was a mix of human and alien faces. Overseeing the station's emergency ward was Dr. Grote Maxwell, played by veteran actor Morton. He was an emergency physician whose keen skill and knowledge won the admiration and respect of his colleagues and patients. He was calm and solid as a rock. His boss, Dr. Haylen Breslauer, the station's Director of Medicine, played by Del Mar, was a very attractive woman and she was also Maxwell's trusted friend. Haylen's younger sister, Dru Breslauer, played by Alexandra Wilson, was the station's newest resident. Aside from being raw and under pressure, Dru had the unfortunate task of attempting to live up to her sister's expectations and standards. Her past had also caught up to her present: An old boyfriend from Med School was serving aboard the station. Dr. Caleb ("C.J.") Jurado, played by Brian McNamara, just happened to be romantically involved in the present with Kim (played by Salli Richardson) and was torn between the women, even as he tried to convince Kim that Dru was far behind him. The resident psycho-surgeon from Earth, Dr. Rema Cook, played by Gay Thomas, was eager to serve aboard the station.

Non-humans on the staff included Dr. Batung (played by Jordan Lund), who was a slug-like creature; his species was known as the Shenn. His was a prickly personality and working among humans was new to him and those from his world. Serving as a nurse was the young woman "ANI" (Android Nurse Interface), played by Julia Pennington; ANI was an android designed to assist wherever she could. She had just started learning to experience emotions, with tears and laughter being evoked on the job. Her programming was not perfect by any means. She continued to be fascinated by human behavior. When a nearby couple embraced and kissed, ANI later asked a young man in Admitting, "Are you seeing anyone?" startling the man.

Making sure everything was running smoothly was the station's chief of staff, Dr. Harris DeMilla, played by Joe Spano (assuming the role played by John DeLancie in the pilot). He trusted his people but when the sick and the powerful came aboard his station, conjuring up ethical problems, he had to make the difficult decisions.

Typically, each episode had two or three plot threads dealing with personal or professional dilemmas. As the series progressed, stories became less about the alien disease of the week and more about the interpersonal relationships of the staff. In the series pilot "New Arrivals," a computer virus has somehow jumped into humans and Maxwell uses ANI as the means to develop an antidote. "Last Resort" involved a powerful and influential man bringing his son to *Mercy Point* for a life-saving treatment, but the doctors object until the alien whose blood may save the son, agrees. The results startle everyone: The alien is the one who benefits, not the young boy. In "No Mercy," a series of puzzling deaths of non-humans prompts an investigation, and the clues points to Dr. Maxwell as the killer. Elsewhere, Dru jeopardizes her career as a doctor by performing an illegal procedure without parental consent on a young girl. In the series finale, "Persistence of Vision," a deranged man arrives on the station and talks in riddles and prophecies. The doctors are convinced he has discovered a new world to be explored. C.J. is determined to help prove his experiences, but matters are complicated when Kim wants the man's memories intact to be turned over to the military.

To film the series at a practical cost, Vancouver, Canada, was selected. Many genre TV series had used Vancouver with success; *The X-Files, Stargate, Battlestar Galactica* and *Smallville* were all SF series filmed in and around that city.

Because *Mercy Point* was a space station, the entire series would be shot on soundstages and so the production design and sets were critical to the show's success. "The sets were phenomenal!" says Callaway. "You could walk in and mess around. They had been all painstakingly created.

Everywhere you looked, there was constant activity. It was very active. That was always a positive memory for me, just walking into the sets."

The show's production designers, Greg Loewen and Graeme Murray, envisioned the hospital as a circular hub with offices and rooms radiating outward. There was even a second floor where the chief of staff could look through his window and down to the bay where ambulances arrived with patients.

Mercy Point was a show with good behind-the-scenes genes. "We were very lucky in that we inherited the crew, almost in its entirety, from *The X-Files*," notes Callaway. "They were seasoned filmmakers. We were very happy to have those guys at our disposal."

Callaway also ended up voicing Hippocrates, *Mercy Point*'s all-seeing, all-knowing mainframe medical computer. "I had voiced the role for free in the original pilot presentation and the network just kinda never got me out of their heads," says Callaway ruefully. "Even though we cast about for a replacement, I still got saddled with it for series. And I do mean saddled because as much as I may enjoy acting, running a show is hard enough without having to provide voice cues for every single episode, especially when they're that full of gobbledygook med-tech speak! I'm still not sure how I got some of that stuff to flow out of my mouth."

In a similar vein, the on-screen actors themselves had to grapple with the medical technobabble for every emergency room scene they had to act out. And Callaway was right there, off camera, listening in on the protests. "One of my favorite things was listening to the on-set sound feed which was always on — the cast always forgot — between takes. Suffice it to say, a big source of their constant exasperation and my subsequent (if surreptitious) entertainment was listening to them gripe about having to deliver all that stuff with feeling. Granted, I was somewhat sympathetic since I had to spew a bunch of it myself as Hippocrates."

Director Joe Napolitano, who helmed the series' third episode, "Last Resort," calls *Mercy Point* as "a good candy store for a director" because of the care with which the sets were designed. He wasn't forced to shoot in close-ups, hiding the deficiencies of the hospital environment. Indeed, he could do extended "walk 'n' talk" scenes with the doctors and show off the size and scope of the hospital. "The first time I saw the sets, I was amazed how much of it actually functioned," says Napolitano. "It was designed so that we could shoot through things so that you always felt the [spacial] depth, scope and size of the station. This was a hospital in space. There was one scene I did that just kept on going and it was like two or three scenes put together. It was continuous. It's long takes and long scenes without cuts. They're fun to design and do. This particular set afforded that."

Having previously directed contemporary medical dramas like *Chicago Hope*, Napolitano had that experience under his belt, but because this show was science fiction, it meant there were new layers added on top of the usual characters and drama. "We were talking [author Michael Crichton's NBC-TV series] 'E.R. in outer space.' But by saying 'outer space,' you were opening up a whole new world. The only thing that you brought from *E.R.* was the pacing and maybe the camera direction. Everything else was new and interesting. A couple of things that were very different about this show than doing a regular medical show is that you have aliens. That's the first thing. Then you have all the futuristic toys that you don't have on a current show. It makes a big difference when you're doing the show."

As an example of the complexity added by the show's science fiction elements, Napolitano points to the hospital staff's non-humanoid Dr. Batung (played by actor Jordan Lund) as a complicated affair in prosthetics makeup preparation. "His character was extremely difficult," says Napolitano. "Hours of prosthetics that he had to have done every day and it would wreak havoc on the production schedules." A slug-like creature that moved about the hospital on a mobile sled, Dr. Batung's skin and appearance were truly alien, complete with an undulating tail that snaked up and down on his shoulders and neck. Designing and applying that special effects makeup took time — and stamina on Lund's part. "His movement was always a complicated question," recalls Napolitano. "Is he moving in this shot or is he just static? Did he need the prosthetics below his chest? There were different rigs and setups."

A simple "guest star alien" appearing as a patient was also complicated for the filmmakers. An extraterrestrial named Jeel, who was a Goling species alien, was a *Mercy Point* patient with a terminal illness. Under his chin were a series of round sacs that slowly expanded and contracted in a regular rhythm, representing alien gills. Underneath the hospital bed where the actor reclined, there was a makeup artist supplying the sacs' pulsating activity. "You could put those gills anywhere," Napolitano says. "We talked about putting them on the sides of his chest, but in retrospect it was better putting them under the chin because you see them all the time. No matter how close you got, you saw those gills."

Mercy Point's life and death came quickly. The series premiered on October 6, 1998, with "New Arrivals" but just three weeks later, after the broadcast of "Last Resort," it was canceled by UPN.

No one was more shocked than Callaway, who, on the day he received the cancellation phone call, had spent the morning getting approvals of the season finale storylines. "That came as a huge shock not only to myself and my cast and crew but even to the studio, Columbia Tri-Star," says Callaway. "They were footing most of the bills for the show. They were flabbergasted by the whole thing. The studio was very supportive considering they had in me a first-time creator-showrunner."

Callaway attributes *Mercy Point*'s quick death to three factors, all beyond his control:

(1) Cost. As with most typical science fiction shows, creating a fantasy world beyond today's reality is expensive. "It was very challenging, financially speaking," says Callaway. "It was a very large ensemble cast. Even though we were up in Vancouver, those savings still required a large crew. The production design and visual effects was extremely expensive."

(2) Bad timing. The first episode, "New Arrivals," aired opposite the World Series. "A lot of those viewers we'd hoped would be watching us were watching baseball," sighs Callaway.

(3) UPN affiliates. "It was on a network that, historically, was struggling to find itself," points out Callaway. "And that season, probably more so than any other season, the UPN affiliates around the country got together and had a little mini-revolt and said to the network, 'No, no! We don't want any more science fiction! We want more *Moesha!*'"

Moesha was the six-season teen sitcom starring the pop singer Brandy. When *Mercy Point* premiered, it was *Moesha*'s third season. Although on paper *Mercy Point* was supposed to be coupled with *Star Trek: Voyager*, it was actually *Seven Days* that snagged the in-tandem timeslot. *Mercy Point* was linked, instead, on Tuesday night with *Moesha*. "Not only did we not get our audience, we got next to no money for marketing," says Callaway.

Being connected with a teen audience timeslot actually imposed a shift in the nature of *Mercy Point*'s plotting. "We spent a lot less time involved in the dramatic, ethical and technological issues of futuristic medicine," says Callaway. "We spent a lot more time on 'who was sleeping with who.' Which is fine, because I love a good soap opera as much as the next guy, if not more so. We were forced to evolve so quickly."

If the UPN affiliates were opposed to more science fiction programming (*Seven Days* was also on the network at the time), how did *Mercy Point*'s presentation pilot pass muster with affiliates before the 13 episodes was greenlighted? The only explanation that makes sense is that the affiliates did not have those feelings about science fiction until after the series went on the air. Callaway agrees with this theory. "There's often a big 'Rahrah, go team go' drive mounted by the networks that carries new programs into their splashy upfront presentations each season — but it's usually not until the party's over that they get a chance to see how the affiliates and advertisers really feel. And by that point, for people in my position, it's usually too late to turn the train (or space station) around, creatively speaking."

Reviewer Joanne Weintraub, writing for the *Milwaukee Journal Sentinel*, said, "I haven't been this happily surprised by a show since *Buffy the Vampire Slayer*. This UPN hour ... works for the same reasons *Buffy* does: both series takes their special effects seriously and their often tongue-in-cheek dialogue lightly."

On the other hand, an SF webzine called "The Sci-Fi Guys" had the opposite reaction. "Boring and stupid," wrote Kevin Wagner. "It is neither compelling drama or interesting science fiction. A deadly combination for network television. The pilot introduces our hero physicians in their space hospital as they battle a mysterious lethal virus that spreads by touch. Despite people dying, it's strangely unmoving. More puzzling are the advanced containment efforts that appear to consist of rubber gloves. Just don't notice the bare forearms that appear to be touching the contagious patients. They must be super gloves."

Callaway has his own perspective on the feedback: "It ran the gamut. You want to be talked about — period. Within days of the debut of the show, hardcore fans — God love them — started up websites devoted to the show. They were posting more information than I even knew!

"We had great reviews from people who really understood what I was after, which is just try and envision how medicine would be better and worse. And how it could be exactly the same. These issues of life and death are infinite and universal. They lent themselves well to a science fiction show. The people who 'got it' seemed to be cheering us on, critically speaking. But I remember this one reviewer referred to the show as 'fish Jell-O.' It was his way of saying, 'I like fish. I like Jell-O. I know, let's put the two together and make fish Jell-O!' His contention was that a medical show and an SF show didn't belong together. There was no reason in my mind that those two genres couldn't creatively, dramatically co-exist together."

Whomever that reviewer was, he was not aware that in literature science fiction, there are many novels and short stories dealing with exactly this type of storytelling. One of the most famous in the field are the 12 James White books in the "Sector General" series, also about a hospital space station inhabited by human and alien doctors and patients. Another writer, Murray Leinster, wrote stories about a "Doctor to the Stars" (a physician with his spaceship traveling to different planets). Lee Correy (a.k.a. G. Harry Stine) wrote a book called *Space Doctor* which was about an Earth-orbiting hospital station.

When the show was declared officially dead in its third broadcast, cast and crew were in the midst of filming its eighth episode. There was enough time given afterwards for the producers and editors to consolidate and edit into the seventh — and now final — episode, storylines and scenes originally intended for the eighth episode. It would be a very short and bittersweet swan song. The final four episodes was packaged as two two-hour movies and broadcast on the network the following July. "We were able to bring some form of closure to the series," says Callaway. "When you watch them as a whole, even though each one stands on its own, there is definitely an arc to the seven episodes. In retrospect, I think about it as a limited-run series."

Looking back, Callaway feels that many things about the show worked well. "What worked was the extremely relatable issues of life and death. Those are universal and timeless and drove well the stories that we told episodically. Even if you weren't an SF fan, if you gave us ten minutes of your patient time, you would have been drawn into the interpersonal dynamics of a universal and timeless issue.

"What didn't work, outside the factors out of my control, [was] probably me just because it was my inaugural production, trying too hard to please so many people at one time. I remember one of the notes I got from the network, who were running scared from the affiliates, was, 'Instead of thinking of this as a futuristic hospital, just think of this as a hospital that happens to be in space...' I remember thinking, 'Well, if you put *St. Elsewhere* up in deep space, it's kind of a different hospital. All the same rules don't apply!' I don't think people expect, or necessarily want to see their typical TV hospital. It's a different entity."

Had *Mercy Point* continued to the end of its first season, many intriguing stories were planned. "There were several primary story arcs that were going to be heavily explored through the remainder of the season. One was Haylen's continuing struggle with homesickness, a crippling interstellar condition unique to humans that ultimately linked their survival to returning to Earth. That particular story fascinated me in the way it literally grounded our species, no matter how ambitiously we tried to explore the great beyond. Another revolved around the fallout from Dr. Batung's decision to not return to the protective fold of his species, the Shen. I planned to continue the evolution of ANI after being used to create an antidote to the computer virus which skipped into humans in the pilot story. I envisioned her character as the ultimate clash between the organic and technological worlds. And I also wanted to continue planting seeds about Grote's missing family — specifically revealing more about exactly *why* they'd gone missing — through a story that involved both Grote and C.J. embarking on a dangerous rescue mission into the unexplored and mysterious 'Sahartic Divide.' In and around those major arcs, of course, I would've continued the downward spiral of Dru's character into a new battle with old addictions — as well as further exploration of Dr. Cook's burgeoning theory that the temporal lobe was the home of the human 'soul,' which would've also played directly into Haylen's homesickness. And as you can imagine, we had a plethora of new and exciting medical cases to treat, as well."

CAST NOTES

Joe Morton (Dr. Grote Maxwell): Morton was born in New York. He acted in daytime dramas in the late '70s and early '80s before breaking out in the independent film *The Brother from Another Planet* (1984). He played roles in many films including his notable supporting role in 1991's *Terminator 2: Judgment Day*. He appeared in *Speed* (1994), *Executive Decision* (1996), *Blues Brothers 2000* (1998), *Ali* (2001), *Paycheck* (2003) and *Stealth* (2005). He was part of the cast of the series *E-Ring* before joining the cast of The Sci Fi Channel's series *Eureka*.

Maria Del Mar (Dr. Haylen Breslauer): See the Cast Notes for *TekWar*.

Alexandra Wilson (Dr. Dru Breslauer): Wilson was born in Pasadena, California. She gained fame as Josie Watts in the daytime drama *Another World*. After leaving that show, she starred in the dramatic series *Homefront*. She also appeared as a recurring character on *Beverly Hills 90210*. Since *Mercy Point* she has been seen as a guest star on a number of television series including *Curb Your Enthusiasm*.

Jordan Lund (Dr. Batung): Lund was born in Long Island, New York. He began acting in the early '80s appearing in such television series as *The Street* and (in 1989) the original *Lonesome Dove*. He has made guest appearances on *Murphy Brown*, *The Flash* and *Cop Rock* and has acted in the films *The Adventures of Ford Fairlane* (1990) and *Doc Hollywood* (1991). He appeared on *Star Trek: The Next Generation* and *Star Trek: Deep Space Nine* as well as the TV movie *Alien Nation: Dark Horizon*, *Law & Order* and *Seven Days*. After *Mercy Point*, Lund has been seen in *Firefly*, *Star Trek: Enterprise* and in the movie *Alex & Emma* (2003).

Julia Pennington (ANI): American actress Pennington has appeared on *Seinfeld*, *Veronica's Closet* and *Dharma and Greg*. Since *Mercy Point* she has appeared in two episodes of *Rude Awakening* and in one episode of *JAG*.

Gay Thomas (Dr. Rema Cook): Thomas is an American actress who began her career with a small role in the original *Battlestar Galactica*. She made appearances in *Another World*, *Freddy's Nightmares*, *Homicide: Life on the Street*, *The Pretender*, *Cracker* and the final episode of *Seinfeld*. Since *Mercy Point* she has appeared in the movies *Dancing in September* (2000) and *Boys and Girls* (2000). She has also made guest appearances on *The Sopranos* and *Nip/Tuck*.

Brian McNamara (Dr. Jurado): Born in New York, McNamara is best known for his role in the TV movie *Billionaire Boys Club* for which he was nominated for a Golden Globe award. He starred in the Disney SF movie of the week *Earth Star Voyager* and has had lead roles in numerous motion pictures including *Arachnophobia* (1990). On television he has had guest starring roles on *Seinfeld*, *NYPD Blue*, *St. Elsewhere*, *Star Trek: Voyager*, and *The Suite Life of Zack and Cody*. He also starred in the film *Tillamook Treasure* (2006).

SOURCES

Wagner, Kevin. "TV: Mercy Point Review." Sci-Fi Guys online.

Weintraub, Joanne. "Mercifully, 'Mercy Point' a Pleasant Surprise." *Milwaukee Journal-Sentinel*, October 6, 1998.

Mysterious Ways

(2000–2002)

A university anthropologist is fascinated with "miraculous phenomenon" and with his psychiatrist friend they investigate the weird, the unusual and amazing events that may — or may not — be explained by traditional means.

Cast: Adrian Pasdar (Declan Dunn), Rae Dawn Chong (Dr. Peggy Fowler), Alisen Down (Miranda), Sarah Brown (Emma Shepherd) *Year 2*
Created by: Peter O'Fallon; **Executive Producers:** Peter O'Fallon, Carl Binder, Kevin L. Beggs, Harold Tichenor; **Producers:** Jonathan Goodwill, David Willson; **Co-Producers:** Melissa R. Byer, Treena Hancock, Kira Domaschuk, Dawn Ritchie, Keri Young; **Directors of Photography:** Attila Szalay, Kevin Hall, Scott Williams; **Writers included:** Melissa R. Byer and Treena Hancock, Barbara Covington, Dawn Ritchie, Eric Tuchman, Carl Binder; **Directors included:** Peter O'Fallon, Brad Turner, Anne Wheeler, Michael Robison, Allan Kroeker; **Mysterious Ways Main Theme:** "Fabric of Dreams"—Lindsay Tomasic; **Guest Stars**

included: Jerry Wasserman, Ken Pogue, Andrew Arlie, Jim Byrnes, Dale Midkiff, Katie Stuart, Camille Mitchell, Barry Corbin, Colin Cunningham, Winston Rekert, Rob LaBelle, Brent Stait, Kathleen Duborg

NBC/Pax Television/Crescent Entertainment/ Lions Gate Television; 2000–2002; 60 minutes; 44 episodes

In a nutshell, *Mysterious Ways* was "*X-Files* lite." Instead of mysteries that lead into the darkness, ensuing events swiveled into the bright light. When writer/director Peter O'Fallon developed the idea for this series, which he first dubbed "One Clear Moment," he wanted a family-friendly science fiction drama that would explore warm, humanistic themes. (The series title was inspired by the rock band U2's song of the same name.)

Oregon university anthropologist Declan Dunn formed a friendship with Dr. Peggy Fowler, a psychiatrist at the local hospital. Together with a physics student, Miranda, the three got involved in and investigated weird, unusual events that could be construed as "miracles." Events would come to the protagonists sometimes by way of Peggy's job at the hospital, or Declan's position at the university, but often miracles would become publicized and the trio would express interest in learning more.

For example, in "Ties that Bind," a mystery surfaces when the bizarre, compulsive behaviors of three people comes to a head when Peggy and Declan realize they're all connected in some fashion. Miranda inexplicably finds herself on the ledge of a building. A grandfather sees the number 528 all over the place. And a third person, Paul, also sees the number 528 and he changes his hairstyle for no reason. And they all have a very strong urge to travel to Alaska. What's the common denominator and what can be done to restore their everyday lives?

Inspiration for the show's premise came from O'Fallon's life-threatening events as a child.

"I've always had weird things happen in my life," says O'Fallon. "I've had a couple of near misses and things like that, and I was always surprised that things worked out the way they did. I grew up in Colorado. I had a couple of close calls skiing when I was a young kid. We used to ski, backcountry, all the time. I felt fortunate and lucky and I was trying to figure out why. I thought that would make an interesting show if anyone spent his time trying to find out the scientific reasons for things that happened. Was there

some unknown 'X factor' that would have explained how it all worked? Declan was intrigued by that."

Using his skiing experiences as a jumping off point, O'Fallon gave Declan Dunn a similar experience. Because Declan had survived an avalanche, he became obsessed with and pursued miraculous phenomenon in a search for understanding the forces of the universe.

In casting the character, O'Fallon says that he was simply looking for "an everyman" and found it in Adrian Pasdar, who had appeared in TV shows like *Profit, Judging Amy* and *The Outer Limits'* "In the Zone."

"Sometimes he doesn't say the right thing. Sometimes he's a little clumsy," says O'Fallon. "But he has an intriguing and open mind. Adrian came in and we got along really well. He brings an element of dry humor which I really liked."

In casting for Peggy Fowler, the producers found the right actor in the renowned and attractive Rae Dawn Chong, whose many film appearances include *Quest for Fire, The Color Purple* and *Commando.* Her television appearances included *The Outer Limits'* "The Second Soul" and *Poltergeist the Legacy* with her sister Robbi Chong. "We needed someone who could match wits with Adrian. And Rae Dawn obviously handled that well," says O'Fallon.

Actor chemistry was very important for the show because this was, effectively, a three-lead cast. The producers were hoping for, and found, a strong and entertaining chemistry between the three actors.

Peggy was skeptical about miraculous phenomenon but her curiosity was so heightened that she joined forces with Declan to explore these incidents. They also became good friends. Peggy's relationship with Declan was compared as being the skeptical Scully to Declan's believing Mulder.

Alisen Down essayed Miranda, Declan's physicist student friend who tested a suspected miracle's veracity. Declan would ask Miranda to see if it was possible to recreate or find a real-world explanation for a miraculous event.

"The series premise was a very interesting idea and it was something that hadn't been done," remarks Alisen Down. "I thought it was a good mixture of the scientific and the miraculous. It made for an interesting show that tried to meld the two together." Down's casting, at age 24, as Miranda, was her "first big job," she says.

"I really believe that I get the job that I'm

The *Mysterious Ways* cast: From left: Rae Dawn Chong, series executive producer Carl Binder, Adrian Pasdar, Alisen Down, and series executive producer, creator and director Peter O'Fallon.

supposed to," she says. "Even if I'm in a terrible time or something. When I lose a job it's not as bad because I know that is the purpose of it. The universe will put in front of me what it's supposed to be. I auditioned for another series before I got *Mysterious Ways*, about a week before I booked it. I got a callback, and I think it was between me and someone else. I was devastated when I didn't book that show. Devastated! A week later I got *Mysterious Ways* and if I had booked the other show, I would not have worked half as much on half as good a show. Things like that happen to me. Just stepping back and believing that as long as I'm pursuing, as long as I'm pro-active, the universe is going to provide."

Once cast in the role, Down recalls her emotions during this time. "I don't recall the exact first day of shooting, but I recall the first few days

and the feeling attached to them: I was *so* excited, I was over the moon and nervous as hell and bubbly and happy, everything all rolled into one," Down said, chuckling. "The mood on the set was similar, everyone was really excited to be there, creative juices were flowing, there were a lot of smiles. Everyone was truly happy to be there."

Down recalls that Miranda's character was written as a reserved, intellectual university physics student but with a very dry wit. "At first I stuck very much to the dry wit," she admits. "And stuck very much to her not giving much to anybody. But as I went along, I found outlets to her that made her more quirky and kept that dry wit to her. But she had the ability to reach out to people in need. She wasn't great around people. People weren't her forte, but physics investigations were her forte. I had a conversation with

Peter about six or seven episodes into the show, and we talked about letting her out a little bit, expanding her. As we went along, she kind of became who she was."

Certain episodes allowed Down to widen the character's palette considerably. In the final scenes of "Ties that Bind," it was written that Miranda would belt out the R&B pop standard "Midnight Train to Georgia." Although Down did get to record the song, in the final episode, the voice wasn't hers. "I can't imagine what was the problem when they heard that. But they were sweet to me about it," she says.

"Ties that Bind," written by Melissa Byer and Treena Hancock, was an interesting episode because it explored the notion that medical patients who received blood transfusion or organ transplants take on characteristics from the donors. "Treena and Melissa did a lot of research about that and based the story on it," explained Down. "There were cases of food cravings. Suddenly people would have a craving for a particular food that they've never had a craving for before. The writers were constantly doing research on interesting phenomenon."

In the episode "Free Spirit," Miranda's personality swung wildly as a result of an electrical shock accident. Previously introverted and quiet, she was now exuberant and outgoing. This afforded two challenges for Down. The first was how to make that personality switch. "I found it a difficult episode because I spent so long with Miranda not coming out of her shell that when 'Free Spirit' came along, I found that I didn't know how to get out of the Miranda spirit suddenly," Down admits. "I found it a welcome challenge to do a 180 degree turn."

For a scene in the same episode, Miranda took up the violin, and this was Down's second challenge. For the long shots, she had to appear facile at masterfully playing the instrument. "It was hard because they had a double for me in the close-ups. From far away I could play it, but for close-ups finger work, that takes years to get."

Peter O'Fallon reports that the stories' percentages were about 60 percent explained and about 40 percent unexplained and unknown.

From the outset, the show's humanistic themes were deliberate. "It wasn't sappy," notes O'Fallon. "It just left you with a warm feeling in the heart. As filmmakers, you can take a twist in the end that goes dark or take that twist and go bright — that humanity will live out. It was to make you

wonder about life and how it all works. Life is complex but ultimately it can be a good thing.

"I did a movie called *Suicide Kings* which was a very dark, edgy film," notes O'Fallon. "I also did the pilot of a series called *American Gothic* [starring *Crusade*'s Gary Cole]. It was dark and horror. I was very good at that. But it's also very interesting to play, as a writer and director, the better part of people's hearts. It's a nice feeling to watch."

As an example of how the viewer's emotions were stirred by the show's "miraculous" drama, witness the teaser of the series' pilot, "Amazing Grace." In it, viewers witnessed a young boy drowning at a frozen lake nearby his log cabin. But he survived. Somehow he was pulled out and was discovered lying face-up next to the ice hole where he fell. As the scene played out, it was juxtaposed with Declan Dunn in his anthropology class conveying to the students the origins of the Christian hymn poem, "Amazing Grace." As Declan played the song to his students, we witnessed the boy thrashing in the water.

"Years ago, I was watching PBS with Bill Moyers," explains O'Fallon. "He had loved the song 'Amazing Grace.' I had a spiritual connection to it. It's just a beautiful song. Bill Moyers talked about the guy who composed the poem — a slave trader. I thought it was such a fascinating idea about this guy on his last voyage across the Atlantic. He realized he was an affront to mankind. He supposedly looked to the heavens and said 'Amazing grace, how sweet the sound, that sav'd a wretch like me.... I was once lost, but now am found, was blind, but now I see.' I found it intriguing. He had done such evil, awful things, but stood the wherewithal to find something in his heart, to write something that has lasted so many years."

In an uncredited contribution, the singer of the song in the pilot was none other than Adrian Pasdar's wife, Natalie Maines, one-third of the Dixie Chicks musical group. She had read the script of her husband's new TV series and quickly suggested, "Why don't I sing the song?" and O'Fallon could only reply, "Sure!"

"We got lucky," notes O'Fallon. "She did an unbelievable version of it. When she said she wanted to do this, I was incredibly excited. The studio and the record company wanted to do it. The network was worried about all sorts of things, but finally, Natalie just went ahead and did it."

"It was a very powerful idea to have Natalie sing 'Amazing Grace' in the pilot," agrees Alisen Down. "Her voice is quite unique and ethereal."

Filmed in and around Vancouver, Canada, *Mysterious Ways*' themes about coincidences, supernatural occurrences, near-death experiences and premonitions actually was not such far-out fiction as one might come to believe. O'Fallon recalled a real-life incident that occurred during filming that made just about everyone think twice about the show's content.

In the episode "Crystal Clear" a skyscraper window washer falls from his scaffolding, but survives. Just after having filmed that segment, O'Fallon found out that a window washer, just like the episode's character, had fallen while on the job, but he survived and there wasn't an explanation of what had happened.

The show's first eight episodes started on NBC in July 2000. The show returned in January 2001 (five episodes) and July 2001 (four episodes). By August 2001, NBC pulled the show because of poor ratings. Meanwhile, the show's primary run was seen on PAX TV, which simultaneously aired it from August 2000 to September 2002, including reruns. (In 2001 NBC owned 32 percent of PAX.) This transfer worked in *Mysterious Ways*' favor creatively. "It turned out to be a godsend in a weird way, because they pretty much left us alone," says O'Fallon. "That was great because we were able to pretty much tell the stories we wanted."

Alisen Down vividly recalled the day to shoot what ultimately became the series' final episode at the end of the second season. "The last day of shooting is always bittersweet on anything, no matter what happens after. We were all pretty hopeful that we would have a third season, so speaking for myself, I was trying to think of it not as a goodbye, but a small break."

But the *Mysterious Ways* experience for Down was very rewarding. "I couldn't have asked for two better people to work with on a job like that. Adrian and Rae Dawn will always hold very special places for me. They were really good to me. They were professional, focused and passionate for what they did."

The ax fell only because Lions Gate Television and PAX could not agree on the show's budget. Although ratings on PAX were good, the negotiations were $20,000 per episode apart from a renewal. But once added up, that's a season shortfall of about $440,000. With a planned 44 episodes (two season's worth) that was about $880,000 in total needed to keep the show going.

Alisen Down confirms that there were also discussions to moving the show either to Australia or Calgary, Alberta. "Nothing was solidified."

O'Fallon says that out of the 44 unproduced story ideas that were waiting in the wings, one of his favorites was about a man who had gone to Hawaii and spent a considerable time alone. When he returned to civilization, he was stunned to realize that three years had passed. He had only believed that he was gone for about three months. "The thought was that the Earth spun beneath him. He got caught in a vortex somewhere," says O'Fallon.

Mysterious Ways does well in international broadcasts and a DVD release of the show was being considered.

Years after the show was cancelled, the feedback keeps on coming.

Down continues to receive mail from fans who are discovering the show from countries around the world. "I think it's got international appeal," says Down. More than that, fans have been expressing themselves to Down, talking about how the show has been impacting them. And this has taken Down completely by surprise. "Normally, I don't feel what I do for a living is making a big difference in the world. The mail that I really responded to emotionally was mail I'd get from young girls who would say, 'I felt like I was outcast until I saw Miranda.' Another girl said that she was dying her dark hair and she was letting it grow longer, because of Miranda.

"Those responses made me feel like I somehow made a difference. I think what I do for a living does have the potential to help people and if I can do that through a character or a circumstance in a movie or television show then that makes me feel like I can make a difference and, big or small, that is important to me.

"It was incredible. People related to her. At first people didn't know how to take Miranda. Or what to do with her. But as she went along, people liked her."

In 2005, in a return to Vancouver to direct the pilot of the Sci-Fi Channel TV series *Eureka*, O'Fallon was approached by a production crew member who told him, "I just want to thank you for your show because I always felt good when I watched it."

O'Fallon says, grinning, "That's why we do what we do. You want to make them laugh or scare them. As a storyteller, that's exciting when people are understanding the story."

Cast Notes

Adrian Pasdar (Declan Dunn): Director Tony Scott created the character Chipper in the hit feature *Top Gun* (1986) for Pasdar when he was just 19 years old. This led to roles in *Solar Babies* (1986), *Streets of Gold* (1986) and *Near Dark* (1987). He also appeared in Brian DePalma's *Carlito's Way* (1993). Pasdar wrote and directed a short film, "Beyond Belief," and directed a feature, *Cement* (1999), starring Chris Penn and Jeffrey Wright. Pasdar starred in the short-lived series *Profit* (2000) and *Judging Amy* (2004). His most recent role was politician Nathan Petrelli in *Heroes* (2006). He's appeared on stage in *The Glass Menagerie*. He's married to Dixie Chicks singer Natalie Maines, and they have two children.

Rae Dawn Chong (Dr. Peggy Fowler): A Canadian actress and the daughter of comedian and actor Tommy Chong, she first caught attention with her role in *Quest for Fire* (1981), garnering her the Canadian Genie award for the performance. She continued staying busy with film roles in *Beat Street* (1984) and *Fear City* (1984), *Commando* (1985) with Arnold Schwarzenegger and

Steven Spielberg's *The Color Purple* (1985). On television, she guest-starred in *St. Elsewhere* (1983) and had a recurring role on *Melrose Place* (1992). She's appeared in *The Outer Limits* ("The Second Soul"), *Highlander* ("Timeless") and *Poltergeist: The Legacy* (1997). Chong is also a writer and director and filmed *Cursed Part Three* and *The Babylon Sisters*.

Alisen Down (Miranda): Born and raised in Langley, British Columbia. After graduating high school, Down studied acting at the American Academy of Dramatic Arts in Los Angeles and at the British American Academy in Oxford, England. Her TV appearances includes the Canadian-produced series *Cold Squad* (for which she won a Leo and a Gemini Award), *Stargate SG-1*, *The Dead Zone*, *Smallville* (as Lex Luthor's mother), and *DaVinci's Inquest*. She starred in the TV movies *The Life* (2004) and *Tripping the Wire: A Stephen Tree Mystery* (2005). She was also one of the survivors rescued from Caprica in *Battlestar Galactica* (2006). Her character, Jean, appeared in five of the *Battlestar Galactica* "webisodes" leading up to the third season that was posted at the Sci-Fi Channel's website.

Night Visions
(2001–2002)

Premise: An anthology series that deals with alternate dimensions, visions, ghosts and strange mysteries.

Host: Henry Rollins
Created by: Billy Brown, Dan Angel; **Executive Producers:** Dan Angel, Billy Brown; **Co-Executive Producers:** Naren Shankar, Steven Aspis; **Producer:** Robert Petrovicz; **Co-Producers:** Erin Maher, Kay Reindl, Drew Matich; **Consulting Producers:** Yves Simoneau, Jim Leonard; **Executive Consultant:** Scott Shepherd; **Directors of Photography:** Danny Nowak, Andreas Poulsson; **Writers included:** Julie Siege, Ted Humphrey, Billy Brown, Dan Angel, Steven Aspis, Kay Reindl, Erin Maher, Naren Shankar, Jim Leonard, Earl Hamner Jr., Wendy MacLeod, Sophie C. Hopkins; **Directors included:** Tobe Hooper, Joe Dante, Michael Watkins, Brian Dennehy, Bill Pullman, Philip Sgriccia, Po-Chih Leong, JoBeth Williams, Nick Gomez, Ernest Dickerson, Thomas

Wright, Jeffrey Levy; **Guest Stars include:** Joanna Pacula, Jack Palance, Lou Diamond Phillips, Mare Winningham, Karen Austin, Luke Perry, Miguel Ferrer, Malcolm McDowell, Natasha Gregson Wagner, Pam Grier, Chad Lowe, Marla Sokoloff, Bridget Fonda, Sherilyn Fenn, Bill Pullman, Brian Dennehy, Cary Elwes, Adrian Quinn, Alison Matthews, Ty Olsson, Allison Hossack, Emily Holmes, Shirley Knight, Meghan Black, Jerry O'Connell, Randy Quaid, M. Emmett Walsh.

Fox Network/Angel/Brown Productions/Warner Bros. Television/; July 2001– September 2002; 60 minutes; 13 episodes

Night Visions might have made a bigger impact had it premiered 30 years earlier. But it followed in the wake of classics such as *Twilight Zone, The*

Outer Limits and *Night Gallery*, and more recent anthologies such as James Coburn's *Darkroom* (1981), *Tales from the Darkside* (1983–1988), and the new *Twilight Zone* (1985–1987).

The Fox Network had great hopes for the series and called it "a special show" but its debut date in October 2000 was suddenly rescinded. The reality show *Police Chases* and the supernatural *Freakylinks* went into the 8–9 P.M. Friday slot.

Was Fox uneasy about *Night Visions'* unpredictable nature? "I don't have a clue," says co-creator Billy Brown. "They said many conflicting things. We had a chance to option an incredible Dean Koontz short story that was just terrifying, and they nixed that because it was too scary. And yet they complained that other stories weren't scary enough. Did I say the network gods are a fickle lot? Am I whining yet?"

Doomed by indifferent scheduling, *Night Visions* ended up as summer filler in 2001. Three other episodes were aired in September 2002.

"There was a changing of the guard at Fox between the time we filmed the pilot and by the time the network was ready to order the series," says Brown. "The new regime wasn't convinced an anthology would work, yet everyone agreed that the pilot was good. I had the feeling the network didn't think the show was hip enough. Who knows? The network gods are capricious and unfathomable. There's no doubt that Fox buried the show, even though it had decent ratings considering its time slot and complete lack of promotion."

Like *Twilight Zone*, *Night Visions* was more of a fantasy, occasionally broaching science fiction, and often delivered twist endings. Each episode was comprised of two half-hour stories and featured big-name actors.

"I love anthologies because it's a chance to create cinematic short stories every week," says Brown, who, with his partner Dan Angel, had previously created the highly successful Fox Kids series *Goosebumps*, based on the R.L. Stine novels. "Of course I was inspired by *Twilight Zone*. I'll never forget seeing that show as a pre-adolescent, and having my mind completely blown. I can't tell you how creepy it was to a nine year-old, I never saw the twist endings coming. It's a different audience now and it's very hard to surprise anyone. In *Night Visions* we tried for a wider palette of weird and scary stories—some that were psychological, some straight horror, some surreal nightmarish stories, some sci-fi, and some a mixture of all those styles within one episode. My own tastes and talents were weighted toward horrific fantasy arising out of character. My favorite horror movies are *Don't Look Now*, Roman Polanski's *Repulsion*, *Rosemary's Baby*—all character pieces in some respect, all shot through with dread and irony. In a half-hour with a limited budget and limited time, it's tough to achieve those heights, but I think 'The Passenger List' [Aidan Quinn investigating a fatal plane crash] and 'The Occupant' [Bridget Fonda trying to find a mysterious resident in her home] were neat little tales. Aidan Quinn and Bridget Fonda were terrific. 'Patterns' [Malcolm McDowell as an obsessive-compulsive man whose actions keep the world in order], written by Phillip Levin, and 'When a Tree Falls' [dead teenagers trapped in a lake] by Steve Aspis, were two of the more original ideas I've come across."

What puzzled many viewers was the presence of muscular singer-musician Henry Rollins as the show's host. Tattooed and dressed in a black T-shirt, Rollins stepped into frame and took a combat stance as he opened each episode with two or three terse lines. When a newspaper reporter asked Rollins if he was the new Rod Serling, he replied, "Naw, I'm just this little newcomer. Serling was the man."

Serling was indeed the man. "Having a host was a mistake," says writer Kay Reindl. "The latest *Twilight Zone* series [2002] had a host as well [Forrest Whitaker] and all that does is make you think of Rod Serling. Serling worked as a host because it was *his* show. A host who isn't the show's creator just doesn't work."

Rollins, a former rock singer for the 1980s punk rock band Black Flag, looked more like a barroom bouncer as he stood in front of a giant eyeball. In fairness, some of his tough-guy closing bits, delivered with humorless, flat conviction, actually provided a chilling footnote to the stories.

Writer Steve Aspis recalls that the creative team protested, telling Fox that Rollins was no Rod Serling. "He just wasn't right for the show," says Aspis.

"I never wanted a host," states Brown. "There should have been an introductory voice-over, à la *Outer Limits*. But the network said, 'No host, no show.' So we started looking, and actually got a commitment from Gary Oldman. Having played Dracula, and being a fantastic actor, he would have brought a real presence. The network said no. They wanted Henry Rollins. Huh? What? I didn't get it, nor did anyone else on the show's staff. What did the punk-rage-protest poet of

Black Flag have to do with a collection of imaginative, scary tales? It seemed like someone's desperate idea to make the show 'hip.' That was an indication that the network didn't really believe in the show. Needless to say, Henry seemed out of place on the show. In retrospect, having seen Henry interviewed on documentaries about the punk movement, I see that he is a funny and witty guy. We should have let him just improv his segments."

Miscast host aside, the series allowed writers like Steve Aspis to flex their imagination. Aspis, who grew up reading stories by Ray Bradbury and Rod Serling, enjoyed writing for the series but says, "The nature of an anthology is hit and miss. They blessed us with a very large budget and cursed us with a large amount of creative interference."

One of Aspis' more SF-oriented stories was "A View Through the Window," where a 19th-century prairie house suddenly materializes in a desert. A pioneer family of five lives there, and an electro-magnetic field keeps U. S. soldiers from entering the site. "It's like a Norman Rockwell painting come to life," gasps one soldier at the bizarre setting.

The major in command (played by Bill Pullman) is unhappy with his personal life and has turned to drinking. Obsessed with this prairie house, he penetrates the barrier, and is hugged by the beautiful pioneer woman. Suddenly, she and her cannibalistic brood devour him.

Based on a story by Bob Leman, the episode went way over budget. Aspis recalls vigorously clashing over his script for about "eight hours" with its director (and leading man) Bill Pullman. "Bill felt the character was too flawed and weak," recalls Aspis. "He wanted him to be stronger, more Captain Kirk-ish. I saw him as a man desperate to get away from his life. So we compromised in-between."

Another highlight was Julie Siege's "Bitter Harvest," with Jack Palance as an old farmer named Jennings who is chasing Shane, a trespassing teen, from his farm when he trips into an auger and has his arms cut off. Shane is forced to work on Jennings' ranch as punishment, and Jennings torments the guilt-ridden boy with sly threats. When the boy's pet horse has a foal, born without limbs, Shane realizes Jennings is a warlock and had cursed the animal. The episode ends with Shane's mom announcing that she's pregnant and she'll soon have a baby brother for Shane. Shane looks over to see Jennings' sinister smile. "How vindic-

tive is old man Jennings?" asks host Henry Rollins at the end. "Shane will have his answer...in nine months." A suspenseful script and strong performances by Palance and Brendan Fletcher (as Shane) made this a first-rate thriller.

"'Bitter Harvest' was perhaps my favorite tale in the series," says Brown. "It doesn't have death or insanity at the end, but it does end on a deeply disturbing note. It's truly creepy, and quite original. The best horror makes us feel that there is something fundamentally askew in the cosmos, that everything we've relied on to give us comfort and security has been an illusion all along."

Night Visions could also be haunting without being outwardly gruesome. "If a Tree Falls" has three college students accidentally plunge their car into a lake. The three swim to shore as their car sinks but in reality, their bodies remain trapped in the car. The young people learn they will remain alive only as long as their bodies remain hidden under the lake. But sensitive Devin (Jonathan Jackson) questions whether he's cheated God by escaping death and he wrestles with guilt. He decides it's unnatural to escape destiny and he dives underwater to free his body. But by accident, he frees his two friends' bodies instead, and the car goes plunging over a ledge, with Devin's body still wedged in the driver's seat. His girlfriend and buddy run to stop Devin and both disappear the moment a fisherman sees their bodies floating in the lake. An anguished Devin, now alone, walks to the edge of the lake, lamenting that he should have left well enough alone and embraced this "miracle" of rebirth.

The location photography in a foreboding lake well conveys the claustrophobia of being trapped in a submerged car. It was reminiscent of some true-life news stories. In 1948, a car carrying a family of four plunged into a remote mountain lake in British Columbia, Canada. As a distraught trucker watched helplessly, the car sank, its victims pounding frantically against the windows as the car slipped under the dark water. They were never seen again. And months after "If a Tree Falls" aired, Lake Crescent, Washington, divers found a car which had been submerged with its occupants since 1929.

Director Po-Chih Leong captured that watery dread and writer Steve Aspis concedes Leong provided the episode with "wonderful visuals." However, Aspis wrote "If a Tree Falls" not to terrify but rather to illustrate the dramatic power of human denial and ego—in this case, ignoring one's own death by pretending it never took place.

But Aspis wasn't totally satisfied with the finished product.

"I really disagreed with the casting of Natasha Lyonne as the girlfriend. She was incredibly wrong for the role. I wanted someone intellectually intense and thoughtful and Natasha had a laid-back, stoner persona. We had Kirsten Dunst lined up but we had to go with Natasha."

The episode concludes with the body of Devin's girlfriend Bethany lying on shore, a tear of blood seeping from her eye. The final fade-out is on Devin's motionless body, trapped in the submerged car, his eyes wide open.

Disappointed with Lyonne's interpretation of her role, Aspis tried to salvage the story by spending hours editing the footage. "There's a scene where the boyfriend is talking about his conflicted feelings about being alive. The girlfriend is supposed to be very moved by what he's saying but instead, she laughs at him! I had to edit a lot of that out."

Considering that *Night Visions* emphasized horror, it kept up the genre tradition of having evil triumph over good people. In "Used Car," Sherilyn Fenn was a kind young woman named Charlotte who tries to befriend the ghost of a woman who is out to wreak vengeance on Charlotte's philandering husband. But for all her compassion, Charlotte is killed by the ghost. And the young crewman in "Cargo" is concerned for the welfare of trapped stowaways in the cargo hold. He tries to free them and ends up torn apart by the cannibalistic immigrants.

Luke Perry understood that he had to be careful in "Now He's Coming Up the Stairs" since his powers of healing people are taking a physical toll on him. But when he tries to cure a boy who has visions of a walking dead man, Perry's character ends up with visions of the zombie coming after *him*.

"The characters on *Night Visions* do have unfortunate demises," agrees Brown. "It's very hard to avoid this in horror. These types of stories demand something other than a happy ending."

Another retribution tale was "Dead Air," where Lou Diamond Phillips played an uncaring radio DJ who mocks his listeners until one of them turns the tables on him. Kay Reindl, who scripted the segment with writing partner Erin Maher, notes, "*Night Visions* was inspired by *Twilight Zone* and any time you're doing an anthology, you're evoking Serling's show. *Twilight Zone* was a morality play at its core, where bad things happen to the people who deserve it. While the DJ in

'Dead Air' didn't exactly deserve what happened to him, his behavior doesn't make the viewer totally sympathetic to the guy."

"Dead Air" is one of the series' best episodes, with Phillips a standout. His performance underscores one of *Night Visions'* continual strengths: solid acting by actors who broke away from typecasting to have some fun.

"'Dead Air' was one of the best anthology episodes we have ever written," says Reindl. "It took place in essentially one indoor location and relied more on the actors and the story than on effects. We required a strong actor to carry what was basically a play, and Lou Diamond Phillips could not have given a better performance. He was exceptional. He's one of our most underrated actors."

Phillips' persona changes from arrogance to true terror as he searches for the deadly intruder hiding somewhere in his late-night radio station. As old music tunes such as "I Think We're Alone Now," by Tommy James and the Shondells, "Downtown" by Petula Clark and "Up, Up and Away" by the Fifth Dimension, echo through the dark halls, Phillips discovers two dead bodies, victims of the crazed killer. "We always wanted to kill someone to the tune of 'Downtown,' and we finally got the chance!" laughs Reindl. "The episode was strongly directed by Jeff Levy and wonderfully edited by our consulting producer, Scott Shepherd. It was a fun episode to write and produce. It wasn't trying to tell some larger story, or tackle issues. It was supposed to be fun and scary and it succeeded."

Also featured in the episode is Canadian actress Meghan Black, as the voice of Laura, a frightened college student who calls up the insensitive DJ and pleads for help. Black is never seen but her voice conveys Laura's cascading emotions, from being lonely, pensive, indignant, scared, sobbing and finally to a crescendo of fear as she finds a rat in her pizza and a dead body lying nearby.

"I put my heart into that performance," says Black of her vocal portrayal, which is so heartfelt and intense that even the cold-hearted DJ soon fears for Laura's life. "I tried to put myself in Laura's shoes. Had these things happened to me in real life, that's how I would have reacted. My husband thought I did a great job! I loved how that show turned out."

Black appeared in another *Night Visions*, "After-Life," where she played the young daughter of Randy Quaid, whose crazed character tries to pull her into another dimension. "There was one intense scene where I run into the bathroom to get away from my dad. Randy kicked open the door and grabbed me and dragged me across the house. What you're seeing isn't acting! Randy was really grabbing me hard. I'm all of 5'1" and he's a big guy." It was a scary experience for Black but she says, "The most important thing is we got the job done and it looked great."

A high-budgeted show, *Night Visions* had a look of quality: Locations were varied, the photography created an ambiance of dread, and even when an ending was predictable, more often than not, it worked. "*Night Visions* is one of the best horror anthologies to hit the tube in a long, long time," said SCIFI.com critic Kathie Huddleston. "The focus is on the psychological elements of suspense without giving in to the easier and sloppier gore.... [I]t's all-around good television."

"The show would have been a success if the network had supported it," concludes Brown. "About a third of the episodes were good to excellent, a third were fair to good, and the other third were fair except for a couple of stinkers. But I run into people who like episodes I didn't care for and vice versa. My 12-year-old boy, Nemo, and my seven-year-old boy, Elias, like them all though. That's good enough for me. Although, I must admit, they do have *some* notes."

But whether stories were good or bad, Henry Rollins was there with his bulldog delivery, which sounded like fortune cookies gone sour. "When the truth is too ugly to face, we tell ourselves lies," he says in one show. Or, "We all like to think we control our own destinies but there's always somebody pulling the strings." Or after DJ Lou Diamond Phillips gets his just desserts, "For all of you pain in the asses out there, remember — you can only irritate so many people before you piss off the wrong one."

CAST NOTES

Henry Rollins (host): Born in Washington DC, Rollins began his career in hardcore music bands as a young man and was lead singer of the 1980s punk band Black Flag. He had another group in the 1990s, The Rollins Band. He was also a columnist for *Details* magazine. His films include *Heat* (1995), *Bad Boys II* (2003) and *Feast* (2005).

SOURCES

Huddleston, Kathie. *Night Visions* Review. "Spine-tingling Tales of Terror Arrive with Goosebumps to Chill a Long, Hot Summer." Sci-Fi.com, 2001.

Odyssey 5
(2002, 2004)

The crew of the orbiting space shuttle Odyssey 5 is shocked to witness the destruction of the Earth. An alien being saves the crew and transports them back in time five years ago, to discover who — or what — is responsible for the planet's explosion.

Cast: Peter Weller (Col. Chuck Taggart), Sebastian Roche (Kurt Mendel), Christopher Gorham (Neil Taggart), Leslie Silva (Sarah Forbes), Tamara Craig Thomas (Angela Perry); **Created by:** Manny Coto; **Executive Producers:** Manny Coto, Jonathan Glassner, Tracy Torme; **Supervising Producers:** Nicholas J. Gray (Pilot), Larry Gross; **Producer:** Jim Michaels; **Co-Producers:** Edithe Swenson, Adam J. Shully; **Associate Producer:** Gary Mueller; **Consulting Producers:** Alan Brennert, Tommy Thompson; **Writers included:** Tracy Torme, Tommy Thompson, Edithe Swenson, Alan Brennert, Lindsay Sturman, Michael Cassutt, Jonathan Glassner, Melinda Snodgrass; **Directors included:** David Straiton, Randy Zisk, Peter Weller, Stephen Williams, George Mendeluk, Ken Girotti, Bryan Spicer; **Directors of Photography:** Victor Goss, Henry S. Chan; **Production Designers:** Jeffrey Ginn (Pilot), Oleg Savytski; **Special Effects:** Sundog Films, Inc.; **Guest Stars included:** Jonathan and Matthew Langford, Ted Raimi, Victoria Snow, Jonathan Higgins, John Neville (as The Seeker)

Showtime Networks/Columbia/Tri-Star Television; 2002 (final six episodes in 2004); 60 minutes; 20 episodes; DVD status: Complete series

What's a desperate writer to do for ideas and stories? The well was dry. Manny Coto looked up to the skies and it was there he found the answer he was seeking and energy flowed through his brain once more. "What was the worst thing that could happen?" he asked himself.

"It was really a light bulb going off in my head," says series creator and executive producer Coto. "I thought of the world blowing up, then I thought, 'How do you get out of that?' and then I envisioned, 'What if people were orbiting around the Earth in a shuttle and managed to survive it, and then where do you go?' Then I hit on the idea, 'What if an alien species shows up and moves them back in time to prevent the destruction,' and from that point on, I had a series. So it was a step-by-step process. What made it stand out for me was the process of time travel, that they didn't physically go back in time but that their consciousness was downloaded into their bodies of the past. So it allowed them to literally wake up five years ago and relive those years. And with them being the only ones who know they're from the future."

Odyssey 5 was originally a one-hour TV pilot developed at NBC for actor George Clooney's production company, and at one point was set as a feature film at Warner Bros. When that didn't pan out, the script languished for a while until Showtime expressed interest. And then Columbia/Tri-Star jumped in.

About six years elapsed between the writing of the script and the green light of a two-hour series pilot in the summer of 2000, proving that patience was another important part of being a successful screenwriter-producer in Hollywood.

Initially, the show was going to be *Odyssey 7*, reflecting on seven astronauts aboard the space shuttle, but that later got whittled down to five characters.

"I set out consciously to make an SF series that SF fans and non–SF fans could fall in love with, a series that was grounded in reality," explains Coto. "There were almost two different series in the same package. One dealing with personal issues of what would an individual do if they had five years to live over again. And also, in a more SF technological sense, the reality of the world about to be exploded in five years and having to solve that very large-scale SF premise. I envisioned it as a SF show for adults."

In the series pilot, Col. Chuck Taggart, commander of the space shuttle *Odyssey*, and his son Neil were in orbit around the planet with several colleagues: mission specialist Dr. Kurt Mendel, pilot Angela Perry and journalist Sarah Forbes. The Earth beneath them exploded, sending shockwaves across space and damaging the shuttle. With only nine hours of oxygen left aboard the ship, their final fate seemed inevitable.

An unexpected reprieve presented itself when an alien being named "The Seeker" snatched them to safety. The alien revealed that civilizations across the galaxy had met the same fate as Earth. He used his vast powers and projected the consciousness of the crew back five years in time so that they could use their knowledge to discover why Earth was destroyed. The *Odyssey 5* now also had the opportunity to rewrite and improve their recent personal lives.

"I was very happy and proud with the way the show turned out, how the stories developed and the way it was shot and edited," says Coto. The pilot and series, for budget reasons, were filmed in Toronto, Canada. "We basically moved up there and it was a great shooting environment. We had a tough time making Toronto look like Houston, but we pulled it off!" he chuckles.

For the pilot, the interior of a space shuttle had to be built, and that was expensive; also, the actors' "weightless" scenes had to be believable and effective. "We found a company in L.A. that had stock space shuttle interiors that were actually designed by NASA, which actually work," explains Coto. "You have the cockpit with all the light boards and the switches and these are sets used in a lot of movies. *Space Cowboys* had used that set. So we basically grabbed the space shuttle sets and trucked them Toronto."

Weightless conditions inside the shuttle were visually simulated by slow-moving actors. "Zero gravity is very difficult to do," notes Coto. "We talked about flying rigs and wiring, which we all found very expensive. So we brought in a choreographer, a mime artist, who coached the cast on simply pretending to be in Zero-Gs. We created a really tremendous effect, I thought it worked beautifully. I remember Showtime was concerned about the Zero-G photography and said to me, 'Why can't there be artificial gravity on the space shuttle?' That blew my mind, I was like, 'Forget about it!'"

Stylistically, Coto wanted and got a handheld-camera shooting style that was reminiscent of *Hill Street Blues* and *NYPD Blue*. "I wanted a conscious, handheld feeling for the show, to make it dramatic, immediate and believable, and now you see it everywhere. I was quite proud of that, that we led the way in that sense." Also, *O5* was one of the earliest shows to be filmed using a new wave of camera technology. The series joined *Earth Final Conflict* and a fantasy-adventure series called *The Secret Adventures of Jules Verne*, in discarding the traditional method of shooting on film. The series was shot in what is known as "24P high-definition" video. Coto says, "It was quite a leap to do that at the time. I wanted it to look pristine. And when they made that switch on *Enterprise* [where Coto served as an executive producer] for the fourth year to high-def, the other producers were concerned but I wasn't concerned, I knew how good it looked. 24P looks like film, not video, so I liked the results."

Being a program on the pay cable Showtime also afforded the filmmakers an unusual advantage over "the big three" networks: The freedom to use stronger language. "The characters could speak more believably than they could on network television," says Coto. "They could curse, so there was more freedom in that respect." Let's just say that their dialogue was not limited to "Heck!" That could become "Hell!"—and stronger. "But also there was simply much less interference from Showtime in regards to the show creatively. We could go where we wanted to go, do the stories we wanted to do, there were very few network notes and we didn't have to worry about commercial breaks," says Coto.

Although the pilot was filmed in the summer of 2000, it took another year for the series to begin shooting (Showtime made the decision to proceed in the winter of 2001).

Melinda Snodgrass, who contributed a freelance script, "Vanishing Point," recalls her reaction upon screening the series pilot. "I was just blown away by it," she says. "Manny did a great job of putting every dime on the screen. It was a really interesting cast. They were so much fun to write for. They had such distinctive voices. It was a show that I would have loved to have been on staff."

With a full-blown five-year saga in mind, Coto plotted ahead as far as he could, "in a sweeping, broad arc, all the way through the first four or five seasons. I knew where the show was going and where it would end up, in broad strokes. It would have also allowed me to go in different directions within the body of the piece, but still being able to circle back to the ending that I had originally envisioned."

Actor Peter Weller stepped into the role that George Clooney would have played, in a different incarnation. "We needed a very magnetic character to lead the team. Originally, I envisioned a kind of Tom Hanks from *Apollo 13,* a kind of straight-arrow astronaut fly-boy type who was in over his head in this kind of strange SF situation, but Peter brought a darker, more edgy sense to the role and he was just perfect for the part."

The supporting players were all previously unknown to Coto. "Christopher Gorham [cast as Taggart's son Neil] hadn't done any series up to that point," notes Coto. "He gave a terrific read and had a great boyish quality but you can see him being a really smart individual, who would, in five years, go from this stoner kid to an astronaut."

For the role of Kurt Mendel, actor Paul McCrane from *E.R.* was initially considered but was unavailable because of his commitment to that hit NBC medical drama series. (McCrane had already appeared in *RoboCop* with Weller, as one of the bad guys.) At the last minute, French actor Sebastian Roche was signed to play the part. "We were trying to find a good-looking scientist and unfortunately, most of the good-looking guys who came in didn't sound very smart," chuckles Coto. "We ended up with Sebastian Roche, who was terrific, and all these other people who came into read and who I fell in love with. That's how we put the cast together."

With five years to relive, Chuck Taggart found that he had continuing relationship problems with his wife, and the challenges of being a parent to Marc and Neil. In his mind, Neil saw himself as a NASA astronaut but he was bewildered to find himself back in high school and with his old girlfriend.

It was Kurt who was most interested in using five years' knowledge to his own advantage, going as far as marrying a future rock star to gain the riches. In Sarah's case, the opportunity to relive the years was darker: She was reunited with her husband but also had to face the emotional pain of being together again with her young son, who had died of cancer in the original timeline. But Sarah also had a heart. When the story of a serial child killer resurfaced in the news, she recalled details about the crimes from the original timeline and was determined to take steps and make sure it would not happen again. Angela had to deal with her father, a senator, and was able to use her knowledge and change the course of their lives.

In each episode the producers carefully balanced the private lives of the *Odyssey* crew with

Odyssey 5's Leslie Silva, left, Tamara Craig Thomas, Peter Weller, Sebastian Roche and Christopher Gorham (© Columbia/Tri-Star).

their ongoing mission to hunt down Sentients and Synthetics. Sentients were nano-technological creatures living inside computers, created and let loose by Dr. Naran Chandra. Synthetics were human-looking beings with a mysterious and deadly agenda that could be tied in with the fate of the planet five years in the future. "The whole concept behind it was that there were races of artificial beings that were generated by intelligence that formed on the Internet and were living amongst us, so what you were seeing was the rise of artificial life that would somehow lead to the destruction of the world," explains Coto.

Coto compares these beings with Cylons on the new *Battlestar Galactica*. In that show, the villainous Baltar believes that he sees the humanoid Number Six because of an implanted chip in his head. Notes Coto, "For second season we had planned out a whole arc where some of these artificial life forms appear only in your mind, which is interesting, because that's what's happening on *Battlestar Galactica*. So we were kind of playing in the same sandbox."

As an example of how the *Odyssey 5* team would cross swords with Synthetics and Sentients, consulting producer Alan Brennert turned in a script he called "The Trouble with Harry," an off-beat series episode because it was, essentially, a comedy.

"The thing that appealed to me about *Odyssey 5* was that it was to some extent a character-driven show, and those character stories actually grew organically out of the central premise," says Brennert, a veteran genre screenwriter who also worked on *Twilight Zone* and *The Outer Limits*. "It wasn't just a show about people going back in time five years to save the earth—the *Odyssey* crew also couldn't resist trying to fix what went wrong in their own lives in those five years. The characters' private lives and personal tragedies are given added urgency and poignancy by the central premise. The best-remembered SF-fantasy on television has had that combination of character drama wedded to a core SF concept."

In Brennert's story, a Sentient inhabiting a Synthetic body named Harry Mudd locates the *Odyssey 5* team to warn them that a Sentient named Phaedra is preparing to destroy the planet by hijacking a SuperCollider physics experiment. The *Odyssey 5* team found themselves pursued by other Synthetics attempting to stop Harry in his efforts. A *Star Trek* fan will recognize that the Sentient has taken on the name of one of Trekdom's favorite characters, Harry Mudd, as played by

Roger C. Carmel in two of the original series' episodes.

Playing Harry was actor Ted Raimi, who was a regular in the *Xena* fantasy television series. Raimi played Harry in a very goofy way, experiencing life as a human for the first time and absorbing life around him with wide-eyed wonder, resulting in quite a few comedic situations.

There are numerous in-jokes and comics references embedded in the story. In a scene where the *O5* team is escaping from Synthetics pursuing them in a van, Harry ran alongside the *O5* team's van and pulled himself in. The familiar "Bionic" sound effect used by Steve Austin in *The Six Million Dollar Man* accompanied Harry's jog. Later, Harry uttered a snide Spider-Man joke to Sarah's son at a playground. Years later, Raimi's brother, Sam, directed the blockbuster *Spider-Man* feature film, in which Ted appeared in a cameo.

"We just auditioned a bunch of actors, and Ted was far and away the best of them," recalled Brennert. "Most of the actors played Harry as a cartoonish nerd, but Ted had a grounded quality about his performance that I thought was essential. Even though he was playing what was, let's face it, a pretty outlandish character — a sentient computer program in humanoid form — the audience needed to feel empathy for him, and Ted brought a very endearing, vulnerable quality to the role, along with his considerable comic talent."

"Trouble with Harry" also challenged Brennert to believably supply "technobabble" dialogue describing the nature of the SuperCollider physics experiment, which had the potential of creating a massive planetary implosion. Researching all that physics jargon, says Brennert, made his head hurt. "All [of it] is taken from real experiments with particle accelerators. Strangelets, gluons, strange matter ... you think I could make this stuff up? I showed the episode to my friend [SF novelist and scientist] Greg Bear and he was impressed by the use of science in the story."

Because *Odyssey 5* was on a pay cable network, the writers had wider latitude in how scenes could be written. Brennert points out, "I would never have even considered writing the *menage-a-quatre* scene with Harry, Kurt, Sherry and Shari had the series not been on Showtime, and yet I think it proved to be an essential step in Harry's understanding of humankind — and pretty damn funny, too."

Melinda Snodgrass remarks, "The characters didn't have to be as pleasant as they had to be on network television. They could have harder, rougher edges. People like Steven Bochco get to do that, but oftentimes, it's not as easy to have strife between your main characters. You can use stronger language and you can also dig a little deeper into the characters and into some uncomfortable places that network television doesn't generally go. It frees you up to present people in many more facets, and some of those facets are very attractive."

"Overall the series went a little overboard at times on language, though it was nice having the freedom to use the words if you felt the scene warranted them," says Brennert.

Odyssey 5 ended at 20 episodes not because of poor ratings, but because Showtime made a decision to get out of science fiction and progress into urban dramas. "It's kind of like what happened with *Enterprise* on UPN. They've made similar decisions," says Coto.

"The show was doing very well for them in the ratings," says Coto, "So it was kind of an odd decision not to bring the show back. We later found out that SF was being phased out." As a package, the last six episodes were held back by Columbia/Tri-Star's corporate parent. "Sony wanted to sell the show somewhere else," explains Coto. "Showtime wanted to air those six episodes immediately, but Sony asked them not to. They wanted to hold those episodes in a package for whomever might pick up the show."

But the marketing effort to sell *Odyssey 5* elsewhere failed, and the only remaining option was allowing Showtime to air the remaining episodes—*25 months later*! In its original run, *Odyssey 5* ended with "Skin" in September 2002, then returned to the airwaves as two-hour episodes over a three-week period on October 2004.

"I'm just heartsick that Showtime didn't continue with the show," says Melinda Snodgrass. "I just keep hoping they'll bring it back. I thought it was growing and getting ever more interesting. I keep hoping that someone will look again at *Odyssey 5* and go, 'You know, this is really good. We really didn't explore the promises of this show....' I would be there in a heartbeat if I had the chance to write for the show. It was a great idea and what a terrific cast."

Coto remarks, "It was a very intelligent, adult science fiction series for people who not only didn't like SF but for people who loved to read SF. We were trying to get away from simple plots of aliens and using bug-eyed monsters and

Sebastian Roche and Tamara Craig Thomas *in Odyssey 5* (© Columbia/Tri-Star).

Star Trek Enterprise, Coto appeared at a Star Trek convention, he was lobbed many questions about *Odyssey 5* by fans. "That was kind of surprising because I was there to talk about *Star Trek*. And those people all commented on how they felt it was a smart show that challenged them."

Star Peter Weller appeared in two episodes of *Star Trek Enterprise* and got to reminisce with Coto. "He said a lot of people still stop him and talk about *Odyssey 5*. And it's the same with the other actors, who are recognized and the question they are always asked is, 'How does it end?'"

That remains a closely guarded secret. "I'm still holding out hope there may be ways to resurrect the show in another form, maybe," Coto says. "I'll let a few years go by and I may try to restart the show. I still think it was a great premise. It was on the wrong network. If I get it started somewhere else, even if it means I have to use a new cast, I'll just start off from scratch. I would still want to hold onto that concept."

The notion of *Odyssey 5* returning to the airwaves to complete their mission is not unusual. Kenneth Johnson's *Alien Nation*, another SF series that was cut down after one season, managed to return as a series of five movies-of-the-week in 1995, five years after its demise. Bill Bixby's *Incredible Hulk* returned as three movies-of-the-week six years after the series' 1982 cancellation. Steve Austin and Jaime Sommars returned in three "Bionic" movies-of-the-week in the 1990s. The most spectacular example of this trend was Joss Whedon's short-lived 2002 series *Firefly*: The show was revived as a moderately successful 2005 feature film titled *Serenity*.

One day, if all goes well, *Odyssey 5* will launch again.

phasers and try to tell really challenging SF concepts, mixed with wrenching personal stories. And a lot of people have seen the show. It kind of got me on to *Enterprise*. So there are many fans of the show out there who know how good it was."

Snodgrass says that if there was one quibble she had about the show's evolution, she would have urged Coto not to introduce the Synthetics so early. "I think they got bodies to use and go among the world a little sooner than I wanted," she says. "I wanted that sense of creepy unknown, without knowing exactly what's going on. I would have wanted that to go on a little longer."

Years later when, as an executive producer on

Cast Notes

Peter Weller (Capt. Chuck Taggart): A graduate of the American Academy of Dramatic Arts,

Peter became a member of the Actor's Studio in New York. He's appeared on stage in *Full Circle* and *Summer Brave*. Genre fans know him as the title characters in *RoboCop* (1987) and *The Adventures of Buckaroo Banzai: Across the Eighth Dimension* (1985); he also starred in *Naked Lunch* (1991) and *Mighty Aphrodite* (1995). Also a director, Peter helmed episodes of *Odyssey 5*, *Homicide: Life on the Street* and *Monk*. He was Capt. Paul Gallico in a 2005 TV mini-series remake of *The Poseidon Adventure*. In addition to acting, Peter has lectured at Syracuse University on the history of Hollywood and the Roman Empire. He has a Masters degree in Roman and Renaissance Art.

Sebastian Roche (Kurt Mendel): A French actor, Sebastian is a graduate of Conservative National Superieur d'Art Dramatique in Paris. On TV he's starred in *Roar*, *Earthsea* (2004), a Sci-Fi Channel mini-series based on Ursula LeGuin's novel of the same name, and played a recurring role on *General Hospital*. A recent film credit was *Beowulf* (2007).

Christopher Gorham (Neil Taggart): See *Jake 2.0* Cast Notes.

Leslie Silva (Sarah Forbes): Leslie has appeared in a wide variety of TV series: *Cosby*, *Providence*, *Gideon's Crossing* and *Star Trek: Enterprise* ("Daedalus"). She had a recurring role on *The Agency*.

Tamara Craig Thomas (Angela Perry): An actress from Toronto, Tamara is a founding member of the Blue Sphere Alliance Theater Company. Her strong theater background includes performances in *The Great Experiment*, *Absence in the Afternoon*, and Ted Tally's Off-Broadway production *Hooters*. In film, she starred in *Tromeo and Juliet* and *Terra Incognita*. On TV she's guest starred on *Star Trek: Voyager* ("Life Line") and *The Dead Zone* ("Symmetry").

The Outer Limits

(1995–2002)

An anthology series based on the original 1960s show created by Leslie Stevens. Stories explored the human condition in the face of monsters, aliens, time travel, space travel and cutting-edge technology.

Narrator: Kevin Conway ("The Control Voice"); *Creator–Program Consultant:* Leslie Stevens; *Executive Producers:* Pen Densham, Richard Barton Lewis, John K. Watson, Jonathan Glassner *Year 3–4*, Sam Egan *Year 5–6*, Mark Stern *Year 6–7*, Matthew Hastings, Steve Aspis, Michael Sloan *Year 7*; *Co-Executive Producers:* Manny Coto *Year 1*, Michael Cassutt, Jonathan Glassner *Year 2*, Scott Shepherd *Year 2*, Sam Egan *Year 3*, Brad Wright *Year 3–4*, Carleton Eastlake *Year 4*, Chris Ruppenthal *Year 5*, Grant Rosenberg, Alan Katz, Brent Karl-Clackson *Year 6–7*; *Supervising Producers:* Brad Wright *Year 2*, Brad Markowitz, Chris Ruppenthal *Year 4*, James Crocker *Year 7*; *Producers:* Justis Greene *Year 1*, Brent Karl-Clackson *Year 1–5*; *Associate Producers:* Fiona Duncanson *Year 1*, Sally Dixon *Year 2–3*, Ben Brafman *Year 4–6*, Diane Panozzo *Year 7*, Roger Mattiussi; *Co-Producers:* Will Dixon *Year 5*, Robert Habros *Year 5–6*, Ron McLeod, Scott Peters *Year 6*; Gordon Smith, Nora O'Brien

Year 7, *Executive Consultant:* Joseph Stefano; *Creative Consultants:* Manny Coto, Jonathan Glassner *Year 1*, Scott Shepherd *Year 2*; *Advisors:* A.L. Katz *Year 5*, Naren Shankar *Year 5*, Steve Aspis *Year 7*; *Senior Advisor:* Joseph Stefano *Year 6*; *Directors of Photography:* Phil Linzey, Attila Szalay, Richard Wincenty; *Writers included:* Melinda Snodgrass, Jonathan Glassner, Alan Brennert, James Crocker, Sam Egan, Scott Shepherd, Carleton Eastlake, Chris Ruppenthal, Alan Katz, Scott Peters, Grant Rosenberg; *Directors included:* Stuart Gillard, Paul Lynch, Allan Eastman, Brad Turner, Michael Robison, Mario Azzopardi, Rebecca DeMornay, Neill Fearnley, Peter DeLuise, Ken Girotti, Adam Nimoy, Helen Shaver, Steven Weber, James Head, Jeff Woolnough, Mike Rohl, Brent Karl-Clackson; *Guest Stars included:* Beau Bridges, Lloyd Bridges, William Sadler, Bruce Davison, Robert Patrick, Nicole DeBoer, Michael Dorn, Alyssa Milano, Nick Mancuso, Robert Foxworth, Brent Spiner,

Howie Mandel, David McCallum, Melissa Gilbert, Robert Hays, Cliff Robertson, David Ogden Stiers, Michael Ironside, John DeLancie, Sean Patrick Flanery, Bruce Boxleitner, Jessica Steen, Kristin Lehman, Laura Harris, Alex Diakun, Robert Duncan McNeill, Marlee Matlin, Leonard Nimoy, Mark Hamill, Greg Evigan, Saul Rubinek, Kevin Nealon, Nicholas Lea, Charlton Heston, Hal Holbrook, Amanda Plummer, Heather Graham, Bruce Harwood, Eric McCormack, Kirsten Dunst, Cynthia Nixon, Nathan Fillion, Dennis Haysbert

Showtime/Sci-Fi Channel/Trilogy Entertainment Group/Alliance-Atlantis Communications/ MGM Television Distribution; 1995–2002; 60 minutes; 153 episodes; DVD status: Seasons 1–4, 7 "Theme Collections"

Against great odds, one of television's unique SFTV series was resurrected for modern audiences in the spring of 1995. *The Outer Limits,* a black-and-white series created in 1963 by Leslie Stevens and produced by Joseph Stefano for the ABC network, had become known over the years as one of the genre's most iconic creations. It stood with *The Twilight Zone* as one of the 1960s' most memorable efforts. The new *Outer Limits* that scrambled the television sets of Showtime subscribers in 1995, and ran for a solid seven years, is the longest-running SF anthology in television history.

Viewers today are trained to watch series with continuing characters, not thematic anthologies with stand-alone stories each week. "Television audiences are by and large resistant to the anthology format, and because of that, studios and networks are resistant to developing them," notes writer Alan Brennert. "You see this reflected in so many aspects of popular culture. Look at the feature film business. Endless numbers of sequels, attempts to take something that by rights can support only one movie and turn it into a 'brand.' Did we really need three *Matrix* films? Did *Rush Hour* really cry out for two more hours in which to expand on its weighty theses, hence *Rush Hour 2?* Book business, same thing, you have endless numbers of fantasy series, trilogies, quatrologies."

But this show succeeded where many others have failed. How—and why—did *The Outer Limits* return to television? First of all, this was a show with a pedigree. Many 1960s kids watched the show, grew into adults in the 1990s and had fond (and nightmarish) memories of it. MGM-TV's strategy was to tap that audience as well as attract new ones who would look upon their *Outer Limits* as a new concept (and perhaps rediscover the original show on home video as well). This is typical corporate branding of their assets, hoping for synergy in both directions.

In 1991, MGM-UA, one of Hollywood's most prestigious film studios, was in financial crisis. Pieces of the company were being sold to various buyers. But in 1994 Frank Mancuso, formerly the president of Paramount, bought the company from Credit Lyonnais, a bank in France. He hired John Symes away from Paramount and anointed him as president of MGM-TV, with a goal to rebuild the company. "Frank Mancuso was searching for a recognizable name or title that could be turned into a TV series, *à la Friday the 13th,*" recalls co-executive producer Michael Cassutt. "He zeroed in on *Outer Limits,* which others had tried to revive for a decade or more, only to fail when they couldn't get Joe Stefano or Leslie Stevens to agree to a deal.

"Stevens had created *Outer Limits,* then brought in Stefano to run it. If you look at the original credits, you see the names 'Villa-diStefano and Daystar'—their two companies. It wasn't impossible to make a deal with either Stevens or Stefano individually, but agreements kept falling apart when each man had to agree to the other's involvement. I don't know how Mancuso finally persuaded them to agree, but he did."

MGM-TV's deal with Showtime to provide 150 films over seven years helped guarantee that the series would return. That the company finally decided to do something with the property was fitting because there had already been ill-fated attempts to bring the show back in various forms. In 1983, MGM-UA asked Stevens for a feature idea, and Stefano tried taking the property to Paramount, but MGM-UA wouldn't sell the title. In 1985, ABC wanted a "backdoor pilot" movie but when the TV series *Amazing Stories* and *Twilight Zone* didn't fare well, the notion was abandoned.

It took 10 years for the idea of a revival to catch TV executives' interest; this time it was an effort to discover if the series could help rebuild the company's television division.

To recreate the series, John Symes and MGM-TV approached one of Hollywood's busiest production companies, the Trilogy Entertainment Group, as managed by partners Pen Densham, Richard Barton Lewis and John Watson. They were high-profile film producers on major feature projects like Kevin Costner's *Robin Hood: Prince of Thieves* (1991), director Ron Howard's

Backdraft (1991) and Jeff Bridges' *Blown Away* (1994). They were also known for producing the short-lived science fiction series *Space Rangers* (1993).

"We've been primarily a feature company," said former Trilogy partner and series executive producer Richard Barton Lewis. "The TV area we wanted to explore. The economics of it is extremely competitive. It's gotten more and more competitive on a financial level. There's so much risk involved in mounting a show. What a great opportunity. We have this huge platform to play with. What a great way to tell these stories we want to tell and get a message across."

In his first step to building up the show, Pen Densham, a fan of the original series, wrote what he envisioned as the series bible. He wasn't aware of, and didn't see until later, Joseph Stefano's original "Canons of the Outer Limits" as reprinted in David Schow's book *The Outer Limits Companion*.

Densham's bible set the tone and style of the modern incarnation. In all, he wrote about 15 pages of material, including revisions of the initial four-page document. In its original draft, Densham challenged those who would create the show to (figuratively and literally) push the boundaries of the storytelling beyond what had already been seen on television, because we live in a modern technological age, and because for today's audience the show would be a "celebration of the human imagination."

The new *Outer Limits* was defined as tales of "science gone wrong." Stories generally focused on scientists experimenting with the latest cutting edge technology, time travel, encounters with hostile aliens or fantastic flights to other worlds. It also included science fiction "gothic horror," a mood or tension that permeated many episodes of the original 1960s series. The producers strove to be as original as they could with their storytelling, willing to take risks and being prepared to fail in the process.

Kevin Conway took on the narrating chores performed in the original series by Vic Perrin. "God, how we've evolved over the last 30 years, is incredible," said Conway. "The subject matters of the old shows were more about aliens— us-versus-them kind of thing. These [new] shows are more about human beings against themselves. In a sense, we've become less willing to paint everyone coming from outer space as a bad guy. Which we were in the 1960s. That show was, in a way, 'black and white.' This one, you're never really sure until the show was over, who the bad guys are.

It may look like the bad guys are the microbes, or some sort of alien force. Sometimes it's the human beings themselves that cause the problem."

The original series was often assailed by such criticisms, of being little more than a creature feature. But while the black-and-white series had its share of marauding extraterrestrials, placed there as ratings grabbers by a nervous network, it also had stories such as reluctant aliens who were being coerced by the U.S. military to conduct mind-bending tests on unsuspecting soldiers, disabled and mentally challenged children being brought together by aliens so they could live out their lives on a planet free from their limitations, an android of the future seeking the whereabouts of the entire human race and a secret agent who infiltrates a party of stranded aliens by being transformed into one of the creatures— only to decide to return to their home planet, where he finds personal peace of mind. Actors such as Martin Sheen, Martin Landau, Robert Duvall, William Shatner and Sally Kellerman were cast. Writer Mark Holcomb of *Salon* categorized the 1960s *Outer Limits* as a series that "confronted audiences with edgy inquiries into the human predicament, supercharged with expressionistic visuals, eye-popping monsters and resolutely adult themes," claiming it was "deceptively influential and virtually impossible to duplicate."

Often, when the next generation re-imagines an old series, the new producers are cautious not to reveal any negative feelings they had towards the original, for fear of alienating older viewers. But Atlantis Films co-founder (and production partner in the new *Outer Limits*) Seaton MacLean offered a politically incorrect comment to *TV Guide* in 1994. "Boy, were they ever bad!" he exclaimed after screening several old episodes. "I can't believe these shows scared me as a kid."

Because the resurrection was ported into a pay cable station, producers had freer rein to ramp up the suspenseful intensity (conveyed via monster makeup) of the stories. A new element was also added: occasional female nudity. In a number of episodes, notably "Caught in the Act" with Alyssa Milano and "Valerie 23" with Sofia Shinas, nudity was used as part of the storytelling. "We only did nudity if it was integral to the story," recalls executive producer Jonathan Glassner. "We averaged maybe four or five episodes a season that had it. A lot of times, frankly, it's for shock value. A robot who's built to be a companion, and suddenly takes off her clothes and is willing to do anything, literally, is shocking." As the series progressed, this element was abandoned for more pure storytelling.

Producers also weren't shy about mounting remakes of their favorite episodes from the original series ("I, Robot," "Nightmare," "The Inheritors," and "A Feasibility Study").

"It's this notion of a bridge to the past," explained writer and co-executive producer Sam Egan. "The kind of storytelling that made the original series a success is really the same kind of storytelling that we're involved with in this series. We've got a lot more bells and whistles today in terms of visual effects and in 1990s prosthetics, all of the camera trickery that's part of the new technology. But, what it comes down to in the end is good ideas and good storytelling which is the heart of science fiction and it just seems a natural to go back to the original series and [wonder] what's compelling then that would be compelling today?"

MGM-TV decided that the production would film in Vancouver, Canada, and so the Canadian production entity Atlantis Films (now Alliance-Atlantis) joined the team. For the first six episodes, writer Michael Cassutt became the series' co-executive producer, the showrunner on location. But he was faced with a situation where the program had just a series bible and no scripts. It all had to be built from scratch.

The series' premiere episode was a Melinda Snodgrass adaptation of SF novelist George R.R. Martin's novella, "Sandkings." It starred Beau Bridges, Lloyd Bridges and Helen Shaver. This story depicted how one man stole some alien sand from a laboratory and conducted his own unauthorized experiments in his barn. He descended into madness, trying to play god with alien creatures with tragic consequences. It echoed original series episodes like "The Zanti Misfits" (alien insects with human heads) and "The Invisible Enemy" (a "sand shark" on an alien world). There were also, unfortunately, echoes of a 1975 William Castle film called *Bug* starring Bradford Dillman, with a similar storyline of a scientist studying intelligent cockroaches in his basement.

The Oscar-winning feature film actress Marlee Matlin was originally going to play the wife in "Sandkings" according to Snodgrass, who had worked with, and gotten to know Matlin in the 1991 legal drama *Reasonable Doubts*. "I was the perfect person to do it because it's very difficult to write for a non-hearing actress. Mike Cassutt and I talked a lot about the difficulties with 'Sandkings'

because while George's novella is brilliant, it's not really terribly filmable. You have a loathsome leading character. He's just a horrible human being. No one is going to be spending two hours talking with this person. That was just not going to work."

As a result, the marching orders were to take a futuristic story that took place on another planet, and custom tailor it especially for present-day Earth and for Matlin. "Having Marlee, it became about communication," notes Snodgrass. "Communication between the husband and wife, the father and the son, and the Sandkings and their 'creator.' That's what was in my mind when I wrote my draft of the script."

Then something unexpected happened. "MGM panicked," she said. "They got cold feet about going with Marlee. Because it was the two-hour series opener, MGM said, 'No, no! We don't want to open with Marlee!' I suppose their feeling was that it was a new show, a weird setup, and you add a deaf actress. I thought it was unfortunate because she's a terrific actress. And I really liked what I had done with the script. I had to go back and rewrite it for a speaking actress."*

At this juncture, the script was adjusted to accommodate the Bridges acting family as the featured players. Trilogy producer John Watson had a relationship with the Bridges, having worked with Jeff Bridges on *Blown Away,* and he thought bringing them into the project would be a good audience grabber.

Story editor Chris Dickie shares insights into how stories were selected for the series. He got the job on March 1996, and found the last six scripts of second season awaiting him.

Life had changed for Dickie when he enrolled in a continuing education night school course in screenwriting, and his assignment was to write a one-hour script. "I'd always enjoyed science fiction and wrote it!" says Dickie.

"'Worlds Apart' was a space story," he says. "I heard a remake of a Carpenters song, called 'Superstar,' which had been remade by Sonic Youth, an alternative rock band. They used sound distortion techniques. They made the song sound as if it came from long distances.... And I thought 'What if...?'—and all these stories begin with 'What if...?'—a message came from somewhere in space? And was in fact, a piece of music? It was a way of connecting to lovers who had been separated by time and space. How does one say to the other, 'I love you,' unless you can say goodbye

---

*Marlee Matlin later appeared in an episode titled "The Message."

in the most effective way? And I thought, 'Maybe it's with a piece of music.'"

These ideas sparked Dickie to write a script where an astronaut passes through a wormhole in space and crashlands into the ocean of a planet light years away from Earth. Thanks to the wormhole's space-time distortion and a communications device, Lieutenant Christopher Lindy is able to communicate with his superiors on Earth — and to his lover, Nancy McDonald.

"[Lt. Lindy] has the song that they loved when they were together," explains Dickie. "Most relationships have a song that both like. Somehow, music plays an integral part in human love relationships. That's why he had the piece of music with him and played it in the end when he knew he wasn't going back.

"And I hadn't really thought it would be an *Outer Limits* script, although I suppose maybe, in the back of my mind, I was being very aware of the program. I realized that it might certainly work," says Dickie.

In the fall of 1995, with a script in hand, Dickie submitted a story titled "Remittance Man" which was accepted and put into production in January 1996 under the title "Worlds Apart." "That was the very first thing I ever sold!" says Dickie.

Dickie is a rare Hollywood success story: He was someone who managed to walk through the guarded door on his first try. In the process, he made a remarkably seamless transition from one successful career to another. Prior to landing this position, he was a successful entertainment lawyer for Atlantis Films, one of the series' production partners. Dickie had the advantage of not being a total stranger to the staffers on the series. "I was lucky to be able to get it in and get it read. Brad Wright and Jonathan Glassner, they all liked it," he says.

Dickie was given an opportunity to rewrite a script titled "Paradise," and on the strength of that work he was offered the story editor staff position. One of the first things that Dickie had to do was get clear in his mind, "What is an *Outer Limits* story?"

"We're first concerned with what the script will *not* be: That it's not a *Twilight Zone* story, that it's not a *Poltergeist*-type story. We looked for stories that have a science basis that could be explained to a certain extent. Generally, most stories tend to extrapolate from sciences we know now. We looked for stories that had a strong parable. Most of the stories are small morality tales. We all looked for twists as well.

"The greatest challenge among the staffers was to find that fresh idea, that unique science fiction twist that was never been done before on television but one that's within the scope of the budget.

"The great thing about science fiction now is that it doesn't have to be limited to alien invasions. We've done a lot of stories— we pride ourselves on the diversity of the tales we told —from medical stories to transformation stories to time travel stories to alien to far-future stories to space stories."

Taking story "pitches" from prospective *Outer Limits* writers was another part of the job. "We had a script coordinator who read a lot of submissions that came in from agents' writing samples. Some, but very few, unsolicited scripts had a very good eye for what we're looking for."

The greatest problem with outsiders who never pitched to the show before, said Dickie, was that at least 50 percent of them failed to watch more than a few *Outer Limits* segments. Dickie said that one out of 20 prospective writers were successful in selling a story idea. (And Dickie belonged to this exclusive club.)

"One out of 20 was a bit low," Dickie says. "Sometimes you got germs of ideas. For example, from the writer of 'From Within,' we got pitched an idea. In its entirety it didn't really work. Either it was too clichéd, or it didn't fit into what we're doing. You may have an element that is so neat you talk about it. That can sometimes lead to some great tales.... I've been approached by friends ... who thought, 'Oh, I've got a great idea for a story!'" They would proceed to tell a story but as Dickie absorbed the content, he would ask the simple question, "How does he manage this? How is this character able to bring people back from the dead all the time?"

"Oh, he's an alien!"

Raised eyebrow.

"That's a bad pitch," says Dickie wryly. "You can't explain everything just by saying 'Oh, he's an alien.'"

In another instance, someone pitched a story about a young couple that moves into a new neighborhood and discovers their host is being haunted by a troll. "First of all, is it a haunted story?" wondered Dickie. "If it is, then it doesn't belong here, unless you have some sort of scientific exploration. Where does this troll come from? Why is it there? Some people get fantasy and science fiction mixed up. They do share a border, but they are two distinct beasts. *Twilight Zone* played more with both camps very successfully."

As the show developed, many episodes emerged as SF-TV genre classics. Arguably, "Sandkings" successfully recaptured the mood and tenor of the original series with modern special effects. "Quality of Mercy" featured *tour de force* performances by its lead actors, Robert Patrick and Nicole DeBoer, as human POWs thrown into an alien prison. Brad Wright's story, designed to be a "bottle" episode, leads to a shocking conclusion.

"I loved doing 'Quality of Mercy," says DeBoer. "For an actor it was so great, because it was like a little play. It was just a two-hander, myself and the actor Robert Patrick in a room. And the director, Brad Turner, was so great too, because that's a challenge for a director as well, to just be stuck in this one room all the time and keep it interesting for an hour. That script was very strong. It was really well written — it had a great sort of twist ending to it. I was quite proud about that one."

Author Steven Barnes turned in "A Stitch in Time," where actress Amanda Plummer was a time-traveling executioner and Michelle Forbes was the FBI agent in pursuit. "We succeeded in telling a story that had a strong emotional hook," says executive producer Richard Barton Lewis. "This was a woman's story almost exclusively. You had not just Amanda Plummer, but you had [Michelle Forbes] playing opposite her. It really is a woman's investigative detective who's trying to piece together a series of crimes. You have one woman tracking down another woman who's killing men before they commit horrible crimes. It's a real interesting morality tale and it's a real good character story. Amanda gave us a great performance and that's why she won [the Emmy]. It's a very emotional and hard-driving story."

In "Trial by Fire," Robert Foxworth played a president of the United States who, on the eve of his inauguration, entered an emergency situation where an extraterrestrial ship was detected on its way to Earth. The question was: Was it hostile or friendly? His decision-making determined Earth's fate.

"I thought Robert Foxworth was great," says director Jonathan Glassner. "I couldn't have asked for a better actor. The whole cast was wonderful, which made my job easier as a director. It was a tough episode to do because basically we had five actors in a room for an hour. And that's really hard to sustain, for an hour of television, and not have it get boring.

"I insisted that we have multiple levels, different heights, on the set. And ramps and stairs and railings, and things that the actors could play with and move around. So that helped quite a bit. We also did about 75 percent of the show on Stead-icam. Which is something that's not usually done."

SF novelist Larry Niven's short story "Inconstant Moon," adapted by Wright, was an exploration of how to spend the final moments before Armageddon. "It's a very prophetic story," noted Lewis. "What if you had one day to live and what if you're afraid to tell everyone else? That's quite a burden. It's like *On the Beach* by Nevil Shute which became the film with Gregory Peck. It's very compelling.

"I loved the visuals on that. What we're doing on television is extraordinary looking. That whole skyline bursting into flames was incredible. [Visual effects supervisor] Steve Anker and all those guys in special effects really nailed it. It was a little slow, but it was a challenge."

A remake of one of the original series' most celebrated episodes, "A Feasibility Study," featured actor David McCallum, who had appeared two times in the original series. In this Joseph Stefano story, an entire neighborhood was snatched by aliens for slave labor, and the Earthlings gathered together to make a fateful decision, one that would save Earth from destruction.

In "Feasibility's" chilling climax, the kidnapped humans decided to end their lives in order to save humanity. They allowed themselves to be infected by an alien disease so that the aliens couldn't use them as slaves. Said producer Sam Egan, "Even in rehearsals when we were casting, every time we hear the line, 'I've taken my daughter's hand. Will someone take mine?' you get a chill down your spine because you realize its significance. It's human sacrifice that's involved. It's a very powerful moment."

Egan added that having the original writer, Stefano, orchestrate the remake story was exciting for all those connected with the production. "He's a wonderful talent and has a remarkable imagination. He's been something of a patriarch and an inspiration to all of the writers on the current show."

"Pen [Densham] asked me if I was interested in doing a remake of one of the original stories, and that got me excited," said Stefano. "I hadn't been inclined to write an episode, so this seemed a good way." But interestingly, says Stefano, the writer's freedoms today are not any different than in the 1960s as far as content. "The same rules and laws apply today as they did then. There are still things they don't like and won't have in the script. There's a great myth about the freedom of cable television. It's bullshit, frankly. It's not there. It depends on who is running what. The people who are running these have their own attitudes, their own tastes, about what should be on television. So we're no different today than we were in the early 1960s. As a matter of fact, there are more people today censoring and telling us what we should do."

For the series' 100th episode, in its fifth season, Sam Egan penned one of its most emotional and resonant episodes ever. He wrote a story titled "Tribunal," about Aaron Zgierski, a modern-day Nazi hunter (actor Saul Rubinek) who pursues an old man named Robert Greene, whom he believes was a Nazi lieutenant. Karl Rademacher is a terrible Auschwitz concentration camp commandant responsible for the death of Zgierski's father's wife and child. But without any direct evidence, how could he bring the man to justice? Because of Nicholas Prentice, a meddling time traveler (actor Alex Diakun), the opportunity suddenly presents itself and the evidence he wants becomes available under mysterious circumstances. Curious about the man, Aaron follows him to a local hotel where he discovers Nazi paraphernalia. Because of a mysterious antique watch—the source of the time traveler's ability to transverse the ages—Aaron accidentally transports himself back to March 1944 and the Auschwitz camps where his father was incarcerated. There, he witnesses firsthand, the horrors of the Nazis' crimes.

Still in possession of the watch, Nicholas realizes what has happened and whisks Aaron back to the present age. He explains to a frustrated Aaron that his allowances to adjust the timestream are limited. But another problem is created when an enraged Aaron takes the Nazi gun in desperation and goes to execute Robert Greene (formerly Rademacher). In a confrontational scene under gunpoint, Aaron accuses Robert of being Karl Rademacher, and threatens to shoot him, but Nicholas offers a different solution.

Dressed in Nazi uniforms, Aaron and Nicholas transport a disoriented Robert Greene, now clad as an Auschwitz "resident," back to the camps in 1944. In an ironic twist of fate, his younger self, the commandant, executes his older self. But Aaron has one last legacy in mind: He snatches his father's young daughter and orders Nicholas to return them to the present. In the story's coda, the girl is presented to his father who is astonished to discover his child ... still alive....

What made the episode emotional and resonant for Egan was the fact that his own father, Leo

Egan, was a survivor of the camp. Sam wrote this episode as a tribute to his parent and to the wife and daughter who did not survive.

"Tribunal" was filmed in February 1999, at a chicken farm in Port Coquitlam, in the outskirts of Vancouver Canada. Actor Alex Zahara played Karl Rademacher, the young lieutenant running the camps. "We had 150 people playing Auschwitz internees," recalls Zahara. "It was very realistic. They rebuilt the gates of Auschwitz. It was hundreds of feet long. 'Arbeit Macht Frie' 'Work will set you free' written on the gates. It was very cold. It was snowing. Up to our ankles in mud."

Egan's work was so powerful that Zahara admits the script evoked strong emotions from him. "I read it and cried. As an actor who reads a lot of scripts, it was the first time I've ever just started crying. I've watched the episode and you can't *not* cry. I read that the same thing happened to Stephen Geaghan, the production designer.

"Singularly, this is the piece I am the most proud of as an actor, that I've ever done. There was truth of the man's life and I was trying to bring justice to that—to *reveal* that life. And to not make this Nazi, this man, a caricature. Make him a real human being as well because Nazis are always portrayed as animals. This monster was a man, he was responsible for his actions, as was everyone else. I had to bring forth the inhumanity of this man, and that's hopefully what I did."

Director Mario Azzopardi simply told Zahara, "This man is bored! He's bored!" That one-liner that gave Zahara a strong view of the soldier. "I played this guy like a heartless, cold son of a bitch," says Zahara. "I felt this guy was a warrior who was a garbage man. He wanted to be in the front, killing for the Third Reich. But instead, he has to take the garbage out. He's so freakin' bored that to amuse himself every morning, he picks one of the prisoners out, kills him and then goes and eats his breakfast.

"The toughest and most memorable part was the opening sequence. My character rides out on a horse, and this man would do this every day. He takes a riding crop, and he would run it over the prisoners, until he picked the lucky one. 'You're the lucky one!' He would execute them in front of everybody. That was our first day of filming.

"I had to commit all this violence! Murdering a Jewish prisoner. Having to shoot my future self in the head. There are feelings that come up having to shoot somebody. It's acting. It's not real. But nonetheless, you have to bring that into your

Actors Alex Diakun, Roman Danylo and Kyra Azzopardi, director Mario Azzopardi and actor Alex Zahara on the set of the *Outer Limits* episode "Tribunal" (courtesy Alex Zahara).

soul — the need to kill. I had some pretty weird dreams, very frightening for about three weeks after that."

The location, the freezing environment, the many extras — all served to starkly evoke the tragedies of ages past. "They cast a lot of European extras," says Zahara. "They wanted people with Russian backgrounds, very much fresh off the boat. They did that as much as possible. There were a lot of people who didn't speak a lot of English. They had an authentic look. When I came out there and rode, and did my riding crop thing, people were really, actually kind of scared. They were standing out in the freezing cold with garbage bags underneath their clothes. We had to give them that because it was so freaking cold.

"When I put my riding crop down, and you see it go, *whack* at the beginning, this woman flinched. That was for real. She wasn't acting. They were being hustled around like prisoners. We had guards around them. People were pushing and shoving."

What made the shoot especially poignant and emotional for Zahara and the production crew, was that Sam Egan invited his father Leo, the

Auschwitz survivor, to the location. Leo's reaction to the proceedings was very strong. "When I first met Leo, he looked like a little man, but as we spoke I realized he was a great man, in strength and survival," recalls Zahara. "When he saw me walk out [in my wardrobe], some of which was actual Nazi memorabilia, I'll never forget it. He just looked up at me, and his eyes just flinched and he turned away, and took a minute. When he came back, he told me all kinds of stuff that just made your hair turn white, stuff we could never show."

Later, Sam Egan told Zahara about further comments made by Leo. "Leo said, 'Samuel, how — how did you do this?! How did you bring this from Germany to here?!'" Zahara recounts. "And Sam said, 'No, Dad, we rebuilt this.' 'How?! It is just like I am standing where I was! How did you do it?!'

"Steve Geaghan is incredible. The art department did all the research. They reproduced the barracks, so much so that a man who had actually stood there, thought they picked up the building and brought it from Germany."

Remarking on his script, Sam Egan quietly says, "I think 'Tribunal' was the finest work we did in seven years of the show and my father couldn't agree more."

The series' sixth season finale, at the time intended to be the series finale, "Final Appeal" brought together Charlton Heston, Robert Loggia, Cicely Tyson, Hal Holbrook and Swoosie Kurtz as Supreme Court justices hearing one of the strangest cases in judicial history: They would decide to review, or support, the ban of technology. The defendant: Dr. Theresa Givens, Amanda Plummer's character from "A Stitch in Time," who was on trial for murder. In this story, writer Sam Egan presented a clever two-hour "clips" show, looking at previous episodes, with the setting of a futuristic courtroom drama in a world where technology and science were outlawed. He used this as a "wraparound" device. "They use technology to 'view' old episodes and their technological uses," explains Egan. "Dr. Theresa Givens used the time travel device, not only to go forward into the future, she brought with her a dozen of the touchstones of science and technology, which our audience will remember as the devices used in six years of *Outer Limits*. One of those devices, being in the presence of an object, can transport those in the proximity to re-experience the history of that object. As exhibits are brought in, the minds of the Supreme Court justices are taken over and are transported back to see these moments in their minds where these devices are used. It is an opportunity for us to go back and re-experience these dramatic moments in which these particular objects are the fulcrum, the crux, of the drama of an episode. It's almost as if the gestalt of the object is being re-experienced. It's a bit of a conceit that the justices of the court literally go through the experience of that objects' life."

"It's a perfect finale to the series," said executive producer Mark Stern in 2000, at the end of the Showtime run. "It's an incredibly well considered, written script that does not take a side on this debate. It tries to discuss and debate what went on in the six years. The performances were amazing. I like the fact that we found a way to do a show that brings clips in from previous shows so that we could end by seeing a lot of what we've done in six years, and see how its relevant to the underlying themes over six years. The show works as its own, as a dramatic episode. But it's a real fitting summary of what we've been trying to do for six years."

Although "Final Appeal" was designed as a series finale, the show returned to the airwaves for a seventh season on the Sci-Fi Channel. "We were told Sci-Fi had enough shows. They didn't need more," says Densham. "They said that the episodes got the same audience ratings, no matter whether they were new ones or reruns. So Sci-Fi made a deal: If we lowered the budget, they would continue to shoot shows. We didn't want to give up on the show because we felt we had a lot of great stories to do. So we worked really hard to try and figure out how we could squeeze the same quality out of a slightly smaller budget. So we got Sci-Fi to agree to let us do that."

Showtime ended the series because of a desire to "freshen up" the programming slate with new material. "They kind of sacrificed us even though they kept the term 'No Limits' as their slogan for years afterward!" says Densham.

After Showtime, the series later ran in syndication, allowing a larger, general audience to be exposed to the anthology. And then, there was the inevitable videotape and DVD aftermarket product sales.

Sci-Fi Channel continued the series as it previously had done with Showtime's *Stargate SG-1* and *Poltergeist: The Legacy*. Behind the scenes, Mark Stern joined the series as executive producer in year six and seven. In contrast to the Showtime run of the series, seventh season had a smaller budget, and one less day shooting for each episode. The seventh season became more of a talky drama, with actors in strong dramatic scenes.

Certain segments were strong enough to spawn sequels, and sometimes with the same characters. For example, "Quality of Mercy" was so popular that writer Brad Wright resurrected Robert Patrick's character and used him in "The Light Brigade." "The Camp," in which humans are corralled by aliens after several generations, spawned "Promised Land" which continued the story but without the original characters. "Valerie 23" explored a female android as a companion and it inspired "Mary 25" as a child nanny. Actor Alex Diakun's character, Nicholas Prentice, who debuted as a time traveler in "Tribunal," reappeared two more times, in "Gettysburg" at the American Civil War and in "Time to Time" where we had a flipside, a glimpse of his futureworld era and how he operated. (Look fast for *Battlestar Galactica*'s Grace Park in a supporting role.)

In the end, the outer limit of the show was found and it ended after seven seasons and 154 episodes.

"I'm incredibly proud that I was able to bring

back a show I had admired," says Densham. "I was able to put imagination on the screen when there was no other show like it. Although I didn't create *The Outer Limits*, I felt I was carrying on a legacy. To me, the concept was to take what the guys who had created it originally and extend it into the future, in a way that honored what they had done. I was a fan of Heinlein, Asimov and Sheckley's short stories. I ate SF as a kid. One thing I made very clear on *Outer Limits*, I don't want to control this. I want to create a structure, a groundwork, where people can go and create the most imaginative things possible. I wrote things, like the Ten Commandments, which was to take risks and do things differently and not to get trapped into cookie cutter-ing. What we did really well was to be innovative and get a great creative team together, and to make a show that was close to impossible. Every costume is different, every character is different, every set is different, every week and yet we were able to maintain that kind of quality. I can't say I did anything more than try to inspire people to succeed. I wanted to be a mentor.

"Mark Stern was there, my partner Richard Lewis had a large role in it, and so did my partner John Watson, but I was the person who had to figure out how to convince both MGM and Showtime that this could be done."

Adds Richard Lewis: "I believe both the original *Outer Limits* series as well as the more contemporary run that I had the pleasure of working on, successfully mined the power of science fiction parables in questioning the human journey. Where can science help advance the human condition and the planet as a whole, and where does man's manipulation of science cross the line ethically, and potentially cause irreparable harm?"

The show received many nominations and awards. Beau Bridges was nominated for an Emmy award for his guest appearance in "Sandkings." Later, Amanda Plummer won the guest star Emmy for "A Stitch in Time." The Cable Ace awards gave the series Best Dramatic Series in 1996 and gave director Stuart Gillard an award for "Sandkings" in 1995.

The Academy of Science Fiction, Fantasy, and Horror Films, which hands out the genre-focused Saturn Awards, gave the series three Saturns for Best Genre Series between 1996 and 1998, and continued to nominate it in the same category from 1999 until 2001. Writers Guild of America gave two awards to Naren Shankar and Harlan Ellison for their teleplay "The Human Operators" (based on Ellison's story), and Scott Peters for "Simon Says." Director Mike Rohl won a Canadian Leo Award for helming "Down to Earth."

The Outer Limits also won several "Canadian Emmys," the Gemini awards, with a total of three statutes (Best Music Score by John Van Tongeren in "Simon Says" and "Tribunal," and Best Short Dramatic Program, "A Stitch in Time") plus 24 nominations.

In all, *The Outer Limits* received 13 awards and 34 nominations which includes the International Monitor Awards, the Canadian Leo awards and the Motion Picture Sound Editors of America.

Notes writer Alan Brennert, "The success of *The Outer Limits* has really brought back MGM-TV from limbo. It was the right name, at the right place and at the right time."

CAST NOTES

Kevin Conway (The Control Voice narrator): A veteran film, stage and voice actor, Kevin has appeared in off-Broadway productions of *One Flew Over the Cuckoo's Nest*, *The Elephant Man*, and *Other People's Money*. On Broadway he's appeared in *Of Mice and Men*. In film, he's had starring roles in *F.I.S.T.*, *Paradise Alley*, *Scarlet Letter*, the 1980 PBS TV movie adaptation of Ursula K. LeGuin's *The Lathe of Heaven* (as Dr. William Haber), and *Thirteen Days* (as a general). He was also Kahless the Klingon in *Star Trek: The Next Generation*'s "Rightful Heir."

SOURCES

Garcia, Frank. "Outer Limits— Reinventing Sci-fi's Classic Anthology for the '90s." *Cinefantastique*, 30:5/6, September 1998.
Holcomb, Mark. "The Outer Limits." Salon.com, April 2002.
Slotek, Jim. "Sci-Fi Boom." *TV Guide* (Canada), May 27, 1995.

Prey
(1998)

*The world is threatened by a superior and deadly new species of man. Dr. Sloane Parker
risks her life trying to learn more about this mysterious race and save her species.*

Cast: Debra Messing (Dr. Sloane Parker), Adam Storke (Tom Daniels), Vincent Ventresca (Dr. Edward Tate), Frankie R. Faison (Ray Peterson), Larry Drake (Dr. Walter Attwood)

Created by: William Schmidt; **Executive Producers:** Charlie Craig, William Schmidt, Rob Thompson; **Co-Executive Producer:** Peter O'Fallon; **Supervising Producer:** Jeremy R. Littman; **Producers:** Phil Parslow, Donald Marcus; **Associate Producer:** Drew Matich; **Writers included:** Chris Levinson, Laurence Andries, William Schmidt, Donald Marcus, Charlie Craig, Jeremy R. Littman; **Directors included:** Winrich Kolbe, Dan Lerner, Bill Corcoran, Jim Charleston, James A. Contner, Ian Toynton, Martha Mitchell, Terrence O'Hara; **Guest Stars included:** Alexandra Hedison, Brian McNamara, Patrick Gorman, Susanna Thompson, Michelle Joyner, Shelley Morrison, Vanessa Bell Calloway, James Morrison, Jennifer Sonnerfield, Kaj-Erik Eriksen, Dwier Brown, Roger Howarth (as Lynch)

ABC-TV/Warner Bros.; January 1998–July 1998; 60 minutes; 13 episodes

Forty thousand years ago, the most advanced species on Earth was wiped out by a powerful new life form — *us*. Now, another new species has evolved — stronger, smarter and dedicated to our annihilation. Leading the fight against them is Dr. Sloane Parker, the bioanthropologist who uncovered their existence. Once again it is survival of the fittest — and this time we are the prey.

That was the weekly narration of *Prey*. The premise postulated that our homo sapiens species developed during the Ice Age and wiped out the inferior Neanderthal Man. Now, global warming has created a similar evolutionary process: A new species of dangerous man has evolved and plans to destroy our "inferior" human race.

The original 1997 pilot film was called *Hungry for Survival*, with *Twin Peaks* actress Sherilyn Fenn cast as Dr. Sloane Parker and Michael Stuhlbarg as her colleague. ABC loved the basic idea but asked for a re-tooled pilot. Debra Messing, the future star of *Will and Grace*, was cast as Sloane and 13 episodes were ordered.

Dr. Parker, a young woman working at Whitney University in California, has her world turned upside down when her mentor, Dr. Ann Coulter (Natalija Nogulich), is murdered in her office. Parker finds the body and sits in a state of shock, tears in her eyes, as police try to piece together the evidence. Parker discovers Coulter's research files have been mysteriously deleted and that the lead FBI detective, Daniels, is bogus— he's actually one of the new species of mankind who has orders to kill her. These supermen want their existence kept secret until they've infiltrated society and arranged for mankind's destruction. However, Daniels is attracted to the resilient Sloane and he can't kill her. Instead, he joins up with her to expose his own race.

But his help doesn't make Sloane's life any easier. Not only is she chased through stairways by a killer, almost blown up in a car and shot at by machine-guns from passing cars, she finds herself falling in love with this emotionally remote species man. And he experiences love for her, a new emotion for him.

One murderous species man named Lynch, who has cut off the heads of five men, targets Sloane. He eventually dies in a ball of flame but his clone continues the hunt.

"People love to be scared," executive producer Charlie Craig noted during *Prey*'s production. "And if you can scare people in a believable way, then they're interested in coming back every week. I like making people think, 'This could happen to me.' We're trying to make it as realistic as possible."

Writer Tracy Torme had high hopes when he agreed to work with his friend, *Prey* creator William Schmidt. But things quickly turned sour. "I had just signed an overall deal with Warner Bros. to create television when they asked me to join the staff of *Prey* in a series of brainstorming sessions that were being used to map out the entire season of episodes," says Torme. "I recall that ABC wanted the show to be serialized. I spent many hot, air conditioner-less days in a large conference room beating out stories for the season. I was going to take a consulting producer credit and write a couple of the episodes at twice the normal scale. Then, Bill Schmidt was fired before shooting began. I had very little respect for the back stabbers on the show who had caused him to be fired and taken his place, so I shocked everyone, who thought I'd just take the money and run, by walking away. I also declined to take a year-long credit because I saw that the show was going to be a very short-lived turkey. I assume some of my ideas were used during the year but I can't say for sure since I never watched the show."

Faryl Saliman Reingold, who currently works as a researcher and writer at the University of Southern California, has fonder memories of the show, but his stint as a *Prey* researcher was also brief. "Bill Schmidt had pitched a few things to ABC, and they were most intrigued by his initial ideas about doing a futuristic series about a new species of dangerously superior humans emerging on Earth. He wrote a pilot filmed as *Hungry for Survival*. Trouble was, Bill was not all that familiar with the genre. Bill and I had been friends for years and knowing I was a genre fan, Bill contacted me to brainstorm ways that the genre could be used for more than just, 'aliens bad, Earth heroes handsome and good.' I sent Bill some favorite *Star Trek: The Next Generation* episodes and in no time flat, Bill had absorbed the 'best of' television, film and published science fiction. His *Hungry for Survival* script was about a species 99.6 percent related to humans. They were 'beyond' humans as we are 'beyond' chimps, who are about 99.6 percent related to us, genetically. The pilot was set about 17 years in the future. Sherilyn Fenn starred as Dr. Sloan Parker, and Sloan's colleague and best friend was Edin Kozarak, a Muslim man who escaped the Bosnian genocide as a child. Ms. Fenn was great, the moodiness of this near-future setting was compelling, and the plot about a human-but-not-human species represented by a charismatic double-agent, played by Adam Storke, was intriguing. ABC picked up the series for 13 episodes, and Bill had the opportunity to staff the show. Bill hired me as a researcher, since the show would be exploring scientific issues and would need some factual grounding. It also gave me an opportunity to work with the writers and perhaps eventually write a script myself."

But those hopes dissolved. "ABC soon wanted Bill to revisit his vision, and coupled him with other writer-producers to make the sweeping changes they wanted, including recasting all the lead actors except Adam. Among the changes were moving the show to the present-day and changing Sloane's best friend from a Muslim man to an all–American guy. With other writer-producers working on the show, it was no longer 'politically correct' to have a researcher who was 'Bill's person,' so my job was eliminated. However, to keep his promise to me, Bill offered me an opportunity to continue working with him as his assistant, mostly developing new projects."

Looking back on his minimal involvement with *Prey*, Reingold notes, "I did like one theme from the original pilot. I didn't think it was as well developed in the scripts of the series. That was, the purpose of the Dominants was first and foremost survival, and only secondarily was that to be 'by any means necessary.' There were times when they seemed more 'evil' in the series, which isn't as interesting to me as 'fighting for survival.' The Dominants thought they were 'doing God's work' in eliminating homo sapiens in favor of themselves, making them deadly and 'right' in their own minds. I also liked the themes of racial tolerance in the original pilot. The series made parallels with systematic 'ethnic cleansing,' such as Germany in the 1940s, and Bosnia, when the series was being made, and Darfur and Tibet today. But I felt the original pilot was more direct by incorporating a character who was a Muslim survivor of the Bosnian genocide. This character was later transformed into Ed Tate in the series."

Indeed, Reingold applauded the original pilot's choice of presenting a Muslim man as a regular. "Bill wanted to have a character who was Muslim and very sympathetic and likable to the audience. This was post–Gulf War and Bill wanted to make a point about racial tolerance, as well as explore many caring, wise and just plain not 'Judeo-Christian' ideas in the Islamic religion and culture. He was also aware that we needed to relate instantly to this man, not just see a 'foreign' face and fear that maybe he wasn't trustworthy. In our brainstorming, I suggested making the character a Bosnian. This would also give the character a very visceral experience of genocide, which was what the Dominants were ominously moving toward committing. And so Sloane's best friend was Edin 'Ed' Kozarak, cast with an actor with a Balkan-Bosnian-type accent. He was later reconfigured to all–American Ed Tate. Edin would have been cool, but so was Ed."

Just before the series got rolling, Reingold provided some interesting input. "I had two particularly interesting and enjoyable research projects during my tenure as researcher.... The first was one I suggested: I prepared a dossier for the writers on how much popular culture and technology can change in just 17 years. With the series originally planned to be set in the near future, the idea was to show a society very close to the one in which we live, but slightly askew from our current reality."

Reingold compiled a time capsule dossier of 1980–1982 to show the writers how things had changed in the past 15 years, giving them an idea of how the next 15 years *might* change. "I had just distributed it to the writers' assistants when we got word that the 'set in the future' concept had been scrapped. It was too expensive for wardrobe, props, picture cars, etc. The other particularly interesting research I had done was on daily practice for a Muslim man, and the history of Muslim culture, especially as experienced in Bosnia. Although the role of Edin Kozarak had been changed to Ed Tate and recast with the wonderful actor Vincent Ventresca, Tate was still supposed to be of Bosnian heritage and still supposed to be a Muslim. Vincent called me to talk to me about Islamic culture. He was very committed to portraying the character's religious beliefs and practices accurately. He asked me to help him to find material and even to meet with Muslim practitioners and teachers who could guide him to making the character real. I was impressed by his desire to make Ed real and to respect Islamic culture and religion. Before we set up any meetings for him, the network changed the character to a regular American guy, 'converting' him from Muslim to, well, not Muslim. That was that."

As for the lead actress of *Prey*, Reingold recalls, "Bill became great friends with Debra Messing. She respected that he had cast her in a role as a very intelligent and courageous scientist. Her previous work was largely in comedies like *Ned and Stacey*. Debra trusted that Bill would 'protect' her character, and make sure she stayed heroic, never becoming a 'damsel in distress.' It was a promise he kept to her. When the show was canceled, everyone was very sad, of course. Bill later told me that he and Debra had a long talk, and she said that she was thinking she needed to go into a comedy to help lighten the unhappiness of losing such a promising series. She had been offered a very offbeat pilot that seemed like a long shot because of its somewhat controversial subject matter, a friendship between a straight woman and a gay man. Bill was very supportive of her taking the offer to do the pilot, and thus Debra became Grace Adler, and TV history was made with *Will & Grace!*"

Although Reingold feels global warming is a legitimate concern, he says in *Prey*'s premise, "That was really a background issue, as far as I'm concerned. Global warming was simply a reason presented that justified why this new species had emerged. Bill certainly did have concerns about global warming and if *Prey* raised some people's consciousness about global warming, great. But it wasn't a primary aim of the show. Frankly, I thought *Prey* was a show about racial tolerance, about asking if we can't all 'just get along' and it was a great vehicle for exploring that issue."

The series debuted to promising ratings, which slowly tapered off. Messing proved herself to be an excellent dramatic actress. She projected a sense of vulnerability, humor and genuine fear. With her wonderfully expressive eyes, she peered into a scary world that had targeted her. But at the same time, she had the courage to fight and save her species.

"She is an unlikely heroine," Messing said in 1998. "She is fundamentally a lab rat who is very passionate and dedicated to her science work and she's thrust into the middle of this thing. She's not really equipped to handle it but she finds a resolve to forge ahead and explore, discover and ultimately thwart this new species." Messing liked the series' premise too: "I love that it's not really sci-fi. We call it science fact."

Parker's teammates include Dr. Edward Tate, a genetic engineering and computer expert. He loves Sloane but realizes she's in love with Daniels. Dr. Walter Attwood is their boss but he's secretly getting orders from a mysterious woman (played by Alexandra Hedison), head of a secret organization. She's manipulating Attwood in hopes of bringing both races to the brink of war. Meanwhile, detective Ray Peterson is a family man who is fired from his job after publicly expressing his belief in Sloane's war, that supermen are going to take over our world.

"I loved doing *Prey*," says director William Corcoran. "It was the very best kind of cerebral sci-fi that reaches into the very possible and takes science to its next stage. All of us are aware — except perhaps the Neo-Christian right in Los Angeles — that evolution is a powerful force that has guided mankind from pond scum to some of the truly wonderful and deceitful things man does to man. Evolution does not stop and rest on its laurels. It continues, always, and the basis for this simple premise was *Prey*."

At the time of filming, Corcoran hadn't seen Messing's work in comedies. "I was not aware of Debra Messing in anything other than dramatic work," he says. "It was only later, several months into the show, that she mentioned *Ned and Stacy*, another comedy she had done long before *Will and Grace*. She was marvelous to work with. She had a deep grasp of the subject matter and yet always tried to keep the 'science' of the show immediate and exciting. She was generous with all the other cast members and crew and she was never a diva. Though she was the 'star' of the show, she was totally collaborative and very hard-working."

The early episodes in particular, where Sloane was unsure whom to trust, are atmospheric and moody. As the series progressed, the creepiness gave way to more of a procedural plotting by the team of Sloane, Daniels, Tate and Dr. Attwood.

In one episode, they recover a mummified body from Mexico, revealing that this new species can give birth to four babies at a time. Ancient underground pillars contain a code that says something "bad" will happen in the second week of October, 1998. Detective Peterson is bewildered by the weekly revelations of doom. "I should have been paying closer attention in sixth grade when Mrs. Roberts taught evolution," he laments.

That episode, "Origins," was directed by Corcoran on location at Vasquez Rocks; many other classic SF productions over the years have used the craggy landscape to simulate alien worlds. "I was blown away as my mind flashed to the first days of *Star Trek*," says Corcoran. "These were the same rocks where Spock and Captain Kirk had fought so many aliens. It made me feel a part of the wonderful world of science fiction storytelling. Especially since I, a kid from Canada, had fought the producers to let me come to their town and shoot this series."

The producers claimed to be paying attention to real anthropologists, who offered technical advice. Yet the series' premise, that blamed global warming for creating this new species, raised some critical eyebrows.

"In talking with anthropologists, they do say that the climatic change will bring about genetic changes in people," affirmed Charlie Craig during production. "And a species more adaptable to rising temperatures *would* be a superior species."

He was upfront that *Prey* carried a cautionary message. "These [new species] guys are the result of bad things happening to our environment and the lack of regard for our world. So there is a subtle message here."

Prey also wanted mankind to realize that their domination is transitory, that there's always a bully-boy species lurking around the corner. "It at-tacks the egocentric approach that people have today, that we're the last, best model of human beings," pointed out Craig. "But you know, a new car comes out every year!"

Writer Peter Huston of *The Skeptical Inquirer* wasn't impressed with *Prey*. "It isn't particularly good and sadly, is most certainly not literate or intelligent," he said in 1998. "The entire notion of a new species springing into place, achieving adulthood and developing a group identity overnight without being noticed is very illogical ... and why do they look exactly like us, to the point of all of them (so far) being Caucasian?"

In one of *Prey*'s later stories, Sloane and her friends tried to protect a reporter who is targeted by the species. Surprisingly, their efforts fail and the reporter is shot dead by a female assassin. Later on, Dr. Tate finds a way he can change the species' dominant DNA into the same as human beings. Tom Daniels volunteers to be a test subject and at first the serum works. He becomes human, which flames his passion for Sloane, but the effect is only temporary.

Despite the growing romance between Sloane and Daniels and their various escapades, the ratings kept sinking. After eight episodes, ABC pulled the series in March 1998. Protests by viewers resulted in the last five episodes being aired that summer.

"*Prey* was a show troubled by inner politics at Warner Bros. from its very beginning," says Corcoran. "It was intellectual science fiction, launching somewhat into the world that *The X-Files* had re-invented. It was TV for geeks. But it was smart and had a forbidden love affair holding it together. As I understand it, the creator of the show, William Schmidt, and the management at Warner Bros. had a parting of the ways shortly after or during the shooting of the pilot. People left and new people were brought in. Charlie Craig has a tremendous pedigree and was a former *X-Files* writer but he wasn't really given a chance to make the show his own. Despite increasingly strong ratings, the slow death of the show rang out on the set. It was a sad time to see a wonderful show with so much potential die. It was not given a fair shot."

The last episode sets up a cliffhanger: Species man Tom Daniels is kidnapped by military men and the camera pulls back to show him alone in a cage, in the middle of a giant, dark warehouse. That's how it all ended. Tom imprisoned, mankind still imperiled by this new species and a secret human organization seemingly out to implement their own agenda.

Corcoran, who directed this concluding segment, says, "When we did the last episode, we did not know for sure that the series would be canceled. We felt it was a great show and hoped it would continue. That episode was left as a cliffhanger, hoping that the studio and ABC and the fans would be excited enough by the episode for the show to be renewed. Alas, it was not to be. My dear friend Phil Parslow was the show's producer and he offered me a job as director-producer of the show if it came back. It saddened all of us to see the show disappear. We all knew we had a hit show and a winning cast. We just couldn't make the network believe how wonderful a show it really was."

Prey at least highlighted Debra Messing's star potential and she was immediately signed up for *Will and Grace.* That new series ended fans' hopes that a second season of *Prey* might result from their fevered letter-writing campaign (insiders reported that a deluge of angry emails to ABC about *Prey*'s cancellation annoyed, rather than impressed, the network). Reruns of *Prey* on The Sci-Fi Channel have been successful but at this late date, Dr. Parker and her teammates have been permanently frozen in time.

CAST NOTES

Debra Messing (Sloane Parker): The Brooklyn-born actress was a self-admitted fan of *The X-Files.* Messing thought *Prey* was equally scary: "What I like about our show is that it's very intelligent and because it's fact-based, it's much scarier." Right after *Prey* was canceled, she beat out Nicolette Sheridan for the role of Grace Adler on the NBC sitcom *Will and Grace* (1998–2006).

Adam Storke (Tom Daniels): Before *Prey*, Storke was seen in the TV films *Phantom of the Opera* (1990) and *Attack of the 5ft 2" Women* (1994). The New York City–born actor later appeared in *The Invisible Man, Law and Order,* and the 2005 Iraq war series *Over There.*

Vincent Ventresca (Edward Tate): See *The Invisible Man* entry.

Frankie R. Faison (Ray Peterson): Some of his earliest film credits include *The Cat People* (1982), *Coming to America* (1988) and *Silence of the Lambs* (1991). He was also a Tony Award nominee for his role in Broadway's *Fences* (1987). His later film credits include *In Good Company* (2004) and *Premium* (2006).

Larry Drake (Dr. Walter Attwood): Drake won two Emmy Awards for his portrayal of Benny, the mentally impaired office worker in the *L.A. Law* series in the late 1980s. Benny was a far cry from his role on *Prey* as the very professorial-looking genius, Dr. Attwood. He was the villain in the 1990 film, *Darkman.* His later credits include guest shots on *Firefly* and *Crossing Jordan* and the movie *Living the Dream* (2006).

SOURCES

Huston, Peter. *Prey* review. *The Skeptical Inquirer,* 1998.

Psi-Factor: Chronicles of the Paranormal
(1996–2000)

Follow the adventures of the investigative team from the Office of Scientific Investigation and Research (OSIR) as they probe paranormal, extraterrestrial and creature sightings.

Cast: Dan Aykroyd (The Host), Paul Miller (Prof. Connor Doyle) *Year 1*, Matt Frewer (Matt Praeger) *Year 2–4*, Maurice Dean Wint (Dr. Curtis Rollins) *Year 1*, Nancy Anne Sakovich (Lindsay Donner), Colin Fox (Prof. Anton Hendricks), Barclay Hope (Peter Axon), Peter MacNeill (Ray Donohue) *Year 1–3*, Nigel Bennett (Frank Elsinger) *Year 1–3*, Michael Moriarty (Michael Kelly) *Year 2–3*, Joanne Vannicola (Dr. Mia Stone) *Year 4*, Soo Garay (Dr. Claire Davison) *Year 4*;

Developed for Television by: James Nadler; ***Created by:*** Peter Aykroyd, Christopher Chacon, Peter Ventrella; ***Executive Producers:*** Seaton McLean, Peter Aykroyd, Christopher Chacon, James Nadler *Year 1–3*; ***Producers:*** John Calvert *Year 1*, Jan Peter Meyboom *Year 2*, David N. Rosen

Year 2–4, Damian Kindler *Year 1; 3–4*; **Creative Producer:** Larry Raskin *Year 4*; **Line Producer:** Neill Browne *Year 3–4*; **Co-Producer:** Will Dixon *Year 1–2*; **Associate Producers:** Matt Frewer *Year 3*, Caird Urquhart *Year 3–4*; **Consulting Producers:** Rick Drew *Year 2–3*, Damian Kindler, Will Dixon *Year 4*; **Writers included:** Christopher Chacon, Damian Kindler, Robert C. Cooper, Larry Raskin, James Nadler, Mark Leiren-Young, Ian Weir, Rick Drew, Sherman Snukal, Peter Aykroyd; **Directors included:** John Bell, Allen Kroeker, Clay Borris, Stephen Williams, Ken Girotti, Ross Clyde, Vincenzo Natali, Milan Cheylov; **Directors of Photography:** Michael Mc-Murray, John Holosko; **Production Designers:** Gordon Barnes, Jacques Bradette; **Visual Special Effects:** C.O.R.E. Digital Pictures; **Music Theme:** Lou Natale; **Guest Stars included:** Ryan Gosling, Nicole DeBoer, Andrew Jackson, Lynda Mason Green, Kristin Lehman, Tori Higginson, Karl Pruner, Harlan Ellison, Margot Kidder, Christina Cox, Nicholas Campbell, Lisa LaCroix (as Natasha Constantine), Peter Blais (as Lennox Q. Cooper), Elizabeth Shepherd (as Smithwick), Tamara Gorski (as Corliss), Lindsay Collins (as Miles)

U.S. Syndication/Alliance-Atlantis Communications/Atlantis Films/First Television/Paranormal Productions/CanWest Global/Eyemark Entertainment/KingWorld Productions; 1996–2000; 60 Minutes; 88 episodes

When *Psi-Factor: Chronicles of the Paranormal* debuted in syndication in the fall of 1996, critics immediately labeled it as an *X-Files* clone. But the series' genesis was more sophisticated than that. Film and TV actor Dan Aykroyd and his brother Peter were developing the series at the Toronto-based film production company, Atlantis Films, with Christopher Chacon. Peter Aykroyd and Chacon were members of a real-life organization called the Office of Scientific Investigation and Research (OSIR) and wanted to adapt the organization's work in a dramatic television treatment. "Dan and his brother Peter are huge believers in the paranormal and *Psi-Factor* was a pet project of theirs," explains Larry Raskin, who served as creative producer in the fourth year. "As the creative contact to Dan, I was developing the original project and acting as point person on all things

Psi-Factor until I finally handed that off to James Nadler at Atlantis when *Psi-Factor* started to become real. It was too much on my plate at the time as I had several development projects on the go."

One of the problems of making this translation, notes executive producer and showrunner James Nadler, was that the actual OSIR case investigations were fairly mundane in nature. "Most of the time they go and they find out, 'Oh yes, it's just the pipes! There is no ghost. It's just the pipes!' The case studies weren't that exciting. They didn't have stories. They didn't have scientists mentioned within them. That's not the most exciting television show!"

But the development continued when other production entities entered into the mix. The syndicator, Eyemark Entertainment, a CBS company, wanted to do a show with Atlantis Films. The series' development and sale was made at NATPE (the National Association of Television Program Executives) which is an annual "buy and sell" television industry convention. Nadler was first introduced to the series while he was on vacation and he received a frantic phone call from Peter Sussman, one of the partners at Atlantis Films, who needed a series bible in just five days. Nadler brought it with him to NATPE. "The bible was thrown together very quickly as a sales document. At the same time, Will Dixon, who was on the show's first two years, was brought in to write a script," recalls Nadler.

The series' development had been a continuous series of conversations among the interested parties over a six-month period, primarily because it took a long time for everyone to get on the same page of what the show could be.

When the series finally arrived at NATPE, it came together very quickly. "That's January [1996] and filming began in May for the first year," says Nadler.

The initial goal was to create a one-hour dramatic series presenting two half-hour stories about the OSIR investigators investigating things that went bump in the night.*

The series' focus, initially, was predominantly on the phenomenon that was being investigated, not the characters. In its first year, the OSIR team explored UFOs, demons, creatures in sewers, the Devil's Triangle, reincarnation, possession, ghosts and psychic powers.

Atlantis Films, which subsequently merged with Alliance Communications in September 1998 to become Alliance-Atlantis, initially felt that two years of half-hour stories would generate 88 individual stories that could be packaged for strip syndication, but that wasn't quite how the show eventually played out.

Dan Aykroyd served as a continuity spine as the host-narrator, opening and closing each episode with a few words about OSIR's mission. Producers rotated the characters, with different "case manager" team leaders. The rationale was to convey that the OSIR was a large organization. "That was an unusual thought," recalls Nadler. "I resisted that because I have a very traditional view of television. I believe audiences tune in for the characters. There are very few shows, like *Law & Order* and *Mission: Impossible*, where it's completely plot-driven and the recurring characters are secondary."

This resulted in Canadian actor Paul Miller leading the series as Prof. Connor Doyle with character support from Lisa LaCroix, Elizabeth Shepherd, Tamara Gorski, Lindsay Collins and Maurice Dean Wint. The actors who eventually formed the core group — Barclay Hope, Peter MacNeill, Colin Fox and Nancy Anne Sakovich — were also present from the beginning.

Hope, who was Peter Axon throughout the series, says he was unhappy with the half-hour story format in the first year. "I don't feel there's enough time," he says. "There's Dan Aykroyd's intro and extro which takes up a minute on top and bottom. There's commercials and you're left with about 18 minutes to tell and resolve the story. Find out something about the people telling the story. There's just not enough time.

"One of the best things about the show was that it did evolve. It started out fairly dry, fairly documentary. Once we really got into it, it evolved to an extent where we were actually doing a piece of entertainment."

As the year progressed, the producers realized their initial approach was not working out. "We were adding characters even as we went into production," recalls Nadler, "in part, because originally the characters were not important. Some characters just didn't work and then we found out we had too many characters. Originally we had three case managers and they were supposed to rotate. One of them, a really wonderful actress named Elizabeth Shepherd, only appeared in one episode. Tamara Gorski was the other and Paul Miller. These characters were supposed to rotate equally."

When Maurice Dean Wint gave consistently strong performances, the producers went to Shepherd and apologized that they had to let her go because "we had to consolidate and get it down to a fewer number of characters," says Nadler. "Nancy Ann Sakovich's character, Lindsay Don-

ner, was added very last-minute because someone else was unavailable. And we really liked her. So she ended up being a mainstay of the show."

Dan Aykroyd and Chris Chacon felt that the investigators should be older, more "traditional" scientists. "We didn't feel that was the most exciting or commercial [way to go]," says Nadler. He recalls that the ages of the characters became an ongoing debate among the producers. "We'd be talking about a particular actor. They would say, 'This person is great!' and I'd say 'This person is great!' and we'd go around the room, and then we'd get to Chris Chacon and he would say, 'Too young!' That happened over and over again. It was very frustrating."

Nadler says that making the transition to second year was fairly easy because "we'd done well in the States. In Canada we'd always done well in ratings. In the States it was a very competitive time for first-run syndication. We were doing as well as we'd hoped."

However, there were two major changes. The first was a cast shakeup. "We had to pare it back going into year two. Lisa LaCroix did a really good job. We never found a place for her to come back. And Maurice Dean Wint, we did find places for him to come back, but as a guest star. Unfortunately Paul Miller had to be dropped for commercial reasons. He did a great job. But we needed another name for second year.

"We brought in Matt Frewer as a new case manager and brought in his fan base also and used his character as a way of shaking up the series and the relationships between the characters. We had new ways of attracting conflict within the team, which was a big change."

Frewer was a good choice for the new lead for the series. Professor Connor Doyle was killed off in the first-year finale, paving the way for Frewer's entry. Frewer had a following because of previous series like *Max Headroom* (1987), and was able to bring a sardonic wit to the character Matt Praeger. His interaction with the team created compelling personality conflicts as he and Peter Axon often disagreed with investigative methods.

"When Matt Frewer came on, he added a whole other dimension to it. He was absolutely wonderful in not accepting mediocrity," says Hope. "He started to demand that the scripts had more work put into them, to have a more dramatic context to it. He really pushed for scenes that were good, and not just people talking about a bunch of different things."

Frewer said during production in 1998, "[I was

responsible for] the design of the blueprint of Matt Praeger on a weekly basis. I'm the associate producer of the show too. My contributions are largely creative on a script standpoint and continually tinkering with them and changing them, trying to make them better. Trying to make each season better than the last. It's an ongoing process."

Another interesting addition was actor Michael Moriarty (*Law and Order*), who played Praeger's enigmatic boss Michael Kelly. The purpose of the character was to create friction and added conspiracies, "which I actually based on internal Atlantis corporate politics!" chuckles Nadler.

In the second year, the characters' interactions were given as much attention as the paranormal investigating. This year the team looked into UFO reports, psychokinetic powers, people returning from the dead, suspended animation and people growing younger.

"We really looked for character actors that had a certain liveliness and electricity for the parts," says Nadler. "That's why the humanity, especially in year two, really comes through. These are guys going down there and seeing horrible things. But at the same time, they have these moments where the actors are warmer and have quite a bit of humor. It makes it that much more believable as drama."

The second major change was restructuring the show from two half-hour stories into a more traditional one-hour, one-story structure and this time the emphasis was no longer just on the plots but the characters as well.

"We worked with the writers and asked them to bring a sense of life of our characters into our jobs," says Hope. "Whereas the jobs sort of dictated the show in year one, in year two we started to bring life to the characters. In year three we brought more life which helped us stay fresh from show to show.

"If you have to deal with a UFO, for instance, you have the undercurrents of perhaps, say, a relationship with your father that adds a different element to how you play the scenes. That's the way we try and change it. That's what's interesting — to see people."

Hope offers an example of how this newfound approach was used for his character, Peter Axon. "I tried to get them to bring more life history into the character," Hope continues. "When confronted by a situation, it's not just the situation to deal with but also memories of the previous situation. Maybe the night before I received a call from a girl I was engaged to. And left. And maybe I had that in the back of my mind, and that context served as the means of how the character dealt with his current situation."

Hope points to a Praeger-centric episode titled "Happy Birthday Matt Praeger" where "he ended up on a game show. It was an ethereal thing where it was all about his fears and his personality. How he would avoid emotional contact with people, and how he would push people away because that was something in his character that he wasn't equipped to deal with. What they did was, they forced him to deal with his own emotions. It was using SF to get into the character. To make Matt Praeger be a person and deal with things."

The second year would attack other topics inspired by the real-life case files. "I moved the show away from any hint of docu-drama," says Nadler. "I wanted to work with specific actors and performers and develop characters that audiences could tune into. Some of our characters were popping off the screen. Viewers were saying, 'I like him! I like Donner!' They developed really big fan bases."

At the end of the second year, Hope recalls the state of affairs among the OSIR team before the turnover to third year: "At the end of year two, Praeger quits," he says. "Donner is considered a mole and is outcast. [As Peter Axon] I move up to case manager. And Anton Hendricks is missing. All that has to do with the internal workings of the OSIR people. There are people higher up pulling strings. We don't know what their agendas are. Michael Moriarty's character was one of the guys feeding us information about stuff going on but we weren't supposed to know about it. Bosses in big corporations don't tell everyone what their plans are. OSIR has bosses up there somewhere. They're pulling strings and flying us in directions we don't understand."

It's this kind of material that made working on the series engaging for Hope. "It was a lot more interesting in the end to get the scripts," he says. "They started to get into story arcs that would go from the beginning of a season to the next season. And then lead on to the following season so the stories weren't just plucked from the thin air. The stories were quite directed towards the characters, which is always much more interesting for the actors than spaceships. That happens to a lot of shows. It happened on *Stargate* and *The X-Files*. They got away from the SF aspect and got into the lead characters and the stories of their lives. That's way more interesting for actors."

By the third year, it was increasingly difficult to stay focused on the real-life OSIR files, says producer Larry Raskin. "We've pushed the show more cinematically," adds Nadler. "We continued with a very classic style and look. We made the stories less talky and more visual."

One of the major themes in the third year was the Afterlife. "What happens after you die and what doesn't and so forth," notes Nadler. "Whether you go to heaven or hell or just nowhere."

As an example of how the series was organized for the characters, Nadler remembers that in third year, "we divided the year into thirds," he says. "The first third was really very much Praeger and Hendricks. The middle third was a bit of Praeger and Donner. The final third was Axon and Praeger."

Nadler recalls how stressful the job was. "It's the first show I worked on as a showrunner. I got pneumonia a few times! The best thing I got to do was meet [writer] Harlan Ellison. The lawyer on *Outer Limits* phoned me and said, 'Look, I've got Harlan Ellison's email. We've just optioned a short story from him. I know you're an SF fan. Would you like to contact him?' And I did, and I offered him a role on the show. And he said, well, he was intrigued. 'But I think you'd better see what I look like before you do that!' So he sent me some tape. I looked at the tape and said, 'You know what? We can write him in. This guy can actually carry a scene.' I got Damian Kindler to write the particular episode ["The Observer Effect"] with the instruction, 'Write it so that if we have to cut him out, we can't!' Harlan came up and my wife and I went out to dinner with him and talked about *A Boy and His Dog* [a novella that later became a 1975 film] and he was just a real gentleman. And he did a good job! That was quite a thrill for me."

Nadler also recalls that the show once "lost" a snake in an Ontario library after it guest starred at the location in an episode. And it was six weeks before the production company was notified that the snake was finally found. "We had to phone up the snake wrangler and tell him, 'You gotta go pick up your snake. You left him in a potted plant!'" chuckles Nadler. "There was another snake in year one that ran for it, and got to the roof of a garage, and our first assistant director had to hang onto the end of it."

As the third year came to a close, Nadler realized he'd burned out. He'd written ten episodes over three years and was anxious to do something else. But he also became aware of two issues that seriously affected the life of the series. First, Alliance-Atlantis was getting out of television, so that limited the future life of the show. Alliance-Atlantis once had 350 hours of television production, but in 2007, the company was completely out of that business. "That's a huge drop in volume and opportunities," laments Nadler.

Secondly, because of his background as a lawyer, Nadler was involved with the series' financing as well as being the showrunner and he looked at "the numbers" for the fourth year. "I knew the budget was going to have to be cut by about a third," he says. "I knew that the only way you could cut the budget that significantly — we were not a really expensive show — was by firing people. And I just couldn't do it."

Barclay Hope sympathizes. "The further along in this business I go, the more I can see how budgets dictate the outcome of a show."

Although both the production company and the syndicator asked him to reconsider, Nadler rebuffed the offers and stepped away. "I didn't earn any money for a year, which was probably not the best thing to do!"

Stepping in to take over was Larry Raskin, who had been busy developing Anne McCaffrey's *Dragonriders of Pern* novels for television (the project was later aborted). He says, "With Atlantis, Eyemark, and Global [the Canadian broadcaster] in Canada all acknowledging that this would be the final year, and the budget being reduced, producer David Rosen and I discussed various ways to proceed. David had produced the previous year as well. I brought back Will Dixon and Damian Kindler, and added story editor Andrea Moodie to the mix. We brainstormed for about a week on how to approach the year, keeping in mind the budgetary constraints."

The map that was plotted out was this:

- Make better use of the cast (Matt Frewer, Barclay Hope, Nancy Anne Sakovich, Peter MacNeill). "Previous years had started to focus stories on the investigators more and that seemed like a good thing to continue," says Raskin. "We were paying them a lot and they were all good actors so we wanted them to carry the show more — not just investigate the phenomena but experience them as well. We felt that these OSIR investigators should be magnets for paranormal activity."
- Due to the budgetary restraints, Matt Frewer was cut loose. "We gave him a six-episode arc and a royal send-off," says Raskin.

"Praeger was chosen to help populate a new race [in the episode "883" where Praeger must choose between dying on Earth or surviving by helping colonize a new world] and we added a new young investigator played by Joanne Vannicola."

- Adjust the tone of the show. "We didn't take everything so seriously," says Raskin. "In fact, we sometimes went for high camp. Our stories were inspired by the case files but no longer so closely based on them. We pushed the envelope more in the outrageous direction but also tried to make all the characters more grounded in some reality; sometimes it was an alternative reality.
- Structure the show to work with the reduced budget. "We limited stories to fewer characters and locations and tried to adhere to a mystery-suspense structure wherein the investigators pursued various leads and angles but didn't clue in to what was really going on until the fourth act," says Raskin. "And, we put them in the line of fire or allowed them to get more emotionally involved."

Raskin says the plan was successful and all the parties were pleased with the results.

One of the fourth-year episodes, 'Once Upon a Time in the Old West," was a favorite for Hope. "Three bank robbers from the past and also the future, came to steal some gold from a bank," he recalls. "The whole reality of our world had shifted once they had entered our dimension. Peter Axon came back from the future as an older man in his 70s. He had invented this time machine that these guys had stolen. [The bank robbers] had used it to jump around time to steal gold. That was a lot of fun simply because I got to play myself at two different ages. I had to go through a complete makeup process. It put us in a different reality. Lindsay Donner was married to this cop and she ends up dying in this episode. But at the end of the episode she's back to life because the [true] reality was restored. And I got to talk with myself. The younger self talked to the older and the older talked to the younger. We were also dealing with some great character actors who were playing cowboys."

Having looked again at various *Psi-Factor* videotapes in preparation for his interview, Barclay Hope reflects, "It was a lot of fun. A lot of people really enjoyed it because people still come up to me and say, 'Wait! *Psi-Factor*! I remember you!' I find that of all the things I've done, science

fiction seems to stick. SF fans are more devoted fans. They know more about the facts. They know the show, the storylines, all that stuff. [One time, a fan in a music store] looked at me and he said, '*Prometheus*, right?' and that was the ship I was the captain, in *Stargate*. He knew the ship. He knew who I was. Then he mentioned *Psi-Factor* because he knew me from *Psi-Factor*. I think SF is an interesting genre in that respect. Fans know their stuff. I honestly feel there's a difference between SF fans and other genres. They're very dedicated. I don't really know why that is, I just think it's different from the genre of a movie of the week or comedies."

In the end, Nadler says he's proud of the show. "Given the resources we had, we accomplished a really good show," he says. "We won the Gemini [award] for editing. We were nominated for some of the acting in year two and three, which for a SF show in Canada, that's pretty good. The show did extremely well internationally. The show sold to about 150 countries. Every European country. Every South American country. South Africa."

The international distribution and exposure of a science fiction show is a fascinating subject. Can science fiction cross cultural barriers? "There's actually a Russian trailer for *Psi-Factor* on YouTube," says Nadler. "I know some episodes about snakes never aired because of cultural sensitivities there. In the Middle East some episodes about religious icons never aired. There weren't major controversies. I don't think we ever did anything really offensive.

"It did well with audiences in Canada. We were put all over the map in scheduling as was every Canadian show, but the audience really found it. Occasionally I'll wear my *Psi-Factor* jacket and people remember the show. It's proof that it's a very good show. It hasn't inspired the cult reaction that some other shows have. I don't think we'll ever see a convention for *Psi-Factor* but I like it a lot and I had a good time."

CAST NOTES

Dan Aykroyd (Host): Aykroyd was born in Ottawa, Canada. After beginning his career in Canadian television, he joined the famous Second City Theater company in Toronto. While working there as an improvisational actor, he was cast in *Saturday Night Live* where he created some of his most memorable characters and met John Belushi. Together they formed the duo The Blues Brothers and released an album and then the hit movie *The Blues Brothers* (1980). Aykroyd teamed with Belushi in Steven Spielberg's *1941* (1979) and again in *Neighbors* (1981) before Belushi's untimely death in 1982. Aykroyd's subsequent credits include *Twilight Zone: The Movie* (1983), *Ghostbusters* (1984) and *Ghostbusters 2* (1989). His lifelong interest in the paranormal led him to *Psi-Factor* as well as a number of other documentaries on the subject.

Paul Miller (Prof. Connor Doyle): Miller was born in Canada. He appeared in an episode of the series *Friday the 13th*, a 1993 film version of *Romeo and Juliet*, the Canadian series *Traders* and the Canadian films *Execution of Justice* (1998) and *H2O* (2004).

Matt Frewer (Matt Praeger): Born in Washington, DC, Frewer shot to fame portraying the iconic 1980s character Max Headroom. Since then he has played the lead in the sitcom *Doctor, Doctor* and made guest appearances on *Star Trek: The Next Generation* and in the mini-series Stephen King's *The Stand*. His voice has been heard in a number of animated series, from *Tiny Toon Adventures* to *Batman: The Animated Series*. He was also the voice of Panic in Disney's *Hercules* before joining the cast of *Psi-Factor*. Since then he has appeared in a number of TV movies as Sherlock Holmes, and acted in the Steven Spielberg mini-series *Taken* and in Stephen King's *Desperation*. He has had roles on the TV series *Eureka* as well as on the CBC drama *Intelligence*.

Maurice Dean Wint (Dr. Curtis Rollins): Wint has appeared in numerous movies (*The Sweetest Gift, Cube, TekWar*) and TV shows (*Friday the 13th, Robocop, Due South, Secret Service*).

Nancy Anne Sakovich (Lindsay Donner): Sakovich was born in Belleville, Ontario. After a career as an international fashion model, she turned to acting. She appeared in *Kung Fu: The Legend Continues* and *The Commish* before landing her role on *Psi-Factor*. Since then she has appeared in *Relic Hunter, Queer as Folk* and in the TV movie *Category 6: Day of Destruction*. She played a recurring role on the TV series *Doc*.

Colin Fox (Prof. Anton Hendricks): An actor in Canada for many years, Fox was featured in a series called *Strange Paradise* on the CBC in 1969, and has appeared in numerous shows and has voiced many animated characters since. After *Psi-Factor*, Fox was best known playing Fritz the chef in A&E's short-lived *Nero Wolfe* series. He lives just outside of Toronto.

Barclay Hope (Peter Axon): Hope recently starred in ABC's *Path to 9/11* opposite Harvey Keitel. He has had recurring roles on *Smallville, The L Word, and Stargate SG-1*. He also starred in *The Stranger Game* with Mimi Rogers and in the indie hits *Fetching Cody* and *The Truth About Miranda*. Barclay has acted on stage at the Royal Alexandra Theatre in Toronto, the Manitoba Theatre Center in Winnipeg and at Stratford's Shakespeare Festival.

Peter MacNeill (Ray Donohue): MacNeill's feature film roles include *Crash* and *The Hanging Garden*, for which he won a Genie Award for Best Supporting Actor. He also had principal roles in *A Small Miracle* and *Blind Faith*. His TV-movies include *Lives of Girls and Women, Giant Mine, Love and Hate, Too Close to Home, My Own Country*, and *Gross Misconduct*, for which he received a Gemini nomination for Best Supporting Actor. His TV series work includes *Road to Avonlea, Beyond Reality*, and *War of the Worlds*. He lives with his family in Toronto.

Nigel Bennett (Elsinger): Bennett was born in Staffordshire, England but has been based in Canada since 1986. He is best known for playing the *vampire* patriarch Lucien LaCroix in the TV series *Forever Knight*. He has also been in a number of major films such as *Murder at 1600* and *The Skulls*. He had recurring roles in *Kung Fu: The Legend Continues* and *LEXX*. He was also the star of many Oatmeal Crisp commercials in the 1990s. Teaming up with writer P.N. Elrod, Bennett co-authored a series of acclaimed vampire adventure novels for Baen Books.

Michael Moriarty (Michael Kelly): Born in Detroit, Michigan, he began his acting career in 1973 in the movie *Bang the Drum Slowly* alongside Robert DeNiro. He went on to star in a TV adaptation of *The Glass Menagerie* for which he won an Emmy. He appeared in the television mini-series *Holocaust*, a role which earned him another Emmy. On the big screen he appeared in a series of Larry Cohen films including *Q, The Stuff, It's Alive 3* and *A Return to Salem's Lot*, as well as in Clint Eastwood's *Pale Rider* and the prisoner of war drama *Hanoi Hilton*. He is best known for his role as Benjamin Stone in the TV series *Law & Order*. Moriarty left the show in 1994 after his political views put him at odds with the series producers. He moved to Canada. He has since appeared in such films as *Courage Under Fire, Along Came a Spider* and the television series *Emily of New Moon*.

Joanne Vannicola (Dr. Mia Stone): Canadian

actress Vannicola is most notable for her role as Dr. Mia Stone in *Psi-Factor* and as the voice of Willy Zilla in Gene Simmons' animated television show *My Dad the Rock Star*. Vannicola has also appeared in many other shows such as *Relic Hunter, Mutant X, Kung Fu: The Legend Continues* and *Night Heat*. In 1990, she won an *Emmy* for Outstanding Performance in a Children's Special (*Maggie's Secret*).

Soo Garay (Dr. Claire Davison): Born in Toronto, she spent her childhood and teens as a nationally ranked competitive swimmer. Garay began her acting career working extensively in theater and has made over 20 appearances with major Canadian companies in Toronto and on tour across the country. She has appeared in *Jacob the Liar, Shot Through the Heart, Blues Brothers 2000, Man in My Microwave, The Mao Lounge* and *Storm of the Century*. She has also been seen guesting on TV series, including *Forever Knight*.

Quantum Leap
(1989–1993)

Dr. Samuel Beckett spearheads Project Quantum Leap in the year 1999. Before the time apparatus can be perfected, funding for the project is threatened, so he jumps back into time. Unable to control his time leaps, Beckett materializes into the bodies of various people during his travels, correcting problems in their lives and in history. Beckett hopes one day to make the leap back to his own time in New Mexico.

Cast: Scott Bakula (Dr. Samuel Beckett), Dean Stockwell (Admiral Al Calavicci), Deborah Pratt (Main Title Narrator)

Created by: Donald P. Bellisario; *Executive Producer:* Donald P. Bellisario *Year 1–5*; *Co-Executive Producers:* Deborah Pratt *Year 2–5*, Michael Zinberg *Year 3*, Charles Floyd Johnson; *Supervising Producers:* Scott Shepherd, Paul M. Belous, Robert Wolterstorff, Harker Wade, Tommy Thompson, Richard C. Okie, John Hill; *Producers:* Harker Wade, Chris Ruppenthal, Robin Jill Bernheim; *Co-Producers:* Chris Ruppenthal, Paul Brown, Jeff Gourson; *Associate Producers:* David Bellisario, Julie Bellisario, Jimmy Giritlian, Scott Ejercito; *Assistant Associate Producer:* Joanne Oboyski-Battelene; *Writers included:* Deborah Arakelian, Sam Rolfe, Paris Qualles, Richard C. Okie, Sandy Fries, Donald Bellisario, John D'Aquino, Tammy Ader, Randy Holland, Deborah Pratt, Toni Graphia, Beverly Bridges; *Directors included:* David Hemmings, Ivan Dixon, Gilbert Shilton, Michael Vejar, Alan J. Levi, Aaron Lipstadt, James Whitmore Jr., Michael Zinberg, Donald P. Bellisario, Christopher Welch, Joe Napolitano, Debbie Allen, Andy Cadiff, Scott Bakula, Virgil W. Vogel, Eric Laneuville, Anita Addison, Stuart Margolin, Christopher Hibler, Bob Hulme, Michael Watkins, Gus Trikonis; *Guest Stars included:* Lauren Woodland, Teri Hatcher, Jennifer Aniston, Kristoffer Tabori, Anne Lockhart, Chubby Checker, Neil Patrick Harris, Dr. Ruth Westheimer, Meg Foster, Brooke Shields, Terry Farrell, Bob Saget, Maggie Egan, Andrea Thompson, Michael Madsen, Jason Priestley, Claudia Christian, Katie Sagal, Guy Stockwell, Teri Copley, Nancy Kulp, Nick Cassavetes, Russ Tamblyn, Janine Turner, Marcia Cross, Joseph Gordon-Levitt, Amy Yasbeck, Dr. Laura Schlessinger, Robert Duncan McNeill, Marjorie Monaghan, Renee Coleman, Carolyn Seymour, Peter Noone, Josie Bissett, Kristen Cloke, Roddy McDowall

Universal/NBC; March 1989–August 1993; 60 minutes; 95 episodes; DVD status: Complete series

Quantum Leap went beyond entertainment. "We received phone calls from schools across the country, asking to use our episodes to teach kids about issues like prejudice, violence and animal rights," says creator Donald P. Bellisario. "Lives were literally changed by the series."

Bellisario classified *Quantum Leap* as the only TV series in history that needed an instruction manual to understand its premise. NBC president Brandon Tartikoff pleaded for Bellisario to explain the show in terms that his own mother could understand. "I never did explain the show successfully to anybody," star Scott Bakula would later quip.

Bellisario, a writer-producer-director, had previously created such shows as *Airwolf* and *Magnum P.I.* (and later *JAG* and *Navy NCIS*). He didn't want a time travel series where Sam Beckett met ancient Romans or landed aboard Christopher Columbus' ship. "Audiences of today won't accept the hero walking around ancient Rome," he said. Beckett's travels were confined to his own lifetime (1953 onward). Bellisario waived this rule only twice: a 1945 visit to World War II, and 1862, where Sam leaped into the Civil War body of his great-grandfather.

Beckett had no control over his travels. He would appear as a convict on a chain gang in 1956 or as a New York City cop on his honeymoon in 1960. Instead of materializing as himself, he would "leap" into the body of another person and accomplish that episode's mission. TV audiences saw him as Beckett but the people around him would see the person Sam had leaped into. Meanwhile, the person Sam was inhabiting would be transported to Project Quantum Leap's Waiting Room in 1999 until Sam's adventure was over.

Tartikoff was right — pass the instruction manual!

NBC had previously tried and failed with a time travel series called *Voyagers*, with Jon-Erik Hexum and young Meeno Peluce fixing anomalies in time as they met famous people. The 1982–83 series failed to click with audiences. It was the success of the *Back to the Future* movies in the 1980s that partly persuaded NBC to try again.

When NBC president Warren Littlefield listened to Bellisario's pitch, the network executive admitted, "It's a strange idea," but he saw the series' potential. Bellisario encouraged believable scenarios for *Quantum Leap*. "I wanted stories about real people, not historical figures," he says. That meant Beckett's leaps took him into the lives of a black man in the bigoted south, a Vietnam soldier, a paraplegic, a pregnant woman, a rape victim, an American Indian, a Mafia don, a boxer, a high school nerd, a crazy radio DJ, a trapeze artist and a TV star. Beckett's trademark quip whenever he leaped into a new body was, "Oh boy!"

He could also appear in the bodies of women and even materialized as a space-borne chimpanzee (again, TV audiences would see actor Bakula pretending to be the ape).

Most of Beckett's time-tripping was confined to America but on occasion he materialized abroad.

He met a vampire in England, a mummy in Egypt and slogged through the Vietnam jungles in "The Leap Home, Part II."

Helping Sam avoid danger was Al, his friend back at the Project who accompanied Sam as a holographic image. Al supplied Sam with background information every week, using a handheld link device to Project Quantum Leap's supercomputer, Ziggy.

Al was a last-minute addition to the series. Sam needed someone to bounce things off of; when Bellisario saw Dean Stockwell's comedic performance in the film *Married to the Mob* (1988), he knew he was perfect for the part.

Al and Sam soon realized that the time leaps were not being directed by Project Quantum Leap but rather by a "higher" power. They never ascertained who that was. However, Sam could only leap to the next time period once he corrected whatever was wrong in his present adventure.

Whenever the show was labeled as science fiction, Bellisatio bristled. "Our show used the concept of time travel but it was not about time travel," he explains today. "It was more of an anthology show. We weren't locked into an action-adventure format. I wanted warm, humanistic stories, sometimes as a comedy, sometimes fantasy drama, sometimes as an action-adventure and sometimes as a romantic story."

Stockwell agreed. "It's really stories about people and their problems," he said during production. "We get into social problems too, so the SF aspect is quite minor."

The Hollywood Reporter considered the series an SF milestone. "Its concept is something viewers have never seen before," it stated. "It's expanded the boundaries of traditional science fiction on TV."

The show's executive producer, Deborah Pratt (a former dancer-actress, and Bellisario's wife during *Quantum Leap*), smiles as she recalls how one angry critic, an SF fan, got into a flap over the series' premise. "One of the reviewers said that we 'defied all of the rules of time travel.' My response was, 'What rules of time travel?'"

She was more interested in addressing real issues of the day. In her script, "Black and White on Fire," Sam is a black man in love with a white woman during the 1965 Watts riots in Los Angeles. The episode caused controversy. "All of the sponsors pulled out of the show and several states banned the episode from airing," she says. "To NBC's credit, they aired the episode anyway."

The series' ratings took a dip in its Friday night

slot and the show was never a ratings powerhouse. It finished 58th out of 96 shows for its second year, 1989–1990. A change to Wednesdays resulted in better ratings and ratings-wise it continually beat out its competition, *China Beach* and *Wiseguy*.

Bakula called the series "the best acting job on TV," and became fast friends with Dean Stockwell. Their comedic camaraderie was perfectly suited for the family-oriented show.

"Scott was the ultimate everyman," Pratt says of her star. "You believed him in every situation. He brought a commonality to Sam Beckett that made viewers feel they wanted him to come into their lives, walk in their shoes and make their lives a little better. Scott and Dean had a great spark of chemistry between them."

Al, the know-it-all hologram, served an important purpose. "Al has a perspective on history that carried the weight of pathos and humor," says Pratt. "And Dean Stockwell was such a consummate actor, he made Al both guardian angel and tempestuous devil."

Some of Sam's other leaps included into a woman who is

In this early publicity photo, Scott Bakula, left, and Dean Stockwell sit in a 1950s convertible.

being sexually harassed, a blind concert pianist, a mentally challenged youth and a pregnant teenager. "Cheers to *Quantum Leap* for turning a gimmicky premise into one with promise," *TV Guide* raved. "While the show could have stuck with safe storylines, it has instead taken risks. It sure beats *The Time Tunnel*."

Interestingly, one of the visitors on the *Quantum Leap* set was James Darren, who had starred in the 1960s *Time Tunnel* series. He and Bakula joked over their respective time adventures. *Time Tunnel* had been one of Bakula's favorite shows as a youngster.

"What makes the show work is Bakula's acting, mixed with Dean Stockwell, plus some superbly written scripts," said critic John Peel. "The show hasn't given us any low points yet."

On the other hand, Paul Mount of the British

magazine *Starburst*, couldn't understand all of the fuss. "*Quantum Leap* is deadly dull," he observed. "The format is a strait-jacket that chokes out almost all imagination. We're left to run through the same situation time and time again."

Director Joe Napolitano considered *Quantum Leap* far from routine. "That was my first show as a director," he says. "Each episode was like a little film. Don Bellisario wanted little movies, not television. The cleverness of the art department, the writing, and the photography, was amazing."

The show required ingenuity. "The sets were completely different for every episode," Napolitano says. "The first episode I did, 'Pool Hall Blues'—our pool room set later ended up as a school room for another episode. That's the way that show was done, efficient and creative. Change *those* walls into *these* walls, and repaint

Dean Stockwell, left, and Scott Bakula in the episode "A Single Drop of Rain — September 7, 1953."

them, that was the challenge! Both Scott and Dean were very dedicated to the show, a dream to work with. I learned a lot from both of them. [Director of photography] Michael Watkins was also very helpful."

The network wanted to pump up the ratings by having Beckett occasionally encounter famous people. This resulted in visits with a young Buddy Holly, Stephen King and Elvis Presley. Beckett once even leaped into the body of the chauffeur for

Marilyn Monroe. These were called "kisses with history." In the most controversial episode, Sam leaped into the body of Lee Harvey Oswald, the alleged assassin of President John F. Kennedy. Beckett tries to stop himself from carrying out the assassination, but he loses more and more of his identity to Oswald as November 22, 1963, wears on. Just as Oswald is about to fire, Sam leaps from Oswald to a Secret Service man, who saves Jackie Kennedy from the sniper's fire.

Despite the conspiracy theories, the drama postulated that Oswald was the lone gunman. (Coincidentally, Bellisario and Oswald had served together as Marines in Santa Ana in the mid–1950s.) But many fans didn't like the episode, feeling it was exploitative. Others were turned off by its morbid and confusing storyline.

"It was too diffuse and didn't work as a whole," says its director, James Whitmore Jr. "It was very confusing. The response I got was that no one knew what the hell was going on. "

Despite those misgivings, Whitmore was a fan of the series. "*Quantum Leap*'s stories were about people and their emotional situations. That was its core and that's what I found exciting."

Robin Bernheim wrote another offbeat episode, "Deliver Us from Evil," where Sam confronts an evil female time traveler who is out to create chaos and undo all of Sam's good deeds.

Other ideas never make it to film: Sam leaping into the bodies of Robert F. Kennedy, a baby, a dog, and even a cartoon character. There were also plans for Sam to leap into the TV show *Magnum P.I.* (the 1980s Tom Selleck crime drama).

Had the show gone the historical route, Bakula would have liked playing two characters: the captain of the *Titanic* and the spiritual and political leader of India, Mahatma Gandhi. However, the actor agreed that it was wise to ignore the historical past.

Quantum Leap continued to get bounced all over the schedule. When the show was moved to Fridays at 8 P.M., the ratings suffered. Protesting fans sent in over 50,000 pieces of mail. An advocacy group, Viewers for Quality Television, organized even more protests. NBC president Warren Littlefield was surprised by the attention and the series was moved back to Wednesdays. The network at least had a sense of humor, running a series of TV ads showing a NBC executive buried under piles of mail from fans as he tries to announce *Quantum Leap*'s new Wednesday time slot. NBC dubbed the fans "Leapheads" but fans preferred to be called "Leapers."

The show was also recognized by the industry, receiving Emmy nominations as best drama series. Bakula and Stockwell received nominations as well.

There was also a 1991–1993 comic book version produced by Innovation Comics. According to Pratt, the series changed people's lives. "I remember a letter from a family whose daughter was dying of cancer. The family came together in the ward to watch *Quantum Leap* and at the end of the episode, they realized they had given up hope of their little girl living. The episode gave them the will to believe and when they wrote the letter, it was seven months later and the girl was in remission. The power of thought."

On another occasion, Pratt says, "I wrote the episode 'Eight and a Half Months,' where Sam leaped into a teenage pregnant girl whose father was going to disown her. I received a moving letter from a girl who told me a similar thing had happened between her and her father and she stopped talking to him. She never understood his side of the story until she saw the episode. Even though he was dead now, she was able to forgive him and let go of the anger she held all those years against him."

Budget cuts in the show's fifth year and a shift to Tuesdays at 8 o'clock doomed the show. The series, crawling along with a dismal 11 ratings share, was finally canceled. Warren Littlefield later called *Quantum Leap* "an outstanding series," and admitted the network should have nurtured it better by keeping it in one time period.

The last episode, "Mirror Image," had Beckett materialize in a coal mining town in Pennsylvania (1953) on his birthday, and he meets a mysterious bartender who may be the intelligence behind his leapings. For the first time, Sam can see his own reflection in a mirror and meets people from his past, all of whom have different names. Its meaning is left ambiguous since the episode was originally intended as a cliffhanger for a sixth year. When the cancellation was announced, the episode was edited as a final show, leaving questions. As it ends, a female narrator states, "Dr. Sam Beckett never returned home." Many fans were disappointed, wanting Beckett to be reunited with his wife and daughter. "Half of the fans loved it," Bellisario said of the finale. "And half hated it. They wanted to see him get home." Bellisario chose the bar locale because he had grown up in a small Pennsylvania coal town where his father owned a bar. He even made a cameo in the episode.

Pratt wanted Beckett to remain lost because there was talk of doing a movie sequel. "Don and I had a huge 'discussion' over that ending. Don wanted to bring him home. I said that was a huge mistake. I cited the *Fugitive* series, where he finally got the one-armed man and that killed any sequel. If Sam went home, we wouldn't have a motion picture. Don agreed and so Sam is still out there, waiting for his daughter. When Universal is ready, I have the script."

Reruns leaped over to the USA Network and later to The Sci-Fi Channel. *TV Guide* later ranked Sam Beckett as #12 in their "25 Greatest Sci-Fi Legends" issue.

Bakula considered Beckett his favorite role, and remains proud of the series. "There were a wide variety of issues and situations that we were able to examine," he told *The Washington Post* in 2006. "We all worked unbelievably hard for four and a half seasons. And the show still holds up."

There was talk of resolving *Quantum Leap*'s premise and creating a new series that would feature Sam's daughter and Al traveling through time. *Quantum Leap: A Bold Leap Home* was to be filmed in Australia for The Sci-Fi Channel. Trey Callaway was to executive produce this new pilot and he says, "I was a huge fan of the original series. The premise of the new show was that Sam's daughter teams up with Dean Stockwell, not only to continue the work of Project Quantum Leap, but also to find out where her Dad went. It was supposed to kick off with Scott Bakula making an appearance at the beginning. It would have done the original series justice and took the material to a new place for a new audience. Everyone was geared up and excited about it. For reasons I don't understand, it just stalled."

Pratt was not involved in that effort but says, "I did hear that The Sci-Fi Channel wanted that version to have more special effects and be more fantastic. But the wonderful thing about *Quantum Leap* was, it was about real people and that Sam could make a difference in their lives. That was the real heart of the show."

Bellisario still has hope of a revival. "There will be some form of the show coming back," he says. "Too many people love it, it touched an emotional core for them. It's too interesting of a show for it to disappear."

Quantum Leap remains an exhilarating journey for Pratt. "I wrote over 20 episodes and got to explore character, history, relationships, family, friendship, pain and love. The series touched many people, who found their own special rea-son for loving it. Even today, my favorite thing is when people meet me and recognize my name. They'll say, 'I don't watch TV but I watched your show,' or 'It changed my life!' That's a great feeling of satisfaction."

Cast Notes

Scott Bakula (Sam Beckett): Born in St. Louis, the actor formed his own rock band in fourth grade. He had planned to be a lawyer but decided on an acting career and moved to New York City in 1976. He made his Broadway debut as Joe DiMaggio in *Marilyn: An American Fable* and received a Tony nomination in 1988 for his performance in the Broadway musical, *Romance/Romance*. He entered the TV world by doing commercials for Canada Dry and Folgers Coffee. An accomplished singer, dancer, pianist and composer, he was also a recurring reporter in *Murphy Brown* from 1993 until 1996. Bakula later starred as Captain Jonathan Archer on *Star Trek: Enterprise* (2001–2005).

Dean Stockwell (Al): As a child actor he appeared in such films as *Anchors Aweigh* (1945) and *The Boy With Green Hair* (1948). He quit acting at the age of 16 but after a series of odd jobs he returned to show business. He worked as a young man in films like *Compulsion* (1959) and made guest appearances on Rod Serling's *Twilight Zone* and *Night Gallery* but once again, when worked slowed down, he decided to retire from acting and go into real estate. Acting jobs soon returned. and he made his movie comeback in such popular 1980s films as *Dune*, *To Live and Die in LA* and *Blue Velvet*. At the time he was offered *Quantum Leap*, he was also offered a starring role in a TV version of *Married to the Mob*. He picked *Quantum Leap* (*Married to the Mob* would later bomb). Stockwell said he had only one wish, that *Quantum Leap* had gone on for just one more year. His more recent work includes appearances on *Stargate SG-1*, the new *Battlestar Galactica* and *JAG*. He was reunited with Scott Bakula in the 2002 *Star Trek: Enterprise* episode "Detained."

Sources

Mount, Paul. *Starburst*, May 1990

Peel, John. *Starburst*, 1990.

Phillips, Mark, and Frank Garcia. *Science Fiction Television Series: Episode Guides, Histories, and Casts and Credits For 62 Prime-Time Shows, 1959 through 1989*. Jefferson, NC: McFarland, 1996.

RoboCop

(1994)

In the near future, Delta City police officer Alex Murphy is reborn as a half-man–half-machine, encased in a silver metal suit. He strikes fear in the hearts of evildoers everywhere as RoboCop.

Stars: Richard Eden (Alex Murphy/RoboCop), Yvette Nipar (Det. Lisa Madigan), Blu Mankuma (Sgt. Stanley Parks), Andrea Roth (Diana Powers), David Gardner (OCP Chairman), Sarah Campbell (Gadget)

Based on Characters Created by: Ed Neumeier, Michael Miner; **Executive Producers:** Steve Downing, Kevin Gillis, Brian K. Ross; **Producer:** J. Miles Dale; **Line Producer:** Robert Wertheimer; **Co-Producer:** John Sheppard; **Director of Photography:** William Gereghty; **Writers included:** Ed Neumeier, Michael Miner, Alison Lea Bingeman, William Gray, Robert Hopkins, John Sheppard, John Considine, Mary Crawford, Alan Templeton; **Directors included:** Mike Vejar, T.J. Scott, Paul Lynch, Allan Eastman, Mario Azzopardi, William Gereghty, Alan J. Levi, Timothy Bond; **Guest Stars included:** John Rubenstein, Cliff DeYoung, Richard Waugh, Ann Turkel, Roger Mosley, Geriant Wyn Davies, Nigel Bennett, Lisa Howard, Dan Duran (Bo Harlan), Erica Ehm (Rocky Crenshaw), James Kidnie ("Pudface" Morgan), Wayne Robson (Shorty), Jason Blicker (Aubrey Fox), Martin Milner (Russell Murphy)

Syndication/RoboCop Productions Limited Partnership/Rysher TPE, and produced by Skyvision Entertainment and Rigel; 1994; 60 minutes; 23 episodes

RoboCop's three prime directives:
1. <u>SERVE THE PUBLIC TRUST</u>
2. Protect the Innocent
3. Uphold the Law

RoboCop the series was an attempt by Hollywood to do more with an SF character that had progressively deteriorated as a feature film franchise. RoboCop first hit the big screen in director Paul Verhoeven's 1987 R-rated SF actioner starring Peter Weller, Nancy Allen, and Dan O'Herlihy. The film, a big hit, grossed $53 million in the U.S. alone. It was later followed by a 1990 sequel directed by Irvin Kershner also starring Weller and Allen. The second one was also tough and gritty and had visceral action from a screenplay by comic book legend Frank Miller and Walon

Green. But it wasn't as creatively satisfying, and grossed $45 million in the U.S. In 1993, *RoboCop* returned for a third time but without Weller, who didn't want to be tied down to the series. Robert John Burke took over the lead role and it was directed by Fred Dekker, who tapped Frank Miller to co-write the script with him. This film did less business than its predecessors with only a $10 million U.S. gross.

What else was there to do with RoboCop? Of course — go straight to television!

Making the leap from big screen to small has always had mixed results. Successful feature titles such as *Logan's Run*, *Planet of the Apes*, *Timecop*, *Westworld* and *Starman* spawned similar TV efforts that lasted just one season and did not meet expectations. However *The Dead Zone* and *Stargate* were two highly creative success stories.

For this RoboCop incarnation, the two screenwriters who had created RoboCop, Ed Neumeier and Michael Miner, pulled out a sequel script they had planned for the second film, and adapted it for television.

In the course of retooling their creation, a few adjustments were made. A deliberate tonal shift to social satire was the mission on television. To emphasize this, two news break newscasters, Bo Harlan and Rocky Crenshaw, were invented. In each episode their broadcasts would tie into the plot and their sometimes wacky news items would strike the viewer with a point of absurd satire. Their slogan was "Give us three minutes and we'll give you the world!"

The series was filmed in Toronto, Canada; cast in these two roles were a pair of popular Toronto VJs at MuchMusic, Dan Duran and Erica Ehm. Today, Ehm recalls her time on the show. "Shooting *RoboCop* was a blast," she says. "I remember laughing so hard that tears streamed down my cheeks. On several occasions we had to stop filming to redo my waterlogged makeup. Part of what would set us off was the very funny satirical 'news' we had to read with straight faces. The other part was the incredibly insipid character I was playing. Rocky the newscaster was so devoid

Richard Eden as Robocop, filming in Toronto, Canada (© Rysher Entertainment).

of any intelligence, she reacted inappropriately to the disastrous news she was reading, which in many cases is true on TV today. Let's face it, how many newscasters know what they're talking about when they read the teleprompter? If anything, hosts, anchors and other news media types are becoming more vapid as the years go on. In the near future, I predict they'll be using more cyborg hosts to read the news."

In spite of the comedic effects via witty dialogue and over-the-top campy villains, *RoboCop* had strong action, stunts, explosions, gun firefights, matte paintings and computer-generated special effects. The action-adventure format was designed to attract, primarily, a very young male demographic.

In a near future when greedy, predatory corporations dominated the landscape, RoboCop was still police officer Alex Murphy, who had been riddled with bullets and left for dead by sadistic bank robbers. But because of a secret project undertaken by the OCP (Omni-Consumer Products) corporation, Murphy's life was saved by encasing him into a shining silver robot suit and they dubbed him "RoboCop," the best police officer the world has ever seen. Thanks to sophis-

ticated technological design, RoboCop had infrared spectrum vision, could tell if someone was lying via their heartbeat, could record audio and video of everything he saw, was an excellent marksman and could withstand a hail of bullets. He was not fast and nimble but he definitely was a walking and talking tank. Beneath the metallic exterior was the shell of a human being trying to continue his life without letting his wife and son (who believed he was dead) become aware that was now "serving the public trust" as RoboCop.

Detective Lisa Madigan, who essentially served the same role and function as Officer Lewis in the feature, was a loyal friend and partner. Occasionally she would try and prod Alex to let his wife and son know that he was alive as RoboCop, but Alex consistently dissented. He did not want to burden them with his existence.

Sergeant Parks ran the Metro South police station and was Madigan's boss. Hanging out at the station with him was his adopted daughter, Gadget, who occasionally got into trouble. But Gadget was smart and sometimes she stumbled on the right clue or piece of information that would help the officers crack a case.

Running the giant corporation, the OCP chairman tried hard to be a friend to RoboCop, but underneath him were many varied OCP projects that were frequently shepherded by greedy or evil corporate wonks.

RoboCop's greatest adversary, or biggest pain in the ass, was the twisted "Pudface" Morgan, a man out for revenge against RoboCop because of an incident that gave him physical scars when he fell into a vat of toxic chemicals. (These were events that took place in Verhoeven's original film.)

In the series pilot "The Future of Law Enforcement," directed by Paul Lynch, Delta City faces dire consequences when "Pudface" Morgan teams up with a corrupt scientist and his corporate lackey in a plan to install a majordomo computer system capable of controlling every facet of the city from power supply to computer systems. This system, which they called NeuroBrain, would be their ticket to blackmail and ultimate power. But NeuroBrain literally needs a human brain to operate. Dr. Cray Mallardo and his partner in crime, Chip Chayken, found that brain in their beautiful blond assistant Diana Powers. They kill her and she becomes a hologram with direct access to just about everything in Delta City. Throughout the series, Diana (RoboCop's secret friend and partner) had access to the city's electronic infrastructure and helped Robo however she could. Only the OCP chairman was aware of her existence.

"The pilot was gritty, violent and closer to the themes of the movie," says series line producer Robert Wertheimer. The pilot's writers Neumier and Miner adapted an unused script that they had originally intended as a sequel to the feature *RoboCop*. Their intention, as well as those who picked up the mantle for television, was to faithfully render the character for the small screen. But working in television is very different than feature movie-making. "The entire production was radically altered to be more cartoonish," reveals Wertheimer. "Less realistic and less dark in order to satisfy the watered-down TV marketplace as perceived by the market buyers, who are usually out of touch with reality. There were certain things the censors wouldn't permit.

"None of us had signed on to do a light Saturday afternoon show. We all wanted a tougher mainstream show similar to the first movie. What we ended up having to do was something much softer and none of us were happy about it."

It was inevitable that an R-rated property like *RoboCop* would be subject to the limits that television imposes on its dramatic content. In fact,

prior to the shooting of the pilot, the word came down to the filmmakers of what they *couldn't* do.

"This was right at the time we were in a last-minute prep of a big shootout with 'Pudface' Morgan," says Wertheimer. He refers to a sequence when "Pudface" and a gang of bad guys set fires to draw in RoboCop. And when he arrives, "Pudface" launches a missile at him. "Huge sequences with cars, massive barricades, and motorcycles flying through rings of fire," Wertheimer continues. "And then the decision was made we couldn't actually kill anybody. That was dictated to us by the owners, who basically caved in to the buyers, who said, 'You'll have trouble with the German market if it's too violent.'"

Unlike Verhoeven's approach where RoboCop would aim directly and fire his gun at bad guys, he would now engage his internal targeting computer and calculate the trajectory of a bullet fired at, say, a chandelier, which would fall and knock over a bookcase onto the bad guy. This was a clever, albeit very indirect, method of crimefighting.

"I'm sure the syndicator was the one who communicated the temerity and anxiety over the sensitivities of foreign markets to violence," says Wertheimer. "It's a standard problem that you have in the industry." To convey their relationship with the syndication marketers, Wertheimer uses an analogy: "You have to make a tomato, design a tomato, and we're presenting a tomato, and [they] say, 'Gee, I really wanted a watermelon...' Well, it isn't a watermelon. 'That's what I really want.' But, you ordered a tomato! That's a classic example of how the guts and the legs of the series creatively were chopped out from under it." But the producers did devise a variety of distinctive characters and lots of action.

"[We made] a noble attempt to make [the series] as entertaining and as realistic as humanly possible," says Wertheimer. "My memories are about how tough it was for Richard [Eden] and Ken [Quinn], his stunt double, to work in those suits in the Toronto winter. I remember one segment all about motorcycles. It was one of the worst Canadian blizzards. The actors were all frostbitten. And the dialogue couldn't be said because the actors' mouths were literally frozen shut. Shooting in winter conditions in 10, 15 to 20 degrees below zero for exteriors is inhuman.

"Mike Kavanaugh [series special effects coordinator] was quite the 'powder guy,'" says Wertheimer. "We blew up a few buildings. We'd constantly work 20, 21-hour workdays. We'd have all-day nights. We had a second unit shoot where an attack bomb would stick on the wall and blow up. We'd sit there, exhausted and freezing, and the attack bomb would not stick on the wall." The shot was finally achieved, 24 takes later.

Beyond freezing temperatures, Richard Eden was very restricted in not just what he could do physically, but limited by the emotional range that he was allowed to bring to the character. He was, after all, playing a man rebuilt as a robot. "Richard tried desperately to bring his talent to the role. And the producers tried desperately for him not to bring his talent to the role," notes Wertheimer. "It was quite an issue because naturally Richard had a lot to offer. And the producers, justifiably, said that the story arc is of someone whose emotions and essence has been ripped out by surgery so they were not interested in the emotional range that he was capable of bringing to bear. Richard was pretty frustrated by the restrictions emotionally."

In the supporting cast, Wertheimer was most pleased with how Diana, Delta City's secret NeuroBrain, contributed to the story arc. "[Andrea Roth] was very young and very beautiful at the time. You could tell she was going somewhere. She had an ambition and drive about her. She approached her work very professionally. She was very focused on the work. She did a great job.

"I think we had a lot of character in the virtual girl, which was excellent, an attempt to give RoboCop a conscience. His relationship to his family was interesting character development. 'Pudface' Morgan was a terrific villain, he was kind of a Lex Luthor, or a Spider-Man supervillain."

The design and execution of RoboCop's action sequences were quite admirable, despite the restrictions of a television schedule and budget. "I thought Richard Eden's stunt double, Ken Quinn, did some of the best work that anyone has done in Canada," says Wertheimer. He points to two vehicle-related stunts that illustrated the grand scope of the show's action.

The first gag, his favorite, is what he calls "the bus stunt." In the episode "Nano," "nano-technology" (a real-world developing science in which, hypothetically, scientists can use molecular-level engineering to create "nano-robots") is used as a weapon. The bad guy injects a public transit bus with the nano-tech weapon, enabling it to take off under its own power. When Lisa Madigan sees the runaway bus, she runs after it and climbs aboard. Now running at high speed, it hits a

barrier and flips over on its side and bursts into flames, skidding into another vehicle.

Wertheimer was on the set with T.J. Scott, the series' second-unit action director. They had six or seven cameras strategically placed in various corners to capture as much detail as they could. "None of us really knew what was going to happen," recalls Wertheimer. "I'm standing behind T.J.'s shoulder and we were about 50 yards away from where the bus was supposed to plow into [a] truck, get in the air and flip, and blow up and land on its side." The stunt went well and the footage was used in the episode. "The bus stunt was quite legendary," says Wertheimer.

The second gag was a variation of one of the oldest vehicular stunt gags in movie history (and was famously redone in Steven Spielberg's 1981 blockbuster Raiders of the Lost Ark). And that stunt was a homage to one executed by legendary stuntman Yakima Canutt in John Ford's 1939 film Stagecoach. It's the stunt where the character is in front of the moving vehicle and he falls underneath the vehicle but is able to save himself by grabbing the undercarriage even as the vehicle continues moving at a fast pace. To escape from this position, the character hitches himself downward to the tail of the vehicle and climbs back inside from the rear entrance. He would then rush to the front, defeat the driver, and take over the controls himself. And this was all accomplished without special effects or cheats of any kind. The stunt performer would plan, prepare and execute the stunt as seen on film.

In the RoboCop episode "Officer Missing," the vehicle was a very large military-style truck driven by a bad guy (actor Maurice Dean Witt from TekWar). Witt's character sees RoboCop ahead of him and he gleefully increases speed in an attempt to ram Robo. Robo grabs onto the front of the truck and rides with it as it careens forward at high speed. Conveniently, a tow rope spool is available in the front of this truck. Robo grabs onto the rope and allows himself to be dragged underneath the truck. The smooth steel of his robotic body serves as protection. At the tail end of the truck, Robo spins himself 180 degrees, and now he can look up facing the rear of the truck. By pulling the rope, he's able to raise himself back up to a standing position and, using his two titanium steel legs, "braces" himself into ramming position. Immovable object meets irresistible momentum: The truck screeches to an abrupt halt. The driver without a seat belt crashes forward into the windshield and lands right into the feet of Sgt. Parks, who was standing there, in shock, witnessing the events.

"And all this is done live," notes Wertheimer. "And this is Ken Quinn in a plastic suit, freezing to death in the wet cold, on pavement!"

Wertheimer points out that in a feature film "you'd have anywhere from five to ten days to plan for something like that," he says. "We'd have five hours. People don't understand when you do action television, you have to be ten times more creative, better and faster just because there's no time and no money.

"The fact that no one actually got hurt on the show is absolutely remarkable. The stunt requirements were massive. Ken Quinn did almost all the stunt doubling for Richard. The guy was fearless. He was also a skydiver. Fearless and an unbelievable guy to work with."

Lasting just one season, *RoboCop* was a ratings disappointment. Wertheimer shrugs and says, "It ran its course. There wasn't a lot of energy to do another season. It was not as good as it could have been because the writing was rushed.

"The brief for the show was altered in a way that made it very difficult for [executive producer] Steve [Downing] to deliver a type of product that he wanted to deliver so he was caught trying to be really creative and interesting, and be commercial. I also don't feel that the show lent itself very well to commercial television. It lends itself to one, two, and three good movies where it could be as edgy or as dark as you wanted it to be. [On TV] it became more of a kid's younger demographic. It's not RoboCop. It's something else. My biggest lasting impression was the lost potential. The clay was there. The franchise was there. The [robot] suit was there. The pieces were there to make something interesting."

Wertheimer was frustrated by the inability to present a RoboCop that was on a par with other superheroic icons. "It's very hard to compete unless your characters are very well developed and people sign on with the character," he says. "In the case of RoboCop, if your lead guy is not permitted a full emotional range, you're handicapping your show's relationship with the audience's response."

RoboCop's story doesn't end here. In 1998 a short-lived animated series was made, and in 2001 a stronger, tougher Canadian-produced mini-series titled *RoboCop: Prime Directives* (under a new creative team and a new lead actor) extended the life of the character. Although they offered the role to Richard Eden, it was actor Page Fletcher (*The HitchHiker*) who ended up as RoboCop. Writers Brad Abraham, Joseph O'Brien and producer-director Julian Grant took the reins. While the satiric elements were there, *Prime Directives* was considerably stronger in tone and approach than the 1994 series. The mini-series' three parts were titled "Meltdown," "Resurrection," and "Crash and Burn."

CAST NOTES

Richard Eden (Alex Murphy/RoboCop): A busy Canadian actor who has appeared in a wide variety of episodic television series, Richard had recurring roles on *Emerald Point N.A.S.*, *Tales from the Crypt*, *Freddy's Nightmares* and *Tarzan*. After *RoboCop*, he continued with episodic appearances in *Total Recall 2070* ("Brain Fever") and *Earth Final Conflict* ("Emancipation"). His feature work includes *Public Enemies* (1996), Most recently he appeared in *The Intervention* (2007), and *Disappearing in America* (2007).

Yvette Nipar (Det. Lisa Madigan): Coming to prime-time from daytime soaps, Yvette started out in *General Hospital* and *Days of Our Lives*, and then gained notice as Johnny Depp's girlfriend in *21 Jump Street*. She also guest starred on *The Flash* and *The Human Target*, and had a recurring role on *Adventures of Brisco County Jr.* with Bruce Campbell. After *RoboCop*, Yvette starred in the horror feature *Phantoms* (1998) and *Stranded* (2001). Recently she landed co-starring gigs in *Walking Tall 2* (2006) and *3* (2007) with Kevin Sorbo.

Blu Mankuma (Sgt. Stanley Parks): A native of Seattle, Washington, Blu is one of Canada's busiest actors in film, television, theater and voice work. His film credits include *Bird on a Wire* (1990), *The Russia House* (1990), *Another Stakeout* (1993), and *The Final Cut* (2004). On TV he's appeared in the MOWs *Miracle on I-880* (1993) and *Body of Evidence* (1988). SF and fantasy-wise, he was seen in *M.A.N.T.I.S.* as Chief Grant, *Forever Knight*, *Earth Final Conflict*, *The X-Files* and three episodes of *The Outer Limits*. He's also a musician, singer and songwriter.

Andrea Roth (Diana Powers): A native of Woodstock, Ontario, of Scotch-Dutch-Canadian ancestry, Andrea first appeared in *Alfred Hitchcock Presents* (1988) and then later in the acclaimed mini-series *Spoils of War* (1994) and *A Woman of Independent Means* (1995). She's guest-starred on *Nash Bridges*, *Highlander*, *The Outer Limits* ("The Sentence"), *Parker Lewis Can't Lose*,

Earth: Final Conflict ("The Journey") and *CSI*. More recently she had a regular role on *Rescue Me* (2004–2006).

David Gardner (OCP Chairman): An experienced theater actor, David was also a television director at Canada's CBC-TV and he directed 75 productions over nine years. He's one of the founders of the National Theater School in Montreal, Quebec. He's starred in TV's *Street Legal* (1989–1993), *JFK: Reckless Youth* (1993 miniseries), and *Captain Power and the Soldiers of the Future* (1988). In features he starred in *Murder at 1600* (1997) and *The Familiar Stranger* (1997).

Sarah Campbell (Gadget): Sarah has guest-starred on *Kung Fu: The Legend Continues, Psi-Factor: Chronicles of the Paranormal, Stingers, Quintuplets* and *American Dreams*.

Roswell
(1999–2002)

In Roswell, New Mexico, the lives of three human-alien hybrid teenagers, Max and Isabel Evans and Michael Guerin, are complicated when their deepest secret is exposed to their closest friends, Liz, Maria and Alex. Their identities are jeopardized when the town's sheriff, Jim Valenti watches them all very closely.

Cast: Shiri Appleby (Liz Parker), Jason Behr (Max Evans), Katherine Heigl (Isabel Evans), Majandra Delfino (Maria DeLuca), Brendan Fehr (Michael Guerin), Colin Hanks (Alex Whitman) *Year 1–2*, Nick Weschler (Kyle Valenti), William Sadler (Sheriff Jim Valenti), Emilie DeRaven (Tess Harding) *Year 2*, Adam Rodriguez (Jesse Ramirez) *Year 3*

Recurring cast: Diane Farr (Amy DeLuca), John Doe (Jeff Parker), Jo Anderson (Nancy Parker), Garrett M. Brown (Philip Evans), Mary Ellen Trainor (Diane Evans), Devon Gummersall (Sean DeLuca), Desmond Askew (Brody); **Based on the Roswell High book series by:** Melinda Metz; **Developed for Television by:** Jason Katims; **Executive Producers:** Kevin Kelly Brown, Jonathan Frakes, Jason Katims, David Nutter *Year 1*, Lisa J. Olin; **Co-Executive Producers:** Thania St. John *Year 1–2*, Ronald D. Moore *Year 2–3*; **Producers:** Philip J. Goldfarb (pilot), John Heath, Christopher Seitz, Carol Dunn Trussell, Aaron Harberts, Gretchen J. Berg *Year 2–3*, Tracey D'Arcy *Year 3*; **Co-Producers:** Tracey D'Arcy *Year 1–2*, Fred Golan, Lisa Klink *Year 2*, Christopher Seitz; **Consulting Producers:** David Simkins, Tonia Graphia; **Writers included:** Thania St. John, Jason Katims, Toni Graphia, Ronald D. Moore, Gretchen J. Berg, Aaron Harberts, Lisa Klink, David Simkins, Melinda Metz, Laura J. Burns; **Directors included:** David Nutter, Jonathan Frakes, Nick Marck, Paul Shapiro, James Whitmore Jr., Patrick Norris, Bruce Seth Green, James A. Contner, Allan Kroeker, Bill L. Norton, William Sadler; **Director of Photography:** John Bartley; **Guest stars included:** John Cullum, Genie Francis, Charles Napier, Allison Lange, Jason Peck, Jonathan Frakes (as himself), David Conrad (as Agent Daniel Pierce), Ned Romero (as River Dog), Jim Ortlieb (as Nasedo), Julie Benz (as Kathleen Topolsky)

October 1999-May 2002; The WB Network/ United Paramount Network/20th Century–Fox/ Jason Katims Productions/Regency Television; 60 minutes; 61 episodes; DVD status: Complete series

One of the greatest modern mysteries is "Did an extraterrestrial flying saucer crash-land at Roswell, New Mexico, in July 1947?" This burning question has confounded generations of UFO buffs and has spawned a vast mythological industry that has generated books, museums, documentaries and films over the past 60 years. Allegedly, the government's top mandate is "Deny Everything!" "Don't trust the government" is a catchphrase in mainstream usage today.

Roswell High, the ten books from Pocket Books, and this TV series are products of this ongoing fascination with the Roswell event.

In 1997, Laura Burns and Melinda Metz were editors at Parachute Publishing in New York City. It was a company specializing in children's books, notably R.L. Stine's bestselling *Goosebumps* series and the *Adventures of Mary Kate and Ashley* series. Burns and Metz became good friends and began working on projects together. When Burns moved to another company, 17th Street Productions, a teen-oriented book packager, a request came in from Pocket Books for a series with just a title — *Roswell High*, a series about teenage aliens. Burns took that concept and developed the core characters and a Romeo and Juliet romance story with a primary story arc that would thread throughout the book volumes. When it came time to assign an author to actually write the series, Burns tapped Metz, who by this time was out on her own as a freelance writer.

The TV rights were sold and a pilot was ordered before the first book was even in the stores. The rights were sold on the basis of the first draft of the first manuscript, says Metz and Burns. "It happened so quickly it didn't feel quite real. It was a complete thrill!" says Metz. "It was unexpected. I'd worked on book series before that had received interest from Hollywood, and it always went nowhere," adds Burns.

Roswell High told the story of three high school teenagers, Michael Guerin and the siblings Max and Isabel Evans, who were the survivors of the Roswell crash in 1947. While growing up, the trio had come to realize they were very different from everyone else. They possessed extraordinary powers and, in fear of being discovered, kept this secret to themselves. Max and Isabel didn't even tell their adoptive parents of their capabilities. And none of them understood why they had powers or where they came from. But one day, by accident, an incident occurred that changed everyone's lives.

The Crashdown Cafe in Roswell was a favorite teen hangout and the proprietors were the parents of classmate Liz Ortecho. Maria DeLuca, another classmate, also worked at the Crashdown and she was Liz's best friend. At the Crashdown, Liz and Maria worked as waitresses. One day when Max and Michael entered the Crashdown for a drink, an argument ensued between two patrons, and one of them had a gun. In a struggle between the two, a shot was fired and Liz was hit in the abdomen. Max immediately rushed to Liz and he saw the blood on her stomach. Covertly, he placed his hand on the wound and with his powers he erased any sign of the wound. However, in this process, he experienced mental "flashes" of her life growing up. A psychic connection was established. Grabbing a ketchup bottle, and smashing it, Max spread some of it over Liz, and he implored her to say she was not wounded and had only been hit with the condiment.

To avoid the local law, Max and Michael dashed out of the café. Liz came to and realized what had just happened, as she too experienced the flashes when Max made physical contact with her. She was stunned to realize that Max was not an ordinary human being.

The next day at school, Liz asked Max for an explanation. The residue of his lifesaving intervention was a "silver hand print" on her stomach. Reluctantly, Max revealed to her that he was an alien. Later, when a suspicious Maria grilled Liz, she was also told that Max, Isabel and Michael were aliens. Eventually a third classmate, Alex Manes, was also allowed into the circle. When the local sheriff, James Valenti, grew suspicious of Liz's recovery, he became a real threat to the lives of the three very special teenagers.

Over the course of the ten books, the six teenagers' lives intertwined in very complex ways with a love relationship between Max and Liz at its core. Michael and Maria had their own push-pull type of a boyfriend-girlfriend relationship and Isabel became very fond of Alex. Constant threats of exposure kept the group very busy.

Thematically, *Roswell* explored three distinct areas simultaneously: It was a quest for identity among the teenage aliens: "Does where you come from define who you are? Is it right to use power just because you possess it? Everyone feels like an alien sometimes," says Metz and Burns. Additionally, there was the Roswell sheriff and the government trying to find and capture them. And it was a teen drama romance between three sets of teenagers. Three of them were ordinary teenagers but the other three were human-alien hybrids.

From a pragmatic and commercial viewpoint there were also echoes of two other popular teen dramas: *Beverly Hills 90210* and *Melrose Place*.

The *Roswell High* book property fell to producer-writer Jason Katims, who had made his name with the short-lived cult series *My So-Called Life* starring Claire Danes. An ideal person to adapt the books for television, he was very faithful to the material. Katims only slightly adjusted a few things: Liz would no longer be a Latino named Ortecho but a Caucasian girl named Parker. The physical descriptions of the teen characters didn't have to match the actors who were cast. In the TV series, Sheriff Valenti evolved into a character who was not a "black hat" villain as he was drawn in the book series.

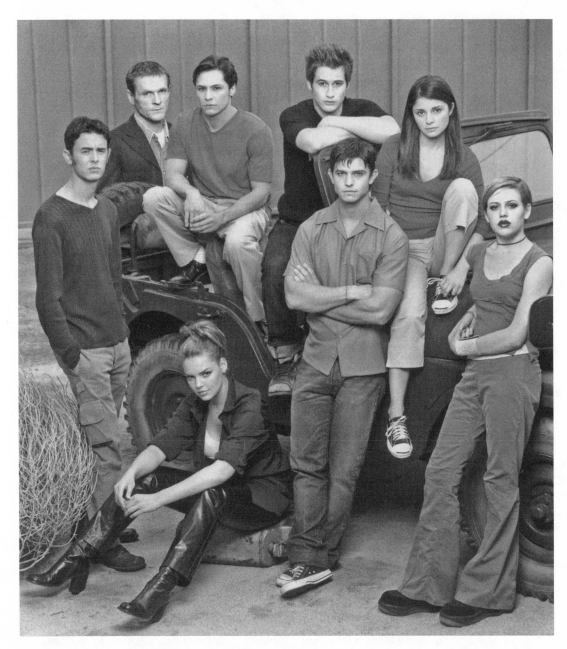

Roswell players: sitting Katherine Heigl; from left, Colin Hanks, William Sadler, Nick Wechsler, Brendan Fehr, Jason Behr, Shiri Appleby and Majandra Delfino (© Warner Bros. Television).

Retained were the characterizations and relationships between the human and alien teenagers. "Since we both tend to focus more on character than plot, we were perfectly happy about this!" say Metz and Burns. It allowed producers and writers to build their own universe and allow the stories and characters to organically grow into their own.

Although the series was initially developed by Fox Television for the Fox Network, it was ultimately sold to the WB Network, who felt the show would appeal to the audience they were interested in reaching. The WB Network gave the producers a full 22-episode order for the first season. (Had *Roswell* aired on Fox TV, the show would have likely received an initial 13-episode order.)

Actor-director Jonathan Frakes recalls his introduction to *Roswell*: "I had a healthy respect for all things alien. I had hosted the *Alien Autopsy* and had also done another show on Roswell, so for better or worse I was attached, in people's minds to that genre." Frakes appeared on the series three times as himself and directed five episodes. "What I didn't know was how wonderful this show ... would turn out to be. Fox hired Jason Katims, a very clever writer, and he took over as the show-runner, as I'm not a writer."

At that moment in time, Frakes was finishing up a *Star Trek* film, *Insurrection*, and he had been primed to direct the pilot, but "the head of 20th Century–Fox thought it would be a good idea if I did just one job, so David Nutter ended up shooting the pilot, and it was a great success."

When the pilot aired on October 9, 1999, Metz and Burns were ecstatic. "It was so cool. I felt like I was collaborating with a bunch of people I'd never met — Jason Katims and the writing staff, the actors, the producers, the director, the costume and set people," says Metz.

"There was a sense of heightened excitement in watching it, knowing that it was truly the starting point for a whole different version of *Roswell*," says Burns. "I don't think there was a single thing about it that we didn't love. It had a very similar tone to the books (and of course the plot was very close to the plot of our first book), and the touristy goofiness of the place mixed with the romance between Max and Liz was exactly in keeping with what we'd envisioned for the books. I still think it's one of the best pilots out there."

David Nutter, who had a television development deal with 20th Century–Fox, arrived on *Roswell* after having completed a MGM feature film, *Disturbing Behavior* starring Katie Holmes and James Marsden where he did not have a good time. "That movie was something that they wanted, 'X-Files with teenagers,' and I attempted to give them that but they ended up not wanting that," says Nutter. "I was creatively crushed and needed a pick-up. Then Fox came to me with this *Roswell* idea, which was exactly what they had tried to do with *Disturbing Behavior* so I really wanted to be involved with this."

When Nutter met up with Katims, they hit it off together and collaborated on the pilot. What attracted Nutter was, foremost, the Romeo and Juliet component between Liz and Max. These were two characters who wanted to be together but could not, primarily because of Max's alien heritage.

"It was the highest-testing pilot ever made for 20th Century–Fox Television and I was very proud of that," says Nutter, who also became the series' executive producer in its first year. "When directing a pilot, you're really involved in every creative decision, from casting of the leads to the look and tone of the show. Jason and I worked a lot on the story together and it was a wonderfully creative experience."

When the *Roswell* producers began casting, it wasn't yet pilot season in Hollywood. This meant that the acting pool to draw from was larger than usual. Nutter was instrumental in casting the series' leads. The search spanned from Los Angeles to New York, but having worked many times in Vancouver (where *Disturbing Behavior* was filmed) Nutter encouraged that casting also look there for candidates. Brendan Fehr was cast in Vancouver.

"We loved all the actors on the show," says Metz and Burns. "They never condescended to the characters or played them as just a gimmick. Instead, they all focused on the humanity at the core of the characters, even when the characters were aliens."

When Jason Behr was cast as Max, he brought a vulnerability and, often, a very understated acting style to the role. But as the series progressed, the character grew stronger and more decisive. "Jason Behr really captured Max's seriousness, and the responsibility he had to carry," say Metz and Burns. "And when he looked at Liz — wow. You could really feel the longing."

"Shiri Appleby brought so much soul to the part, and such a feeling of an ordinary girl thrown into an extraordinary situation. She did a wonderful job, and her depiction of the relationships with Max and with Maria were exactly what we'd pictured."

Katherine Heigl, as Isabel, was the blond beauty among the cast. Isabel had, in the words of the authors, bits of "aloofness, bitchiness and coldness," but the actress brought out her soft heart "and she was able to show that vulnerability to the cameras."

Colin Hanks (as Alex, one of the three teenagers entrusted with knowledge of the aliens' identities) was just what the authors wanted: a "goofy boy-next-door with the strength to back his convictions with absolutely everything he had."

Brendan Fehr, a Canadian import, served as the impulsive, emotional foil against Jason's Max. As Michael, he was the most defensive alien. It took Michael a long time to open up emotionally and to allow Maria to enter his life. But what came with that were the complexities of a love relationship. When they were together, Michael and Maria were a very hot and cold dynamic. Say Metz and Burns, "Brendan always found ways to show that streak of vulnerability Michael had. But he also brought a sense of humor to the character that constantly cracked us up."

Majandra Delfino (Maria) did much with the "best friend" supporting player and found her own very complicated love life with Michael. "Majandra brought such sparkle and humor to Maria," say Metz and Burns. "The scenes with Shiri and Majandra really made you feel that best-friend bond between Liz and Maria. There was one scene where Shiri was resting her head in Majandra's lap that just made you go 'Awww!' So sweet."

Serving as antagonists in the first season against the alien teenagers, Sheriff Valenti and his son Kyle were played by William Sadler and Nick Weschler. "We loved the shades of gray [Sadler] brought to the character," say Metz and Burns. "He's a phenomenal actor, and his very presence brought a sense of gravitas to the show. Nick's Kyle is so funny and sweet, and the relationship between him and Bill Sadler as his father was always touching and frequently hilarious." As a contrast from the novels, the TV Valentis evolved into sympathetic and heroic personas.

Jason Katims, the executive producer who adapted Metz's books for television, was very candid at the Television Critics Association Press Tour, which was held on July 20, 1999 in Pasadena, California. He told the assembled press that although the first season had generally been plotted out, they were mostly just "totally winging it" on a daily basis. "To me, one of the exciting things about the premise of the show is that three alien characters in the show don't know about their history, which makes [things], from a writing point of view, exciting because as they discover their backstory, the audience is discovering it.

"We have a way of doing it that can be personal and hopefully very emotional. It's something that we're going to discover with them and it will be a long ride and hopefully a really fulfilling journey."

David Nutter added, "It's a very timeless story about unrequited love. That's something that emotionally will bring the audience into making them want to watch the show and get involved in these characters."

Actress Shiri Appleby, also talking at the press

tour, said, "I actually auditioned for all three of the girl parts numerous times. I think what really drew me was the writing. It really spoke to me and it is written in a really realistic way, so for people my age, it's easy to understand. And I got really lucky in working with a really good group of talented young people and so we're able to work together and bounce ideas off of each other. That's what really appealed me to the entire show."

In its first season, *Roswell* began exploring the burgeoning relationships between the three alien teenagers and their new-found friends who were let in on their secrets. But at the same time, they became even more protective and private. They were fearful of an inquisitive sheriff, government agents, curious UFO buffs, and even another classmate: Kyle Valenti.

Over the course of the first season, Liz found clues to the aliens' secret origins at an Native American reservation. Michael became independent of his abusive adoptive father and a new girl, Tess, arrived at Roswell High; Max found himself very attracted to her. Liz became suspicious and planted a camera inside her house and was shocked that Tess also possessed alien powers. At the end of the season, Max was snatched by government agents convinced that he was an alien and tortured in a "white room." Nasedo — who was a shapeshifter alien — was Tess' father, and she was "the fourth alien" that incubated along with the other three after the Roswell crash. Her power to cloud minds and plant images was useful in penetrating the government base to retrieve Max. This was called "mind-warping."

In the season's finale, "Destiny," Sheriff Valenti and Kyle learned of the teenagers' alien nature when Kyle was struck by a bullet. Max saved Kyle's life in the same way he had saved Liz's life — he placed his hands on Kyle and used his powers to repair the damage that the bullet had done. The sheriff and his son now became grateful allies.

Although the first season did well and attracted a loyal fan following, the WB network admitted it was on the fence about renewal for a second year. This instigated a fan campaign. On April 10, 2000, a $2,500 full-page ad was bought in *Variety*, the Hollywood industry trade magazine, by fans who called themselves the "Alien Blast"; in the ad copy, the fans wrote, "We would like to thank The WB for the hottest show on television. We are looking forward to next season!" The graphics used were the *Roswell* series logo and a glowing hand-print (the one left by Max Evans on Liz Parker's abdomen when he saved her, as seen in the series' main titles).

As part of the campaign, fans mailed thousands of Tabasco sauce mini-bottles to WB executives, as an attention-getting gimmick that would help draw the attention of the media and non-viewers to the show's plight and help get the show renewed. Why Tabasco hot sauce? It was the dietary favorite of the three hybrid aliens, who loved to use it on almost everything. The WB redirected some of the bottles to newspapers such as the *New York Daily News* to help publicize the effort.

Various news reports from the *Washington Post* cited "over 3,000 bottles" were sent (the Associated Press said 6,000 bottles). There was a publicity photo of Katherine Heigl holding a Tabasco bottle while surrounded with mail bags full of them.

When The WB announced their fall schedule on May 16, 2000, all of their dramatic programs survived including *Roswell*. Susanne Daniels, president of the Entertainment division, said in a press release, "*Roswell* and *Felicity* came into their own creatively and ratings-wise the last eight episodes of the year and they both earned their way onto the schedule. The Tabasco sauce, e-mail campaigns and demonstrations also got our attention."

Series producer Kevin Kelly Brown wrote an open letter to fans on the same day; it was posted at the Crashdown website, a clearinghouse for all things *Roswell* the TV series. He said, in part, "[T]he fans of *Roswell* proved that they are the most powerful fans of any show on television. I don't think anyone in or out of television has seen anything like your 'Roswell Is Hot' Tabasco campaign. It grabbed more attention in the press than any save-the-show campaign anyone can recall."

Aaron Harberts and Gretchen Berg, a writer-producer team on the series, recalled the first year as a character and universe-building time. "I think [series creator Jason Katims] was just setting up the world," says Harberts. "It was a very emotional season. It was the humans interacting with the aliens." "It was very heart-wrenching, romantic and sweeping. It was really well-executed," agrees Berg.

Harberts and Berg joined the writing staff at the start of the second year. Their first script was "The Summer of '47," a serio-comic look at the Roswell crash from the point of view of a military officer who was there. "Summer of '47" was a departure for the cast, an opportunity to play other roles in the year 1947 during the time of the spaceship crash.

"It was a period piece where we went back to the original Roswell crash," says Harberts. "The cast really got into it. They got to wear 1940s costumes. That was just a lot of fun because we were writing about what allegedly took place back at that time and we did a lot of research on it. Some characters were composites of some real people who were there. We kind of blended a lot of the myths and legends together. It was really neat to have turned the soundstages at Paramount into a military base for several scenes and just watching the actors walk around in their period costumes."

The writers' job was to blend the historical research together with the characters and situations of the TV series. "To make the story work there was some poetic license in some places, but at the same time it was kind of neat how we were able to dovetail," says Berg. "It was exciting to be able to pick and choose from history and execute it with our actors that we were already familiar with. It was a very fun episode to do and it was a great introduction to the show."

Roswell's second year emphasized the science fiction, and leaned more towards serialized storytelling. *Star Trek* writer Ronald D. Moore joined the show as a producer and writer and he brought his talents to the fore.

In terms of plot, the second year focused on the existence of alien enemies dubbed "the skins," who were out to get the alien teenagers. In subsequent episodes, the Roswell aliens learned they had a "duplicate set" of themselves living in New York, and that Max was "the king" of the planet Antar. "Two batches" of the four were purposely sent to Earth as human-alien hybrids "to be reborn." Genetically, they were representations of "the Royal Four," and were in exile as a result of planetary war.

Later, when Alex was killed as a result of an apparent automobile accident, the entire group fell into enormous grief. As the events unfolded over a series of episodes, Liz investigated the nature of the accident and in the final episode of the second year, just when the Roswell aliens returned to their secret incubation chamber in the desert, to leave Earth via the hidden "Granilith" (a device that could send them home), Liz, Maria and Kyle frantically arrived and accused Tess of orchestrating and hiding Alex's death. In the end, Tess left Earth and left behind the Royal trio. As a result of her departure, Max was in great pain. She was pregnant with his child.

"We did have more focus on science fiction,"

says Harberts. "There was [a] push to develop an SF mythology, get more into the world of the aliens and start building that out. That was actually fun. But it was a change from what they were doing on the first season. When Gretchen and I came to the show, we never considered ourselves SF writers, we came to the show being huge fans of Jason's writing. We came in loving the show because it was very emotional and dealt with the relationships."

Killing off Alex was actually for behind-the-scenes reasons: Actor Colin Hanks had received an offer to do a feature and the producers didn't want to hold him back, so they arranged to write the character out of the series. "He didn't want to leave," notes Harberts. "He got an opportunity to do this movie with [director] Mike White, *Orange County*. That was just the way the story had to be told to make the [work schedules] all work out. Alex's death had a huge effect on that season."

"Alex was a huge character," adds Berg. "It was great that we were able to use him when we could, to come back and be an angel on Isabel's shoulder. She missed her friend and he was able to be there for her" as a ghost.

Harberts says, "Everyone was sad because Colin was somebody that everyone loved. He's a joy to work with and a joy to write for. We were sad to see him go."

With the loss of two recurring characters, the third year was a new page. The show flipped from the WB network to UPN. During the transition, loyal fans mobilized once again. On April 2001, as the final six episodes of the second year were airing, the network told Sci-Fi Wire (the Sci-Fi Channel's newswire service) that a decision whether to renew or cancel the show would be announced on May 15. By early May, rumors circulated that if WB canceled *Roswell*, the show would migrate to UPN along with *Buffy the Vampire Slayer* and *Angel*, two series that UPN promised to pick up if WB axed them. (With an average of four million viewers per episode, the show was vulnerable.) This time around, fans targeted UPN and Fox with a renewed Tabasco bottle campaign. According to Sci-Fi Wire, 12,000 bottles were sent to UPN and *The New York Post* reported that series producers sent the network an online petition signed by 30,000 fans urging that the show be saved.

On May 14, The WB officially canceled the series but kept *Angel*. On May 15, UPN announced it was picking up *Roswell* and airing it on Tuesdays at 9 P.M. after *Buffy the Vampire Slayer*, another WB series they had picked up. Apparently these decisions were made at the last minute. According to an interview with Zap2it.com, an online newswire service, executive producer Ronald D. Moore and series creator Jason Katims were on the phones with the networks and their agents on May 14. And it all worked out to the delight of series fans everywhere.

In its third year, complicated relationships abounded. Max and Liz were back together again, but Max was obsessed with finding his son who left the planet with Tess. Believing a spaceship was hidden in a secret facility underneath a convenience store, Max and Liz pretended to hold up the place in order to access the ship. But they got arrested, and Liz's father forbade her from seeing Max again. Meanwhile, Isabel wrestled with her grief over the death of Alex and her newfound love for Jesse, a lawyer working in her father's office. Maria and Michael grew closer to each other, just as Maria pursued a musical career.

As the season progressed, Liz developed precognitive powers as a result of her physical interactions with Max. Isabel became engaged to Jesse, in an attempt at a normal life, but withheld her alien heritage from him. When her "true identity" was finally revealed, Jesse was bewildered and frightened. Max's father and Liz's father colluded together in an investigation of Max's background.

In the end, numerous plots were wrapped up: Max and Isabel's parents learned the truth about their adopted children's heritage and Tess returned with Max's son. Frightened of placing the child constantly in danger, Max very reluctantly had it put up for adoption.

In the series' final episode, all six teens decided to leave Roswell immediately after their high school graduation (Liz's precog powers had foreseen the FBI's Special Unit assassination of them all). In an effort to protect themselves and all their loved ones, Max, Isabel, Michael, Maria, Liz and Kyle stepped into a Volkswagen bus and tearfully left Roswell for an unknown, nomadic future. But Liz and Max did get married....

Reflecting on the third year, Harberts notes, "There was focus on a lot of the aliens and a lot on the 'mythology' that season," he says. "The stories tended to be bigger. Sometimes more science fiction and sometimes more action, more special effects. It's always fun to blow things up. The best is when Michael and Max come to blows ["Who

Died and Made You King?"] when Michael takes over Max's powers. They get into this huge fight at Isabel's house. Jason Behr was really strong in that arc to find his son. And Shiri Appleby had to do a lot of crying! The pain that she had to channel in that season was really good, too. They were doing some really good acting in that year."

Coming full circle, *Roswell* book creators Melinda Metz and Laura Burns joined the series as staff writers. "We were in L.A., hoping to get a staff job on a TV show, and we met with Jason Katims just to chat and ask him for some advice," says Metz. "At that point, the WB had decided not to pick up *Roswell* for a third season, and the UPN hadn't picked it up yet, so there was no chance of a job on that show. When *Roswell* did get added to UPN's schedule, Jason offered us a job."

The TV show "was kind of like an alternate universe to the books," says Metz. "We got a great welcome from the *Roswell* writing staff and it was wonderful to sit in a room with them and help figure out what could happen next in the *Roswell* universe."

"We had no extremely possessive feelings about *Roswell*, although many writers might have, I guess," Burns says candidly. "We understood from the start that the television show would have its own life and would create its own world. We were, therefore, pleasantly surprised to see that it started out being so close to the world we'd created! We'd expected it to change more than it did. And, of course, we watched it the whole time it was on — even before we ever worked on it. So we were just as familiar with the TV plots and characters as we were with the book ones. By the time we joined the writing staff of the show, we were thrilled to be able to discuss and plot for our 'baby' with lots of smart, funny, talented writers."

Jonathan Frakes sums up, "I was very proud of the show. *Roswell* was a fascinating show with a very loyal fan base. It had such survival instincts. It was a great experience directing it. It had a maturity. I'm a big fan."

If there was one aspect of the show that Frakes regretted, it was that too many characters were aware of the aliens' secrets. "I was concerned that we, as producers, writers and the network, let too many of the regular characters in on the secret, as to who was an alien," he says. "There wasn't a lot of surprise and there wasn't much opportunity for conflict and revelation and all the things that would come with not knowing that.

"Once that mistake had been made, by all of us, it was hard to write for because their intimate friends knew their secret. It would have been more interesting had they not."

Two years after the series' cancellation, the Season One DVD box set was released on February 2004 (subsequently, Seasons Two and Three were also released). But first, a number of the songs heard in the series had to be replaced for licensing reasons. One of the gimmicks used to attract a youthful audience to the show was the inclusion of pop songs from contemporary artists such as Sarah McLachlan, Nelly Furtado, and Coldplay. (A series soundtrack album was released in February 2002.) The series' catchy and memorable theme song, "Here With Me," was a song previously released by British pop star Dido. (The song appears on her "No Angel" album.) The lyrics were warm and romantic and applied to the Romeo and Juliet component of the story.

"There's something so evocative in Dido's voice and in the melody," notes Melinda Metz. "But I almost think Sarah McLachlan's 'Fear,' which was used elsewhere in the show, has lyrics that fit the star-crossed love part of *Roswell* better. Yet at this point I can't imagine anything but 'Here With Me' as the show's theme song."

"Jason Katims loves music; all the music on *Roswell* reflects his great taste, and 'Here With Me' is no exception," says Burns.

As a merchandising spin-off, Pocket Books published three novels, "Loose Ends," "No Good Deed" and "Little Green Men" when the show was on the air.

After the series ended, Simon Spotlight Entertainment published a series of eight novels. The first four ("Shades," "Skeletons in the Closet," "Dreamwalk," and "Quarantine" by Laura Burns) acted as a bridge between year two and three. The final four ("A New Beginning," "Nightscape," "Pursuit," and "Turnabout") picked up where the final episode left off. The last two books proposed a resolution to the outstanding plots and issues that had prevented the kids from returning to Roswell.

"[The show] had a lot more life in it," notes Harberts. "It was sad. The writers really got the characters sent to such a great place and then it was over. I think there could have been a lot more interesting stories and dilemmas to tell with Michael and Maria, and with Liz and Max. It's too bad it ended when it ended. They were moving along in a very nice direction."

Berg's final observation of the series: "It was just fantastic. It was really good fun, creative and [telling] a lot of stories. We got to see characters grow a lot. It was really fulfilling."

According to Harberts, "It was a fun and fulfilling experience because we had fans who loved it. They lived and died by the show. We had a cast who we knew were all going to be big stars. You could feel that you were getting in the ground floor of something exciting and special. It was a time when I felt everyone was doing their best work."

"I wish it was back," Jonathan Frakes sighs. "I still hold out hopes there is a *Roswell* movie that would answer all the questions that were asked but not answered. It may all be in my mind, but it's something to be considered. It would make a wonderful film. Because of the cast, and Jason [Katims'] talent and Ron Moore ... they got the mythology. The relationships were wonderful. They had a sense of humor which a lot of these teen shows didn't have."

Cast Notes

Shiri Appleby (Liz Parker): She began her acting career at the young age of four. After appearing in various national commercials (Cheerios, Taco Bell, M&Ms), she landed her first television job in daytime appearing on *Santa Barbara*. Next came roles on *thirtysomething, Xena: Warrior Princess, Doogie Howser, M.D.*, and *7th Heaven*, among others. After *Roswell*, Appleby appeared in the TV series *Six Degrees*. She has also been seen in numerous films including *The Other Sister* (1999), *Swimfan* (2002), *What Love Is* (2007) and *Charlie Wilson's War* (2007), the latter written by Aaron Sorkin and produced by Tom Hanks. Her name Shiri means "song of mine" in Hebrew.

Jason Behr (Max Evans): Familiar to fans of The WB via his roles on *Dawson's Creek, Buffy the Vampire Slayer, 7th Heaven, JAG*, and *Profiler*, Behr is a native of Minneapolis who began acting when he was only five. A veteran of over 75 commercials, Behr was in *Pleasantville* (1998) and *Rites of Passage* (1999). After *Roswell* he did more feature work: *The Grudge* (2004), *Happily Ever After* (2004) and *The Tattooist* (2007).

William Sadler (Sheriff Jim Valenti): Sadler's 30-year acting career includes *The Shawshank Redemption* (1994) on film and *Biloxi Blues* on stage. He's a veteran of the New York stage, appearing in over 75 productions in 12 years. He's famous for a villainous role in *Die Hard 2* (1990), as the Grim Reaper in *Bill and Ted's Bogus Journey* (1991) and

for his work in *Disturbing Behavior* (1998), directed by David Nutter. On TV he's appeared in *St. Elsewhere, The Outer Limits, Tales from the Crypt*, and *Star Trek: Deep Space Nine*. After *Roswell*, Sadler's television appearances included *Law & Order: Criminal Intent, JAG, Thirdwatch, Tru Calling*, and *CSI*. On the Broadway stage in 2005, he appeared in *Julius Caesar*'s title role.

Katherine Heigl (Isabel Evans): Born in Washington D.C., Katherine began acting at the age of nine and had a breakout role as a rebellious teenager in *My Father the Hero* (1994) with Gerard Depardieu. She starred in the action-thriller *Under Siege 2: Dark Territory* (1995) and in the horror film *Bride of Chucky* (1998). In 1998 she co-starred with Peter Fonda in a movie of the week reworking of Shakespeare's *The Tempest*. After *Roswell*, Heigl was featured in a movie of the week, *Critical Assembly* (2003) and a *Twilight Zone* episode, and in 2005 got cast as a regular in *Grey's Anatomy* as Dr. Isobel "Izzie" Stevens. In 2007, she won her first Emmy award as Best Supporting Actress in a Drama for that medical series.

Majandra Delfino (Maria DeLuca): When she was cast in *Roswell*, 18-year-old Majandra had just completed her senior year of high school, but was already an experienced actress. Daughter of a Venezuelan father and a Cuban-American mother, Majandra danced in *The Nutcracker* when she was just ten years old and sang in an all-girl quartet, "China Doll," opening for The Bee Gees. Her first music album, "The Sicks" sold 12,000 copies on the Internet and was popular in Paris. At 14, she won the role of Kathleen Quinlan's daughter in *Zeus & Roxanne*; in her first television series, she played Tony's eldest daughter on *The Tony Danza Show*. Her big-screen credits included *Traffic* (2000), *I Know What You Screamed Last Summer* (2000), *Fluorescent* (2006) and *I Remember* (2006). After *Roswell*, she had the lead role in the romantic comedy movie of the week *Celeste in the City* (2004).

Brendan Fehr (Michael Guerin): A Canadian raised in New Westminster, British Columbia, Brendan had his eye on sports but eventually he moved on to print modeling work for sportswear catalogues. When he signed with a talent agent in Vancouver, he landed a guest-starring role in *Breaker High*. That appearance led to many other Vancouver-based film productions such as *Millennium*, and he caught the attention of director David Nutter and appeared in his 2001 feature *Disturbing Behavior*. He also had a brief role in the cult hit *Final Destination* (2000). After *Roswell*, in 2004–2005 Brendan had a major recurring role on *CSI: Miami* as Dan Cooper for 24 episodes. His feature work includes *The Long Weekend* (2005), *Comeback Season* (2006) and *The Fifth Patient* (2006).

Colin Hanks (Alex Whitman): Born in Sacramento and the son of actor Tom Hanks, Colin's star rose quickly. After *Roswell*'s second season, Colin was immediately cast in a feature comedy, *Orange County* (2002), and that led him to other roles: *Rx* (2005), *Standing Still* (2005), and *King Kong* (2005), the latter directed by Peter Jackson. Other films include *Tenacious D: The Pick of Destiny* (2006), *The Great Buck Howard* (2007), *Homeland Security* (2007) and *Barry Munday* (2007).

Nick Weschler (Kyle Valenti): A native of Albuquerque, New Mexico, Nick started his acting career in high school plays. His Hollywood adventure began with the movie of the week *Full Circle* (1996), which led to appearances in *Team Knightrider, Silk Stalkings* and *Lazarus Man*. After *Roswell*, Nick made guest appearances in *Tru Calling, Malcolm in the Middle* and *Crossing Jordan*.

Emilie DeRaven (Tess Harding): After seven episodes of the Australian-filmed fantasy series *Beastmaster*, Emilie spent just one month in Hollywood before being cast in *Roswell*. She next landed a succession of guest-starring roles (*Navy NCIS, CSI: Miami*, etc.) and appeared in the movie of the week version of Stephen King's *Carrie* (2002). She hit it big with a role in ABC's monster hit TV series *Lost* (as Claire).

Adam Rodriguez (Jesse Ramirez): An American actor of Puerto Rican and Cuban heritage, Adam dreamed of being a professional baseball player but turned to performing in children's theater in New York. His Hollywood break was a role on *NYPD Blue*. He's made guest appearances in *Brooklyn South, Felicity* and *Resurrection Boulevard*. After *Roswell*, he landed the role of Eric Delko in *CSI: Miami*. He was featured in *People* magazine's "Sexiest Men Alive" issue.

SOURCES

Bauder, David. "ABC, WB Networks Present New Schedules." Associated Press, May 19, 2000.

Roberts, Chris. "New WB Series Ups the Ante on Teen Angst." Associated Press, September 29, 1999.

"Roswell Officially Picked Up." UltimateTV.com May 12, 2000.

Scott, Tracy L. "WB TV's Roswell Series is Saved by Aliens' Tabasco Sauce." *Washington Post*, December 2000.

Starr, Michael. "Roswell's on the Ropes ... Can Hot Sauce Save This Show?" *New York Post*, April 7, 2000.

seaQuest DSV

(1993–1996)

The submarine seaQuest DSV patrols the colonized oceans of 2018 (and in a follow-up series, 2032).

Cast: Roy Scheider (Capt. Nathan Bridger) *Year 1–2*, Michael Ironside (Capt. Oliver Hudson) *Year 3*, Stephanie Beacham (Dr. Kristin Westphalen) *Year 1*, Jonathan Brandis (Lucas Wolenczak), Don Franklin (Lt. Comdr. Jonathan Ford), Ted Raimi (Lt. O'Neill), Stacy Haiduk (Lt. Comdr. Katherine Hitchcock) *Year 1*, John D'Aquino (Lt. Benjamin Krieg) *Year 1*, Royce D. Applegate (Security Chief Manilow Crocker) *Year 1*, Edward Kerr (Lt. James Brody) *Year 2–3*, Rosalind Allen (Dr. Wendy Smith) *Year 2*, Marco Sanchez (Miguel Ortiz) *Year 2*, Kathy Evison (Ensign Lonnie Henderson) *Year 2–3*, Michael DeLuise (Tony Piccolo) *Year 2–3*, Peter DeLuise (Dagwood) *Year 2–3*, Elise Neal (Lt. JJ Fredericks) *Year 3*

Created by: Rockne S. O'Bannon; **Executive Producers:** Rockne S. O'Bannon, Tommy Thompson *Year 1*, Steven Spielberg, Philip Segal, David J. Burke *Year 1–2*, Clifton Campbell, Patrick Hasburgh *Year 2–3*; **Co-Executive Producers:** Clifton Campbell *Year 2*, Carleton Eastlake *Year 3*; **Supervising Producers:** Les Sheldon, Hans Tobeason, Kerry Lenhart, John J. Sakmar *Year 1*, Clifton

Campbell, Lawrence Hertzog, Carleton Eastlake, *Year 2*, Lee Goldberg, William Rabkin *Year 3*; ***Producers:*** David Kemper *Year 1*, Clifton Campbell, Philip Carr Neel, Carleton Eastlake, Les Sheldon, Oscar L. Costo *Year 2*, Steve Beers Year *2–3*, Gregg D. Fienberg; ***Co-Producers:*** Philip Carr Neel *Year 2–3*, Harker Wade, David Kemper *Year 3*; ***Associate Producer:*** Philip Carr Neel *Year 2*, Peter Mavromates *Year 3*; ***Coordinating Producer:*** Lindsley Parsons III; ***Consulting Producer:*** Les Sheldon *Year 2*; ***Technical Consultant:*** Dr. Robert D. Ballard *Year 1*; ***Executive in Charge of Production:*** Philip David Segal; ***Writers included:*** Carleton Eastlake, Naren Shankar, Melinda Snodgrass, John J. Sakmar, Kerry Lenhart, Michael Cassutt, Ted Raimi, Jonathan Brandis, Lee Goldberg, William Rabkin, Patrick Hasburgh, Javier Grillo-Marxauch; ***Directors included:*** Irvin Kershner, Les Landau, Anson Williams, Bill L. Norton, Bryan Spicer, Gus Trikonis, Oscar L. Costo, Bruce Seth Green, Jesus Salvador Trevino, Burt Brinkerhoff, Gabrielle Beaumont, Les Sheldon; ***Guest Stars included:*** Charlton Heston, William Shatner, David McCallum, Brittany Murphy, Turhan Bey, Roscoe Lee Browne, Yaphet Kotto, Kellie Martin, Udo Kier, David Morse, Tim Russ, James Shigeta, Jonathan Banks, Dennis Lipscomb, Bonnie Bartlett, Mark Hamill, Dom DeLuise, Robert Foxworth, Kristoffer Tabori, Seth Green, Michael York (as President Bourne), Kent McCord (as Commander Scott Keller), Richard Herd (as Admiral Noyce); ***Production Designer:*** Richard Lewis; ***Music Theme:*** John Debney *Year 1 and 2*, Russ Mitchell Landau *Year 3*; ***Special Vocal Effects (Voice of Darwin):*** Frank Welker

Amblin Entertainment and Universal Television/NBC; September 1993–January 1996; 60 minutes; 58 episodes; DVD status: Seasons 1–2

"As soon as that dolphin opened its mouth and started jabbering, I knew its life would be short-lived." That was an online fan talking about *seaQuest.* The series had famous actors, talented producers, big budgets and a pilot that opened with an inspiring voice-over by President John F. Kennedy. Even *The National Education Association* recommended *seaQuest*— at first. But it sank as a terrible kids' submarine saga, punctuated by a talking dolphin. "*seaQuest* was always a troubled show," observes writer Carleton Eastlake.

The year is 2018 and, on the surface, the overpopulated world's natural resources have been used up. The ocean is more essential to human survival than ever and pioneer families, farmers and miners have colonized the ocean floor. The series focused on Captain Nathan Bridger, who created the submarine *seaQuest DSV*. After his son was killed in battle, he made an oath to his wife to quit the military and conduct research with his super-intelligent dolphin, Darwin.

When a fanatical submarine commander named Marilyn Stark (Shelley Hack) attacks undersea settlements in the first episode, the reluctant Bridger (now a widower) is convinced by The United Earth Ocean Organization (UEO) to command *seaQuest* again. His crew includes young black Commander Ford, nerdy communications officer O'Neill, genius teenager Lucas Wolenczak and British doctor Kristin Westphalen.

Stark's enemy sub is sunk in a climactic battle and Bridger agrees to stay on *seaQuest* and continue its explorations. The two-hour pilot racked up spectacular ratings but Shelley Hack as the raving villain and Michael Parks as a nefarious Frenchman were straight from pulp fiction.

Rockne S. O'Bannon, who had previously worked on the 1980s *Twilight Zone* TV series, created *seaQuest.* "When I first met with Steven [Spielberg] regarding arenas for doing a potential television project together, he expressed a particular interest in doing an undersea adventure series. The idea I brought back to him was to do a series that took place in the relatively near future — no more than 25 years. A very accessible future, positive future, where humankind had developed the technology that would allow them to more fully explore and utilize and inhabit the world's oceans. An undersea series instantly presents challenges, but the premise Steven and I built steered clear of the claustrophobia, prohibitive production costs, etc. We worked very hard to present the ocean as the expansive, wide-open space that it is. Although it was never going to be an inexpensive show, we went into it with a design to make for a very manageable production.

"[Spielberg] was very involved during the creation of the series, vital in bringing Roy Scheider to television, and was an amazing force in selling the series. There's nothing quite like pitching a series to a network with Steven Spielberg sitting next to you and jumping in with his own enthusiasm."

Patrick Hasburgh, one of the show's producer-writers, was approached after the pilot was completed. "I was offered the executive producer-showrunner position after the pilot was filmed," he recalls, "but I had just finished writing and directing *Aspen Extreme* for Hollywood Pictures/ Disney and decided to turn down the *seaQuest* offer. Even then, it was clear the execs and the creative guys were having trouble figuring out what the series was going to be. The pilot was big and pretty but very boring — a bunch of handsome folks floating around, looking for magic seaweed. When I first saw the pilot, I asked the guys at Amblin [Spielberg's company] who the 'bad guys' were going to be. They told me there weren't going to be any 'bad guys' in the traditional dramatic sense. Right then, I knew they'd be in deep trouble and that they'd come back to me with even more money. I ultimately took the show over around episode 10 or 12 of the first season. We spent the next two seasons trying to fix the series' setup. I made more dough off of *seaQuest* in the next two and a half years than I had ever made on any other Hollywood project, before or since! It seems *seaQuest* was a disaster for everyone but me."

All first-year episodes concluded with science factoids presented by Dr. Robert Ballard, the famed oceanographer who discovered the *Titanic*'s wreckage in 1985. Ballard was approached by producer Phil Segal at an early stage in the development of the series and given a lot of latitude in keeping the series scientifically oriented. "I loved the concept of stretching science into the future, without breaking its link to reality," says Ballard today. "It was not to be a science-fiction series but a science-stretch series. The purpose of the segment at the end of each show was to reinforce the show's connection to science. Roy Scheider and all of the actors were very excited about this new concept."

Ballard told *The Los Angeles Times* before the show's premiere, "The ocean is truly the last frontier. We're going to go there for recreation, food, natural resources, geothermal energy and waste management." Ballard and Scheider became good friends and both shared the vision of making *seaQuest* a human-oriented yet scientifically feasible show for the entire family. In fact, Captain Bridger was loosely based on Ballard, who had worked on Navy submarines.

According to Ballard, the early loss of O'Bannon, who left the series for personal reasons, and Spielberg's focus on his films *Jurassic Park* and *Schindler's List*, left a void, and led to more fantasy storylines. "The studio began making a series of tragic decisions that drove *seaQuest* away from science and toward science fiction," says Ballard. "Unfortunately, the loyal viewers of *seaQuest*

were far more intelligent than the studio and quickly lost interest and the series died. I had in my contract that should the series cross this line, I was out, and out I went. It was a tragic loss of an excellent opportunity that will never come to me again."

Ballard's on-screen presence gave *seaQuest* the appearance of being grounded in science. And while the series had the pedigree of being produced by Spielberg's Amblin company, Hasburgh says, "Steven had nothing to do with the series beyond that his company co-produced it with NBC and he was charmed by the original concept."

The first year became the butt of critical barbs. Jay Leno of *The Tonight Show* dubbed the series *seaQuest PMS*, noting that the female characters were always in a bad mood. In the pilot alone, Lt. Katherine Hitchcock chews out Bridger, Dr. Westphalen snarls at Comdr. Ford and crazed Capt. Marilyn Stark orders torpedo attacks on peaceful communities.

"The first guys who ran the show never 'got it' creatively, whatever the *it* was," says Hasburgh. "Their one defense was that *seaQuest* originally took place only 25 years in the future and that sci-fi was impossible to distinguish from today." As an example, Hasburgh notes, "Before I took over, there was an episode where people were driving everyday golf carts around mine shafts under the sea. Golf carts! It was ludicrous."

Capt. Bridger's primary goal was to research the ocean depths for future generations. Roy Scheider liked the personal dimensions of the character, expressing cautious optimism to *The L.A. Times* in 1993 that Bridger would become a cross between Jacques Cousteau and Popeye. "Cousteau because of the science and exploration involved, and Popeye because he's eccentric," he said. He also envisioned the series as an adventurous cross between the best of *Star Trek* and *20,000 Leagues Under the Sea*. But as the series veered into fantasy, he made it clear he was not happy.

"Roy pretty much hated my guts," says Hasburgh. "I saw my job as reining in a show that had been wildly and irresponsibly over-budget, creatively vacuous and pretty much just un-entertaining. I wanted to fix it and make the show much more mainstream and commercial. Roy is a remarkably talented man and I love his work; but on *seaQuest* we had a different view." Hasburgh pauses. "We didn't exchange Christmas cards."

Episodes involved commandos taking over the *seaQuest*, officers lost at sea on a raft, and the submarine racing to rescue astronauts whose ship has crashed into the Atlantic Ocean. A successful example of early fantasy included the surrealistic "Knights of Shadows" where the crew falls under the spell of the ghosts who haunt a sunken ocean liner. SF icons William Shatner and Charlton Heston made guest appearances on the series.

For comic relief, Lt. Krieg was always conniving, whether to grab a rare beef hamburger or conspiring to stockpile undersea gems (which turn out to be petrified animal poop). And there was Darwin, the talking dolphin, hated by most of the show's writers but liked by a dedicated few.

"I loved Darwin!" Carleton Eastlake declares bravely. "He was my favorite character. I probably wrote more for Darwin than anyone else. Darwin was innocent. He was not a social or political or psychological rival, so people would always listen to Darwin." But the man who created the nattering mammal has a different view. "Darwin is one of the great disappointments of my career," confesses Rockne S. O'Bannon. "I originally conceived Darwin to serve the series in the same way that Mr. Spock distinguished the original *Star Trek*. Mr. Spock may have been an alien, but he was a ranking member of the crew, and his nonhuman status gave him an always fascinating outsider's point of view on human actions, foibles, etc. Darwin was originally conceived as Ensign Darwin — the premise being that the Navy had finally seen the wisdom of including another intelligent Earth species as a member of the crew, a notion that promised a fascinating examination of how humans act and interact with the other lifeforms with whom we share our planet. The translator-aided 'dialogue' from Darwin was always supposed to be thoughtful, intelligent, with a certain Spock-like unique wryness about humanity. Unfortunately, after I had passed the project off to the folks who were to run the day-to-day series, all of this was jettisoned in favor of making Darwin more of a ship's mascot. And instead of speaking articulately, he spoke *Day of the Dolphin*—'fa loves pa' baby talk. All in all, a horrible missed opportunity."

"It's obviously derived from *Voyage to the Bottom of the Sea*," said *The Washington (D.C.) Science Fiction Association Journal* review. "I'm not sure 30 years of improved technology have resulted in a better show. Most of the major characters are not only stereotypical but poorly done."

British author John Clute noted, "It's a high-budget return to the watery world of *Voyage to the Bottom of the Sea*. It's simply more of the same, with a seasoning of ecological concern." Both Spielberg and producer Philip Segal were fans of the Irwin Allen 1960s series *Voyage to the Bottom of the Sea* and were essentially updating it for the 1990s. But as *TV Guide* critic Nicholas Aistone noted, "*Voyage* had a tension that *seaQuest* has never achieved."

Another undersea forerunner was the disastrous *Man from Atlantis* (1977–1978), whose marine hero (Patrick Duffy) battled a two-headed seahorse, a crazed elf and an amphibian gunslinger from the 1880s. Was *seaQuest* similarly doomed by its briny format, since much of the underwater world had been explored?

"The failure of *seaQuest* didn't have anything to do with the premise being flawed," stresses writer Javier Grillo-Marxauch. "It's really about the execution. Unlike *Man from Atlantis*, which was essentially a superhero show, *seaQuest* established a futuristic underwater world of colonies and a fairly well-developed political landscape, as well as a myriad of stories about scientific discovery, search and rescue. *seaQuest* was able to sustain three seasons of such wildly divergent storytelling and that is a testament to the viability of the premise. Its failure was an inability to establish a continuity of tone, stakes and, most importantly, the characters and the story premises never coalesced into a consistent and believable whole. If you look at the best episodes, the DNA for a successful series was there."

And then there were the special effects. When television depicted an underwater world on *Voyage to the Bottom of the Sea* (1964–68), twenty-foot submarine models were filmed on Lake Sersen and smaller models maneuvered in a deep water tank at Fox. The series won multiple Emmys for its effects.

seaQuest eschewed real underwater work in favor of computer generated images. But the skeletal-looking submarine, designed as a cross between a shark and squid, was hard to see in the first season. It remained frustratingly hazy to fans of miniature model work. Other undersea effects, particularly explosions, were often cartoony. Clearly, CGI had limitations in creating an undersea environment.

"I asked why the CGI images were so dark and I was told that under the sea, it *would* be dark and murky," Patrick Hasburgh told *SF Universe* magazine in 1994. "I told them, 'I don't care — these people are tuning in to see cool stuff!'" Today, he says much of that disappointing work came down to expense. "To do the CGI right would have cost millions of dollars per episode. And it would have taken months for each segment. The CGI was pretty bad but considering the realities, we were lucky the show wasn't rendered in crayon." By the second and third season, the undersea effects were lightened up, so viewers could at least *see* the sub.

"The state of computer technology was too primitive and expensive to make the intended effects doable in the first season," says Eastlake. "I heard that the first year was a nightmare and what contributed to that was the lack of CG technology. This forced the show to spend more time in the submarine rather than in any elaborate undersea world. The irony is, by the end of the series, CG had gotten much cheaper and much more effective, so the show was finally doable — but it was canceled. When we started the show, we could not do particle animation. We couldn't even do the surface of the ocean. When I needed to show a cavern flooding around stranded submersibles, I had to buy old-fashioned miniature work, with little physical models of our normally CG submersibles, because we couldn't animate the water flooding in."

Creating a futuristic world above the sea was expensive too. "They had futuristic cars under contract but it was too expensive to deploy them," recalls Eastlake. "Instead of futuristic electric cars, you had people going around in ordinary taxi cabs. The same thing happened with Darwin the dolphin. He worked fairly well, except when they were controlling him underwater, because he was radio-controlled and radio waves don't travel well underwater. Darwin took three trucks to transport. He was, after all, a heavy, robotic submarine. You needed a truck for Darwin, a truck for the crane and a truck for the control modules. And [for all this] you needed a large crew. Deploying Darwin was really expensive."

And time-consuming. When Darwin was tested early on, he sank straight to the bottom of a lake, the result of low batteries.

Yet, some people regarded *seaQuest* as a grand experience, including director John T. Kretchmer. "*seaQuest* was very dear to my heart," he says warmly. "Most importantly, it was where I became a director. I had been the assistant director on *Jurassic Park*, and when I heard that Amblin was preparing a new TV show, I went to Kathy Kennedy and said that I would volunteer as an assistant director for the first season if I could direct an episode. She checked with Tony Tho-

mopolous, the head of the television division, and within 24 hours, said okay. Steven Spielberg also gave his blessing. What was to have been a nine-month commitment turned into a 17-month commitment, because of delays due to three changes in the producing teams and a very large earthquake. Nonetheless, it was an exciting show to work on, with a great crew. I had worked with Roy Scheider on *Jaws 2*, and when I started to direct, he could not have been more helpful or gracious. He was kind enough to say complimentary things to Steven Spielberg about me, which never hurts."

Kretchmer felt many episodes came off looking well, noting, "My favorite episodes of the first season were directed by Bryan Spicer. He gave the show a sophisticated visual look and succeeded in making it one of the best-looking shows on TV."

With a budget of $1.3 million per episode, *seaQuest* began well against *Lois and Clark: The New Adventures of Superman* on ABC and *Murder She Wrote* on CBS, but ratings-wise it soon sank into perilous depths that didn't justify the show's expense.

NBC and Universal recognized one of the series' strengths was Jonathan Brandis, who was receiving thousands of letters per week as young Lucas. Teen magazines ranked *seaQuest* as the most popular show with kids 10–17 and young Brandis began to feature prominently in TV ads for the show.

The last episode of year one, "Ocean on Fire," has the world threatened by an errant power plant that has created a chasm in the sea floor. Bridger seals the fissure, but the cliffhanger has the *seaQuest* blowing up in the process.

The second year, *seaQuest* moved to the production facilities of Universal Studios in Orlando, Florida — a budget-saving condition required to ensure a second year.

Science guru Robert Ballard was dropped as science consultant. "If you want facts, watch the Discovery Channel," urges Hasburgh. "Ballard is a smart guy but there was no place for the scientific nuance the original creators had hoped for in *seaQuest*. The 8 P.M. audience could care less that a sea mollusk tastes like chicken or that an eel might cure blindness. They want to see shit blown up or folks voted off islands or pretty girls with big boobs...."

In year two, Stephanie Beacham, Royce D. Applegate, John D'Aquino and Stacy Haiduk were out while a younger group was brought in. Kathy

Evison was cast as energetic young ensign Lonnie Henderson, but three other new characters were wired with gimmicks— a telepath (Rosalind Allen), a feisty amphibian (Michael DeLuise) and a genetically engineered man (Peter DeLuise). This gentle giant, nicknamed Dagwood, is the sub's janitor and speaks in simple sentences, trying to fathom human behavior.

Year two had a new *seaQuest* submarine and presented even more fantastic adventures— killer plants, a prehistoric crocodile, space aliens, several super-powered humanoids, a trip 250 years into the future and even an encounter with the Greek god Neptune. Many segments moved away from the submarine, including a trip inside a giant video game (where robots chased the crew). Sometimes the land-lubber adventures teed off real people. An ambassador from Brazil angrily wrote to the producers, taking umbrage to an episode that depicted a villain as a nasty South American dictator. Critics remained unimpressed. "When *seaQuest* began last year, the world shuddered," said Mike Hughes of *The Gannet News Service*. "It ducks emotions and gives us characters we don't care about."

Roy Scheider, unhappy with the show's new direction, was quoted as saying that *seaQuest* was "childish trash" and "*21 Jump Street* meets *Star Trek*." *TV Guide* editorialized that the star should be "more graceful" about voicing his displeasure.

However, Hasburgh didn't care for the new approach either. "It bored the hell out of everyone but particularly bored me. I'm pretty much a straight-ahead comedic dramatist. I'm writing novels now, I probably never should have done TV. To me, *seaQuest* was a weak *Star Trek* rip-off. We certainly made *some* entertaining episodes. The best episode was 'Whale Song,' guest-starring Jonathan Banks. It was about whale-poaching and eco-terrorism. It is a great hour of TV and I was lucky enough to write it. It was what the series should have been from the onset. But most of us doing TV are idiots and cowards and we rarely fight for what's good and right. There's too much money to be made playing dumb. Overall, the series was a bust."

The strangest thing Hasburgh was asked to do during *seaQuest*: "It was hard to top being asked to write dialogue for a dolphin," he says dryly.

Other highlights of the second year included Carleton Eastlake's "Dead End," a tense survival story set in a deep undersea cavern where several *seaQuest* characters and an explorer are trapped. For them to escape to the surface, one of them must remain behind and die. Eastlake came up with a provocative way for the characters to address that dilemma.

"Then, as now, some people were complaining how religion wasn't shown with respect on television or wasn't shown at all," he says. "So when they're all trapped and someone will have to remain behind, I had a scene where Ted Raimi's character of O'Neill says, 'You guys don't have faith, but I'm a Catholic. I'll stay behind and die. I'm going to Heaven. It's easier for me to stay and die. I have faith in something ahead of me, but it's a horror for you, so I'll stay.' And you know, no one noticed. There wasn't any reaction to that scene."

The president of NBC believed in *seaQuest*. "Warren Littlefield at NBC was brilliant," says Eastlake. "He was one of the most literate, intelligent senior network people that I have ever dealt with. He read the first five scripts for the second season and made notes on them. My first script ['Sympathy for the Deep,' about people going crazy with evil] was assigned to me as a one-line concept. I settled on a Jungian psychological model, where the Shadow Side of each person had been drained away, but remained in this cloud of evil, because denial is not a solution, only psychological integration is. Of course, I disguised all of this. But when Warren got to my script, he said, 'You're really writing about Jungian psychology here, aren't you?' I was astounded. And I was even more astounded when he said, 'Don't be afraid to say it. You can put it in the script.'"

Despite the occasional successes, fans were unhappy with the show. They wrote an open letter to NBC and Amblin as the second year closed. "Viewers who had looked forward to *seaQuest* became disenchanted with the inaccurate science and second-rate scripting," said the letter. "How could a series, with a good cast, sizable financing and Steven Spielberg's backing, be given such short-shrift on scripts?" Scheider was quoted around the same time as saying many fans had fled the show because it had grown "too fantastic and childish."

The last episode of the second year had the *seaQuest* transported to an alien water planet, where a civil war is raging. The submarine is destroyed and Lucas and Dagwood are left adrift on an alien sea, their shipmates apparently lost. Having finished the season in 57th place in the ratings, cancellation was a near-certainty, so writing the characters into such a corner wasn't a problem.

When an empty spot on NBC's 1995–96 schedule opened up, executives decided that *seaQuest*'s male demographics were worth going after and it was surprisingly renewed for 13 more episodes. This time, the network and studio wanted to do it right. "We pissed off our core viewers," admitted an anonymous NBC executive.

Its third season would be more military-oriented, forsaking weird storylines. Scheider, still unhappy, left the series. He would say years later, on a Prodigy chat, that although he had liked Bridger's human and scientific side in the early shows, he disliked the character's presentation as a "combat commander" in later episodes.

Michael Ironside was offered the role of the new captain, Oliver Hudson. But when the actor screened six episodes, representative of "the best" of the past two years, he was horrified. Calling the episodes "awful and dull," he turned it down.

Terry O'Quinn and Jonathan Banks were considered for the role of Hudson but when Ironside was given an opportunity to make suggestions on how to improve *seaQuest*, he signed up. New supervising producers included Lee Goldberg and William Rabkin.

There was the problem of resolving year two's outer space cliffhanger. It was decided to have the *seaQuest* re-appear magically in a cornfield in Iowa and get on with new adventures as fast as possible.

The new episodes were set several years later, in the year 2032. The crew (unaged) has no memory of what happened. This allows hard-nosed Captain Hudson to come in and take command. Scheider guest-starred as Bridger in the year 3 kick-off, "Brave New World," and he would return for a couple of other guest shots, but he was happy to be otherwise done with the series.

"Adding Michael Ironside was an attempt to make the show more entertaining, tougher and more action-orientated," says Hasburgh. "He is a great actor. Where the series was going in the third season is where the series should have started. If it had been, *seaQuest* would probably still be on the air. But it was too little, too late."

seaQuest newcomers Goldberg and Rabkin had to find their own way on this troubled show. "Although we were supervising producers, we were essentially ranked fourth in the power structure behind Patrick Hasburgh, Clifton Campbell, and Carlton Eastlake," Rabkin says. "So we weren't in a position to determine the direction of the show. In fact, all such decisions were Patrick's. That being said, it was pretty clear that season two was

not a success. It had no clear direction, the monster-of-the-week scenario was silly, and the show was struggling. When we were brought on, Patrick described his vision for year three—a move into the future, with the world at the brink of war, and *seaQuest* as the last chance to prevent global conflict. That sounded like the first solid franchise the show had ever had and gave it the chance to find its footing."

Gone was John Debney's Emmy award–winning main-title theme, one of the most engaging TV adventure themes ever recorded. Russ Landau's provided a robust title theme, better suited for this new season.

Now under the auspices of United Earth Oceans, *seaQuest* took off on missions that involved runaway icebergs controlled by bad guys and a speeding underwater train sabotaged by evil-doers. Captain Bridger re-appeared in "Equilibrium," where he clashed with Lucas over ways to deal with a dangerous underwater organism.

"'Equilibrium' and 'Weapons of War' [the series' last episode] are, to this day, two of my favorite scripts," says Grillo-Marxauch. "In the case of 'Equilibrium,' I had a great mentor and co-writer in Naren Shankar [the show's executive story editor]. Naren is not only a very accomplished and talented writer, but also a very patient teacher."

By the third season, Commander Ford (a black man) and Ensign Lonnie Henderson (a white woman) had become romantically involved. That was Carleton Eastlake's intention. "I had just done a pilot on a different network in which I had implied that a white girl was just hanging out with a black boy, not even on a date, and the network heads freaked out. People forget that this was the early 1990s, and having a romance between Don Franklin's character [as Ford] and Kathy Evison [as Henderson] was different for television. Patrick Hasburgh wanted to attack racism and he had us write a love story for Don and Kathy. All the same, we thought we better discuss the issue with Warren Littlefield. But he just looked at us and said something like, 'It's time to get over that sort of racism on TV. It's a good story. I'm glad you're doing it and we aren't going to even discuss it further—just do it.'"

So in Eastlake's "Second Chance," the *seaQuest* materializes in 1962 to prevent a nuclear holocaust during the Cuban Missile Crisis. "The right wing was making a lot of noise about affirmative action for women and blacks at the time, implying that sexism and racism were such ancient history that no further remedies for them were justified," states Eastlake. "So in 'Second Chance,' I wanted to send a female sub-fighter pilot and a black second-in-command back to the 1960s, to the Cuban Missile Crisis. When they meet the Intelligence officer who arrests them, the real reason he doesn't believe them is not because of what they're telling him about being time travelers, but because [to him] it would be impossible that these two people could ever be in the U.S. Navy. To him, even in the future, there would *never* be a black second-in-command or a woman pilot. And that's why I wrote the episode, to remind people of that mind set only 30 years earlier."

As *seaQuest* progressed, Goldberg and Rabkin steered clear of network politics. "We were well insulated from the network and studio," says Rabkin. "Patrick Hasburgh is an incredibly strong showrunner, and all of the serious creative decisions were his. When the studio or the network had an issue, he was the one they called, and he fought those battles himself. I do remember Lee [Goldberg] complaining to a studio exec that he hated writing for a talking dolphin and getting absolutely no sympathy back. Not that he deserved any! Lee always referred to Darwin as 'that fish,' and no amount of correction would ever get him to stop."

John J. O'Connor, critic for *The New York Times*, praised the new team for fixing the series: "*seaQuest* is emitting considerably more energy. The new and improved *seaQuest* is a generally nifty adventure series for younger audiences [and] at least takes swipes at serious issues." But O'Connor also felt it was too late. Year three's episodes averaged around 80th in the ratings, with a paltry 10 share.

Many of the fans had abandoned ship. "Sadly, I don't remember a single positive bit of feedback from the 'fans,'" Rabkin notes. "The only ones we ever heard from were a group that believed that they should have creative control over the series, and that we were screwing up their vision. We were also informed that the fanfic was infinitely superior to our work because we were 'only doing it for money' while the fans were writing 'for love.'"

"*seaQuest* was one of the first shows to be subject to an Internet campaign," says Grillo-Marxauch. "A group of fans who disliked the second season actively used the web to campaign for the show to return to its roots, the serious, science-based storytelling of the first season. This was 1994 and the Internet was very new to the general populace. I, for one, was completely blindsided by how much heat and attention they were able to generate. It was my first exposure to the good, the bad, and sometimes the ugly of Internet fandom."

"We had this wacky chick on the Internet that had launched this 'we hate the new *seaQuest*' campaign," Hasburgh recalls. "It was quite damaging. I can't remember her name but she actually made it into *USA Today*. I invited her down to the set and welcomed her input. I even offered to hire her as a consultant but she refused."

By this time, Steven Spielberg was far from the series, busy with other projects. "Spielberg had checked out of the show long before we were there," says Rabkin. "Whether that was due to the show's creative direction, or that was his intent all along, I have no way of knowing. In the third season, there was even talk about Amblin's logo being taken off the show. I do know Spielberg visited the set in Florida because Universal was eager to show off their new facilities there. Bruce Seth Green was directing that episode, and he was both thrilled and terrified that Spielberg was coming to his set."

Constant pre-emptions worsened the situation. Michael Ironside (and some critics) felt the show was improving but viewers didn't trust the show anymore and stayed away. Sinking with moribund ratings, *seaQuest* was canceled in the middle of its third season.

Carleton Eastlake observes, "There was very little organization. There was NBC, Amblin, Universal, one showrunner in Florida, another in Los Angeles and the star. Those are six parties that could destroy a show, yet none of them had the power to make the show. In the second season, each writer-producer shepherded their own shows. But it did not make for a uniformity of storylines. There was a constant change of direction and a tremendous struggle for power on the show. So *seaQuest* was whatever the writers wrote each week. The third season was an unexpected season, no one thought the show would be renewed. There was an attempt at an arc story with Michael York and the Macronesia storyline [York played the ruthless dictator of a belligerent renegade federation, which sought to rule the ocean] and that gave them some opposition and antagonism. But it didn't work particularly well, creatively."

"I think the path to a fourth season was set out in the last episode 'Weapons of War,' written by Javier Grillo-Marxauch," says Rabkin. "He introduced a new enemy, the Chaodai, who were essentially North Korea's political leadership, combined with China's size and power. It was a force of unknown strength and intention, and a mystery that could take seasons to unravel. We were excited about the episode, although by the time it was shot, we knew we weren't coming back."

Grillo-Marxauch says, "The first bunch of episodes had aired to less-than-stellar ratings. However, Patrick Hasburgh gave me a mandate to create a nemesis that could be used for possibly nine more episodes, as well as to create a new series regular. I jumped into the assignment with full faith that it would help save the show."

That new character was Kimura, played well by Julia Nickson. This final episode has the nerdy O'Neill falling for a mysterious woman over the Internet. It turns out to be Kimura, who is simply using him. "After working on the show for three years — two as a network executive and one as a writer — I wanted to give Ted Raimi something to do other than comedy relief," says Grillo-Marxauch. "I had always liked him as an actor, and felt a certain kind of kinship with the character — big geek that I am — so I wanted to show O'Neill's potential as a hero. It is one of my favorite pieces of writing and Julia Nickson and Ted Raimi were great together. Steve Beers, who was the show's producer in Florida, did an amazing job directing. It was probably a good sign that the cancellation was a fait accompli because, on the last day of shooting, the pyro crew loaded the bridge set with so many explosives for the climactic battle that it caused permanent damage to the structure!"

"The show was better in its third year than ever before," says Rabkin. "It had real conflicts and real stakes. Although many of the characters were still fairly indistinct, the presence of Michael Ironside as Captain Hudson tended to clarify them by putting them into conflict. We still had silly holdovers from the initial seasons — that damn talking dolphin, for one — but they were being minimized."

But Rabkin well understood how viewers had been "burned" by previous episodes and weren't coming back. "Whatever we did, that season was hopeless, no matter how much better it was."

"It was just dumb, and every season was dumb in its own way," says Hasburgh. "I am no science fiction guy. I think even the best sci-fi is basically crap. I hated 2001: A Space Odyssey. The movie was a pompous, finger-pointing bore compared to what was really going on in the real world of 2001."

"The series' greatest strength was its initial concept of presenting a positive view of the future, in direct contrast to the steady stream of apocalyptic futures that we so often see," says creator Rockne S. O'Bannon. "I wanted to show people, especially kids, that the future wasn't destined to be some bleak, distressed place, but a bright, exciting world offering fascination and adventure, where the greatest frontier on earth — the sea — still remained to be explored. The weakness of the series was the erosion from this original concept to the uninspired, simpled-down 8 P.M. gimmick show it became. Each season grew progressively further away from that initial concept which had gotten Steven, Roy, and NBC excited in the first place."

But as Grillo-Marxauch says, they all *tried* to make *seaQuest* work. "The third season was an earnest attempt to bring the show back to earth and give it a believable and consistent tone," he says. "Given where the show had gone and that the second season finale had been designed as a *series* finale — the ship destroyed, the entire crew either dead or stranded on an alien planet — restoring any credibility to *seaQuest* was an impossible task. There was much baggage attached to the series at this point, so much tinkering and changing and recasting and redeveloping. For better and for worse, we picked a hill to die on, planted our flag and went down swinging."

Cast Notes

Roy Scheider (Capt. Nathan Bridger): The New Jersey–born actor's feature debut was in the horror film *The Curse of the Living Corpse* (1963). He went on to co-star in *The French Connection* (1972) and the summer blockbuster *Jaws* (1975) and earned an Oscar nomination as Bob Fosse in *All That Jazz* (1979). He's appeared in the films *The Punisher* (2004) and *Dracula III: Legacy* (2005). He died in 2007.

Michael Ironside (Capt. Oliver Hudson): Born in Toronto, Canada, he made his first genre splash as a mind-altering villain in *Scanners* (1981) and co-starred as the rambunctious Ham Tyler in the alien invasion mini-series *V* in the mid–1980s. Many fans recall him as Richter, the relentless assassin pursuing Arnold Schwarzenegger in *Total Recall* (1990). He's also co-starred in features such as *Mindstorm* (2001), *Maximum Velocity* (2003) and *Guy X* (2005).

Stephanie Beacham (Dr. Kristin Westphalen): Born in Casablanca, Morocco, her earliest British appearances include Gerry Anderson's *UFO* series (1970) and as the heroine in films like *Dracula A.D.* (1972) and *And Now the Screaming Starts* (1973). In the 1980s she played Sable on *Dynasty* and *The Colbys*. With only 40 percent hearing, she once planned a career teaching mime and dance to deaf students. She also appeared in the films *Witches Hammer* (2004) and *Love and Other Disasters* (2006).

Jonathan Brandis (Lucas Wolenczak): He began acting in commercials at age five, eventually appearing in nearly 100. He also had a bit role in the hit movie *Fatal Attraction* (1987). After *seaQuest*, he unsuccessfully auditioned for the role of Anakin Skywalker in *Star Wars II: Attack of the Clones*. His other credits include the feature *Hart's War* (2002). He was preparing to direct his first movie when he died in November 2003, a suicide.

Don Franklin (Lt. Comdr. Ford): The Chicago-born actor began as a dancer but an injury forced him to give that up and pursue acting. One of his earliest roles was a bit part in Christopher Reeve's *Somewhere in Time* (1980). He starred in *Fast Forward* (1984), directed by Sidney Poitier. He later co-starred in *Seven Days* (1998–2001) as Captain Donovan and had guest shots in *CSI Miami* and *The District*. Of *seaQuest*, Franklin says today, "It was the time of my life, with really great scripts. I liked how they successfully interwove all of the characters into the plot, so that you got to see all of us deal with the stories individually and then collectively. It was an awesome time."

Ted Raimi (Lt. O'Neill): The Detroit-born brother of filmmaker Sam (*Spider-Man*) Raimi, Ted says he was picked on mercilessly in school but found escape in humor and acting. He studied acting at Michigan State University and the University of Detroit. He joined the cast of *Xena: Warrior Princess* as Joxer during 1996–2001. His film work includes *Spider-Man* (2002) and *Nice Guys* (2006).

Stacy Haiduk (Lt. Comdr. Katherine Hitchcock): Born in Grand Rapids, Michigan, she co-starred as Lana Lang in the TV series *Superboy* (1988–1992) and later guest-starred on *Navy NCIS*, *The X-Files*, *CSI Miami* and *Heroes*. *The Darwin Conspiracy* (1999) and *Attack of the Sabretooth* (2005) are some of her TV movie credits.

John D'Aquino (Lt. Benjamin Krieg): A self-admitted TV junkie as a kid, he would memorize every page of *TV Guide* magazine. Raised in Queens and Brooklyn, he has had roles in the films *Cowboys and Angels* (1999) and *It's All About You* (2002). He became a semi-regular on TVs *JAG* in 2001.

Edward Kerr (Lt. James Brody): A western buff, his idols while growing up on a Kansas farm included John Wayne and Clint Eastwood. After *seaQuest*, he remained busy, including guest shots on *Sex in the City*, *House M.D.* and *CSI Miami*.

Rosalind Allen (Dr. Wendy Smith): Allen is a New Zealand–born actress. Before *seaQuest*, she appeared in the daytime dramas *All My Children* and *Santa Barbara* and guest-starred on *Star Trek: The Next Generation* ("Outrageous Okona") under her previous name, Rosalind Ingledew. She teaches drama and does TV commercials and has appeared in the TV movie *Dallas: JR Returns* (1996) and the movie *Hijack* (1999).

Royce D. Applegate (Security Chief Crocker): He began his career as a radio DJ in Texas and did comedy routines on stage. Some of his earliest appearances were on TV's *Mayberry RFD* (1970) and the feature film *Fuzz* (1972). He was also a writer, including scripts for *Welcome Back, Kotter*. Just before his death in a house fire (at age 63 in January 2003), he appeared in the horse-racing film *Seabiscuit* (2003).

Marco Sanchez (Ortiz): His parents came to America from Cuba. He grew up in Palm Desert, California and graduated from UCLA. His work includes guest shots on *24*, *CSI:NY*, and *Enterprise*. His movies include *The Rookie* (2002), *Illusion* (2004) and *Edison* (2005).

Kathy Evison (Ensign Lonnie Henderson): Her father was a park ranger and Evison, who was born in Boulder City, Nevada, was a shy child who drifted toward acting. She began as a model in magazines like *Seventeen* and *Shape*. She was saved from drowning while an exchange student in New Zealand and was still afraid of the water when she did *seaQuest*. She originally read for the Dr. Wendy Smith role on *seaQuest* but was too young for the part. Her post–*seaQuest* credits include *Seventh Heaven*, *The Pretender*, *Flipper*, *Diagnosis Murder* and the TV film *Murder She Wrote: A Story to Die For* (2000).

Michael DeLuise (Tony Piccolo): The son of actor Dom DeLuise, he grew up as a monster buff, collecting *Famous Monsters of Filmland* magazine. He has appeared on *Stargate SG-1*, *CSI-NY* and *The Gilmore Girls*. His movie credits include *Comedy Hell* (2005). He's also a producer and director.

Peter DeLuise (Dagwood): The brother of Michael DeLuise, he had previously spent five years playing a cop on the series *21 Jump Street*. He made his acting debut at age one on his father's

Dom DeLuise Show in 1968. He also appeared on the new *Outer Limits*, *Friends* and *Third Rock from the Sun*, and later turned to writing, directing and producing. He directed several episodes of *Stargate SG-I*, *Stargate Atlantis*, *Andromeda* and *Jeremiah*.

Elise Neal (Lt. JJ Fredericks): Born in Memphis, Tennessee, she dreamed of being a dancer before moving to Hollywood and establishing an acting career. Her later TV credits included *CSI* and *All of Us*. She also appeared in the films *Scream 2* (1997) and *Mission to Mars* (2000).

SOURCES

Aist, Nicholas. *seaQuest* review. TV Guide (Canada), May 1995.

Cerone, Daniel. "NBC Takes Risky Plunge: Steven Spielberg's Expensive 'seaQuest DSV' has an Oceanful of Expectations to Fill." *Los Angeles Times*, 1993.

Clute, John. *Science Fiction: The Illustrated Encyclopedia*. New York: Dorling Kindersley, 1995.

Goldberg, Lee. "How *seaQuest* Sank." *Starlog* no. 229, August 1996.

Hughes, Mike. "Earth 2: Better Than Expected." Gannett News Service, November 3, 1994.

Millman, Joyce. *San Francisco Free Press*, 1994.

O'Connor, John J. *seaQuest* Review. "Never Mind the Dolphin, Check Out the Bald Guy." *New York Times*, November 15, 1995.

TV Guide, July 1993 and October 1994.

Warren, Bill. "Altered Voyages—Now Refitted for Science Fiction Adventure, Will *seaQuest* Sink or Swim in its Second Season?" *Starlog* no. 208, November 1994.

_____. "Prepare to submerge—For the Men and Women of *seaQuest* the New Frontier is Below the Waves." *Starlog* no. 196, November 1993.

Seven Days

(1998–2001)

The chronicles of Frank Parker, a "Chrononaut" who travels back in time in a silver sphere, to a maximum of seven days to prevent cataclysmic disasters.

Cast: Jonathan LaPaglia (Lt. Frank Parker), Don Franklin (Capt. Craig Donovan), Norman Lloyd (Dr. Isaac Mentnor) *Year 1–2*, Justina Vail (Dr. Olga Vukavitch), Nick Searcy (Nathan Ramsey), Sam Whipple (Dr. John Ballard) *Year 1–2*, Alan Scarfe (Dr. Bradley Talmadge), Kevin Christy (Andrew "Hooter" Owsley) *Year 3*

Created by: Christopher Crowe, Zachary Crowe; **Executive Producers:** Christopher Crowe, Reuben Leder, John McPherson, Thomas Ropelewski *Year 3*; **Co-Executive Producers:** James Crocker *Year 1*, John McPherson, Brad Markowitz, Thomas Ropelewski, Alphonese Ruggiero, Jr., *Year 2*; **Supervising Producers:** Thomas Ropelewski *Year 1*, John McPherson *Year 1*; **Producers:** Chip Scott Laughlin, John McPherson, Phillips Wylly *Year 1*, Ron Binkowski *Year 2*, David Roessell *Year 3*; **Co-Producer:** Tim Finch *Year 3*; **Associate Producers:** Keira Morrisette, Ron Binkowski, Walter Dornisch *Year 1*; **Consulting Producers:** Michael Cassutt, Evan Katz, Alfonse Ruggiero Jr. *Year 1*, Paul Barber, Larry Barber *Year 3*; **Writers included:** Stephen Beck, James Crocker, Tim Finch, Dan York, Tom Ropelewski, Harry Cason, Paulette Polinski; **Directors included:** Kenneth Johnson, David Livingston, Michael Vejar, John McPherson, Charles Correll, Chip Scott Laughlin, Charles Picerni, Jeannot Szwarc; **Director of Photography:** Richard M. Rawlings; **Production Designer:** Bill Malley; **Visual Special Effects:** Metrolight Studios, Velocity Visuals; **Music Theme:** Scott Gilman; **Guest Stars included:** Jenna Lyn Ward, Katherine Cannon, Tom Amandes, Kirk Baltz, Holmes Osborne, Ned Romero, Stacey Stone, Charley Lang, Jerome Butler, Keegan Connor Tracy, Alessandro Juliani, Roxanne Dawson, Blu Mankuma, Anne Marie Loder, Kristen Dalton, Gary Graham, Robert Picardo, Phil Morris

UPN; 1998–2001; 60 minutes; 65 episodes

If you had the ability to travel back in time at will to a maximum of seven days, would you? Would you go back and say yes instead of no? Go back and turn left instead of right? Change that decision that turned out to be disastrous? Save the life of someone who was run over by a car?

Try and stop that plane that should not have lifted off?

At its very core, *Seven Days* is a time-travel wish-fulfillment fantasy. It is a series that focuses on the ability of a "Chrononaut" to step into a time machine and turn back the clock to prevent a cataclysmic disaster. And the "Chrononaut" is not an ordinary citizen but an ex–CIA operative with the resources of a secret military organization at his command.

In contrast with other time travel-based TV series, *Seven Days* is distinguished by the limits imposed on the premise by the creators. Unlike *Time Tunnel* where two scientists bounced back and forth in time hundreds (or thousands) of years, or *Time Trax* where the hero traveled 200 years to a particular year, *Seven Days'* uniqueness was that the time machine had a limitation of transporting someone for a maximum of seven days into the past.

Hidden inside Never-Never Land a top-secret military base in the Nevada desert, was Operation Backstep, an organization that answered directly to the president. Operation Backstep used a gigantic sphere, the "Chronosphere," as their time-traveling device. The technology was "reverse engineered" from the mysterious alien spacecraft that crashed in Roswell, New Mexico, in July 1947. Whenever a major disaster struck, the White House would order "a backstep" and the sphere's pilot would go back and do everything in his power to avert the disastrous event.

The ride into the past is always violently bumpy and the landing is very unpredictable. Wherever he lands, he must contact his colleagues at Never-Never Land and announce to the switchboard operator that he is "Conundrum!" a code word that signifies that the project has backstepped, and that a crisis is imminent. Reconnecting with his Area 51 colleagues, Parker debriefs them on the mission.

In the series pilot, a small plane crashed into the White House, killing the president and the vice president. The Area 51 staff was preparing for their first "backstep" and were considering different military-based candidates as their first time-traveling pilot. Captain Craig Donovan (Don Franklin), the project's military advisor, supported selecting an ex–CIA operative named Frank Parker (Jonathan LaPaglia), a man with a photographic memory, a high threshold for pain, and a bad-ass attitude. Aboard the time-traveling sphere, he must use a joystick to navigate his way into the past. It was not just the task of trav-

eling from one point in time to another that was at issue. The Earth travels through space and the sphere must compensate for the physical distance that is displaced as a result of the Earth's orbit around the sun. The sphere's landing point is always unpredictable because of this.

Scientists at Operation Backstep who approved of Parker's selection included team leader Dr. Bradley Talmadge (Alan Scarfe). Working for the National Security Agency, Talmadge interfaced with the government and activated the Backstep when needed. The two scientists connected with the project were Dr. Isaac Mentnor (Norman Lloyd), the wise and experienced creator of the Backstep, and astrophysicist Dr. John Ballard (Sam Whipple), an invalid in a wheelchair, whose theoretical physics made the sphere possible. He was the project's nuts 'n' bolts man. Dr. Olga Vukavitch (Justina Vail), a Russian-born scientist whose job was to look after the well-being of the Chrononaut, also favored Parker's selection. The one dissenter was Nate Ramsey (Nick Searcy), the project's security officer, who saw Parker's flaws and declared him unfit for the job. But he was outvoted in the matter.

In the series pilot, Parker's first Backstep involves preventing a terrorist attack; among the victims was his young son, who was in a school play near the area destroyed. From information supplied by Parker, Talmadge and his team located the terrorists' hotel room. After a firefight between the terrorists and the U.S. military, three bad guys are dead and three others still at large. Further intelligence revealed that the terrorists' alternate plan was to release poisonous gas as near as possible to the White House. In the streets of Washington D.C., our heroes successfully avert a different disaster scenario.

Pleased with Parker's performance in this, the first official Backstep, Talmadge and his team were now confident that future Backsteps were possible and that redirecting their future was within their reach.

Each episode's disaster story was a self-contained scenario, but to give the show a sense of ongoing continuity, the producers developed an ongoing arc of personal relationships between the Operation Backstep team. Nate Ramsey was constantly disgusted with Parker. Parker was constantly trying to get himself into the good graces (and perhaps the arms?) of Olga, who was constantly fending off his advances. Donovan had his strong friendship bond with Parker and his support was unswerving. The two scientists, Mentnor and Ballard, were supportive with their technical knowledge, propelling the plots forward. And standing back watching it all play out was Talmadge, the team's loyal and experienced leader.

Seven Days' scripting was often inventive and clever. Some of the various disaster scenarios played out on the program included:

- An outbreak of the Ebola virus;
- As a result of an experiment, Frank, Olga, Hooter and a military man are the only survivors on the planet. They must trek back to Never-Never Land to initiate a Backstep;
- A tanker truck spills deadly acid that kills North Korean diplomats;
- Inexplicable homicidal behavior erupts from residents of a small town and Mentnor recognizes it as World War II bio-weapons research;
- During a Backstep, a "time gremlin" alien attaches itself to the Sphere and wreaks havoc with Parker and everyone at the base.

The ability may have been there but the technology was never perfect. More than just occasionally, a spate of "Backstep glitches" interfered with the success of a mission. In particular episodes we saw Parker believing he was a 10-year-old boy ("HAARP Attack") and become split into two beings ("Doppelganger,"). In a wry homage to *Quantum Leap*, Parker "leaped into" the Pope! Other glitches had Parker becoming a ghost and entering an alternate reality.

Seven Days had two recurring story threads: The first dealt with the Roswell aliens (the source of the Chronosphere's technology). Three episodes explored the aliens: "EBEs," "Lifeboat," and "Walk Away." The other recurring story thread was an evil Russian double for Olga, who was actually smitten with Frank. Two episodes dealt with this: "Something About Olga" and "Two Weddings and a Funeral."

The idea for *Seven Days* came from Kerry McCluggage, the then-president of Paramount Television (and running the UPN Network). He had mentioned the concept of a time machine able to travel back seven days to executive producer and director Christopher Crowe, who loved the idea. Coincidentally, Crowe had been doing research about the military's secretive Area 51 base for film producer Don Simpson and, armed with that knowledge, he developed the concept as a series.

The fact that *Seven Days* lasted as long as three seasons, notes veteran producer-director Kenneth Johnson, is a credit to McCluggage's loyalty. "The

order of the show came from Kerry so that's the reason it was nurtured and kept even though the audience wasn't very large for it," he says.

Recalling his three years on the show, Alan Scarfe says that it was a fun experience. "I thought we'd run five seasons. It had many scenarios," he says. "They weren't running out of plots or writers. It was a good, very enjoyable show. I didn't have to wear any peculiar makeup. I could wear my tie loose and walk around looking boss-like in a double-breasted suit. I couldn't have been more comfortable. I just enjoyed doing it. Being a regular is a nice way to do television.

"*Quantum Leap* had vastly more flexibility in its plots than *Seven Days* did because we were limited by the seven days thing. But they could have made more of the technology, so maybe he could have gone back nine days or whatever."

Justina Vail, who essayed the role of Dr. Vukavitch, says, "I thought they did extremely well considering that you could really only go so far with the idea of cleaning up a disaster week after week. The other part of it is the on-and-off ... *Moonlighting*-type of a relationship between Frank Parker and Olga. That was, again, something that ... could only go so far. It always seemed to be a matter of finding a new angle on both the time-travel and romance."

"The scripts were quite well conceived," says Johnson, who came on board the show at the behest of his friend and director colleague John McPherson, the series' co-executive producer. "Clever. Each one of them, I had an opportunity of directing a different style. Each of the episodes I did seemed to have its own set of unique characteristics. That gave me an opportunity to do a different kind of filmmaking."

As a demonstration of this elasticity, Johnson points to "Mr. Donovan's Neighborhood" as a "very gritty urban piece which I decided would be mostly hand-held cameras for close-up action or very long lenses that would compress the neighborhood and give it a claustrophobic feel."

For "Time Gremlin," which echoes *Twilight Zone*'s classic "Nightmare at 20,000 Feet," it was a challenge to show the Sphere floating in space "and having to shoot in a weightless environment. It was a very spacey, strange piece," says Johnson. The episode "Raven" was a sweet love story. "It [had] a very slick kind of a *Mission: Impossible* feel," he says. Two episodes were filmed on location in Las Vegas. "I thought it to be a huge amount of fun to be able to go and direct without having to worry about executive producing. It was like a bandwagon and I got to go out to the playground. It was terrific."

The appeal of the show's premise was very simple. We all want, at one time or another in our lives, to rewind our bad days and start over. "For instance, my wife slipped on the front steps and broke her wrist," explains Scarfe. "And I didn't say, 'Hold the rail as you go down.' But what if I could reverse that tape and say, 'Hold the rail'? She wouldn't be in that predicament of falling. So there are many instances where we would all like to replay the tape. It's a wish fulfillment."

The series' two-hour pilot was partially filmed on location in Washington D.C. and cost the company $13 million. "I've heard rumors that it was the most expensive pilot made up to that time," says Vail. "There was a lot of pressure on everyone to make the movie work." Written by Christopher Crowe and filmed in 1998, its haunting image of a White House in flames could very well have occurred in the real world during the events of 9/11; on that day, the airliner that crashed in a field in Pennsylvania was, ostensibly, bound for the White House. *Seven Days* graphically showed us an alternate reality that "could have been" our reality.

Throughout the history of Hollywood filmmaking, we've been exposed to "disaster" stories: the 1970s motion picture *The Towering Inferno*, the *Airport* movies, James Cameron's 1997 megablockbuster *Titanic*. As consumers and viewers we watch and enjoy these films as entertainment. But when something happens in the real world that is similar to fiction, it is eerie and creates echoes. "It was very timely," notes Scarfe. "When [then–United States National Security Adviser] Condoleezza Rice later said, 'Well, nobody ever envisioned anybody flying a plane into a building.' I thought, 'What!? We just had it on television.'"*

Today, natural disasters, terrorism and large-scale wars are on the forefront of our consciousness. More than ever, our wish-fulfillment desire to rewind history is heightened. *Seven Days* has become more pertinent than during its original broadcast.

But *Seven Days* was not a show to be watched with your hands gripping your armchair in rapt tension. It was a science fiction show. Wild 'n' crazy disaster scenarios were played out at the beginning of every episode, and in each story, a wild 'n' crazy gambit would prevent the future calamity. Each plot would have built-in tensions illustrating that even if Parker had all the relevant information needed to thwart a doomsday moment, events would play out uniquely and we would still be headed towards potential danger.

"He only solves the problem at the last conceivable second," chuckles Scarfe. "If he had a luxurious amount of time to solve these issues, it wouldn't be so tense or suspenseful. Normally, it took us six days to find out what he was supposed to do before we sent him, so we had already run out of six days because we needed to research it, so he had even less than seven days to solve the problem."

When the series was being cast, Justina Vail was contemplating leaving the business altogether. But when she read Christopher Crowe's script, she was impressed. She had just finished reading Philip Cosco's book *The Day after Roswell*, and this was a series with a UFO-related component. "I've always enjoyed the science fiction genre," says Vail. "The script appealed to me. I thought it was very well-written. It was a nice enough pilot that I thought, 'Okay, I'll go for it.'"

Over the course of three seasons, Vail got to watch and contribute to Dr. Olga Vukavitch's character growth. "She was a very interesting character to me. There was a lot underneath the surface that I could play with. Originally she wasn't written in very fleshed-out form, but there was enough there that we had a skeleton on which to work," she says.

But Olga's talents expanded to a level that stretched credulity. "She started the series as a physicist, and, as the series progressed, she also turned out to be a psychiatrist, a biologist, an M.D., a UFOlogist and it went on," Vail says wryly. "I began to ask, 'What does this woman actually do?' It would be impossible for someone to have that many roles in life. You can't have that many PhDs in one lifetime. Certainly not at that age. For me it was a little bit of a discipline to keep going to the writers and saying, 'Okay, she's something else now. Let's get clear about this character!'"

Scarfe says that in one episode he recalls vividly, Vail played her own evil twin, a Russian double who infiltrates the top secret base and has a strong

---

In another dramatic example that proved to be prescient, on the first episode of Chris Carter's short-lived X-Files spin-off The Lone Gunmen, *which aired on March 2001, a commercial jetliner was aimed at the Twin Towers in New York by remote control, but our three heroes were able to avert the disaster.*

attraction to Frank Parker. "It gave her tremendous opportunities for acting," he says. "That was a good one. And she won a Sci-Fi [Saturn] award for that."

Says Vail, "It was fun and it was very challenging at the same time. Galina was a really disturbed character. The way I used to work as an actor was to go into the emotional aspect of all of my roles. Probably too much. This character was the darkest and most troubled personality that I'd ever stepped into. I had to reach into those parts of myself and pull them out. It took me a number of months to recover!"

Scarfe admits that sometimes it was necessary to get pragmatic about the way things got done on the stage. "There was always a boardroom scene where there was a close-up of me as I was describing the scenario of the Backsteps," says Scarfe. "And the others would be off-screen and as I would go on, they would start to behave badly and try to make me crack up. So I would say, 'Look kids, it would be much easier if you all just cleared the room. I'll just imagine that you're there. That will make my life a lot simpler.' Most of the time that's fun but sometimes when you're under the pressure of the schedule, with a lot of expository dialogue that you can hardly remember anyway, and someone is trying to crack you up, it can waste a lot of time."

But there were genuinely hilarious moments on the show that Justina Vail wishes had been preserved. "Nick Searcy's character, Nathan Ramsey, had just been punched in the face by Frank Parker. He had these cotton balls stuffed up his nose. He was in a very foul mood which was not unusual for that character. So Ramsey, myself and I believe Talmadge, were standing around by a chalkboard and talking very seriously about the situation at hand. Ramsey snorted in disdain and the cotton balls flew out of his nostrils like torpedoes. It was the funniest thing. It was such a serious scene. I always wished that they kept that for an outtakes reel!"

One shot that *could* have been an outtake was kept in the final edit. "It was during the shooting of an episode ["As Time Goes By"] where we discover that Olga has a long-lost, presumed-dead husband," says Vail. "Olga had been in the operations booth watching a scene in the hangar unfold where her husband had been discovered in a crashed craft. I rushed out of the booth and came running into the craft. The ground was slippery and I slipped and fell really hard on my behind. I though the director would yell 'cut' but he didn't

and I kept going. That was my training — to keep going. They kept it in the episode. It worked. It was a very spontaneous moment.

"[Shooting in Las Vegas] was fairly chaotic because there were crowds of people everywhere making a lot of noise. We certainly didn't have the floor to ourselves. We shot in and around the public. Those big gambling halls are so loud! It was hard to think. We were shooting scenes in there knowing that we would have to do voice-over work at a later date, because we couldn't hear each other speak. Vegas has a lot of exciting energy."

In one very elaborate scene in "Sister's Keeper," directed by Kenneth Johnson, Vail had to sprint through a very crowded public area and then do a powerful emotional scene inside a glass elevator. "Kenny was very, very quick," recalls Vail. "He really maps out ahead of time and choreographs it. The great thing about working with Kenny is that he is so adept at choreographing scenes, without directing traffic as it were. A lot of directors forget about the human aspect of a scene because they're so inundated with the need to choreograph. They become traffic cops. Kenny has this extraordinary capability to include, in all of that, the human aspect of a scene.

"You really have to be emotionally 'in the moment' for a scene like that. Especially that kind of a scenario. Kenny was great just at making eye contact in the moments before 'action' and triggering all the work you've prepared, and then he'd make space for it to go where it needed to. He treated us with respect. He'd stand back and let the camera people work with you in that moment."

Initially filmed in Los Angeles, the *Seven Days* company moved north to Vancouver, Canada, for its second and third season for budgetary reasons. Vail recalls making some adjustments: "When you're in California, especially where we were shooting, it was dry and the light is so sharp. It was clear and the physical experience was different. When we got to Vancouver, immediately we had to find ways to stay warm and work with the different light. It changes your mood and your vibrational energy. It was a shock to the system. But it was also really lovely because I remember as soon as I arrived on the set to meet the hairdressers, makeup artists and the crew, they were such sweet, friendly and down-to-earth people and very welcoming. It was like going to a happy, friendly family that just took you into their arms immediately and said, 'You're one of us!'

And that was a complete shock! You wouldn't experience that in California so much. I thought, 'Oh, great, this is going to be so much easier than we thought!' It became a different lifestyle. We adapted quite well.

"You'll notice in some of the later episodes when we shot outside, I looked about 40 pounds heavier and the reason is, I had about six layers of clothing underneath!" she laughs.

Seven Days wasn't embraced by television critics. The *South Florida Sun–Sentinel* remarked, "The level of gratuitous violence is so far off the charts that even the producers conceded this summer that it needed to be toned down.... *Seven Days* is easily the goriest newcomer of the season.... In addition to numerous fire fights and a combatant getting his neck snapped, viewers will be treated to the stomach-turning spectacle of dozens of murdered school children being placed in body bags. When you're on an 'emerging' network, you do what it takes to emerge from the pack...."

As noted by Jason Snell (writing for the web site TeeVee), "If the premise made any sense, there wouldn't be a show. For instance, if you go back seven days in time to your office, wouldn't you run into yourself there? And then a month later, when you needed to go back in time to prevent your best friend from joining the *Mercy Point* fan club, wouldn't you run into two of yourself? One season into *Seven Days*, we'd have enough Jonathan LaPaglias to make a football team."

Actually, this aspect of the time travel situation is sidestepped by a quick explanation in the series pilot. Whenever Parker goes back seven days, he doesn't run into his original self. His original self actually *disappears*. In the pilot, after the first successful Backstep, the original Frank Parker vanished from the military hospital where he was incarcerated before he was recruited into the program. The show doesn't explore this.

There are two interesting side effects of being a Chrononaut. One is that Parker is aging faster than his colleagues. If you go back in time one week, you must re-live that week. And so you age an extra week. Parker, who must travel back in time frequently, re-lives his weeks again and again and accumulates more weeks than anyone else. After three years of adventures, that's a lot of weeks to re-live! Eventually his birthday will arrive earlier for him than if he had not been time-traveling.

Second is that contained in his brain are *all* of the disaster scenarios and the consequences of those events, plus the related emotional trauma. Parker's colleagues are only informed of the totality of all the disaster universes from his reports.

Four episodes into the third season, Sam Whipple's character, Dr. John Ballard, was written out and his replacement was a young scientific genius named Andrew "Hooter" Owsley, as played by Kevin Christy. The switch was necessary because Whipple had become ill with cancer; in 2002 he passed away.

Justina Vail and Whipple were close friends and she remembers him very fondly. "From the day we started to work together, we were pretty much together most of the time," she says. "He was such a very funny, smart and sensitive person. We got along so well. It was great that we had each other because some of the difficulties on the show would have been very tough for either of us if we didn't have each other to talk to about it. He was a mentor in some ways when it came to the craft of acting. He expanded me in my craft and he also expanded me as a person.

"He would keep us laughing. He would do these characters on the set in between takes. He would have me in tears. [One day] when we were in the makeup trailer together, there was a short brown wig on the counter. He put it on and started to pretend he was Al Pacino in *Scarface*. This is his versatility. Suddenly, he was 'Scarface.' And had us all howling."

Series creator Christopher Crowe at this point unexpectedly showed up on the set and didn't expect to see Whipple in a mad Pacino "riff." "And Sam didn't leave that character," continues Vail. "He stayed in character. It freaked Chris out a little bit to the point where he left very shortly afterwards!" she laughed.

"Kevin [Christy] was wonderful and I enjoyed introducing him," says Johnson. However he also felt that Christopher Crowe missed an opportunity to introduce a better gender balance in the show's cast. "I thought it suffered heavily from not having more than one female character. They should have made the young geek a hottie young woman who develops a crush on Jonathan. That would've added a much-needed additional female to the boy's club cast, provided a new sexual shot for the young guys in the audience and created a wonderful triangle with Justina's character."

Justina Vail quit the series just prior to the end of the third season, and she had already left the production before filming ceased. This departure is not readily apparent when viewing the episodes because, at Paramount's request, she filmed a few scenes for the final episodes for continuity purposes and to "wrap up" the character. "The circumstances were just not good for me," notes Vail. "And Paramount just ... it wasn't in their power to change the situation. So they agreed to let me go and it was a big relief. The show was very tough for everybody. It needed to complete itself somehow and they realized it was just too hard."

Johnson reveals, "There were some tensions between Jonathan and Justina. Jonathan and Justina grew apart as the series went on although they were supposed to have a very hot, sexual chemistry between them. Personally, they didn't like each other very much. That made things very difficult at times. But the stories they got were interesting enough that they kept everybody hanging together."

Alan Scarfe also hints that these tensions may have contributed to the series' demise. "There was a lot of friction with the cast, that may have had something to do with it."

Scarfe says he was dismayed that UPN didn't pick the series up for a fourth season. "Chris [Crowe] was very surprised," he says. "He fought very hard for its continuation. The ratings were never that good. Surprising, since it has such a following now."

"It never really found much of an audience," notes Johnson. "Indeed UPN as a network never found much of an audience. That's why UPN has now gone away. I thought it was a shame. They spent quite a bit of money on each of the shows. An episode was over $2 million, which is pretty hefty considering there were no big stars. I felt it did have a potential to go on longer."

"I would say that every episode would get a different rating from me," Vail says. "That was one of the downsides of the whole series. To me there wasn't enough consistency. Some episodes I thought were terrific. Every now and then we'd get a good one. And then some mediocre and then some episodes that were a bit of a struggle and we didn't quite pull it off. So I'm not sure I could rate the whole series. I know everyone worked as hard as they knew how to work. It was a good cast. We were up against so many odds. It just amazes me that we pulled it off at all. I would say [it was] the best work that everyone could possibly do under the circumstances."

In the end, although the series garnered two Saturn Award nominations from the Academy of Science Fiction, Fantasy and Horror Films in 1999 and 2000 for Best Genre Series, and Jonathan La-Paglia got a nomination for Best Actor, it was Justina Vail who walked away with a statue for Best Supporting Actress in 2000. "I was very surprised and honored by that," she says. "I enjoyed playing the part and to get a little gold statue is just a bonus."

Today, whenever she walks into her office, the gleaming, golden rings of Saturn sparkle. Vail chuckles, "I kept it hidden in a trunk in the living room until my husband insisted I put it out!"

CAST NOTES

Jonathan LaPaglia (Frank Parker): After working for 10 years as an emergency room physician, LaPaglia changed the course of his career to look for new outlets of creativity. Born in Australia, he practiced medicine in Australia and in the U.K. before moving to New York, where he spent two years training to be an actor in the Circle in the Square Theater School. His major acting break was a job as a series regular on *New York Undercover* (1996–97). He also guest starred in a 1998 episode of *Law & Order* and a UPN movie titled *Inferno* (1998). He worked with filmmaker Woody Allen in *Deconstructing Harry* (1997). After *Seven Days* he landed a regular role in *The District* (2001–2004) and appeared in *Brothers and Sisters* (2006). His older brother Anthony is the star of CBS' *Without a Trace*.

Justina Vail (Olga): Born in Malaysia, Vail was raised there until she was nine years old and her family moved to Hong Kong and then to England. While visiting her sister in Hong Kong, on a whim she walked into the production office of a television series filming there and landed an audition for a guest star role. Later, she performed in theater productions in England. She was one of Tom Cruise's ex-girlfriends in *Jerry Maguire* (1996), co-starred with Morgan Freeman in *Kiss the Girls* (1997), and was a vampire in *The X-Files*. SF fans will remember her as Odessa in multiple episodes of *The Adventures of Superboy* (1992). She was also in a series pilot of Jules Verne's *Journey to the Center of the Earth* and in 1997 tried out for a *Highlander* spin-off pilot. After *Seven Days*, in 2001, she quit acting, got married and is now a transpersonal therapist with workshops around California.

Don Franklin (Capt. Craig Donovan): Franklin began acting in grade school plays and musicals. His first professional acting job was in a play, *Amen Corner* by James Baldwin, performed in New York. He went on to star in *The Tempest,*

A Chorus Line, and *Pippin.* His first television series was the crime drama *Knightwatch* (1988). He later starred in *The Nasty Boys* (1989) and *Young Riders* (1990). SF fans will remember Franklin as Commander Jonathan Ford in *seaQuest* (1993–96). After *Seven Days* he appeared in various television series: *She Spies, The District, Navy: NCIS* and *CSI: Miami.*

Nick Searcy (Nate Ramsey): Born and raised in Cullowhee, North Carolina, Searcy began acting in the fifth grade and later performed in high school, college and off–Broadway productions. His film debut was in *Days of Thunder* (1990) with Tom Cruise. He portrayed real-life astronaut Deke Slayton in the Emmy award–winning HBO mini-series *From the Earth to the Moon.* After *Seven Days* he appeared on *CSI: Miami* and *The West Wing.* His other credits include *The Assassination of Richard Nixon* (2004), *Flicka* (2006), *The Dead Girl* (2007) and *An American Crime* (2007).

Norman Lloyd (Dr. Isaac Mentor): A veteran actor, producer and director whose career spans eight decades, Lloyd was actually in the original Mercury Theater Group with Orson Welles and John Houseman in 1938. He's worked with Alfred Hitchcock, Charlie Chaplin, and Martin Scorsese. Best known as Dr. Auschlander in *St. Elsewhere* (1982–88), he is also a theater and television director (he produced and directed the *Alfred Hitchcock Presents* and *Alfred Hitchcock Hour* television series). After *Seven Days* he appeared in the television remake *Fail Safe* (2000) and multiple episodes of *The Practice.*

Sam Whipple (Dr. John Ballard): Whipple began acting in sketch comedy at the age of 17. He's appeared in such films as *The Rock, The Great White Hope, The Doors* and *This is Spinal Tap.* He was in the SF made-for-TV film *Lifepod* (1993). On television, he had guest roles in *Seinfeld, NYPD Blue, Space Rangers, The Pretender* and *Dark Skies.* He was Jughead Jones in a MOW titled *Archie: To Riverdale and Back Again* (1990). Whipple became ill with cancer during the filming of *Seven Days* and his character was written out. He died on June 3, 2002, at age 41.

Alan Scarfe (Dr. Bradley Talmadge): He began his acting career in the early 1960s, doing theater work in the U.K. and Canada. He is very experienced in performing Shakespeare, has appeared in more than 150 stage roles and has directed stage productions of *King Lear* and *Romeo and Juliet.* His SF TV credits include *Andromeda, The Outer Limits, Star Trek Voyager, Star Trek: The Next Generation, Highlander, seaQuest* and *The Ray Bradbury Theater.* Since *Seven Days* he's appeared in *Kingdom Hospital, Stargate Atlantis* and the *Earthsea* mini-series.

Kevin Christy (Andrew "Hooter" Owsley): He began acting in commercials for Dodge Chrysler, 7-Up and Burger King, then made appearances in various comedies: *Malcolm in the Middle* (2000), *Dude, Where's My Car?* (2000), etc. After *Seven Days,* Christy acted on *Buffy the Vampire Slayer* and *CSI.*

SOURCES

Jicha, Tom. "There's No Time Like The Past: Violent Seven Days Sends Slightly Unhinged Agent Back In Time To Prevent Disasters." *South Florida Sun–Sentinel* (Fort Lauderdale, FL), October 7, 1998.

Sleepwalkers

(1997–1998)

A scientist-psychologist and his team of specialists use advanced technology to treat and cure patients by entering into their dreams and solving their problems from within.

Cast: Bruce Greenwood (Dr. Nathan Bradford), Naomi Watts (Kate Russell), Abraham Benrubi (Vince Konefke), Kathrin Nicholson (Gail Bradford), Jeffrey D. Sams (Ben Costigan)

Created by: David S. Goyer, Stephen Kronish; **Executive Producers:** Stephen Kronish, David S. Goyer; **Supervising Producers:** Steve Beers (pilot), Tim Iacofano; **Co-Producers:** Sara B. Charno, Stephen Gaghan, Robert Parigi, Harker Wade; **Associate Producer:** Gianna Rubin; **Consulting Producers:** David Nutter, Jennifer Faltings; **Writers included:** Steve Gaghan, David S.

Goyer, Sara B. Charno, Steven Kronish, Connie Kaplan, David Weinstein; *Directors included:* David Nutter, Kristoffer Tabori, James Whitmore, Jr., Jeff Woolnough, Cliff Bole; *Director of Photography:* Philip Linzey; *Production Designer:* Greg Melton; *Special Effects Makeup:* Toby Lindala; *Visual Special Effects:* Elan Soltes, Paul Cox; *Music Theme:* Jeff Rona; *Guest Stars included:* Lewis Arquette, Ray Wise, Harry Groener, Paul Dooley, Sarah Jane Redmond, Jeff Doucette, Suki Kaiser, April Telek, Rachel Luttrell, Michael McCarty

NBC Studios/Columbia Tri-Star Television/ Tree Putt Productions; November 1997/February-May 1998 (some West Coast NBC stations); 60 minutes; 9 episodes

Got a series of recurring nightmares that make you jump up in the middle of the night in a cold sweat? Don't know what to do or who to talk to? No problem! Put yourself into the hands of Dr. Nathan Bradford, a "neuropsychologist." He's got a revolutionary dream analysis machine. Lie down and let the medical team hook up the wires to your head. Watch Dr. Bradford lie down on the pallet next to you and as you drift off to sleep, boom, thanks to a virtual reality environment, he's right there in your nightmare. It is his job to observe, interpret, advise and, if all goes well, cure you.

Dr. Bradford has the ultimate hi-tech psychoanalysis tool.

Now, of course, if you've got a weird sexual hang-up that's interfering with your life, good luck having the courage to walk into the doctor's office and explain it all to him ... because for him to treat you, he would have to ... well....

Sleepwalkers, which is unrelated to Stephen King's novel of the same title, was created by producer-writers Stephen Kronish and David S. Goyer. It was a short-lived NBC-TV series airing in November 1997, and canceled after just two episodes (although nine episodes were filmed).

Dr. Nathan Bradford (played by Bruce Greenwood), a former professor at Stanford University, is now the director of the Morpheus Institute. Their work is dangerous and highly experimental. Their analyses and conclusions need to be as accurate as possible. Any misinterpretation of the nature of the problem inside the patient's mind, can be deadly for all participants. There's an additional risk for the doctors diving into a patient's dreamworld: They are gripped by their own private fears and anxieties that they bring with them into the journey.

Bradford's team members are Kate Russell (Naomi Watts), the leading psychologist and dream interpreter; Steve Turner (played by guest star Michael Watson), the Institute's risk-taking co-founder; and Vince Konefke (Abraham Benrubi), the technical support expert.

In the first episode, a former Air Force marine pilot, Ben Costigan, became Bradford's patient because of nightmares in which he is pursued by a shadowy figure across forbidding landscapes. In his dreams, a raven haunts him while riding a subway train. Kate and Steve enter Ben's nightmare and gain some clues, but Steve becomes a victim of Ben's pain and is hit by the train while in the dream. The result: Steve falls into a coma. In a second attempt, Nathan and Kate follow Ben as he walks toward his childhood home, and there, he remembers burying a toy soldier. Pulling the clues together, Nathan realizes that Ben actually has a twin brother who did not survive childbirth, and that his mother's recent death brought back to the surface his survivor's guilt. Armed with that knowledge, Ben conquers the "shadow man" and finds peace. In the end, the Morpheus team offers Ben a job with them.

When he screened the series pilot, veteran director (and former actor) Kristoffer Tabori says that he was impressed. "I remember thinking that they used up the best plot in the pilot and that it would be interesting to see how, and if, they could top themselves. Mind detectives going into the victim's psyche to find out who his tormentor is, only to discover the opponent is the victim himself — and his dark side must be confronted. This is a great story for a series that uses the psyche as its geography — so Freudian. Secretly, I remember I said to myself, 'What the hell are they going to do now?'"

Consulting producer–director David Nutter says he got involved when NBC president Warren Littlefield asked him to consider the series. "You had two very talented writers from two very different worlds," recalls Nutter. "One was steeped in the SF-horror genre, which was David Goyer, and [the other was] a wonderful dramatist in Stephen Kronish, who created shows like *The Commish*. So they looked at drama from different perspectives. They had a wonderful idea for a series and had written a script. But it was a little bit of this, a little bit of that."

Nutter says that he sat down with the show creators and streamlined the series' concept. "We all worked together to make it a tactile, dramatic show," he says.

One of the main difficulties was that, because a lot of time was going to be spent inside the minds of various patients, that promoted surrealism which is not a very "accessible" form of storytelling for the ordinary viewer who tunes in.

According to Kathrin Nicholson, who played Nathan's comatose wife Gail, this was the crux of a creative tussle. Just how deeply was dream surrealism allowed to be incorporated into the stories? As Nutter has explained, Goyer and Kronish were from "different worlds" and because of that, there were differing views of how much dream surrealism viewers would accept. "David [Goyer] is very intelligent, creative and stubborn," says Nicholson. "He thought the audience should be given more credit for understanding, rather than feeding them typical, easy stuff. But he didn't want input, and Bruce being the star wanted to give that, as of course did Kronish. Because it was television, [Goyer's] progressive ideas were shut down quite a bit and that led to a lot of tension.

"Bruce just wanted the writing and the characters to be good no matter what was going on, but as the star he wanted to give his input as well. I don't think Goyer was always amenable to that. He had his vision and thought Bruce was just being difficult.

"TV is so much about committee, but typically the best shows have a really strong creator and vision. Goyer was that, but unfortunately he didn't start the process. He was brought in because Kronish had never done sci-fi so he couldn't be 'The Guy' by himself. [Goyer] also never done TV, and Kronish had years of experience on successful shows. So [you had] two completely different personalities and sensibilities."

Another difficulty was making sure there was sufficient tension in the dramas. "Nothing realistic ever takes place in them," says Nutter. "It is hard to really dramatize some of this stuff. We wanted to create an empathy for this character, who was involved in this quandary, this pilot who was having terrible nightmares, and finding what it was all about. To me it was getting behind the story and making it as believable, as plausible and as relatable as possible."

To help sell the series' drama, it was important to have a credible actor portraying the lead character and fronting the action. Everyone agreed on their first choice. "Bruce Greenwood was someone viewers really respected as a lead of a TV series," says Nutter. "He had just finished *Nowhere Man* and didn't want to jump back into a TV show, unless it was something with some quality to it. Basically, Goyer and Kronish and I sat down and talked him into it."

In other casting, Nutter remembers snagging a British actress who was just new in Los Angeles, as she hailed from Australia. "The most exciting part of the casting process was someone we all agreed on and felt would be a great addition to the show—Naomi Watts," says Nutter. The blond, attractive actress was later cast by film director David Lynch in his 2001 TV pilot *Mulholland Drive* which ended up being released as a feature film. From there, she launched a successful feature film career.

The pilot introduces us to Kate Russell as she tries to overcome her fear of darkness by approaching a mineshaft cave in an dreamworld with Steve. "They were rediscovering themselves and getting into their own psyches, testing out the equipment," says Nutter. "Each of them had their own psyche and emotional being that are missing."

Although each episode presented a stand-alone mystery, the series' overall arc dealt with Nathan's private pain. His wife Gail was in a coma as a result of a car accident but thanks to the Institute's apparatus, he's able to visit her inside the dreams. The cruel irony is that although Nathan helps cure patients by day, he remains powerless to restore his own wife. "This isn't a show about medical miracles," explains Nutter. "Her brain damage was such that it was inoperable. She was closed off and in a sense, brain-dead. All he could do was communicate with her [via the dream world]."

Kathrin Nicholson says that playing Gail was fun and she liked the series' premise. "I thought the cast was terrific," she says. "We shot the pilot in Los Angeles, but when the show shot in Vancouver we did a couple of group trips together up to Whistler, mountain biking, etc. We all got along well.

"*TV Guide* called us a 'must watch' show for the season, so they liked it. It did have a bit of a cult following in Europe as well. Some people thought it a bit dark and weird, but most thought the premise was fascinating and were curious as to where it would go.

"We were given this book on dreams by the producers. They were taking actual symbolism from real dreams that people have, so if it had continued it could have been really fascinating to fans who like to become really involved."

Nicholson reveals that the cast members had

their own issues about the development of their characters. "Naomi hated the fact that she felt like a talking head all the time, just spouting facts," she says. "Bruce is a perfectionist, so he wanted to rewrite things to add to the character development, but the producers had their own timeline for that. We didn't know where we were going, which is often how it is in TV. He and I had a scene in the park, and he felt it could really be a revealing moment about our relationship so we spent an hour at the hotel before work rewriting it. It was good, but the producers didn't want to reveal too much too soon."

In the series' second episode, "Night Terrors," Nathan and his team were presented with another alluring mystery: A young boy named Keith experiences nightmares and expresses them in violent behavior. His father, a deacon, and aunt approach the Institute for help. Entering the young boy's mind to investigate, they arrive at a darkly lit cathedral. Nathan and Kate encounter "the smiling man," a figure who appears to stand in the way of solving the mystery. Eerily, "the smiling man" seems to know Nathan and taunts him.

During a second attempt, the cathedral shimmers into a brightly lit lake. Keith becomes frightened and exits the dream. Upset at the lack of progress, Keith's father takes him home. But that night Keith narrowly misses stabbing his sleeping aunt with a knife.

Nathan learns that as a toddler, Keith accidentally pushed his sister's carriage into the lake. The father believes his son has no memory of having a sister but Nathan disagrees. Kate visits Keith's mother, who is in a mental institution. The mother is wracked with guilt over the incident.

In their third trip into the dreamworld, Nathan revisits the lake with Keith and discovers "the smiling man" waiting for them. He spars with Nathan and Keith. Keith is forced to relive a scenario experienced as a toddler which resulted in his sister's carriage sinking into the lake.

In the fourth visit to the lake, the truth of the trauma is revealed: Keith's aunt safely removed the baby from the carriage before she pushed it into the lake. The young girl with whom Keith has grown up, and thought was his cousin, is actually his very alive sister. The aunt, Angie, breaks down and confesses that she wanted to be a better mother to the child than the mentally unstable biological mother.

Before directing this episode, which he calls "ambitious," Kristoffer Tabori sat down with the writer. "It was written by Stephen Gaghan, who went on to write *Traffic* and then wrote and directed *Syriana*. When I started prep, the script was a mess—a talented mess. But a mess nonetheless. The interesting and talented parts were obscured by sequences that were either hokey or sensationalistic. The problems that Stephen hadn't solved were structural. But the [script] was also imaginative and talented, clearly penned by someone with fresh ideas.

"Stephen was a smart young guy, very engaging, very self-assured. I remember him being complimentary to me after a notes session. His ego was secure. Rare in my business. I gave him a lot of notes addressing logic, clarity, things paying off, ways we could do things that were more cinematic, ways to use less exposition. Often times people are resentful and especially in television feel it is not the director's place. But Stephen wasn't like that at all. He was really cool, not threatened. I remember thinking, 'This is a guy on his way up.'"

One of Tabori's major challenges was filming the very surrealistic dreamscapes that complemented the storytelling. Due to budget, recreating a cathedral was impossible, so Tabori suggested a "impressionistic" version. He admits that wasn't a perfect solution. "I said, 'Let's just surround the church elements with drapes and have the background all fall off and have the church essentially be just *elements* of a church. Let's not worry about having all the specifics of a church because that's going to cost a fortune.'"

Recalling Bruce Greenwood, Tabori says, "Bruce is incredibly accomplished and talented. He has very strong ideas about his character. I tend to work in a very loose manner. I don't like to stage in the conventional way. I don't think people should stand and talk to each other. I like moving them and having them do things. I remember Bruce found me a little hard to swallow because I was always pushing and had a different style than he was used to. At least that was my impression. But he is a gentleman and we got along fine."

Tabori cast the guest stars in his episode, including a pair of favorite actors that he'd admired for a long time. The antagonist in this tale was "the smiling man" inside the dreamscape and Tabori knew exactly whom he wanted. "I kept thinking about that part," says Tabori. "It's a tough part. A lemon in that part, I'd be sunk. It required an actor of great sophistication." And the person who answered the call was Harry Groener. "I was so excited to learn he had accepted this part," says

Tabori. "I had been a fan of Harry Groener's for 15 years or so from his work in theater. Harry's skill set is both refined and superior. And he's such a fabulous guy! He's very available as an actor. He comes out of the theater so he's ready to work, prepared and knowledgeable."

Tabori also says he was pleased to have Sarah Jane Redmond (*Harsh Realm*) in his cast, playing the role of Keith's biological mother who was sequestered in the mental hospital. "I admit I had had a crush on her," he says. "I think she's an amazing actress. She's incredibly sexy and a really interesting woman. She is, and was in that show, brilliant."

Tabori also hired friends Anna Gunn (of *Deadwood* fame) to play Keith's aunt and Pepper Sweeney to play the deacon. The most important role went to Michal Suchánek, playing the ten-year-old Keith. Tabori had high praise for his performance. "The little boy was amazing," says Tabori excitedly. "He was an old soul which is what you always want from a kid who has to play a child who has suffered greatly. And those children are often wise beyond their years. Michal came with such a sophisticated spirit inside of him. The boy worked his ass off. I pushed and pushed him. I never felt I had to worry about him or had to take care of him. The kid was here to work and learn and he was tremendous."

Tabori is very candid about his assessment of the finished product. "For me, the episode fell apart," he says. "It may be that it was due to my skill set. The episode was too rational. What's interesting about dreams is that they're not rational. The episode tended towards the didactic. It over-rationalized and explained everything. The irony is that some sequences in it are some of my best work. There are sequences that have great vitality and energy. I thought a lot of my camerawork, and staging pushed things along well. But the story was hokey! I remember thinking, 'This scene is too pat! Too literal. It's not mad enough! There's chaos in our dreamscapes....'

"I was under enormous pressure. The expectations didn't match the reality of what needed to be accomplished in that eight-day schedule, and compromising things that I think could have been much better. But you always compromise."

In other episodes, the plotlines were quite esoteric. In "Counting Sheep," the Morpheus Institute is asked to get information from a dying killer to save the life of one of his victims. In "Passed Perfection," Gail's estranged father is dying and Nathan uses the dream machine to bring them together one last time ... with deadly consequences when Nathan's consciousness becomes trapped in the father's brain. Nicholson says she recalls shooting this story. "I thought the episode called for some drama in Gail's confrontation with her father," says Nicholson. "This was huge for her. I asked to do a take when we got the blocking and ran through it, so I could get to where I thought I should be emotionally. We did two takes. The second was right on. However, in editing, the producers decided they wanted Gail to remain a somewhat cool character for awhile so they started with the second take and switched to the first at the key moment. As a result, the scene didn't work for me as an actress, and it was frustrating to watch."

Had the show run longer, we would have learned that comatose Gail was not just a running subplot that would be seen in various episodes. Gail would eventually become something greater. "Actually, she was very integral to the whole show," explains Nicholson. "They were going to make her like Diana the Oracle who can see things and give insights that others couldn't see." Nicholson says that the Neuropsychologists would actually consult Gail for answers to mysteries that they were investigating. There were also additional plots that would integrate the character as part of the show's mythology. "There was a triangle between Gail, Nathan and McCaig [actor Ray Wise], who used to be Nathan's partner, but who was responsible for Gail's coma. Either she picked Nathan over him, or they had an affair, something the producers had yet to figure out. Kate also had an affection for Nathan, so the possibility of my waking up became more of a threat to her."

In "Sub Sub-Conscious" a horror author's nightmares are interfering with his creativity and he asks for Nathan's help in relieving the pressure. The strange part is that the author seems to be enjoying himself....

Bruce Greenwood says he was intrigued by the series' "limitless possibilities" of entering the unknowable terrain of the subconscious/unconscious. "Not in visual terms exactly, as the constraints of budget dictated the extent to which the writers could explore that aspect but more along the lines of modes of thought, and the idea that stories could develop in nonlinear ways, reflecting the synaptic leaps that provided us with ingredients for thought and feeling. Great in concept, tricky to execute.

"There were a couple of scripts that seemed to work pretty well and where the production design team had sufficient funds and time to make something special, and then of course there were the clunkers that came in late, underwritten or overwritten and asked too much of the visuals, but that's not uncommon. I do remember thinking the main lab room was very well-designed, elegant and seemingly purpose-driven. What they dreamed up was pretty impressive."

Sleepwalkers had a very short life history. Just two episodes aired before it was canceled. "I think it could have worked but Warren Littlefield, NBC president at the time, just hated it, so it was doomed from the start if the ratings were anything but stellar," notes Nicholson.

The series pilot had aired in November 1997, two months after the fall premiere season; "[The network] waited until after the World Series [to air the series] and it's tough. Viewers already have their 'must watch.' I think cable was also encroaching and networks weren't sure what was happening and blamed the shows. We had a 10 share [rating], I think, which for today would have been good."

Episodes three to seven aired by some West Coast NBC stations from February to May 1998. Its final two episodes have gone unaired.

Regarding the series' quick cancellation, David Nutter says, "*Sleepwalkers* was given a coveted slot by NBC because another show had been canceled. But it was frustrating that they didn't give it much of a chance. It was almost DOA. It was really sad. Networks play to the lowest common denominator. They don't believe in quality. They only believe in audience."

An NTSC Region-1 German-distributed DVD box set edition of the series, titled *The Sleepwalker Project*, contains the first six episodes; it is available via the German edition of the online retail seller Amazon.com. A Region-2 DVD U.K. box set containing three episodes is also available from Play.com.

CAST NOTES

Bruce Greenwood (Dr. Nathan Bradford): Born in Quebec, Bruce graduated high school in Switzerland. He developed his love for acting at the University of British Columbia in Vancouver, Canada, trained at the American Academy of Dramatic Arts and has proven to be a versatile actor. In television he's starred in *St. Elsewhere* (1986–88) and *Nowhere Man* (1995) and made a TV movie appearance in *The Life* (2000). In fea-

tures he's starred in *Exotica* (1994), *Double Jeopardy* (1999), *Thirteen Days* (2000) (as President John F. Kennedy), *The Core* (2003), and *I Robot* (2004).

Naomi Watts (Kate Russell): Naomi was born and raised in England; her family later moved to Australia and it was there she began studying acting. Her earliest credits are in Australian commercials and television. Her first feature films were the Australian indie flick *Flirting* (1991) with Nicole Kidman and *Tank Girl* (1995). After *Sleepwalkers* she was cast in David Lynch's *Mulholland Drive* (2001) which got her a lot of attention at the Cannes Film Festival. She starred in two popular horror films, *The Ring* (2002) and *The Ring 2* (2005). She received her first Oscar nomination for *21 Grams* (2003). Her career reached new heights when she was cast as Ann Darrow in Peter Jackson's *King Kong* (2005).

Abraham Benrubi (Vince Konefke): A 6'7" actor from Bloomington, Indiana, Abraham is best known as Jerry Markovic on *E.R.* (1994–2006). In his early acting days, he guest-starred on *Growing Pains* and *Parker Lewis Can't Lose*. In features he's starred in *The Shadow* (1994), *Open Range* (2003), and *Miss Congeniality: Armed & Fabulous* (2005). Recent TV credits include *The X-Files* ("Arcadia") and *Dark Angel* ("Flushed").

Kathrin Nicholson (Gail Bradford): Born in Solihull, England, and raised in Canada, Kathrin attended the University of Toronto, modeled in Europe, and graduated from the Academy of Dramatic Arts in 1989. She's guest starred on *The Outer Limits* ("The First Anniversary"), *First Wave* ("The Aftertime"), *Melrose Place* and *Profiler*. After ten years as a successful actress in TV, theater and commercials, Nicholson's passion for home design and renovation took center stage and she pursued her real estate license, turning her favorite hobby into a full-time career. In 2004, Nicholson sold the entire penthouse floor of most exclusive condominium building to one client; it remains the highest sale on the famed "Wilshire Corridor" to date. She recently co-starred in the television documentary *The Fabulous Life: Really Rich Real Estate* (2006) on VH-1.

Jeffrey D. Sams (Ben Costigan): A native of Ohio, Sams has appeared in a wide variety of television parts. He's had recurring roles on *Law & Order*, *Wasteland*, *Strong Medicine*, *CSI: Miami*, and *Veronica Mars*. He's also done voice work. He was the Black Panther in *Ultimate Avengers II: Rise of the Panther* (2006), an animated DVD feature.

Sliders

(1995–2000)

The adventures of four travelers who jump through a "wormhole" transporting them to parallel Earths which are different in small or large ways from their original world, Earth Prime.

Cast: Jerry O'Connell (Quinn Mallory) *Year 1–4*, Sabrina Lloyd (Wade Welles) *Year 1–3*, John Rhys-Davies (Professor Maximilian Arturo) *Year 1–3*, Cleavant Derricks (Rembrandt Brown), Kari Wuhrer (Maggie Beckett) *Year 3–5*, Charlie O'-Connell (Colin Mallory) *Year 4*, Robert Floyd (Quinn Mallory) *Year 5*, Tembi Locke (Dr. Diana Davis) *Year 5*; **Created by:** Tracy Torme, Robert K. Weiss; **Executive Producers:** Robert K. Weiss, John Landis, Leslie Belzberg *Year 1*, Jacob Epstein *Year 2*, Tracy Torme, Alan Barnette *Year 2–3*, David E. Peckinpah *Year 3–4*, Bill Dial *Year 5*; **Co-Executive Producers:** Tracy Torme, Jacob Epstein *Year 1*, Paul Jackson, Tony Blake *Year 3*, Bill Dial *Year 4*; **Supervising Producers:** Tony Blake, Paul Jackson *Year 2*; **Producers:** Steve Ecclesine *Year 1*, Les Kimber *Year 1*, Jon Povill, Tim Iacofano *Year 2*, Mychelle Deschamps *Year 2–3*, Richard Compton *Year 3*, Marc Scott Zicree, Jerry O'Connell, Edward Ledding *Year 4*, Chris Black, Paul Cajero *Year 5*; **Co-Producers:** Jeffrey Barmash, Janice Cooke-Leonard, Murray Shostak, George Erschbamer *Year 1*, George Grieve *Year 2*, Bruce Golin *Year 3*, Chris Black *Year 4*; **Associate Producers:** Cathy M. Frank, Marianne Canera *Year 1*, Bruce Golin *Year 2*, Peter Chomsky *Year 4*, Paul M. Leonard *Year 5*; **Consulting Producers:** Josef Anderson Year 3, David Peckinpah *Year 5*; **Writers included:** Lee Goldberg, William Rabkin, Chris Black, Tracy Torme, Richard Manning, Marc Scott Zicree, Jon Povill, Tony Blake, Paul Jackson, Nan Hagen, Josef Anderson, Bill Dial, Michael Reaves; **Directors included:** Adam Nimoy, Richard Compton, Mario Azzopardi, John McPherson, Jeff Woolnough, Jim Johnston, Jerry O'Connell, Mark Sobel, Reza Badiyi, Paul Lynch; **Production Designers:** Anthony Brockliss, Steve Geaghan, Colin Irwin, Michael Nemirsky; Visual Special Effects: Digital Muse, The Post Group; **Guest Stars included:** Robert Englund, Roger Daltrey, Mel Torme, John D'Aquino, Adrienne Barbeau, Kristen Dalton, Peter Jurasik, Jerry Doyle, Julie Caitlin Brown, Jay Acovone, Michael York, Lester Barrie (as Elston Diggs), Linda Henning (as Mrs. Mallory), Neil Dickson (as Col. Angus Rickman)

Fox Television/Sci-Fi Channel/St. Clare Entertainment/Cinevu Films/Studios USA Television/Universal Television; March 1995-February 2000; 60 minutes; 88 episodes; DVD status: Seasons 1–4

What if you could travel to parallel worlds? The same year, the same Earth, only different dimensions.

A world where the Russians rule America, or where your dreams of being a superstar came true, or where San Francisco was a maximum security prison?

My friends and I have found the gateway. Now the problem is finding a way back home!

—*Sliders* opening narration by Quinn Mallory (Jerry O'Connell)

Sliders was an exciting television series concept that studied permutations. It was a fantastic idea explored in science fiction literature and comics, but untapped in film. What would it be like to travel from one earth to another and find yourself in another universe?

Sliders explored the life and adventures of young genius Quinn Mallory, a student who engaged in revolutionary quantum physics experiments in his basement. He was obsessed with inventing anti-gravity, but discovered something else. Because of a freak accident while demonstrating his device, Mallory was flung into another universe along with Professor Maximilian Arturo, his blustery physics teacher; Wade Welles, Quinn's girlfriend; and Rembrandt Brown, a passionate African-American blues singer (the latter whisked into the wormhole's event horizon when he was just driving by the area).

Quinn's hand-held device "The Timer" (at first glance it looked like a TV remote control) counted down the amount of time left before the next wormhole gateway could be engaged. Upon activation, the "Timer" emitted a beam creating a gigantic, circular portal between universes. With a running jump into the vortex, the travelers would land on the other side, in another Earthly dimension and another new adventure. If the Timer was not activated when the numbers reached zero, another wormhole could not be created for 29.7 years.

In the series' two-hour premiere, the four travelers were stuck in an "Ice Age" Earth. The Timer's settings were advanced ahead of time and the consequence was that coordinates for the original Earth got erased. And, because quantum physics mathematics says that there are an infinite number of Earths, the chances of the Sliders ever returning home to "Earth Prime" was infinitesimal.

For five seasons, the Sliders endured the joys and traumas of Sliding, and searched for their way home. Not all of them survived. When Sliding to alternate Earths, the travelers would often encounter ... themselves! That is, their "doppelgangers," or duplicates, who are living in that world's environment.

The alternate Earths that were visited by the Sliders were as wildly diverse as the imagination. In just their third Slide, the travelers slammed right into a Communist Russia–dominated United States of America. It was a universe where democracy had failed.

In its first season we visited worlds where...

... smart people are treated like rock stars;

... women dominated the cultural landscape and men were second-class citizens;

... a voluntary lottery controls planetary population;

... and the British won the Revolutionary War.

The seeds for Sliders were planted in the heads of writer-producers Tracy Torme and Robert K. Weiss when they became involved in a project for film director Joe Dante.

"I'd got the idea about visiting parallel universes and I'd been looking for someone who could get the science fiction angle of it and also provide what I had hoped would be some humor as well," recalls co-creator Weiss. "One of the opportunities of Sliders was to turn culture upside down with things we were familiar with.

"I had known Tracy casually before creating the series," he continues. "I had a television company called St. Clare Entertainment that I'd formed with John Landis and Leslie Belzberg. Our mission at Universal was to create TV series. What premise could be milked for potentially 100 episodes?

"One of my inspirations for Sliders was a story called 'By His Bootstraps' [by famed SF author Robert A. Heinlein, writing as Anson MacDonald; it explored time travel paradoxes]. I had read this story about a guy going back in time

and chasing himself. I thought, 'What if this could be applied to parallel universes?' And just by myself, I began thinking of Sliders as Time Tunnel only sideways. Instead of going back and forth in time, we'd be going across the same year but different world. Time Tunnel was a show I grew up loving, and so when Tracy came in, I told him about my reference with this. He had read a story that was tied in to the Revolutionary War."

Tracy Torme recalls that his idea about parallel universes came from a reading of a book about President George Washington. The book "talked about how he had almost been killed early in the Revolutionary War," says Torme. "And I began fantasizing, what would happen at the Revolutionary War had Washington been killed? And I think there never would have been a United States. The whole history of the entire world would have been completely different. That one moment in time, six British pickets shot at point blank range at Washington up at his horse and missed him. But what if one of them had hit him? The whole world would be different. It was from that moment, 'What if?' that I came up with the original concept for Sliders."

"We, right away, thought this would be great," says Weiss. "It just started clicking. From the beginning we thought this would be a great collaboration."

In its original incarnation, Sliders was considerably different from the final construction. "Quinn and his mom and all the people living in the boarding house. They were all the people who had gotten affected [they became Sliders]," says Weiss.

In the development of the concept, Torme and Weiss wrestled with the show's tenor: Should it be a black comedy or a pure SF show? Says Torme, "We ultimately decided, 'Let's be really ambitious and do both! Let's do 80 percent straight SF and 20 percent satirical dark comedy.' That was my model that I was very committed [to] in my two and a half years there, but which the network was never comfortable [with]."

Once the development of the series revved up, it was marketed to two networks: NBC and Fox Television.

"We went to NBC first," says Torme. "They didn't know what the hell we were talking about. They looked at each other, 'Are these guys crazy?' It was Warren Littlefield and other guys. And they said, 'We don't get it....' They had just committed to Steven Spielberg's seaQuest. The next place we pitched was Fox Television. We saw Peter Chernin. He was interested. I was convinced that NBC was going to buy it and Fox was going to pass on it. And it was exactly the other way around."

The series was blessed in some ways because Weiss recalls that the network underwent three management changes in the time between the pilot and the green-lighting of the series. "A lot of times your project can get flushed down the toilet. Two guys can come in and say, 'Why should I have this baggage? I'm not going to be held responsible!' It's crazy because it could be something really good. We were lucky."

While choosing a parallel world to be visited during the series' two-hour pilot, "we had suggested, 'Let's do the one where capitalism had been defeated by Communism,'" says Weiss. "The Fox TV executive suggested that was old news and no one would care."

It was just a few years earlier that the death of Communism and the fall of the Berlin Wall had occurred in Eastern European countries. And here came along two series developers suggesting a flip-flop—a Communist-dominated world where democracy had failed. "It was funny to think they thought that was too retro," grins Torme.

"I'm glad we did it because we felt that it was an easy way to show the contrasts between the two different worlds. And we could get to have some fun," says Weiss.

An example of that "fun" was presenting in the pilot a Communist-themed parody of the daytime court TV show *The People's Court* with Judge Joseph Wapner. "The network was just horrified by that whole concept," chuckles Torme. "'You're putting in this whole satirical humor in the middle of a science fiction show. It will completely confuse the audience. They're going to be turned off by it,' [said the network]. We had a big fight with them over that."

"We wanted, for the lead Quinn Mallory, a guy who could be both hunky and good-looking, and you could believe he could be this brain," says Weiss. "A lot of times you get a really smart guy on a show, he's portrayed too much of a nerd, or a geek. You don't have the other element. We wanted to mix the two."

Jerry O'Connell snatched the role. He was already well-known in the business for an acclaimed performance in Rob Reiner's feature film *Stand By Me*. "When we met him, it was like, 'Wow!' He was good-looking, he was a great

actor, he was smart," continues Weiss. "He got the concept. He was enthusiastic. He wasn't, at that time, the traditional network mold for a guy."

For the role of Professor Maximilian Arturo, a few actors were considered, including *MASH*'s David Ogden Stiers, but the role ultimately went to a highly respected Welsh actor who co-starred in Steven Spielberg's *Raiders of the Lost Ark*. "I wanted to make sure we got an actor who lent an air of legitimacy," says Weiss. "I knew all the other parts would be people not well-known. I was keen to getting someone with some real chops and real experience. I'd always loved John Rhys-Davies. He comes ready-made with all the pomposity and seriousness and he can be cantankerous and funny. And he was really wonderful."

As Wade Welles, Quinn's girlfriend, the producers knew exactly who they wanted but were met with opposition. "The network did not want to cast Sabrina Lloyd," explains Weiss. "'Oh, what are you doing there? Don't you want someone else with blond hair and giant breasts?' 'No we don't! Here's what we like about this part.' We browbeated the network to let us cast Sabrina. We really thought she brought great values and was a good actor. She was really against type."

The role of Rembrandt Brown required an actor with some very specialized skills. "When you do casting, you see a lot of people over and over," sighed Weiss. "After a while it becomes mind-numbing. You're looking for someone who has their own original voice they can bring to the character you've created. This guy was a performer and we were looking for someone who could sing. When Cleavant Derricks read, we were excited. He said, 'Hey, aren't you going to ask me to sing "The Star Spangled Banner?" In the material, Rembrandt was on his way to the ball park to sing "The Star Spangled Banner." Would you like to hear me do that?' 'Sure!' said Tracy. He belted out his version which was really funny, made us laugh and helped us really see how he would be great for the series."

In an unused scene shot for the pilot, Derricks did sing a funny eight-minute version of the National Anthem at Candlestick Park in San Francisco in front of about 40,000 people.

Visiting other universes that had histories vastly different from our own, allowed the creators an opportunity to inject social commentary into the storylines. "Sometimes it was satirical, sometimes it was parody," notes Weiss. "I'm not sure how much of that played out as the show went on. We wanted to do a lot of it with humor.

Sliders cast members Cleavant Derricks, Sabrina Lloyd, John Rhys-Davies and Jerry O'Connell (© Fox Television).

We didn't want to hit people over the head with it. But if we could make the social commentary in a humorous context, you get the best of everything."

"I wrote a lot of music for the show," notes Torme, son of the legendary singer Mel Torme, who cameoed in a *Sliders* episode ("Greatfellas") as himself. "I would write fake commercials and fake rap songs. I wrote a fake rap song about going to the library in the show 'Eggheads.' It was so realistic that a lot of people thought it was a public service announcement. My idea was a bunch of gangsta rappers singing about the ben-

efits of going to the library and reading. I loved injecting that into the show because I knew that it infuriated the network but I was interested in doing it anyway."

Although the show had a high-concept setup, clearly explained in the flashy main titles, some viewers in the media circles still didn't quite comprehend. There were some reports, initially, that the show dealt with time travel. "I remember there was a little bit of it," agrees Weiss. "It really boggled our minds. We went out of our way, even when you look at the main titles, explaining the premise. I thought, 'Oh my god, we're just hitting people over the head. I don't want to be pedantic!' I would say 90 percent of the people got the premise of the show."

This notion of alternate universes, is not pure fiction. It's based on real-world quantum physics — specifically String Theory. Physicists write that they have great difficulty in explaining the universe without the presence of a multiverse. In the many-worlds interpretation of quantum mechanics, all possible universes exist simultaneously. It gives *you* the probability of being in *one* of an infinite number of branches, each representing a different universe.

Albert Einstein, considered history's greatest physicist, recognized this in his papers. "I've always been interested in, and studied, quantum physics," says Weiss. "In my own mind, I thought about — and this is *outside* the theory — 'What if there's a way to connect these parallel universes as if they're all linked together with a string and you could slide down the string?'"

Weiss says he was encouraged to pursue the concept when he spotted a copy of the latest issue of a science publication, *Discover* magazine, that had on its cover "All of These Earths" which was a discussion on the physics of parallel universes. "I showed it to Tracy and said, 'Here it is! We're not making it up!' That was mainstream thinking and that was very satisfying for us."

When it came time to design "The Timer's" (special effects) wormhole vortex, Weiss says they asked themselves, "How do you do it in a way that's not a million dollars and we don't have to reinvent the wheel every week?" He continues, "In reading the literature, some scientists speculated that on the other side of a wormhole you'd actually see a distorted picture of the opening on your side. These were the things that were cool but we had to abandon because it was too much trouble to do. But we thought about it a lot." Eventually the design chosen proved to be successful and visually exciting each week; the wormhole vortex became the show's visual signature.

The producers made Vancouver, Canada, their home base, and the city's varied landscape helped them tell stories based in San Francisco and other locations.

Fox was not overly enthusiastic about the show. "They weren't quite sure about us and couldn't put a handle on us," says Torme. "I was battling pretty regularly with them about the content of the show. It was kind of a headache for them. There's a lot of other shows they wanted to replace us with." He recalls that the network was surprised when then they looked at the numbers for the first season. "It did really well in the ratings. It surprised the hell out of them. They very reluctantly ordered 13 episodes. From that moment on, for the first few seasons, we were always on the edge of cancellation. And always found a way to come back. But we always did a little better than everybody else. They always reluctantly put us back."

The series' second season premiered in the spring of 1996, and ran for a sold four months from March to June. In this 13-episode season the Sliders visited worlds where ...

... the government of Texas has taken over and the "old west" traditions continue;

... San Francisco is a maximum security prison;

... an allosarus has survived the prehistoric age;

... and psychics dominate the society and one of them has fallen in love with Wade.

In the interim between the first and second season, a major behind-the-scenes shift occurred that had far-reaching consequences. "John Landis, Leslie Belzberg and I stepped down to executive consultants with other people running the show," says Weiss, who moved on to a television series based on the *Weird Science* fantasy-comedy feature film. "Universal had a team of guys they wanted to bring in. We weren't sure that was the way to go. There were other shows we wanted to get off the ground. We said, 'We have to do this 100 percent or not do it. Maybe it's better to let others go on with the show.' With some regret, we stepped out as executive producers. I had high hopes that Tracy would still impart those values we had. But Tracy was not the showrunner. There were other guys that were brought in as showrunners."

To this day, Weiss has mixed feelings about his departure. Soon he began seeing changes that he was not happy with. "In the third year the show started to feel different. I was not watching it regularly. It became harder for me to watch because it departed more from what the original values of the show were."

The third season premiered in September 1996 and ran for 25 episodes to May 1997. The production company moved from Vancouver and back down to Los Angeles.

The Sliders visited worlds where ...

... Quinn meets a younger version of himself and plays bodyguard;

... dragons and castles exists;

... the world is threatened by a pulsar;

... and Wade falls in love with a rock singer, but he is ... a vampire!

Weiss was experienced enough in Hollywood to know that a series' evolution was natural and often needed. He had to ask himself if he was too fixated on the show's original incarnation. "Just because it was not exactly what it would have been as envisioned, does that make it wrong? I had to examine that. As it turned out, I really didn't like a lot of it!" he laughs. "It could have been so much better."

To crystallize what he saw as unwanted changes in the show, Weiss points to the nature of the villains each week. "They took the low, or easy, road in terms of the nemesis," says Weiss. "It got a little arch for me. It became, in some ways, not as smart. It didn't have the humor, the social commentary, the parody. I'm not faulting anybody. I can't think of another show to compare it with that has those kinds of levels. That, I think, was the biggest disappointment."

Sharing this sentiment was Tracy Torme, who had his own beef. He says that for a second season episode titled "Invasion" (one of his favorites), he invented an alien species called "Kromaggs." It was how these aliens were subsequently handled by other writers that irked Torme. "It was my attempt to create a villain that was unique in Sliding," he says. "My original attempt was, here's some guys that developed from a different kind of ape that became dominant on several of the Earths.

"They were savage and warlike. They hated homo sapiens and found out homo sapiens were living on other Earths. They were Sliders. They were very unique villains for the show and we worked very carefully with some of the makeup guys from *The X-Files*, who were up in Vancouver with us."

Change in how the Kromaggs were depicted annoyed Torme. "I didn't want them to be, like, really bad Klingons. They were like bald-headed guys, bad skin, bad teeth, who ran around growling and speaking in perfect English. They had static, stupid lines like 'You must be destroyed!' I was horrified. [Producer] Peckinpah came in and decided the Kromaggs should be like Nazis. In the original episode they didn't speak English. That was an example, to me, of the way the show went downhill."

However, Weiss does acknowledge how hard it was to conjure up the "multi-levels" of the show's construction. "It takes more work," he says. "The pressures to write that kind of material every week. To make it fresh yet be a formula. To try and meet people's expectations and try to surpass them. That's tough."

Torme's analysis of the show's progression was very simple. "The main reason the show went downhill in the last two and a half seasons is, there were very few people there who really cared about the show," he says. "It became, sort of, 'Let's churn out a bunch of episodes that will be enough for syndication.' There was a lot of continuity errors, carelessness, there was just a lot of stuff where it didn't have a look that anyone who was caring was involved any more."

This "lack of care," as Torme puts it, extended to the cast of the series. Beginning with the departure of John Rhys-Davies in the middle of third season, the show would see a cast changeover in the following two seasons that radically altered the character dynamics.

In a two-parter titled "The Exodus" (from a story contributed by Davies), Professor Arturo was written out of the series, dying in a heroic effort to save human lives. Actress Kari Wuhrer served as his replacement; her character, former military officer Maggie Beckett, joined Quinn Mallory and his friends in their Sliding adventures.

Fox TV canceled the series at the end of its third season, on May 20, 1997, but on June 23, USA Networks picked up the series for 22 episodes. Sci-Fi Channel aired the fourth season.

Another original member of the cast, Sabrina Lloyd, also did not return to the show for the fourth season. Wade Welles, Sabrina's character, was written out as having been captured and killed by the Kromaggs. Sabrina was not available for the filming of the end of her character, and only supplied a voiceover for one episode as a means of resolving the character. There was reportedly friction between Lloyd and Wuhrer on the set during filming. In a September 1999 America Online chat, Lloyd revealed the reason of her departure: "I left because I wasn't creatively challenged any more. I felt I had gone as far as I could with the character, and I was ready for something new."

"Both Sabrina and John Rhys-Davies were treated horribly. They were both forced out of the show," claims Torme. Allegedly, the network wanted someone else more "MTV-friendly" than Davies. In a 1998 interview, Rhys-Davies acknowledged to *Sci-Fi Universe* magazine that he was fired and that he was upset with the show's direction and writing quality.

"When David Peckinpah joined the show he was given a mandate. The show was too cerebral," says Torme. "It basically needed to be dumbed down. He made it clear to everybody that he didn't understand the show. He didn't like the show. He was just there as a caretaker until he moved on to his next project.

"I spent the third season trying to get him to discuss the characters with me. I kept saying, 'When do you want to talk about the characters?' 'Oh, we'll get to it!' This went on for weeks. We never did have a single meeting to discuss the characters or what my vision of the show was. When I realized I was going to be leaving, in the middle of the third season, I wrote my best episode, 'The Guardian,' prior to leaving. I had a feeling this show was going to go into a terrible direction. What I didn't know, and I found out recently, was the two executive producers that were still in the show when I left, Alan Barnette and David Peckinpah, were very upfront with everybody that they really didn't like or care about the show.

"Ron Meyer, who ran Universal, came in and gave them a mandate: go to video stores and check out different movies like *Twister, Island of Dr. Moreau,* or whatever.

"The actors were still trying hard and putting in their best efforts. The people at the top had no sense of what we were trying to do in the first few years. All the political satire and black humor left. All the social satire and pop culture references, everything went out the window. It just became a very exceedingly dumb show.

"There's just nobody minding the store at the top of the food chain. Had I been more aware of that at the time, I would have exploded." Torme went off to Warner Bros. for other projects, leaving the series in the hands of other people.

Midway through the fourth season, Jerry O'Connell's real-life brother Charlie, who was also an actor, was introduced as Quinn's "long-lost brother" living in an "Amish world"; he joined them in the Sliding adventures. It was in this season that Jerry became more creatively involved with the show as a producer, writer ("Way Out West") and director of two episodes.

At this juncture, the screenwriter and author of the *Magic Time* series of SF novels and *The Twilight Zone Companion*, Marc Scott Zicree, joined up as a writer-producer. He says the network's mandate was to "Fix it, make it better!" To that end, says Zicree, "the first thing we did was sit down with the cast and ask them one on one, 'What do you think is working? What isn't working? Where do you want to see your character go?'

"Those conversations were very useful and collaborative. I thought the actors were terrific and very eager for us to bring the show to its potential. *Sliders* was a great idea for a show that had not reached its potential. At the time I was hired, I had only seen the pilot. Once I came aboard, I started watching episodes from previous seasons. The whole notion of jumping from parallel world to parallel world was wonderful.

"But by the third season, some of the actors were unhappy and John Rhys-Davies had left by that point. And I had heard there had been a lot of infighting in the writing staff. The only person on the writing staff who was still there was David Peckinpah. Basically, I watched third season and I was appalled. They were ripping off movies week after week. One week it was *Twister,* another would be *Jurassic Park,* and another would be *Island of Doctor Moreau,* and on and on. The characters weren't there for each other. There were huge logic holes."

Zicree also says he recognized that fans didn't like Kari Wuhrer and wanted her out of the series. But after carefully evaluating her work both on and off the show, he concluded, "There were a lot of things she could do. The actress was fine. It was the way they were writing her. So I just sat down with the other writers and said, 'We shouldn't rip off movies any more. Stories should stem from our characters and the strong SF premise that we have. Be fresh and original and utilize these characters in an exciting way.' Fortunately, the other writers felt the same way. So we were off and running."

One of Zicree's other challenges was finding a way to incorporate Charlie O'Connell into the cast as he would be appearing in 17 of the 22 episodes. What kind of a character would he play? "He looked so much like Jerry, we wondered if he should play Jerry's brother," says Zicree. "It was unavoidable. For weeks we batted it around, 'How do we make his character different from Quinn?' And someone came up with the idea of making him from an Amish world, the innocent coming from a non-technological society, who would be asking a lot of questions, and that allowed us to have a character to use for exposition. Someone who could ask 'What is this? How does this work?' and Quinn could explain it to him."

One of Zicree's first scripts was "World Killer" where Quinn's doppelganger was responsible for inadvertently sliding all the inhabitants of one world into another (doubling its population) and leaving them stranded there for a number of years. "There's the issue: Can we morally take responsibility for sliding half of the population back, when they've been there for a number of years and have established lives there?" says Zicree. "And it was about responsibility and second chances, all the things I like to write about. Everyone loved that script. And I was thrilled by how it turned out."

During the Zicree season of *Sliders*, a real variety of stories were told. "One episode would be straight SF, such as 'Slide Cage,' of a prison on an alien world, and we actually used sets from [the TV series] *TimeCop*. I said, 'Don't tear those sets down. We can use them!' We got a half-million dollar set for that episode. And we used costumes from *12 Monkeys* and *Waterworld*. Again, knowing what Rod Serling had done on *Twilight Zone*, where he could use all the sets, props and costumes from MGM productions, the first thing I asked when I got on the show, was, 'Okay, what's our budget? And can we use things from other Universal productions?' The answer was yes, with very few exceptions. It was great to be on the Universal lot."

At the end of the fourth season, Zicree decided to leave the series to pursue other projects. "My wife and I were writing and producing a pilot. And also I had gotten a deal to write three *Magic Time* novels. As much as I enjoyed *Sliders*, I had a feeling it was time to move on. I didn't see the fifth season but I heard it was not as good. I don't want to sound egotistical, but in the fourth season I had a feeling of, 'Let's push for quality. Let's push for inventiveness.' And when you change the mix on a writing staff and you don't have that one guy who is sort of a gadfly, then it becomes, 'Okay, we have a show to make, let's get it done!' I also think the budget was lower on the fifth season. And I think the people at Sci-Fi Channel were not necessarily encouraging the show so I think there were a lot of factors to make it weaker."

When the show was renewed for a fifth season, both Jerry and Charlie O'Connell decided to depart because negotiations over their contracts had collapsed. Only Wuhrer and original cast member Derricks remained. In the opening scene of the fifth season premiere, "The Unstuck Man," Quinn, Colin, Rembrandt and Maggie fall out of a Sliding vortex. But a major accident occurs: While the Sliders are inside the vortex, lightning strikes. Quinn undergoes an astounding transformation: He's merged with an Alternate Earth's Quinn Mallory, but this person did not look like the original Quinn, as he was played by actor Robert Floyd. "I don't think that worked particularly well," notes Zicree.

Two Quinns inside the Vortex at the same time created a dimensional nexus that fused the two men together. "The merged Quinn" retained the personalities of both the original Slider Quinn and the alternate Quinn. The merging was a consequence of an experiment conducted by Dr. Diana Davis (played by Tembi Locke), who joined the team as a Slider and became the resident scientist on the trips. Colin Mallory was lost in the vortex, never to be seen again. This was an efficient, painless way to write out the character.

In this fifth season, the Sliders leaped to many different worlds where ...

... they became trapped in a place between dimensions, and battled the Kromaggs;

... tabloid journalism has run amok and is the news standard;

... Rembrandt was contacted by the lost Wade and traced her to a Kromagg lair;

... the Sliders land on a pirate ship and drift away from their next portal;

... and Maggie and Diana are caught in a virtual reality scenario and are forced to relive death over and over.

In the series' final episode, "The Seer," the Sliders meet a man who professes psychic powers, has been following the Sliders' adventures from one dimension to the next and knows everything about them. Their sliding exploits are legend in his world (where they're called "Slidology"). At the end of the story, Rembrandt injects himself with an anti–Kromagg virus and leaps into the vortex by himself, leaving behind Diana, Quinn and Maggie. He is determined to defeat Kromaggs once and for all.

Typically for a series finale, the final scenes set up a cliffhanger, leaving us with the question, "Did Rembrandt survive and live on to defeat the Kromaggs?"

In retrospect, the excitement of the show came from the viewers' anticipation: "What kind of a different, scrambled Earth will we see this week?" Torme says his favorite Alternate Earth was their very first one, the Soviet America. "It was a good, over-the-top satire," he says. "It was also a message to people that we have freedoms that people don't treasure and take seriously. What would it be like to have a totalitarian state instead of what we have now? That was a good blend of the two—serious SF with the satirical topics."

But what about the Alternate Earths that the

series *never* visited? One of Torme's aborted ideas was a script titled "Savoir," which is a French word to mean "to know." "It was a really interesting show where some water that was discovered in the French Alps enabled mind-reading," he says. "So the government immediately put out a campaign against this water. We did commercials like 'This is your brain and this is your brain on Savoir Waters.' It was an allegory about the drug wars. The only way they could police knowing which people were using Savoir Water illegally was having these *Blade Runner*–like guys who have to take it themselves and read people's minds and know who was taking it. The whole show was about this draconian effort to ban this substance. It was an allegory about the fallacies of the drug wars. What happens when things are demonized and when prohibition kicks in and how wrong it is. That was something that Fox was very uncomfortable with. They took it wrongly, thinking it would be a pro-drug message. And they killed that show."

In another unused Torme script, "Heart of the Moment," the Earth is four months away from falling into the sun. Quinn and Wade are married and Rembrandt gets killed. Right after the wedding scene, a vortex opens and our Sliders arrive and we suddenly realize that we've been watching doppelgangers. The story was unused because it was written at a time when John Rhys-Davies was leaving the series and Torme refused to rewrite the story without Professor Arturo.

Tracy Torme reflects on the show's evolving history. "I feel very satisfied with the first three seasons," he says. "When I see them on repeats, I feel very proud of them. They actually stand up pretty well. The vision was pretty well explored in those years. And then, it morphed into something different — Kromaggs chasing people in every show, they brought in an actress [Kari Wuhrer] that they thought would appeal to the MTV generation, and they fired Rhys-Davies. Those were calculated choices made by the network and studio.

"I really liked the idea that these four characters were a difficult mix. Two of them had unrequited love. One had a big ego problem, sort of a pompous character, and the other was just a fish out of water.

"I wanted to see the four of them evolve over the course of the show. There was a lot of dysfunction and disagreement going on. That's the way I wanted to play the show. We did the show that way in the first two and a half years. In the later two and a half years, they were all one big happy family, just classic action heroes. They did a lot of fistfighting and karate punching. The characters were not anything like the characters that they originally were. They just became bland action heroes. That wasn't what I wanted to do."

CAST NOTES

Jerry O'Connell (Quinn Mallory): Born in New York, O'Connell is best remembered as a child actor playing Vern Tesio in the film *Stand By Me* (1986). He went on to star in the Canadian television series *My Secret Identity* (1988–1991). As an adult he appeared in a number of series and movies for television before being cast in *Sliders*. Since then he has appeared in numerous films including *Joe's Apartment* (1996), *Jerry Maguire* (1996), *Scream 2* (1997), *Mission to Mars* (2000) and *Kangaroo Jack* (2003). Most recently his voice has been heard as Captain Marvel in the animated series *Justice League Unlimited* and as Nightwing on *The Batman*. He was in the cast of the crime drama *Crossing Jordan*.

Sabrina Lloyd (Wade Welles): Lloyd was born in Fairfax, Virginia. Her television career began in 1988 when the 14-year-old had a small role in an episode of *Superboy*. After that came roles in the series *Law & Order* and in the movies *Chain of Desire* (1992), *Father Hood* (1993) and *Iris* (1994). Post-*Sliders*, she has appeared in the series *Sports Night*, *Madigan Men*, *My Sexiest Mistake*, and *NUMB3RS*.

John Rhys-Davies (Professor Maximilian Arturo): The Welsh-born Rhys-Davies first gained widespread popularity for his role in the much-touted drama series *I, Claudius*. In 1980 he played a supporting role in the epic mini-series *Shogun* and was cast as Sallah in *Raiders of the Lost Ark* (1981). His other movies include *Victor/Victoria* (1982), *King Solomon's Mines* (1985), the James Bond film *The Living Daylights* (1987), and *The Lost World* (1992). Since *Sliders*, his voice has been heard in *Aladdin and the King of Thieves* (1996) and *Cats Don't Dance* (1997). He received acclaim for playing the dwarf Gimli (and furnishing the voice of Treebeard) in the three *Lord of the Rings* films (2001–2003). He has also been seen in *The Princess Diaries 2: Royal Engagement* (2004) and *In the Name of the King: A Dungeon Siege Tale* (2007).

Cleavant Derricks (Rembrandt Brown): Born in Knoxville, Tennessee, Derricks began his career as a Nashville gospel songwriter with his father before moving to New York to take up acting. There he created the role of James "Thunder" Early in the original Broadway production of *Dreamgirls*, winning a Tony award for best actor. Derricks appeared in films such as *Moscow on the Hudson* (1984), Neil Simon's *The Slugger's Wife* (1985) and Wes Craven's *Carnival of Souls* (1998). He was a regular on the television series *Thea* and *Good Sports* and had guest-starring roles in the series *A Different World, Miami Vice,* and *Spenser: For Hire.*

Kari Wuhrer (Maggie Beckett): Born in Connecticut, Wuhrer is of Cherokee and German descent. She began her career as a singer in her teen years. She also studied acting. Her first break came in 1987 when she appeared on MTV as a VJ and as the co-host of *Remote Control.* After appearing in Andrew Dice Clay's *The Adventures of Ford Fairlane* (1990) and in the leading lady role of *Beastmaster 2: Through the Portal of Time* (1991), she starred in over a dozen straight-to-video sexploitation movies, most notably *Sex and the Other Man* (1996), *Vivid* (1997) and *Spider's Web* (2001). Wuhrer appeared in the television series *Swamp Thing* as Abigail from 1991 to 1993. After *Sliders*, she acted in 1997's *Anaconda* and 2002's *Eight Legged Freaks.* On television she guest-starred on a number of shows, including *CSI*, and briefly joined the cast of *General Hospi-*

tal. She also released a music album entitled *Shiny.*

Charlie O'Connell (Colin Mallory): The younger brother of Jerry O'Connell, he was born in New York and began his career in 1981 as an announcer on the show *Small World.* He made guest appearances on *V.I.P., Wasteland* and *Cruel Intentions.* Since *Sliders* he has been seen in the movies *Dude, Where's My Car?* (2000), *Devil's Prey* (2001) and *Kiss the Bride* (2002). He has guest-starred in *Without a Trace* and *Love, Inc.* and also appeared in the TV movie *Kraken: Tentacles of the Deep* (2006).

Robert Floyd (Quinn Mallory): Floyd's first roles were in mid–1990s shows such as *Law & Order, The Famous Jett Jackson* and *V.I.P.* After *Sliders,* Floyd appeared in *Walker, Texas Ranger* and *Dark Angel* and in the films *Rebound* (2005) and *Soul's Midnight* (2006).

Tembi Locke (Dr. Diana Davis): This prolific actress' first role was in *The Fresh Prince of Bel Air* in 1994, followed by TV shows and films including *Beverly Hills 90210, Star Command, Friends* and *The Hughleys.* Since *Sliders* she has been seen in *Touched by an Angel, The Bernie Mac Show, Windfall* and *Born in the USA.*

SOURCES

"Sci-Fi Cancels Sliders." Sci-Fi Wire, July 20, 1999.

Space: *Above and Beyond*

(1995–1996)

It's the year 2063. When Earth colonies are attacked by aliens called Chigs, Lt. Col. "T.C." McQueen and a group of raw fighter pilots, the 58th Marine Corps Squadron "Wild Cards," climb into their Hammerhead attack jets and battle the aliens in space.

Cast: Morgan Weisser (Lt. Nathan West), Kristen Cloke (Lt. Shane Vansen), Rodney Rowland (Lt. Cooper Hawkes), Joel de la Fuente (Lt. Paul Wang), Lanei Chapman (Lt. Vanessa Damphousse), James Morrison (Lt. Col. Tyrus Cassius "T.C." McQueen)

Created by: Glen Morgan, James Wong; ***Executive Producers:*** Glen Morgan, James Wong; ***Co-Executive Producer:*** Stephen Zito; ***Supervising Producer:*** Tom Towler; ***Producers:*** Glen Morgan, James Wong, Tim McHugh, Howard Grigsby,

Michael Lake (pilot film only); ***Co-Producer:*** Herb Adelman; ***Associate Producer:*** Ken Dennis; ***Writers included:*** Marilyn Osborn, Peyton Webb, Matt Kiene, Joe Reinkemeyer, Glen Morgan, James Wong, Richard Whitley, Julie Selbo; ***Directors included:*** David Nutter, Thomas J. Wright, Charles Martin Smith, Winrich Kolbe, Felix Alcala, Jesus Salvador Treviño, Stephen Posey, Jim Charleston; ***Guest Stars included:*** Gail O'Grady, Harriet Sansom Harris, Doug Hutchison, Kimberly Patton, Tasia Valenza, Michael Mantell,

David-Jean Thomas, David St. James, Richard Fancy, R. Lee Ermey, Alan Dale, Adam Goldberg, David Barrera, David Duchovny, French Stewart, Richard Kind, Tony Amendola, Steve Rankin, Scott MacDonald, Michael Reilly Burke, Janet Gunn, Granville Van Dusen, Robin Curtis, Tucker Smallwood (as Commodore Ross); *Original Music:* Shirley Walker; *Visual Effects:* Area 51

20th Century–Fox/Fox Network; September 1995–June 1996; 60 minutes; 24 episodes; DVD status: Complete series

"Hit the beach at Celestial Body 20-64-K." That gung-ho military terminology was deliberate: The idea was to take the Pacific Island war action of World War II between the Americans and Japanese and transpose it into space. This action would resonate with younger fans who were raised on violent video games. Even Col. McQueen's opening narration is drenched in patriotism: "To surrender is to never go home. All of us must rise to the call. Above and beyond!"

"The series had that large-scale World War II feeling," says director David Nutter, who filmed the series' two-hour pilot. "It was the future, but with a retro tone. All of these Marines were pulling together to fight evil, a clear cut good versus evil story. Many episodes were based on World War II fighter-pilot films."

But when raw recruits hot-dog it against alien foes, you're going to take some flack. "It's simply *Beverly Hills 90210* in space," one critic sniped. Others likened it to a galactic *Top Gun* (Tom Cruise's 1986 film). Ed Martin of Inside Media found the kickoff reminiscent of *Melrose Place*, "laced with enough political correctness to irritate even a Chig." But he found later episodes "engrossing" and concluded that creators Glen Morgan and James Wong had a good chance of creating a Sunday night SF franchise.

Fox originally wanted an "academy in space" show but writers Morgan and Wong, who had previously collaborated on many *X-Files* stories, delivered a war series inspired by John Ford westerns and the 1986 James Cameron film, *Aliens.* They also acknowledged 1950s films such as *The Red Badge of Courage* and *The Naked and the Dead.* Literary SF fans pointed to Robert Heinlein's *Starship Troopers* (1959) as a possible influence; that novel which followed the military life of a space-age recruit, culminating in a battle with insectoids called The Bugs.

Fox didn't want *Space* to be labeled square SF,

so they reissued a press release: "This is *not* the final frontier. It's more *Star Wars* than *Star Trek.*"

Morgan and Wong met during their high school days in San Diego and, as college sophomores, they took a history class called The Fiction of War. This gave the young writers the idea of one day doing a war drama set in space. *Space: Above and Beyond* set up a world in 2063 where mankind has begun to colonize the galaxy. The Vesta Earth colony is suddenly destroyed by a powerful alien race the humans call "Chigs" (because their armor resembled a Chigoe, a tropical flea). In the resulting battle, Earth's top pilots are killed. Young, inexperienced pilots of the 58th Marine Corps squadron must move to the front lines.

The series pilot was filmed in Australia and the remaining episodes were lensed in Culver City, California. Morgan and Wong hoped for at least a three-year run, to show the Wild Cards gaining more experience and displaying deeper character arcs. Nutter, who directed the pilot, already had a fantastic track record for launching popular TV series (his other genre pilots include *Smallville, Dark Angel* and *Roswell*).

"Glen Morgan and Jim Wong had been my champions on *The X-Files,*" says Nutter. "They had pushed for me to direct episodes of that show and they were the ones who really forged my career. I was very fortunate and pleased when they asked me to direct the pilot of *Space.* They had written a great script. Not since the days of *Combat!* [1962–67] had there been an all-out war show. Knowing how well Glen and Jim could write, I felt it could be a real success."

Morgan and Wong wanted the title *Above and Beyond* but Fox demanded *Space* be added. The producers also wanted the 8 P.M. slot on Fridays, which had worked so well for *The X-Files,* but when *Strange Luck* got the slot, *Space Above and Beyond* dug in Sunday nights at 7 P.M., up against *60 Minutes* on CBS. Both writers felt the series never got the promotion or scheduling it deserved.

A fresh-faced cast was a necessity. "Jim and Glen were looking for a lead actor who wasn't well-known and Morgan Weisser fit the bill very well," says Nutter. Weisser's character of Nathan West joined the Marine Corps in hopes of finding his girlfriend, who might have survived an attack by the Chigs. "We also found some really interesting types of actors who hadn't done much but they really kicked butt and did a great job for us."

This included Kristen Cloke as Shane Vansen,

who saw her parents murdered years ago and had to raise her two younger sisters. Tired of responsibility, she's opted for a military world where she can follow orders. Vansen can present a soft demeanor off the battlefield but in her cockpit, she's a hellcat.

Cooper Hawkes (Rodney Rowland) is one of the In-Vitros, manufactured in a gestation tank and born at the age of 18. He's experienced prejudice — he was nearly hanged by bigoted thugs and then thrown into jail for fighting the ruffians. Sentenced to boot camp, he decides to become a pilot. He's still adjusting to his newly awakened emotions and learning about trust and teamwork.

The Wild Cards' leader is Lt. Col. "T.C." McQueen (James Morrison) who, like Hawkes, was created In-Vitro. McQueen is brilliant on tactical warfare and fiercely protective of his young charges. McQueen will chew out his recruits but deep down, he admires their bravery. "We needed someone to be the leader, and that's when we found James Morrison," says Nutter. "He hadn't done that much but he was absolutely tremendous in that role."

Morrison knew he was part of a special show. "Glen Morgan is one of the most generous and talented writers I've ever worked with," says Morrison today. "He was deeply in touch with his muse — often aggressively so — on *Space* and I'm grateful I was chosen to benefit from his friendship and trust. He allowed to me to be a fellow worker/warrior among an enormously dedicated and talented cast of actors/soldiers and made me their heroically flawed leader. I'll always be indebted to him for that."

All of the actors had to prepare for real physical and mental stress. "Since they were playing newly enlisted Marines, we put the actors through a world-renowned obstacle course in Brisbane, Australia," recalls Nutter. "This was used for special training of SEALS, Rangers and other armies. We took our people through this thing, supervised by a sergeant from Sydney. They had two days of very serious training. The fun part was that Jim, Glen and I went through the course ourselves. The last task was to climb up a 40-foot ladder and jump off a platform into a lake. And we did! We were with the actors all the way."

The series depicted a depressing-looking future: The spacecraft carrier *Saratoga* is dark and cramped, like a submarine. Targets in space are zeroed in on by a periscope device, and objects on scanners are called "bogeys." There are also whoops of joy when Chigs are blown up and cries of "objective achieved" when enemy forces are destroyed.

Nutter wanted it to look as realistic as possible. "I contacted [production designer] Simon Murton, who had done work on films such as *The Abyss* [1989], to help us put together the feel and concept of the show. We also needed a design for the alien ships and American fleets. Simon basically took that under his auspices. We had some of the best conceptual artists in the country working on the pilot. We also brought in Bernard Hides, an Australian production designer. He had done a lot of World War II work and research with the Navy, so he understood that world."

Meanwhile, the show's Wild Card pilots had to psych themselves up for extremely hazardous missions and they gained strength by bonding with each other. "These are the only people I care about," Hawkes says quietly. Not everything is so somber. As they talk on their bunks, one Marine lets loose a fart and everyone playfully buries their faces in their pillows. But they also wonder among themselves, "If this war had never happened, would we have been friends?"

"People often say how much they appreciated the chemistry between us on the show, that we seemed to be a close-knit group, like a real squadron," notes actor Joel de la Fuente (Lt. Paul Wang). "This is because we did our training together in Australia. We were five young adults more than 10,000 miles away from home in a place called Surfer's Paradise. We began with a common experience and became much closer as a result. The time we spent on the east coast of Australia comprises some of my fondest memories of a very special time."

Yet the actors had their own problems as the series marched on. They sweated like crazy on the hot soundstages, smothered in their heavy flightsuits. They found it difficult to breathe, as well as having to fight claustrophobia. But they got used to the hardships.

Meanwhile, the alien Chigs remained camouflaged in space, hidden within their mysterious spaceships or marauding nocturnally on planets. "We intentionally decided not to show too much of the aliens early on," Wong told *Cinescape* magazine. "We thought it would be better to keep the audiences wanting more."

In the suspenseful episode "The Enemy," written by Marilyn Osborn, the Chigs devise a new way to destroy the Marines. The Wild Cards land to deliver supplies and come under fire by a crazed Marine who has killed his fellow soldiers. Soon the pilots begin hallucinating and exhibiting odd behavior: Wang thinks the radio is a cockroach and smashes it, leaving them cut off from the *Saratoga*. Damphousse panics when she sees her hand bleeding, and Hawkes tries to rip off his helmet in the poisonous atmosphere. They fight to regain their sanity and learn that they're the victims of an electronic nerve gas that is tapping into each person's fear factor.

"Ray Butts" was another well-written episode (by Morgan and Wong), highlighted by an excellent performance by guest star Steve Rankin as a tough but warped officer who listens to Johnny Cash tunes. At one point, he physically beats up the entire 58th Squadron after berating them with insults. But Colonel Butts is impressed with the team's camaraderie and wants to take them on a classified mission. The Wild Cards hate his aggressive style. "I'm in a squad where I'd rather shoot the C.O. than the enemy," mutters Hawkes. They parachute onto a desert planet and Butts reveals their mission: to recover and bury the bodies of his crew, who lost a battle with the Chigs. Butts feels guilty over their deaths because he left his young troops behind so that he could go ahead and complete their mission solo. He and the Wild Cards escape in his dead crew's planes, but they're pursued by Chigs. Butts manages to drive them off but his plane is pulled into a nearby black hole and as his power systems fail, he bids them farewell. One by one, the Marines, who now respect him, say goodbye. His plane begins to disintegrate as a Johnny Cash tune, "I Walk the Line," fades into eternity.

In "Stardust," written by Howard Grigsby, the 58th Squadron is in the middle of a secret counter-offensive against the enemy (where the key is to supply the Chigs with misinformation). Meanwhile, the *Saratoga* has three new passengers: a famous general, a no-nonsense colonel and the body of an executed criminal. The dead man, encased in ice, is Navajo James Dark Moon (Pato Hoffmann), who was lethally injected for killing an officer.

"I reviewed the episode and found it still holds up as good drama," says its director, Jesus Treviño. "I particularly liked how I handled the execution scene in the opening of the episode. I also remember discussing the portrayal of Native Americans. A story about a Native American murderer at first blush perhaps sounds racist and certainly plays into stereotypes of Native Americans but the redeeming elements were the allusions to Ira Hayes [a Native American who was one of the five Marines photographed raising the flag on Iwo Jima in World War II] and the laudable roles that Native Americans played in World War II." (Navajo Indians used their native language to convey secret information, thereby confounding German wiretappers.)

Treviño also liked how the story kept viewers guessing. "There was a possible reason as for why the Native American had killed the female officer. She had taunted him and it is left unclear exactly how her death occurred. It made the storyline workable and made the Native American who gets executed much less of a villain."

Apparently, the Chigs had once visited Earth and were hailed as gods. "That was the most intriguing aspect of the episode, the possible link of Native Americans to the Chigs," says Treviño, "that the Chigs visited Earth previously, leaving an imprint in the culture of Southwest Indians and even on their language. Had the series continued, it would have been great to find out more about this early interaction between Earth people and Chigs."

Treviño recalls a memorable moment during filming. "To simulate the dead Native American in a frozen condition, we had to cover the actor with wax and this proved an ordeal for Pato Hoffmann, who was forced to lie perfectly still and pretend he was dead, with layers of wax on him that caused insufferable discomfort and itching. He told me it took days before he got all the wax out of his hair!"

"Toy Soldiers," written by Marilyn Osborn, had Nathan West's brother Neil (played by Marc Worden) enlist in the Marine Corps, where his life is endangered by a risk-taking lieutenant. Director Stephen Posey, who had been a cinematographer and director for the acclaimed 1980s war series *Tour of Duty*, recalls conflict over the casting of actor David Barrera, who played Lt. Herrick. "I felt he should be sort of Ivy League, snotty, full of himself," recalls Posey of the character. "Glen and James were bowled over by David Barrera's reading of an inspirational speech from the script and wanted to cast him. I thought he was too blue collar and I argued, perhaps too vehemently, for another actor. I think that casting session queered my relationship with the execs. It was frustrating that I could never get David to deliver the speech on camera as well as he had done it in the office!"

There were also production challenges for Posey. "We were rained out one night on location in a rock quarry and ended up having to recreate the planet's surface on stage. We shot the climactic battle sequence in close shots to hide our surroundings. The Chigs were also a nightmare to work with. They could barely move in their suits and it was extremely difficult to make them believable as a dangerous foe. That's probably why you see so little of them."

Jeff Jarvis of *TV Guide* liked the action of *Space: Above and Beyond* and noted, "It isn't about lofty thoughts, it's about saving humankind with tough talk and big weapons. If *Space* can keep up its tension and create truly scary bad guys, this could mark the end of namby-pamby sci-fi shows and return us to the *Buck Rogers* era of space action."

Another critic, Michael Logan, called *Space* "a gritty, gutsy vision of the future." But that vision was clouded by lackluster ratings. Although it did well in the male demographic range (ages 18–48), its overall ratings lagged. "I know we have a good show," said Glen Morgan. "We can't help but wish our work was seen by more people."

The pessimistic dialogue by war-zone rookies seemed appropriate. "This is the first time I've seen a dead body," says one. "It won't be the last," says another.

That grim-jawed war-time banter may have been the series' undoing. Perhaps it was too retro and down for younger SF fans and yet too familiar to older fans, who had seen the same storylines on the late, late show.

"I think one of its great flaws was being too true to the World War II prototype," observes Treviño. "For instance, the manner in which the shipboard planning was demonstrated, that felt really anachronistic. In the planning room they had a table with a floor diagram of space and tiny vessel replicas representing the various carriers of the space fleet and where they were positioned. For an audience that was familiar with sophisticated CGI graphics, this seemed really old-fashioned. There's a scene in 'Stardust' where McQueen and Ross are briefing the Wild Cards on where to deliver their subterfuge cargo to the planet Eris. All we see is a wall drawing, showing Eris and proximate space. Again, for an audience that was familiar with cool graphics, this appeared to be anachronistic at best and just plain silly at worst."

But he says some of the retro-tailoring was effective. "The flight deck on the *Saratoga* was patterned after the flight decks on a World War II carrier and because of the cool hydraulics that lowered the pilot capsule into the waiting squadron jets, the conceit worked well. I remember walking the set on my first day of prep and being really impressed with the scope and vision of the flight deck. It was a really cool toy and I was getting paid to play with it!"

The 7 P.M. time slot also meant some censorship. Characters couldn't use the word "ass" too often and bloody scenes were limited. Morgan and Wong hated it when critics called the show "*Top Gun* meets *Melrose Place*." But Jeff Jarvis of *TV Guide* supported the show and was pained by its poor ratings (ranking 72nd in the Nielsen tally by early spring). "It's better than the competing SF shows," said Jarvis. "It's different, with more action and less thumb-sucking."

In the last episode, "... Tell Our Moms We Done Our Best," written by Morgan and Wong, an alien fighter approaches the *Saratoga*'s hangar bay and out steps a Chig, with overtures of peace. A ceasefire is called and negotiations begin to retrieve human hostages. But McQueen is wary: "This is either a beginning or an end." The peace process turns out to be a gimmick by the enemy to circumvent Earth's secret attack plan, Project Roundhammer. It leads to a big showdown in space and there are surprising casualties. Vansen's plane loses power and the last we see of her and Damphousse, their Hammerhead is spiraling down towards a planet, and presumably their deaths.

"The series was very popular in Germany, it was the number one show on television there," relates Nutter. "There was some discussion about picking the series up for a second season just for that reason." Had a second year happened, an injured McQueen would have left for Earth and a female commander would have temporarily taken over the 58th. But the April 1996 ratings continued to tumble, putting the series at 87th out of 110 shows. Cancellation was inevitable. Morgan and Wong therefore ended the series with a bleaker scenario, with the Wild Cards engulfed in that aforementioned, explosive battle.

Space: Above and Beyond, despite its loyal fan base, just didn't deliver. "Our plan had been to go in at 8 P.M. Friday, right before *The X-Files*," says Nutter. "But Fox loved the *Space: Above and Beyond* pilot so much, they said, 'Let's put it on at 7 P.M. Sundays.' That was a really tough slot. It was like we were being damned for having done such a great job on the pilot. But the show did, at least, last the entire season." The series also received two Emmy nominations, for original music and visual effects.

Morgan and Wong were hailed as "The Lennon and McCartney of SF-TV" by *The Houston Chronicle*'s David Martindale in 1998. Fans pushed for a TV reunion movie but cost factors were a detriment. The flight deck of the *Saratoga* had cost $200,000 to build for the Australian pilot and another $200,000 to recreate in Los Angeles. The sets had since been destroyed.

Reruns later showed up on The Sci-Fi Channel (U.S.), Canada's Space: The Imagination Station, and the U.K.'s Sky One, all to good ratings. The series was also released on DVD and, on the Web, fans still speculate over what happened to the fighting 58th.

CAST NOTES

James Morrison (Lt. Col. "T.C." McQueen): Born in Utah and raised in Alaska, he began his acting career as a clown and wire walker for Carson and Barnes' Wild Animal Circus. Stage trained, he has an extensive theater résumé. He's also a playwright, director and yoga instructor. Morrison can be seen in the films *Abilene* (1999), *The One* (2001), and *American Gun* (2005), among others. His television credits include *Quantum Leap*, *L.A. Law*, *Millennium*, *The Others*, *Prey*, and *The West Wing*. He joined the cast of *24* in 2005.

Morgan Weisser (Lt. Nathan West): Born in Venice, California, his father is actor Norbert Weisser. After *Space*, he appeared on *The X-Files*, *Alias*, *Charmed* and *The Division*. His film credits include *Murder Without Conviction* (2004) and *Cool Air* (2006).

Rodney Rowland (Lt. Cooper Hawkes): Born in Newport Beach, California, he was a print model for Calvin Klein and J. Crew. He auditioned twice for the producers of *Space: Above and Beyond* but didn't impress them. Randy Stone, the VP of talent at 20th Century–Fox Television, recognized Rowland's talent and had him audition directly for Fox executives, which won him the role. He guest-starred on *The X-Files*, *Dark Angel*, *Charmed* and *Angel*, was a regular in *Pensacola: Wings of Gold* (1997), and had a recurring role in *Veronica Mars*. His film credits include *The 6th Day* (2000), *Soulkeeper* (2001) and *Run for the Money* (2002).

Kristen Cloke (Lt., later Capt. Shane Vansen): The Van Nuys, California–born actress' films include *Final Destination* (2000) and the remake *Black Christmas* (2006). Her television guest credits include *Quantum Leap*, *The X-Files*, and *Cheers*. She was a regular in *Winnetka Road* (1994) and had recurring roles in the series *Silk Stalkings*, *Millennium* and *The Others*. She married *Space: Above and Beyond* producer Glen Morgan in 1998. Cloke skillfully balanced strength and vulnerability as Shane Vansen for *Space: Above and Beyond*, which remains special to her. "Shane was a rich, complex, tough, kind, strong, soft, sad, loyal, faithful Marine," she says today. "I don't know that I conveyed that, but I tried. I miss her."

Lanai Chapman (Lt. Vanessa Damphousse): Before *Space*, the Los Angeles native appeared as Ensign Sariel Rager on *Star Trek: The Next Generation* and was featured in the mini-series *The Jacksons: An American Dream* (1992) and the film *White Men Can't Jump* (1992). After *Space*, she played Whoopi Goldberg's daughter in the feature film *Rat Race* (2001) and had guest star roles on *Judging Amy* and *The District*. As for *Space*, Chapman (her first name was spelled Lanei during the series' run) offers a philosophical, poetic look back on it today. "Just as [its characters] explored unknown territory, confronted fears, forged friendships and found personal truths, so too did we, as cast and crew, battle to construct something that held meaning for each of us. There was a sense of ownership. We fought for our space, for our right to expand the idea of who we were as men, as women. We created a voice, hurled it into the atmosphere and hoped that it would find eternal life amidst the stars. That it would bear witness to our journey and all that we discovered about life and ourselves along the way."

Joel de la Fuente (Lt. Paul Wang): Born in New Hartford, New York, he grew up in the outskirts of Chicago. The actor recalls signing up for *Space: Above and Beyond*: "Before I even got the role, we had to agree to terms with the network," explains de la Fuente, who was excited over the prospect of filming in another country. "I signed my contract with the understanding that, if the pilot were picked up, the series would be shot in Australia. The commitment, I believe, was for six and a half years. Having just graduated from acting school and intent on doing theater in New York, this was a major, scary commitment, a leap of faith. I remember exactly where I was when I heard from my agents that the deal had been agreed upon: I was visiting my girlfriend (and now my wife) at the Shakespeare Theater in Washington D.C. I dropped to my knees, both in gratitude and in utter fear: what would the future hold?" He's guest-starred on *Due South* and *ER*, and had recurring roles on *High Incident* and *100 Centre Street*. In 2002, he signed up as recurring character Ruben Morales in *Law & Order: Special Victims Unit*. His film credits include *Return to Paradise* (1998), *Personal Velocity* (2002) and *From Other Worlds* (2004).

Tucker Smallwood (Commodore Glen van Ross): Born in Washington DC, Smallwood was a lieutenant in the U.S. Army during the Vietnam War. He later studied acting in New York at the Neighborhood Playhouse. His film credits include *The Cotton Club* (1984), *Contact* (1997), *Deep Impact* (1998) and *False Prophets* (2006). On television, he guest starred on *JAG*, *Enterprise*, *Seven Days*, *The X-Files*, and *Millennium*.

But it's *Space: Above and Beyond* that carries a special meaning for the actor. He was the dedicated skipper of the *Saratoga*, a role originally designed for only one show but Smallwood made such an impression that the producers expanded his character to recurring status. "My involvement with Glen Morgan and Jim Wong while shooting *Space: Above and Beyond* remains a high point in my career," he says today. "It was clear from the outset that they had a deep respect for those who serve this country and were dedicated to 'getting it right.' As a former commander and military advisor in Vietnam, I was allowed to contribute, making this for me a uniquely collaborative experience. As I traveled around the country during the show's run, there were numerous encounters with active duty personnel and their reception was always positive about the work and their depiction." Smallwood is the author of *Return to Eden*, an anthology of essays about his wartime experiences and subsequent return to Vietnam.

SOURCES

Cinescape: Science Fiction Television Yearbook, 1995.

Jarvis, Jeff. *Space: Above and Beyond* Review. *TV Guide*, 1995.

Johnson, Allan. *Chicago Tribune*, November 1995.

Logan, Michael. *Space: Above and Beyond* Review. "'Space' Odyssey — A Feisty Platoon of Futuristic Marines Does Battle with Aliens — and Sunday-night Ratings." *TV Guide*, January 20–26, 1996.

Martin, Ed. *Space: Above and Beyond* Review. *Inside Media*, October 1995.

Shapiro, Marc. Interview with James Wong and Glen Morgan. *Starlog's SF Explorer* no. 10, 1996.

Spelling, Ian. "Space: Above and Beyond." *Starlog* no. 220, November 1995.

Space Precinct

(1994–1995)

In the year 2040, a New York police lieutenant moves his family to a crime-ridden planet called Altor near the Milky Way, where he works as a cop on the orbiting Space Precinct 88.

Cast: Ted Shackelford (Lt. Patrick Brogan), Rob Youngblood (Jack Haldane), Nancy Paul (Sally Brogan), Jerome Willis (Capt. Padly), Simone Bendix (Jane Castle), Nic Klein (Matt Brogan), Megan Olive (Liz Brogan), David Quilter (Sgt. Fredo), Mary Woodvine (Officer Took), Richard James (Officer Orrin), Leo Hirsch (Officer Romek), Joseph Mydell (Officer Carson), Gary Martin (voice of Slo Mo, the robot)
Created by: Gerry Anderson; *Executive Producer:* Tom Gutteridge; *Co-Executive Producers:* Roger Lefkon, John Needham; *Producer:* Gerry Anderson; *Line Producer:* Tom Bachs; *Associate Producers:* Richard Grove, Jeffrey Brunner; *Creature Effects Design:* Neill Gorton; *Tarn and Creon Alien Design:* Richard Gregory; *Senior Model Maker:* Steve Howarth; *Visual Effects Director:* Steven Begg; *Writers included:* Chris Hubbell, Philip Morrow, J. Larry Carroll, Hans Beimler, Richard Manning, Burt Prelutsky, Philip Morrow, Arthur Sellers, Steve Brown, Mark Harris, Marc Scott Zicree, David Bennett Carren; *Directors included:* Colin Bucksey, John Glen, Sidney Hayers, Alan Birkinshaw, Peter Duffell, Piers Haggard; *Guest Stars included:* Nikolas Grace, Lana Citron, Jade Punt, Andrew Tiernan, Michael

Shannon, Nigel Gregory, Pippa Guard, Steven Berkoff, Stephen Billington, Alison Rose, Sheila Ruskin, Alison Fielding, Suzanne Bertish, Stephen Grief, Maryam D'Abo, Todd Boyce, Kate Harper, Rolf Saxon, Christopher Fairbank, Jacqueline Defferary, Francis Barber, Anne Kristen, Cecilia Noble, Natalie Roles, and Kiran Shah

Mentorn Films and Gerry Anderson Productions, in association with Space Precinct L.P. and Gilman Securities Corporation for Grove Television Enterprises; American Syndicated run: 1994–1995; 60 minutes; 24 episodes

"The name is Brogan. Lt. Brogan. For 20 years, I was with the N.Y.P.D. And now ... let's just say I've transferred to another precinct."

In 2040 A.D., Brogan and his family enter an interplanetary exchange program that takes them to Demeter City, on a planet of crime called Altor. As his wife Sally and two kids settle in an orbiting "Space Suburb," Brogan and his human partner, Jack, patrol the city in their flying space cruiser.

Demeter City is a trading center crowded with aliens, primarily two races who colonized here long ago, the Creons (wide-faced, reptilian creatures) and the Tarns (telepathic beings, with a third eye in their forehead). Other aliens live here as well, which allowed for stories that examined prejudice.

"It's a brilliantly simple but original idea of combining two of the most popular television genres, the American cop show and the outer space series," raved the London paper *The Independent*. "It's inventive and witty, with much of the humorous charm that *Thunderbirds* had."

Filmed at the U.K.'s Pinewood and Shepperton studios, *Space Precinct* was a brainchild of Gerry Anderson, the producer famous for his British marionette shows of the 1960s—*Thunderbirds*, *Captain Scarlet* and *Fireball X-5*. He later created the live action series *UFO* and *Space 1999*. The original *Space Precinct* pilot, filmed in 1986 under the title of *Space Police*, starred Shane Rimmer as Brogan and Catherine Chevalier as Officer Cathy Costello. In this pilot, puppets were used as aliens. A lack of financing dashed plans for a weekly series.

In 1993, Anderson tried to revive the premise. The show's cost factor was enormous, since most of the characters were aliens. It meant CGI, robotics, animatronics, makeup and stop motion in every episode. The BBC was interested in bankrolling the show, but at a cost of $1.5 million

(U.S.) per episode (making it the most expensive TV program in the U.K.), they backed out.

The American-based Grove Television Company picked up the tab and wanted an American star as its lead. Ted Shackelford, best known as Gary Ewing on TV's *Knots Landing*, was selected. Shackelford could handle action but was ordinary enough for viewers to accept him as a family man. Brogan weeps when his friend is killed in a car bomb explosion, gets angry when a trusted pal betrays him, shows fear when his wife is held at gunpoint and is quick-witted about shooting a bad guy in self-defense. "How was I to know his armpit was where his brain was?" Brogan replies.

At other times, Shackelford looks tired, reminiscent of Nick Adams' appearances in those mind-numbing Japanese monster films of the 1960s. At the time, Shackelford was impressed with the show. "I've never seen anything like this on television," he said during production. "The kind of special effects they're doing is really feature film quality ... it's incredible stuff."

Anderson strived to reach a large audience. "I want to make a cop show for adults that children would watch," he said during production. "I'm absolutely fascinated by the New York police, in cinematic terms, with their squad cars, sirens and loudhailers. They're fabulous." He also made sure that villains on *Space Precinct* could be anybody. "We don't say that all humans are good and all of the aliens are bad. They share crime across the board."

The show tried to balance adult drama with comedy. When his workload threatens his marriage, Brogan confides to his wife, "My marriage to you is the luckiest thing that ever happened to me." But in another show, as Brogan is chasing after villains in his flying cruiser, silly officer Jack is sitting in the passenger seat, trying to get a ketchup dispenser to work.

Anderson felt American writers would best capture the world of space-age cops he was aiming for and one writer he recruited was Marc Scott Zicree, who scripted three segments. "A human cop and his family on an alien world is a great premise but it was abominably executed," says Zicree. "Gerry Anderson was relentlessly determined to make it a 1970s kids show. David Carren, Larry Carroll and I wanted it to be an adult *Blade Runner* kind of show. While some of the basic storylines were good, there was a lack of creative vision and it totally missed its potential. The remote-controlled alien heads were interesting, but they put their money in the wrong places. For example, we were told they were spending money to build a swimming pool for the hero's house, even though there were no scenes of him using the pool."

Some stories got better but others were rehashed cop sagas. Storylines included a search for a rare female beetle, stolen by a friend of Brogan's. The friend is apprehended and the beetle metamorphoses into a beautiful butterfly.

In another show, an alien girl has visions of a rogue cop killing vigilantes and Brogan has to protect the girl from the killer. In the last episode filmed, "Deathwatch," Brogan is injected with an enzyme that will kill him in 52 hours unless he locates and contains a space-borne parasite. The creature is finally destroyed as its plant-like tentacles spread outward towards the city.

Absolutely crucial to all Gerry Anderson productions were the sets and models. Fantastic explosions, a mainstay of other Anderson productions, were common. "Whenever a craft crashes, it crashes as if it's loaded with thousands of tons of TNT," said visual effects director Steve Begg. "It doesn't just blow up once, it blows up a dozen times!"

Steve Howarth, senior model maker on the show, had grown up watching Anderson's marionette shows; *Space Precinct* gave him a chance to help create flying space cruisers and space-age buildings. "Bill Pearson was the head of the modelshop on *Space Precinct* and is a designer-modelmaker, as were John Wellar and myself, the two supervisors on the show. Bill trusted *us* get on with it, which freed him up to deal with the art department. Main items like the Space Suburb and the Precinct itself, had a lot of the surface detailing done by myself, even though Steve Begg had done the concept illustrations."

They also scavenged London's shops to find odds and ends that would go into making Demeter City. "Bill saved much time and money by buying stuff from the one-pound stores," says Steve. "A lot of it ended up in the city model, one being the CD rack building. Making up stuff as you go along is always much faster than following drawings."

Steve would also use pieces of model kits to create his own vehicles. "I would go to car-boot sales every weekend and hunt for suitable toys or even find household objects. Transformer robots were always good. This kind of stuff was cheap and if you told the seller that their plastic '60s domed lampshade was going to be on television,

The *Space Precinct* suburb during construction (courtesy Steve Howarth).

you'd often get it even cheaper. A favorite was a baby's rattle that I'd converted into a hover workbee. Once you've combined two or three different toys together, added some other chunky pieces and a few pipe-runs and sprayed it gray and thrown some black powder at it, no one would ever recognize the toys in a million years. Half the time, the stuff is never seen anyway. I don't think you can see my Rattlemobile anywhere, and believe me, I've looked!"

He also created a flying car that he grew protective of. "I was a bit precious about this one," he admits. "Everybody knew it. But in designing it, I had gone too far into the future with its propulsion. That implied it had some sort of anti-gravity devices with rings of illuminated green perspex. Steve Begg said, 'I can't film this,' explaining that the *Space Precinct* police cruiser had to be the *star* vehicle in the show. Anything that was of a higher technology, such as my streamlined model, might show it up. My model was originally meant to be flown on wires in the same shot as the cruisers but Steve said, 'I'll film it, but it'll have to be parked on a roof or something.'

"The next day I went to see the rushes and towards the end, Steve Begg said, 'There's your little vehicle.' Sure enough, there it was, parked on a rooftop. The camera stayed on it for a time and suddenly, KABOOM! It exploded right before my eyes! Steve Begg had blown up my flying car! I couldn't believe what he had done. Then Peter Chiang handed me a piece of my car. The stunned look on my face must have been worth it because Steve said, after they'd all stopped laughing, 'Do you really think I would do that? It's a jump-cut!' Steve explained that a 'jump-cut' is where they take some frames of the vehicle on the roof and then stop the film. They remove the vehicle, place a pile of debris and a pyrotechnic charge in its place and then start the camera. It looked so convincing, I took it hook, line and sinker. To clinch the gag, someone had snuck into the workshop when I wasn't there, taken one of the vacuum formings of my car and manufactured a fake piece of debris, complete with charring and everything, which is what they had handed to me."

Green-screen techniques allowed the actors to be superimposed into intricate models of the city that were only a few feet high. The aliens (actors wearing big prosthetic heads) looked unintentionally lovable as they committed mayhem. Some aliens had smooth skin, like the coneheads of *Saturday Night Live*, while others had faces with bumps and groves. There was also a giant blue alien who left a gooey mass of slime whenever he shook people's hands and he

Most of the widgets for the show came from flea markets that *Space Precinct* modelmaker Steve Howarth attended on weekends (courtesy Steve Howarth).

emitted an odor that attracted swamp flies, which he lapped up with his tongue. The alien makeup was uniformly good and many of the actors under these weird faces gave excellent performances. But it was grueling work. The masks were filled with complex electronics, the eyes, eyebrows and other features controlled by off-camera technicians operating remote-controlled radios. The actors would often gasp from a lack of air and swelter under the hot studio lights.

As Brogan, Ted Shackelford brought humor and feeling to the role but Zicree observes, "As a lead, he just wasn't that strong. You wanted somebody kind of gritty and rough around the edges and our lead certainly was not that." Zicree was also disappointed in the way his stories turned out. "One was originally supposed to be about a boxer and they made him into a wrestler instead. When I saw it, I was appalled. They hired this tub-of-lard kind of guy. It wasn't credible at all and the drama was totally lost."

David Bennett Carren, who scripted five segments with writing partner J. Larry Carroll, liked the show's basic premise. "It was a great idea, *Hill Street Blues* in space, shot in an original manner," he says. His first episode, "Double Duty," had Brogan searching for an alien killer who is targeting sellers of an illegal substance called Black Crystal. "That was fun to write and that episode got us hired. It also helped to sell the series. We had extraordinary freedom to explore just about any idea we wanted. The show was great fun to write for and we explored themes with some weight."

Another writer, Burt Prelutsky, had previously written for TV shows as diverse as *M*A*S*H*, *The Mary Tyler Moore Show* and *McMillan and Wife*, as well as writing many articles for *TV Guide* magazine. He had never tackled science fiction before but his writing partner, Steve Brown, convinced him to collaborate on *Space Precinct*'s two-parter "Fire Within," where Brogan investigates a religious cult.

"Once I turned 50 in 1990, I found it nearly impossible to get work in TV," Prelutsky says of industry ageism. "I needed the money." He good-naturedly calls the series "an English bit of hokum," and confides that the show had specific challenges. "The producers were in England and we weren't. The larger problem was that the show had a limited budget, so even the modest effects we came up with were out of the question. As a result, you couldn't help get the feeling that you were working on a rather schlocky series. In the

U.S. it never had a regular time slot — it wound up airing whenever an hour of filler was needed."

Gerry Anderson had high hopes for the show. Before production, he noted, "*Space Precinct* is the ultimate combination of a proven formula of New York cop action-drama and SF. Typically, series set in space promote the notion that space travel and exploration will provide an answer to our worldly problems. *Space Precinct* rejects that. Demeter City has all of the problems we have and more. However, the philosophy of the show is not a negative or depressing one. It is in tune with contemporary 1990s positive thinking."

Roger Lefkon, co-executive producer, thought the show would be a huge hit. "We've taken no shortcuts and spared no expense in mounting what we expect will become a major worldwide franchise," he said in 1994.

There would be three paperback books based on the series, published by Harper Prism, and nine action figures, including ones of Brogan and officer Jane Castle. But despite vigorous promotion by Anderson and his team, and good ratings in Europe, erratic scheduling in American markets doomed it. The website Eofftv.com observed, "It can't make up its mind — is it a children's show or one aimed at adults? This indecision results in a bland and forgettable show."

Steve Howarth was at least excited over meeting Anderson. "My main contact with Gerry was in the early stages of *Space Precinct* when it was still called *Space Police*," he says. "Bill Pearson had put my name forward to go to Miami, Florida, with the models to promote the show at NATPE [National Association of Television Program Executives, the annual industry trade show where series are bought and sold in the international marketplace]. It was my job to unpack the models, secure them on the stand, make sure that the lights worked properly and talk to people about the models. Gerry was there most days and I had brief chats with him. This was the legendary Gerry Anderson, so I wasn't that bold with him and I came away as star-struck as I was before. That feeling kind of disappeared when he visited the model workshops one time. I was expecting him to walk around and have a look over our shoulders and see what we were doing. But nothing. He wouldn't have had to compliment our work, just a show of interest, that would have been motivational enough. But Gerry Anderson, not interested in models? How is that possible?"

Zicree felt Anderson missed an opportunity with *Space Precinct*. "I talked with Gerry directly and admired his past work. I grew up watching his wonderful shows like *Supercar* and *Thunderbirds*. He was a visionary when it came to his marionette shows. I was saddened that he wasn't willing to explore *Space Precinct* with the critical and technical expertise that I felt was warranted. He wanted *Kojak* [the 1970s Telly Savalas cop show] in space and this was after *Hill Street Blues* and *Blade Runner*. We wanted something gritty and dark but Gerry Anderson and his people in England didn't want that. Also, the effects were outmoded. They were doing a lot of modelwork and while it was fun, blue screen was now the dominant SFX form for spaceships. We were told they didn't have the budget for blue screen work. There was also the problem of having the writing staff here in the States and the production staff in England. There was a lot of miscommunication and that hurt things. It would have been smarter to move the entire writing staff over to England."

At one point, Zicree was offered the writer-producer job on the show but he turned it down. "By that time it was clear the show was not going to meet its potential. I didn't want to be constantly butting heads creatively. *Space Precinct* was designed in such a way that many of the stories were meaningless. It was about nothing and that's why it was disappointing for me."

"I wouldn't even attempt to psychoanalyze the show and talk about the deeper levels beneath the cheesiness, etc.," says Steve Howarth. "It's hard to be objective when you've been so close to a project. Considering the time it was made, and how much money was spent per episode, I was expecting the show to *look* a lot better than it did. I don't know where the money was going, but it wasn't going to the effects department as much as it should have been. Certain sequences were fantastic, considering a lot of it was still on wires. The animatronic heads were also good, but the sound department couldn't afford to remove the sounds of the servos when the eyes blinked, so often you can hear them go zzzz-ing, blowing the illusion completely and destroying all that department's good work. Technical issues aside, I thought that the concept itself was ridiculous. You have a police station in space but yet you deal with problems on the planet's surface? Surely if you can afford to build a station in space, you can afford to have stations built on the planet's *surface* to deal with the surfaces' problems."

David Bennett Carren has a fond memory of *Space Precinct*. "They flew us out to London and we toured Pinewood Studios, where all the live action was shot. We also toured Shepperton where they did the table-top model sequences. I remember putting on a safety helmet when they blew up some buildings on the model. Gerry was a terrific host, and we had a wonderful time. I went to college at London University for one semester so it was old home week for me. What a great city to do a series in."

Anderson considered it a fine series but those early morning time slots in America resulted in poor ratings that killed any financial incentive to continue *Space Precinct*. Anderson continued his work in television, including a CGI-version update of *Captain Scarlet*, which premiered to critical and financial success in 2005.

CAST NOTES

Ted Shackelford (Brogan): The actor had to move to England to do *Space Precinct*, leaving his family behind for the nine months of filming. Shackelford was raised in Tulsa, Oklahoma, where his father, a military man, was stationed. He began his TV career on daytime's *Another World* (1975–77) and had guest shots on *Wonder Woman* and *The Rockford Files*. He then starred as Gary Ewing on *Knots Landing* (1979–1993). "People asked me what I wanted to do next," he said during *Space Precinct*'s production. "I said I wanted to run around with a big gun and kill bad guys. Well...here I am!" His later TV films include *Miracle Dog* (2003) and *Officer Down* (2005). He signed up on daytime's *The Young and the Restless* in 2006.

Rob Youngblood (Jack): The Indiana-born actor appeared on *MacGyver*, *JAG*, and *Sliders*. He was also in the TV films *Murder One* (1997) and *Twice Upon a Time* (1998).

Nancy Paul (Sally Brogan): She appeared in the fantasy films *Sheena* (1984) and *Lifeforce* (1985) and made TV appearances on *Beverly Hills 90210* and *LA Law*.

Jerome Willis (Capt. Padly): *Space Precinct* was fortunate to have veteran British actor Willis, who agreed to wear the heavy makeup as the alien captain. His career stretches back to 1950s TV series such as *Bleak House* and *Adventures of Sir Lancelot*. Other early TV credits include *The Avengers*, *Z Cars*, *Dr. Who* and *Danger Man*. He also appeared in the films *Khartoum* (1966), *Lifeforce* (1985), *Alibi* (2003) and *Global Conspiracy* (2004).

Simone Bendix (Jane Castle): A Danish-born actress whose TV credits include *The Young Indiana Jones Chronicles*, *Noah's Ark* and *The Last Detective*. She co-starred in one of the *Inspector Lynley Mysteries*, "In the Presence of the Enemy" (2003).

SOURCES

Hughes, Mike. *The Gannett News*, 1994.
Lister, Scott. *The Independent* (newspaper), 1995.
Weaver, Tom. "Puppetual Motion." *Starlog* no. 307, February 2003.

Space Rangers
(1993)

The Space Rangers, a team of futuristic peacekeepers based on the planet Avalon, streak across space in their Ranger Slingship.

Cast: Jeff Kaake (Captain John Boon), Marjorie Monaghan (JoJo), Cary-Hiroyuki Tagawa (Zylyn), Jack McGee (Doc Kreugar), Clint Howard (Mimmer), Danny Quinn (Danny Kincaid), Gottfried John (Erik Weiss), Linda Hunt (Commander Chennault)
Created by: Pen Densham; *Executive Producers:* Richard B. Lewis, John Watson, Pen Densham, Scott Brazil; *Senior Producer:* Robert Halmi, Jr.; *Producers:* Rachel Talalay (pilot), Herbert J. Wright; *Co-Producer:* M. Jay Roach; *Line Producer:* Tim Harbert; *Associate Producers:* Bob Weber, Martin Cohen; *Coordinating Producer:* Mark A. Stern; *Writers included:* Pen Densham, Herbert J. Wright, Gregory Widen, Gavin Scott, Ed Spielman, Howard Spielman, Jess Hugh Mann; *Directors included:* Mikael Salomon, David Burton Moss, Ben Bolt, Thom Eberhardt; *Directors of Photography:* Don Burgess (pilot), Robert Steadman; *Production Designers:* C.J. Strawn (pilot), Curtis A. Schnell; *Costumes:* Kathleen Detoro (pilot), Katherine K. D. Dover; *Special Effects Makeup:* Tony Gardner, Alterian Studios (pilot), Ed French, Mary Westmore; *Visual Special Effects:* Chuck Comisky (pilot), Scott Squires (pilot), Industrial Light & Magic (pilot), Stargate Films Inc., Sam Nicholson, Kevin Haug, Rick Kerrigan; *Music Theme:* Hans Zimmer, Mark Mancina; *Guest Stars included:* Pat Morita, Amy Steel, Tony Amendola, Leon Russom, Buddy Hackett, Claudia Christian, Sherman Howard, Sam Whipple, Wings Hauser
CBS/Trilogy Entertainment Group/Ranger Productions, Inc./RHI Entertainment, Inc.; January 1993; 60 minutes; 6 episodes

As a contrast to the hi-tech, sleek technology on *Star Trek* or *Babylon 5*, *Space Rangers* took a decidedly low-tech approach to science fiction storytelling. It was a space western-style drama. Series creator and executive producer Pen Densham wanted a gritty, visceral science fiction television series for a change, as he puts it, to play "rock 'n' roll" to *Star Trek*'s "classical music." "We wanted to tell adventure stories," says Densham. "I loved the original *Star Trek* because they were adventurous. And I wanted to take a little bit of *Star Wars* and a little bit of *Star Trek* and inject it into *Space Rangers*. This way you had the philosophy and adventure. That's why the machinery on the ship broke down, and they were working with second-hand parts. People were improvising to find solutions. There was a frontier planet, where not everything was known yet."

Space Rangers premiered on CBS-TV in January 1993, just entering an era where the technological breakthroughs would make computer-generated visual special effects practical on television budgets. P-TEN's *Babylon 5* ended up pioneering that at the same time.

It's the year 2104, Earth has reached into deep space and on a distant planet, Avalon, Fort Hope is a thriving frontier town. The Space Rangers are a small group of diverse law enforcement officers dedicated to the task of protecting colonists against crime and the hazards of extraterrestrial exploration.

Capt. John Boon (Jeff Kaake) is the hard-nosed but experienced commander of the Ranger Slingship #377. "In the pilot, we gave Boon a wife and child, and then we realized we had completely cut ourselves off from any opportunity to have female relationships with the hero," says Densham. "Every time he would see a woman, because he was married, he would be a schmuck. So we made that error in the pilot. The lady playing his wife [guest star Amy Steel, who co-starred in 1982's *The Powers of Matthew Star*] did a fantastic job, it had nothing to do with her work, but we had eliminated any opportunity for the robustness of his sexuality, so we had to change that bit.

"I felt Jeff Kaake embodied everything I wanted — rough edges, strength, and vulnerability, and he looked great on camera but he didn't look Hollywood soft-pretty, he looked strong-rugged-handsome, the kind of guy you would follow into a nest of aliens."

Joining Boon on the missions was a band of disparate officers: Jojo Thorsen (Marjorie Monaghan) was tall, attractive, blond and tough — and the best pilot in the Rangers Corps. "Marjorie was a joy," says Densham. "She was physically taller than most women but in a perfectly formed figure. Marjorie was game to play someone whose sensitivities, abilities and strengths were strong without losing her femininity."

The ship's engineer, Doc Kreuger (Jack McGee), had been injured so many times on missions that he was outfitted with an artificial mechanical left arm that oftentimes malfunctioned and required constant fine-tuning and repair. He also had a removable heart. He was loud and brash, and constantly smoked a cigar. It was Doc who nicknamed the starship "Tin Lizzie."

"Jack McGee was someone we had worked with before and he was someone we really wanted from the beginning," says Densham. "In a sense, he's Scotty [from *Star Trek*] but he actually isn't, because he carries a gun and gets into it but he keeps things running, and fixes things by hammering rather than with exquisite finesse."*

An imposing and intimidating warrior monk from the planet Graaka, Zylyn (Cary-Hiroyuki Tagawa) used a "cybernetic pacifier" around his neck to control his aggressive tendencies. He removed the pacifier when it was time to enter into battle. But he declared himself as a peaceful man except in self-defense. Densham describes Zylyn as a Zen-like priest who controls his own violence. "I thought that was really cool," he says.

Rounding out the team was Danny Kincaid (Danny Quinn), a rookie straight out of the Academy. The son of a general in Earth's Central Command, he was the team's very green backup man. Densham says that Kincaid was modeled after actor Horst Buchholz's character in the classic western *The Magnificent Seven*.

Working with the Rangers at Fort Hope were three principal figures: Commander Chennault (Linda Hunt), a petite woman who also served as head magistrate. Says Dancham, "We wanted to have Linda Hunt represent the dignity of women in an age where women's skills were revered, so her leadership would be natural. We got Linda involved and I thought that was a fantastic breakthrough." Hunt's character was based on a real-life World War II man, Col. Claire Lee Chennault, who served as a civilian advisor to the Chinese against the Japanese and commanded a unit known as the American Volunteer Group. "We used his name and modeled some of [Linda Hunt's character] belief systems off that [man]," notes Densham.

Dr. Mimmer (Clint Howard), an irritating, nonstop-talking chief medic and forensics scientist, "was a little bit Q from James Bond," admits Densham.

And Col. Erich Weiss (Gottfried John), second in command, was someone who longed to return to Earth. His relationship with Chennault was sometimes quarrelsome and other times respectful. But he believed in the Ranger program. Once, he tried unsuccessfully to introduce androids into the team. Densham reports that Weiss's name is actually famed magician Harry Houdini's real name, "which shows you some of the tongue in cheek. We made him a foil, made him an antagonist within the group, which helped with story construction."

Once all these actors got together, jumped into their costumes, and personified the characters, they meshed as an ensemble quite well. "We were all constantly growing and exploring as we went on," notes Densham. "Even though I didn't direct the pilot, as the writer I was able to bring a lot of control to the elements and share my discoveries with the cast. We were trying to give confidence to the actors, to take control of their characters right away, and also wanted to create a world that felt closer to our own in some ways. We shot with a lot of motion and physicality, so there was an energy to these people. We wanted to

---

*When Trilogy Entertainment Group (the series' production company, headed by Densham, Watson and Lewis) got the green light to go to pilot, Densham consulted with Mattel, the toy maker, about action toys to tie in with the series. "Out of that came some ideas, like a character who has a removable heart — Jack McGee's character."

keep them very up, very in your face. They understood that and got it. We were using what we called *Hill Street Blues* shooting, trying to get away from the very static, boring *Star Trek* style."

Ready to launch into missions, the Rangers clambered aboard a long silver Slingship. Once in orbit above Avalon, the ship used a "lightspeed ring," a gigantic object hanging in space, to launch ships into hyperspace to other planets or regions of space.

Instead of landing the ship at every planetary destination, the Slingships were equipped with "Bellysnappers"—one-man escape pods in which the Rangers could "beam down" to a planet surface.

Among the Rangers' most formidable foes were the Banshees, a predatory species that attacked vessels as they traveled in hyperspace. Their weapon was a "sonic scream" capable of disorienting any human in the vicinity.

Over the course of the six episodes that were produced, the Rangers embarked on a variety of challenging missions: An ex–Ranger crash-landed on a planet that was a Graaska burial site; a famous comedian was stranded on a perilous prison planet; the ferocious Banshees attacked civilians aboard a starship; a new android officer was assigned to the team during an investigation of a crime lord; Zylyn was accused of murdering another Graakan, and Boon became his defense attorney; and Capt. Boon accidentally offended an alien warrior, and challenged the official to a duel in order to save the Fort Hope colony and Central Command from retribution.

In an alien planet's jungles, *Space Rangers'* Marjorie Monaghan (as Jojo) and Jeff Kaake (as Boon) (courtesy Trilogy Entertainment Group).

The idea of *Space Rangers* was to drop humans into different planetary environments and various adventurous situations. "This idea stayed in my files for a long time," Densham says. "Originally, we started off by calling it *Space Marines*. That's a title I wish we had kept now." The series' original treatment by Densham was titled "Planet Busters" and it offers some interesting contrasts to the finished product.

For starters, "Grunt" was the prototype for Doc, a man described as a practical joker who could fix anything. An experimental mechanic who carries an ancient projectile device, he died once but carries a mechanical heart that gives him extraordinary strength. He "can be frozen on a planet and revived. Not easily killed."

Grunt has a robotic canine companion called a slug, operated via a wristwatch-like device. The slug also flies and Grunt can see where it is via the watch-device.

A character described as "Denim" was surely the prototype for Jojo. She's a communications chief–backup medic from a planet where women

Jeff Kaake with Linda Hunt in Fort Hope, the Space Rangers' base (courtesy Trilogy Entertainment Group).

have always been leaders, a planet where brutal jousting and gladiatorial battles are the sports of choice. "Her philosophy is, you go out and make your money then come back and settle down," wrote Densham. "Good with animals. She keeps a pet — a little mouselike thing which is very intelligent."

In this original concept, there was a second woman on the team, "a rich woman" who doesn't talk about her past. "Was in love with somebody — got jilted and went into marines," wrote Densham. "She's wanted for something, we don't know what it is. People don't ask questions about her past unless they're very careful." This character did not make it into the series.

At Fort Hope, we would have seen a proprietor running a *Casablanca*-like restaurant ("Rick's Place") who is involved in illegal activities. "He's got his own sense of honor and ethics, but he's always a little shady. He's always looking to trade different and illegal things with them for what they need," wrote Densham. Again, a character and aspect of the series not seen.

The prototype of the Ranger Slingship, originally referred as the APC (Armored Personnel Carrier), was a spacecraft that was much more esoteric than what we were given. Densham wrote: "Relies on speed and agility. Very fast and maneuverable. Can move so fast that [it] seems to disappear and reappear. Can also make itself look like it's actually somewhere else (like three miles away). If chased for too long, it runs out of power. Projected from home base with a sling. Travels very quickly to trouble areas. Marines have to be strapped in. Because it doesn't have much armor, Grunt has figured out ways to disguise it — to change its shape and color — plant on planet and make skin move to hide on planet."

Densham often referenced classic titles as inspiration for the series' own plots. An exciting idea was a *Guns of Navarone*–like story, the blowing-up of a bridge. Another idea was having our space Marines confronting "zombie troops," but they were actually clones. Other story references included *Day of the Triffids* — and *Scarlet Pimpernel* — like ideas.

The military themes were actually stronger in the initial vision, an "Annapolis in space" where cadets would be trained for an ongoing war. The influence of famed SF author Robert A. Heinlein's *Starship Troopers* novel was clear here.

In Densham's teenage years when he was devouring science fiction literature, "I loved Robert Sheckley's short stories more than those of any other SF writer. His darkly humorous, offbeat but deeply human, imagination caused me to search out every word he wrote. When I was formulating my approach to *Space Rangers*, Sheckley's work inspired me. I wanted *Space Rangers* to be more like Sheckley's work: fast, funny and irreverent. With just a hidden touch of a parable."

It wasn't until Densham began working with Jeff Sagansky, who was the production president of TriStar Pictures in the 1980s, that *Space Rangers* was born. Densham had directed a 1988 horror film titled *The Kiss*, and so when Sagansky migrated to CBS in 1990 as head of programming, Densham and his production company, Trilogy Entertainment Group, were invited to pitch TV series ideas. "And I sold him four pilots in a row, which is apparently not normal! My agent said, 'That's enough, Pen — you have to stop pitching!'" *Space Rangers* was one of those titles.

To launch the series, Densham joined forces with his friend Jay Roach (who would later gain fame as the director of the *Austin Powers* comedy features starring Mike Myers), who contributed as a co-producer and co-writer.

Filming in a warehouse in Culver City in April 1992, the series pilot had a novice director, Mikael Salomon, a noted feature film cinematographer. Production of "Fort Hope," the pilot, brought together a company of creative artists to build a brand new universe from scratch. However, just as filming got underway, the Rodney King riots broke out on Wednesday, April 29. The L.A. riots were ignited when a jury acquitted four white police officers of beating up black motorist Rodney King. The case was infamous because the beating had been videotaped by a witness and was broadcast by the media. Thousands of people were angry that the officers had escaped conviction and the rioting went on for days.

Producer Rachel Talalay recalls her experiences at the time. "We had to shut down in the middle of the shoot because the riots had happened. The rioting was spreading. The moment that we shut down the production was when one of our employees came in and had been hit on the head with a baseball bat a block from the studio. He was bleeding and they smashed his car window and had hit him. A couple of blocks away was a large retail store that had a lot of looting. There was a fire about two blocks away. At that point I thought it was unsafe to keep filming. I called the producers. I said, 'We have to shut the production down!' and they were in Beverly Hills, going, 'What are you talking about?'

"I said, 'There's rioting about a block away!'

"'You can't shut down! What are you talking about?' replied the Trilogy producers.

"I said, 'You don't understand, there's a building burning a block away!' and I had to send someone to the hospital. And then [they said,] 'Okay!'" sighs Talalay.

"I pulled the plug in the middle of the day, which is a huge deal," continues Talalay. "It could be very expensive. Unfortunately, I was correct. There was a curfew in the next couple of hours. I remember watching the city burn on TV. It was very dramatic to be responsible for a crew and to have someone come in and to have his car smashed with a baseball bat for absolutely no reason except stopping at an intersection."

After several days, the city returned to normal and filming resumed. But it was hard for the company even after the violence had subsided, according to Talalay. "It made a couple of days of shooting very difficult to focus and shoot," she says. "Even when we came back, it was such a shocking thing for the city. When we came back, the National Guard was patrolling everything. It was hard to keep people focused."

It was estimated that approximately 10,000 people were arrested in the melee. In the end, almost $1 billion in material damage was done to the city. Pen Densham remarks, "I do remember abandoning the stages with our spaceship builds to a crew of security men and taking off for safer areas. Only to be in my backyard in Hancock Park, drinking a glass of wine, and looking at the smoke that was on all four sides of our community!"

But back to shooting. Talalay recalls that in making the pilot, the company experienced growing pains with a new director who had vast feature film experience. "Trilogy had been making all these huge movies, *Robin Hood* and *Backdraft*, and this was their first time being personally responsible for making a [TV] pilot. They brought me on to be responsible to make something at this level.

"Mikael always had this big-budget attitude. He would come in and say, 'I want this, this and *this*!' and we really didn't have the money. This was not a very well-funded pilot at all. He wanted his spaceship to look like a Jim Cameron spaceship."

But Talalay did recognize Salomon's talents.

"Mikael has a beautiful eye — he's a beautiful cinematographer [but] the production side just wasn't able to provide to him all the beautiful things that came from him having shot *The Abyss*, one of Cameron's movies," she says. "Mikael was not ready [for television]. He was obsessed with 50 times the size and scope of what we could afford.*

"I definitely remember that as being the most tension on the show, not be able to provide," says Talalay. "The other thing was that Trilogy was absolutely insistent that all the spaceships being CGI [computer generated] visual effects instead of models."

The extensive visual effects requirements were frustrating for the producers. Their first step was going north to San Rafael to pay a visit to George Lucas' visual effects facility, Industrial Light & Magic. (Although ILM had a reputation for providing some of the best visual effects in the feature film business, their experiences in television at the time were minimal: a couple of *Ewoks* made-for-TV movies in the 1980s, *Amazing Stories* in 1985, and the *Young Indiana Jones Chronicles* for ABC in 1992.) Says Talalay, "It was one of the first shows that had an entire digital budget. ILM said, 'We'll do this if you let us do everything in CGI because we want it to be our showcase.' I remember seeing some early tests and thinking, 'Oh, I don't know if this is going to work. Are digital spaceships going to hold up? I think we should film some models. I'm not sure if we have the time and money to make this work.'"

The Trilogy producers also sensed that ILM's participation in their project wasn't going to work. Although the company did provide the effects for the series pilot, the issue became how to achieve the effects needed for the series. The roadblocks were time, money and flexibility. Computer-generated effects were expensive: ILM was literally "counting frames" of their output, and every single shot cost money. "CGI was still too slow and cumbersome for the kind of action stories and turnaround that we intended," explains Densham. "So we ended up trying to make our own models, we built our own special effects division, and that failed miserably," he says.

Trilogy found themselves at the door of Stargate Films, Inc., run by visual effects producer and supervisor Sam Nicholson. "We literally said to them, 'We are desperate. We need help,'" recalls

<hr>

*Salomon has subsequently launched a successful directing career: He's helmed episodic television (Alias), high-profile miniseries (Salem's Lot, Nightmares and Dreamscapes, Band of Brothers) and other pilots (The Fugitive).

Densham. "And they came in and built our models and filmed them in ways that would never have occurred to me. They shot them in real time and made them feel like they were in the same tonal texture of filming as the rest of the material. They had an inventive and irreverent approach to the process, and they would shoot any way they could to make these models feel alive. It was a very exciting process and to this day I'm still incredibly grateful to Sam and his team at Stargate."

Densham was so grateful that later, when he filmed the feature *Moll Flanders*, he made sure that Stargate Films got the job of supplying the visual effects of a storm sequence. "His team gave me three times what I had thought possible for my budget!" exclaimed Densham.

Looking back, Densham is candid when he assesses the finished product (just six episodes, by any standard an unsuccessful show). He lays the blame on CBS, which aired just four of the six episodes before canceling the series. The fourth episode aired was the series pilot, "Fort Hope." (*Firefly* was not the only show that ran the series pilot as the final episode upon cancellation.) "I've often wondered how the show would have fared if we had started in the normal way by introducing our characters and environment," says Densham. Sagansky decided to dive into the show with a regular episodic story instead of a real introduction. The episodes "Death by Dishonor" and "The Entertainer" (which guest-starred comedian Buddy Hackett) never aired in the United States. All six episodes were later released on videotape and given a Region 2 DVD release. "I believe there were politics on CBS at that time," says Densham. "There were different people with different perspectives, about where the network should go. We had very strong advertiser support. I've often thought if we had been on cable or WB or USA, we would have continued running. We also made another strategic mistake, we were offered to be on Saturday nights and one of my partners said, 'That's not good enough for us,' and he pushed to get us in the middle of the week. If we had stayed on Saturdays, I think we would have done really well."

CAST NOTES

Jeff Kaake (John Boon): Kaake was born in Detroit, Michigan. He moved to Southern California in 1979 and in the early '80s began to make appearances on various shows including *Three's a Crowd*, *Club Med*, *Hunter* and *Houston Knights*.

A recurring role on *Dynasty* was followed by guest appearances on *Murder She Wrote*, *Silk Stalkings*, *Melrose Place*, and *The Sentinel*. He appeared in the television series *The Dream Team* and in *Hollywood Wives: The New Generation* (2003).

Marjorie Monaghan (Jojo): Before her role in *Space Rangers*, Monaghan appeared in the series *Quantum Leap*, *Law & Order*, and *Murder, She Wrote* and played small roles in the films *Bonfire of the Vanities* (1990) and *Regarding Henry* (1991). Since then she has appeared on *Cheers*, *LA Law*, *Star Trek: Voyager*, *The Pretender*, *JAG*, *Babylon 5* (as "Number One"), *Becker* and *Gene Roddenberry's Andromeda*. She was at one time considered for the role of T'Pol on *Star Trek: Enterprise*.

Cary-Hiroyuki Tagawa (Zylyn): Born in Tokyo, Japan, he was raised in various cities before settling in California, where he began acting as a teen. His big break came with a role in Bernardo Bertolucci's *The Last Emperor* (1987). He also appeared in the first *Star Trek: The Next Generation* episode, "Encounter at Farpoint." His movies include *Twins* (1988), the James Bond flick *Licence to Kill* (1989), *Nemesis* (1993), *Rising Sun* (1993), *The Phantom* (1996), *Vampires* (1989), *Pearl Harbor* (2001), *Planet of the Apes* (2001) and *Memoirs of a Geisha* (2005).

Jack McGee (Doc): McGee is a former New York City firefighter. Since 1985 when he appeared in a small role in *Turk 182!*, he has been working steadily. He moved to Hollywood in 1986 and has had small roles in many feature films and television shows. Since *Space Rangers* McGee has become better recognized through his commercial work (campaigns for Budweiser and Barrons). He has also turned up in *seaQuest DSV*, *The X Files*, *Buffy the Vampire Slayer*, *CSI*, *Carnivale*, and *Law & Order: Special Victims Unit*.

Clint Howard (Mimmer): Born in Burbank California, he is the son of actor Rance Howard and the younger brother of actor-director Ron Howard. Clint began his career as a child actor in the television series *Gentle Ben* (1967–69) and would sometimes appear on *The Andy Griffith Show*. He is best remembered for playing the diminutive alien Balok in the original *Star Trek*. His was also the voice of the young elephant Hathi Jr. in the 1967 version of *The Jungle Book* and of the original Baby Roo from *The Many Adventures of Winnie the Pooh*. He has had small roles in many of his brother Ron's movies including *Cocoon* (1985), *Parenthood* (1989), *Backdraft* (1991) and *Apollo 13* (1995). Howard has also appeared in guest roles in two other *Star Trek* series, *Star Trek:*

Deep Space Nine and *Star Trek: Enterprise.* He has had roles in all three of the *Austin Powers* movies and has been seen most recently in 2006's *How to Eat Fried Worms.*

Danny Quinn (Danny Kincaid): Born in Rome, Italy, he is the son of actor Anthony Quinn. He began acting in Italy but soon moved to America where he appeared in the 1986 movie *Band of the Hand.* He moved back and forth between Italian and American cinema before being cast in *Space Rangers.* After that series, he was seen in *Code Name: Wolverine* and in a *Rockford Files* TV movie in 1997. Quinn has subsequently appeared mostly in Italian-language films and television and has moved into directing, writing and producing.

Gottfried John (Erik Weiss): Born in Berlin, he has worked primarily in Germany, particularly for the famed German director Werner Rainer Fassbinder. He is most well known internationally for the role of General Ourumov in the James Bond film *Goldeneye* (1995).

Linda Hunt (Commander Chennault): The New Jersey-born Hunt made her film debut in Robert Altman's musical comedy *Popeye* (1980). She won the Oscar as Best Supporting Actress as the male Chinese-Australian dwarf Billy Kwan in the film *The Year of Living Dangerously* (1982). This made her the first actor to ever win an Oscar for playing a character of the opposite gender. Since that time she has appeared steadily in movies and television programs. She played the Shadout Mapes in David Lynch's *Dune* (1984) and also had roles in *Silverado* (1985), *Kindergarten Cop* (1990), *The Relic* (1997), *Yours, Mine and Ours* (2005) and *Stranger Than Fiction* (2006). Her rich, resonant voice has been used effectively in numerous documentaries, cartoons, and commercials. She was the voice of Grandmother Willow in Disney's *Pocahontas* (1995), voiced the character of "Management" in the TV series *Carnivàle*, and voiced the character of Gaia, who narrates the *God of War* video games.

Special Unit 2

(2001–2002)

The adventures of two officers who work for the Chicago Police Department's secret branch, obliquely named Special Unit 2. Their task is to combat "Links"— mythological creatures of the night that the public are not aware of.

Cast: Michael Landes (Det. Nicholas O'Malley), Alexondra Lee (Det. Kate Benson), Richard Gant (Capt. Richard Page), Danny Woodburn (Carl the Gnome), Jonathan Togo (Jonathan) *Year 2*

Created by: Evan Katz; **Executive Producer:** Evan Katz; **Producers:** John T. Kretchmer, Roee Sharon, Ron Binkowski *Year 2*; **Co-Producer:** Mike Spadone; **Associate Producers:** Suzanne Lauer, Keira Morrisette; **Consulting Producers:** Martin Weiss, Jack Bernstein, Paul Bernbaum *Year 2*; **Writers included:** Evan Katz, Joel Surnow, Paul Bernbaum, James Krieg; **Directors included:** John T. Kretchmer, Oscar T. Costo, David Straiton, Michael Lange; **Directors of Photography:** Eric Haase, Karl Herrmann; **Production Designers:** Patrick Tatopoulos *Year 1*, Jill Scott *Year 2*; **Special Effects Makeup:** Mike Fields; **Creatures Designed, Fabricated and Su-**

pervised by: Patrick Tatopoulos; **Visual Special Effects:** Jim Finn, Michael Morreale, Paul R. Cox; **Music Theme:** Mark Snow, Mark Morgan; **Guest Stars included:** Willie Garson, Cameron Bancroft, Dominic Keating, Tom Welling, Amy Acker, Stefan Arngrim, John DeLancie, Sebastian Spence, Jack Coleman, Deanna Milligan, April Telek, Sam Whipple, Sean Whalen (as Sean Redmon)

UPN/Rego Park/Paramount Television; April 2001-February 2002; 60 minutes; 19 episodes

Do you remember as a child being haunted by frightening storybook creatures and monsters that lurked in a dark alley, or waited to jump out at you from under your bed? Well, in the universe of this series, all of them are ... real! And the Chicago Police Department has a special covert organization that has been empowered to deal with these creatures and monsters. They're called Special Unit 2. These creatures (the Boogeyman, the Sandman, a Black Widow Spider, Werewolves and Gargoyles) all live and pounce under the cover of darkness. They're called "Links." As in "missing links" from Man's distant past. It's the job of Nick O'Malley and his new partner, Det. Kate Benson, to protect us.

In the series' pilot, written by Evan Katz, Chicago PD officer Kate Benson watched as a Gargoyle kidnapped a young girl—and then as SU2 officer Nick O'Malley, armed with a futuristic rifle, intervened in an attempt to save the girl. Later, when Benson's captain suspended her as a result of reading her report of the fantastic incident, she encountered O'Malley once again. Intrigued by her dedication and honesty, O'Malley escorted Benson into the SU2 headquarters, hidden underneath a dry cleaning business. Capt. Richard Page tells her, "Benson, we're impressed with you! Consider yourself temporarily assigned to Special Unit 2...." To convey that "Links" were real, Captain Page grabbed a pistol and shot the "Link" informant Carl the Gnome several times in point blank range. Benson was shocked at the shooting and was also bewildered when Carl picked himself off the floor unharmed and as cheerful as ever, with bullet holes in his shirt. "You're going to pay for this shirt, aren't you?" he asked the captain.

Benson and O'Malley joined forces to locate the missing 12 human victims of the Gargoyle's rampage. To entice the Gargoyle out of hiding and into custody, Benson set herself up as bait in a late-night stakeout at a local park. When the creature "bites," O'Malley and his team capture their prey. Later, after an interrogation (which involved a bazooka that shrank the Gargoyle to tiny size), they knew the location where the victims were held. But it was just a trap and O'Malley himself was kidnapped by another Gargoyle. It was left to Benson to engage in the detective work and find O'Malley and the other victims. When clues pointed to an abandoned coal mining factory, the SU2 team rushed to the location. Inside the dark and musty lair, Benson tossed a rifle to O'Malley, who was in the middle of a battle with the formidable Gargoyle. Snatching the rifle, O'Malley shot at the creature, blasting him into thousands of pieces. O'Malley and Benson are now officially an SU2 team.

According to the series' creator and executive producer, Evan Katz, *SU2* was first pitched to the Fox Television Network. "It was all done ver-

bally," says Katz. "They were going to pass on the script, but I got a chance to do a last-minute pass, addressing their concerns. I did a 'Hail Mary' three-day rewrite, and they picked up the pilot. They ultimately passed on ordering it to series, and a year later, UPN picked up six episodes."

There were some bumps in the road before it would receive a prime-time premiere broadcast. After seeing the pilot, which was filmed by director D.J. Caruso, UPN asked for a recasting of the female lead role before the company would carry on to the remaining five episodes. In the pilot, a young, blond-haired actress named Christina Moore played Kate Benson. (Her name and image was used on a 1999 promotional card issued by Paramount.) "So the original pilot was thrown out," continues Katz. "It has never aired, and has a different story."

A few minor plot and character details were different in this lost pilot from the final rendition. Captain Page's first name was William, not Richard. The city was New York, not Chicago, and Carl the Gnome had a different makeup design. The unseen pilot also featured a puppet constructed by famed special effects makeup wizard Stan Winston, who made his name building dinosaurs for Steven Spielberg's *Jurassic Park* and aliens for James Cameron's *Aliens*. A Gargoyle informant played by actor Sam Whipple (Dr. John Ballard in *Seven Days*) was another "lost feature" from this presentation.

"In the original pilot, the 'Links' had loaded a subway train with explosives, to blow up a Cubs Game," says Katz. "I took a splinter unit to New York to shoot Shea Stadium and the subway cars. It was great. The story was changed for the new episode to the Gargoyle story, to make the series revolve more around creatures. The change had nothing to do with the events of [9/11]—that hadn't happened yet. But of course these days, that original story would never fly."

The revised pilot directed by series producer John T. Kretchmer, featured only two shots from the Caruso pilot. (The two shots retained: a police van exploding and the final shot of O'Malley's Chrysler swerving as it headed down a highway off-ramp as O'Malley tiffed with Carl in the back seat.) "Much of the same dialogue and plot elements exist in the aired version, although I had to reshoot them," explains Kretchmer. "I should say that D.J. Caruso, who shot the initial pilot, did a very good job."

Kretchmer says the female lead had to be recast because "I felt that the original actress' energy level was too low. There wasn't a large sense of fun about her, qualities that Alexondra Lee, her replacement, brought in spades.

"I don't think that there was more creature presence in the show I shot; however Evan and I agreed that the puppet of the little gargoyle was not very effective. I also prefer the resolution of the story in the script I shot. The original fight on the elevated train was not nearly as scary as seeing a large gargoyle attack and be blown to bits."

Kretchmer also isn't sure why a change was made from New York to Chicago but he has a theory. "Chicago has a city under the city — a series of streets and tunnels below street level that is used by delivery trucks." This probably aided the storytelling by making it easier for "underground creatures" to be hidden in the shadows, and to locate SU2's secret headquarters in an abandoned subway station. "The aired script is much, much stronger," says Kretchmer. "I think that Evan took advantage of the recasting to improve those aspects of the story that weren't as successful."

Because he was both the new pilot's director and producer of the series, Kretchmer was involved with the casting of Kate Benson and "read every actress in Hollywood for Kate, who qualified for the role." He says, "We were very lucky to have Alex do the role.

"Michael and Alex were simply terrific to work with — they had many long scenes with snappy repartee, and they always came prepared and were letter-perfect, which is a tremendous help when you have so little time to shoot complicated scenes. I bless them for everything I ever shot with them. Richard Gant was a unique presence. His process was different than Michael or Alex's, but he was always a happy person on the set, very gracious and warm. And the results are remarkable. He gives his character a weird, unique, scary spin that somehow works. Danny has remained a good friend — I have cast him in two other shows I have worked on [Charmed and She Spies], and he is truly one of the finest actors I have ever worked with. He always came to each day's work with an idea that would invariably crack me up."

Katz says he had to prod actor Danny Woodburn to do the Carl the Gnome part. "He really didn't want roles that had anything to do with him being a little person. But I think he realized my heart was in the right place — realized that Carl usually had the last laugh and the last word — and I think it was a good job."

One of the hallmarks of the series was its humorous, tongue-in-cheek dialogue. Sample these typical lines from the pilot:

> In her second encounter with Nick, Kate holds him at gunpoint and attempts to search him. "I'm putting my hands in your pocket!" she declares. Nick replies sardonically, "And I didn't even have to invite you to dinner!"

In another episode we have this exchange:

> After Carl helps Kate and Nick break into an office by snaking his way through the air vents and opening the door for them, Nick quips, "Thanks for taking your time." Carl replies, "Hey, those vents were disgusting. We're talking rats."
> Nick asks, "How'd they taste?"
> "I'm a vegetarian. Unlike yourself, I don't survive on the suffering of others," snaps the Gnome.
> Nick charges, "No, you just rob people blind!"
> Kate interjects, "You guys want to work or insult each other all night?!"
> "Give me a minute," replies Nick.

"Michael and Alex always got along, and seemed to genuinely like each other, which is a godsend on a series," says Kretchmer. "If the leads don't get along, it can be poisonous. Their mutual respect comes across in their scenes, and was evident from their very first reading together in a casting session in Evan's office. It was there from the start to the finish. The network also recognized it when we took them to UPN together.

"Michael and Alex immediately recognized Danny's great talent. He was just so damned funny. It was difficult not to like him. Michael had the advantage of having worked with Danny on the first pilot, and so was comfortable already. It wasn't difficult at all for Alex to loosen up in her first scene with Danny."

One of the most interesting characteristics of *SU2* is its similarity to director Barry Sonnefeld's 1997 SF action epic *Men in Black* starring Will Smith and Tommy Lee Jones. Both take place in a contemporary society that is oblivious to creatures and aliens that lurk in their midst. A secret organization has been assembled to corral these creatures and aliens who frequently wreak havoc. Dramatically, we follow the dynamic interpersonal relationship of a pair of agents and their boss. Both the film and TV series are categorized as science fiction action comedies. Tonally, the two share a very similar humorous tone. Both feature hi-tech futuristic weapons and gadgets (*Men in Black* just has the bigger budget). The introductory story of both involves one partner becoming initiated into the secret organization and we witness (with bemusement and laughter) their bewilderment in learning the true facts of life around them.

How the two are *dis*similar: The Men in Black are so secret, not even the federal government is aware of them. MiB agents carry silver pen-like devices called "Neuralizers" which wipe out the memories of victims (in a blinding flash) for a pre-determined length of time, in an effort to keep the public oblivious to the aliens in their presence. SU2, on the other hand, is a covert agency under the aegis of Chicago PD. Whenever they respond to unusual cases, they merely have to identify themselves to the local authorities as SU2 detectives, and that gives them access to the crime scenes. SU2's organization clearly operates under a smaller budget (of TV proportions, of course) and the creatures are not extraterrestrial but mythological beings such as "the Sandman" or "Gorgons."

"Of course there are similarities with *Men in Black*, but they weren't the first to do cops chasing monsters, and *SU2* won't be the last," says Katz. "I tried very hard to distinguish the series from the film, but the fact is, the premises exist in similar universes."

"Tonally, I think that *Men in Black* served as a touchstone," says Kretchmer. "But from my standpoint, I don't think the movie affected my visual style. They had so much more money than we did, but I am pleased with what were able to accomplish with the budget we were given. We did not consciously refer to the film or screen it."

To spice up the show's look, Evan Katz developed a "time compression" visual that served as *Special Unit 2*'s signature transitional device. A regular feature in every episode, it was used as a means to "enter" the beginning of an episode and, sometimes, reversed as a device to "exit" the story to the end credits.

For instance, rather than a standard-speed shot of characters entering the dry cleaners, we see a sky-high shot looking straight down at Chicago and the film "rushes" into super-speed mode, and dissolves into a helicopter shot of the Chicago river, into the street facade of the dry cleaners, into the hallway, rushing down the stairs, and turns into the SU2 bullpen, and *then* slows down to "normal speed" and follows two characters as they walk together....

This is a super-speed form of establishing the setting. Technically speaking, it is increasing the number of frames per second so that a great amount of film material is viewed in a shorter amount of time. It can be done in two different ways: In the camera or in post-production, in the editing stage. Evan Katz was inspired by the German film *Run Lola, Run*, written and directed by Tom Tykwer, for this "rushed exposition" says Kretchmer.

The reason that a dry cleaning business was the front for SU2's headquarters was to tip the hat to the 1960s cult spy TV series *The Man from U.N.C.L.E.* (the U.N.C.L.E. headquarters had a similar front).

The six-episode season's finale aired in May 2001; Katz reports that a renewal order came in from UPN. "They ordered 13 episodes," says Katz. "They filled out the order to the full season order of 22. But then UPN management changed, and they cut back the order to the original 13. A shame."

At that point, scripts #14–#18 had already been written, and the company was preparing a story that took place in 1976. "I had bought car chase footage from a 1970s movie called *The Seven-Ups*," says Katz. "And we had tracked down matching cars, and were going to do a period car chase in the middle of it. Carl the Gnome was a pimp. Say no more."

The remaining scripts were going to deal with a leprechaun, Bigfoot, a super-fast creature and one other Link that Katz says he doesn't remember.

Looking back, Kretchmer says the series was a rewarding, pleasant project for him because of the quality of the scripts and that it was well cast. "Evan gave me a tremendous amount of freedom to create the visual style of the show, and supported me down the line in my duties as a producer and overseer of the other directors," he says.

"I should compliment the production designer–creature designer, Patrick Tatopoulos, a wonderfully creative guy who loved his job and gave so much to the look of the show. The dragon from 'The Drag' is the revamped *Godzilla* that Patrick had designed for the eponymous movie. I had a great deal of fun filming that episode.

"His work was complemented by our two cameramen: Eric Haase in Los Angeles (who had shot the wonderful short, *George Lucas in Love*) and, in Canada, Karl Hermann. Both men 'got' the show and worked incredibly hard giving it a consistent visual scheme."

Series cancellation came when there was a change in UPN management. "I was prepping episode 14 of the second season," recalls Kretchmer. "I was about five days into prep when the word came down, which means that there were three more days of shooting. Morale was poor, but everyone pulled it together and finished the last episode."

Paramount's chairman Kerry McCluggage who shepherded the series to broadcast, was pushed out and Les Moonves walked in. "And Les Moonves did not support the show," says Kretchmer. "This is not unheard of; a new regime wishes to distance itself from the previous regime's shows, whether or not they are successful. The ratings were good. We were at the time the number two show on UPN [behind *Smackdown*], and every show that UPN replaced ours with received lower ratings in the same time slot. We were not canceled for reasons having to do with ratings or budget — we were notoriously on budget and schedule. We were in the middle of a titanic power struggle. We had recently been picked up for another nine episodes, and crew and cast members had proceeded with that assumption — some had bought new cars, etc. I had extended the lease on my house in Vancouver until May, and was stuck holding the bag when we heard the news. We all took it very hard, because we were not only proud of the work we were doing, we were having such a good time doing it, and knew how rare an occurrence that is in this line of work. Evan took it very hard. It was his baby, and he had done such a fabulous job of realizing his dream. He was an excellent boss, and to this day, I miss working with him on the show."

"Les either didn't like the show, his people didn't like it, or it didn't fit in with his vision of a new UPN," notes Katz. "I was very sad when the show got canceled. But I then went on to work on [Fox TV's serialized suspense drama] *24*."

CAST NOTES

Michael Landes (Nick): Born and raised in New York, Michael began acting at 16 years old and played Winnie Cooper's boyfriend on *The Wonder Years* (1989–91). He was the "first" Jimmy

Olsen on *Lois & Clark: The New Adventures of Superman* (1993). After *SU2*, he starred in a TV movie (a "back door pilot") titled *Max Knight: Ultra Spy* (2000). He starred in the feature *Final Destination 2* (2003) and guest-starred on TV's *thirtysomething, Providence, CSI: Crime Scene Investigation* and *Ghost Whisperer*. He's married to actress Wendy Benson-Landes.

Alexondra Lee (Kate): Before *SU2*, Alexondra guest-starred on TV's *Picket Fences* and *L.A. Law*, and had recurring roles on *Party of Five* and *Boston Public*. After *SU2*, she appeared in *Robbery Homicide Division, What I Like About You*, and *CSI: Crime Scene Investigation*.

Danny Woodburn (Carl): A veteran of film, TV and stage, Danny is a graduate of Temple University School of Communications and Theater. He has made over 100 TV appearances. He's had recurring roles on *Seinfeld, Conan the Adventurer, Baywatch* and *Charmed*. In film he's appeared with Arnold Schwarznegger in *Jingle All the Way* (1996) and Robin Williams in *Death to Smoochy* (2002). He's an advocate for the disabled and for Little People and is on the Screen Actors Guild Performers with Disabilities Committee.

Richard Gant (Capt. Page): A prolific and experienced actor, Richard is a veteran of film and television roles reaching back to 1980. His feature roles include *Rocky V* (1990) and *Godzilla* (1998). His TV credits include *The Cosby Show, Diagnosis: Murder, Lois & Clark: The New Adventures of Superman, Babylon 5* ("The Face of the Enemy" and "No Surrender, No Retreat"), *Smallville, JAG* and *Deadwood*.

Jonathan Togo (Jonathan): Raised in Massachusetts, a graduate of Vassar College, Jonathan has an Bachelors of Arts in Theater. He's performed in *Suburbia, Conduct of Life*, and *Romeo & Juliet*. His film credits include *Mystic River* (2003) and *Raccoon* (2004). Other TV credits include *Judging Amy, Law & Order*, and *The Jury*. Most recently he joined the cast of *CSI: Miami* as Ryan Wolfe.

Star Trek: Deep Space Nine
(1993–1999)

The life and times of the crew of the Cardassian-made space station Deep Space Nine.

Cast: Avery Brooks (Commander/Captain Benjamin Sisko), Rene Auberjonois (Odo), Terry Farrell (Jadzia Dax) *Year 1–6*, Nana Visitor (Maj./Col. Kira Nerys), Colm Meaney (Chief Miles O'Brien), Armin Shimerman (Quark), Siddig El Fadil/Alexander Siddig (Dr. Julian Bashir), Cirroc Lofton (Jake Sisko), Michael Dorn (Lt. Commander Worf) *Year 4–7*, Nicole deBoer (Lt. Ezri Dax) *Year 7*

Recurring Cast: Andrew Robinson (Garak), Marc Alaimo (Gul Dukat), Robert O'Reilly (Gowron), Aron Eisenberg (Nog), Jeffrey Combs (Weyoun/Brunt), Rosalind Chao (Keiko O'Brien), J.G. Hertzler (General Martok), Max Grodenchik (Rom), Chase Masterson (Leeta), Louise Fletcher (Kai Winn Adami), Casey Biggs (Damar), Barry Jenner (Adm. Bill Ross), Salome Jens (Founder Shapeshifter), Brock Peters (Joseph Sisko), James Darren (Vic Fontane), William Sadler (Sloan), Penny Johnson (Kasidy Yates); **Created by:** Rick Berman, Michael Piller (based on Gene Roddenberry's TV series *Star Trek*); **Executive Producers:** Rick Berman, Michael Piller *Year 1–3*, Ira Steven Behr *Year 3–7*; **Co-Executive Producers:** Ira Steven Behr *Year 1–2*, Ronald D. Moore *Year 5–7*, Hans Beimler *Year 7*; **Supervising Producers:** Ira Steven Behr *Year 1*, James Crocker *Year 1–2*, David Livingston *Year 1–3*, Ronald D. Moore *Year 2–5*, Peter Lauritson *Year 3–7*, Hans Beimler *Year 6–7*, Rene Echevarria *Year 7*; **Co-Supervising Producers:** Hans Beimler *Year 5*, Rene Echevarria *Year 5–6*; **Producers:** Steve Oster, Peter Allan Fields *Year 1–2*, Peter Lauritson *Year 1–3*, Rene Echevarria *Year 2–5*, Hans Beimler *Year 4*, Robert Hewitt Wolfe *Year 4–5*; **Co-Producers:** J.P. Farrell; Peter Allan Fields *Year 1*, Robert Hewitt Wolfe *Year 3–4*; **Associate Producer:** Terri Potts; **Coordinating Producer:** Robert Della Santina; **Writers included:** Michael Piller, Ronald D. Moore, Ira Steven Behr, Joe Menosky, Rene Echevarria, Robert Hewitt Wolfe, Hilary Bader, Bradley Thompson, David Weddle, Hans Beimler, Michael Taylor; **Directors included:** Paul Lynch, David Livingston, Corey Allen, Rene Auberjonois, Andrew Robinson, Avery Brooks, LeVar Burton, Jonathan Frakes, James L. Conway, David Carson, Allan Eastman, Jesus Salvador Trevino, Michael Vejar, Les Landau, Alexander Siddig/Siddig El Fadil; **Directors of Photography:** Marvin V. Rush, Jonathan West; **Visual Special Effects:** Digital Muse, Image G, Foundation Imaging, Digital Magic Company, CIS Hollywood, Howard Granite Films, Makeup Effects Laboratories, Newkirk Special Effects, Pacific Ocean Post Digital Film Group, Question Mark FX; **Production Designer:** Herman Zimmerman; **Main Theme:** Dennis McCarthy; **Guest Stars included:** Bill Mumy, Bernie Casey, Patricia Tallman, Ron Canada, Eric Pierpoint, Frank Langella (as Jaro), William Campbell (as Koloth), Michael Ansara (as Kang), John Colicos (as Kor), Philip Anglim (as Vedek Barell)

Syndicated/Paramount Television; 1993–1999; 60 minutes; 176 episodes; DVD status: Complete series

In the summer of 1991, at the behest of Paramount Studios chairman Brandon Tartikoff, producer Rick Berman began preparing another *Star Trek* series. (*Star Trek: The Next Generation* was then wrapping up its fourth year.) To help him design the show, Berman tapped writer-producer Michael Piller; together, they conjured up the most complicated and dense *Star Trek* series to date. It was populated with more characters (both alien and human) than its predecessor, *The Next Generation*. Arguably, *DS9* also had more action, explosions and special effects than *TNG*. Over the course of seven years, *DS9* intimately explored characters and their interactions with each other, and involved them in a brutal intergalactic war.

Deep Space Nine was a Cardassian-built space station in the Alpha Quadrant. (The Cardassians were a ruthless military-dominated humanoid race who became one of the greatest enemies of the United Federation of Planets and the Klingon Empire.) The station was situated near a Federation-protected world, Bajor, and the UFP inherited the administration of the station formerly named *Terok Nor*. When Benjamin Sisko walked into the station with his young son Jake to take command, he found it in ruins, carnage left by the Cardassians at the end of their occupation of Bajor. Aboard the station, there were three people who would play pivotal roles in his life for the next seven years: Major Kira Nerys, a Bajoran woman who became his second-in-command; Quark, a mischievous and profit-grabbing male Ferengi who ran the bar; and the security officer Odo, an odd shape-shifting being who didn't know where he came from.

Others from the Federation filled out the various positions required for the so-called transfer of power from the Cardassians. Dr. Julian Bashir, from Starfleet and Earth, was a young officer on his first field assignment. He found himself attracted to Science Officer Jazdia Dax; she was a "joined" species, partly Trill, partly a slug-like creature secreted inside the body. Chief Miles O'Brien was a talented and hard-working engineer who transferred over from Captain Picard's *Enterprise* to restore the station to tiptop working order. Bashir and O'Brien soon became good friends.

With this setting and these characters, *DS9* became a very strong SF-action-adventure drama in which every character evolved and experienced life-changing events. Their work on *DS9* had galactic-reaching consequences.

Ingeniously, Piller and Berman were able to solve a fundamental problem that plagued them on *TNG*: How to create dramatic conflict without having their main Starfleet characters fighting amongst themselves? Gene Roddenberry maintained that by the 24th century, humankind would have progressed as better, more professional people and would be above petty squabbles. New *TNG* writers had to cope with that restriction during the series' first and second year. With *DS9*, Piller and Berman planted Starfleet officers in an alien landscape where they could clash with the Bajorans, the Cardassians, the Vorta, and all the other aliens they would encounter. (Berman and Piller briefly considered a planetary-based Starbase, to be filmed on location, but that was too expensive.)

Inspiration came from some key *TNG* episodes. In *TNG's* fourth-year episode "The Wounded," we were introduced to the Cardassians. Later, "Ensign Ro" introduced actress Michelle Forbes in the role of a besmirched Starfleet officer from the planet Bajor, who had knowledge of the world that Captain Picard needed for an important mission. Ro Laren stayed aboard the *Enterprise* for several episodes. Piller and Berman wanted to bring Ro over to *DS9* in the second-in-command position, but when Forbes didn't want to be tied down to a series, Kira Nerys, a new character, was created.

"The Price" posited the notion of "wormholes," celestial phenomena that could be used as a transportation shortcut from one end of the galaxy to another. Piller and Berman thought that the alien space station should have a *stable* wormhole nearby for easy access. It would become an important region for denizens of the galaxy to engage in trade and exploration. *DS9* would be a location where everyone would visit. Consequently, more background players walk around in the hallways than you ever saw on the original *Star Trek*.

Simply put, ideas for *DS9's* concept and characters grew out of some creative work that was explored in *TNG*. And in the series pilot, the *Enterprise* briefly appeared and Captain Picard made an appearance. As depicted in the pivotal *TNG* two-parter "The Best of Both Worlds," Captain Picard's Borgified self, Locutus, had assaulted the starship in which Sisko was stationed. And it was there, in the battle of Wolf 359, that Sisko lost his wife Jennifer. When he met Picard for the first time, his pain surfaced because it was Locutus who was responsible.

Many members of *TNG's* creative team jumped starship in order to reinvent *Star Trek* again. Production designer Herman Zimmerman, scenic designer Michael Okuda, conceptual illustrator Rick Sternbach, composer Dennis McCarthy, makeup wizard Michael Westmore, and veterans from the writing staff combined forces to extend the franchise beyond *TNG*. At the center of it all was Rick Berman, who had to manage both shows.

One of the most important building blocks of a successful series is a group of actors with good interactive dynamics. If the actors didn't have chemistry with each other, the audience would immediately take notice. Fortunately, *DS9* rounded up some professional actors with distinctive personalities. Actors also were pulled in from *TNG*—faces that audiences already knew. Colm Meaney as Chief Miles O'Brien is an example.

Piller and Berman felt it was time for a black Starfleet officer to take the lead. A number of different actors were auditioned, including Tony Todd (who appeared earlier on *TNG* as Worf's lost brother, Kurn), James Earl Jones, Carl Weathers, and Bernie Casey (who later showed up as a Starfleet officer himself). But Caucasian actors from Germany, England and America were still considered. Allegedly, *MacGyver's* Richard Dean Anderson was a contender. *Automan's* Chuck Wagner also claims that he auditioned for the role. *Alien Nation*'s Gary Graham says he was one of three finalists.

Ultimately, "the man named Hawk" was cast. Avery Brooks was actor Robert Urich's partner in the *Spenser: For Hire* crime drama series, and he came to *Star Trek* with a strong, authoritative presence and a voice to match.

Terry Farrell was working heavily in the audition circuit at the time and hadn't expected to be cast as Dax, but got the part after three auditions. Other actresses who tried out had difficulty understanding the Trill concept.

Although her agent cautioned her about trying out for a syndicated TV series, Nana Visitor was intrigued by Kira Nerys because she was a strong, commanding woman and was unlike other stereotypical roles that she was constantly reading for. In just two auditions, she was given the role.

Cirroc Lofton was selected out of a pack of 200 kids and was given the part of Jake, Benjamin Sisko's son, on his 14th birthday.

Andrew Robinson read for Odo, but he was given the plum role of Garak, the lone Cardassian who stayed aboard the station.

The *DS9* station was Cardassian in construction, and Federation technology was grafted onto many of its control systems ("Thanks, Mr. O'Brien!"). Dramatically, the purpose was to make life messier, harder to manage and the polar opposite of the *Enterprise*'s plush and comfy hotel-like environment.

Michael Piller integrated a creative plot thread that ran through seven years and culminated in the show's final episode, "What You Leave Behind." Benjamin Sisko became, as illustrated in the series pilot "The Emissary," a religious figure among the Bajorans.

Initially, Sisko felt as though his new job was an assignment to a frontier town at the edge of space. He was ready to resign from Starfleet until the astonishing discovery of the stable wormhole which led to another corner of the galaxy, the Gamma Quadrant. It was inside the wormhole that Sisko made contact with aliens who live beyond the time spectrum. Their presence became a religion on Bajor, and they were referred as "the Prophets." Sisko's successful communication with the Prophets led the Bajorans to give him the title "The Emissary." As a result of his first contact with the Prophets, Sisko realized the importance of the assignment to usher Bajor into the Federation as a member. But due to complicated events, it didn't quite work out that way.

"I thought it was a really cool show," says veteran *TNG* writer Robert Hewitt Wolfe, who was invited to join *DS9*. (Wolfe would rise through the ranks to co-producer and producer, up to the fifth year.) He was impressed with how different *DS9* was from *TNG* and was surprised that "the show was a little less edgy than I thought it was going to be in some ways. We weren't really driving these characters until the episode 'Dax.' Peter Allan Fields wrote and Michael [Piller] did some work on [that episode] which took it to the next level. 'Dax' was really eye-opening. I get the show. I understand what Michael [Piller] and Ira [Steven Behr] are going for. Our heroes don't have to be innocent all the time. Our heroes are fallible, interesting and complicated people. I really started seeing the enormous potential of the show." In its first two or three years, *DS9* developed characters and story plots, trying to find its footing and identity.

Wolfe says he admired the way the series was cast. "As a writer, it was always wonderful to know that when you write down words on a page, you have actors on the stage who are not only going to do those words justice but actually make you look better as a writer. They're going to elevate that material. That was something we could always count on. And not just from the main cast, but from all the great recurring guys we had—like Andy [Robinson], Max [Grodenchik] and Louise Fletcher. It goes on and on. We never had to write around anybody. It was never, 'Ohhh, he won't work, we can't use that guy!' On a lot of shows, that does happen. [On *DS9*] it was strong actors from top to bottom.

"They were all experienced drama actors except for Terry [Farrell], who was sort of the least trained actress. But the great thing about Terry was, she worked to get better every year. And we learned how to write her character a little better too, and got to understand her personality a little better. No one was lazy on that show."

Michael Piller shepherded the show for its first three years. "Michael was a really talented writer," notes Wolfe. "I learned to appreciate Michael's focus on character, theme and relationships. I learned a lot from him. A really decent human being even when we disagreed. He was the boss, so I did what he wanted me to do [*laughs*]! That was a tremendous learning experience. Not just working with Michael but also with [producer-writer] Ira [Steven Behr] and all the other guys."

At the end of his three years on the series, Piller left to co-create *Star Trek Voyager* with Berman and Jeri Taylor, leaving *DS9* in the hands of *TNG* veteran and co-executive producer Ira Steven Behr.

In the third year's premiere episode "The Search," a new starship vessel, the *Defiant*, was introduced as a means of allowing the *DS9* command crew to embark upon "away missions" and not be stuck aboard the station all the time. The ship had a new design that would be used in almost every episode thereafter and it contained one very different element from all the starships: It possessed a Romulan Cloaking Device, which made it invisible. (The ship also came with a Romulan observer, but seen only briefly.) By the last episode of its third year, Benjamin Sisko was promoted to the rank of captain.

In the series' run from fourth to seventh year, Behr made a pact with himself to "do whatever we wanted!" During his tenure, Behr gave Kira something of a makeover. She was given high heels, a sexier uniform, and of course, a change of hairstyle. In the premiere episode of the series' fourth year, Sisko shaved his head and sprouted a goatee (a look that Brooks had when he filmed his previous TV series *Hawk*) and played a stronger, more aggressive commander. Behr also brought in Lt. Commander Worf at the top of the fourth year (in "The Way of the Warrior"), as the station's new security officer, to deal with a nasty Klingon problem. In truth, the ratings were not good, and Paramount requested something to shake up the proceedings. Worf added new sparks and introduced a Klingon story thread. The Klingon stories were continuations of relationships and political affairs set up on *TNG*.

"You had a very well-delineated character," notes writer Hans Beimler, a veteran *TNG* staffer who served as co-supervising producer in this fourth year (and later graduated to co-executive producer). "The audience already knew him and had expectations of him. That was the obvious benefit. When you put a Klingon in a room, it tends to heighten everything. The tension and everything gets elevated. They're not exactly nice, you know? Michael [Dorn] plays it well and does a very good job of delivering what we used to refer to as the 'unexpected Klingon.'"

Beimler already had a long history with Behr, having worked on four TV series with him. "Michael Piller was no longer running the show on a day-to-day level," he says. "He was still a consultant. He really let Ira run with the ball. He would read every script and read every draft of every script and give copious notes."

This year also introduced the war with the Dominion, aliens who were situated in the Gamma Quadrant. They consisted of several races, dominated by "the Founders" or Changelings, Odo's shape-shifting species. They declared war against "the solids" (humanoids who did not have the ability to shape-shift) and developed genetically engineered shocktroops called Jem'hadar. Jem'hadar worshipped the Founders as gods. In between the Jem'hadar and Founders were the Vorta, who managed the troops and also dealt directly with other "solid" species.

All this character development and plotting became very complicated, serialized, three-dimensional and "dense" in its layers. And this is typical of a space opera, but unusual for *Star Trek*'s standard "stand-alone episodic" format. "When you're on a space station and you don't go away, you can't fly away from your problems every week," explains Wolfe. "It just becomes organic to the storytelling, naturally, that you start accumulating recurring characters. *TNG* was about coming to a world and solving a problem in some 40-odd minutes plus commercials and then flying away. *DS9* was more about digging in, rolling up your sleeves and doing the hard work. After Picard and those guys fly off, people like Sisko have to show up, and actually make the thing work for the next three to five years.

"It's just like the real world. Going into Iraq and blowing things up is a lot easier than staying in Iraq and trying to make sense out of the situation. Sometimes that works out and sometimes it doesn't work out. We really tried to tell those stories and in telling those stories you needed to have those levels of complications. We were basically trying to say, 'Yes, it's complicated. It's hard. It's difficult.' It's real life. Federation *is* paradise but paradise isn't free, it takes a lot of work.

"Sisko really is like a general in charge of Iraq, Afghanistan or Bosnia. Pick your place. We were sort of aware of historical attempts to rebuild places after wars and the chaos. It's interesting that we did that show before Bosnia, I think. And certainly before Iraq. The whole U.N. Mission sort of approach [to] the whole thing was kind of prescient in some ways."

But there were still many stand-alone episodes, he says, that could be enjoyed in their own right. "You can still down and watch 'Little Green Men' today. And you don't need to know what's going on in the war and where you are with 'Call to Arms.' That episode still works great. You can watch 'In the Cards,' or even some of the heavier episodes like 'Duet' or 'The Wire,' those episodes work. Yes, the show definitely has more continuity than an episode of *CSI* but it's got less than *Lost*!" As an example of the personal dramas that were taking place during the war, in the sixth year Worf married Dax in an episode titled "You Are Cordially Invited."

Almost as an indulgence, Quark's Holosuite was used frequently for offbeat stories. Inside the holosuite we had spy spoofs ("Our Man Bashir"), baseball games ("Take Me Out to the Holosuite"), and homages to Frank Sinatra movies ("Badda-Bing, Badda-Bang"). This episode introduced another recurring character: Vegas lounge singer Vic Fontane (James Darren). Variously, Vic would help Odo serenade Kira so that he could get closer to her ("His Way"), console Nog after losing a leg in battle ("The Siege of AR-558"), and in the series' final episode, help his friends say goodbye. These were designed as "taking a break" episodes from the heavy-duty war dramas.

Burned out, with a desire to do other things, Robert Wolfe left the series at the end of the fifth year (but not without giving himself a brief cameo as a wounded Starfleet officer in "Call to Arms," an episode he co-wrote with Ira Behr). "It was a great experience," says Wolfe. "It was five terrific years. I learned a lot. A lot of what I know about the business I learned on that show from Michael and Ira and Rick."

When Terry Farrell, in the sixth year, began hinting that she wanted to leave the show, producers and writers were unsure how Jadzia's storyline would be played out. The decision was made to kill off the character.

"I loved Terry Farrell, she's very funny, but Terry had a hard time doing the technobabble dialogue," says Beimler. "She'd stumble on scientific words. She had other assets but handling tech-talk wasn't her strength. Since Dax was supposed to be the science officer, it always seemed to me it was never a good fit. On the other hand, Terry was incredibly sexy, human and alluring. She was fun to be around with. She wanted to get out of the makeup and into [Ted Danson's sitcom] *Becker*." In the episode "Tears of the Prophets," Cardassian bad guy Gul Dukat released a Pah Wraith (an evil Bajoran prophet) from an ancient Bajoran relic, and was possessed by the non-corporeal being. In the process of attempting to destroy another of the Bajoran Orbs aboard *DS9*, Jadzia lost her life in an encounter with Dukat.

In the seventh year, Berman and Behr created a new character replacing Jadzia Dax. It was written that Dax, the Trill portion of the character, had survived, and was placed into another Trill. Ezri Tigan, a young female psychologist, was played by Nicole deBoer. Later, Ezri transferred to *DS9* and joined the team as Ezri Dax.

"I take credit for Nikki," says Beimler. "I threw her name in the hat because I'd worked with her on other shows. I basically gave her first job on a show called *Beyond Reality* years ago, kept in touch with her, and used her on *TekWar*. She's just a terrific talent."

As the Dominion War grew more complex, Sisko realized that in order to achieve his goals, his ethics were tested and stretched to the limit. Screenwriter Michael Taylor's "In the Pale Moonlight" emphasized this: Sisko deliberately, and with Starfleet's knowledge, brought Romulans into the Dominion war via deception. Jadzia's death was one of many sacrifices.

DS9's final ten episodes were one long serialized war drama, exploring many facets of a war from various points of view.

"Everyone was so nervous about that arc," says Beimler. An earlier four-story arc was like a preparation for what was in store for all the writers. "It was an excited nervousness. We put up big [white slate] boards up around my office, actually. We had six boards and we literally plotted the ten episodes so we knew where we were going. Frankly, if you don't know where you're going, any road won't get you there. So it was important to know where we were going and tried to keep that amongst ourselves where the ending was going to be."

The final result, says Beimler, was an epic television event. "If you take any ten episodes, 'Which ones are your favorites?' it would probably be those! If I had to show *DS9* to someone who had never seen the show, that's what I'd show them!"

Sisko's fate in the final episode, "What You Leave Behind," was intended to be a bookend to the first episode, when he picked up the title "The Emissary." It was revealed that his mother was an incarnation of a prophet and that he was born, literally, to be the emissary.

Sisko also battled with Gul Dukat, the evil Cardassian, who was possessed by a Pah' Wraith, and shoved him into a fiery pit. Sisko's final fate laid with the Prophets. After saying his goodbyes to his family and friends, Captain Benjamin Sisko went into the wormhole and "lived with the prophets."

Thematically the show's finest hours high-lighted personal dramas ("Duet," "Far Beyond the Stars," "Rejoined," "The Visitor"), epic action drama ("The Way of the Warrior," "For the Uniform"), comedy ("Trials and Tribble-ations," "Little Green Men") and even musicals ("Badda Bing, Badda Bang," "His Way").

"What DS9 gave us was 'lower decks' so to speak," notes Beimler. "It gave us two things: The view of 'the little guy.' It didn't focus all the time on the eight principals who were the heads of department. It focused on obscure characters, the little guy and what their role in society was. To me, the guy that embodied the show was Garak. He was a fuckin' spy, man! He was a bad guy, in a way. But you got to know and understand him. And he got to know us and understand us. Even appreciate us. He wasn't such a bad guy at the end of the show.

"At the same time, it focused on the big issues of life. A lot of our discussions were about big issues. Marriage, religion, faith, destiny. The discussions we had amongst the writers were about those issues. And the characters wrestled with those issues.

"What does it mean to be a god, to have a destiny, and a destiny that you'll fulfill and a destiny that you'd author. All those wonderful questions that Star Trek can bring up in a kind of heightened reality [are] its great legacy."

But in the mass of SF-TV shows over the years, DS9 seemed to get lost in the shuffle. Beginning as TNG was still on the air, and continuing in syndication while Voyager became the flagship show for the new UPN network, DS9 never got the promotion or support of the other Trek series.

"I thought it would be more appreciated than it has by now," says Beimler. "There are people who love it. It's not the most popular show of them all. I'm surprised it hasn't come into more recognition. But it's still early in the game. I think Ira's vision for the show will be appreciated."

On a more personal level, Beimler says that his time on DS9 was more than just playing in the sand box of a science fiction universe. It was also a personal journey, working with close friends. "One of the great things DS9 had in its favor was that the five writer-producers, Ira Behr, Ron Moore, Rene Echevarria, Robert Wolfe and myself, actually liked each other. And we'd go to lunch with each other practically every day. Not because we had to, but because we liked each other. There was a lot of respect. Ira insisted on it and set the tone. We all had different talents and

brought different skills to the party. We accomplished a lot of things people said couldn't be done.

"And that was part of Ira's design. He put us together and formed the team. He knew how to use each one of the horses. He had five different horses and he had to know how to run the races."

Not all fans warmed to DS9's increasingly dark themes, the large ensemble cast and the complicated multi-character story arcs. Plus, the fundamental fact that the show took place aboard a space station and was not "out there" exploring space. Piller and Berman used the wormhole to fulfill this function.

However, many critics have also praised DS9's complexity and large ensemble cast as indicators of Star Trek's maturity and its best assets.

"I think we left behind some very sophisticated storytelling with some really compelling characters," says Wolfe. "It's a show that doesn't give you a lot of easy answers. It's a show that challenges the audience to think a little deeper about morality and choices and consequences of actions. I'm very proud of the show. I think it really is in the best spirit of what Gene Roddenberry set out to create in Star Trek. It really is a show that challenges the audience to think more about their lives, their times and their world. I think it's a really nice some 170-odd episodes of some really good television."

CAST NOTES

Avery Brooks (Commander/Captain Benjamin Sisko): Brooks was born in Evansville, Indiana. Aside from being an accomplished stage and screen actor, Brooks is also a jazz and opera singer. He has also been a tenured professor of theater at the Mason Gross School of the Arts of Rutgers University for more than three decades. Brooks worked in the New York theater through the '70s and '80s and did a one-man show about the life of actor Paul Robeson. In 1984 he appeared in PBS's American Playhouse production of "Half Slave, Half Free: Solomon Northrup's Odyssey," for which he won critical praise. In 1985 he was cast as Hawk in the television series Spenser: For Hire. That led to the short lived spin-off series A Man Called Hawk. After Deep Space Nine Brooks appeared in the 1998 picture American History X. He has also narrated many documentaries including Walking with Dinosaurs and Jesus: The Complete Story. He continues to work in theater and to prepare an album of ballads and love songs.

Terry Farrell (Jadzia Dax): Farrell was born in Cedar Rapids, Iowa. At 16 she became a model and moved to New York. While under exclusive contract to *Mademoiselle* magazine, she studied acting. Her first major roles were in the short-lived 1983 television series *Paper Dolls* and in the feature film *Back to School*. Farrell also had guest-starring roles in *Quantum Leap*, the new *Twilight Zone* and *The Cosby Show*. Since *DS9* she has appeared in the television series *Becker* (1998–2002) as Reggie (she played the role until the producers decided to replace her). She has been heard as the voice of Six in the Sci-Fi Channel's *Tripping the Rift* and appeared in the films *Gleason: The Jackie Gleason Story* (2002) and *Code 11–14* (2003). She has also voiced a number of video games including two based on *Star Trek: Deep Space Nine*.

Nana Visitor (Kira Nerys): Born in New York, Visitor was originally Nana Tucker, and is the niece of actress-dancer Cyd Charisse. Visitor began her acting career in the 1970s on the Broadway stage in such productions as *The One and Only*. Her film debut (billed as Nana Tucker) came in the 1977 film *The Sentinel*. On television, Visitor co-starred in the short-lived 1976 sitcom *Ivan the Terrible* and from 1978 to 1982 she had regular roles on three soap operas: *Ryan's Hope*, *The Doctors*, and *One Life to Live*. She also co-starred in a short-lived sitcom based upon the film *Working Girl* and appeared in a failed television pilot for a series based upon the comic strip character, The Spirit. After *DS9* ended, she had a recurring role as a villain on the series *Dark Angel* and starred as Roxie Hart in the touring company of the musical *Chicago* to exceptionally favorable reviews. Visitor was then cast as Jean Ritter on the ABC Family series *Wildfire* in 2005. She was briefly married to her *DS9* co-star Alexander Siddig. The two divorced in 2001 after having a son.

Colm Meaney (Chief Miles O'Brien): Born in Dublin, Ireland, he began to study acting when he was 14. He became a member of the Irish National Theater and spent the next eight years in England, touring with several theater companies. He also guest-starred on TV's *Remington Steele* and *Moonlighting*. Meaney appeared in the *Star Trek: The Next Generation* series pilot (1987); his character was eventually given the name of Miles O'Brien. In 1993, Meaney left *The Next Generation* for *DS9*. Since then he has played a minor recurring role on the Sci-Fi Channel series *Stargate Atlantis*, and guest-starred on *Law & Order: Criminal Intent*. His numerous feature films include

The Commitments (1991), *Con-Air* (1997), *Mystery, Alaska* (1999) and *Five Fingers* (2006).

Rene Auberjonois (Odo): Auberjonois was born in New York. He began acting in theater and landed many coveted roles on Broadway. He received numerous accolades and awards for his stage work. Auberjonois appeared in many motion pictures and television series throughout the seventies. He is best remembered for the role of Father Mulcahy in the 1970 film *MASH*. He also had roles in *Brewster McCloud* (1970), *McCabe and Mrs. Miller* (1971), *The Hindenberg* (1976), *King Kong* (1976) and *The Eyes of Laura Mars* (1978). On television he guest-starred on many series including *The Rockford Files*. He played Clayton Endicott III on the hit series *Benson* for which he received an Emmy nomination. He played a role in *Star Trek VI: The Undiscovered Country* and played guest roles on *Star Trek: Enterprise*, *Stargate SG-1* and *The Practice*. He was in the cast of *Boston Legal* alongside *Star Trek* alumnus William Shatner for three years.

Armin Shimerman (Quark): Shimerman was born in New Jersey. He began his career at a young age in the Los Angeles theater. He played guest roles on a number of television series including *Beauty and the Beast*, *Buffy the Vampire Slayer* and *Stargate SG-1*. Since *DS9* Shimerman has appeared in *Boston Legal*, *Numb3rs*, and *The West Wing*.

Siddig El Fadil/Alexander Siddig (Dr. Julian Bashir): Born in Sudan, he spent most of his life in England. He is the nephew of actor Malcom McDowell on his mother's side and of former Sudanese Prime Minister Sadiq al-Mahdi on his father's. His acting career began in England where he appeared in a small role in *Sammy and Rosie Get Laid* (1987) and as Emir Feisel in *A Dangerous Man: Lawrence After Arabia* (1990). Since *DS9* Siddig has appeared in *Reign of Fire* (2002), an episode of the English series *Spooks* (seen in America as *MI-5*), *Kingdom of Heaven* (2005) and *The Nativity Story* (2006). He has recently guest-starred on the series *24*.

Cirroc Lofton (Jake Sisko): Born in Los Angeles, Lofton was a child actor and appeared on a number of shows before joining the cast of *DS9*. Since then he has had a regular role in Showtime's *The Hoop Life* and has made a guest appearance on *CSI Miami*.

Michael Dorn (Lt. Commander Worf): Dorn was born in Luling, Texas, grew up in Pasadena, California, and studied radio and television production at the Pasadena City College. From there he pursued a career in music as a performer with several different rock music bands. His first television role was a guest appearance on *W.E.B.* in 1978. After that he had a regular role (1979–82) in the series *CHiPS* and had a small part in 1976's *Rocky*. He was cast as Lieutenant Worf on *Star Trek: The Next Generation*, the role he took with him to *DS9* and for which he is best known. He also played the character's own grandfather in *Star Trek VI: The Undiscovered Country* (1991). More recently Dorn has been seen in the movies *The Santa Clause 2* (2002) and *Ali* (2001) and has voiced animated characters in the series *I Am Weasel*, *Gargoyles*, *Megas XLR*, *Superman: The Animated Series* and *Justice League Unlimited*.

Nicole deBoer (Ezri Dax): See Cast Notes for *Beyond Reality*.

SOURCES

StarTrek.com.
Guatteri, Mario. "Jadzia Dax." http://mario.lapam. mo.it/ds9/dax.htm.

(Star Trek) Enterprise
(2001–2005)

In the mid–22nd century (100 years before the days of Captain Kirk), Captain Jonathan Archer and his crew begin space exploration aboard the Enterprise NX-01.

Cast: Scott Bakula (Captain Jonathan Archer), Jolene Blalock (T'Pol), Connor Trinneer (Cmdr. Charles "Trip" Tucker), Dominic Keating (Lt. Malcolm Reed), John Billingsley (Phlox), Linda Park (Ensign Hoshi Sato), Anthony Montgomery (Ensign Travis Mayweather)

Based on Star Trek by: Gene Roddenberry; **Created by:** Rick Berman, Brannon Braga; **Executive Producers:** Rick Berman *Year 1–4*, Brannon Braga *Year 1–4*, Manny Coto *Year 4*; **Co-Executive Producers:** John Shiban *Year 2*, Chris Black *Year 2–3*, Manny Coto *Year 3*; **Supervising Producers:** Merri D. Howard *Year 1–4*, Peter Lauritson *Year 1–4*, Ken LaZebnik *Year 4*, Chris Black; **Producers:** Antoinette Stella *Year 1*, Dawn Velazquez *Year 1–4*, J.P. Farrell *Year 1–4*, Mike Sussman, Tim Finch; **Co-Producers:** Tim Finch *Year 1*, Stephen Welke *Year 1–4*, Brad Yacobian *Year 1–4*, Phyllis Strong *Year 2–3*, Mike Sussman *Year 2–4*, André Bormanis *Year 4*, Garfield Reeves-Stevens *Year 4*, Judith Reeves-Stevens *Year 4*; **Associate Producer:** David Rossi *Year 1*; **Consulting Producers:** Fred Dekker *Year 1*, David A. Goodman *Year 2–3*, Brent V. Friedman *Year 3*, Alan Brennert *Year 4*; **Writers included:** Phyllis Strong, Andre Jacquemetton, Maria Jacquemetton, Fred Dekker, Chris Black, David A. Goodman, Andre Bormanis, Manny Coto, Rick Berman, Brannon Braga; **Directors included:** James L. Conway, Allan Kroeker, Mike Vejar, LeVar Burton, Roxann Dawson, Michael Dorn, Terry Windell, Robert Duncan McNeill, Les Landau, David Livingston, James Contner, David Straiton; **Guest Stars included:** Dean Stockwell, Peter Weller, Brent Spiner, Joanna Cassidy, Clint Howard, Robert Pine, Fionnula Flanagan, Bruce Davison, Gregg Henry, Andreas Katsulas, Daniel Dae Kim, Roger R. Cross, Jack Donner, Bobbi Sue Luther, John Schuck, Eric Pierpoint, Marina Sirtis, Jonathan Frakes, Michael Nouri, Scott MacDonald, Christopher Shea, Melinda Page Hamilton, James Cromwell, Matt Winston (as Daniels), Gary Graham (as Soval), Jeffrey Combs (as Shran), Vaughn Armstrong (as Admiral Forrest), Kellie Waymire (as Ensign Elizabeth Cutler); **Director of Photography:** Marvin V. Rush

UPN/Paramount; 2001–2005; 60 minutes; 98 episodes; DVD status: Complete series

"Relax. This series will run seven years. Guaranteed." Those were the words from a studio executive to a nervous Scott Bakula. *TV Guide* also affirmed it would be a hit: "If *Trek*'s past is any indication, *Enterprise* is in for a sure-fire seven year mission."

Enterprise was the fifth *Star Trek* series, designed to rescue the flagging *Trek* franchise. After you've been "where no one has gone before," where do you go next? After *Star Trek: The Next Generation*, there were the spin-offs *Deep Space 9*

in 1993 and *Voyager* in 1995. But it was time to grab back viewers who had been turned off by *DS9*'s dark visages and *Voyager*'s lost-in-space escapades.

Rick Berman proposed a series set 100 years before Captain Kirk, as humans were setting out to explore the galaxy. Transporters were so experimental and dangerous that people were loathe to step into them, force fields were in early development and Vulcans looked on from afar, dubious of humanity's abilities. Starfleet existed but the Federation of Planets had yet to be created. Paramount hyped the show with the line "First Captain. First Crew. First Mission."

Captain Archer was created as a cross between aerospace pioneer Chuck Yeager and *Star Wars* rogue Han Solo. Bakula, best known as Samuel Beckett in *Quantum Leap*, was a solid choice. "We wanted someone who had a contemporary feel," Berman said of Bakula. "Someone who is extraordinarily likable."

Jolene Blalock was officer T'Pol, the first Vulcan to live amongst humans. "Trip" Tucker (Connor Trinneer) was the easy-going engineer from the Florida Keys. There was also a Denobulan alien, Dr. Phlox (John Billingsley), and the British-accented Lt. Reed (Dominic Keating). The supporting characters included Hoshi Sato (Linda Park), who dealt with alien languages (the universal translator had yet to be developed). She was also terrified of space, a vulnerability rarely seen in *Star Trek*. Helmsman Mayweather (Anthony Montgomery) stoically manned the helm.

The production designers, led by Herman Zimmerman, visited nuclear submarines to get inspirations for the *Enterprise*'s cramped, claustrophobic military quarters. Co-creator Brannon Braga wanted to avoid any similarity to the 1960s *Enterprise*. "The original ship looked like a model on strings," he sneered.

To keep it real, costumes were designed like NASA jumpsuits. As for humor, there was Captain Archer's pet dog, Porthos, who in one show leaps out of a space shuttle and takes a pee on a sacred alien tree.

The first episode had Archer trying to rescue a kidnapped Klingon from aggressive aliens. This debut was the second highest rated show in UPN history, drawing 12.5 million viewers. Some of the reviews were surprisingly hopeful. "It's hot, it's sexy, it's kinda funny — would you believe it's *Star Trek*?" asked *Entertainment Weekly*. "This is the first Trek spin-off that appeals to both Trekkies and non-fans. It can lift a straggling network out of the intergalactic crapper."

UPN chief Dean Valentine was optimistic, calling it "a re-energizing of the *Star Trek* franchise." But the words *Star Trek* were not included in *Enterprise*'s title for the first two years, a gambit to break away from the *Star Trek* mantle, which was perceived as square.

Controversies arose. The opening title sequence for *Enterprise* infuriated many fans. The beautifully edited montage encapsulated the early days of American exploration and flight, including clips of Alan B. Shepard (the first American in space) and aviatrix Amelia Earhart. The lyrics for the theme "Faith of the Heart" (written by Diane Warren and sung by Russell Watson) was condemned by fans as sappy. A petition was started to have the song removed. Yet the theme and montage was actually an inventive way to launch this prequel series and some fans warmed up to it as the series progressed.

Two of the show's early writers were husband and wife Andre and Maria Jacquemetton. "We were huge fans of the original *Star Trek* series, but watched the following incarnations sporadically," says Maria. "We were classified as non–Trekkies and that actually played in our favor in getting hired. One network mandate was to cut down on the technobabble, which they felt made *Trek* less accessible to new viewers. They wanted fresh stories and voices. Brannon Braga read some of our original sci-fi–horror pieces and hired us, even though we were coming off *Baywatch Hawaii*, a series which carried a certain stigma."

The actors were instructed to follow the scripts to the letter. Any last-minute changes or ad-libs were rejected or vigorously scrutinized before being approved.

"Initially, we were very excited about writing for the first ship out there," say the Jacquemettons. "We wanted it to be markedly different from the other series. After all, this crew was untested and uncertain. There was no Prime Directive to dictate their actions. We wanted them to be heroic, but we also wanted them to make mistakes, show vulnerabilities, and make un–Trek decisions. With the usual bravado, we wanted confusion, fights, trysts, insubordination, all the juicy stuff that should happen when you're flying across the universe in a tin can with no fixed destination. We also wanted to mirror some of the hardships and tragedies that the NASA program had encountered over the years. Exploration had to come at a cost. We wanted the first season to end with the *Enterprise* limping back to port, with blast holes across the hull and half the crew missing. Ultimately, our ambitions were tempered by the powers-that-be."

Enterprise was a unique series for the writing team. "The challenge of working on *Trek* was that we were dealing with a huge franchise with a library of hundreds of episodes, many of which were considered classics in the genre. There was also the hurdle of having a large fan base, which was very critical and protective of the *Trek* universe, a culture very resistant to change. Under these circumstances, coming up with, and getting others to accept, something fresh and new, proved very difficult."

The couple wrote three episodes for the first year, including "Breaking the Ice," where Archer investigates a strange comet. "Brannon Braga was intrigued by the idea of landing on a comet and exploring the crew's excitement at being the first to do this. We combined that with T'Pol having a fiancé back on Vulcan, an arranged marriage which she was obligated to go through with, and how this could drive a rift between herself and her human relationships."

They also wrote "Dear Doctor," where the crew finds a planet inhabited by two humanoid races. One species is being genetically wiped out by a disease and needs medical help. The question: Should the crew step in and save this race? "The script's original ending had Dr. Phlox disobeying Captain Archer's orders to administer a cure to the Valakian race, whose species was facing extinction," the Jacquemettons recall. "Archer believed that if humans could help an alien race from dying, we had an obligation to do so. Phlox, on the other hand, although appreciative of human compassion, felt it was wrong to interfere with nature and was willing to go against his captain if necessary, to protect this belief. This ending didn't go down well with the powers-that-be. They felt the captain's authority was undermined by a crew member. Thus, the ending was changed." Archer ultimately decides that he and his crew can't play God and lets nature take its course.

In "Acquisition," Ferengi pirates overcome the *Enterprise* crew and scavenge for valuables, unaware Trip is spying on them as he tries to regain control of the starship. "We intended to write the entire episode in Ferengi," say the Jacquemettons. "But only the first act ended up in the Ferengi tongue. Since there wasn't a lexicon, as was the case with Klingons, we had to construct the language from scratch. We first wrote the alien dialogue in English, then translated it to French, then broke down syllables into a language that became Ferengi. It was fun to write."

Despite highlights and challenges, much of the first year was a predictable blend of drama and science fiction. "Strange New World" was a redux of past *Trek* clichés where alien pollen causes the crew to hallucinate. In "Shuttlepod One," Tucker and Reed are adrift in a damaged shuttlepod, and struggle for survival as their air supply runs low. "Unexpected" had a twist, as Trip unwittingly becomes pregnant after encountering an alien female engineer.

The crew also met hostile Andorians, aliens called the Vissians (a three-gender race) and an aggressive race from the future, the Suliban.

Kellie Waymire appeared in three episodes as Ensign Elizabeth Cutler, delivering a low-key but warmly engaging characterization. Tragically, the young actress died of heart problems in 2003 at the age of 36, two years before *Enterprise* ended.

One guest star playing a Vulcan had tremendous difficulties with his makeup. The exasperated actor finally ripped off his Vulcan ears, threw them in the trash can and stormed off the set and quit. The other actors, unaware of the situation, waited in vain for their Vulcan guest to return. Another actor was hastily brought in and the scenes were completed.

Critical reaction to the early episodes was mixed. "It's one of the best *Star Trek* series," the *New York Daily News* said. *The Washington Post*'s David Segal wasn't convinced: "It has a bargain basement feel that lands this side of camp."

When a half-naked Trip and T'Pol scrubbed each other's bodies with decontamination gel in the pilot ("Broken Bow"), some fans were disgusted, feeling it was a crass effort to woo viewers by sexual innuendo.

The Jacquemettons' look back candidly on their *Enterprise* experience. "In the beginning, we tried to make *Enterprise* different from the previous *Trek* series," they say. "But we fell back on old habits and found ourselves revisiting previous episodes. Ultimately, it proved very hard to deviate or tear ourselves away from the original formula. The series never attracted the new viewership we hoped for. Still, being a part of *Star Trek* was a great honor and a privilege. We will always be grateful for the opportunity."

Actor Vaughn Armstrong played Captain Archer's friend, Admiral Forrest, during *Enterprise*'s first two (and fourth) years. The actor had played various alien characters in previous *Star Trek* series but playing the admiral was special. "This character was what I would have liked to be under similar circumstances," says Armstrong. "He was a man of principle, vision, and heart. He cared deeply about the exploration program and wanted to see it work. He believed that contact with, and understanding of many alien nations, could only bring about a better life for all. He felt as though Archer was his favorite son and the best man for the job of captain. He also chose Archer because he felt he was the most human. Forrest was a military man who ruled with an iron hand but also had a heart of gold. He would have loved to be the man in the captain's chair but realized he had too much responsibility to the rest of Starfleet to spend all his time in space. These are rich and rare qualities for a role on TV to possess."

Armstrong quickly recognized how good the role was. "Most actors in my position, recurring or guest roles, are relegated to a few moments that never allow any real depth to develop. I feel privileged to have been given the opportunity to investigate the admiral's personality. He was the consoling father in one episode and the politician in the next and the drill sergeant in the next, etc."

He also found the working atmosphere to be warm and supportive. "I had worked with many of the people on this crew for many, many years. They treated me quite well and seemed genuinely happy to have me on the set. The prop man used to announce my arrival with a hearty 'Vaughn's in the house!'"

Enterprise's ratings began to fall during year one and by year two, one-third of the audience had abandoned the show. Only the die-hard fans were watching. The stand-alone stories of year two (such as "Dawn," where Trip is trapped on a distant moon with a hostile alien, or "Marauders," where Archer protects miners from nasty Klingons) didn't stir much interest. Whereas *The Next Generation* had reached a peak of 20 million viewers a week in 1993, *Enterprise* now drifted with four million. Its second year ranked a disastrous 135 out of 159 shows. Even fan reaction was tepid. "It's dead, Jim ... almost," announced *Entertainment Weekly*.

"What can you say?" a dejected Brannon Braga told *TV Guide* magazine. "We're bummed."

The magazine didn't pull punches on what ailed *Enterprise*, noting its "whiny crew," "predictable endings" and "endless babble" by the characters. The most stinging remarks were aimed at Captain Archer. "As written, Scott Bakula has as much commanding presence as Cap'n Crunch," *TV Guide* charged. They suggested he be "more heroic."

The ratings stupor resulted in a story shakeup. At the end of year two, a powerful energy beam rips across the state of Florida to Venezuela, killing seven million people. This sneak attack on Earth was launched by a mysterious alien race, the Xindi; Trip's sister is one of the casualties. As the heavily armed *Enterprise* takes off in pursuit of the aggressors, a tormented Trip is out for blood. "I can't wait to find the people who did this," he rages to Archer. "Tell me we won't be tiptoeing around any of that non-interference crap!"

The story arc for the third year had the *Enterprise* enter the Delphi Expanse, from where the Xindi plan another attack that will annihilate the human race. This unexplored region of space provided the crew with additional adventures as they tracked the aliens.

Archer was now more decisive, having changed from optimistic space explorer to obsessed pursuer. Unfortunately, his new style of command became almost labored. Rather than leading through quiet strength, he now barked his commands and often froze his facial features in a hawk-like grimace.

Enterprise reclaimed the *Star Trek* title in its third season and featured good work, such as "Similitude," where Trip is critically injured and Dr. Phlox must create another Trip via cloning, so that he can use his organs for a vital transplant. In the end, the reluctant clone must die to save the original.

Competing against *Smallville* and *American Idol* on Wednesdays, the series continued to lose over half its audience from the pilot's debut. The entire *Star Trek* franchise took another blow because of the poor box office performance of the *Next Generation* film, *Star Trek: Nemesis*, in 2002.

In the third year finale "Zero Hour," Archer destroys the Xindi doomsday weapon as it hurtles to Earth. The captain then vanishes in an explosion and reappears on Earth, where aliens and Nazis have joined forces during World War II and now occupy America in 1944.

Many of the cast braced for an expected cancellation. Surprisingly, a fourth year of *Enterprise* was ordered but with a reduced budget. Paramount agreed to charge UPN less for the series in exchange for a renewal. This would give the series four years' worth of episodes for syndication and keep the merchandise going.

This also meant a switch to cheaper high-definition video instead of film. Manny Coto (as executive producer) was now the show's driving force. Coto, who once stood in line as an eighth grader in 1979 at a Florida convention to get Walter Koenig's autograph, knew what was ailing the series.

"My main diagnosis was that some episodes seemed lackadaisical," he says. "Sometimes there didn't seem to be enough story in the episodes, or they didn't start off with a bang or there wasn't a clear concept of jeopardy. Also, the way the ship would roam around the galaxy, 'Maybe we'll go over here and look at this star cluster,' hurt it a lot. There was no real urgency in the show."

Coto liked the premise but says, "It should have shown us more of Star Trek's world before Kirk and Spock. There were no Orions, very few Andorians, and Tellerites and Vulcans. That's what I wanted to bring to the show. The cast was largely good but there wasn't a lot of chemistry going on. A lot of that comes from the writing. Each character was operating in a vacuum and I tried to create more sparks between them. Towards the end of season four, the characters had real camaraderie and that's important in a TV show."

Coto felt the series should have been a big hit. "The pilot had 12 million viewers. Unfortunately, they didn't like what they were seeing. But the concept of a prequel was a very valid one. It could have been an interesting way to see the forming of the Federation and the Romulan wars. A lot of those things weren't touched on."

Coto accepted that the mainstream audience was permanently gone. He tried to regain the Star Trek fans by writing stories that examined the Vulcan philosophy and provided more background on classic races such as the Andorians.

"It's a very rich world and amazingly coherent. A lot of Star Trek fans pick apart the continuity but when you really look at it, it's amazing how well the continuity holds up. We're talking 700 episodes of Star Trek and the teams of writers over 40 years have managed to build a universe that is pretty coherent. That's very hard to do."

The fourth year kicked off with a two-parter, "Storm Front," where Archer joins a resistance group to battle Nazis and aliens who occupy America in an alternate timeline in 1944. Archer restores the timeline, paving the way for a last year of stand-alone adventures.

Despite the falling ratings, world-wide Star Trek conventions welcomed the Enterprise cast. "In Germany, at the Galileo 7 convention,

there was a moment in the opening ceremony where about a thousand people in the audience stopped applauding when I walked on stage," recalls Vaughn Armstrong. "I was troubled, I didn't think they knew who I was. Then they all began singing the theme song to Enterprise to me. I looked at the screen behind me and there was a tribute to me, via a montage, of all my characters on a giant viewing screen. I was moved beyond words."

Armstrong recalls meeting many fans at other conventions. "A young man told me that my Admiral Forrest character stopped him from committing suicide. A couple wanted me to be the best man at their wedding — the bride had little chance of living much longer. And I walked another young lady down the aisle at her wedding when her father couldn't make it. There was something about the character I had played that made them want me to be an important part of their lives for just a moment. These moments are gratifying and humbling. I'm proud to be a part of a show that has moved people to this degree."

But there was also the flip-side: "A man at a convention in Vegas once stood in line for half an hour and said, 'I'd love to have your photo but ... who the hell are you?'"

In the year four episode "The Forge," Admiral Forrest is killed by a terrorist bombing at a Earth embassy on planet Vulcan. "The production crew and I were quite close, especially the makeup people," says Armstrong. "So Admiral Forrest had died and I wasn't happy about it. It was like losing an old friend, not to mention a healthy income. I was driving home that night and stopped in the middle of the street behind a van that was parked in the road. I assumed they would move forward. To my surprise they slammed their van into reverse, slamming into the front of my wife's new car (my truck had been stolen the week before). That did it! I got out, and was ready to confront the driver, doing my best to hold my temper. Three gangland types got out of the van and approached me. I didn't care. I had it. 'I've got to see your license and your proof of insurance,' I said. 'We've got it!' they retorted. One of them walked to their car (I assumed to get the required documents) as I reached into the glove box to get mine. The other two walked around the back of my car. Then I saw the guy who went for the documents leaving. 'Wait a minute,' I said. 'Let me see your license!' They all took off running. Like an idiot, I chased all three of them! There I was, chasing three young men down the middle of the street. I was tired and mad and finally yelled. 'If you don't stop right now I'm going to beat the @#$% out of you.' They must have believed me because they didn't stop. It was probably fortunate for me. But I was filled with adrenaline. I had just died in the role I had enjoyed most to date and my truck was stolen the week before. I was mad as hell and I wasn't going to take it anymore. I realize now that I'm fortunate I didn't die twice in the same day. The van they were in turned out to be stolen. At least I saved that for the owner."

As the fourth year of *Enterprise* progressed, the ratings stayed frustratingly sub-cellar. *TV Zone*'s Gareth Wigmore felt the show remained timid: "*Enterprise* isn't so much reacting to current world events as it is lazily picking items from the news to produce stories."

In 2004, Scott Bakula spoke to astronaut Michael Fincke, who was aboard the International Space Station. Fincke would later call that conversation "one of the highlights" of his space voyage and praised *Enterprise* for depicting "the peaceful exploration of space and that's what we do here at NASA."

Meanwhile, Manny Coto found a change in the viewer mail. Instead of complaints, there was praise. "I had boxes of fan mail, mostly saying, 'Thank you for making *Enterprise Star Trek* again.' Many people thought *Enterprise* wasn't *Star Trek* until the last year."

The fourth year included a much heralded three-episode appearance by Brent Spiner: In "Borderland," Spiner played Arik Soong, the distant relative of the creator of *Next Generation*'s Data android. Rick Berman, pulling no punches, admitted Spiner's guest appearance was another effort to encourage *Next Generation* fans to sample *Enterprise*.

Peter Weller was memorable as Paxton, a bigoted fanatic who tries to stop Archer from creating a coalition of planets in the two-parter "Demons' and "Terra Prime." Paxton capitalizes on people's fear and hatred of aliens, brewing since the destructive Xindi attack, and demands all aliens leave Earth or he will destroy Starfleet Command.

There was also "In a Mirror Darkly," where a power-mad, parallel universe Commander Archer captures a starship from an alternate future. Vaughn Armstrong played the manipulative *Captain* Forrest in this hostile parallel world where he and Hoshi Sato have a passionate relationship. "My first day of shooting involved several hours of intimate contact with Linda Park," recalls Armstrong. "Now, I'm a 55-year-old man and Linda is a beautiful young lady in her 20s. It was something of a dream job in that respect. I was enthusiastic about it when I got home that night, eager to share my good fortune with my wife. Big mistake! She's a third grade teacher and she works from the moment she gets up in the morning until the moment she goes to bed at night. She was correcting papers that night when I came home. I happily related my day. Her reply was something like this: 'You made more today than I make in a week ... and .... you ... spent *all day* making out with *Hoshi*!!!? ARGGGG!' I've learned more discretion in what I share about my workday."

There was speculation that William Shatner would reprise his role as Captain Kirk in an episode, and the actor had submitted a story idea, but the series' cancellation squashed that.

"We were shunted off to Friday in the last year," says Coto. "That's always a death knell. However, if you look at our ratings, it was the first year where our ratings didn't fall. They were consistent all season. So people who tuned in at the beginning of the season stayed around. Also, in its first three years, the show received an incredible amount of negative press and that was very difficult to surmount. *Enterprise* also didn't fit into UPN's corporate mold. They were going for an urban, hip, younger, black audience. *Enterprise* didn't belong on UPN."

The last episode, "These Are the Voyages," is a holographic recreation of Captain Archer's final days aboard the *Enterprise* as his crew return to Earth to be decommissioned. Archer prepares to celebrate the birth of a United Federation amongst humans and aliens.

The scenario is viewed by Commander William Riker from *The Next Generation* who is using the holodeck to investigate a mysterious event that occured during Archer's command. As Riker observes the holo-story, Archer tries to rescue an Andorian girl from sinister criminals and we witness Trip's ultimate sacrifice to blow up the kidnappers.

Some of the cast members were upset over *Next Generation* characters being brought in for the final episode. The always outspoken Jolene Blalock told *The Boston Herald*, "I assumed the ending would be about our show and not a wrap-up of the conglomerate ... it was just insulting," she noted of the finale's attention on Riker and Troi.

TV Guide agreed, stating, "Most of the regulars were cheated out of airtime to make room for

Jonathan Frakes and Marina Sirtis." *Dreamwatch* magazine noted, "It was a poorly constructed plotline, a bad send-off that should have been about the entire crew."

In *TV Guide*, Conner Trinneer lamented, "I wanted us to have a big *M*A*S*H* moment, a really memorable farewell." But he appreciated that his character had a death scene. "I'm the only one who went out with a bang!"

The Vancouver Sun critic Alex Strachan was glad to see *Enterprise* wrap up. "Seeing Riker and Counselor Troi reminded this former Trekker of better days—and better *Star Trek*s—from the past," he said. "The villain in this piece looks like David Bowie gone wrong and sounds unmistakably like Krusty the Clown."

Rick Berman said the farewell had to encompass all *Trek*s, not just *Enterprise*. Indeed, the last seconds of the episode included famous voice-overs from Captains Kirk and Picard.

On the last day of filming, two surprise guests visited the set, Majel Barrett Roddenberry and her son, Rod, who thanked the cast and crew for working hard to keep Gene Roddenberry's legacy alive.

Fans tried to save the series by mounting a letter campaign and attempted to raise $32 million to help subsidize a fifth season. There was hope the *Trek*-friendly Spike TV, which had aired *Next Generation* reruns to good ratings, would be interested. Despite three million pledged by anonymous donors in the aerospace industry (they felt *Enterprise* did a lot of good promoting space exploration), it was to no avail.

"A lot of critics dumped on the show, and even though word was out that season four was different and better, it wasn't enough," says Coto. "By the end of season four, we had 98 episodes, which was good enough for syndication. But I was disappointed. I had a lot of great ideas for season five."

Cliff Bole, who directed many episodes of *The Next Generation*, *Deep Space Nine* and *Voyager*, feels that *Enterprise* came along too soon. "*Star Trek* needed some breathing room. *Enterprise* seemed a bit much and became redundant. You run into a wall after awhile, even though you're trying to keep the interest up with new ideas."

"The next series should move into the 25th century, with a younger cast," Coto theorizes. "Nothing against the past captains, they've been great actors, but for some reason we've had 40–45 year-old captains. It should be a youthful crew

and more like the Horatio Hornblower novels, where you follow a group of youngsters through the service, as they grow and get promoted. By season six, they would all be commanding their own ships. It would be a fascinating take about their experiences in Starfleet. Or begin with the Federation having fallen apart and the task is to put the pieces back together."

While *Star Trek*'s future on television is unknown, writer/director J.J. Abrams (co-creator of TV's *Lost* and director of *Mission: Impossible III*) was given the green-light in 2006 to co-produce and direct the 11th *Star Trek* feature film, which will introduce a young James Kirk and Spock in their earliest adventures.

CAST NOTES

Scott Bakula (Captain Jonathan Archer): Bakula began a rock band in the fourth grade and wrote his own songs. He won a Golden Globe for playing time traveler Sam Beckett in *Quantum Leap* (1990–1994) and was very effective as Candace Bergen's love interest in the comedy series *Murphy Brown* (1993–94). His TV films have included *I-Man* (a 1986 superhero pilot) and the 1995 TV-movie remake of the '60s series *The Invaders*. He also starred in Clive Barker's 1995 film *Lord of Illusion*. Bakula admitted he was more of a *Lost in Space* and *Time Tunnel* fan as a kid, only catching up with classic *Star Trek* in college. His youngest son (age four in 2003) refused to visit the *Enterprise* set whenever the alien Andorians were there, because he was terrified of their blue faces.

Jolene Blalock (T'Pol): She was a fan of Mr. Spock since childhood and had a poster of him up on her wall. Originally, her *Enterprise* character was going to be a younger version of T'Pau, the Vulcan leader from classic *Trek*'s episode, "Amok Time." She was grateful for the opportunity to do *Enterprise* and liked her fellow castmates but she was never happy with the way her character developed, especially T'Pol's teasing relationship with Tucker. "Nothing ever happened," she said to *The Boston Herald* in 2005. "We repeated the same story over and over. Either make it a relationship or don't ... it got boring."

Jolene always wanted to be an actress and started her career as a model in Europe and Asia. She moved to Los Angeles to do TV commercials and made her acting debut in a segment of Kirstie Alley's *Veronica's Closet* in 1998. Her films include *First Fear* (2007).

Connor Trinneer (Cmdr. Charles 'Trip'

Tucker): Born in Walla Walla, Washington, he grew up in Kelso, Washington. The New York daytime soap *One Life to Live* was one of his first credits, and *Sliders* was his first Hollywood job. Playing Tucker on *Enterprise* was one of his favorite roles and the personable actor quickly bonded with fans at *Star Trek* conventions. When Tucker becomes pregnant with an alien life form in "Unexpected," Trinneer called it "an awesome experience. Where else would I ever get a chance to do this?" (*TV Guide* interview). He appeared in several *Stargate Atlantis* episodes during 2007.

Dominic Keating (**Lt. Malcolm Reed**): Born and raised in England, Keating wanted to be an actor at the age of nine. He got started in the business in Vidal Sassoon commercials in the 1980s and later made appearances on *Buffy the Vampire Slayer* and *Poltergeist the Legacy*. He was a well-known comedy actor in England, but grew frustrated when his initial forays in Hollywood met with rejection. The discouraged actor was about to open a restaurant when he auditioned for the role of a prince on *Star Trek: Voyager*. He didn't get the role but producer Rick Berman decided Keating would be perfect for his upcoming *Enterprise* series. Keating admits that as a youngster he was traumatized by seeing the flying jellyfish in classic *Trek*'s "Operation Annihilate" and he stopped watching the series.

John Billingsley (**Phlox**): Billingsley was another actor terrified by the original *Star Trek* as a kid. He studied theater at Bennington College in Vermont and later did such shows as *The Others*, *Cold Case* and *The X-Files* and the TV movie *Man from Earth* (2007). He was saddened by the tepid reaction to *Enterprise* in North America but was surprised when he attended conventions in Europe and found fans much more enthusiastic about the series. One German *Star Trek* convention he attended had over 3,000 fans.

Linda Park (**Ensign Hoshi Sato**): Born in Korea but raised in California, she is also an accomplished international ballroom dancer. She had roles in the mini-series *Taken* (2003) and the films *Jurassic Park III* (2001) and *Honor* (2006). Her favorite *Enterprise* episode was "In a Mirror, Darkly," the two-parter where she played the wicked mirror-universe version of Hoshi who poisons a scheming Archer. She appeared in several episodes of the TV series *Raines* in 2007.

Anthony Montgomery (**Ensign Travis Mayweather**): He had auditioned for the role of Lt. Tuvok for *Star Trek: Voyager* and although he didn't get it, he remained in the minds of the cast-ing people when *Enterprise* came along. He played a recurring role on the TV series *Popular* (2000–2001) and guested on *Charmed* and *JAG*. He's the grandson of jazz guitarist great Wes Montgomery.

Vaughn Armstrong (**Admiral Maxwell Forrest**): Although it was only a recurring role, Armstrong found true simpatico with his character of Admiral Forrest and says today, "I don't know that I will ever find a role more enjoyable or a company more fun to work with."

His early TV work includes appearances on the 1970s hits *Wonder Woman* and *Lou Grant*. He later appeared on *Quantum Leap*, *Seven Days* and *Buffy the Vampire Slayer* and in the TV movie *Trail End* (2007). His first *Trek* appearance was in *Next Generation*'s first-year "Heart of Glory" as Commander Korris, a Klingon. In all, he played 13 different characters on four *Star Trek* series. Armstrong is also a musician. "I am in a band called the Enterprise Blues Band. It's comprised of Casey Biggs, Richard Herd, Steve Rankin, Ron B. Moore, Bill Jones and myself. Ron is the five-time Emmy award–winning special effects director of *Enterprise*. Casey, Steve and Richard have all done multiple characters on various *Trek*s. And Bill is the percussionist who is also a very fine actor that I have worked with for years. We have a ball."

SOURCES

Amatangelo, Amy. "The Finale Frontier: Vulcan Star of 'Star Trek: Enterprise' Complains About Ending: It's Not Logical." *Boston Herald*, May 2005.

Chapman, Matt. *Star Trek: Enterprise* Season Four DVD Review. *Dreamwatch* no. 135, December 2005.

"How to Fix Star Trek?" *TV Guide*, 2003.

Itzkoff, Dave. "Its Long Trek Over, the Enterprise Pulls Into Dry Dock." *New York Times*, May 1, 2005.

Jablon, Robert. "'Star Trek: Enterprise' Ends, Along With an E." Associated Press, May 13, 2005.

Logan, Michael. "Trek Star Fires off Parting Shots." *TV Guide*, May 23, 2005.

Mangels, Andy, and Michael A. Martin. "Tucker's Luck — From Taking His Shirt Off to Getting Pregnant with an Alien Offspring, Enterprise's Leading Hunk Connor Trinneer is Ready for Anything the Star Trek Universe Can Throw at Him." *Dreamwatch*, June 2002.

Shapiro, Marc. "Archer's View." *Starlog* no. 306, January 2003.

Snierson, Dan. Enterprise review. "2001: A New
  Space Odyssey — EW Goes Behind the Scenes of
  the UPN Prequel That's Shaking Up the Sci-fi
  Universe." Entertainment Weekly, October 2001.
Spelling, Ian. Interview with Scott Bakula. Starlog
  no. 317, December 2003.

_____. "The Last Days of Enterprise." Starlog no.
  335, June 2005.
Strachan, Alex. The Vancouver Sun, 2005.
Wigmore, Gareth. Enterprise Review. TV Zone no.
  186, 2005.

Star Trek: The Next Generation
(1987–1994)

*The adventures of the crew of the starship U. S. S. Enterprise, under the command of
Captain Jean-Luc Picard, as they explore the far reaches of space in the twenty-fourth
century.*

Cast: Patrick Stewart (Captain Jean Luc-Picard), Jonathan Frakes (Commander William
Riker), Brent Spiner (Lt. Commander Data),
LeVar Burton (Geordi La Forge), Gates McFadden (Dr. Beverly Crusher) *Year 1* and *3–7*, Marina
Sirtis (Counselor Deanna Troi), Michael Dorn
(Lt. Worf), Wil Wheaton (Wesley Crusher) *Year
1–5*, Denise Crosby (Lt. Tasha Yar) *Year 1*, Diana
Muldaur (Dr. Katherine Pulaski) *Year 2*, Whoopi
Goldberg (Guinan) *Year 2–7*, Majel Barrett
(Computer Voice)

Recurring Cast: Colm Meaney (Chief
O'Brien), Dwight Schultz (Lt. Barclay), Michelle
Forbes (Ensign Ro Laren), Majel Barrett (Lwaxana Troi), John de Lancie ("Q"); *Created by:*
Gene Roddenberry; *Executive Producers:* Gene
Roddenberry *Year 1–5*, Rick Berman *Year 3–7*,
Michael Piller *Year 4–7*, Jeri Taylor *Year 7*; *Co-
Executive Producers:* Rick Berman, Maurice
Hurley *Year 1–2*, Michael Wagner, Michael Piller
Year 3, Jeri Taylor *Year 6–7*; *Supervising Producers:* Robert H. Justman *Year 1*, Jeri Taylor *Year 4
-5*, David Livingston *Year 6–7*; *Producers:* Maurice Hurley *Year 1*, David Livingston *Year 1–5*,
Burton Armus, Robert L. McCullough, John
Mason, Mike Gray *Year 2*, Ira Steven Behr *Year 3*,
Peter Lauritson, Merri D. Howard *Year 6–7*,
Ronald D. Moore *Year 7*; *Line Producer:* Merri
D. Howard *Year 6–7*; *Associate Producers:* D. C.
Fontana *Year 1*, Peter Lauritson *Year 1–2*, Wendy
Neuss *Year 4–5*; *Co-Producers:* Robert Lewin
Year 1, Herbert Wright *Year 1*, Hans Beimler,
Richard Manning *Year 3*, Peter Lauritson *Year
3–5*, Joe Menosky *Year 5*, Ronald D. Moore *Year
5–6*, Wendy Neuss *Year 6–7*, Brannon Braga *Year

7*; *Consulting Producers:* Robert Justman *Year 1*,
Peter Lauritson *Year 7*; *Creative Consultant:*
Tracy Torme *Year 2*; *Writers included:* Joe
Menosky, Rene Echevarria, Naren Shankar, Peter
Allan Fields, Herbert J. Wright, Hilary J. Badler,
Ronald D. Moore, Michael Piller, Jeri Taylor,
David Bennett Carren, Richard Manning, Brannon Braga, Melinda Snodgrass, Hannah Louise
Shearer, Tracy Torme; *Directors included:* Corey
Allen, Paul Lynch, Rob Bowman, Kim Manners,
James L. Conway, Cliff Bole, Joseph Scanlan,
Winrich Kolbe, Les Landau, Gabrielle Beaumont,
Jonathan Frakes, Gates McFadden, LeVar Burton,
Patrick Stewart, David Carson, Adam Nimoy;
Guest Stars included: Kirsten Dunst, Ashley
Judd, Terry O'Quinn, Ronny Cox, Famke
Janssen, Linda Thorson, Ben Vereen, Robin Curtis, Kelsey Grammar, John Tesh, Lawrence Tierney, Jean Simmons, Ray Walston, Clive Revill,
Professor Stephen Hawking, Bebe Neuwirth, Rosalind Chao, Suzi Plakston, James Cromwell,
Kathryn Leigh Scott, Nick Tate, Elizabeth Hoffman; *Original Production Design:* Herman Zimmerman; *Special Effects Makeup Supervisor:*
Michael Westmore; *Music Theme Composed by:*
Alexander Courage, Jerry Goldsmith (orchestrated-conducted by Dennis McCarthy)

September 1987-May 1994; Syndicated/Paramount; 60 minutes; 176 episodes; DVD status:
Complete series

"*Star Trek* has been fatally dead for a long
time," DeLap's *Fantasy and SF Review* magazine
snapped in early 1978. "After nearly 10 years, there
is little life left in the old cadaver." In retrospect,

it sounds like a ridiculous pronouncement. But at the time, classic *Trek* merchandising such as the Poster Book series and Mandala photonovels had died and despite constant announcements by Paramount, a new *Star Trek* just didn't materialize.

The original *Star Trek* (1966–69) ran for 79 episodes on NBC, occasionally cracking the top 40 during its first year. Dedicated fans helped to keep it on the air for three years. Shortly after the first (and hugely successful) *Star Trek* convention in 1972, and with reruns on 145 American TV stations, Paramount and creator Gene Roddenberry discussed reviving the series.

A *Star Trek II* series was almost launched but after *Star Wars* opened in 1977, Paramount instead announced *Star Trek: The Motion Picture* (1979). More films followed but fans really wanted a new TV show. Roddenberry was adamant that he would never produce a TV series again, due to the time and stress. "Nothing would make me happier than for someone else to make a better *Star Trek*," he said. That someone turned out to be Roddenberry.

It was the challenge of doing a new *Star Trek* for syndication, to correct the creative and production mistakes of the original, that changed his mind. In 1986, he recruited classic *Trek* writers David Gerrold, Dorothy C. Fontana and producer Robert Justman to work on the new series. Paramount offered Leonard Nimoy the job of executive producer, which Nimoy turned down (he would later categorize *Next Generation* as "a fine body of work").

Roddenberry also solicited Rick Berman, a Paramount executive, to help produce the two-hour pilot. Berman had only seen a couple of the original episodes but after he screened *Star Trek: The Voyage Home*, where the crew transports whales from the 20th century, he jumped aboard.

Paramount suggested a series about Starfleet cadets but Roddenberry hated the idea. Instead, he created a new *Enterprise* crew to continue the exploration of space 100 years after the original. He wanted Stephen Macht as Captain Jean-Luc Picard but reluctantly considered Justman's suggestion of British actor Patrick Stewart as a middle-aged bald Frenchman. Stewart, with his powerful presence and resonant voice, won over everyone.

A female Vulcan officer was conceived as the great-great granddaughter of Mr. Spock but that character was dropped in favor of a teenage girl named Leslie. Ultimately, Roddenberry decided on a teenage boy, Wesley.

Also aboard was Data (Brent Spiner), a sentient android fascinated by human characteristics, Tasha Yar (Denise Crosby) the tough security officer and Counselor Troi (Marina Sirtis), a half–Betazoid psychologist with empathic abilities. LeVar Burton played helmsman Geordi La Forge, who wore an electronic visor to enable him to see. There was also Wesley's mother, Dr. Crusher (Gates McFadden), and Klingon security officer Worf (Michael Dorn).

Jonathan Frakes won the role of first officer Riker over Christopher McDonald and Bill Campbell. Patrick Stewart had been considered for the role of Data before Brent Spiner landed the role (Eric Menyuk and Colm Meaney were also considered). Denise Crosby originally read for Troi and Marina Sirtis was considered as Tasha Yar.

Proposed titles for the new series included *Star Trek: The Mission Continues, Future Trek, A New Beginning, The New Generation* and *The Second Generation*. Finally, Roddenberry and Paramount announced that *Star Trek: The Next Generation* would premiere in the fall of 1987.

This *Star Trek* was updated for the 1980s: Females would wear jumpsuits rather than 1960s mini-skirts and Captain Picard would remain on ship while his "away" teams beamed down to investigate unknown planets. While the classic *Trek* characters had clashed over moral dilemmas, Roddenberry wanted this crew to be harmonious. Rick Berman's ignorance of the original *Trek* resulted in some peculiar observations. "There was very little conflict amongst the [old] *Star Trek* characters," he stated early on.

The Prime Directive (the Federation's law not to interfere with alien worlds) had been routinely ignored by Captain Kirk for dramatic and moral purposes. When, for example, Kirk violated the Prime Directive to free humanoids from a giant computer in "The Apple," it was to illustrate to TV viewers that people are entitled to flourish in a free environment.

Next Generation strictly enforced the Prime Directive as a matter of principle and often ingeniously circumvented deadly situations without yanking a society up by its cultural roots. Gunplay was also discouraged. "The *Enterprise* was never a warship," Roddenberry bristled. "It is a ship of exploration."

Roddenberry also perceived a difference in maturity between Captain Kirk and Captain Picard. He characterized Kirk as "a guy who wanted to end up with a piece of ass." Kirk expected aliens to adapt to his American values, whereas Captain Picard and his *Next Generation* crew tried to learn from extraterrestrials.

The new model of the *Enterprise* divided critics. Some thought it looked sleek, others claimed it resembled an overstuffed turkey. However, no one could disparage the dazzling interior, brimming with realistic technology. Herman Zimmerman did the original design and production designer Richard D. James and his team later won an Emmy award for their outstanding work and even received praise from NASA. There were even bathrooms aboard the new *Enterprise* (taboo in the 1960s version).

But there were still doubts about *Next Generation.* "You can reanimate a corpse but that doesn't necessary means it lives," noted novelist Robert Bloch. William Shatner said succinctly, "It's a mistake."

The pilot "Encounter at Farpoint" had a lot to prove. The crew faces Q (John de Lancie), an obnoxious, omnipotent being who thinks mankind is too childish to be exploring space. He subjects Picard and his crew to a hostile tribunal of aliens. Critical reaction was mixed. "*The Next Generation* soars with the spirit of the original," beamed *The Dallas Morning News. USA Today* raved, "A fabulous meshing of story, character and FX." *The Wall Street Journal* was dismissive: "Full-blown kitsch."

"You couldn't match the original TV series," says frequent *Next Generation* director Rob Bowman. "Everybody was very open to starting fresh. We said, 'Let's just be ourselves and make our own *Star Trek*.' By the second year we had a great deal more confidence and we were proud of our work."

However, it struck some fans as strange that *Next Generation* avoided many contemporary issues. Whereas the original show featured two interracial kisses (between black Lieutenant Uhura and white Nurse Chapel in "What Are Little Girls Made Of," and later between Kirk and Uhura in "Plato's Stepchildren"), as well as examining birth control, racism, the Vietnam war and slavery, *Next Generation* was passive and politically correct. Author Peter David observed, "If anything, *Next Generation* leans towards over-caution. Storylines of more daring occur in an average *episode* of *L.A. Law* or *China Beach* than in the average *season* of *Next Generation*."

An early *TV Guide* review by Lee Anne Nicholson was particularly harsh, noting, "Captain Jean-Luc Picard is visibly frustrated by his ineffective crew—a blind navigator, a trigger-happy Klingon, a half-human, half–Betazoid empath who can read others' emotions but is lamentably inept at turning her readings into useful advice and a first officer who is impossibly stiff."

However, *TV Week*'s J. K. Malmgren loathed the 1960s series, calling it "hokey," and added, "Unlike the original series, *Next Generation* shows the kind of plot complexity and thought-provoking writing that is the stuff of real speculative fiction. Gone are the one-dimensional characters."

What frustrated some *Next Generation* writers and directors was that the series wasn't as good as it could be. "When Gene was running *Next Generation*, it wasn't as strong," says director Paul Lynch. "He wanted sexy women's bodies on the show. He had a very 1950s attitude towards female characters. He was stuck in a time warp that didn't measure up to today's world."

Writer Tracy Torme found other restrictions. "When I was there [during the first two years], the characters were too agreeable. Nobody had any conflicts. As it evolved, they put a harder edge to the show. That was a very good choice. That early lack of conflict was Gene's idealized future. Before I joined the staff, I pitched an addiction story called 'The Dream Pool.' A device is brought aboard the *Enterprise* where the characters start spending more of their time remembering their dreams instead of working on the ship. Gene didn't want people having addictions in this *TNG* world and that story was never made. He felt it was a very dark human foible and he didn't want to explore it."

The early days of *Next Generation* were uncertain for the actors as well. Patrick Stewart lived out of his suitcase for the first few weeks because he didn't think the show would survive. The sign outside his trailer read, "Beware of Unknown Shakespearean actor." He began to receive hundreds of letters from love-sick female fans. Picard's lines of "Engage!" and "Make it so" became catch-phrases. Stewart chuckled when a scientist told him there was a moon crater named Picard!

"I remember Patrick and Jonathan [Frakes] saying we would last 13 episodes or *maybe* a year," recalls Lynch. "I said 'Five years.' I was closest to being correct. It was an entertaining fantasy-family show, well-acted and -written."

Despite great ratings, there were rough times behind the scenes for the first two years. David Gerrold, who had first suggested a holodeck (where the crew could indulge in VR-like fantasies) and Away teams for *Star Trek* landing parties, quit the series when his allegorical script on AIDS was rejected. Dorothy C. Fontana and several other writers also clashed with Roddenberry and angrily left the show.

But there were early highlights, including "Conspiracy," a frightening tale of paralytic aliens who take over key Federation personnel. This sets the stage for a gruesome finale as the crab-like beings are destroyed by phasers but not before they send out a coded message to their home world, leaving Earth open to a further invasion.

"'Conspiracy' was an effort to do something different," says Tracy Torme. "The *TNG* characters at that point got along too well, they were too willing to surrender. 'Conspiracy' had some darker, rougher edges to it."

What develops in Torme's story is pure paranoia as Picard is baffled by the strange behavior of top Starfleet officers. He learns they're being controlled by aliens. "The original concept was to do *Seven Days in May* [the 1964 film about a covert military coup of the U.S. government] inside the Federation. Gene didn't want to go that far. So to explain why some Starfleet people were treacherous, I brought in the alien element. But the show still caused a lot of controversy. Half of the fans said, 'This is great, this is exactly what we need to be doing more of,' and the other half were disturbed by the darker imagery and tone. It also had a slightly negative, nebulous ending. It didn't wrap everything up neatly like most *Star Trek*s do. I'm proud of that show."

Another interesting show, "Symbiosis," has been much-maligned for a brief but silly "just say no" discussion between Tasha and Wesley about drug use. But it presented an interesting tale of an obsessed, drug-craved culture, tragically underscored by the emaciated-looking appearance of actor Merritt Butrick (playing an alien addict) who died of AIDS shortly afterward.

Richard Manning, who co-wrote the script with Hans Beimler, has an apologetic attitude about it. "The Anti-Drug Public Service Announcement scene was a later addition to the script. We protested, but our bosses wanted it, so we wrote it. Wil and Denise did the best they could with it, but not even their considerable talents could overcome the subtle-as-an-anvil writing. *Mea culpa, mea maxima culpa.*"

In Tracy Torme's "The Big Goodbye," Captain Picard visited 1940s San Francisco as detective Dixon Hill via the holodeck. The episode won the Peabody Award, the prestigious annual international prize given for radio and television.

"Why they chose that particular show for a Peabody award, I can't tell you," says Torme. "It was a great honor. The production people took the script and did a great job in realizing it. The Dixon Hill character ended up appearing several times later."

Most of the 1960s *Star Trek* cast had been skeptical or actively hostile towards *Next Generation* (with the exception of Leonard Nimoy and Nichelle Nichols). Classic fans had gone from scoffing at *Next Generation*'s flaws to vigorously promoting the series' emerging virtues. When Walter Koenig (Chekov) lampooned *Next Generation* at a convention, one fan angrily admonished him and a chastened Koenig later watched several episodes and he agreed the show was improving.

But many devotees of the 1960s *Trek* were still annoyed whenever a *Next Generation* person would rave about how "their" show had been more successful than the "old" show. *The Next Generation*'s cast and crew celebrated when they reached their 80th episode, surpassing the original's 79th segment. Yet Classic *Trek* had struggled in a more restrictive TV world, where survival depended on attracting the anti–SF, mainstream audience. Between 1971 and '79 it broke all syndication records with 79 heavily edited and yellowing reruns. Without this trailblazer, *The Next Generation* would have never existed.

The ratings continued to soar, putting *The Next Generation* just behind *Wheel of Fortune* and *Jeopardy* as the most-viewed show in syndication. Roddenberry's control over the series lessened by the third year due to poor health, and executive producer Rick Berman and his team of writers, including Michael Piller and Jeri Taylor, produced some high-quality, imaginative scripts.

While Berman and Piller were not classic *Trek* fans, many of *Next Generation*'s writers were, including Joe Menosky. "I was obsessed with first-run *TOS* [The Original Series] as a young child and it had a deep effect on me at a very psychologically receptive time," he says. "Nothing else in the franchise could ever come close to that, not the movies and not any of the other *Star Trek* series. But I am sympathetic when I read arguments for *TNG* as the 'maturation' or 'culmination' of *Star Trek*. Michael Piller brought another dimension into what was still old-school action adventure, giving *Trek* characters an inner life and emotional development they had never seen before, certainly not on the original television series. *TNG* ended up having the same universal appeal that *TOS* had. That has not been the case with the other, subsequent *Trek* series, no matter how successful they might have been creatively or otherwise."

As *The Next Generation* continued, there were inevitable cast changes. Denise Crosby left after the first year, discouraged by Tasha's lack of humor and character development. Her character is killed off by a gooey alien in "Skin of Evil." Whoopi Goldberg joined in year two as Guinan, bartender of the Ten Forward lounge. Gates McFadden was replaced in year two by an abrasive Dr. Pulaski (Diana Muldaur) but fans mounted a letter-writing campaign, and McFadden was reinstated by year three. Commander Riker grew a beard, Geordi was promoted to chief engineer, and Troi, whose hair was wild and woolly during year one, was given a more conservative do.

The cast also learned to be cautious when it came to judging *Star Trek* fans. When Jonathan Frakes appeared on *The Arsenio Hall Show* in 1990, he talked about his first *Star Trek* convention and laughed that the fans were "really weird." Fans were outraged by his comments. "It was a slip of the tongue that I really came to regret," a chastened Frakes confessed to journalist Ian Spelling. "It was inappropriate and I've tried to apologize to the fans."

The producers also paid close attention to fan mail. Rick Berman received over 200 letters when the *Enterprise* mistakenly fired a phaser from its photon torpedo port. Female fans were annoyed that while the males battled the villains with swords in "Q-Pid," Dr. Crusher and Trois resorted to a girly defense of throwing ceramics! "*Next Generation* is the most intellectually challenging of the *Trek* series, yet one populated by docile women," *TV Guide*'s Michael Logan wrote of the show's chauvinism. "They are caregivers to the male members of Starfleet."

Even some of the show's writers admitted that many *Next Generation* staples, including malfunctioning holo-decks, time travel stories, all-powerful aliens, politically correct speeches and mind-numbing technobabble, had been overdone.

And then there were the fans who simply enjoyed the show, among them Robin Williams and General Colin Powell.

The cast had their own challenges. In "Power Play," Marina Sirtis refused to be doubled by a stuntwoman so that she could fling herself backwards on the set as wind engulfed her. She broke her tail bone and couldn't walk for several weeks (this shot remains in the final cut). And when

Patrick Stewart and Gates McFadden were trapped in a planetary sandpit in "Arsenal of Freedom," sand fleas nibbled at them, making the scene torturous for the pair.

Jonathan Frakes directed eight episodes and recalls that his first job, "Offspring," where Data creates his own daughter, had him shaking in his boots. "As a director, I was a nervous wreck," he admits. "Brent Spiner couldn't have been more helpful. He's incredibly talented and probably has the biggest acting range of anyone on the show."

In "Drumhead," Frakes directed Jean Simmons, who played a tough admiral investigating a conspiracy that became a witch hunt. "She was a two-time Oscar nominee and was also a *Star Trek* fan. She watched our show every Wednesday in Los Angeles and she would call her friends to discuss the episodes."

Patrick Stewart liked to have fun with Captain Picard by acting out fantasy scenes off-camera. "I had this alternate Picard I would sometimes do when we were setting up shots," he says. "In rehearsals, I'd make him this knee-trembling coward and I'd say, 'We're all going to die! We're all going to die!' and occasionally I'd leap into Jonathan Frakes' arms."

By the third year, *Next Generation* was airing on over 230 affiliate stations. The show had begun by feeding parasitically on classic *Trek*'s creativity but was now a force to be reckoned with. "Television has grown up a lot since the 1960s," Berman stated. "Our show is much more believable than the old show. Old *Star Trek* had people who wore togas, standing under arches. Our *Star Trek* is much more contemporary and believable."

Critic John Peel observed, "By the second season, plots began making sense, characters started to become real and the show became very enjoyable. *The Next Generation* was dreadful for its first year and has steadily progressed to where it's as good as the old show ever was."

Ronald D. Moore, who began writing for the series during its third year (and who later wrote and executive-produced the re-imagined *Battlestar Galactica*), told Anna L Kaplan of Fandom.com that when he first came aboard, there was still a lot of fan flack to contend with. "There wasn't a lot of support in the [*Star Trek*] community. At conventions, people were still selling bumper stickers that said, 'Kirk and Spock forever, Picard and the bunch — to hell with them!'" Moore credited a lot of the turnaround to Michael Piller. "What Michael brought was a determination to make the show about characters and not just about the aliens of the week...."

Writer David Bennett Carren says, "*Next Generation* was very well-produced and acted and during the third season found its own voice. Unlike *TOS*, the series tended to focus on dramatic character pieces rather than shoot-'em-up adventures. Piller and Berman were quite brilliant to focus on character-driven stories almost exclusively. That was highly unusual for science fiction series at that time, and it's still a difficult feat."

Carren and J. Larry Carroll worked on the series as story editors during 1990 and 1991. Their script "Future Imperfect" has Riker thrust 16 years into the future, where he finds himself captain of the *Enterprise*; a peace treaty between Romulans and the Federation is about to be signed. He also finds he has a young son, Jean-Luc (played by Chris Demetral). The twist ending reveals the whole adventure is the creation of an alien child named Barash. Nevertheless, Riker is touched by the experience of having had a son and he invites the lonely alien aboard the *Enterprise*. "To me you will always be Jean-Luc," he tells the alien boy.

"Larry pitched the idea to Michael Piller, who immediately asked one question — are Romulans behind the plot?" recalls Carren. "When we told him it was a lonely little alien boy, he grinned and said, 'Story with option for teleplay.' We wrote an outline and had a break session where the staff got together and put all the story beats on the board. We then wrote the first draft, which fell apart in act four. The problem was, we vamped for five acts on the *Enterprise*, with the alien boy acting more and more suspicious, and it just didn't sustain. Piller called a meeting, and my memory is that I tossed in the idea that the Romulans step out from behind the curtain at the end of act three, in what appears to be a Romulan plot, but it's still just another part of Barash's fantasy. Piller went for it, and we wrote it. They shot our script and loved it so much, they put us on staff."

Carren is still pleased with the final result. "It's one of the two best things I've ever done in television. The performances were excellent. [Director] Les Landau did a great job, and the production values were superb. Les directed so efficiently that every day the show came in short. We were 'a minute short today, we're two minutes short today,' and so it went through the entire shoot. By the next-to-last day of production, we were still two minutes short! We wrote and added new scenes every day, but they had to be limited to cast and sets we already had in place. By the last day, we had run out of stuff we could legitimately add, so Piller, Larry, and I trooped over to Berman's office that night and discussed our options. We settled on the turbolift scene where Riker bares his soul to young Jean Luc and they decide to go fishing. It was a joint effort. Berman offered the 'I missed your first tooth' stuff, and Larry the fishing and Curtis Creek business. The line where Jean Luc says 'You've never let me down,' I said that to my dad shortly before he died. I can't imagine that episode without that scene. To me, it's the most important beat in the episode, and perhaps one of the most revealing moments, emotionally, about Riker that the series ever did. That isn't surprising when you consider that scene came from the hearts of everyone who worked on it."

Other writers had their favorite shows. "I still have a soft spot for 'Who Watches the Watchers?'" says Richard Manning, whose script depicted Picard wrestling with the Prime Directive after aliens mistake him for a god. "It was a controversial subject, with a dynamite guest cast: Kathryn Leigh Scott, Ray Wise, Pamela Segall, James Greene, and some wonderful thunder from the exceptional Patrick Stewart. The cast and crew were excited to get off the Paramount lot for once. We shot on location at Vasquez Rocks, a time-honored location for Westerns and for the original *Trek* as well." That location proved truly dangerous for everyone, with poisonous snakes and scorpions lurking around. "Unfortunately, it was also one hundred degrees that day," says Manning. "They were all wearing heavy wool costumes. If the foot chase seems a little slow, that's the reason."

There were still ties to the classic series. In the first episode, DeForest Kelley had made a cameo as an ancient Dr. McCoy. Mr. Spock (Leonard Nimoy) appeared in "Unification" (a two-parter that was dedicated to Gene Roddenberry) and Scotty (James Doohan) stepped aboard the *Enterprise* in "Relics." Mark Lenard, playing Spock's father, gave a poignant performance in "Sarek," as his memory is affected by an Alzheimer's-like degenerative disease.

Yet *Next Generation* still had its misfires, such as "Rascals," where technobabble tried to explain how Picard and his officers were transformed into children. And fans were spared from a threatened 1991 comedy spin-off of *Next Generation*, starring Majel Barrett as Lwaxana.

"*Next Generation* can be both intoxicating and

inspiring," said *Sci-Fi Universe* magazine, "but when it does things wrong, it can be downright insipid."

Writer Joe Menosky has a couple of favorites. "In terms of ideas, 'Darmok' [Picard and an alien leader try to communicate with each other, without knowing each other's language] is at the top of the list. In terms of fun, I really like 'The Nth Degree' [Lt. Barclay is given mental powers by an alien force]."

He's surprised that some fans like 'Legacy,' where Beth Toussaint excellently portrayed the late Tasha Yar's sister, who betrays Data during a rescue mission. "It just proves, no matter how apparently weak the episode, there is always somebody who sees something in it," he muses. "Maybe they see what we intended in the script, but thought had been lost in production. Maybe they see *more* than we intended, but there's always some positive response from somewhere. I had high hopes but it just never really came together for me. There is one really nice moment at the end, all on Brent's face, where you get the sense of a hint of a shadow of loss in Data. That was sort of what the whole thing was about. But that's pretty much all that was left of my original intentions. It's not through any fault of the rewriting process or production. It's just that sometimes what you think you're putting into the script doesn't translate to the screen."

"The Best of Both Worlds," a two-parter where Picard is captured and assimilated by the mechanized Borg, has frequently been cited as *TNG*'s finest hour, and has landed on many of TNG's "best episodes" lists. Also noteworthy was the episode "Frame of Mind," with Frakes outstanding as Riker desperately battles for his sanity against an outside force.

"Tapestry" had Q guide Picard through an alternate reality where Picard has made choices that have trapped him in a bleak and unproductive life. "Measure of a Man" was an interesting examination as to whether Data had any rights as an android or whether he was just a machine, ripe for disassembling by Starfleet.

"Cause and Effect," where the crew become aware of their ship's future destruction and try to avoid it, was another interesting show. The teaser, which shows the *Enterprise* and its crew perishing in an explosion, was heralded as unique ("You will *never* beat that teaser," Ron D. Moore opined later) but it wasn't that innovative. The very last episode of TV's *Voyage to the Bottom of the Sea* (1968) stunned audiences by opening with its heroes and submarine being blown to bits, a shocking event for 1960s television. Like in "Cause and Effect," the submarine's crew had to manipulate time to avoid their destruction.

In 1993, "The Inner Light" (where Picard lives the life of an ordinary farmer on a drought-stricken planet) won a coveted Hugo award, the first Hugo for televised SF since classic *Trek*.

Data provided good comedy relief throughout the series. In the episode "Haven," he remarks, "Could you please continue the petty bickering? I find it most intriguing." The series received an Emmy nomination as best dramatic series for the 1993–94 season.

In the seventh year, with *TNG*'s production and salary costs rising, Paramount decided to retire the series. Ronald Moore felt it was time. "Everybody was getting really tired," he told writer Anna Kaplan in 2000. "The quality of the show suffered that last year."

Next Generation reruns proved a goldmine and a spin-off series, *Deep Space 9*, was successfully launched. It also allowed Paramount to get a *Next Generation* feature film, *Generations* (1994), into production.

The last episode, "All Good Things," written by Moore and Brannon Braga, was something of a homage to Kurt Vonnegut's time-tripping protagonist in the novel *Slaughterhouse-Five*. Picard tries to stop a space anomaly from destroying humanity by enlisting his past and future selves. Q, who is bouncing Picard back and forth through time, gains a new respect for Picard when the captain manages to avoid the catastrophe. As a bored-sounding Q says, "You saved humanity ... once again." The very last scene has Picard sitting down to play cards with his officers and as he deals five card stud, he looks around warmly at his friends and says, "The sky's the limit." This Hugo award–winning episode was a solid and satisfying capper. There would be several *Next Generation* motion pictures, starting with *Star Trek Generations*, where Picard meets William Shatner's Captain Kirk, *Star Trek: First Contact* (1996), *Star Trek: Insurrection* (1998) and the last to date, *Star Trek: Nemesis* (2002), which cost $60 million but grossed only $43 million.

Critical evaluations of the TV series remain laudatory. "Expectations were cosmic, but even die-hard Trekkers came to acknowledge that *The Next Generation* not only equaled but surpassed the original," said *TV Guide* in 2002.

"It was one of the best shows of its time," AP writer Robert Jablon noted in 2004. "A strong cast, good special effects, terrific storytelling and the toughest Trek villains ever, The Borg."

British author John Clute observed, "It was a child more sophisticated than its parent ... some found it marginally less fun than the original but this was because *Star Trek* had grown up."

Tracy Torme agrees. "It's a very respected show. A lot of the credit goes to Rick Berman and the exceptional group of actors. They portrayed their characters with a lot of depth and emotion."

The Next Generation indeed broke new syndication barriers for modern science fiction television, clearing a path for a host of new genre shows.

CAST NOTES

Patrick Stewart (Captain Jean Luc-Picard): As a child growing up in the English town of Mirfield, his happiest times were watching movies in the cinema. He left school at the age of 15 and worked for a local newspaper before discovering the world of acting. He spent 25 years with the Royal Shakespeare Company, developing a reputation as one of the finest actors around. His early film credits include *Excalibur* (1981), *Dune* (1984) and *Lifeforce* (1985). Stewart was fiercely protective of *The Next Generation* and he wouldn't let the series be demeaned. When a weatherman from *Good Morning, America* did his schtick while wearing a *Next Generation* outfit, prior to Stewart being interviewed, Stewart angrily walked off the set. He wasn't overjoyed with the way Picard was written during the early years of *Next Generation*, feeling the captain was "too narrow and desk-bound." He asked for more humor and romance and when he got it, he was a lot happier with the character.

His later work includes the TV films *Moby Dick* (1998, as Captain Ahab) and *A Christmas Carol* (1997, as Scrooge). He starred as Professor Xavier in the *X-Men* films (including *The Last Stand*, 2006).

Jonathan Frakes (Riker): "I'm not getting laid nearly as much as Kirk did in the old show," joked Frakes to *Starlog* magazine early on. One of his first jobs in the 1970s was to dress up as Marvel Comics' Captain America to visit kids in hospitals and even to attend an environmental lawn party at Jimmy Carter's White House. He gave himself five years to make it as an actor, working as a waiter and furniture mover. He finally nabbed a continuing role on the daytime soap *The Doctors* (1977–78). He also did the mini-series *North*

and South (1985) but he remained typecast in bad-guy roles until *Star Trek*. Married to actress Genie Francis, Frakes is also a director (including *Thunderbirds* in 2004).

Brent Spiner (Data): As a teen he watched three movies a day and fantasized about becoming an actor. He moved to New York, where he appeared in off-Broadway plays. He began acting professionally in 1969 and made his TV debut in the 1970 telefilm *My Sweet Charlie*. He noted a curious phenomenon after doing seven years of *Next Generation*: "*Star Trek* is not something Hollywood producers and casting people watch," he told writer Marc Shapiro. "When *Next Generation* was over, Hollywood wanted to know where I had been for the last seven years." He received the most fan mail of any *Next Generation* cast member. His later TV credits included *Enterprise*, *Outer Limits*, and *Law and Order*; he was a regular on *Threshold* (2005–2006). One of Spiner's dreams is to reunite the *Next Generation* cast for a non–*Trek* film.

LeVar Burton (Geordi La Forge): Born in Landstuhl, West Germany, he became famous for his starring role as the African slave Kunte Kinte in the TV mini-series *Roots* (1977). He has hosted PBS's *Reading Rainbow* since 1983. Burton, a classic *Trek* fan, wasn't fond of the visor he wore as Geordi, feeling it robbed him of eye contact with his co-stars (as well as being painful to wear). But it provided humor. When he and the other cast members appeared on *The CBS Morning Show* before *Next Generation*'s premiere in 1987, it was explained that the starship was on a 15-year mission. When Burton revealed his character was blind, wore a visor and that he flew the ship, Patrick Stewart joked, 'That's why it's taking 15 years!" Real-life science caught up to *The Next Generation* in 2004, where experimental "retinal prostheses" were surgically implanted into the eyes of blind people, giving them the opportunity to see light and shapes. Their visors resembled the ones worn by Burton's character.

Gates McFadden (Dr. Beverly Crusher): She attended Brandeis University in Waltham, Massachusetts, before heading to Manhattan to appear on the New York stage. She also worked as a Muppeteer for Jim Henson and choreographed his Muppet films *The Dark Crystal* (1983) and *Labyrinth* (1986). One of her earliest film roles was in *The Muppets Take Manhattan* (in 1984, billed as Cheryl McFadden). She also appeared in the 1990 suspense film, *The Hunt for Red October*.

Marina Sirtis (Deanna Troi): Born in London

to Greek parents, three-year-old Marina would sing to passengers on the bus. She acted in musical theater and British TV shows before moving to America in 1986. She found sporadic work and was packing her bags to return to England when she got the role of Troi. Her later guest work includes *The Outer Limits*, *Earth: Final Conflict*, and *Stargate SG-1*. She also appeared in the Oscar-winning film, *Crash* (2004) and the TV movie *Grendel* (2007).

Michael Dorn (Worf): Born in Texas and raised in Pasadena, California, he was a rock singer in high school. One of his earliest movie appearances was as Apollo Creed's bodyguard in the Sylvester Stallone hit, *Rocky* (1976). He also had a bit role in *Demon Seed* (1977). He then became a regular on *CHiPs* (1980–1982) as one of the motor cops. He also played Worf's grandfather in *Star Trek VI: The Undiscovered Country* (1991) and reprised Worf in the later years of *Star Trek: Deep Space 9* (1995–1999). He starred in the TV film *Night Skies* in 2007.

Wil Wheaton (Wesley Crusher): He was born in a hospital across from Disney studios and made his show biz debut in a Jell-O commercial with Bill Cosby. He was a fan of classic *Trek* (he owned all 79 episodes on video), but it was the Patrick McGoohan series *The Prisoner* that Wheaton considered his favorite show. The young actor made his movie mark in Rob Reiner's *Stand By Me* (1986) but his role as Wesley brought mixed reactions. He endured fierce backlash from fans who considered Wesley a know-it-all brat. He was hurt to see "Nuke Wesley" signs at one of his first *Trek* conventions. Although he left the series in its fifth year, he returned for three additional guest shots. His early guest work included *Highway to Heaven* and *Family Ties* and later appearances on *The Invisible Man* and *CSI*. He's also a book author.

Denise Crosby (Tasha Yar): The granddaughter of Bing Crosby, she appeared in such films as *48 Hours* (1982) and *Curse of the Pink Panther* (1983). She left *The Next Generation*, unhappy that the women's roles on the show weren't being expanded. She later returned for guest shots ("Yesterday's Enterprise," "Redemption" and "Unification") and was back as Tasha Yar in the final episode, "All Good Things." Her other TV guest roles include *The X Files* and *The Flash*. She appeared in the movies *Pet Sematary* (1989), *Deep Impact* (1998) and *Born* (2007).

Diana Muldaur (Dr. Katherine Pulaski): Born in New York City, her early work included the sci-ence fiction show *The Invaders* and two episodes of classic *Trek* ("Return to Tomorrow" and "Is There in Truth No Beauty?"). She had a recurring role as Dennis Weaver's girlfriend in *Mc-Cloud* (1970–1977) and another as lawyer Rosalind Shays in *LA Law* (1989–1991), where her character's demise (a surprise plunge down an elevator shaft) drew national attention. She was the first woman to serve as president of the Academy of Television Arts and Sciences.

Whoopi Goldberg (Guinan): At first everyone thought this Oscar winner (for *Ghost* in 1990) was kidding when she said she wanted to be a recurring character on *The Next Generation*. She was a fan of the classic series and inspired by Nichelle Nichols' portrayal of Uhura. Goldberg was born in Manhattan and held a job in a funeral parlor while playing small roles on Broadway. She started as a stand-up comedienne and received rave reviews for her performance in Steven Spielberg's *The Color Purple* (1985). She resided in the center square on *The Hollywood Squares* from 1998 until 2002, and now co-hosts *The View*.

Sources

Alexander, David. *Star Trek Creator: Authorized Biography of Gene Roddenberry*. New York: Penguin, 1994.

Berman, Rick. Interview. *TV Guide*, January 1993.

Christenson, Gary D. *TV Guide*, July 1988.

David, Peter. *Comic Buyers Guide*. 1991.

Delap's Fantasy and SF Review. 1978.

Gross, Edward, and Mark Altman. *Captain's Logs*. London: Boxtree, 1995.

Letters, *Starlog* no. 167, June 1991

Logan, Michael. *TV Guide*, 1997.

Malmgren, J.K. *TV Week* (Canada), May 2001.

Nemecek, Larry. *Star Trek: The Next Generation Companion*. New York: Pocket, 2003.

Nicholson, Lee Anne. *Star Trek: The Next Generation Review*. *TV Guide*, November 1987.

Nimoy, Leonard. *I Am Spock*. New York: Hyperion, 1995.

Okuda, Michael, and Denise Okuda. *The Star Trek Encyclopedia*. New York: Pocket, 1997.

Phillips, Mark, and Frank Garcia. *Science Fiction Television Series: Episode Guides, Histories, and Casts and Credits For 62 Prime-Time Shows, 1959 through 1989*. Jefferson, NC: McFarland, 1996.

Shapiro, Marc. "Independence Data — It's the World According to Brent Spiner: Star Trek, Star Trips and Starting Over." *Starlog* no. 221, December 1995.

Spelling, Ian. "First Officer and a Gentleman — After Years of Service Jonathan Frakes is Now at

the Helm." *Starlog* no. 173, December 1991.
_____. "Wil Wheaton Token Teenager — He Gained a Uniform and Lost His Mom but He's Still Part of 'The Next Generation.'" *Starlog* no. 140, March 1989.
Roush, Matt. *USA Today*, 1991.
Staples, Sarah. "Implants Offer Hope to People Who Have Lost Their Sight — Retinal Prostheses Allow Test Subjects to See Light and Movement." Canwest News Service, May 6, 2005.
Starlog no 113, December 1986.
Starlog no. 118, May 1987.
Starlog no. 177, April 1992.
Time, November 1994.

Star Trek: Voyager

(1995–2001)

In the 24th century, the starship Voyager is pursing a Maquis rebel ship when both vessels are transported to the other side of the galaxy by an alien intelligence. The Voyager and Maquis crews must now undertake the trip home, which will take 70 years.

Cast: Kate Mulgrew (Capt. Janeway), Robert Beltran (Commander Chakotay), Tim Russ (Tuvok), Roxann Biggs-Dawson (Lt. B'Elanna Torres), Robert Duncan McNeill (Lt. Tom Paris), Robert Picardo (The Doctor), Garrett Wang (Ensign Harry Kim), Ethan Phillips (Neelix), Jennifer Lien (Kes) *Year 1–3*, Jeri Ryan (Seven of Nine) *Year 3–7*

Based on Star Trek by: Gene Roddenberry; **Created by:** Rick Berman, Michael Piller, Jeri Taylor; **Executive Producers:** Rick Berman *Year 1–7*, Michael Piller *Year 1–2*, Jeri Taylor *Year 1–4*, Brannon Braga *Year 5–6*, Kenneth Biller *Year 7*; **Co-Executive Producers:** Brannon Braga *Year 4*, Kenneth Biller, Joe Menosky, *Year 6*; **Supervising Producers:** David Livingston *Year 1*, Peter Lauritson *Year 2–7*, Brannon Braga *Year 2–3*, Kenneth Biller, Joe Menosky, *Year 5*, Merri D. Howard *Year 6–7*, James Kahn *Year 7*; **Co-Supervising Producer:** Merri D. Howard *Year 4–5*; **Producers:** Brannon Braga, Peter Lauritson *Year 1*, Merri D. Howard *Year 1–3*, Wendy Neuss *Year 2–4*, Joe Menosky *Year 3–4*, Kenneth Biller *Year 4*, Robin Bernheim *Year 6*, JP Farrell *Year 6–7*; **Line Producer:** Brad Yacobian *Year 2–5*; **Co-Producers:** Wendy Neuss *Year 1*, Kenneth Biller *Year 2–3*, J.P. Farrell *Year 3–5*, Dawn Velazquez *Year 5–7*, Bryan Fuller *Year 7*; **Associate Producers:** Dawn Valazquez *Year 4*, Stephen Welke *Year 5–7*; **Consulting Producer:** Brannon Braga *Year 7*; **Creative Consultants:** Michael Piller *Year 3–7*, Jeri Taylor *Year 5–7*; **Writers included:** Jeri Taylor, Brannon Braga, Rick Berman, Naren Shankar, Carleton Eastlake, Kenneth Biller, Mike Sussman, Larry Nemecek, Andre Borman, Nick Sagan; **Directors included:** Winrich Kolbe, Terry Windell, Cliff Bole, Jesus Salvador Trevino, LeVar Burton, Allan Kroeker, Les Landau, Nancy Malone, Allison Liddi, David Livingston, Alex Singer, Michael Vejar; **Guest Stars included:** Judy Geeson, Michael Ansara, Marjorie Monaghan, Kellie Waymire, Rob La Belle, Gary Graham, John Savage, Joel Grey, Brad Dourif, Grace Lee Whitney, Basil Langton, Terry Lester, Susie Plakson, Patricia Tallman, Alan Oppenheimer, Ed Begley Jr., Jonathan Frakes, John de Lancie, Gerrit Graham, Ray Walston, Zach Galligan, Kate Vernon, John Rhys-Davies, Lori Petty, Jason Alexander, Kevin Tighe, Karen Austin, Eric Pierpoint, Jeffrey Coombs, Ron Glass, Jeff Yagher, Donny Most, Joseph Campanella, Alice Krige; **Music Theme:** Jerry Goldsmith; **Makeup Designed and Supervised by:** Michael Westmore

UPN/Paramount; January 1995–May 2001; 60 minutes; 172 episodes; DVD status: Complete series

When *The Cleveland Press* previewed the original *Star Trek* in 1966, they explained the premise as, "The starship *Enterprise* loses contact with Earth and becomes lost in space. A malfunction makes a return trip home impossible." That was an error but the newspaper was unwittingly 30 years ahead of its time because they had approximated the premise of *Star Trek: Voyager*.

After *Star Trek: Deep Space Nine* launched in

early 1993 with unspectacular ratings, there was a feeling that its static space-station format and darker stories were taking the adrenaline out of *Star Trek*. "Paramount wanted a show very much like *Star Trek: The Next Generation*," Michael Piller told *Omni* magazine in 1995. "We had to take the universe that Gene [Roddenberry] had given us and find a different perspective on it."

So they took a lost starship and had it commanded by a woman, Captain Kathryn Janeway. Unlike *Next Generation* and *Deep Space Nine*, which were produced for syndication, *Voyager* was on a single network, UPN, and the network made it clear that they wanted lots of action and no story arcs.

In the series' opener, "Caretaker," the starship *Voyager* pursues a Maquis ship, helmed by a group of self-declared freedom fighters considered as terrorists by the Federation. Both ships are suddenly engulfed by a mysterious plasma beam and transported 70,000 light-years across the galaxy to the uncharted Delta Quadrant.

Janeway confronts the alien responsible, a benevolent-looking old man. When she demands he return them to Earth, he snaps, "You're rather contentious for a minor bi-pedal species!"

The Caretaker is presiding over the Ocampan race, whom he feels responsible for. His technology laid waste to their planet's surface centuries ago. The Ocampan are now living underground in a world created for them by the ailing Caretaker. He has been kidnapping aliens, hoping to find a compatible life form that he can mate with, and leave behind a new generation of Caregivers.

When the Caretaker's transporter Array is about to fall into the hands of an aggressive Kazon race, Janeway altruistically destroys the Array — ending *Voyager*'s chances of using it to get home.

The crew must now set sail for a 70-year journey to Earth (on a ship that was designed to be in space for only one year at a time). Unless they can find a wormhole or alien technology that will shorten the voyage, many of the crew will not live to see Earth again. The *Maquis* officers, with their ship destroyed, agree to travel back home with the *Voyager* crew. One of those officers, a native American named Chakotay, who was once a Starfleet officer, agrees to become Janeway's first officer. He and his *Maquis* cohorts will drop their differences in favor of mutual cooperation and a way home. It was here that a source of interesting conflict between the two disparate crews was lost. Piller, feeling there was already too much char-

acter conflict on *Deep Space Nine*, opted for the Roddenberry approach of heroic people working together. A potentially rich tapestry of conflict between *Maquis* and *Voyager* officers was jettisoned. "To have Chakotay and his crew fall into place so quickly and eagerly was the wrong choice," actor Robert Beltran (Chakotay) said to *TV Zone* magazine. "The writers short-changed themselves."

And while the half human-half Klingon B'Elanna Torres angrily questions why Janeway is being allowed to make decisions for everyone, Chakotay assumes the subservient profile of a henpecked husband: "Because she's the captain," he says. Thus, the Maquis officers compliantly slipped on *Voyager* outfits and took orders from Janeway without blinking an eye.

There were also no tears shed for members of Janeway's crew, who perished during the pilot episode. Ensign Rollins (Scott MacDonald) dutifully executes several life-saving orders for Janeway but when he's blown to bits during a Kazon attack, no one mourns his loss. It was onward to the Alpha Quadrant for the long journey back to Earth, "seeking new life and exploring" along the way. That first episode was a hit, with over 20 million viewers.

"In retrospect, the one script that stands out for me is the pilot script," says co-creator Jeri Taylor, who started out writing for 1970s shows such as *The Incredible Hulk* and *Salvage One* (and as writer-producer on the 1980s series *Quincy M.E*). She later produced *Star Trek: The Next Generation*. She watched all of the classic episodes of *Star Trek*, which she had never seen, to better prepare herself for *Voyager*.

"Writing a pilot is always a daunting challenge," she says, "as it must satisfy so many requirements: establishing the franchise of the series, positioning the main characters, and of course being a rip-roaring yarn that will entice viewers to return. Michael Piller and I, working together, accomplished all those tasks. The franchise was certainly established, the characters seemed to jump off the page, and it was a terrific story, with all of the elements that make drama work."

The characters aboard *Voyager* were a mixed bunch. In addition to the Maquis' officers (Chakotay and Torres), there was Janeway's crew: Commander Tuvok (a Vulcan security officer), Ensign Kim (fresh out of the Academy) and Lt. Paris (a former bad boy who matures into a loyal bridge officer). Neelix was a Talaxian, a golden-skinned, comedic fellow who serves as chef and guide. His Ocampan girlfriend, Kes, has a nine-year lifespan. The ship's doctor had died during the plasma-beam transfer and his replacement was a fussy holographic Doctor.

Casting Captain Janeway turned out to be the real nightmare. Janeway was described in the story outline as a "Lindsay Wagner" type. Wagner, along with Chelsea Field, Lindsay Crouse, Blythe Danner, Dana Delany, Linda Hamilton, Kate Jackson, Joanna Cassidy, Tracy Scoggins, Patty Duke, Susan Gibney and Patsy Kensit, were some of the actresses considered for the role. Hundreds of other actresses, from the ages of 30–65, were tested. Genevieve Bujold was finally selected, as she was physically right for the part. However, unaired footage of Bujold on the set reveals an actress unhappy and uncomfortable with the role. She interpreted Janeway as a scientist rather than a tough captain and generated passive energy. When Bujold told the producers that she was wrong for the role, she was encouraged to continue. By the second day, she voluntarily withdrew from the series. The actress's publicist later stated, "She realized it wasn't for her. She wanted to let people know sooner than later." Bujold reportedly said later on, "I did not study acting all of these years to play a cartoon character."

The producers momentarily abandoned the idea of a female captain and looked at male actors (including Gary Graham and Britisher Nigel Havers) until they found Kate Mulgrew, who, with her husky Katharine Hepburn–type voice and strong presence, seemed perfect. This first female TV captain was accompanied by writing challenges.

"They were myriad!" exclaims Taylor. "The studio and the network were very nervous, and reserved the right to cast a male unless we could find absolutely the right woman. Part of that was that *Star Trek* has always enjoyed a very high demographic among young men, a very prized audience. The powers-that-be didn't want to risk alienating that audience by giving them a captain that they wouldn't find credible. Our catch phrase was: 'Would you follow this woman into battle?' She had to be an unqualified leader, one that men as well as women would respect. However, I felt strongly that she should be a woman, not just a man being played by a woman. I wanted the full range of her emotional components to come into play, all of her female instincts at her fingertips. This was a delicate balance but one that I feel we largely achieved. Finding Kate Mulgrew to portray her solved a lot of our problems."

Writer Joe Menosky offers a male perspective. "Writing for Janeway was mostly gender-blind, at least in my experience on the show. Almost any given episode or scene would have been conceived and executed regardless of her gender. Kate was a pleasure to write for—she had a way with dialogue and personal charisma."

However, Paramount executives didn't like Janeway's shoulder-length hair in the pilot, so those scenes were re-shot and she was given a bun. Piller joked, "This is probably the only *Star Trek* pilot in which the hairdressing cost more than the special effects."

Native-American actor Graham Greene was approached to play Chakotay and when he turned it down, Robert Beltran was cast. Actor Robert Picardo liked the mischievous nature of Neelix but when he lost that role, he reluctantly accepted the part of the Doctor (which Dwight Schultz had been considered for).

Picardo had called the Doctor "the worst role on the entire show" but he made it a break-out character. This "electronic man" (as Neelix once called him) displayed a witty, acerbic manner ("It seems I've found myself on the voyage of the damned"). "Certain aspects of my own personality did crop up in playing the Doctor," says Picardo today. "But his very aggressive physical posture, and his precise, even occasionally fruity way of delivering lines, is not me. But I always admired the doctor's desire to expand his abilities."

Picardo turned the fussy doctor into one the show's most popular characters. "Bob Picardo is a consummate actor," says Jeri Taylor. "We read so many people for that part and he was literally the only one who 'got' the character. It was a delight to write for him!"

Menosky agrees. "The Doctor was a great character and Picardo is an amazing actor."

Some actors joked that the series was *Gilligan's Island* in space, while fans pointed to the 1960s hit, *Lost in Space*.

The series downplayed the real fear, frustration and isolation that humans would feel trapped in an uncharted area of the galaxy (having lost everything they knew) and instead dealt with a host of aliens, most of them replete with attitude.

"The 70-year journey represented the injection of chronological time into a stand-alone premise," observes Menosky. "That could have allowed for a continuing arc series. Yet the show really was always meant to be stand-alone."

One of the most entertaining segments was "Prime Factors," where the crew enjoys shore leave on a planet where citizens "extract pleasure from every moment." The leader of this group, Gath (a perfectly cast Ronald Guttman), has a device that could send *Voyager* home but he refuses to share it. Janeway tries to win him over with pecan pie ("Most pleasurable") and with volumes of literature, downloaded from *Voyager*'s library. But Gath is a game player and has no intentions of helping *Voyager*. When she admonishes him for his selfish behavior, Gath is genuinely annoyed. "I don't enjoy being judged," he protests. "It is not at all pleasurable."

Lt. Torres and another crew member, Seska (Martha Hackett), barter with Gath's people behind Janeway's back and, with Lt. Tuvok's help, secure the device. However, their surreptitious efforts to use the alien technology fail and an angry Janeway confronts Tuvok with a stern, "You are the one I turn to when I need my moral compass checked ... don't ever go behind my back again." Well-written and suspenseful, with many witty and amusing touches, this early show delineated Janeway's loyalty to the Prime Directive and conveyed the desperation of her crew to get home.

But even as the ship finished its second year, the show's creators continued to fine-tune the product. "*Voyager* has a really good crew," Taylor told *Cinescape* magazine, "but they don't laugh together, they don't joke together, they don't have fun. They have these sort of serious, dire adventures." She was on the money; early marketing research showed that viewers accepted the crew as authentic professionals but didn't find their "whiny" personalities appealing.

That began to change with episodes like "Bride of Chaotica!" a black-and-white spoof of old movie serials. Here, aliens inhabit holodeck characters, including the evil Dr. Chaotica! (Martin Rayner), who must be stopped by *Voyager*'s crew (who also appear as pulp fiction characters).

There were also laughs with "Q and the Grey," where John de Lancie appeared as Q, the omnipotent alien from *Next Generation*. He desperately needed the crew's advice on how to "break through Kathy's cold exterior" so that he could mate with her and have a child. "I've been single for billions of years," he laments. "I'm lonely." The wise Janeway doesn't believe a word he says.

On the other hand, the show's efforts to do high-concept stories produced what Kate Mulgrew considered the worst of the series, "Threshold," where Tom Paris is transformed into a lizard creature. Another dubious entry was "The 37s," a gimmicky story which begins like the famous *Star Trek* skit on *Saturday Night Live* where the *Voyager* encounters not only a phony-looking, 1936 Ford truck floating in space but long-lost aviatrix Amelia Earhart.

As a tribute to the 30th anniversary of *Star Trek*, George Takei appeared as Captain Sulu in "Flashback" aboard the *Excelsior*.

Taylor's most unusual fan mail dealt with Captain Janeway. "It was from the Kate Mulgrew fan club," she says. "These were highly organized, militant, even strident people who seemed to feel it was their right to dictate who Janeway was and how she would behave in any situation. We didn't always see eye to eye! When I wrote *Mosaic*, Janeway's backstory [for Pocket Books], they hated it and let me know that. They refused to believe their beloved captain could ever have had moments of weakness or problems to overcome. They were wrong, of course."

Mulgrew thought it was a bold step for television to have a female captain and she loved her role. "A lot of Janeway is me," she revealed to *TV Zone* during production. "I've had this broad under my belt for five years. I own her." *The Chicago Sun–Times* agreed she was perfect: "Kate Mulgrew adds real chutzpah to the character of Captain Janeway."

But in the fourth year, there were changes. In the two-part episode "Scorpion" the crew encounters the mechanical Borg race and meet a hybrid–Borg named Seven of Nine. This human female had been assimilated into the Borg collective as a child. Now separated from the collective, she permanently boarded *Voyager* and sought to understand and experience human life once more.

Seven of Nine gave the show a much-needed boost. Her arrival coincided with the departure of Kes (whose storyline had dried up). Jeri Ryan had originally turned down the role, concerned over typecasting. Other actresses, including Claudia Christian, Justina Vail and Hudson Leick, were considered. Ryan finally accepted, and her character was designed to create conflict. Seven of Nine wasn't interested going to Earth, she was incapable of lying and grew amused by human foibles and their humor.

Seven of Nine's real purpose was to cater to the snickering demographic of young male viewers and it worked. Episodes featuring her did better in ratings and no wonder: Ryan was a startling sight in her constricting catsuit (which took the actress thirty minutes to get into every day). "Jeri Ryan was hot!" joked comedian Owen Burke. "She made *Star Trek* sexy — and no one thought that could happen."

"Intelligence comes in every possible package and it's time we showed that," Ryan said of Seven of Nine's provocative appearance. However, the actress was disheartened when she learned that Internet fans were busy analyzing Seven of Nine's bust size. Some other cast members didn't hide their thoughts of this new addition. "Let's face it, sex sells, and UPN wants to see it," said Tim Russ. Some fans resented the new character's presence, calling the series *Star Trek: Seven of Nine.* But most fans embraced her and Ryan was touched by many supportive letters from women viewers. Ryan knew little of *Star Trek* and wasn't an SF fan. She had to screen the movie *Star Trek: First Contact* to get a better idea of what the Borg were.

"There was a female contingent which had been fully prepared to hate her," Ryan told *Star Trek Monthly*. "But they couldn't because she is a very strong personality and they responded to that."

"Jeri brought the show a tremendous amount of publicity," raved Rick Berman to journalist Ian Spelling after she was brought aboard. "She got real popular, real fast, which was terrific." But *Voyager* still didn't get much respect from the media. Reviews continued to be lukewarm or downright hostile.

"It's lame," said the AP's Robert Jablon. "It has re-treaded aliens, goofy aliens and the weak leadership of Kathryn Janeway.... [I]t has upped the silliness ante with a Borg who wears skin tight catsuits and high heels."

"The show is awful," groaned *Sci-Fi Universe* magazine. "The premise is inherently flawed. Kate Mulgrew has gotten so over-earnest and self-important that in every dramatic scene, she either stops to whisper or sounds like she's going to cry."

But it also had its proponents. Julia Houston of About.com was initially cautious about *Voyager* but by the third season said, "*Voyager* is now putting out some really high quality entertainment."

Anna Kaplan's later retrospective for *Cinefantastique* noted, "*Star Trek: Voyager*'s strengths were in its appearance, its stunning visual effects, its high-concept episodes and its two-parters.... Its weaknesses involved the characters, who, until the final season, demonstrated no arcs and built no personal relationships."

If there was one constant criticism of the show, it was the incredibly dense technobabble. "Take warp drive off-line, re-modulate the shields and get ready to emit the anti-protons" was a typical line. Even writer Ronald D. Moore, who worked on *The Next Generation* and *Deep Space Nine* (and briefly for *Voyager*), was appalled by *Voyager*'s reliance on jargon. He confessed to Fandom.com in late 1999, "When I was studying *Voyager* to work on it, I was watching the episodes and the technobabble was just enervating, it was just soul-sapping. Vast chunks of scenes would go by and I had no idea what was going on. I write this stuff. I live this stuff. I do know the difference between the shields and the deflectors and ODN conduits and plasma tubes. If I can't tell what's going on, I know the audience has no idea what's going on."

Meanwhile, *Voyager* sailed on. Nancy Malone is an actress* turned Emmy award-winning director who was instantly attracted to *Voyager*. "It had a great premise," she says. "I had no experience with special effects but the producers and effects boys were wonderfully encouraging." Kate Mulgrew asked that Malone be hired (they had worked together on the 1988 series *Heartbeat*). "We had gotten along famously and I adored her professional demeanor and luminous talent," says Malone. "Two words of direction can generate volumes of ideas for her." She also enjoyed working with the ship's residential hologram. "Bob Picardo made me laugh. He has an amazing detachment that he can turn it on and off in the blink of an eye."

Malone especially liked how her episode, "Coda" (where Janeway, hovering near death, has a vision of her late father), turned out, and she received a lot of positive mail from *Voyager* fans. Her other segment, "Message in a Bottle," had the Doctor transported to a Federation ship near home. Wacky comedian Andy Dick played an advanced medical hologram who considers the Doctor outdated. "That episode was a bit more difficult," she admits. "Andy Dick had not done any drama at that point and he had a load of difficult dialogue. He was wonderful to work with but he had to fight some nervousness."

Surprisingly, for a show that championed a female starship captain, there was still some earthbound chauvinism for Malone to deal with. "One

In the 1960s, Malone starred in the Outer Limits *episode "Fun and Games" and in* Twilight Zone's *"Stopover in a Quiet Town."*

of the challenges was working with a director of photography who didn't care to work with a woman director," she says. "That's not unusual for women directors."

Allison Liddi, another of the show's female directors, observes, "It's unfortunate in the DGA today only nine percent of its female members are working in the guild. People think women cannot do certain jobs. To be honest, we all feel pressured to do well not only for our own work but also so producers will feel more open to continue to hire other women. I have had it said to me, 'We tried a woman director once and it didn't work.' I have seen men do mediocre jobs and they get hired again. As a female director, I tend to get pigeonholed with all females. If a female director does not produce a stellar show, then all female directors are held as suspect. Strangely, if a female director does an amazing job, only that female is held in esteem. There are countless shows that have never had a female director. They never had a female director on The X-Files. Several other action shows have similar track histories. It's frustrating."

Liddi helmed "The Collective," where Chakotay, Kim, Paris and Neelix are taken hostage aboard a Borg Cube ship, where five Borg "children" try to assimilate them into the collective. These young Borgs are considered damaged goods by mature Borgs and they will never rejoin their race. The Doctor removes the implants from the children and they recover their identities.

"My brother loved Voyager," says Liddi. "I thought he was a little nerdy but when I sat down and watched it with him, I found they were fascinating stories. I remember calling him from the Voyager set and being very excited that I was on 'the bridge.' The show seemed timeless to me because it dealt with universal themes such as racism, globalization, political power, and of being an outsider. That was its appeal.

"I liked [my] episode ... well, my cut. The producers had other ideas in mind. They cut out a beautiful crane shot with all of the children surrounding the big light [in the Borg ship]. I also didn't agree with the producer's choice for the lead kid. I thought that his voice was odd. I come from the theater and I thought his voice was immature and didn't land."

The old adage is never to work with kids and dogs but Liddi enjoyed it. "I have always loved working with kids. It depends on the kid but generally they can give you very fresh and true performances. I loved the little girl [Marley McClean]

and they kept these kids on for several more episodes. And Kate Mulgrew is a wonderful actress. She gave the character a lot of depth, levels that a lesser actress would not have. Jeri Ryan is smart and sexy. I loved what she brought to the show. As a kid, all we had was Lieutenant Uhura."

The holographic Doctor was highlighted in "The Swarm," where he suffers from an electronic form of Alzheimer's. His memory program begins to crash and he forgets things. "I particularly liked an exchange between Kes and the Doctor, when the Doctor doesn't even remember that he doesn't have a name," says Picardo. "It was very frustrating and emotional for him. I suggested that scene to Jeri [Taylor] and she wrote it into the script."

From most accounts, Voyager was also a fun set to work on, with a cast that bonded well. The show's technicians tirelessly created worlds of the future. Inside the five-foot Voyager model were photo-slides of the Voyager's sets, to give the model more realism. For mess hall scenes, Fernando Sepulveda's job was to find exotic-looking fruits and vegetables like horned melons and opal squashes. He once found a thorn-covered South-Asian fruit called Durian that, under the hot studio lights, gave off a horrible odor that sent people scrambling, spoiling the sharpest of appetites.

Another director who worked on the show was Jesus Trevino, a veteran of SFTV but with a genuine affection for the Star Trek universe. "I had been a fan of the original Star Trek series and it was a delight to be able to join in this modern extension of the franchise," he says. "Perhaps most meaningful for me was the fact that I have been reading science fiction since I was 10 years old. I grew up with the ABCs of SF—Asimov, Bradbury and Clarke. Being raised in the east side of Los Angeles, science fiction permitted me to see a world beyond that of the barrio. The knowledge of worlds beyond our own probably kept me from going down the road of gang life that so many of my peer group followed. Particularly important to me was the sense of wonder that comes with science fiction. I remember the first time I grasped the concept of time travel or parallel universes and how I felt my head explode with the possibilities. That is what attracted me to all the science fiction shows I have directed—Star Trek Voyager, Deep Space Nine, Babylon 5, seaQuest, Space: Above and Beyond, etc.—that sense of wonder. That is what I try to convey in my storytelling as a director."

Trevino recently viewed two of his episodes,

including "Fair Trade," where Neelix joins up with his former smuggler buddy (played by James Nardini) to secure a star map of the area — unwittingly putting Neelix back into a smuggling life. "That was my initiation into the *Star Trek* family and unlike most episodes, where one or two alien races are featured, here we created an interstellar marketplace where many races came to trade. We created more than a dozen different alien races for the scenes in the marketplace and that proved to be a challenge. I wanted to give the sense that the marketplace was big but since it was on Paramount's Stage 16, it was rather limited. I had the idea of creating a greenscreen arcade at one end of the marketplace. I first plugged this window and shot a marketplace plate shot full of aliens. Then I took the plug out of the greenscreen and shot another scene with aliens and laid in the previous scene in the greenscreen area, thus doubling the size and depth of the marketplace. I did this again (tripling the apparent depth of the marketplace) and had Paris and Chakotay enter into the scene and look down the center of the scene to emphasize the size of the marketplace. It was great fun to use these technical tricks to help sell the sense of wonder."

In "Day of Honor," B'Elanna and Tom's shuttlecraft is attacked, forcing them into space suits with limited air. Here they finally reveal their deep feelings for each other. "I remember working around Roxanne Dawson's pregnancy," says Trevino. "We had to be inventive in using a body double to show her walking from one place to another. When we had to have full body shots of her, I always positioned Roxanne so that there was always something partially blocking our view of her — having her stand behind a counter or, in a hologram scene, having her stand behind Paris's refurbished car."

Scenes where the pair are adrift in space required on-set ingenuity. Says Trevino, "We tried, at first, to hang Robbie and Roxanne from cables but this proved to be enormously taxing on the actors and not very successful for the visual look I wanted. We settled on a couple of much simpler devices which did the trick. We built a giant Lazy Susan, painted it green and had each actor stand on it, one foot at either end. I then put the camera on a 'hot head,' allowing me to float the camera between them to simulate them floating in space. We also built a teeter-totter type device (also painted green to allow keying-in of CGI space) with a foot rest end. Each actor stood on either end of the teeter-totter and we had it go up and down, simulating motion in space. I was very happy with the final results.

"It was a delight to work with Kate Mulgrew. Her role as Captain Janeway really transcended distinctions of gender. She was simply a great captain of a starship — she brought to the role leadership, tenacity, charisma, compassion and understanding. These are all qualities which a good captain — whether male or female — must have. As an actress, Kate was insightful and demanding when it came to storyline. If it wasn't 'right' in the script, then I knew she would have questions to raise. I tried to catch these concerns with the writers before it came time to rehearse and shoot a scene. I knew I had to have an answer for why we were shooting a scene in a particular way because she, as an actress, would want to know motivation and rationale for everything we were doing and how that affected her character and her crew. Knowing that Kate would let nothing slip by made me pay more attention to my work as a director and kept me honest."

During the fifth season, with a crushing 80-hour-a-week schedule, Mulgrew was unhappy with the toll *Voyager* was taking on her personal life. In addition to missing out on watching her sons grow up, she admitted to *TV Zone*, "I'm in love for the first time in 43 years" (referencing her relationship with Cleveland politician Tim Hagan). "I will be damned if anybody will take that away from me." Scheduling compromises were made so that the actress would get time off.

Mulgrew had a pleasant surprise when she learned that *Voyager* was watched every week in the White House by the daughter of President Bill Clinton. It was Chelsea's favorite show.

The *Voyager* character relationships remained static, although Paris and B'Elanna fell in love and married by the series end. *Voyager* remained UPN's highest-rated show, right to the end of is run. However, in mainstream terms, the series was only a modest hit, ranking 122 out of 150 shows for the 1998–1999 season and 117 out of 150 shows for the 1999–2000 season.

Year six had an episode set on Earth, "Pathfinder," where *The Next Generation*'s recurring character Barclay (Dwight Schultz) becomes obsessed with finding a way to communicate with the long-missing *Voyager* ship and creates a micro-wormhole to contact the ship for brief intervals. This interaction between Barclay and the *Voyager* continued into the seventh year.

But the *Chicago Tribune* later noted that *Star Trek* had taken too many trips to the creative well.

Much of its analysis of *Star Trek*'s weaknesses would be attributable to *Voyager*. The newspaper asked that there be "no more episodes where the holodeck malfunctions, or where they find an alternate reality or where everyone gets a virus that makes them act weird. You might as well put up a sign that says, 'Warning: Writers out of ideas.'"

Voyager's two-hour finale, "End Game" opens in San Francisco 23 years after the crew had returned home. Janeway, now an admiral, nurses some regrets over the death of Chakotay and Seven of Nine. And a hallucinating Tuvok is institutionalized. Janeway goes back in time to when *Voyager* was still lost in space to prevent these tragedies. Upon meeting her younger self, she directs the *Voyager* toward a wormhole that will return them to Earth almost instantly. The Borgs try to prevent the *Voyager*'s trip but the older Janeway sacrifices her life as she manages to destroy the Borg. The *Voyager* gets home and so it ended, completing a successful seven-year mission for another *Star Trek* spin-off. Despite a significant erosion of its fan base during the seven years, "End Game" scored with nine million viewers. "The last episode was a great acting showcase for Kate but there was an abruptness about the final resolution," says Picardo. "Many fans have told me they felt the finale gave short shrift to them getting home."

When Jeri Taylor considers *Voyager* today, she admits, "It seems like another lifetime. I am removed from show business and sci-fi. I'm living another life now.... I feel the [*Star Trek*] franchise and the characters were good, solid strengths for *Voyager*. All the actors brought even more to the characters than we could ever have imagined. If there was a weakness, I think it was that by the time *Voyager* was on the air, *Star Trek* was already suffering from over-exposure. The storytelling wasn't as fresh as it had been on *The Next Generation* because we'd already mined so many kinds of stories. I think it's best that *Star Trek* get a bit of a rest. Let some time go by, and allow people to get hungry for it once more."

Cast Notes

Kate Mulgrew (Capt. Janeway): The Iowa-born actress was the oldest child in an Irish Catholic family. She attended acting school as a teen and at 17 moved to New York City where she again studied acting. She became a regular on the ABC-TV daytime drama *Ryan's Hope* (1975–78) and then spent two seasons as the detective-

housewife in *Mrs. Columbo* in the late 1970s. Her movie credits include *Remo Williams* (1985) and *Star Trek: Nemesis* (as Admiral Janeway). Mulgrew later played Katharine Hepburn in the one-woman play, *Tea at Five*. She admitted her sons preferred *The X Files* to *Voyager* but when she visited the White House, she encountered many teenage girls who were fans of *Voyager* and interested in space and science. It inspired Mulgrew to study up on the technobabble she spouted every week. "I'm now determined to know *what* I'm talking about on the bridge."

Robert Beltran (Cmdr. Chakotay): When he saw the movie *Ben Hur* (1959), he was astonished by the power of film acting. He attended Fresno State University and majored in Theatre Arts. His movie debut was in *Zoot Suit* (1981) and he was the title character in *Eating Raoul* (1982). He had a recurring role as Lt. Soto in the 1994 series *Models Inc.* He developed a reputation for being one of the most outspoken and candid *Voyager* cast member, expressing concern over the writing and lack of character development for Chakotay.

Tim Russ (Tuvok): Born in Washington DC, he grew up on military bases around the world and was a reader of SF classics by Ben Bova, Alan Dean Foster, Arthur C. Clarke and other greats. He began acting in the mid–1980s and was a regular on NBC's adventure series *The Highwayman* (1988). His other TV credits include *seaQuest DSV, Beauty and the Beast,* the 1980s *Twilight Zone, Starman* and *Amazing Stories.* Russ is also a singer and has had several CDs released.

Roxann Biggs-Dawson (Lt. B'Elanna Torres): This Los Angeles native grew up living behind the house of William Shatner and played with his kids as a youngster. As a child, she wrote her own plays and cast neighborhood children in her productions. She grew up to study theater arts at the University of California at Berkeley and began her professional acting career in Broadway's *A Chorus Line.* Her early TV appearances included *Nightingales* and *Baywatch* and more recently she has appeared on *Without a Trace.* She has also directed episodes of *Enterprise* and *Charmed.*

Robert Duncan McNeill (Lt. Tom Paris): He first stepped on stage playing an American pioneer in a bicentennial school play in 1976. He co-starred in a critically acclaimed *Twilight Zone* episode, "A Message from Charity" (1985), but his big break was as a regular on *All My Children* in the mid–1980s. His TV credits encompass *Quantum Leap, The Outer Limits* and *Crossing*

Jordan. Like many of his *Trek* colleagues, he is also a director.

Robert Picardo (The Doctor): The Philadelphia-born actor sang in college, attracting the attention of music composer Leonard Bernstein, who encouraged him to study acting. He was a regular on *China Beach* (1988–91) and was the voice of Johnny Cab, the futuristic taxi driver, in *Total Recall* (1990). Other TV credits include *Amazing Stories*, *The 4400*, *Stargate SG-I*, *The Dead Zone*, *Seven Days* and *The Outer Limits*.

Picardo didn't understand what the appeal of *Star Trek* was before he got the Doctor role, telling journalist Ian Spelling, "I watched the original series and it looked like people in pajamas, standing in front of impossibly fake sets." But thanks to his wife, who was a big *Trek* fan, he did end up watching and appreciating *Star Trek: The Next Generation*. He liked how his character improved as *Voyager* went on. "He became much more human," he says today. "His social skills improved, and he became a more diplomatic and sympathetic individual."

Jeri Ryan (Seven of Nine): Born in Munich, Germany, she attended Northwestern University Chicago, and while there won several beauty contests, including Miss Northwestern Alpha Delta Phi Pageant. She moved to Los Angeles and appeared on *The Sentinel*, *The Flash*, *Melrose Place* and *Time Trax*.

Before *Voyager*, Ryan had co-starred in the series *Dark Skies*, where she received a total of 20 letters from fans. Once she joined *Voyager*, the actress received hundreds of letters before her first episode had even aired. She later co-starred as a teacher in the David E. Kelley series, *Boston Public* (2001–2004).

Garrett Wang (Ensign Harry Kim): He attended UCLA and majored in Asian studies. Encouraged to go into acting, he made his debut in the 1994 comedy pilot *All American Girl*. *People* magazine voted Wang as one of the 50 most beautiful people in 1997.

Ethan Phillips (Neelix): Born in Long Island, New York, Phillips got started acting on Broadway. Also a playwright and author, his original play *Penguin Blues* has been produced many times in North America. He appeared in *Ragtime* (1981) with James Cagney, and later in movies such as *Bad Santa* (2003). His TV credits include the 1980s *Twilight Zone*, *Werewolf*, *Touched by an Angel* and *Arrested Development*.

Jennifer Lien (Kes): She was only 20 years old when she filmed the *Voyager* pilot in 1994. She was drawn to acting as a child, and appeared in summer theater at age 13. The Illinois-born actress made her TV debut in the drama series *Brewster's Place* (1990) and was a regular on daytime's *Another World* (1991–1992).

Sources

Anders, Lou. Interview with Jeri Ryan. *Star Trek Monthly* no. 36, 1997.

Bischoff, David. *Omni*, 1995.

Eramo, Steven. "Tattoo Man." *TV Zone Special* no. 41, 2001.

Greenwald, Jeff. *Future Perfect*. New York: Viking, 1998.

Kaplan, Anna L. "The Big Return — Star Trek: Voyager's Final, Two-Year Mission? To Boldly Tie Up Loose Ends." *Cinefantastique* 33:5, October–November 2001.

_____. "Star Trek Profile: Fan-Writer-Producer Ronald D. Moore." Fandom.com, January 2000.

Poe, Edward Stephen. *Star Trek Voyager: A Vision of the Future*. New York: Pocket, 1998.

Richardson, David. "Kate Mulgrew Facing the Dark Frontier." *TV Zone* no. 112, March 1999.

Segal, David. *Washington Post*, 2001.

Spelling, Ian. "Smoke and Mirrors — Robert Picardo signed on to holo-act on Star Trek Voyager." *Starlog* no. 216, July 1995.

Spelling, Ian. Interview with Rick Berman. *Star Trek Communicator*, 1998.

Taylor, Jeri. Interview. *Cinescape* 2:12, September/October 1996.

Weigel, Tom. "Another Ship Lost in Space." *Cleveland Press*, July 1966.

Stargate: Atlantis
(2004–2008)

An international team from Earth takes control of an alien base (dubbed "Atlantis") in the Pegasus Galaxy. Their mission is to explore, establish diplomatic relations with other races and gather knowledge while thwarting a formidable alien race known as the Wraith.

Cast: Joe Flanigan (Major/Lt. Col. John Sheppard), Torri Higginson (Dr. Elizabeth Weir) *Year 1–3*, Amanda Tapping (Col. Samantha Carter) *Year 4*, Rachel Luttrell (Teyla Emmagan), Paul McGillion (Dr. Carson Beckett) *Year 2–4*, David Hewlett (Dr. Rodney MacKay), Rainbow Sun Francks (Lt. Aiden Ford) *Year 1*, Jason Momoa (Ronon Dex) *Year 2–4*, Jewel Staite (Dr. Jennifer Keller) *Year 5*, Robert Picardo (Richard Wooley) *Year 5*

Recurring Cast: Paul McGillion (Dr. Carson Beckett), Dean Marshall (Sgt. Bates) *Year 1*, Mitch Pileggi (Col. Steven Caldwell, USAF) *Year 2–4*, Jewel Staite (Dr. Jennifer Keller) *Year 4*, Kavan Smith (Maj. Lorne) *Year 2–4* , David Nykl (Dr. Radek Zalenka); **Created by:** Brad Wright, Robert C. Cooper; **Executive Producers:** Brad Wright, Robert C. Cooper, Michael Greenburg *Pilot*, Joseph Mallozzi, Paul Mullie *Year 2–5*, N. John Smith *Year 3–5*; Martin Gero *Year 5*, **Co-Executive Producers:** N. John Smith *Year 1–2*, Carl Binder *Year 2–3*, Martin Gero *Year 4*; **Supervising Producers:** Martin Wood *Year 2–4*, Martin Gero *Year 3*, Alan McCullough *Year 5*; **Producers:** Martin Gero *Year 2*, Andy Mikita *Year 4–5*, John G. Lenic *Year 5*; **Co-Producers:** Martin Wood, Ron French, Peter DeLuise *Year 1*, Martin Gero *Year 2*, Alan McCullough *Year 4*; **Consulting Producers:** Joseph Mallozzi, Paul Mullie *Year 1*; **Associate Producer:** Jennifer Johnson *Year 5*; **Creative Consultant:** Damian Kindler *Year 2–3*; **Writers included:** Kerry Glover, Jill Blotevogel, Peter DeLuise, Alan Brennert, Carl Binder, Damian Kindler, Martin Gero, Robert C. Cooper, Brad Wright, Joseph Mallozzi, Paul Mullie; **Directors included:** Mario Azzopardi, Andy Mikita, William Waring, Peter DeLuise, James Head, Brad Turner, Martin Wood, David Warry-Smith, David Winning; **Guest Stars included:** Robert Davi, Robert Patrick, Colm Meaney, Christopher Heyerdahl, Jewel Staite, Ellie Harvie, Peter Woodward, Alan Scarfe, Don S. Davis (as General Hammond), Amanda Tapping (as Sam Carter), Richard Dean Anderson (as General Jack O'Neill),

Michael Shanks (as Daniel Jackson), Beau Bridges (as Maj. General Landry), Robert Picardo (as Richard Woolsey), Connor Trinnear (as Michael); **Directors of Photography:** Michael C. Blundell, Brenton Spencer; **Production Designers:** Bridget McGuire, James C. Robbins *Year 3*; **Special Visual Effects:** Atmosphere Visual Effects, Rainmaker Special Effects, SPIN West VFX, Zoic Studios, Geoff Anderson; **Music:** Joel Goldsmith

Sci-Fi Channel/The Movie Network (Canada)/MGM Television/Sony Pictures Television/Acme Shark (Cooper/Wright)/Pegasus Productions; July 2004–; 60 minutes; 100 episodes; DVD status: Seasons 1–4

When a television series becomes very successful, it is natural for executives and producers to begin conversations about a spin-off entity that capitalizes on the strengths of their show. Producer Dick Wolf benefited from his successful *Law & Order* TV series, starting three series spinoffs. In *Star Trek*'s case, it took them 18 years of post-series popularity and demand before *Star Trek: The Next Generation* appeared.

The trick of a spin-off series is to retain the identity and familiar aspects of the original show while presenting new characters and premises that are fresh and original. This was precisely the challenge that faced executive producers Brad Wright and Robert C. Cooper when they explored concepts of a *Stargate* spin-off series. There were many curves and detours along the way.

According to Wright, co-creator of the series, when *Stargate SG-1* reached its fifth year, he began considering not a spin-off television series, but a feature film edition to bring the *SG-1* franchise to the big screen. When MGM-TV expressed interest in a leap to a *Stargate* feature, Wright approached writer-producer Cooper, who had been working with him on *SG-1*, and proposed a collaboration.

Showtime, the broadcaster, had only commissioned five years, so there was a certain anticipation that the TV production would be canceled. However, when the series successfully transferred to the Sci-Fi Channel for a sixth year, the feature film plans were put on hold and instead, a series spin-off concept took hold. "Fans became aware of this concept of *Stargate Atlantis* because MGM had reserved the [Internet web page] domain!" chuckles Wright. "Suddenly, there was this [title] called *Stargate Atlantis* because MGM had reserved the domain name. It was funny how that got out. But very little was known about what it was going to be. The plan was that it was going to supplant *SG-1*."

The foundation of a *Stargate: Atlantis* TV series was a revision of a story titled "Lost City," originally intended for the feature film. That story ended up, instead, as a transition film from *SG-1* to the premise of *Stargate: Atlantis*. When planned as a feature, the city of Atlantis was to be found frozen in ice in Antarctica. But with *SG-1* continuing as a series, there couldn't be two teams, one *SG-1* and the other *SG:A*, operating out of Earth. So Wright and Cooper moved the Atlantis base about as far away from Earth as you could imagine.

"It was Robert Cooper that suggested Atlantis actually left Earth in our distant past, and found a home in the Pegasus Galaxy," says Wright. "I resisted the idea at first, as evidenced by O'Neill's line in the pilot episode: 'Flying city?' I had been searching for what the image of the city was going to be, and the idea of it 'rising' from the bottom of the ocean and bursting through the surface of the ocean was compelling."

The dealmaking between Sci-Fi Channel and MGM took a long time. In the interim, before *SG:A* got greenlighted as a series, Wright and Cooper submitted a story titled "Rising" as an *Atlantis* feature film concept. But once the deals were signed and sealed, that story evolved into *SG:A*'s pilot film.

The delayed business action placed greater pressure on the co-creators to conjure up the pilot script. The series' greenlight was given in November 2003, with shooting beginning in February 2004 and a desire to debut the series in July 2004 on the Sci-Fi Channel. To meet this deadline, Wright and Cooper were put in the unusual situation of writing their series script simultaneous with set construction and casting. "Writing a two-hour script for a series that you're going to do isn't something that you can do instantly," says Wright. "I remember celebrating New Year's because we finally had a script. At that point we began casting and it was hard to do because it was pilot season. We had a guarantee of 20 episodes on the air and the track record of *SG-1* to back us up."

Having two *Stargate* series running at the Bridge Studios in Vancouver, Canada, was both hard and easy at the same time. *Stargate* had already been on the air for seven years. Just about everyone behind the camera was an *SG-1* veteran, making for good communication between the various departments. "Bridget McGuire, who is production designer on both shows, worked so hard and I can give nothing but praise, the work that came out of her art department," Wright says. "There were benefits of multiple productions—running two shows alongside each other really paid off. We have nine soundstages between the two shows. We basically have one large production office and one large art department and separate art directors devoted to each show. And this is the kicker: One large writing department. So whenever we broke stories, we'd all break them together. So that's one large group breaking 40 stories each year for the last three years! It's been quite a lot of work. It's very difficult to spawn a television series that way but there are benefits too."

As an example, a set built for one episode of *SG-1*, such as the village from *SG-1*'s "Babylon," could later be redressed for *SG:A*'s "Epiphany." "These are ways we are always trying to get money on the screen," notes Wright. "We make the production values as rich and high as they can be. Certainly not double value, but you get more value. You just have a larger infrastructure."

The vast *SG-1* experience under everyone's belt gave Cooper and Wright confidence that the series would be launched with quality, competence and experience. Cooper remained *SG-1* showrunner, while Wright nurtured *SG:A*'s growth.

In another example of the cross-pollination between the series, the visual effects department worked simultaneously on both shows, and as expensive as generating the VFX were on a per-shot basis, there were also techniques used to pull greater value out of the finished product. "We have a [hyperspace-capable] ship called *Daedalus* that operates in the *Atlantis* universe, and a ship called the *Odyssey* that operates in the *SG-1* universe. They are the same set with different signage, lighting and crew."

Stargate: Atlantis' premise grew out of a story arc that began in *SG-1*. Stargate archaeologist Dr. Daniel Jackson learned that an abandoned Antarctic base, known as Atlantis, was built by the Ancients (builders of the Stargate technology who lived on Earth for a time in the distant past). Jackson determined that eons ago, the Ancients had left Earth and moved their "Lost

City" to the Pegasus galaxy. In the premiere episode, "Rising," General Jack O'Neill visited the Antarctic outpost where Jackson discovered the coordinates for the Atlantis base. To their surprise, Dr. Rodney McKay and Major John Sheppard both had the "ATA gene" that activated the Ancients' technology, qualifying them to join a large expeditionary team of civilian scientists and military personnel preparing to travel to Atlantis. The reason they had the ATA gene was because it meant their ancestors were either Ancients or related to Ancients, who interbred with humans on Earth. Dr. Elizabeth Weir headed the international team as they stepped through the SGC Stargate and landed inside the dormant underwater Atlantis base on a distant planet called Lantea. Under the direction of Dr. McKay, the Atlantis base was reactivated and brought to the ocean surface.

After adapting to life inside the vast Atlantis city, the team explored other worlds in the Pegasus galaxy, using the base's Stargate. One of their main goals was to learn more about the Ancients, their society and their fate.

They soon encountered a benevolent alien race, the Athosians. This includes Teyla, an intelligent woman adept at combat. She joined the mission team headed by Maj. John Sheppard.

Throughout the series, Weir and her SG teams met the galaxy's other inhabitants, both friendly and hostile. One of their most deadly foes were the Wraith, a highly intelligent, telepathic and technologically advanced vampire-like humanoid alien species who "sucked" the life force out of humans to gain their strength. "Robert and I spun the Wraith together," says Wright. "They were really born out of his desire to have a truly scary, truly evil enemy that was far, far away from the Goa'uld."

The Wraiths' DNA is a recombinant of humans and an insect-like species and they were awakened from hibernation in "Rising."

Col. Marshall Sumner (Robert Patrick), the original team leader, and Teyla were beamed up into a sleek Wraith spaceship that was strafing the Athosian planet. Sheppard and Lt. Aiden Ford followed in a shuttle to another planet, locating their friends inside Wraith cells; Sumner was incredibly aged from the Wraith torture he had received during interrogation. Anguished at Sumner's suf-

The cast of *Stargate Atlantis'* first season, from left: Rainbow Sun Francks, Rachel Luttrell, Joe Flanigan, Torri Higginson and David Hewlett (© Sci-Fi Channel).

fering, Sheppard mercifully shot him. Meanwhile, Ford succeeded in detonating the C4 plastic explosives planted throughout the Wraith complex and the Atlantis team were able to escape in the Jumper (a small, but powerful Ancient transport craft designed to travel via the Stargate system) back to the city. But their escape came at a very high cost: The Wraith in hibernation had awakened, ready to wreak havoc on the galaxy once again.

At the end of "Rising," Teyla was very grateful to the Atlantis team for helping her people escape the Wraith and she became a member.

When casting the series, Wright and Cooper essentially chose a fresh-faced cast of unknowns. Joe Flanigan was cast as the square-jawed but laidback team leader, Maj. (and later Col.) John Sheppard.

Torri Higginson, who played Dr. Elizabeth Weir, took over the role from Jessica Steen, who briefly originated the character on *Stargate SG-1*. Weir was a strong and stable source of leadership throughout the series; in the third year finale, she was a victim of a laser beam blast that hit Atlantis from a satellite Stargate platform placed there by their enemies, the Asurans. Consequently, Higginson's role in the fourth season was reduced.

"Dr. Weir is very important in the hearts of our characters," says Wright. "What affected her at the end of season three, and the struggles she's having at the beginning of season four, make it difficult for her to remain as leader of Atlantis."

In place of Weir, Amanda Tapping, as Lt. Col Samantha Carter, joined the *SG:A* team in the series' fourth season.

David Hewlett had already played Dr. Rodney McKay on *Stargate SG-1* as a guest star. When the series was in development, another scientist character was created but it was difficult to cast and the creators realized what they were really looking for was a "Rodney McKay" character. The problem was solved by bringing in Hewlett at the last minute. His characterization of McKay was as a highly intelligent, fast-speaking, arrogant but reliable scientist.

Rachel Luttrell was Teyla, the Athosian who joined the team and eventually gained psychic powers that linked her to the Wraith, providing the team with valuable intelligence. In the fourth year, Luttrell became pregnant in real life and this was incorporated into the storyline.

Paul McGillion, who brought in a Scottish accent, was a recurring character in the first season as Dr. Carson Beckett. He became a regular in the second and third year. His character was killed in a fiery explosion in the third-year episode "Sunday."

Rainbow Sun-Francks was young 1st Lieutenant Marine Aiden Ford, who supported team excursions to other planets. At the end of the first year, both the producers and the actor were not happy with Ford's development so a new idea was hatched. In a battle with a Wraith, Ford became infected with a Wraith enzyme that enhanced his physical prowess, making him more aggressive. His left eye mutated into solid black and there were other physical changes; his body's chemistry now was addicted to the enzyme. Driven to feed the addiction, Ford roamed the Pegasus galaxy using the Stargate network, killing Wraith, and harvesting the chemical.

Essentially, Ford's split with the Atlantis base allowed the character to become an antagonist in the storytelling but appearances were eventually reduced to a recurring role in year two. "That didn't continue because it wasn't working creatively, through no fault of Rainbow," says Wright. By year three, he was written out of the series with no discussion of a return.

In the second year, Jason Momoa strengthened the Atlantis team as Ronon Dex, a military officer of the Sateda, another alien race in the Pegasus galaxy that had suffered under the Wraith. He was a tall, slim, imposing man with a bushy beard who was quick and strong in a fight with a sword and an energy-based handgun. He developed strong, loyal relationships with Teyla and Sheppard. Wright says that as producers they wanted a "Teal'c character" [from *SG-1*], in Atlantis, and Ronan effectively became that strongman.... With Jason being such a gigantic man, and with Teyla walking into the fights, it allowed us, with our stunt coordinators, to do some incredible fights. Together, they make an amazing combination."

Mitch Pileggi joined the series in a recurring role capacity as Col. Stephen Caldwell, commander of the Daedalus, in the second year. The character was a suggestion from the network, which wanted a foil for Dr. Weir. "When we tried to do that with Sheppard, it didn't seem right," Wright says. "You want your team to believe each other and not be fighting with each other. And I wanted to introduce a ship. I felt by season two it was important that Atlantis not be so isolated and have the capability of going back and forth, as difficult as it may be, with the Daedalus. And we needed, to be honest, the cavalry in 'The Siege' storyline which was always planned. It would have been nice to have members of *SG-1* onboard but that became difficult because *SG-1* was picked up again."

The series' first season, the Atlantis expedition had also become enemies of the Genii, a militaristic race of humans who had been under siege by the Wraith. Although outwardly they appeared to be simple farmers, they carefully hid their advanced technology in underground bunkers. Wary of each other at first, the Genii and the Atlantis team agreed to join forces to learn more about the Wraith. But a betrayal by one of the Genii swiftly turned the tide and they, too, became enemies, notably in the two-part "The Storm" and "The Eye."

"We approached that first season knowing it was going to be a hell of a lot of work," says Wright. "Robert [Cooper] was still going to be running *SG-1.* The first season of a series is awfully difficult no matter what because every decision you make is set in canon.

"Season one is quite strong. It was a season that had a nice arc even though I was always struggling with budget. If the audience knew where we started, how we started, they'd know we pulled off a miracle."

"First seasons are interesting," says Torri Higginson. "It's a matter of everybody getting to know each other — the writers getting to know the actors, everyone gets to know their characters. Then, throughout the season, as an actor you begin to get your own footing as to who the characters are. The actors [begin to] own the characters and the writers begin writing for the actors. This series is a different anomaly in that it was spun off from a show that had been on the air for 10 years. So the producers-writers had been working together 10 years. There's something very daunting about walking into that. They all know each other so well, and I think it took us [actors] longer to find our footing, everyone was being a little cautious. By the third episode I still wasn't feeling I was Dr. Weir. I was still feeling, 'What is this Stargate thing?'"

The two-parter "The Storm" and "The Eye" had the Atlantis base caught in the middle of a hurricane. Weir ordered the City evacuated, but then their newfound enemies, the Genii, attempted to take over the facility. When Weir and McKay were captured, Sheppard remained loose, running around the city by himself. This was Wright and Cooper's *Die Hard* on Atlantis.

"I remember it was very wet!" said a laughing Higginson. "There was no acting required in that so it was quite fun. They used these huge fans the size of airplane engine fans and they had these hoses directed at us and we were drenched. You had water being whipped in your face the whole time so we had a lot of ADR [dialogue looping] to do.

"The difficult thing was to get our lines out without shivering, without your teeth chattering and keeping your eyes open. That was the strange challenge of it," she says. "Acting-wise, it was very fun. There were no green screens. It was 'There's the bad guy, there's you, dealing with that conflict face to face.' I got to act with David Hewlett and he's a dream to work with. He also likes to complain a lot," she said, laughing.

"It was very fun watching him getting very frustrated with the buckets of water that were being thrown in our faces."

Brad Wright notes that the visual special effects facility that handled the episode, Rainmaker Digital Effects, had their work cut out for them. "It was very difficult to do visual effects in that environment. Water effects are very difficult, but Rainmaker gave us more than our money's worth in terms of numbers of shots for the episode. I think it's a strong episode too because of Robert Davi's performance. When you get a Robert Davi quality of an actor, it's very helpful. It was a really strong mid-season two-parter."

Coming down from such an arduous shoot was as memorable, says Higginson. "They were very smart — they shot all that just before the summer hiatus. I think they knew if we all got dreadfully sick, that we'd have a month to recover. So we had a month off in July and I went back to Los Angeles and laid in the sun and dried out. But it was definitely exhausting. We were shooting 15–16 hours a day and waking up early and not getting enough hours sleep is very tiring, so when you have that kind of physical strain going as well, being soaking wet for 12 hours a day, it is very easy to get a little run down. I think David spent three weeks in bed after."

In "Before I Sleep," Elizabeth Weir discovered herself as an incredibly frail old woman, frozen in stasis on Atlantis from 10,000 years ago. It was a tremendous acting challenge for Higginson because rather than hire another actress to play the role, Wright and co-executive producer N. John Smith asked Higginson to play both roles. "They knew it would mean about two hours sleep a night for me because of having to shoot both parts of the scene and getting in the prosthetics in the morning, and then have them taken off and then shooting the other half of the scenes," says Higginson. "I was just thrilled they were willing to let me do this because I knew, practically, it meant the production costs would get very high for overtime. It cost them money to allow me to do that and I thought that was really good of them.

"It was also very surreal. The strange thing about science fiction, as actors we're trained to respond to what the other actors offer us. In science fiction, so often you're responding to nothing and having to trust your imagination and trust that the special effects are going to match what you're responding to. A lot of the time, it was a tennis ball that I was really looking at.

"They were also very generous in that they hired my look-alike for whom they would film over the actresses' shoulder to look at me. They hired someone [Holly Elissa Dignard] who was actually an actress, not a photo-double. She was wonderful. She worked very closely with me, she'd come to my trailer and we would rehearse the scenes and she would play both parts, knowing what I was planning to do in the scene and she would do her best to recreate that for me and I really appreciated that."

Dignard, who was "Old Weir" in the scenes when viewers saw "Young Weir" on camera at the same time, had to endure the same trials as Higginson with the special effects prosthetics. She had to rise from her bed at three or four in the morning and report to work. "The process was about six hours," she says. "I fell asleep many times. It was definitely bizarre looking in the mirror and the face being totally and utterly different. I forgot what I looked like as the days wore on because I spent *so* much time in the prosthetic. It was a shock to see my real face at the end of the day. There was definitely a transformation internally once you looked in the mirror and saw 'Old Weir.' Once the contact lenses went in — to look like cataracts— I couldn't really see anything. I had to have people guide me across the set."

With just about half a season "in the can," the series premiered on the Sci-Fi Channel with "Rising" on July 16, 2004. That year's annual San Diego Comic-Con was just a week later. Faithful Sci-Fi and *SG-1* fans had only just seen two episodes as their introduction to the *Atlantis* universe. Higginson admits she was simply not prepared for the feedback she received at the event when members of the cast (including Flanigan, Luttrell, Hewlett and Francks) went to introduce

themselves at panels. "We were working like mad, trying to get into the rhythm of it and understand everything we could about the show and the genre, but I was unaware of the absolute loyalty and fandom that SF creates," she says with strong emotion. "It's such a unique force that way and how vocal and loyal the fans are. None of us had been there before or knew what to expect. It was the first time any of us had been on stage at a convention answering questions and I remember thinking, 'Oh, it will be about 100 people in the room' and we walked in and there was about 5,000 people there. And we thought, 'Oh, we shouldn't have had a cocktail last night!' This is real, it's serious and there are a lot of people here who need our focus and attention. It was a very sharp learning curve.

"There was a football field full of people in this room waiting to speak to us and lineups around the block of people wanting our autographs. We were very, very surprised by that. And it kind of made us go, 'All right, we're doing okay.' Doing a show that is coming off the tails of a successful show is especially daunting. We were concerned that people wouldn't accept us because they might be worried we would take over *Stargate* or *Stargate* wouldn't continue. We were very aware we might get some negative reaction because of that. Instead, we got immense support. The *Stargate* fans just opened their arms and let us in. That gave us a confidence. 'Okay, we're doing a good job here. Just have fun and do your job and don't worry about the politics of it.'"

In the second year, Sheppard was promoted to lieutenant colonel and, thanks to the Asgard, the Daedalus, a hyperspace-traveling starship arrived at Lantea to serve as military firepower support. In this season, Dr. McKay experimented with a Wraith retrovirus, a bioengineering technology that would transform Wraith into humans. An advanced form of the formula was used on one such Wraith, and he was given the human name Michael (Connor Trinneer). At the season's end, the Wraith headed towards Earth in search of new feeding grounds, while holding Ronon and Rodney captive in cocoons.

Higginson notes that the second year was a time for trying to figure out what worked and what didn't on the series. "We missed Rainbow [Sun Francks] but I think they recognized they needed somebody a bit more powerful, and stronger with presence and muscle," she says. "Bringing in [the character] Ronan [played by Jason Momoa] was very smart. His charisma and strength on screen is very striking and very engaging. Mitch Pileggi is such a dream to have around. Because of his résumé and familiarity to the audience, that brought a lot to the show."

In the premiere of the third year, Sheppard saved his teammates from the Wraith's cocoons and succeeded in escaping in a Wraith Dart.

Later, a new enemy appeared: The Asurans, created by the Ancients as an aggressive bio-weapon to defeat the Wraith. They were self-replicating, human-looking "nanites" (microscopic machines). The experiment failed and the Ancients tried deleting the experiment but the Asurans continued to replicate on their own and built their own city, a base almost identical to Atlantis. In a two-part episode, "The Return," written by Martin Gero, the Asurans' succeeded in taking over Atlantis and booted off the Earth team. Against the orders of their superiors, Dr. Weir and the rest of her Atlantis team returned to Atlantis in a stolen Jumper and were able to take back the base from the invaders.

It was in the third year that Higginson began noticing a progressive maturity to the stories and the character development. She said during year three, "People are more excited about it being a different show than Stargate. We own it a bit more. The writers have done some interesting things this year by taking it outside of the norm. We had one episode ["Irresistible"] that was almost a situation comedy and it was nice for a week not having the Wraith coming to get us. They've shook it up a bit this year and made choices that are surprising.

"We've also had interesting, different enemies. The Wraith are an extraordinary enemy. Visually they're stunning. But it's important that they're not the only cause of conflict. And there's been more crossover of characters and history from Stargate this year, which is very smart because they didn't do that for our first two years. They allowed our show to grow on its own and then brought in the crossovers."

"Season three is probably the best season we've done so far, we stepped it up a notch," says Brad Wright. "I think for an SF show to get its legs, to give it a sense of growth, going forward, you have to have a sense of evolution. This season looks more sophisticated, more evolved. If it is a cookie cutter, if there's no difference between episodes in season three and season one, because it's that episodic, the audience is not going to be rewarded.

"My philosophy has always been a balance of series arcing — moving forward and rewarding the audience and acknowledging things that came before — and stand-alone stories. As a writer, there's sort of a desire to serialize because then you're thinking of one big story. Isn't that fun and cool? You end up going down very dangerous roads."

The most successful shows, says Wright, are those that balance careful forethought with make-it-up-as-you-go plotting and character development. "To do one or the other is death to the longevity of the series," he says.

When it came to developing villains for SG:A, Wright reveals that he wanted, initially, the Replicators from SG-1 (first introduced in SG-1's "Unnatural Selection") to be on the show. But the final choice was to create an original villain, the Wraith. In preparing to create the fourth-year villains, he says, "You're going to see something we did quite successfully in SG-1, which was a three-way battle between our two main nemeses. We basically pit the Replicators and the Goa'uld [on SG-1] against each other. And now we're going to be doing it with the Replicators and the Wraith [on SG:A]. That creates an interesting, galactic dynamic that we find ourselves meddling in, and it's fun."

In the series' fourth year, executive producers Paul Mullie and Joseph Mallozzi stepped in as showrunners. Together, they transported Atlantis (quite literally) into uncharted regions of space. In the two-part season premiere "Adrift" and "Lifeline," the entire base itself became a flying city, traveling through hyperspace to escape from the human Replicators' laser attack. A new planet was found and the base remained intact. The human Replicators, personified by guest star David Ogden Stiers, continued to be a formidable enemy to the Atlantis expedition. Later, the Atlantis expedition even allied with a captured Wraith.

Considerable changes were made in the fourth year. Torri Higginson was pulled back to a recurring role. Appearing in just four episodes, her character, Dr. Elizabeth Weir, was critically injured by the Replicators' laser blast. To save her, Drs. Keller and McKay worked together to activate dormant Replicator nanites in her body to engineer the necessarily repairs. She recovered but became, on a genetic level, intimately connected with the Replicators. Later, a Replicator copy of Dr. Weir was found ("This Mortal Coil"). SG:A showrunners had plans to continue the character in a recurring capacity in the fifth year but after consideration, Higginson declined their offer. This created a problem because in the final scene in which we saw Dr. Elizabeth Weir ("Be All My Sins Remember'd"), it was a cliffhanging moment that was resolved in SG:A's fifth year episode "Ghost in the Machine" with a different actress.

In the middle of the series' third season, in the summer 2006, Higginson discussed the depth of her commitment to the series. With *Stargate SG-1* so successful that it ran for an unprecedented 10 years (for an American SF show), how long would Higginson be willing to hang out on a soundstage in Vancouver? "When they first asked us to sign a contract, it was for six years. I panicked at the time and said to my agent, 'No, no, ask for three years!' I mean, six years' commitment to a show you've never seen before? I found that very frightening. I'm sure it's a universal phenomenon but time speeds up when you get older and this year we could not believe we were already in our third year! How did that happen so quickly? There's a part of you as an actor that goes, 'No, I want to play different characters.' And there's also a big part that goes, 'I am so grateful in this very unstable industry to have a regular job. What a gift that is.' And our crew is extraordinary. We just all have a lot of love and respect for each other. So if I'm still receiving a paycheck for year 10 in this job, I will be nothing but grateful. And because we get five months' hiatus, you can still do other work, such as in theater, and keep your acting muscles fresh and heart engaged.

"The wonderful thing about SF is that anything can happen. One week it can be like a sitcom, the next week is full-on action and the next week it can be emotions and drama. You get to cover so many different aspects of a character like where I played a 10,000-year-old lady. That wouldn't happen in *Law & Order*."

Two years later, talking to the Internet radio program *Sci-Fi Guys*, Higginson discussed the reasons behind her departure. "The very last day of filming season three, as I finished filming the last scene on the last day, I was called up to the office and was told that my character was going to become recurring if I chose to be. I thought that was not a very dignified way to deal with it. I was a little bit upset by how it was dealt with."

Executive producer Joseph Mallozzi remarked in his January 31, 2008, online blog that Dr. Weir was always intended to be a supporting player with the rest of the team, just as General Hammond was on *SG-1*. Making the change in the character's direction and participation was simply an outgrowth of the plotting for season four, he says. And they decided, at the end of the season,

to sit down with Higginson to spell out the character's arc, rather than as typically it is in Hollywood, discovering the move from their talent agents between seasons without a face-to-face meeting.

In an interview with the *Stargate* fan website Gateworld, Higginson says she believes that Weir was pulled out of Atlantis in favor of loyalty to *SG-1*'s Amanda Tapping, who had just ended 10 years in the role as Colonel Samantha Carter. She also believes that "finding a place" for Weir among a cast of eight characters was challenging. She told Gateworld, in part, "I think everybody can take a bit of responsibility for that, obviously myself included. They thought 'Here's this woman character that we're not really able to explore to her full right.'

"So many of the episodes I was just there in the background, which wasn't challenging for me. And I think they're going 'Why are we paying this chick when she's only in for a couple of scenes?'.... That's how I hypothesize it."

Stepping in for about half the fourth season and sharing command with Col. Sheppard on the Atlantis base, Col. Carter assisted the expedition in their mission. Since Dr. Carson Beckett was killed in the previous season, a new doctor was recruited to replace him on the base: Dr. Jennifer Keller, played by *Firefly* actress Jewel Staite. Beckett, or rather a version of him, did return in the two-part episode "The Kindred." Plus, new uniforms were issued.

In a July 2007 press conference, series producers and cast members spoke about the new year. Joseph Mallozzi revealed that a new race was introduced: The Travelers, who were highly technologically advanced. "They are nomads, traveling on ships and establishing a civilization," he said. "They are very rustic, and have a very cool look."

Dealing with Rachel Luttrell's pregnancy was one of the major challenges of the year. Would they simply write her out of a number of episodes, or film around her expanding belly? (Such was the case for Gates McFadden on *Star Trek: The Next Generation*.) The decision was simple: Incorporate the real-life event into the series. "We developed a story about Rachel out in the woods with Jewel and it was a fairly violent story," Paull Mullie explained at the press conference. "And we were writing that story when she came in and told us she was pregnant. We were too far down the road with that story to pull back, at that point."

To adapt the real-life with the fiction, Mullie

admitted they just decided, "She doesn't know she's pregnant in this story! We had planned to do a Teyla story arc from the beginning before we knew Rachel was pregnant. We just worked it in."

In the spring of 2008, *SG:A* entered production for their fifth season, bypassing a lengthy Writer's Guild Strike, as it was produced in Canada. Commissioned for a full season of 20 stories, the show's grand total was now 100 episodes.

Taking command of the Atlantis base was Richard Woolsey, played by actor Robert Picardo (*Star Trek: Voyager*), whose character was a bureaucratic representative of the International Oversight Committee. The character appeared in 14 episodes. Jewel Staite was also promoted to full cast member from a semi-regular status. Amanda Tapping and Michael Shanks reprised their long-running roles.

On August 21, 2008, Sci-Fi Channel cancelled *Stargate: Atlantis*, and simultaneously greenlighted an *Atlantis* movie to wrap up the series' plot threads. Later, the movie would be sold as a DVD release. This move follows a successful formula instigated by its sister show, *Stargate SG-1*. That series' two direct-to-DVD movies *Ark of Truth* and *Continuum* were successful and the model has been set. *Atlantis'* future would consist of a DVD movie franchise, with a film produced each year.

On the very next day, MGM announced the commission of a third Stargate TV series, titled *Stargate Universe* to debut in 2009. Like its predecessor, *Stargate Universe*, is co-created and will be executive produced by Brad Wright and Robert C. Cooper. *Universe* will be about a group of explorers who discover an unmanned Ancient spaceship called Destiny. The "young and desperate" crewmembers become trappped aboard the spacecraft that has a built-in, pre-programmed mission. And it takes them to the far reaches of the universe.

Sci Fi Channel president Dave Howe told the *Hollywood Reporter*, "This is an opportunity to reinvent this franchise and make it relevant to a new generation," Howe said. "We really don't want to be more of the same. It's going to build clearly off the existing franchise but with a cast that gives it a younger vibe."

"*Stargate* isn't a series any more. It's a universe [in] which we can tell stories. It's a platform, a franchise quite literally. It's very important to MGM and that's why we're doing the movies and that's why there's a role-playing game called *Stargate Worlds*. We're investing a great deal of money into that. It's a rich ground for storytelling in gaming. Players who haven't even seen the series

before will find a continuity and richness to the mythology that doesn't seem like it's made up on the spot. It's really rooted in 10 years of storytelling."

CAST NOTES

Joe Flanigan (Maj./Col. John Sheppard): Born in Los Angeles, California. Flanigan attended the University of Colorado and then spent a year in Paris studying at the Sorbonne. He began his career as a writer for various New York magazines before moving back to Los Angeles to pursue an acting career. Flanigan had guest roles in numerous television series, including *Murphy Brown*, *Profiler*, *First Monday*, *Birds of Prey* and *CSI: Miami*, then landed his role on *Stargate Atlantis*. He lives in Vancouver, Canada, with his wife and three children.

Torri Higginson (Dr. Elizabeth Weir): Higginson was born in Burlington, Ontario, Canada. Higginson began acting in the early '90s and appeared in *Forever Knight* before landing a semi-regular role in the *TekWar* series. She had a role in *The English Patient* (1996) and guest-starred in *Psi Factor: Chronicles of the Paranormal*, *Highlander: The Raven*, *The Outer Limits* and Stephen King's *Storm of the Century*. In 2004 she took over the role of Dr. Elizabeth Weir on *Stargate SG-1*, replacing actress Jessica Steen.

Amanda Tapping (Col. Samantha Carter): See *Stargate SG-1* cast notes.

Rachel Luttrell (Teyla): Luttrell was born in Tanzania. She was raised in Canada and studied ballet at the prestigious Russian Academy Ballet School. Her professional stage debut began with the Toronto premiere production of *Miss Saigon*. She moved into acting and played Veronica Beck in the CBC series *Street Legal* (1987) and later appeared in guest roles on *ER*, *Charmed*, *Forever Knight* and other television series.

Paul McGillion (Dr. Carson Beckett): McGillion was born in Paisley, Scotland. He moved to Canada and began acting in 1990. He appeared on stage and in many series and movies including *Sliders*, *Viper*, *The X-Files*, *Mercy Point*, *First Wave*, *Smallville* and *The Twilight Zone*.

David Hewlett (Dr. Rodney McKay): Born in Redhill, England, and raised in Canada, Hewlett began acting in the mid '80s. He starred in the cult thriller *Pin* (1988) and became a regular on the series *Kung Fu: The Legend Continues* and *Traders* and starred in the movie *Cube* (1997). He landed the recurring role of Dr. Rodney McKay on

Stargate SG-1 and continued with the role when the character transferred to *Stargate Atlantis*. Hewlett is a self-confessed computer nerd.

Rainbow Sun Francks (Lt. Aiden Ford): Francks was born in Toronto, Canada. He is the son of actor-musician Don Francks and is part Cree. For a brief time, he was an on-air personality on MuchMusic, a Canadian music video channel. He pursued acting and appeared in small roles in movies before being cast in *Stargate Atlantis*. Francks left the show after year two and has since been seen in *This Space for Rent* (2006) and *Aliens vs. Predator: Survival of the Fittest* (2007).

Jason Momoa (Ronan Dex): Momoa was born in Honolulu, Hawaii. His family moved to Iowa, where he was raised. In 1998, he returned to Hawaii, where he was discovered by international designer Takeo and launched his modeling career. In 1999 he was named Hawaii's Model of the Year and hosted the Miss Teen Hawaii contest. Momoa is best known for his role as Jason Ioane (1999–2001) on *Baywatch*. He appeared in *Johnson Family Vacation* (2004) and *North Shore* (2004) before joining the cast of *Stargate Atlantis* in its second year.

Jewel Staite (Dr. Jennifer Keller): See the Cast Notes for *Firefly*.

Stargate SG-1
(1997–2007)

A secret U.S. Air Force military team, designated SG-1, travel the Milky Way galaxy via an interstellar network of ancient alien devices known as "Stargates." As they explore other planets, they meet friends and foes.

Cast: Richard Dean Anderson (Col./Brig. General Jack O'Neill) *Year 1–8*, Amanda Tapping (Capt./Maj./Lt. Col. Samantha Carter), Christopher Judge (Teal'c), Michael Shanks (Dr. Daniel Jackson) *Year 1–5, 7–10*, Don S. Davis (General George Hammond) *Year 1–7*, Corin Nemec (Jonas Quinn) *Year 6*, Ben Browder (Col. Cameron Mitchell) *Year 9–10*, Beau Bridges (General Hank Landry) *Year 9–10*, Claudia Black (Vala) *Year 10*

Developed for Television by: Brad Wright, Jonathan Glassner; **Executive Producers:** Brad Wright *Year 1–6, 8–10*, Jonathan Glassner *Year 1–3*, Richard Dean Anderson *Year 1–8*, Michael Greenburg *Year 1–8*, Robert C. Cooper *Year 5–10*, Joseph Mallozzi *Year 9–10*, Paul Mullie *Year 9–10*, N. John Smith *Year 7–10*; **Co-Executive Producers:** Robert C. Cooper *Year 5*, N. John Smith *Year 6*, Joseph Mallozzi *Year 6–8*, Paul Mullie *Year 6–8*, Damian Kindler *Year 9*; **Producers:** N. John Smith *Year 1–6*, Ron French *Year 1*, Joseph Mallozzi, Paul Mullie *Year 4*, Andy Mikita *Year 5–7, 10*, Damian Kindler *Year 6*, Peter DeLuise *Year 7*, John G. Lenic *Year 8–10*; **Supervising Producers:** Jeff F. King *Year 1*, Joseph Mallozzi, Paul Mullie *Year 5*, Damian Kindler *Year 7–8*, Peter DeLuise *Year 8–9*; **Co-Producers:** Robert C. Cooper *Year 1–4*, Peter DeLuise *Year 1–6*, Martin Wood *Year 6*, Andy Mikita *Year 8–9*; **Associate Producers:** Michael Elliot (uncredited), Jennifer Johnson *Year 8–10*; **Consulting Producer:** Brad Wright *Year 7*; **Creative Consultant:** Damian Kindler *Year 10*; **Writers included:** Robert C. Cooper, Brad Wright, Tor Alexander Valenza, Peter DeLuise, Joseph Mallozzi, Paul Mullie, Damian Kindler, James Tichenor, Christopher Judge; **Directors included:** Mario Azzopardi, Martin Wood, Peter DeLuise, William Gereghty, Andy Mikita, Brad Turner, Peter Woeste, David Warry-Smith, Amanda Tapping, Michael Shanks; **Directors of Photography:** Peter F. Woeste, James Alfred Menard; **Production Designers:** Richard Hudolin, Bridget McGuire; **Visual Special Effects:** Atmosphere Visual Effects, Gajdecki Visual Effects, Image Engine Design, Northwest Imaging & FX, Pinnacle Post, Rainmaker Digital Pictures, Spin West FX, Smoke and Mirrors, Solstice Imaging, XFX, Inc.; **Guest Stars included:** Dean Stockwell, John DeLancie, Alex Zahara, Roger R. Cross, Terry David Mulligan, Jay Brazeau, Brent Stait, Katie Stuart, Christina Cox, Gary Jones (as Sgt. Walter Harriman), Teryl Rothery (as Dr. Janet Fraiser), Carmen Argenziano (as General Jacob Carter/Selmak), Peter Williams (as Apophis), Tony Amendola (as Master Bra'tac), Jay Avocone (as Maj. Charles Kawalsky), Colin Cunningham (as Maj. Paul Davis), Ronny Cox (as Senator/Vice-President Kinsey), William Devane (as President Hayes), Tom McBeath (as Col. Maybourne), JR Bourne (as Martouf), Dan Shea (as Sgt. Siler), Alisen Down (as Dr. Brightman), Jolene Blalock (as Ishta), Garry Chalk (as Col. Chekov), Claudia Black (as Vala), Lexa Doig (as Dr. Carolyn Lam), Louis Gossett Jr. (as Gerak)

Showtime Networks/Sci-Fi Channel/MGM Television/Double Secret Productions/Gekko Film Corp./Kawoosh Productions/Sony Pictures Television; 1997–2007; 60 minutes; 214 episodes; DVD status: Complete series

When *Apollo 11* commander Neil Armstrong stepped from the Lunar Module on July 20, 1969, and onto the surface of the Moon, he said, "That's one small step for man, one giant leap for mankind." The quotation also applies to MGM's *Stargate* franchise, where travelers merely stepped forward through a portal and were instantly transported to other worlds. This alien teleportation device, which tapped into a network of cryptic hieroglyphic "gate addresses," thrust our heroes into many science fiction adventures.

The original *Stargate* feature film (released in 1994) from filmmakers Roland Emmerich and Dean Devlin starred Kurt Russell and James Spader. The $55 million dollar epic was about a military team who traveled to another world using a giant ring-shaped alien device discovered in 1928, buried in the sands of Egypt. After decades of analysis and study, maverick archaeologist Daniel Jackson was recruited into the secret project and helped decipher the puzzling hieroglyphics embedded into the large metal rings' surface. He recognized the symbols as constellations, that the series of symbols denoted dialing coordinates and that the ring served as a "gateway to the stars." It was possible to activate the rings' capabilities by choosing a series of Egyptian symbols in sequence, resulting in a wormhole with an event horizon (a rush of blinding light and water, stretching outward from the ring's center, settling into a bright, blue light of flat, shimmering water). Stepping through this translucent wall of water, the travelers were instantly transported to another world, where another ring received them.

In the film, Air Force Col. Jack O'Neil, as played by Russell, brought with him a team of crack military soldiers and archaeologist Jackson, played by James Spader, to the planet Abydos. They arrived inside a large Egyptian pyramid in a vast desert-like world. There, they discovered a band of villagers who served as slaves for an Egyptian god named Ra, a tall and charismatic leader with glowing eyes. Ra discovered that O'Neil had brought a hydrogen bomb, which was to be used to destroy the receiving gate if a threat to Earth was discovered. Angered, Ra condemned the Earth visitors to death but the rebellion of the villagers thwarted his plans. O'Neil transported the primed bomb up to Ra's orbiting spaceship, destroying it. O'Neil and his team returned to Earth but Daniel Jackson remained behind, to live and study among the villagers. (He had also fallen in love with one of them, a female named Shau'ri.)

Despite some unflattering reviews, the film grossed, according to Box Office Mojo, $196 million worldwide.

Two individuals were so taken by the movie that they had the same idea: "This would make a great TV series!" When writer-producer Brad Wright, who was at the time working on the new *Outer Limits* TV series in Vancouver, Canada, had lunch with MGM-TV vice-president Hank Cohen in Los Angeles, he spoke his mind. "I suggested to Hank that their *Stargate* movie was a natural series, simply because there were 39 symbols on the Gate, and there was no reason it should only go to one planet," recalls Wright.

About the same time, another *Outer Limits* writer-producer, Jonathan Glassner, had a conversation with MGM-TV president John Symes about *Stargate*. "Brad and I had similar ideas about the project before speaking to each other," acknowledges Glassner. "For example, we both noted that the gate had so many symbols on it, which could be dialed in so many combinations, why assume it only went to one place? That pointed to the huge episodic potential of endless places and peoples to explore through the Gate. That is what I pitched to John."

"It's funny, but it was MGM who suggested we become partners to create the series!" chuckles Wright.

Wright and Glassner immediately saw an SF series where the geographical landscape was the entire galaxy. It was an action-adventure format set in the present day with contemporary military characters. It was also an opportunity to create a lot of eye-candy special effects and SF hardware, with the feature film providing a built-in recognition factor with viewers. In terms of merchandising and marketing, the Stargate iconography was all there: a gigantic metal ring with strange hieroglyphics embedded into it, the Egyptian motifs and backdrop plus strange alien weapons and spaceships. It would also be easy to extend into conventions, DVDs, action figures, soundtracks, video games, and novelizations.

Recognizing their shared interest in the property, Glassner and Wright compared notes. They already had a history of working well together on *Outer Limits.* "We were very happy to jump into the project together," recalls Glassner. "I can remember many afternoons pacing around on the MGM campus and on *Outer Limits* sets saying things like, 'But what keeps the aliens from coming through to Earth whenever they want, now that we unburied the gate?'

"'I know! Let's add some sort of shield that closes right at the event horizon...' and thus the Iris was born. Or 'What exactly was the alien character that enslaved Abydos?' Which launched us into the creation of the Goa'uld. And so on. We really did it all together."

Adapting *Stargate* for television meant that certain characters, props, costumes and settings seen in the film could be used in the series. The actual Stargate ring and the main set, the Gate Room (the control room, overlooking the location where teams would step through the Stargate ring and to another galaxy), were rebuilt and reconceived for the series by production designer Richard Hudolin. Everything else had to be invented from scratch.

The producers decided to cast the series as a continuation of the events of the feature. Prior knowledge of the feature was required to understand "Children of the Gods," the series' two-hour pilot introduction.

Fortunately, MGM-TV already had considerable investment and infrastructure set up in Vancouver, Canada, where their TV series *The Outer Limits* and *Poltergeist: The Legacy* were being filmed. Wright and Glassner were still working as writers and producers on *The Outer Limits,* then in its second year.

On the suggestion of MGM-TV president John Symes, actor Richard Dean Anderson was courted to play Col. Jack O'Neill. Anderson was a household name to millions via *MacGyver,* his popular action-adventure ABC-TV series (1985–1992). Wright and Glassner agreed that Anderson was an excellent choice. "John [Symes] made the call," recalls Glassner. "Richard was hesitant at first because he had a bad experience on the show he had

just done [UPN's ill-fated 1995 series *Legend*]. So he insisted on meeting us and discussing how we intended to proceed with the character and to make sure he could spend years working closely with us. Then he wanted to read the pilot script before committing."

Once Anderson's name was on the dotted line, it was on to casting of the rest of the leads. "Our casting directors read people in Los Angeles, New York, Toronto and Vancouver," says Glassner. "They sent the best choices to Brad and me on videotape. We narrowed it down further. Then the studio and network narrowed our choices down further. And in some cases we narrowed the choices down to zero and the casting people had to start from scratch.

"We had narrowed [the role of] Daniel Jackson down to two people — Michael Shanks and another actor. Clearly we made the right choice on that one. I think Michael is a star."

In the role of a female astrophysicist, Glassner says, "We wanted a great actress first and foremost, an actress who read as very intelligent, and could pull off the astrophysics tech-talk in a way that sounded like she knew what she was talking about — a physical presence that was believable as an Air Force pilot and tough soldier, and a beautiful woman. That combo is *very* hard to find!"

When Canadian actress Amanda Tapping appeared, the producers knew they found their Captain Sam Carter. But apparently the studio felt otherwise. "We had to cajole, argue and demand that they cast her," says Glassner. "They finally gave in, thank God. I can't imagine anyone doing better in that role than Amanda."

Casting the role of alien Teal'c, who joins the team in the ongoing battle against the Goa'uld enemies, was the most difficult. "We had asked the casting people to try to find a unique-looking actor — one who is extremely physically fit and imposing — maybe a mix of ethnicities," remembers Glassner. "And first and foremost, he had to be a good actor. You can't believe the wild array of people we saw — and none of them did it for us.

"We had a lot of dreadlocked [hair] people, both African-American and Caucasian. We had a lot of very tall people. We had some guys who were so strange-looking, we weren't sure if they had some sort of deformity. There were a lot of Native Americans. And there were a lot of body builders who could not act at all.

"We were getting closer and closer to the deadline and were actually starting to think we would have to reconceive the part. Then, right before our final screen tests, one of the casting directors found Christopher Judge."

Judge was flown to Los Angeles on the very next day for a final round of auditions in front of studio and network executives. "Rick was there to read with all the actors so we could see how the chemistry worked," says Glassner. "When Chris walked in and we saw him in person for the first time, I remember thinking, 'Wow, what a presence!' and bending over to Brad and whispering, 'Please, God, let him be able to act.' And, of course he did great and the rest is history."

Canadian actor Don S. Davis rounded out the cast as General Hammond, the man in charge of Stargate Command. The two-hour *Stargate* pilot, "Children of the Gods," was filmed in February 1997 and premiered on Showtime Cable in July of that year.

Picking up the story from the conclusion of the feature film, the pilot found Col. Jack O'Neill now retired. The Gate was mothballed and remained unused. One day alien Egyptian soldiers suddenly stepped through the Gate, killed some Earth soldiers, and kidnapped a female sergeant. The Stargate program was reactivated by General George Hammond, who called the retired Col. O'Neill back into duty. O'Neill revealed that Daniel Jackson was still on Abydos with its villagers. O'Neill and his team had reported their hydrogen bomb was used to defeat Ra, but they omitted from their report the fact that the villagers were still alive and that Jackson was among them, so that they could live in peace.

O'Neill's mission was to retrieve Jackson and identify the aliens that attacked them. Captain Samantha Carter, an astrophysicist and the best technical expert on the Stargate, accompanied O'Neill to Abydos. Once there, Jackson revealed he had discovered a "cartouche," a map room revealing thousands of hieroglyphics interpreted as "Gate addresses" that could be used to explore other planets in the galaxy. Suddenly, another attack by the mysterious Egyptian soldiers was mounted on Abydos, and Jackson's wife Sha're and a young boy named Skaara were kidnapped. As O'Neill and the SG-1 team dialed an address to a world called Chulak, where they believed the enemy aliens originated, General Hammond was authorized by the president of the United States to assemble nine Stargate teams on Earth and use the Gate addresses library to assess all future, potential threats to Earth.

On Chulak, the SG-1 team was ambushed and imprisoned in a dungeon by the alien soldiers. The enemy Apophis, named for the Egyptian serpent god, was a Goa'uld. The Goa'uld were a parasitic alien species posing as "gods." They were snake-like creatures that used human hosts to do their megalomaniacal bidding. They had the ability, when a human host expired, to be transferred into another body in order to continue their existences. Jackson was shocked when he realized that his wife Sha're had become Apophis' Goa'uld queen. Her eyes glowed, which indicated she had a Goa'uld inside of her.

Apophis commanded that the SG-1 team members to be killed. As the Jaffa guards were about to comply, O'Neill implored the lead guard, Teal'c, not to follow that order. After a moment's hesitation, Teal'c used his staff weapon and killed his fellow guards and helped the prisoners to escape.

At the Gate, O'Neill and his team helplessly watched as Apophis took their friends Sha're and Skaara, who had become human hosts of the snake-like Goa'uld, through the Stargate. With SG-2's help, all the prisoners and the SG-1 team successfully returned to Earth and Teal'c joined the SG-1 team. Having failed to rescue their friends from the clutches of Apophis, the SG-1 team was more determined than ever to use the Stargate for exploration of the galaxy and the defense of the Earth.

"One of the biggest challenges of science fiction storytelling is the sophistication of the audience," says Brad Wright. "As wonderful as the *Enterprise* is as a means of transporting the characters and the audience from adventure to adventure, Stargate is capable of doing that for the audience in the here and now. It's people from our world in the 20th-21st century, simply stepping into the gate and embarking on an adventure to another world. When we saw the *Stargate* film, we thought, 'What a great device! Every episode we could step through the Stargate and to another world!' Which we began to do. But I swear, had we continued that, we never would have lasted as long as we did. We had to create stories from within the mythology, meaning it wasn't all the transplanted culture of the Romans, or whatever had come from our history, which is how we had set it up in the series." The producers had to go beyond what was established and break new ground. Vancouver, Canada, had forest locations needed to double as alien planets. Every time the SG-1 team stepped through the Gate, on the other side was either a special effects–generated alien landscape or a location-based environment. "The

The cast of *Stargate SG-1* in a sixth season photo: Corin Nemec, Amanda Tapping, Richard Dean Anderson and Christopher Judge (© USA Networks/Sci-Fi Channel).

The cast of *Stargate SG-1*: from left, Beau Bridges, Amanda Tapping, Christopher Judge (front), Michael Shanks, Claudia Black and Ben Browder (©MGM Television, Inc., and Sci-Fi Channel).

only negative of shooting there that I can think of is the weather," notes Glassner. "It changed and rained a lot." As a trivia note, the stock shots of the entrance at the Cheyenne Mountains, where the secret Stargate Command was located, actually show the entrance of the NORAD (North American Aerospace Defense Command) facility. "We had the full cooperation and approval of the U.S. Air Force, they allowed us unprecedented access to shoot there," explains Glassner. "Of course, classified areas were off limits."

The producers also realized the financial burdens of their far-reaching and "big scope" visions. "Every time we stepped through the Stargate, it was quite expensive," continues Wright. Fun fact: It cost $5,000 to create the "wormhole effect" as the Stargate is activated. "We had to find other ways of doing that. That first season was a tough one creatively. To be honest, I'm not 100 percent sure how successful we were creatively. We were very encumbered by budget. Jonathan and I were

very torn because we were also producing *The Outer Limits* and our energies were [exceeded] by the amount of work we had to do. Fortunately, we did find an audience, and had Richard Dean Anderson at the center of our show. And made enough solid episodes to convince our audience and the network that they should keep tuning in. We've grown creatively ever since."

To start with, Wright and Glassner expanded on the feature's villain, Ra, a character inspired by Egyptian mythology. Ra was really one of the parasitic "Goa'ulds." Their race used technology to present themselves as gods and enslaved the inhabitants of many worlds. SG-1's primary villain in the early years was the Goa'uld god Apophis (Peter Williams), who had kidnapped Daniel's wife, Sha're.

SG-1 team member Teal'c would later meet a splinter group of Goa'ulds called the Tok'ra, who covertly assembled to fight against the leaders of the Goa'uld (the System Lords). The Tok'ra battled the System Lords, with SG-1's help, in several adventures.

Other deadly adversaries included the Replicators. These were self-replicating metal machines that were the insidious opponents of a friendly space-faring species, the Asgard.

The Asgard were effectively "the gray aliens" often depicted in UFO-ology lore, and their leader was Thor. They were a highly intelligent and benevolent race who gave SGC the technology needed to construct hyperspace-capable starships such as the *Odyssey* and the *Daedalus* (later used in *Stargate: Atlantis*). This allowed SGC teams to venture forth into other worlds without being dependent on the Stargate rings alone.

By the fifth year, a new enemy was introduced: Anubis. He was a Goa'uld with great powers and had gained partial ascendance. (The Ancients survived extinction by elevating themselves into a higher plane of existence, and Anubis attempted to attain the power and technology but he failed.) His goal was to destroy life in the galaxy using a powerful superweapon. In the sixth year it appeared that Daniel Jackson had died when in fact he had ascended and still lingered as a ghostly figure, only heard and seen by Jack O'Neill. When Daniel attempted to interfere in mortal affairs, the other Ascendents booted him back to the mortal plane, and he rejoined SG-1.

The eighth year's villain was yet another Goa'uld, Ba'al. When he attempted to battle with the other System Lords, the metal Replicators invaded the galaxy and took on the System Lords themselves.

After three arduous seasons of producing, writing and directing *Stargate SG-1* (and producing *The Outer Limits* simultaneously during the first two of those years), Jonathan Glassner left *SG-1* at the end of the third year. It wasn't that he didn't like the job. He enjoyed it immensely. It was simply because he and his wife were homesick for family and friends in California.

Robert C. Cooper, who joined the series as its co-producer in the first year, was promoted in year five to co-executive producer. Later in that same year, he moved up again, to executive producer, writing and directing many scripts and taking the reins of the series as the showrunner for the remainder of its run beginning in the seventh year. That was when Brad Wright stepped back for a one-season sabbatical as consulting producer.

Creatively, the *Stargate* "family" was actually a very small group of people taking on different titles on the organizational chart as the years rolled by. The series' regular directors were producers Martin Wood and Andy Mikita, and actor Peter DeLuise. The team of Paul Mullie and Joseph Mallozzi rapidly worked their way up the ranks from writing duo to producers, supervising producers, co-executive producers and as executive producers in the final two years.

The foundation of the series' creative stability and continuity was this very small, tight-knit "creative family." A good bet why *Stargate* lived a long life was because outside producers didn't come in with their own ideas and declare, "Okay, this season, we're going to take the plot into *this* direction!" bouncing the show creatively on eerie tangents. When the show did evolve, it was because of those who were there from the beginning.

At the end of year five, Michael Shanks departed, despondent because he didn't feel his character was well used. He also yearned for other acting challenges.

"Frankly, Daniel's departure from the show could easily have been permanent," says Wright. "I told Michael when he left that we'd leave the door open for him to return, and when we had stories that fit, we contacted him."

These occasional appearances were made possible because of Daniel Jackson's aforementioned state of "ascendency." His replacement for the sixth year was actor Corin Nemec, as Jonas Quinn, a scientist from another world who became an SG-1 member. "The truth is, Jackson's departure was an interesting turn for the series, and so was his return," says Wright. It was in the seventh year premiere, "Fallen," that Jackson came back as a human, but with amnesia. Jackson's personal journey back to his old self was explored.

To accommodate Richard Dean Anderson's desire for a reduced schedule in order to spend more time with his family in the eighth year, Brad Wright bumped O'Neill up to brigadier general and put him in charge of the Stargate Command facility as Don Davis stepped back.

"We put it off as long as possible because I honestly believed that each season after six was potentially our last," says Wright. "The most difficult seasons in terms of dealing with Rick's schedule fell on Robert [Cooper], since he was the showrunner in seven and eight. Most of the problems were logistical. We often had to shoot scenes of three or four different episodes in the span of a few days, which meant scripts, sets and casts had to be ready to go."

Therefore, O'Neill stayed behind as the SG-1 team went on missions. In the ninth year, Jack O'Neill was promoted to major general and became head of the Department of Homeworld Security.

As Brad Wright explains, a series of three consecutive episodes ("Redemption," "Threads" and "Moebius," where the Replicators and the Goa'ulds were defeated) could each have been series finales. "So Rob [Cooper] said, 'I'm done ending this show. I'm going to start something new!'

At the start of the ninth year, there was a significant reboot in characters and plotting in an effort to keep the series fresh and retain viewership. "'Avalon' is essentially a new series pilot," says Wright. "We even toyed with the idea of rebranding the series, and calling it *Stargate Command*. I think Robert did an amazing job creating a new storyline."

In a bit of inspired casting, Ben Browder and Claudia Black, the lead actors from Sci-Fi's *Farscape*, joined the team. Browder became the new SG-1 leader Col. Cameron Mitchell, and Black played Vala Maldoran, a sexy space pirate who was introduced in the previous season and had a very "intertwined" relationship with Daniel Jackson. Eventually, she would join the SG-1 team as an official member.

Beau Bridges joined as General Hank Landry, and he assumed command of the SGC upon O'Neill's departure. O'Neill, however, did appear occasionally in both year nine and 10. "The network, Robert and I all thought that Ben was a natural fit for the show," says Wright. "That was easy. But we were genuinely surprised and delighted that we were able to land Beau Bridges for the role of Landry. I'm so proud we can say Beau Bridges was on our show. He adds a whole level of class to the series. Seriously, we still exclaim, 'Hey, we've got Beau Bridges in our show!' when we watch him perform in dailies and cuts."

Another difficult task was refreshing the nature of the villains. The producers devised a new and insidious race known as the Ori (pronounced "or-eye"), "ascended" beings who used technology to manipulate other worlds into worshipping them as gods. Their heralds were the Priors, humans who were "enhanced" to serve the Ori with supernatural powers. To fend off the Ori and their Prior, SG-1 followed clues to find Merlin, an "ascended" Ancient working on a powerful weapon against the Ori.

In the tenth year, Vala was transported to the Oris' galaxy and became pregnant with a child, Adria, who became an Ori leader. Over that year, SG-1 searched desperately for the Ori weapon, dealt with Ba'al clones and had to stop Daniel Jackson when he allowed himself to be transformed into a Prior.

"I give Robert Cooper all the praise and credit for the changeover. I was very focused on *Atlantis* at the time," says Wright. "We needed to reinvigorate the series. We had to come up with a new enemy. Because Amanda [Tapping] was having a baby, we needed another guest female lead for six episodes, so enter Claudia Black. Seasons nine and ten are very much a new beginning. The ratings absolutely held. Richard Dean Anderson leaving hurt a little bit but he came back and helped us sometimes. He didn't expect to be with the show for his entire life!"

On April 2006, a press conference was held on the *Stargate SG-1* soundstages, inside the Bridge Studios, in Burnaby, British Columbia, on the occasion of "200," the series' 200th episode. Cast and crew marked the epoch with champagne and cake.

At the event, Anderson remarked, "The only demand I make of a set and a crew and the people I work with is that they have a sense of humor. Life's too short. Nobody's going to live or die by what we do. We're making entertainment for people and if the process of making that isn't fun for us, then it's kind of not worth it. Make sure the work gets done, that we're putting out a quality product but, God, have fun!"

Beau Bridges noted, "Brad and Robert really invite collaboration. Communication is so important and if you have that from the top, that's really important. It's an open door from Brad and Robert to all of us and that's exciting to us as performers."

At the same event, executive producer Cooper remarked, "We know we've had an impact on business here in B.C., with a lot of money brought into the local community and we're very proud of that. We think of *Stargate* as a Canadian show that hires some American actors. We employ a lot of Canadians locally. The visual effects are done here. Not a lot of people in this country recognize that."

Jeannie Bradley, executive vice-president of Sony Pictures Television's Current Programming, said in her speech at the event, "As I was passing through immigration last night at the airport, they asked me, 'What are you here for?' I said,

'On business. I'm going to visit the set of *Stargate*.' The reply was, 'Oh, are you going to cut the cake?' So believe me, all of Vancouver knows. This is such a big deal!"

On August 21, 2006, Sci-Fi Channel announced that the series was canceled and, at the same time, confirmed renewal of *Atlantis* for a fourth year. Several days prior to the public announcement of *Stargate*'s cancellation, key cast members were given the news on the eve of the U.S. broadcast of "200," during a cast-crew party at a lavish Vancouver hotel. Wright knew the show had been axed after receiving a private phone call a week earlier. He found it very difficult to rail against the network because, while they were canceling *SG-1*, they *were* renewing *Atlantis*. The news of cancellation leaking to the press as the cast and crew prepared to celebrate their 200th episode was controversial. Recalls Wright, "I said, 'Your timing is not very good! Next week we have a party celebrating our 200th episode and you've pretty much rained on that parade.' We decided to keep a low key about the subject, but I didn't want to be duplicitous to the crew. As we got closer to the date of the party, we started telling people, privately, just one on one with the crew members. We were celebrating, but we'd grab each actor and pull them aside. Most of our key players and cast knew about it just prior to the party."

The timing of MGM-TV's cancellation of the series was practical, giving the producers lead time to design the final stories with cancellation in mind. The series was still in production and the season finale hadn't yet been filmed. "They didn't want the season to end with a cliffhanger," says Wright.

The reaction from various parties was wide-ranging. "For the cast, they've spent 10 years of their lives so they're going to have very mixed feelings," Wright says. "It was a very good job. Now they have the opportunity to play other roles. With Amanda, she ended up coming over to *Atlantis* and continued to play Carter."

Jonathan Glassner remarks, "It was a mistake for Sci-Fi to cancel it. It was still getting very good ratings—in fact, better than many of their other shows. I think the show was still strong, so did the critics, and the audience still wanted it as shown by the ratings. As long as those two things are true, a show should continue. If either one stops being true, then it's time to end it."

Glassner remains very proud of the series. However, there were some creative decisions he regrets. "Ben Browder is a very good actor," he says.

"But I would not have cast him, simply because he looks way too much like Michael Shanks. I would have promoted Carter to command of SG-1 and brought in a new junior character to fill out the team. But that's just me."

Otherwise, Glassner says he's pleased with the ninth and tenth season revamping and plotting. "They were right in finally wiping out the Goa'uld after all those years, but I'm not sure that the Ori are as interesting an adversary," he says. "They are using the exact same religious 'We are your gods' method of controlling their followers by using technology. But they don't have the interesting human/ethical aspects of a parasitic relationship with human hosts or the enslavery of Jaffa as incubators and warriors."

Looking back at 10 years of stories, Wright sums up his views of the show's longevity and success. "The truth is, our show is a success, but it's not a runaway hit. It took seven years to get on the cover of *TV Guide*. I think we're like a slow burning candle. Never too bright to burn out too quickly. I'd like to think part of the reason we've been around as long as we have is the fact that we've managed to keep much of the same creative team together for so long. Continuity is important in science fiction, and Rob and I have been around from the beginning. [Writer-producers Mullie and Mallozzi] have been around since season four, which is quite a long time too. The great thing about making so many years of *Stargate* is that it'll be around for years to come.

Exciting challenges still remain ahead for Wright and Cooper. A third *Stargate* series, tentatively titled *Stargate Universe*, has been in development. If that proceeds, Wright and Cooper will continue to play in the universe for quite some time to come.

"We like to tell stories and when you create a different palette it's like creating another painting with different colors and a new subject," explains Wright. "It's the same brand as *Stargate*, yes, but it's a new direction for the show. Robert and I are very excited about it."

The fact that *SG-1* reached 10 years of continuous production is a milestone for science fiction television. It is the longest-running SF-TV series in North America and is now a record entry in the Guinness Book of World Records. The UK's *Doctor Who* holds the international record for a single title running for 30 years (but not with the same cast).

Stargate, as a title, has been very good to MGM. There has been merchandise, DVDs (more than

$30 million in sales), conventions, U.S. and German theme park rides, broadcasting in over 120 countries (about 10 million viewers each week), and a Massively Multi-Player Online Role-Playing Game titled *Stargate Worlds*.

MGM continued to have confidence in the future life of the title and, in January 2007, announced the production of two *Stargate* films for exclusive distribution via DVDs to be released in 2008. "MGM would like to do at least two every year [depending] on how well these do," notes Wright. "We have every hope and faith these will do well. Robert and I are having a lot of fun doing these movies."

The DVD movies came about because the storylines for the ninth and tenth year, dealing with the fearsome Ori, needed to be wrapped up. "Robert didn't feel he could squeeze it in, the stories that he was spinning, into the end of the season," explains Wright.

The first DVD movie *The Ark of Truth*, which started production on April 15, 2007, written and directed by Robert C. Cooper, tied up the Ori loose ends. An MGM press release describes the storyline:

> As SG-1 searches for an Ancient artifact which they hope can defeat the armies of the Ori, they learn more Ori ships are about to be sent through the supergate to launch a final assault on Earth. Daniel discovers that the artifact, the Ark of Truth, may be in the Ori home galaxy, and SG-1 embarks aboard the *Odyssey* to find it, and pre-empt the attack. The IOA [International Oversight Advisory] has a plan of their own and SG-1 ends up in a distant galaxy fighting two powerful enemies.

"It's the climax of the Ori story arc. It should be very satisfying for regular viewers of *SG-1*," says Wright.

The second DVD movie, *Continuum*, which began shooting on May 22, 2007, written by Wright and directed by Martin Wood, was a stand-alone adventure that featured Richard Dean Anderson as Maj. General Jack O'Neill. The SG-1 team stood witness to the execution of the Goa'uld Ba'al when suddenly, inexplicably, Teal'c and Vala disappeared. The team returned to Earth and found it radically changed. The Stargate program was wiped from the timeline. When a fleet of Goa'uld starships approached Earth, it was headed by Ba'al, with Teal'c and Vala by his side. The SG-1 team must prevent Earth from being enslaved by the Goa'uld.

"You don't necessarily have to have the whole ton of backstory information about *Stargate* to enjoy [*Continuum*]," explains Wright. "It's a story that stands alone and the characters go through a journey that could have happened at any time in the past several years or some time in the future. We wanted to explore the potential of, 'Okay, there's another big two-hour *SG-1* story that appears as a DVD.'"

The U.S. Navy agreed to incorporate one of their nuclear submarines into a *Stargate* storyline. During the last week of March 2007, MGM sent the *Stargate* team up to the Arctic, approximately 200 miles north of Prudhoe Bay, Alaska, to the U.S. Navy's Applied Physics Laboratory Ice Station. There, director Martin Wood and his team filmed the exterior of a submarine, USS *Alexandria* (SSN-757), pushing through the ice. They were also allowed to film inside the submarine. The U.S. Air Force (who were consulted on every episode of the series) granted the producers permission to shoot footage of four F-15 fighter jets in flight.

Wright was excited about shooting this amazing footage. "It's never been done to the extent we did it just now," he says. "The infrastructure and resources they were able to provide, with an ice camp that allowed us to put up a crew and go up on the ice with helicopters and submarines bursting through the ice ... it's gold. You can't do a visual effect that's going to match the real thing. We shot in the bridge, the wardroom, and corridors. We also put cameras underneath the ice and saw the submarine as it was submerging. This is millions of dollars of production value at our fingertips. We're very grateful to the Navy. We're also very happy that the film turned out as good as it did."

Can there be too much of a good thing? Can the *Stargate* franchise continue beyond 10 years? Wright explains why the *SG-1* sets won't be torn down any time soon:

"We still have soundstages full of sets. We can make a movie that has a million dollar set that is still up. We have all this infrastructure going. We can't do the same thing if we just shut down and decided to do this again five years from now. That would make it prohibitively expensive for the stories that we want to tell. A *Stargate* feature film is very much a possibility, someday. It's still something I hope to do."

Will the gigantic *Stargate* ring prop ever be donated to the famed Smithsonian Institution in Washington, D.C.? "Actually, they've already asked!" Wright laughs. His answer to them was obvious: "We're still using it!"

Cast Notes

Richard Dean Anderson (Col./Brig. General Jack O'Neill): Anderson was born in Minneapolis, Minnesota. He started his acting career appearing on *General Hospital* from 1976 to 1981. He also starred in the television series *Seven Brides for Seven Brothers* (1982–83). Anderson came to fame with the hit television series *MacGyver* which lasted from 1985 to 1992. In 1995 he starred in *Legend*, a comic series of only 12 episodes.

Amanda Tapping (Capt./Maj./Lt. Col. Samantha Carter): Tapping was born in Rochford, Essex, England. She moved to Canada at age three. She studied acting at the University of Windsor in Ontario, played roles on stage, appeared in several television commercials and landed a variety of roles in television and film productions such as *The Outer Limits* and *The X-Files*. She also formed a comedy troupe, The Random Acts, in Toronto in the early '90s. She has also been seen in several movies made in Canada, including *The Void* (2001), and the television mini-series *The Legend of Earthsea* (2006). After several guest appearances on *Stargate Atlantis* she joined the show as a regular, acting in 14 of 20 episodes in its fourth year. She also produced and starred in the science fiction series *Sanctuary*.

Christopher Judge (Teal'c): Born in Los Angeles, California, he attended the University of Oregon on a football scholarship and was an all–Pacific Ten conference player. One of his first roles was in a 1990 episode of *MacGyver*. Judge has done voice acting for animated series and video games, including *X-Men: Evolution* (as Magneto). He wrote several episodes of *Stargate SG-1*.

Michael Shanks (Dr. Daniel Jackson): Shanks was born in Vancouver, Canada. After graduating from the University of British Columbia in 1994, he played in several stage productions, serving a two year apprenticeship with the prestigious Stratford Festival in Ontario. He made guest appearances on the TV series *Highlander, University Hospital,* and *The Outer Limits* and played in the TV movie *A Family Divided* (1995). Post-*Stargate*, he has been seen in episodes of *Andromeda, CSI: Miami* and *24*. He is married to Lexa Doig (*Andromeda*), who played a recurring role in the final two seasons of *SG-1*.

Don S. Davis (General George Hammond): Born in Missouri, he began working in the film industry in the 1980s while teaching at the University of British Columbia. He was a stunt double in *MacGyver*, appeared in the movie *Look Who's Talking* (1989) and joined the cast of the series *Twin Peaks*. There were also roles in the movies *Hook* (1991), *A League of Their Own* (1992) and *Needful Things* (1993) and guest appearances on *The X-Files, The Outer Limits* and *Poltergeist: The Legacy*. Since leaving *SG-1* Davis has been seen in *NCIS* and *The West Wing*. He died of a massive heart attack on June 29, 2008, in Vancouver, Canada. His final performance as Hammond was in *Stargate: Continuum* (2008).

Corin Nemec (Jonas Quinn): A Little Rock, Arkansas, native, he began acting in the early 1980s and appeared in the TV movie *I Know My First Name is Steven* (1989) before being cast as the lead character in the series *Parker Lewis Can't Lose* (1990). He appeared in *The Stand* (1994) and *Operation Dumbo Drop* (1995) and guest starred in *Smallville*. He acted for one season on *SG-1* and wrote the seventh season episode "Fallout." More recent acting jobs include the movie *Three Moons Over Milford* (2006) and TV's *Navy NCIS*.

Ben Browder (Col. Cameron Mitchell): Born in Memphis, Tennessee, Browder played minor feature film and television roles before accepting a lead role on the TV series *Farscape*. He appeared in the 2004 movie *A Killer Within*, and portrayed actor Lee Majors in the made-for-TV film *Behind the Camera: The Unauthorized Story of Charlie's Angels* (2004). He returned to play John Crichton in the 2004 Sci-Fi Channel mini-series *Farscape: The Peacekeeper Wars*, and voiced a character on the animated *Justice League Unlimited* before joining the cast of *SG-1*.

Claudia Black (Vala): Hailing from Sydney, Australia, she began her acting career in the early '90s with TV appearances. In 1998 she guest-starred on *Hercules: the Legendary Journeys* and in 1999 landed the role of Aeryn Sun on *Farscape*. She had a small role in 2000's *Pitch Black* and made guest appearances on *Xena: Warrior Princess* and *Beastmaster*. She also appeared in *Queen of the Damned* (2002) and the mini-series *Farscape: The Peacekeeper Wars* (2004), and lent her voice to a *Neopets* video game.

Starhunter

(2001–2003)

In the 23rd century, bounty hunter Dante Montana and his crew on the spaceship Tulip *make a living capturing criminals. Dante also searches for his young son, who was kidnapped by the villainous Raiders ten years ago. In year two, Dante has vanished into another dimension. His grown son, Travis, takes up a life of bounty hunting and searches for his father.*

Cast: Michael Pare (Dante Montana) *Year 1*, Clive Robertson (Travis Montana) *Year 2*, Tanya Allen (Percy Montana), Stephen Marcus (Rudolpho DeLuna), Claudette Roche (Lucretia Scott) *Year 1*, Murray Melvin (Caravaggio) *Year 1*, Graham Harley (Caravaggio) *Year 2*, Paul Fox (Marcus Fagen) *Year 2*, Dawn Stern (Callista Larkadia) *Year 2*

Created by: G. Philip Jackson, Daniel D'Or; **Original Story:** Nelu Ghiran; **Executive Producers:** Stefan Jonas, Elaine Scott *Year 1*, Tony De Pasquale *Year 2*; **Supervising Producer:** Demerise J. LaFleur *Year 1*; **Producers:** G. Philip Jackson, Daniel D'Or; **Producers:** Boris Bulajic, Richard Jackson, *Year 2*; **Line Producer:** Jessica Daniel *Year 2*; **Co-Producers (France):** Georges Campana and Alain Bordiec *Year 1*; **Co-Producer (U.K.):** Andrew Somper *Year 1*; **Associate Producers:** Rob Mattacchione, Fred Posner, Richard Sniderman, Bernd Hellthaler, Jonathan Olsberg (all *Year 2*); **Writers included:** Nelu Ghiran, Peter I. Horton, Julian Fikus, G. Philip Jackson, Daniel D'Or, Annie Ingham, Peter Campbell, Susannah Brennan, Peter Zorich, Denis McGrath, Mary Rogal-Black, Hudson King, David T. Reilly; **Directors included:** Patrick Malakian, Francois Bassett, David Wheatley, George Mendeluk, Roger Gartland, Luc Chalifour, G. Philip Jackson, Michael Cocker; **Guest stars included:** Nigel Bennett, Ellen Dubin, Alan Van Sprang, Lawrence Bayne, Deborah Odell, Lindy Booth, Natasha Marco, Leon Herbert, Howard Gordon, Laura Landauer, Yves Beneyton, King Kai, Noemie Kocher, Gideon Turner, Angie Hille, Mark Powley, Vincent Winterhalter, Mark Pegg, Caroline Hayes, Gary Cady, Ray Lonnen, James Gaddas, Sam Loggin, Tina Malone, Jennifer Foster, Rachel Sanders, Carla Collins

Year One — Produced with the participation of Canal and TNN–The Movie Network and Super Ecran. And in association with Space: The Imagination Station; Year Two — Citadel Studios and Talisman, in association with Western International Syndication; 2001–2003; 60 minutes; 44 episodes; DVD status: Complete series

"How do you find one small boy in the longest universe? I'm not sure. But I have to keep trying."

The back story for *Starhunter* was a tragic one. On the world of Titan, Dante (a corn farmer), his wife and young son are victims of the Raiders, sterile human savages who kill the wife, leave Dante for dead and kidnap his three-year-old son, one of many children the Raiders need to continue their species.

Ten years later, Dante is now a bounty hunter. As captain of the *Tulip* (a former spaceliner refitted as a creaky bounty hunting vessel) in a solar system colonized by humans by the year 2275, he hunts down bad guys to make a living. His real objective: find his son Travis. "I won't be distracted," he says.

But his crew *is* a distracting and strange bunch. Dante's niece, Percy (a brunette with red pony-tails), lost both of her parents in that Raiders attack and considers Dante a surrogate father. She's a complex package — smart-aleck, obnoxious, spoiled, sullen, giddy, disobedient, surly, childish and alternately brilliant and careless. As the engineer, she keeps the ship running.

Lucretia Scott, a former Marine, is the weapons officer. She's a confident black woman who (at first) is secretly working for her ruthless father, who wants to control an alien gene pool called the Divinity Cluster. Lucretia grows fond of Dante and Percy and finds it hard to obey her father's long-distance edicts to spy on her friends.

For comic relief there is Caravaggio, a glowing yellow A.I. hologram with a proper British accent. He's precise and wry as he offers information with a perpetual electronic frown.

The last regular is Rudolpho, a man of great girth who owns the *Tulip* but never boards her. During year one, he only appears on the viewing screen at the start of every show, giving Dante his bounty hunter assignments. These drunken rants are often incomprehensible, and on some occasions, interspersed with farts and belches. Rudolpho is a cash-strapped businessman and his only goal is to see that Dante's trips are profitable.

The *Tulip* itself is a darkly lit ship, its corridors long and dark, with gray bulkheads, clunky sliding doors and control panels with simple light displays. This gloomy environment was intentional. The producers freely admitted that the show's claustrophobic ambiance was inspired by the look of *Alien* and *Blade Runner*. Two 1960s shows, *The Wild Wild West* and *Lost in Space*, were also acknowledged inspirations.

Michael Pare, who had done such films as *The Philadelphia Experiment* (1984), was intrigued by the show's idea, which was explained to him as "Han Solo hunting criminals."

"I said, 'Wow, that sounds cool." he says today. "And I was told, 'It's also about these super-villains who have kidnapped your son and killed your wife.' It was a wonderful role they described. But when we started shooting, I found out they weren't that wild about the bounty hunting plot." Pare was dismayed that references to Dante's son were less frequent and that the Raiders, initially described to him as a cross between Vikings and Hell's Angels, were softened. "The Raiders ended up looking like hippies instead of bikers," he says. "[The producers] decided they didn't want them to be really bad guys."

The first year of *Starhunter* was funded by several companies, including Canada's Space: The Imagination Station. It was economically filmed in New Brunswick, Canada (some supplemental footage was shot in the U.K.). The seams showed: flat music, dim lighting and jumpy editing. Sets were confined mostly to the *Tulip*. Script-wise, *Starhunter* didn't present itself as a chirpy *Star Trek* clone. Dante's encounters were with other humans, never with prosthetic-looking aliens. (*Firefly*, Joss Whedon's later cowboy series in space, also featured a fractured group of cynical mercenaries and a universe devoid of aliens.)

Producers Daniel D'Or and G. Philip Jackson were known for getting a big bang for their buck in their modest features *The Replikator* and *Millennium Queen*. Working with writer Nelu Ghiran, they created the *Starhunter* series; it had backers in various countries, including France, Germany, Britain and Canada. As one observer quipped, "The production credits run longer than the show!" Europe's prime broadcaster, Canal Plus, picked the first 22 episodes up for prime-time broadcasts in France. There was a last-minute rush into production, meaning that the paint on the sets in the first episode was still wet.

Dante was originally conceived as an overweight, smoking psychologist. But it was decided that audiences would respond better to a good-looking, square-jawed hero. Michael Pare, who had worked for the producers before, brought a laid-back style. He wasn't your typical captain. In one show, as his ship spirals down towards a planet, he is immobilized until Lucretia suggests a solution and Dante yells to himself, "Yes, right! She's right!" And while crawling through an emergency shaft to repair the *Tulip*, he mutters, "Hell, I hope I remember how to do this!"

"I wanted the audience to see the human side of this guy," Pare says today of the hard-nosed but vulnerable captain. "You have to see the hard side of a guy to appreciate the soft side."

Co-creator Philip Jackson felt Pare was right for the role. "Michael did a very strong job," he says. "He was the perfect Dante Montana and was 100 percent dedicated to the series."

Dante's niece, Percy, is bemused by her uncle. She saw her parents killed as a child and uses quirky humor to cope with situations. But her reckless nature can lead to trouble—she almost vaporizes Dante while using the ship's shooting gallery. But what concerns Dante most is that his niece's rebellion signifies that she's leaving childhood—and him—behind.

Dante's command reflects a sense of reality. He has bills to pay, a niece to take care of, and has only a six-month lease left on the ship. He knows Rudolpho can fire him any time he wants.

When a rich man offers Dante a better job as a corrections officer, he refuses. This life is all he knows and in misty-eyed moments, he reflects on his missing son, who would now be a young man, still out there with the Raiders.

"The fact Dante had a vulnerability to his heroic character was very real and compelling, it was not at all a cliché," director George Mendeluk says of Pare's characterization. "Normally, Michael played guys who were tough. Here he was more vulnerable than the stereotypical rock-jawed SF hero, so this was a challenge for him." The director, who had worked with Pare earlier on the film *Men of Means* (1999), says the two developed a strong, mutual trust. "Michael and I had become collaborators as well as good friends," he notes. He praises the star as "a highly underrated actor, very talented and intelligent, and extremely sensitive. He can be very emotional and very tough."

"George Mendeluk is a great director," Pare says. "He had a lot of experience directing television. He could edit the script they handed him and make it into something. I was sorry to see him leave the show."

Mendeluk directed only "Trust," the show's second episode. While he enjoyed working with Pare, he says the overall production "wasn't very cohesive. Everything was up in the air, including who the characters were going to be. So I went off to do other work."

The first-year episodes ranged from the mundane (recovering three million dollars in artwork and jewelry that was stolen from an ambassador ship) to imaginative (an artist is pursued by a strange ship that sweeps her into another dimension). The *Tulip* also transported eccentric passengers, like two naughty teenage girls (played by real-life sisters Anne and Cathy Keenan) who trick Percy into bad behavior, such as getting her high on a giggling pill. Meanwhile, Dante tries to determine if the girls' father is good or bad. (Turns out he's bad and Dante gratefully deposits the father and daughters on Mars.)

The show's humor was in the dialogue: "Just follow my orders, no matter how crazy they sound!" Dante yells to Caravaggio in one scene. The A.I. is puzzled. "Why should today be any different from any other day, captain?" he asks. And when Percy is kidnapped, an exasperated villain says, "Let me think." She needles him: "Yeah, good luck with that!"

"This is an adventure show with attitude," the producers stated at the time. "Our band of merry bounty hunters can be as dysfunctional as any family can get ... and the power of the format is its basic simplicity and the ease at which it will constantly infuse new characters and locales.... [I]t's the wild, wild west of space, where lawlessness and crime have expanded as well."

The show tested the imaginations of the actors. Whenever they spoke to invisible people or holograms, they were really talking to a tennis ball.

One episode cut budget corners by having the crew encounter time bubbles, where people repeat their actions over and over again. To save his ship, Dante must keep trying to change time, which allowed the producers to reuse the same footage half a dozen times. But Dante succeeds in preventing his ship from exploding.

One continuing story arc dealt with the Divinity Cluster, an alien gene pool. It holds the answers to mankind's future, and is coveted by ruthless business people like Darius, Lucretia's father. A bald, humorless man with sunglasses, Darius heads a nasty military group called the Orchard and he seeks power by unlocking the Divinity Cluster, the secrets of which are never truly defined.

In "Half Dense Players," Dante is furious when he learns Lucretia has betrayed him by sending her father secret messages about the *Tulip*'s mission. Dante shouts to her, "Pack your bags and get the hell off my ship!" Lucretia, crying, redeems herself by ending communication with her father and driving off her father's approaching ship.

In the last episode of year one, Dante apparently finds his long-lost son, who is now a teenager with a cool military persona and strange powers. Percy doesn't trust the boy, knowing he's been living with the Raiders all of this time, but Dante is caught up in the reunion. "There were days I thought I would never see you again," he tells Travis.

Meanwhile, the Raiders plan to seed the Earth with deadly Divinity Cluster genes and the only hope is for Travis to mentally transport the seeds somewhere else. But as Dante and Travis speed their shuttle over Earth, it goes out of control. Just before the ship crashes, Dante finds himself back in time with his wife and young son, minutes before the Raiders attacked his family. So ended year one.

It was a deliberate way to get the second year off to a new start. Ratings had been middling and as Philip Jackson says today, "There were commercial, logistical and political forces at play as well as a genuinely creatively motivated desire to make a better series, going into a more fully funded season two." He and Daniel D'Dor carefully studied market reaction in hopes of making *Starhunter* more commercial. It was hoped that new characters and a slight revamp of the premise would increase ratings. A new writing team was recruited and BBC Worldwide Distribution was instrumental in having *Starhunter* adopt a new look, with a bigger budget.

Pare says he was ready to do a second season. "I was excited, but then my agent got a call from [the producers] and said they didn't want me. Maybe they felt it would be cheaper without me or didn't want to work with somebody with more experience? I was very disappointed."

A radical cast change was decided upon for the new year. "Dan and I were also producers of season two," says Jackson, "and we were responsible for the casting changes and for the new production design. We left the show around production of the seventh episode. It was a very difficult decision, prompted because of serious differences in business style with one of the financing parties."

George Mendeluk wasn't privy to the behind-the-scenes issues of *Starhunter* but has a bittersweet memory of "Michael and I sitting on the set together, just talking about our expectations about this particular series and how, hopefully, we were going to work on it for a long time together. Unfortunately, it didn't turn out that way, for him or for me."

The second season, production was moved to larger studios in Mississauga, Ontario. There was more emphasis on character and less on SF story arcs like the Divinity Cluster. "Rebirth" opened the second year. Fifteen years have passed in the blink of an eye and Percy finds herself alone on the *Tulip*. Her Uncle Dante has disappeared into hyperspace, Lucretia is gone and even Caravaggio looks different (actor Graham Harvey replaced Murray Melvin).

Percy claims salvage rights to the ship and becomes its owner. A penniless Rudolpho is forced to serve as one of the crew since his ex-wife now controls him financially. There's also Callista, a weapons expert from the Mars Federation of Special Forces, and a young mechanic named Marcus.

The most surprising newcomer is *Starhunter*'s new protagonist, Travis Montana, the full-grown son of Dante, who has escaped from the Raiders. He wants to use the ship to find his missing father and hunt down criminals for bounty. Travis grew up with the Raiders and wrestles with guilt over participating in their violent activities.

Clive Robertson, a classically trained British performer, was heroic as Travis. *TV Guide* noted that if Pierce Brosnan should ever retire his James Bond role, Robertson could fill 007's shoes "in a heartbeat."

The series was now titled *Starhunter 2300*. The slim budget of year one had contributed to many anemic-looking adventures, but year two had bigger sets, more action, better photography and faster editing as the crew landed on some well-designed sets.

But the production was still thrifty: Each episode was shot in five days and the guest stars were primarily unknowns. Percy was more sullen and Rudolpho showed more vulnerability.

There was more pressure on the writers to study real-life science and incorporate that into the scripts. This meant the latest news in space travel, hyper-dimensions, terraforming, bubble universes and time travel. Year two's adventures included "Stitch in Time," where time anomalies disrupt Travis' attempts to transport a prisoner. In another, a reality TV crew boards the *Tulip* and films its adventures. And in "Kate," Percy lives to regret creating a very troublesome *female* A I.

Travis developed a fierce protectiveness and fondness for Callista; in real life, Clive Robertson displayed the same gallantry. One night, as he walked actress Dawn Stern to her car after filming, two thugs confronted them with a gun. Robertson jumped the robbers, and got slapped across the head with the gun. As the robbers ran off, Robertson bled profusely from a gash on his forehead. He was rushed to the hospital for stitches.

For the record, Michael Pare and Robertson never worked on the series together. In year one, we occasionally saw young Travis in dreams or flashbacks but it was as a boy, played by different young actors.

The series ended with a complex two-parter, "Hyperspace." When Callista is fatally shot in a gunfight, Travis transports the *Tulip* into the hyperspace void so he can change time and save Callista's life. But he has trouble mastering the time-traveling phase, and each time he fails to change the past to save her. As the *Tulip* experiences a molecular degeneration in hyperspace, a strange woman, who turns out to be a vision of Travis's mother, tells him he can only master time by controlling his emotions. This time he does save Callista's life and his ship. But the effects of the void seize the *Tulip*. As the ship careens out of control, Percy says, "I'd rather we blow up than be stuck in some endless space time warp." And that's how it ended, on a cliffhanger. One of the show's press releases noted, "While the stories of *Starhunter* are often dark, they are never without hope." Yet mediocre ratings stranded this dysfunctional family of space travelers in limbo without a resolution.

CAST NOTES

Michael Pare (Dante): Originally he wanted to be a chef. He studied acting with Uta Hagen in the early 1980s, and made his mark as one of the high school kids in the early segments of *The*

Greatest American Hero (1981). That led to starring roles in *Streets of Fire* and *The Philadelphia Experiment*, both 1984, as well as a series of TV commercials in Japan. He also co-starred in the TV cop show *Houston Knights* (1987). He continues starring in independent features films such as *Crash Landing* (2005) and *Bloodrayne* (2006).

Clive Robertson (Travis): He was a rugby player in his native England as a young man and later studied kung fu. He considered going into business but instead went to Africa on an odyssey of self-discovery, torn between becoming a commercial pilot like his father or an actor. He chose acting. Before *Starhunter*, he already had a fan base for his dual role on Aaron Spelling's *Sunset Beach* (1997–1999). His other credits include appearances on daytime's *General Hospital* (2004); he was the voice of a wizard ant in the animated feature *Ant Bully* (2006).

Tanya Allen (Percy): This Toronto-born actress began by doing TV guest shots on *Kung Fu: The Adventure Continues, Outer Limits* and *Tek-War*. She starred in the 1996 Canadian TV film *Lyddie* and starred in the situation comedy series, *The Newsroom* (1996). Her movies include *Chicks with Sticks* (2004) and *Silent Hill* (2006).

Claudette Roche (Lucretia): Born in England, she appeared in the SF films *Short Circuit 2* (1988) and *Millennium* (1989).

Murray Melvin (Caravaggio, Year 1): The London-born actor's career goes back to an early (1961) episode of *The Avengers*. He's also appeared in the films *Alfie* (1966), *Barry Lyndon* (1975), *The Emperor's New Clothes* (2001) and *Phantom of the Opera* (2004).

Graham Harley (Caravaggio, Year 2): His TV credits include *Sue Thomas F.B. Eye, Monk, Secret Adventures of Jules Verne, Relic Hunter, RoboCop* and *Beyond Reality*. He played Davy Jones' father in the TV film *Daydream Believers: The Monkees Story* (2000) and also appeared in the film *Four Minutes* (2005).

Stephen Marcus (Rudolpho): Britisher Marcus has appeared in movies such as *Stage Beauty* (2004) and *The Greatest Game Ever Played* (2005).

Dawn Stern (Callista): Born in Japan but raised in the American Midwest, she studied biology before entering the world of modeling and posing for *Playboy* magazine. She played Dr. Allie Farrow on TV's *Viper* (1996–97) and had guest shots on *Star Trek: Enterprise, Crusade, The Profiler, Ally McBeal* and *The Sentinel*. After *Starhunter*, she had a stint on *The Young and the Restless* (2003–2004).

Paul Fox (Marcus): Born in England, he was a regular on the British soap opera *Coronation Street* for two years before signing up for *Starhunter*. He was also in the U.K. series *The Royal* (2003).

SOURCES

Hall, John S. "Night of the Starhunter." *Starlog* no. 305, December 2002.
Yakir, Dan. "Starhunter's Son." *Starlog* no. 316, November 2003.

Strange World
(1999)

A special investigator for the Army uncovers mysterious cases where scientific discoveries are corrupted by evil conspirators.

Cast: Tim Guinee (Captain Paul Turner), Kristin Lehman (Dr. Sidney MacMillan), Saundra Quarterman (Major Lynne Reese), Vivian Wu (Japanese Woman)

Created by: Howard Gordon, Tim Kring; **Executive Producer:** Howard Gordon; **Co-Executive Producer:** Manny Coto; **Supervising Producer:** Harvey Frand; **Producer:** Tim Minear; **Co-Producers:** Tracy D'Arcy, Ron French, Todd Ellis Kessler; **Consulting Producer:** Thania St. John; **Writers included:** Jessica Scott, Howard Gordon, Manny Coto, Mike Wollaeger, John Chambers; **Directors included:** Joseph L. Scanlan, James Whitmore Jr., Mick Jackson, Tucker Gates, Ian Toynton, Dwight Little; **Director of Photography:** Peter Wunstorf; **Special Makeup Effects:** Rachel Griffin; **Key Special Makeup Effects:** Toby Lindala; **Guest Stars included:** Kevin

Tighe, Sheila Moore, Michael Moriarty, John Finn, Alessandro Juliani, Jerry Hardin, George Wyner, Judith Hoag, Currie Graham, Glynn Turman, Matt Walker, Lauren Velez, Peter Wingfield (as Shepard)

ABC/20th Century–Fox/Teakwood Lane Productions; March 1999 (ABC)/March–April 2002 (Sci-Fi Channel); 60 minutes; 13 episodes

The X-Files inspired a host of imitators but most of them drifted into the backwater of cancellation. *Strange World*, co-created by *X-Files* writer Howard Gordon, went after a similar target audience but they missed. It was gone after three episodes (ten were unaired).

Strange World was set at the United States Army Medical Research Institute for Infectious Diseases (USAMRIID). Captain Paul Turner had had his immune system critically damaged by chemical weapons in Iraq's Gulf War of 1991. As his condition worsened, spots spread over his skin. A mysterious Japanese woman offered him inoculations that temporary halted the spread of the disease.

As a special investigator for the army, Turner pursued cases where science had been corrupted by the government or by other conspiratorial forces. The government considers him a troublemaker and has never forgotten that Turner testified against them over how troops suffered from Gulf War Syndrome disease.

Star Tim Guinee liked the realism of the series. "*Strange World* took place at USAMRIID [a real research institute in Maryland], where the Army keeps ebola and anthrax and other 'hot' diseases. It was a center of germ warfare research prior to the Nixon Accord and is now involved in trying to find defenses against biological weaponry. When I got the *Strange World* job, I called the Army and was granted clearance to visit the facility, which was an absolutely surreal experience. I'm a research junkie, so this was a fantastic experience. Our show was constantly dealing with different subjects — radiation, cloning, genetically engineered food, retro-viruses, etc. So the research never ended, which I found really fun.

"I also enjoyed producer Howard Gordon's conception of my role. He saw Paul Turner as very human. Smart, yes, but frequently out of his element and [in over] his head. He was definitely not a superhero. I personally get bored with shows where a superhero or a computer leaps in and solves everything. I'm interested in seeing a real human being try to come to terms with the challenges facing them. We talked a lot about finding human flaws in the character. Many programs have lead characters who are brilliant and sexy and perfectly dressed and are karate blackbelts and so on. They can do everything. We decided that if Paul was blessed with brains and an inherent inquisitiveness, he would also be cursed with some things he didn't do so well. For example, Larry Drake, the brilliant production designer, put together this amazing messy, cluttered apartment for Paul. The fridge was barely stocked with old food. Paul's car was an old, beat-up wreck. He was not someone who was terribly experienced in a fistfight. I loved not only what he was but what he was not. I loved the humanity with which the writers infused him."

"What struck me most about the series was the lead character's dilemma," says co-executive producer Manny Coto. "He was stricken with a degenerative disease, and his survival was dependent on a serum supplied by a mysterious and powerful underground organization with proprietary access to advanced medical science. This put Paul Turner in a remarkable bind which we tried to exploit at every opportunity."

Turner has a loving wife, Dr. Sidney MacMillan, who is determined to cure Paul. Turner's boss, Major Lynn Reese, has orders to keep him in line but she quickly realizes Turner is often right.

Strange World premiered six years after *The X-Files* and it was impossible for the series not to appear derivative and a minor leaguer. Even its main title sequence and graphics were highly similar to the *X-Files* credits.

But Howard Gordon was enthusiastic. "The scariest things are here on Earth," he told the *Milwaukee Journal-Sentinel* during production. "Scientific progress is going at a pace faster than anyone is aware of."

Turner's cases included a scientist who dies of massive dehydration (the result of a virus created back in 1969), a threat from a bacterial toxin that creates a deadly methane gas in the oil of farmlands, and implants designed to enhance mental and physical performance and create killers. And after investigating several incidents of tragic road rage, Turner suspects something sinister but the military offers a simple philosophy: "The world's a violent place and it grows more violent every day." Turner dismisses that party line and learns that mysterious men injected 200 Cambodian villagers decades ago with "something" which turned them into killers. A survivor of those experiments is now infecting ordinary Americans with a killing rage. The episode concludes with a

SCIFI.COM / STRANGEWORLD

Kristin Lehman starred as Dr. Sidney MacMillan in *Strange World* (© Sci-Fi Channel).

female driver and bus driver getting into a psychotic meltdown over a minor traffic accident. No happy endings here.

"The series was successful in establishing an unrelenting mood of dark paranoia," says Coto. "The stories were always challenging and didn't flinch from showing the worst that science has to offer. Unfortunately, I think these same qualities doomed it. It may have been *too* close to reality. How many Americans want to watch a woman giving birth to a human organ every week? Answer: not enough to sustain a network series."

As a lead character, Captain Turner is refreshingly unpretentious but also so low-key and passive that he can get lost in the dark shadows.

It's a world of secret assassins, where sinister men sit in cars at midnight wearing sunglasses and where meetings are conducted in shadowy halls. People are not whom they seem. Sidney is saved from a car bomb by a man named Shepard, who claims to have Turner's best interests at heart but is actually out to manipulate the human race.

Turner's dealings with the Japanese woman are

equally confusing but she ends up an ally. "Your work with the military threatens to expose my bosses," she warns him and she refuses to obey her superiors' orders to kill Turner. But her nocturnal visits even get on Turner's nerves. "It's getting really old listening to you answer my questions with questions," he snaps.

The truth is out there, somewhere, but in this universe, nobody is talking. When Turner digs to uncover another government plot, he vows, "Whatever they bury, it won't stay buried long." Major Reese grimly replies, "Nothing ever does."

Coto believes the real world is not that mystical. "I'm sorry to disappoint but when it comes to conspiracy theories, I am a hard-nosed skeptic," he affirms. "I believe that Oswald acted alone, what crashed at Roswell was a Mogul balloon, that we really walked on the moon, and that 9/11 was perpetrated by Arab hijackers, not the Trilateral Commission. That said, there's something about these things that I can't get enough of. I attend MUFON [Mutual UFO Network, a scientific study of UFOs] meetings regularly and collect books about the paranormal by the truckload. *JFK* is one of my favorite movies but I watch it in the same way that I watch, say, *Doctor Who*. It's all a pleasant, fantastical joyride that injects some mystery into the world. One takes any of it seriously at one's own peril."

One *Strange World* episode, the Coto-scripted "Azrael's Breed," did get under the skins of the network; some executives felt it went too far. "It was about addicts getting high on memory implants that allowed them to experience other people's violent deaths and it was considered too dark by the network," says Coto. "They were not fans. I must say, though, I was not aware of any pressure from the studio to steer clear from any subject matter."

Strange World remained a challenge. "It was an unusually difficult show to write for," says Coto. "Howard Gordon, Tim Minear and myself spent many weekends in the office, beating out stories. It was tough finding fresh concepts dealing with fringe science that hadn't already been done to death by *X-Files* and the like."

Some critics were harsh. "It's a muddy exercise in paranoia," Joyce Millman of Salon noted in 1999. "It's dark, gloomy and, frankly, not a whole lot of fun."

"We dared to deal with very complicated issues and convoluted plots which really required the audience to participate," says Guinee. "The writing didn't sink down to the lowest common denominator. We presumed we had a thinking audience. But God help you if you went to the kitchen for a ham sandwich halfway through an episode."

The actor is aware that such programs, based on technology and science, are difficult to bring to the screen. "That's one of the challenges of the genre, to introduce the audience to the science on which a plot is driven. Simultaneously, you must find a way not to overwhelm them with that same science."

In the final episode, Turner's condition worsens and the Japanese lady, about to give him another life-saving injection, is knocked out and the serum stolen. Sidney, who has made a pact with Shepard to save her husband's life, learns too late he is a madman with plans to alter human evolution. She sits by Paul's hospital bedside as he is dying. Guinee confirms that Turner's impending death was written as a "next season" cliffhanger, and not as a gratuitous "kill off the lead character."

"As far as I know, the cancellation was based solely on ratings performance, or lack thereof," recalls Coto. "After the first episode's ratings came in, we saw the writing on the wall. The season cliffhanger, rather than representing a real belief that the show would come back for season two, was more wishful thinking on our part."

"I don't think the network quite knew what to do with the show," Guinee observes. "It tested very, very well but ABC only ran three episodes which was a pity because a show like *Strange World* needs time to build a dedicated audience. I was very disappointed by its cancellation."

The series' 13 episodes was later aired on the Sci-Fi Channel in March and April 2002.

CAST NOTES

Tim Guinee (Captain Paul Turner): He studied acting at the American Academy of Dramatic Arts in New York. His earliest TV included appearances on 1980s fare like *Spenser: For Hire* and *Wiseguy*. Later TV assignments included *Stargate SG-1*, *Ghost Whisperer* and *West Wing*. His movie credits include *Broken English* and *American East* (both 2007). His *Strange World* thoughts today: "I enjoyed working with the show's writing staff, the crew and the other actors. Acting with Kristin Lehman, who is an extraordinarily gifted and emotionally available actress, was a wonderful gift in doing the show. Also Mick Jackson, who directed the pilot, is one of the hardest working, most insightful directors it's ever been my joy to work with. And while I've been fortunate to retain many of those friendships, it would be great to get up at five in the morning and go to work and see everybody again."

Kristin Lehman (Dr. Sidney MacMillan): Born in Toronto, Canada and raised in Vancouver, she is also a professional dancer. Some of her earliest credits were the Canadian-filmed shows *Poltergeist*, *Forever Knight*, *The Outer Limits* and *Earth: Final Conflict*. She was a semi-regular on *Judging Amy* (2002–2003) and co-starred on TV's *Drive* (2007).

Saundra Quarterman (Major Lynne Reese): She later guest starred on *Touched By An Angel*, *American Dreams* and *Without a Trace*.

Vivian Wu (Japanese Woman): Born in Shanghai, China, she was featured in the Oscar-winning film *The Last Emperor* (1987). *People* magazine selected her as one of the most beautiful people in 1990. She also co-starred in the murder mystery *Shanghai Red* (2006).

SOURCES

Littlefield, Kinney. "New Sci-fi Wave on TV a Little Tired of Aliens." *Milwaukee Journal Sentinel*, March 11, 1999.

Millman, Joyce. *Strange World* Review. "The Xerox Files—Two New Sci-fi Series from Former X-Files Writers Copy the Original's Formula but Leave Out Main Ingredients." Salon.com, March 8, 1999.

TekWar

(1995–1996)

In the future, Jake Cardigan works at the Cosmos Detective Agency with his partner Sid Gomez. Together they hunt down terrorists, dealers of the illegal virtual reality drug "Tek," and investigate other technological crimes.

Cast: Greg Evigan (Jake Cardigan), Eugene Clark (Sid Gomez), Maria Del Mar (Lt. Sam Houston), William Shatner (Bascom)
Recurring Cast: Lexa Doig (Cowgirl), Torri Higginson (Beth Kitteridge), Maurice Dean Wint (Winger), Natalie Radford (Nika); *Based on the Tek novels by:* William Shatner; *Executive Producers:* William Shatner, Peter Sussman; *Co-Executive Producers:* Hans Beimler, Richard Manning; *Producers:* John Calvert, Stephen Roloff; *Supervising Producers:* Seaton McLean, Jamie Paul Rock; *Supervising Creative Consultant:* Robin Jill Bernheim; *Creative Consultants:* David Bennett Carren, J. Larry Carroll; *Writers included:* Robin Jill Bernheim, James Kahn, David Bennett Carren, J. Larry Carroll, Marc Scott Zicree, Lisabeth Shatner; *Directors included:* Allan Kroeker, Allan Eastman, William Shatner, Bruce Pittman, Ken Girotti, Hans Beimler ; *Director of Photography:* Michael McMurray; *Production Designer:* Stephen Roloff; *Visual Special Effects:* C.O.R.E. Digital Pictures, Gajdecki Visual Effects, Calibre Digital Pictures; *Guest Stars included:* Jennifer Dale, David Cubitt, Kate Trotter, Anita LaSelva, Nicole DeBoer, Julie Khaner, Phil Aiken, Karl Pruner, Melanie Shatner, Richard Comar
Atlantis Films Ltd./Western International Communications, Ltd./LEMLI Productions, Inc./CTV Television Network/USA Network/Universal City Studios, Inc.; January 1995–February 1996; 60 minutes; 22 episodes; DVD status: Complete series

In the late 1980s, when a writer's strike temporarily halted preparation for *Star Trek V: The Final Frontier*, actor-director William Shatner decided to write a novel combining the two things he was well known for: the futuristic science fiction of *Star Trek* and the tough law enforcement of *T.J. Hooker*. *TekWar* was published in 1989 and became a popular multimedia franchise that spawned eight book sequels.

The first two follow-ups *TekLords* and *TekLab* were published in 1991, *TekVengeance* and *TekSecret* in 1993, *TekPower* in 1994, *TekMoney* in 1995, *TekKill* in 1996 and *TekNet* in 1997. The characters' popularity expanded into the 1992–94 Marvel Comics imprint series *TekWorld*, running for 24 issues; it was written by Ron Goulart with art by Lee Sullivan. There was also a CD-ROM game based on the series.

Because of the success of the novels and the comic books, producer Seaton McLean at Atlantis Films bought the rights. Universal Studios looked to *TekWar* as a component of their series package of syndicated TV movies, a combine they called "Universal Action Pack" in 1994. This collection of TV movies included a number of other fantasy and action properties (*Hercules: The Legendary Journeys, Xena: Warrior Princess, Knight Rider: 2010, Vanishing Son*, plus television iterations of two popular action feature films: *Bandit* and *Midnight Run*). An original SF comedy, *The Adventures of Captain Zoom*, was also part of the package.

The first three of the novels were adapted as *TekWar* TV-movies; a fourth (original) movie was titled *TekJustice*. The movies did well; next came a regular one-hour series that debuted in January 1995 on the USA Network.

About 50 years into the future, ex-cop Jake

Cardigan is pulled out of a deep cryogenic sleep, just four years into a 15-year incarceration for being a user of the illegal "Tek" drug. "Tek," a computer chip, is an addictive virtual reality technological device, illegal because the virtual reality is so compelling, the addict who accesses it via a special custom "Tek-helmet" can stay there and forget about the real world. The user can actually die inside the virtual reality environment.

Jake is innocent and is determined to clear his name. In the years since his incarceration, his wife has divorced him, has taken their son Danny with her, and married a businessman with a shady past. Jake also wants to reunite with his son. Cardigan's partner Sid Gomez introduces him to the mysterious Bascom, the owner-operator of a top security firm, the Cosmos agency. Their task is to find Professor Leon Kitteridge and his daughter Beth, scientists who were working on a top secret project that had attracted the attention of prominent "Teklord" Sonny Hokori. Jake is convinced that finding Beth will shed light into the events that led to his incarceration because "she was there" in his drugged state, at the scene of the crime.

Later, Beth reveals that she was in hiding because she knows that vicious Teklords framed Jake for murder and for using "Tek." With Beth's help, Jake's professional reputation is cleared and he's able to continue fighting crime with Gomez and the Cosmos agency.

In the "Tek" future, advanced technology and old architecture intermingle. The Internet has expanded into a three-dimensional virtual reality area called the Matrix (really!). To access the forbidden areas of the Matrix in search of his son, Jake contacts renegade cyber jocks and rides into the electronic space for clues. The "Cowgirl" (played by *Andromeda* actress Lexa Doig) sits in a chair, surrounded by electronic equipment. She dons a rubber glove and a hi-tech electronic helmet and "dives" into the 3D Matrix. She navigates her way using body and chair movements with arm and hand gestures. The Matrix is a graphical visual representation of the global computer network.

William Shatner freely admits he was influenced by the works of SF novelist William Gibson, who coined the term "cyberspace" in *Neuromancer*, his 1984 novel that launched the "Cyber Punk" literary style of science fiction. To help him visualize the series' future history, Shatner assembled scientists and "futurists" to hear their views on what the world might be in 50 years. The re-

sult was not to look at the world as a dystopia. The geopolitical structure of the world isn't really addressed. The emphasis instead is on the pervasiveness of technology upon society and the people who use and abuse its abilities.

To further emphasize the technological advancements in this world, Bascom hands Jake a "Pulse gun." When fired, the gun doesn't spit out a metal projectile; instead it releases a distortion special effect, a "shockwave" that can send a bad guy flying backwards for hundreds of feet.

In the "Tek" future city, driving can be done automatically without a driver's operation; holographic advertising is prevalent throughout the city, and widescreen hi-tech computer screens give access to the Matrix. Donning a "morph mask" allows the wearer to look and sound like another person. A hand-held vid-phone supplies instant communications for users.

The series was filmed in Toronto, Canada, not the most futuristic-looking city in the world. However, thanks to production designer Stephen Roloff's ingenuity, cityscapes looked futuristic via architectural "add-ons" pieces or discreetly placed computer-generated graphics in the background. This strategy worked well.

Brought in as co-executive producers after the four telefilms were completed, Hans Beimler and Richard Manning worked with executive producers Shatner and Peter Sussman. Beimler says that although he's proud of the 18 episodes that was produced, he wanted so much more. "I don't think we ever realized the potential," says Beimler. "We did some good, wonderful things, but it was political and difficult. We felt the Tek drug was the least interesting part of it all. The most interesting part was the new world being presented. It was the closest thing we could see to a kind of ["Cyberpunk" SF author] William Gibson world where people were really affected by the technology and *how* we were going to use that technology."

Beimler says when setting up a series, there has to be a vision, and in *TekWar*'s case, he got about 60 percent of what he wanted. "What we were missing was a kind of unifying style to the whole look," he says. "Something that brought it together and made it its own little world. I don't want to lay blame in terms of the visualization of it, but the writer's conceptions were not quite there yet."

Battling budget woes and trying to stay focused on the storytelling was the primary task. "I like spending money as much as the next producer," says Beimler. "We want every scene in every episode to be as rich in production value as possible. But it has to prioritize itself because there's no time or money to do everything you want. So it's more important to concentrate on what is important — storytelling. Storytelling requires time. You can't cheat that. You can't short-shrift getting the story right."

Realizing *TekWar*'s "look and feel" was one of the most challenging tasks, and that required the services of an imaginative and talented production designer. "What are the gags? What are the toys? How do the effects work? What's our level of technology?" asks producer and production designer Stephen Roloff, hired by Seaton McLean to develop the visual style of Tek's universe. Placing the TV series 200 years into the future as depicted in the novels ("with floating cities") was financially impractical, but 50 years was more realistic. "I did a pitch book with a writer to sort that out and managed to get a nibble from Universal," says Roloff. "As a result of that, I was more conceptually involved than a production designer usually is.

"Twenty years from now, we're looking at such a radical shift from our day-to-day world that we cannot approach this from a logical point of view. It was a matter of saying, 'Okay, what interesting effects and applications of technology can you conceive?' It was a really wonderful little playground."

One major notion was a virtual reality environment that didn't involve the user being jacked into a computer environment (as seen in William Gibson novels) or employing VR goggles where the viewers would see only the POV of the person entering that environment. Instead, another system was developed that would show both the user and his normal surroundings with the VR environment. "I wanted some visual application of the Net," says Roloff. "And in Shatner's books he had adopted the notion of holographic projection, the idea of a translucent three-dimensional image that could be projected in space and maintained there somehow. I thought if that's the case, then instead of having a person going into a visual matrix — what if I literally could find a way of surrounding the operator with a computer-generated universe, the visual universe on the Internet? We came up with the notion of hanging a ring-shaped holographic projector over the operator. So it projects sort of a bubble, like a three-dimensional HUD — 'heads up display' — that they use in fighter aircraft. They now project some technical information directly onto the windshield. Well, instead of that, you have a holographically projected virtual heads up display all around you and you're in a seat that swivels around and you interact with it through a series of hand gestures which make it much more sophisticated. I was also trying to get away from someone sitting at a keyboard. We could have a scene between the two of us because it is projected as a translucent medium around you. You can see me through it and I can see you through it.

"The big Achilles heel in science fiction is transportation," notes Roloff. "We don't have the money to produce a streetscape full of vehicles. [Sylvester Stallone's] *Demolition Man* approached General Motors and got all their prototype vehicles and took out $100 million in insurance, but we can't afford that."

So Jake Cardigan drives ... a Jeep! But Roloff thought long and hard about what the highways of the future would look like. He did some research and discovered that it cost about a million dollars to construct a highway or interstate length as long as a tractor trailer. "So I thought, 'Hmm, the government can't afford this much longer....' And in the U.S. the whole road system infrastructure is falling apart. So I took the notion of privatization; basically you've got a privatized highway. It's got walls around it to keep out any other vehicles. The speed can be quite fast, it is regulated by magnetic strips buried under the road — but you're at the mercy of advertising that is overhead. That's sort of a flip card effect that we're doing to suggest that there are ads flashing by that are actually following your vehicle, so you're a captive audience to the advertising.

"Another thing that will happen in 50 years is, advertising will be much more insidious and it will be predominantly invitational."

When Cardigan walks into Cosmos Detective Agency, he enters an old stone building, but the facade has futuristic "add-ons." "We took an old building and put in this infrastructure of very hitech and they still stand the test of time," says Roloff. "I was showing those images to somebody recently and they said, 'That looks like a nice modern facility,' and that was designed in 1994, so it still holds to some degree.

"A lot of research was going into flat screen monitors in 1994. So when we were creating a series about future societies, we can't have big clunky monitors! We ended up getting fiber optics fabric and used backlight transparencies to be used on flat screens [for the graphics displays]. So when you go look at the offices in *TekWar*, you see these flat screens everywhere. It looks contemporary to [viewers] today, but this was back when flat screens didn't even exist. You can take your best shot at trying to update yourself as far as you can, given everything you know about high technology progress." But Roloff also acknowledges that "you know that you'll still become obsolete."

Says Hans Beimler, "I liked the production design. The 'look' was quite lovely, but I don't think we ever achieved exactly what we wanted."

As Jake Cardigan, Greg Evigan essayed a younger, more vital rendition of the book character (which was actually modeled after author Shatner). The book's Jake was an older, more rugged personality; the artwork on the book covers and in the *TekWorld* comics resembled Shatner. Shatner had initially considered playing the lead role, but finally he decided it was more fun to produce and direct. Instead, Shatner gave himself a supporting role as Comos' enigmatic operator Walter Bascom.

In the transition between print to film, quite a few changes were made. First, the stories lost 75 years from 2120 to 2045, one reason being, the more advanced the futureworld was, the harder it would be on a television budget to depict that future. Losing 75 years put the TekWar future closer to our present.

Evigan's Jake was not quite the hard-boiled detective. He had humor and was the quintessential ex-cop-turned-private eye working for a detective agency. When he began the series, Evigan felt that sustaining Jake's gruff personality as seen in the books, would not be good for the screen. He's joined by his sidekick partner Sid Gomez, a dependable and loyal friend who helped pull Jake out of his cryogenic incarceration and back into the world of the living.

Jake and Sid's liaison at the Cosmos Agency was Nika, a platinum-haired computer whiz who fed them the electronic data they needed to crack the cases. Midway through the series the duo crossed paths with the beautiful and sardonic Police Lt. Sam Houston, and professional sparks flew between them. Later, when Sid got killed in "Killer Instinct," Houston joined Cosmos and became Jake's partner in "Deep Cover" and for the remainder of the series' run.

If an episode didn't revolve around TekLords or Tek-dealing (a clear metaphor for today's societal problems with contemporary drugs), Jake would contend with criminals who used advanced technology or bio-engineering to create havoc. In one case an advanced computer developed the personality of an incarcerated TekLord who was safely "frozen," but it continued the TekLord's murdering rampage; it was up to Jake to unravel the mystery and disconnect the computer. Jake also dealt with his memory being extracted, virtual reality prostitutes, weather terrorists, computer hackers, and "viruses" with the potential of killing millions. TekLords were also powerful enough to manipulate a political election to serve their own nefarious purposes.

"Greg Evigan gave 110 percent day in and day out. Nobody worked harder, nobody was more prepared, and nobody was easier to get along with," says co-executive producer Richard Manning. "He did as many of his own stunts as we'd let him — not out of silly macho, but because he believed (and rightly so) that it looked better on-screen. Eugene Clark was a terrific foil — sly, deadpan, rock-solid. Maria del Mar brought in sass and attitude (and she looks great in leather). And Bill Shatner was marvelous as Bascom, the inscrutable boss who was always one jump ahead of everyone else."

Manning says that one of his favorite segments was a J. Larry Carroll-David Bennett Carren script titled "Deadline." "Maurice Dean Wint had played the humorless, by-the-book, android cop Winger so wonderfully in several guest appearances that we were dying to give him an episode where he could do more than just growl at our hero Jake. The episode was filmed in early December, so it was raining-sleeting in some scenes and snowing in others. What's more, the factory we shot in was a working factory during the day, so we had to do all our interior filming there at night — get in, light the place, shoot some extremely demanding fight scenes, and clear out. Post-production did a fantastic job as well, creating tons of sound effects for the androids such as servos running amok and Winger's haunting electronic scream as he goes berserk.

"*TekWar* was a particular challenge, both writing and production-wise, because it was a curious hybrid: part action, part mystery, part science-fiction. Any action-detective show usually has lots of car chases, gun battles, and fistfights. Well, we only had one futuristically customized car, so we couldn't exactly do car chases!"

Another indicator of the show's limited budget: It was expensive to create the Pulse Gun's distortion visual effects every time Jake pulled the trigger. "Budget-wise, he couldn't shoot the damned thing more than once or twice an episode, which made for rather lopsided gun battles in which the bad guys would be blazing away forever while Jake would lay low, waiting to take his shot," explains Manning. "And even the traditional 'laser blaster' beam-firing gun, though much cheaper to do in CG than Jake's gun, would eat up the CGI budget fast. So many TekWar villains wound up shooting plain old non–CGI 'leadspitters'— traditional bullets."

There was plenty of opportunity to inject both satire and new sociopolitical situations into the plots of various episodes. "We had a throwaway line in one episode where a newscaster referred to President Hillary Clinton which, at the time, seemed a fairly unlikely event. But today, who knows?" chuckles Manning. "Some executive at our Canadian network strongly objected to that line and wanted it excised because it was 'too American.' He insisted that a series filmed in Canada should have Canadian references. We agreed that Canada should get equal time... and in a later episode, the same newscaster made a reference to the 'People's Republic of Quebec.' The executive was silent henceforth.

"Sociological issues tend to be cyclic. 'Tek Posse,' for instance, posited an Untouchables-like government task force that was given free rein to fight the 'war on drugs' by any means necessary ... including torture. Well, scratch out 'drugs' and write in 'terrorism' instead, and you might see one or two slight parallels to what's going on in the U.S. today."

Beimler recalls his television directorial debut with "Skin Deep." "I learned a lot about directing and working with actors," he says. "Greg Evigan was really fun to work with. The one experience that jumps out at me was that we were doing a [camera] dolly shot down this long corridor. I had this image of how it should be done. And Greg started to make fun of me, saying, 'This is the dolly shot that's going to sink the show!' The dolly became something of a character. It became very spontaneous. Everyone started singing 'Hello Dolly.' Everyone got into it. We had a musical number for about two and a half minutes! It was really fun. The energy of the show was really quite exciting. I hate using words like energy, but it really was— the feeling of the show was one of excitement. We tried to encourage that."

Less enthusiastic is veteran television screenwriter and novelist Marc Scott Zicree, who contributed two stories, "Stay of Execution" and "The Gate." "TekWar was a good idea, it had a lot of potential," says Zicree. "Unfortunately, the pro-

duction value was not very great and the lead actor was not good. He just wasn't very strong. It was a series that could have been better than it was in terms of execution, the acting, the visual design of the show."

When his scripts were filmed, Zicree felt they could have been much stronger. "I wasn't very pleased with the outcome," he notes. "Sometimes it's very strange when you're writing a script and then you see the execution and with TekWar, the execution just wasn't up to what was in mind as I was writing it."

From his experience on the show, Zicree understood the challenges that faced all those concerned: "What I was hearing, was that there were so many cooks. Studios, networks and so forth all giving notes. I think the executive producers were being driven crazy, trying to answer all the notes from the interested parties."

Summing up his TekWar experience, Stephen Roloff remarks, "TekWar was a wonderful opportunity to make some projections about the world of the future and there were big changes, like visualizing cyberspace and having a manual interface to navigate data, and the flat screen monitors, communication devices, and Adway. The central metaphor had to do with illusion. William Shatner's idea in his books was this drug that allowed you to experience reality any way you want, so we tried to take that and create many different technologies that would create illusions. One was holographic projections, which is happening today, or hoods that people could pull over their heads that would allow you to morph into the face of a different person, which echoes the prosthetic stuff done later in Mission: Impossible. We tried to create a world where there was adaptive, nimble and lightweight technology, that wasn't cumbersome, and tried to suggest ways technology had evolved elegantly.

"I think where we fell apart was showing transportation. It's very hard to do the future without an enormous budget. That's the death of an SF show about future Earth—cars and fashion. Fashion you can kind of retro fit but cars kind of identify you to a certain time period."

TekWar was canceled because of low ratings. "Our ratings simply didn't justify renewing the show. Atlantis [the production company] couldn't afford to produce the show without USA Network's participation." says Beimler. "It started off terrifically, though. We had like a 3.7 or a 4.0, something very big in the first episode, but we never got back up there."

CAST NOTES

Greg Evigan (Jake Cardigan): Greg became something of a pop idol because of the Glen Larson–produced drama series *B.J. & the Bear* (1979). He later starred in the NBC sitcom *My Two Dads* with Paul Reiser, which ran for two years. Early film roles included *Stripped to Kill* (1987) with Kay Lenz and the underwater epic, *Deep Star Six* (1989). He is also a singer, songwriter and musician with stage roles in *Jesus Christ Superstar, Chicago* and *Grease.*

Eugene Clark (Sid Gomez): A football player with the Toronto Argonauts in the 1970s, Eugene played Detective Colby Burns in *Night Heat* (1985–89), and Ted Garrett in *Sue Thomas: FBEye* (2004). He made guest appearances on *Twilight Zone, E.N.G., Street Legal, Side Effects, Due South, Earth Final Conflict,* and *Robocop: Prime Directives.*

Maria Del Mar (Lt. Sam Houston): Born in Spain, of Venezuelan parents, Del Mar's earliest acting roles included *E.N.G., Forever Knight,* and *Matrix.* She starred in *Street Legal* (1994) before landing *TekWar.* After this series, she co-starred

in UPN's *Mercy Point* as Dr. Haylen Breslauer (1998) and guest-starred on *24* (2004) and *Terminal City* (2005).

William Shatner (Bascom): One of Hollywood's most recognizable and successful Canadian actors, Shatner started his acting career with noted stage performances in Shakespeare Festivals. One of his earliest acting roles on film was *The Brothers Karamazov* (1958). In his first TV series, he played a lawyer on *For the People* (1965). In 1966, he was cast as Captain James T. Kirk on *Star Trek* which ran for three years. Later, he starred in TV's *Barbary Coast* (1975) and *TJ Hooker* (1982–86), and hosted *Rescue 911* (1989–1996). He starred in seven *Star Trek* feature films and directed the series entry, *Star Trek V: The Final Frontier* (1989). More recently, he was Denny Crane in David E. Kelley's *Boston Legal,* a role that garnered him two Emmy awards in 2004 and 2005. In addition to being an actor, singer, writer and director, Shatner is also the co-founder and CEO of C.O.R.E. Digital Effects, the special effects facility that conjured up the *TekWar* visual effects.

Time Trax

(1993–1994)

The adventures of a 22nd century police officer in the 20th century as he chases after fugitives who have traveled back in time to escape from justice.

Cast: Dale Midkiff (Captain Darien Lambert), Elizabeth Alexander (Selma)
Created by: Harve Bennett, Jeffrey M. Hayes, Grant Rosenberg; **Executive Producers:** Harve Bennett, Jeffrey M. Hayes, Gary Nardino, Grant Rosenberg; **Line Producer:** Darryl Sheen; **Co-Producer:** Dean Barnes; **Writers included:** Garner Simmons, Harve Bennett, Jeffrey M. Hayes, Grant Rosenberg, Bill Dial, David Loughery, Ruel Fischmann, Tracy Friedman; **Directors included:** Lewis Teague, Rob Stewart, Colin Budds, Chris Thomson, Jeffrey M. Hayes, Harve Bennett; **Director of Photography:** Barry M. Wilson; **Production Designer:** Stewart Burnside; **Music Theme:** Gary MacDonald, Laurie Stone; **Guest Stars included:** Mia Sara, Michael Warren, Jerry Hardin, Eric Pierpoint, Eddie Albert, Christopher Daniel Barnes, John DeLancie, Tamlyn Tomita, Jeri

Ryan, Priscilla Barnes, Amy Steel, Margaret Avery, Bernie Casey, Henry Darrow (as the Chief), Peter Donat (as Mordecai Sahmbi)
Prime Time Entertainment Network/Warner Bros. Domestic Television/Gary Nardino Productions/Lorimar Television/Warner Bros. Television; 1993–1994; 60 minutes; 44 episodes

The fantasy of time travel is one of the oldest and most popular in science fiction literature. H.G. Wells' seminal novel *The Time Machine* has been adapted several times on film. Who doesn't want an opportunity to use technology and travel in time to witness, and participate in, events that occur in the past or the future?

With *Time Trax,* three veteran Hollywood producers and writers got together and created an action-adventure series that wasn't just science fiction, but also a crime drama.

Time Trax was one of three new television programs for a consortium of independent television stations that banded together under the Prime Time Entertainment Network banner. It was a wheel spoke along with *Kung Fu — The Legend Continues* and *Babylon 5,* all originating from Warner Bros. Television.

Executive producer Grant Rosenberg was an executive at Paramount Studios along with Gary Nardino, and this show was his first as a writer-producer. He had worked with Jeffrey M. Hayes and Harve Bennett at Paramount on various projects; *Time Trax* was a chance to join with them on a TV series project as producing colleagues. Hayes had a long history as a television producer, having been involved with a string of successful crime drama shows (*Vega$, Law & Order,* and *T.J. Hooker*). But it was a successful production experience in Australia with the 1988 revival of the cult spy drama *Mission: Impossible* that set the stage for *Time Trax* to be filmed there.

Like Hayes, Harve Bennett was well known in the industry, having been a writer and producer on a long list of TV series that included *The Mod Squad, Invisible Man, Gemini Man, Powers of Matthew Star,* and the "Bionic" shows. Notably, he revived the *Star Trek* franchise with four feature films beginning with *Star Trek II: The Wrath of Khan* (1982).

"I came up with the original idea for a cop from the future who comes back to our time to chase escaped convicts," says Rosenberg. "Harve helped to flesh out the characters and backstory and Jeff rounded out the trio by bringing in the practical production expertise. It was a terrific partnership."

Working in concert, Rosenberg, Hayes and Bennett crafted a premise that presented Darien Lambert, a young and debonair 22nd century police officer pursuing fugitives in the 20th century. A graduate of West Point military academy, Lambert had extraordinary physical abilities and, as a hobby, had an intense interest in American history. He spoke six languages and was versed in a variety of martial arts skills. He was assisted on his missions by Selma, a 22nd century mainframe computer disguised as an AT&T Master Card credit card; Selma was his intelligence source and connection to the 22nd century. (Selma was an acronym for Specified Encapsulated Limitless Archive.) A product of 22nd century holographic technology, Selma appeared to Darien as a ma-

tronly woman modeled after his biological mother. In her first appearance, Selma shimmered and spoke to him, as he warily waved his arm right through her physical space; since she was only a projection of light, her image crackled and wavered when "touched." On missions, her capabilities were highly advanced but limited. If Lambert needed to listen to a television set that was far away, Selma would augment the audio for him and play it back privately if he held the credit card to his ear. This capability came in very handy if two distant people were having a conversation and he needed to listen in. Similarly, if he needed to see something in the distance, Selma would project for him a holographically magnified view of the scene.

He was also given what appeared to be a small automobile keychain that was actually a futuristic weapon. Called the MPPT (the Miniature Pellet Projection Tube), it served both as a weapon and a device to return escapees to their proper time. A blast from a blue pellet served to stun the target for a few minutes and a blast from the green pellets would render them unconscious for three hours. It was the red pellets, containing a substance called TXP, that prepared the subject, on a molecular level, for return to the future. To complete the process, Selma emitted a "transmission tone" so that the subjects would be sent back to the future.

The series pilot, written by Bennett, features Lambert, as a renowned police captain in the year 2193, working on a series of baffling cases where criminals are mysteriously vanishing. When assassin Sepp Dietrich murders the United Nations president, he is strangely relaxed and gleeful after being captured. He soon disappears from his cell without a trace and Lambert theorizes that time travel was involved. The man responsible is Nobel Prize–winning scientist Mordecai Sahmbi.

The police blast their way into the Trax (Transtime Research and eXperimentation) laboratory to apprehend Sahmbi but he escapes by sending himself back in time. In the process, however, Sahmbi also killed his young and beautiful protégé, Elyssa. Determined to capture Sahmbi and the other fugitives, Lambert follows the fugitive into the Trax chamber and sends himself back 200 years to the year 1993, landing in the ladies room of the Smithsonian. Lambert is startled to find Annie Knox, a splitting image ancestor to the woman he came to love in the future.

With Annie's help, he learns that Sepp Dietrich is planning another assassination, that of the president of the United States in Hawaii. Although Lambert successfully thwarts Dietrich and returns him to the future, Sahmbi and other fugitives, who have been working together, now realize a 'future cop' is dogging their tracks.

To make their new series a reality, the three co-creators hand-picked the one man they felt would be ideal in the role of Lambert. "We'd seen Dale [Midkiff] in a few movies-of-the-week and knew he was on the verge of becoming a series leading man," said Rosenberg. "We presented him to Warner Bros. and to the PTEN board and everyone loved him."

Says Hayes, "Dale was relatively young when he was cast. Very nice soft spoken guy who took his work seriously."

The producers also cast Elizabeth Alexander and Peter Donat as the holographic companion and the arch-villain. "Elizabeth was a joy," says Hayes. "She only worked one day an episode as all her stuff was done on blue screen and then layered into the show. I used her on a remake of Stephen King's *Salem's Lot* [the 2004 mini-series]. We still stay in touch."

Hayes reveals that in an earlier incarnation, Selma was conceptualized as a very different person. "We had talked about Selma being a young knockout Hollywood actress but then decided her character needed the weight of a grounded, more adult woman," he says. "We were fortunate to find Elizabeth in Australia, which also helped with budget concerns. Ultimately, I think it was the right choice as the audience probably wouldn't have bought the typical Hollywood twenty-something actress as Darien's conscience."

"We enjoyed tremendous studio support," says Rosenberg. "We got very lucky, because all of the actors were fantastic to work with, as were our myriad guest stars."

Structurally speaking, *Time Trax* was a semi-anthological format. Each week Captain Lambert would travel anywhere in the world in pursuit of 22nd century fugitives. One week Lambert would have a confrontation with the Japanese Yakuza. Next he would meet up with a U.S. marshal in the west. Other episodes had Lambert battling with a London serial killer, matching wits with a fugitive in the middle of a hurricane, and being trapped in a mine shaft with his archenemy Sahmbi.

"The show was not necessarily typical, given the diversity of criminals who escaped from 2193," notes Rosenberg. "Some were hardened cons, while others were the equivalent of white collar crooks. As such, there was a wide range of

stories that ran throughout the series. At the end of almost every show, Darien would 'zap' the person back to their rightful time, and incarceration."

The filmmakers made an effort to vary the storytelling styles as much as possible so viewers wouldn't get bored. Says Rosenberg, "In one episode, a criminal had fathered a child, who was a great kid. The criminal had gone straight...what does Darien do? Also, it was important to use Darien's unique view of the world — talk about 20/20 hindsight — to make comments on things that were happening today. Some of his observations were based upon his knowledge of events to come, while others were based upon his unfamiliarity with certain customs of the 1990s."

In a restaurant scene in the series pilot, Lambert asks Secret Service agent Annie Knox, "What's a cappuccino?" "We were able to generate a lot of humor as a result of Darien being a kind of 'Connecticut Yankee in King Arthur's Court,'" says Rosenberg.

Catching fugitives was Lambert's task, but there was just one man the filmmakers wouldn't let him capture — Sahmbi. Rosenberg admits that he was their "one-armed man," referencing the elusive killer of Dr. Richard Kimble's wife on the popular 1960s cult show *The Fugitive*. Says Rosenberg, "The plan was to keep him around and then weave him throughout the series as needed. Had we been on the air longer, the intent was for Darien to take Sahmbi back to the 22nd future with him in the final episode."

Time Trax was filmed in Queensland, Australia. "We shot on the Gold Coast, [which] has a varied number of exotic-looking locations. So we had everything from desert (e.g. western episode) to rain forests to beach and oceans," notes executive producer Jeffrey Hayes. "Brisbane, 45 north of the Gold Coast, and surfers paradise served our purposes for an urban look. All of this within a reasonable distance from our base at the Warner/Roadshow Studios."

Hayes also says that occasionally a location was too good to pass up, so a scene or series of scenes in a script would be rewritten to include it in order to showcase the area. As an example, a fantastic waterfall figured prominently in the end of the series pilot.

The only real drawback that the filmmakers discovered by shooting Down Under was that it was necessary to import about a dozen left-hand vehicles (in Australia, you drive on the left side of the road with a right-side wheel). "Australia was fantastic," says Rosenberg. "Not only were we able to stretch our rather meager budget, but the crews and the people were wonderful. Much of the credit has to go to Jeff Hayes, who really was the pioneer American TV producer in Oz. He put together a production team that is still intact today."

Rosenberg says he's amazed at the amount of work that was accomplished given the arduous circumstances under. "I realized at the time that it was an extremely efficient and smooth-running series, but now, having a lot more experience under my belt, I look back and I'm astonished on what we were able to accomplish with such low overhead. Harve and I essentially served as the 'writing staff.' We brought in Garner Simmons as a consultant in the second season and he was a tremendous help in rewriting the freelance scripts. Jeff had the production completely under control."

"A lot of those people who did *Time Trax* still work with me when I shoot in Australia," says Hayes. "Stewart Burnside, our production designer, and John Stokes, our cinematographer, just did *Nightmares and Dreamscapes,* a Stephen King mini-series with me.

"One of our biggest challenges for the pilot was recreating a futuristic Washington D.C. on the Gold Coast. Burnside and I went to D.C. to scout around and see what we could figure out. We built the entire Georgetown Street as a backlot and then matted in [visual special effects] around it. I think one of the better tricks we used was a hanging foreground miniature for the Vietnam Memorial, as seen in the pilot, which was shot on a college campus in Brisbane."

The filmmakers' one creative concession was allowing a couple of "product placement" deals to be made with AT&T Master Card and Continental Airlines. "We needed every dollar we could scrape up for the production," explains Rosenberg. "The AT&T deal was straight cash and to fulfill our end, we needed to show an AT&T Master Card for a certain number of seconds per episode, which is why Darien's computer, Selma, was cleverly disguised as an AT&T credit card. We had a rather complicated formula with Continental, which provided us with tickets to Australia in return for exposure on the series. When you watch the show, you'll notice that there is a very recognizable shot of a Continental jet embedded in the main titles."

Over the course of 44 episodes, Lambert had many adventures and he ultimately sent 19 fugitives back to their future prison. However, he did allow three fugitives (and three non-fugitives) to remain in the 20th century. At least four people learned that he was a time traveler, but only three believed it.

As the series progressed, Lambert and Selma at times argued with each other, but each came to appreciate each other. Quite a strange outcome when you consider that Selma was nothing more than a 22nd century supercomputer that was customized specifically for Lambert's police work.

Darien Lambert's mission was cut short by the PTEN Network after two seasons. "The show was well received by viewers, and we had a plethora of stories left to tell," says Rosenberg. "In the end, it was canceled because PTEN wanted to go with a different show to see if they could increase their viewer base. Instead of a solid 'double,' they wanted to swing for the fences with new programming."

"We all had a good time making the show and were quite sad when it wasn't picked up for one more season," Hayes sighs. "A third season would have been like the first two. Darien catching bad guys and dealing with Sahmbi periodically. The real fun for me doing the series was what kind of a bad guy it was that Darien was chasing. What had they done with their knowledge of the future in the past? How were they surviving? Actually, there was no limit to the types of stories and characters, and ultimately, that's the real test for a good series premise."

If he had a chance to write the series' final episode, Hayes speculates, "That road would have to lead to Sahmbi. It might have been good to weave a love story for Darien into what might have been a two-hour finale. Also, [it] might have been interesting to chase Sahmbi back into the future for his demise or capture."

On the face of it, *Time Trax* is a fairly straightforward action-adventure-SF show. But once you get down to the deeper layers, you might get a headache from the temporal physics involved.

Because Sahmbi "left in a hurry" when the police barged into his laboratory, they gained control of his Trax time machine facility. To stop him from committing his crimes, they sent an investigator to pursue him.

But with a time machine at your disposal, you could send a message back to Darien Lambert and advise him to takes steps to prevent Trax from becoming a reality (a message is the most practical means of changing the events, with the least "contamination" to the timestream). However, if Lambert received the message and prevented Sahmbi from perfecting Trax, all of the events that we witness in the TV series would never happen. And what does that mean? No TV series.

This is where the migraine slaps you in the forehead: If Lambert becomes successful in preventing Sahmbi's Trax from going "online," he wipes out the events of the future and time continues forward with a clean slate. But if he succeeds in doing that, and the Trax future never occurred, how could that future have existed so that a message is sent back asking Lambert to wipe them from existence?

This is what real-life temporal physics tells us: There is a "many worlds theory" of physics which is graphically illustrated on the Fox TV series *Sliders*. It says that time can split into an infinite series of dimensional branches containing some degrees of variation from each other.

When Lambert wipes the Trax future from existence, he only splits his universe into its own branch with a clean slate future. And the Trax future merely "jumps" into a separate branch, never to be seen again.

The show's producers never hint or suggest this direction as a course of action in the series' plotting. It's just too complicated and is not conducive for a simple-to-follow TV series.

The series creators were well aware of the temporal physics but constructed *Time Trax* as they wanted because, if developed any other way, there would not be an ongoing series premise.

However, with about 100 fugitives and a criminal genius running around in the 20th century,

that's an incalculable contamination of the timestream. All of their actions in this era can affect the flow and direction of the future. The series doesn't really go into the consequences of their actions (if you consider the timestream as a river with eddies that impact 200 years ahead), because it's just too complicated.

As it was, even at the end of two seasons, *Time Trax* had a strong format that it could have continued for many more adventures.

CAST NOTES

Dale Midkiff (Capt. Darien Lambert): Born in Chance, Maryland, he has acted in many off-Broadway plays in New York and got his first screen role in Roger Corman's B-movie *Streetwalkin*.' He played John "Jock" Ewing in *Dallas: The Early Years* and went on to play Elvis Presley in the mini-series *Elvis and Me*. He was also in the cast of the 1989 film *Pet Semetary*. Since his role in *Time Trax* he has appeared in the TV series *The Magnificent Seven* and *The Crow: Salvation* and in the movie *Deep Rescue*. He has been seen most recently in the Hallmark Channel movie *Love's Unending Legacy*.

Elizabeth Alexander (Selma): Alexander was born in Adelaide, Australia. She is an actress with a number of high-profile credits in Australian film, television and theater. She has been seen in the films *The Chant of Jimmie Blacksmith* and *Summerfield* and on television has appeared in *Farscape*. She is best known for her recurring role in the medical drama *All Saints*.

Timecop
(1997–1998)

Time cop Jack Logan works for the Time Enforcement Commission in 2007. His job is to bring modern-day criminals back from the past before they can disrupt the present.

Cast: TW King (Jack Logan), Cristi Conaway (Claire Hemmings), Don Stark (Gene Matuzek), Kurt Fuller (Dale Easter)

Based on the comic books by: Mike Richardson, Mark Verheiden; **Created for Television by:** Mark Verheiden; **Executive Producers:** Lawrence Gordon, Robert Singer; **Co-Executive Producers:**

Mike Richardson, Lloyd Levin, Art Monterastelli; **Supervising Producer:** Mark Verheiden; **Producers:** Philip J. Sgriccia, Chris Long; **Associate Producer:** Michael Caplan; **Staff Associate Producer:** Susan J. Spohr; **Writers included:** Miles Millar, Alfred Gough, Mark Verheiden, Art Monterastelli, Linda McGibney; **Directors included:**

Allan Arkush, David Grossman, Chris Long, Robert Singer, Martha Mitchell, Jim Charleston, Philip Sgriccia; **Guest Stars included:** Rena Sofer, Melora Hardin, Nicolas Coster, Bruce Campbell, Joan Pringle, Heidi Schanz, Dick O'Neill, Joshua Devane, Anna Galvin, William Devane, Belinda Waymouth, Tom O'Brien (as Pascoe)

ABC/Universall; September 1997–July 1998; 60 minutes; 9 episodes

"If the public found out that time travel is a reality, it would cause cultural shockwaves," says a scientist. But he had nothing to worry about — the public didn't find out about *Timecop* and after nine low-rated episodes, the series vanished.

It was based on a 1994 Jean-Claude Van Damme film which was based on a Dark Horse comic series. In that film, Van Damme was a timecop who tries to prevent an evil politician from manipulating time to ascend to the presidency.

Three years later, the TV series was picked up by ABC, but then bounced around the schedule and pre-empted. *Timecop* was yet another show that may have fared better had it originally aired on the Sci-Fi Channel.

The series had many successful ingredients, among them a good-looking young hero (with impossibly white teeth) named Jack Logan, and a beautiful blonde colleague, officer Claire Hemmings. And like all cop shows, there was a gruff chief with a heart of gold. Actor Don Stark, whose roly-poly, expressive face was perfect as chief Gene Matuzek, didn't disappoint. His one-liners are so predictable they're amusing: "Cool your jets!" or "What the hell are they doing back there?" and puffer-fish threats like, "I'm gonna have you passing out parking tickets in the mall," and begrudging compliments ("Jack, you're the best I've got!").

"Any changes from the movie were done mostly to create more of a week-to-week franchise," says Mark Verheiden, who created the show for television (and later co-executive produced *Battlestar Galactica*). "Hence giving the main character a female partner. But we stayed fairly true to the movie concept. The success of the feature was probably the main reason we were able to sell the series. ABC really wanted a weekly version of the movie, so a lot of reinvention wasn't required. Action fans may have wanted more martial arts action but that was never in the cards."

He found selling the series a cinch. "The pilot pitch to ABC was pretty amazing. Executive producer Larry Gordon had done a lot of legwork, because the meeting lasted about 15 minutes, involved some perfunctory discussion of story ideas, and ended with the president of the network giving us a 13-episode on-air guarantee. That's almost unheard of today, and it was pretty rare even back then. Since this was my very first TV experience, I figured this must be how it always works. I have since learned otherwise."

But according to producer Chris Long, things soon got rockier. "*Timecop* was damaged goods from the start," he states. "By the time it got on the schedule, new network and studio heads had come in. I don't think anybody likes to pick up someone else's development."

The year is 2007 and Jack, Claire and Matuzek preside over a group of technicians at the Time Enforcement Commission (TEC) in Washington D.C. This is a world where the secret of time travel has been revealed, and criminals and rogue timecops escape into the past and change time. Jack's job is to chase after them. His motto: 'To protect the past and preserve the future." The missions often start with a nameless technician yelling, "Sir, we're picking up a major rift development in the temporal stream." Once the time zone is located, Jack jumps into a rocket-propelled chair and is swept down a blue tunnel as a seductive female voice (supplied by producer Chris Long's wife, a voice-over artist) counts down his departure. He then materializes in the past, sometimes in clothes reflecting the period, and sometimes in his present-day cop clothes, forcing him to make a quick change.

His vitals — heart, respiration and cortex — are monitored by Matuzek and Claire. Meanwhile, a bespectacled historian named Easter provides information on the time period. Despite its TV budget, Jack's visits to eras like the Civil War, World War II and, in particular, moody and misty 19th-century London are convincing.

There was some media curiosity as to why a relative unknown such as T.W. King was cast instead of a marquee name. "We wanted a fresh face, somebody who was physical, a good actor, and somebody we thought would be nice to work with," says producer Robert Singer. "T.W. King fit the bill on all of those."

"I liked T.W. a lot as Jack Logan," says Verheiden, "and Don Stark, who went on to a great run on *That '70s Show*, was great, though Don's character, the head of the Time Enforcement Commission, made some sort of bad decision in almost every episode. We didn't realize we were doing that until a few shows in, when the writers started calling his character, Wrong Again, Matuzek. Cristi came aboard when the network insisted we recast the [original] female lead. While I thought Cristi was fine, I sometimes wonder how things might have gone with the original actress [Allyson Rice-Taylor]."

The stories themselves were a mixture of formula, camp and inventiveness, such as a madman killing Jack the Ripper and then continuing his killing spree. Or a 21st century scientist helping the Nazis speed up their development of the atomic bomb. "If you like comic books, hokey villains and B-grade storylines, this could be your favorite show," remarked *TV Guide*, who labeled it "a juvenile adventure."

The producers also wanted to keep it a "fun action-adventure show. The Holocaust or the [Spanish] Inquisition are not things we're going to get into," said Singer at the time. "We want to do shows that we can have fun with." Singer was also pleased with the way the series looked. "We're spending a lot of money on this show."

In Mark Verheiden's "The Heist," William Devane plays a bitter cop named Langdon, who travels back with Jack to 1977 to solve a diamond heist that ruined the cop's career. As music hits like "Boogie Fever" blare out of radios, the pair meet the cop as a young man (played by Devane's real-life son, Joshua). Langdon decides to stay in 1977 and steal the diamonds himself, since his career ended when he couldn't locate the diamonds after the original heist. But Jack makes sure the younger version of the cop retrieves the diamonds, which makes him a hero and the older, bitter cop no longer exists. It proved that time could be changed for the better.

One recurring villain is Pascoe (Tom O'Brien), an over-the-top nut who, after having had posed as Jack the Ripper, escaped into other time zones, such as 1956, where he plans the murder of a young actress who would give birth to the 44th president of the United States. Jack never caught Pascoe and vowed to continue his hunt for this time-leaping madman.

Jack is a lantern-jawed cop, a likable wise-ass who admits history didn't always interest him. "To me, World War II was nothing more than a scratchy documentary in history class," he says. Born in 1974, Jack admits that the complexities of 2007 scare him ("I'm more comfortable with the past than the present"). He keeps his relationships, especially with Claire, on a teen-boy level, although he matures enough to ask her out for a quiet romantic dinner — which he cancels due

to business. "He has foibles that make him more human," King noted in 1997. "He's good at what he does but doesn't take himself too seriously."

A highlight for Verheiden was the episode "Lost Voyage," where two greedy brothers, hosts of an undersea documentary series in 2007, plan to wreck the *Empress of the Americas* in 1939 so they can claim the luxury liner's salvage rights later and do a ratings-charged TV special.

"In terms of production, that was one of the more fun shows, which we shot almost entirely aboard the *Queen Mary* in Long Beach. I remember doing a location scout with the production manager, who, after climbing the umpteenth staircase and fretting about how he was going to move camera and crew around the ship, looked at me quite seriously and said he wanted to kill me for writing that story. Maybe that says it all about the *Timecop* TV experience. It was, quite frankly, not a happy one."

Chris Long thinks one mistake was setting it in the future. "It had the perfect TV premise, with endless story potential, but we should have set it in 1997, not 2007. Our production designer [Jim Pohl] actually said, 'Let's make it present-day, that way we can film out on the streets and it won't cost as much.' It was an expensive show to make, not only in recreating things like Chicago of the 1930s but with the electric cars." The backlots of Universal Studios helped to recreate the show's past eras.

The most intriguing episode was a present-day tale, told with heart and desperation. In "D.O.A." Linda McGibney's script has an assassin fire a rocket at Jack and Matuzek's car, killing them instantly. A heartbroken Claire travels back in time a few hours and warns Jack that someone is out to kill him. She then vanishes and Jack and Mutuzek work together to prevent their own deaths. As each lead fizzles, and their deaths seem inevitable, Matuzek says, "Maybe this is it. Maybe we're supposed to buy it tonight and there's nothing we can do about it."

The divorced Matuzek wants to see his teenage son one last time, an awkward goodbye that galvanizes both Matuzek and Jack to push one last time to find their killer. They learn the hit man was hired by a beautiful scientist (played by sexy Rena Sofer) who wants Matuzek dead for incarcerating her boyfriend. Jack saves his boss from the gun-toting woman.

Timecop also had its funny moments. When Jack angrily kicks his desk after being dumped by his girlfriend, the tech geeks around him flinch and Matuzek admonishes, "Jack, watch it! You're scaring my computer techs!" And Matuzek is funny as he wrestles with his own sensitivity: "Oh, hell, I'm no good with this touchy-feely stuff." And another timecop (Bruce Campbell) gets tired of the non-interference rules of time and announces to Jack that he's going to bet on the World Series in 1996 because he knows the Yankees will win.

It wasn't long before the producers of *Timecop* knew the series would lose. "We knew we were in trouble when the ABC executives who originally bought the show were replaced about two months into the development process by an all-new regime," says Verheiden. "As usually happens when these seismic shifts occur, the new ABC team was totally not invested in our show. But since we had a 13-episode on-air guarantee, they were forced to deal with us. The first shoe dropped when ABC demanded we recast the female lead after finishing the pilot. Then we were scheduled into the timeslot before and after *Monday Night Football*. In other words, we aired at different times in different areas of the country, and [some] markets ran their own after-game shows instead of network programming. Finally, ABC's promotion for their entire lineup was abysmal. They decided to get cute with their advertising, creating a series of snide, black-on-yellow promos that said nothing about the shows and in fact seemed designed to insult the intelligence of the audience. When the show finally debuted to rather weak numbers, the handwriting was on the wall. And we discovered that a '13-episode guarantee' doesn't always mean you get 13 episodes." *Timecop* was cancelled after nine. One consolation was a series of paperbacks, based on the series, released by Del Rey in 1999.

Assessing the series today, Verheiden says, "The strengths were in the original concept and a mostly great production team. Executive producer Bob Singer had just come off *Lois and Clark* and we were incredibly fortunate to have him on board. In 20/20 hindsight, I wish the show had been darker and grittier both in terms of the storytelling and stylistically. But we were trying to deliver an 8:00 P.M. show. That meant doing something 'suitable for children,' so gritty wasn't

going to happen. We were just getting our sealegs, story-wise, with our last episode, which was a sweet story about Don Stark's character Matuzek trying to reconnect with his teenage son. But we were cancelled as that episode was wrapping production, and that, as they say, was that."

"I was almost relieved when it was cancelled," says Long. "It was a lot of work. It was tough to do something you love but isn't loved by others. You're putting your heart and soul into something you feel is turning out so well and it's not getting a response."

Timecop had the look and energy of a show that could have run for years. But time and destiny were not on its side. Maybe Mutuzek was right all along when he said, "I'm not liking these odds."

CAST NOTES

Ted (T.W.) King (Jack Logan): This Maryland native was a film and video editor before he became an actor. His first big break was as a regular on the daytime show *Loving* (1995). His TV guest shots include *The X-Files* and *JAG*. In 2002, he joined *General Hospital*.

Cristi Conaway (Claire Hemmings): She was a model in Japan before returning to the U.S. for an acting career. The Texas-born actress considered herself a tomboy at heart. Her TV films include *Attack of the 50 Foot Woman* (1993) and *The Expendables* (2000). In 2004 she started her own successful clothing line.

Don Stark (Gene Matuzek): Stark's credits go back to *Baa Baa Black Sheep* (1978) and the 1980s fantasy *Beauty and the Beast*. He was also in the film *Star Trek: First Contact* (1996). New York City–born, he went to acting school on a dare and loved it. After *Timecop*, he co-starred as neighbor Bob Pinciotti on *That '70s Show* (1998–2006).

Kurt Fuller (Dale Easter): His earliest appearances were on the shows *Knight Rider* and *Quantum Leap*. He also appeared in *Ghostbusters II* (1989), *Wayne's World* (1992) and *A Day in the Life* (2006).

SOURCES

Fall preview. *TV Guide*, 1997.

Total Recall 2070
(1999)

In the year 2070, two detectives, one of them an android, protect citizens from technology-based crimes.

Cast: Michael Easton (David Hume), Karl Pruner (Ian Farve), Cynthia Preston (Olivia Hume), Judith Krant (Olan Chang), Matthew Bennett (James Calley), Michael Anthony Rawlins (Martin Ehrenthal)
Created by: Art Monterastelli; **Executive Producers:** Art Monterastelli, Drew S. Levin; **Supervising Producer:** Jeff King; **Line Producer:** Dennis Chapman; **Consulting Producer:** Ted Mann; **Writers included:** Ted Mann, Jeff King, Michael Thoma, Elliot Stern; **Directors included:** Mario Azzopardi, Jorge Montesi, David Warry-Smith, Mark Sobel, Ken Girotti; **Director of Photography:** Derick V. Underschultz; **Production Designer:** Peter Cosco; **Costumes:** Maxyne Baker; **Special Effects Makeup:** Gordon Smith; **Visual Special Effects:** Gajdecki Visual Effects (GVFX); **Guest Stars included:** Kim Coates, Nick Mancuso, Vanessa Williams, Monika Schnarre, David Warner, Anthony Zerbe, Henry Gibson, Ann Marie Loder, Martin Sheen

Showtime/Alliance-Atlantis Communications/Polygram Television/Pro 7/Team Communications Group; January–June 1999; 60 minutes; 22 episodes; DVD status: Complete series

"Forgetting is the Most Dangerous Way to Remember..."—from the Total Recall 2070 series bible

Because of the popularity of his stories, many of his works have been adapted as Hollywood films. But the late SF author Philip K. Dick's fertile imagination was realized on celluloid posthumously, beginning with the most famous adaptation: "Do Androids Dream of Electric Sheep." The novel became the Harrison Ford movie *Blade Runner* in 1982. (Dick, however, did screen scenes with director Ridley Scott prior to the film's release, before he passed away.) Later, the story "We Can Remember It for You Wholesale" became the Arnold Schwarzenegger vehicle *Total Recall* in 1990.

Other films based on Dick's works were also subsequently produced with top-shelf Hollywood actors and directors: *Screamers* (1995), *Imposters* (2001), *Minority Report* (2002), *Paycheck* (2003), *A Scanner Darkly* (2006), and *Next* (2007).

Although Dick is not credited on *Total Recall 2070* the television series, series creator and executive producer Art Monterastelli explains that its setting, tone and atmosphere were modeled after Dick's inventions. The influence, he says, was more about "sensibility." It was a vision of the future, a dark detective noir treatise with generous dollops of science fiction technology. "The look of *Blade Runner* was more of an influence because what we did was more of a paranoid-psychological thriller than an action-adventure series," says Monterastelli. "We thought it would be more cost-effective spending our money up front, creating this moody futuristic city and having the city itself be a character in the series. Trying to pay off the action-adventure elements of the movie, on a week-to-week basis, would be almost impossible to do on our budget. Also, I think doing a paranoid psychological thriller — that is in fact closer to Dick's sensibility in all his work — is more rewarding, creatively, for the writers. I've read most of Dick's stuff and the truth is that ass-kicking world view Schwarzenegger represents is anathema to one of Dick's typical protagonists. His heroes are very much 'anti-heroes,' paranoid everymen just trying to survive the Dystopian worlds they inhabit — whether those worlds are set in the future, in the present, or are in fact largely hallucinatory."

Imagine the dark city landscape and atmosphere of *Blade Runner,* fused with the existence of the Rekall Corporation (from *Total Recall* the feature), whose primary business was to sell virtual reality vacations to customers. The series takes place primarily on Earth although there was a visit to the Martian colonies in the pilot episode "Machine Dreams." "I call our show a futuristic detective noir," says supervising producer-writer Jeff King. "The look and tone of it is more a tip of the hat to the noir genre than it is to the original *Total Recall* movie."

Headlining the series were two detectives from the Citizens Protection Bureau, a federal agency investigating crimes involving uses and abuses of technology. "The CPB has replaced the police departments of our own time as the nature of crime has changed," explains Monterastelli. "It's sort of a combination police department and high-level consumer protection agency — our premise being that 70 years into the future, one of the things people are going to need protection against is technology itself. Technology and the unbridled power of the multi-global corporations have replaced the nation-states of today and basically rule the world.

"Violent crime as we know it today is exceedingly rare and has been replaced by other types of crimes. There's a whole category of 'mind crimes' ranging from manipulation and torture to brainwashing and the outright theft of private memories."

The slim, dark-haired and intense CPB detective David Hume and his partner Ian Farve were portrayed by Michael Easton and Karl Pruner. At the time of its premiere, Easton was most familiar to television audiences for his appearances on *Ally McBeal* (as the nude model), *VR5* (as Duncan, Sydney Bloom's friend) and *Two* (as the good and evil twins).

"Our particular hero is in the tradition of a thinking man's action hero," says Jeff King, referring to David Hume. "In the tradition of a Deckard [*Blade Runner*] or of a Mike Hammer. He's a man of action who operates in a world of intellect and technology that is sometimes bigger than any one man or woman can comprehend."

A Shakespearean stage actor, Karl Pruner is a Canadian whose most visible role was on the long-running Canadian series *E.N.G.* Detective Ian Farve, who becomes Hume's partner after the events of the pilot, was an Alpha-class "Plasma-based" prototype android. "Hume and this new partner are mismatched, very different and Farve is a very unique individual," notes Jeff King. "Most others are based on some bio-mechanical model. Farve is far more developed, from a technology using cloning [rather] than robot building. The cell division used to create him [is] synthetic as opposed to plasma-based flesh and blood."

As illustrated in the pilot, Hume's original partner was killed by rogue androids, a very significant event because "androids are programmed not to hurt human beings," explains King. "And so this is terrifying to the people, since androids mow the lawns, work on the streets. If the general populace thought that for no good reason one might lash out and kill, it would send a panic through the city that would be almost unstoppable. So there's a cover-up to keep this quiet.

"Farve is very different from Hume's original partner — he's trim, polite, well-dressed, very formal, and Hume doesn't like many things about him and he grapples with this. By the end of the two-hour opener, Hume learns he's a very sophisticated android and by the end, they've kicked some ass, had some drinks, solved the murder of Hume's partner, and so Hume's attitude towards technology and androids has undergone a complete rotation. Initially, he would have wanted to kill an android if he was partnered with one. Now, he's bonded with Farve over the things they've done; in fact they've saved each others lives, and the seeds of a working partnership begin to form."

Overseeing the cases at the Bureau was Martin Ehrenthal, played by Michael Anthony Rawlins. "The boss in the Citizens Protection Bureau, he assigns them cases and he is their champion with the bureaucracy above them and is their admonisher when they step out of line," says King.

In the course of their investigations, Hume and Farve often butted heads with James Calley, a representative of the Assessors Office (futurespeak for the Internal Affairs office), played by Matthew Bennett. "I liked him because he played it like a character from an old 1940s picture," notes director Mark Sobel, who helmed two episodes. "You don't really direct him. He just does his thing. It's just fun to watch. When someone's got the character, and you don't even need to say anything to them, it's really fun."

"They're more invasive than Internal Affairs, they don't just police the police, they make sure the police are policing themselves," says King. "They're also the mandarins of information, connected to a source of power that is even bigger than the CPB is."

Also in the character mix was Olan Chang, a multi-talented forensic pathologist, linguist and computer specialist. Her job was assisting Hume and Farve in solving the puzzling cases that confronted them. "She's like our 'Q' character [from James Bond]," chuckles King. "She is the technology specialist, does android autopsies, breaks down computer encryptions, she's our tech expert. Her room is hi-tech futuristic environment and designed so that if anything goes off, the explosion won't take out the entire building." To give Detective Hume a private life, young Canadian actress Cyndy Preston played his very attractive blond wife Olivia.

Meanwhile at work, Hume and Farve's job was to protect ordinary citizens from losing their identity, their valued rights in a society dominated by powerful multinational corporations, who formed "The Consortium." Scattered throughout this world are service worker androids of various classes. As the series progressed, Hume and Farve's growing relationship was examined and their cases were challenging.

Midway through the series, in "Paranoid," Olivia Hume discovered that false memories were implanted into her before she met David. "The world that Phil Dick was writing about, in 'We Can Remember It for You Wholesale,' inspired us," says King. "Dick is writing about something that deep down terrifies us. It's that one day you may wake up and everybody you believe you know, is not who you think they are and not knowing if that's because you are not who you think that you are or whether they aren't who you think they are. That, to me, is a horrifying prospect. It's deep, primal and so basic and primitive that it's got to be something we all share. That's the fascination and fear of the recall experience."

Adds Monterastelli, "A lot of the psychological aspects of the show deal with identity and, specifically in terms of the Rekall machine, the ability a third party has to take your identity away from you and sell or rent it to another person. Maybe they do this in pieces—the memory of one extreme vacation or one intense love affair at a time. Or maybe they steal your entire identity and then wholesale it."

Says King, "It's an opportunity to explore levels of reality and when you pit a hero like Hume against that, it becomes an adventure and that's the larger mystery that will lead us to Mars."

Another ongoing mystery was, who was Detective Farve's creator? Farve came to CBP as an android with amnesia and it wasn't until the final episode "Meet My Maker" that the question was answered.

Every episode dealt with issues pertaining to personal identity, or how a futuretech impacted society and individuals. "A good *Total Recall* story always had a high concept/futuretech hook," says King. "I am interested in futurism. What interested me more is how the technology we invent affects us. Plus I am a bit obsessive. I get interested in things in a way that often borders on compulsion."

King recalls filming a story "about a genetically enhanced call girl of the future being used for industrial espionage by a player who is trading information from one of these major corporations to another. Hume gets involved with one of these women, who is so genetically enhanced that her pheromone level is high because she's been given this enhancement. If she's with you even for a few seconds, it's the sexual experience of your life. It's so overpowering you can't possibly cope with it. We're dealing with the exploitation of these girls, by the people who handle them, of Hume's needs as a human being and as a detective to fight what's been done to these women by bio-enhancement. These are traditional adventures but set in the world of the future, where morality and technology has expanded what is possible. We're transporting the audience to a future reality that they haven't experienced before but these are stories that resonate with audiences, of what's happening today."

In another example of future technology serving as an entertainment device, Olivia purchased from Rekall Inc. a "Sublimator" which allows her to revisit moments with her father (deceased in real life) in three-dimensional realism.

"There are so many ... advances in technology and bio-technology and we use those things to speculate 20, 50, 70 years in the future, that may be real," says King. "We're trying to ground our world in an extrapolated reality, rather than going to a magic of a device *à la Star Trek* like a tricorder. Like, our laser guns are hypothetically possible, laser technology exists now, and that's where we try to come from. We want to ground our show in a believable reality."

"One of the most interesting conceits of the show is that over the first twenty-two episodes Hume becomes increasingly numb to the world around him while his partner Farve, our android, becomes increasingly more human," chuckles Monterastelli.

To pull off the illusion of a futuristic cityscape, digital special effects were provided by John Gajdecki and his team at Gajdecki Visual Effects. Blending a computer-generated cityscape with a live-action soundstage set was the series' signature, as Monterastelli explains. "The futuristic city is supposed to be 180 stories tall," he says. "We built two, and in some places three, levels of this city complete with streets and everything. We were able to match some of the camera moves from the model, through a blue or green screen that allowed us to include our computer-generated images, and right through a window or street grid into the actual city itself. There's a signature move in the two-hour pilot where the camera flies through a computer-generated world, into our model, back into a CGI shot, and then comes out on one of our streets, teeming with people and various modes of transportation. It's really quite an amazing shot."

The production company took over an expansive military base, the Canadian Forces Base Downsview in Toronto, Canada. "It was the best space available in the Toronto area," says Monterastelli. "It was an ideal place because there was so much room and height — it was sometimes a problem finding a warehouse with enough height to accommodate a multi-level set. Our main set is called Vertical City.

"John Campfens, our [visual effects supervisor] at Gajdecki SFX, came up with the idea of taking a city like Chicago— a city that has recognizable buildings, like the Sears Tower and the John Hancock Building — and building a second city right on top of it: hence the name Vertical City," recalls Monterastelli.

"Taavo Soodor, who initially designed our sets and conceptualized our world, was very thorough and specific," says Jeff King. "Rather than mow down and erect something new, they didn't have time for that, so they created methods of construction that allows the city to grow up and out and add on to the original structures."

Director Mark Sobel says that he was pleased with the quality of the performances delivered by the actors. "It was wonderful because these guys are super-professionals," he says. "Michael really is a thinking actor. He's not just a sort of pretty boy. He really loves and cares about the work. As a director it's just so enjoyable to deal with someone like that. And Karl, too, is just a consummate professional. And the two of them had such great chemistry together, both on camera and off. They really were buddies off camera. And you just knew that on film. Both those actors had the ability to play subtle humor. The show had a very dry, black sense of humor going through it. And both those guys got it."

Sobel's memories are especially vivid regarding Cynthia Preston's intimate and emotional "girl talk" scene with Judith Krant in "Bones." "Cynthia was a pleasure. She just had a natural instinct for things. She wasn't pretentious. She didn't have an attitude. She was really nice. As a director coming on for a couple of episodes, I inherit the stars. Whoever made the initial choices really chose a great group of people, which is 90 percent of the battle. Everyone is great to work with. There's a positive vibe, that's the main thing. I've worked on a lot of shows that didn't have a positive vibe. You don't want to go to work in the morning."

In the scene, Olivia was grappling with the knowledge of her implanted memories. She had just separated from her husband, and Olan helped console her. The way in which the scene was prepared garnered Sobel a strong compliment from Preston. "Cynthia came up to me after we did that scene. She said, 'Thank you. That's the most creatively satisfying experience I've ever had as an actor,'" grinned Sobel. "The way we approached it, before we did an official rehearsal, we brought them onto the set and said, 'I want the two of you to spend the next hour here together, just talking along the lines of what the scene is about. I want you to get a feel for each other. Just play with it.' And I walked away. When I came back an hour later, I said, 'Okay, show me the scene,' and we started rehearsing. It just worked great. It wasn't so much that I did a brilliant directing job, it's that I didn't have to direct it because I gave *them* a chance to direct it. I gave them that hour and then I came to see it. Giving them that opportunity, that hour beforehand, really got them into it."

Keeping in line with a noir-ish look and feel, a stylistic decision was made regarding actors' delivery of dialogue. When actors exchanged words in tense and dramatic moments or sequences, often the delivery was ... slow. Pauses aplenty. This was antithetical to how Hollywood's contemporary television was made. "Slow" might create boredom; would the viewer reach for the remote control? "That's how networks see it," Sobel remarks. "As a filmmaker it's exciting to work on a show when the producers tell you, 'Let it play out ... let it be slow....' Nowadays everything on television is fast, fast, *fast*! They're afraid people will change the channel. It's a rare opportunity to work on a show where the producers to have the guts and the conviction of what they are doing to let it play slowly. That was really fun. There's very, very few opportunities to do that any more." The justification here was that slow didn't equate with boredom but depth.

Showtime decided not to pick up the series for a second season; it was canceled at just 22 episodes. "I was so disappointed," says Sobel. "It had a building following. It takes a while to build a cult following.... I came on in the very end of the first season and they really found their direction at that point." A number of different factors contributed to the decision. Essentially, the ratings were not there, and Monterastelli also hints at additional reasons.

Working on the series was quite back-breaking for Monterastelli. He says that Showtime was concerned that he was considering leaving the show if it was renewed for a second season. He had been flying back and forth (Toronto–Los Angeles) for nearly two years. It was enormous pressure on him and his family.

"My biggest regret is that we had too many production entities to answer to, and therefore had a nearly impossible job of finding our dramatic footing," says Monterastelli. "That said, we did some amazing episodes; but we also did some that weren't so amazing — especially when we were bending over trying to please everybody involved.

"Alliance, the Canadian company, had been taken over by Atlantis. Polygram Television, the American production company, was on the verge of basically going out of business, and Showtime's licensing fee was not nearly enough to cover the cost of doing the show."

They might not have total recall 10 years after the series finished, but both Jeff King and Art Monterastelli say that they remain proud of their work on the show. "[It] is and was extraordinarily ambitious," says King. "The series explored big themes and ideas: genetics, globalization, human interaction with artificial intelligence. I think the show succeeded on many levels. Looking now at the power of CGI merged with live action on a series like, say, *Battlestar Galactica*, I'd have to say that we were a few years ahead of our time.... We never quite got the model/CGI integration of the larger city and local streets perfected. But we worked damn hard at it. The studio and network gave us a lot of support. Visually [the series] was pretty impressive when we combined the elements correctly."

"I continue to be most proud of how successful we were building this unique futuristic world," says Monterastelli. "The Emmy nomination for special effects, and the Monitor nomination for post-production are indicative of how effective we were — and the impression we made on our peers in those fields."

Despite all the inspiration derived from the works of Philip K. Dick, the man never received a "based on" or "inspired by" credit. Monterastelli explains: "The demands of early production were so great that it actually came as a great surprise to me when I was informed that the Writers Guild and the Canadian Guild agreed that I should receive 'Created By' credit," he says. "I never wrote an arbitration statement or aggressively sought the credit. I know that from the Guild's POV the biggest issue had to do with any possible credit going to the writers of the *Total Recall* movie. I did know that was being discussed. But I had been hired as executive producer and I had been hired to come up with my own bible. It was never my intention to arbitrate for 'Created By' credit. In fact, at the time, I thought it would be a very unlikely thing.'

His favorite memory of the series is of the 1999 Monte Carlo Film and Television Festival; for five days, cast and crew stayed at the Hotel Du Paris. "The European press responded strongly to our two-hour pilot that premiered at the festival," he says. "Myself, Jeff King, Michael Easton, and Cindy Preston were all flown over there and treated like royalty. We hung out with Prince Albert and went to more parties in four days than I had been to in the previous four years. *Total Recall 2070* was tremendously well received by the French press."

Cast Notes

Michael Easton (David Hume): See the Cast Notes for *VR5*

Karl Pruner (Ian Farve): Pruner lived on numerous army bases in Canada, Europe and the U.S. before finally settling in Kingston, Ontario, Canada. He began his career with an appearance in the film *The Good Mother* (1988). He appeared in small roles in a number of television productions in Canada before being cast in *Total Recall.* Since then he has been seen in small roles in movies and television, including *Welcome to Mooseport, Brave New Girl* and *Open Heart.* He has also appeared on stages across Canada, including the Stratford Festival.

Cynthia Preston (Olivia Hume): Born in Toronto, Ontario, she is best known for playing Faith Rosco on the daytime drama *General Hospital* from 2002 to 2005, and also for providing the voice of Zelda in the *Legend of Zelda* video game. She has appeared in episodes of *The Outer Limits, Neon Rider, Street Legal, Katts and Dog* and *C.S.I.: Crime Scene Investigation.*

Judith Krant (Olan Chang): This Canadian actress began her career in 1994 in the movie *The Significant Other* before being cast in *Total Recall: 2070.* Since then she has appeared in *NYPD Blue.*

Matthew Bennett (James Calley): Bennett was born on Toronto, Canada. He began appearing on television in the early 1990s in a series called *Street Justice.* Appearances in Canadian and American television shows include *The X-Files, Kung Fu: The Legend Continues, Psi Factor, Andromeda* and *Stargate SG-1*. He has a recurring role in the revived *Battlestar Galactica* as a Cylon.

Michael Anthony Rawlins (Martin Ehrenthal): Rawlins is an American actor who is now based in Canada. His first television appearance was in a 1989 episode of *Wolf*. Other TV credits include *Full House, Roseanne, Beverly Hills 90210, NYPD Blue, The Famous Jett Jackson, Relic Hunter, Mutant X, Andromeda, Blade: Trinity* (2004), and *Intelligence*. He was a semi-regular on *The Best Years*.

Tracker

(2001–2002)

An evil scientist transports 218 alien convicts to Earth, where they take over human bodies for purposes of mayhem. An alien prison warden, Daggon, tracks them down one by one.

Cast: Adrian Paul (Cole/Daggon), Amy Price-Francis (Mel Porter), Geraint Wyn-Davis (Dr. Zin), Leanne Wilson (Jess Brown), Richard Yearwood (Nestov), Dean McDermott (Det. Victor Bruno)

Based on the short story by: Gil Grant, Jeannine Renshaw; **Developed for television by:** Gil Grant; **Executive Producers:** Brian Eastman, Gil Grant, Adrian Paul; **Co-Executive Producers:** Peter M. Lenkov, Grant Rosenberg; **Supervising Producer:** Cal Shumiatcher; **Producers:** Sherri Saito, Elaine Scott, Wendy Grean; **Co-Producer:** Carola Ash; **Writers included:** Charles Heit, Scott Peters, Gil Grant, Linda Ptolemy, Leonard Dick, Tracey Forbes, Grant Rosenberg, Peter Lenkov; **Directors included:** Robert Ginty, Holly Dale, Isabelle Fox, George Mendeluk, Neill Fearnley, Rene Bonniere, Bruce Pittman, William Fruet, Ken Girotti, Michael Robison; **Guest Stars included:** Ellen Dubin, Don Francks, Carla Collins, Paul Hopkins, Jason Knight, Deborah Odell, Richard Blackburn, Joanne Kelly, Evan Sobba, Anthony Bekenn

Syndicated; Tracker Productions Corporation and Future Films (Tracker) Limited, in association with Carnival Films and in association with Future Film Financing. Also in production with CHUM Television; Mercury Entertainment/ Lions Gate Television. A Canada–United Kingdom Co-Production; October 2001–June 2002; 60 minutes; 22 episodes

Tracker has the distinction of being the only science fiction series that opens with its hero marching down a road, dressed only in his underwear. Daggon is dazed and confused after taking human form, imperiling his mission — to retrieve 218 escaped criminals from the planet Cyrron 17.

Tracker was another low-budget Canadian series (funded by several financiers) that lasted less than a year. Adrian Paul, best known as the star of the TV series *Highlander*, was supposed to appeal to women but *Tracker* often ended up in early morning slots controlled by bleary-eyed male viewers who craved only action.

Cyrron is 100 light years away from Earth, in the Mygar star system. When an alien scientist named Zin proudly creates a wormhole, the people of Cyrron don't give a rat's whisker. This lack of recognition, which has dogged him for all his life, prompts Dr. Zin to organize a prison breakout for 218 convicts, whom he transports to Earth.

The aliens, who are blobs of energy, take over the bodies of human train passengers bound for Chicago. They disperse to engage in evil deeds, much to the delight of Dr. Zin. But prison warden Daggon arrives on Earth and uses a photo of a male model on a billboard as a template to assume human form. But the model is wearing only underwear, and Daggon, thinking this is appropriate, morphs into a good-looking guy, wearing only briefs.

Mel Porter, a sassy but lonely red-haired woman hurting from a recent breakup, finds him striding down the road. Her car has broken down but he revitalizes the engine with a beam of light and wordlessly continues on his dazed journey. Grateful but wary, Mel gives him a lift, but then asks the big question: "Where are your clothes?" She takes him to her Chicago apartment above her bar, The Watchfire, and helps him master human behavior and language. "Mel is one of those lost souls who really hasn't found her place in life," said actress Amy Price-Francis.

"There is something about his innocence and purity that attracts Mel," said story editor Charles Heit. "He's different from any man she has met before." That's for sure, because he does weird things, like biting ears of corn in half, and eating a candy bar wrapper and all, and getting lost in a revolving door. Nicknamed Cole, he uses computers to uncover the human identities of the 218 space criminals, whom he and Mel hunt down. Cole subdues them and extracts their life force from the human host's body. This alien energy is then downloaded into a secure receptacle.

The characterization of Cole as a slow-to-learn alien didn't impress Holly Dale, who directed the pilot film. "When I got a call to do the pilot, I thought, 'Fabulous.' Then I heard they were shooting episode two first, before doing the pilot. That's a common practice in television. This way you can get the bugs out of a standard episode and you can go on and make a stronger pilot. But it backfired. I watched the dailies of the second episode and I guess Adrian had watched *Starman*, because he made this decision to play the role as a child growing into an adult. That placed a limitation on me, I had to continue that kind of 'retarded' character in the first episode."

Dale found the character annoyingly slow-witted. "It was a very bad call and ultimately, I think, it had something to do with the demise of the show. As I understood it, Adrian had gone to an acting coach to 'find' the character and had decided to go in that direction. Neill Fearnley had directed that second episode and he's a fine director, so this isn't a criticism of him. I'm not sure how much more successful I would have been [trying] to create a more rounded, dimensional character. That second episode had a profound effect on how I could do the pilot. I couldn't go anywhere with that character."

The other characters included Jess, the spunky young woman who works at Mel's bar. It was one of Leanne Wilson's first acting jobs. "It was a great learning experience for me professionally and I loved every minute of it," the British actress reflects. "Adrian, Amy and I all got on really well. My character of Jess was very easy-going and carefree. She had such a great attitude, to love life and if there's anything you want, go out there and get it! She had a great sense of humor and was re-

ally positive. Yet, at times, she was very vulnerable, which made her a joy to play. I wanted Jess to be fun, to contrast with all the seriousness that was happening around her."

Humor is also injected into stories by Cole's confusion over his new environment. "What is train?" he asks. "What is tuxedo?" Or more sophisticated queries like, "Why does your species want to harm us instead of talk with us?" after watching the military attack one of his fellow aliens. Poor Mel spends half of her time helping Cole on missions, and the other half explaining the mundanes and sublimes of human existence.

Tracker played like a by-the-book cable movie— lots of violence (one female alien kills a horny mechanic by hosing him down with gasoline before lighting him afire), lots of fights (choreographed with slow-motion karate chops and *Matrix*-like spins in the air) and many beautiful women who turned out to be evil. One interesting sidelight to the derivative premise is that whenever Cole sucks the alien life-force from a human body, that human dies. It's a tragic exorcism process but it's the only way to rid the Earth of the invaders.

Cole, like many heroes, has emotional baggage: His wife and daughter were killed by the alien Rhee (Joanie Laurer) long ago. Rhee is the first one Cole captures and downloads in the pilot. Cole is also dismayed that his old friend, Dr. Zin, has turned out to be such a space fink. "I trusted you, Zin," Cole deadpans in his heavy European accent. Zin just laughs. Zin is having a great time, even though he fails to kill Cole every week (including one the oldest plots ever, trying to frame Cole for murder). Zin gleefully kills Mel in one show but Cole revives her with a dose of energy and they continue their budget-conscious adventures. (In one show, Cole skulks around a military complex that looks like an empty high school.)

Some stories were conventional—robbers steal Monet paintings, Mel's detective boyfriend (Lt. Bruno) is threatened by thugs. SF scenarios included a possessed German Shepherd that could transform into a bi-pedal monster and an alien drug that causes heart attacks.

Dr. Zin's dialogue has all the zing of Ming the Merciless. "This is the greatest power in all of the solar system," he gloats as he peruses a set of secret blueprints. But when he's outwitted by Cole for the umpteenth time, he rages, "We have been overconfident! We will not make that mistake again."

Make no mistake, Cole is a formidable adversary — he has ESP powers, can scale walls, leap to great heights, rejuvenate wounds on his body and zoom into hyperspeed (turning into a blurred flash as everyone around him stops in their tracks). His Achilles' heal is cold, which slows him down.

"I loved the premise and the characters," says co-executive producer Grant Rosenberg. "Gil Grant wrote a wonderful pilot and created some great, multi-dimensional characters. Plus, once Peter Lenkov and I joined the staff, we brought in a sci-fi sensibility. Unfortunately, *Tracker* turned out to be one of those shows that just didn't translate, for a multitude of reasons. Adrian Paul was not only the star but an executive producer. He had a different take on the character than Gil. In the end, their visions never meshed. It's unfortunate, because I think *Tracker* had unlimited potential. In an ironic way, it was very similar to *Time Trax* [the TV series Rosenberg co-created] in that you had a fish-out-of-water cop who had come to Earth to capture criminals.

"We were shooting in Toronto in January. It was two o'clock in the morning and we were doing exteriors. Snow was on the ground and the wind was taking the temperature into the teens. I was dressed in every piece of clothing I had and standing next to a gas heater, and I was *still* shivering. The actors, in the meantime, were doing their scenes in light jackets or sweaters, and none of them missed a beat. I've always respected actors, but that night, my respect for them soared."

In one of the more offbeat episodes, writer Peter Lenkov's "Native Son," Don Francks played an elderly Indian who uses his tracking skills to help Cole hunt down a killer alien. Director Robert Ginty, who co-starred on TV's *Black Sheep Squadron* and *Paper Chase* before becoming an international director, was very familiar with science fiction. "Interestingly enough, one of my closest collaborators as a writer-producer is Ray Bradbury. We've written a script together based on his novel, *Green Shadows, White Whale*. As a viewer, I certainly enjoyed *The Twilight Zone* and consider Rod Serling one of the masters of the medium."

But *Tracker* was no *Twilight Zone*. "Creators of most science fiction projects aim high and have big ideas," explains Ginty. "Therefore, we have many examples of fantastic SF *motion pictures*. Television, with its budgetary restrictions, makes it very difficult for the writers' concepts to be expressed in a satisfactory way. Fundamentally, as a director, you are trying to achieve an emotional impact but too often the director's hands are tied by decisions he is not given the authority to control.

"There was a real sense of intelligence put into ["Native Son"]. Don Francks is a wonderful old character who has been acting since the 1960s and he brings a wonderful energy to whatever he does. Lions Gate, the Canadian producers, thought it was one of the best episodes of the show and asked me to continue directing. But the series was in a quagmire of creative differences. The studio was not particularly happy with Adrian Paul's performance or his interpretation of the role and Adrian, being one of the executive producers, held his ground. He believed that his interpretation is what suited the show the best. Directors in these situations simply try to create harmony and bring the opposing factions together to create a semblance of a point of view."

But those behind-the-scenes conflicts ultimately doomed the series. "I came to the show at a later stage and the problems between the studio, the producers and Adrian came to some form of Mexican standoff," Ginty continues. "No one was willing to compromise for the sake of the show, thereby leading to its early demise. The series became so divided in terms of direction that it lost its way creatively."

Ginty still laments the lost opportunities. "I had worked in the past as a director with writer-producer Grant Rosenberg quite successfully on *Lois and Clark*, and the concept of *Tracker* was intriguing, as a potential metaphor for how society treats outsiders, whether they be foreigners, illegal immigrants, or in this case, aliens. Overall, I don't think the show succeeded in its reach but strangely enough, there were many talented people connected to it. Gil Grant, its creator, went on to *24* and *NCIS* and Geraint Wyn-Davies is one of the best actors working in any medium today."

Despite Paul's name value, the series didn't click with viewers. "It was not a successful series," notes director Holly Dale. "People aren't running around today, saying, 'Wow, I really loved *Tracker*!'" Especially critics. "The mild sense of wonder wears off quickly," Filmcritic.com said as the series wore on. "It leaves only Adrian Paul's refined good looks and optimism that the special effects team will transform the moronic scripts into something enjoyable."

Paul exerted his influence, making sure rewrites on scripts met his approval. When the series premiered, he told *SF Weekly*'s Kathie Huddleston, "This series is about character development. If the show succeeds, it's not going to be because of the action or special effects. It's going to be because of the relationships."

The last episode, "What Lies Beneath," surprised fans by revealing that Mel's late grandmother had connections to Cole's home planet all this time. A vault under her tavern contains a super weapon. Zin wants to use the weapon on the inhabitants of the Mygar system but Cole locks Zin in the vault and he retrieves the weapon.

Former actress Isabelle Fox directed this last episode, and says, "It turned out as well as can be expected for something that was shot in four days." She also knew the series was deader than a doornail. "It was weird. Directing that last show was like being the coroner at the scene of a crime. Everyone around you is sad and depressed and only days away from unemployment. I felt like I had to shepherd them through the autopsy and funeral. They hired me because I'm a festive and energetic person on the set, I'm not a grouch. I don't feel the need to yell at people to get the job done. But directing that show was funny, frustrating ... and insane."

Tracker ended but one can imagine that Cole will always remain curious about this world called Earth. "What is slow dance? What is mingle? What is telephone?" You can be sure Mel is doing everything she can to answer.

CAST NOTES

Adrian Paul (Cole/Daggon): The London-born and -raised actor is an expert in martial arts and sword fighting. He was a regular during the second year of *War of the Worlds* (1989–1990) and is best known as Duncan MacLeod, the immortal on *Highlander* (1992–1998). During that series, he made headlines when he chased and tackled a fleeing thief and turned him over to the police. "I'm

not attracted to science fiction," he said during *Tracker*'s production. "Science fiction is attracted to me." Paul continues acting in films such as *Little Chicago* (2005). He is also a writer and director.

Amy Price-Francis (Mel): British-born, she later appeared on *Mutant X* and *Sue Thomas F.B. Eye*. She also co-starred in *Pentagon Papers* (2003) and *Cake* (2005). "Amy Price-Francis had marvelous energy and was extremely focused on her role as Mel Porter," says director Robert Ginty. "She was a real pleasure to work with."

Geraint Wyn-Davis (Dr. Zin): He's best known as the 800-year-old vampire in the Canadian series, *Forever Knight* (1992–1996). Born in Wales, he was only seven when his family moved to Canada. At age 12, he starred in a stage production of *Lord of the Rings* and made his professional stage debut in Quebec in 1976. His movies include the TV film *Trudeau* (2002) and *The Cube 2: Hypercube* (2002)

Leanne Wilson (Jess Brown): Mel's bartender, Jess had a lot of insecurities ("I'm 23 years old — the clock is ticking!") but she also radiated a lot of youthful zest. The British-born actress did guest shots on *New Tricks* and *GMTV* after *Tracker*, and played a recurring role on *The Doctors*. She feels *Tracker* was special: "I look back on it with fond memories. It was a great concept, and the show really started to find its way. I loved Adrian's vision on the project and had it been given another year, who knows what we could have made of it?"

Richard Yearwood (Nestov): Cast as Cole's slick ally, Yearwood joined the show early in its run. His credits stretch back to *The Littlest Hobo* (1980). He's co-starred in the TV films *Mayday* and *Webs* (both 2005).

Dean McDermott (Det. Victor Bruno): He began acting in Canadian TV shows such as *My Secret Identity* and *Friday the 13th* (both 1989). After *Tracker*, he did *Earth: Final Conflict* and *The Outer Limits*. His TV movie credits include *H2O* (2004) and *Kojak* (2005).

Tremors: The Series

(2003)

In Perfection Valley, Nevada, a group of residents, led by military survival expert Burt Gummer, try to avoid the hungry, marauding 30-foot worm, the Graboid, and battle other strange creatures that lurk below the desert's surface.

Cast: Michael Gross (Burt Gummer), Victor Browne (Tyler Reed), Marcia Strassman (Nancy Sterngood), Gladise Jimenez (Rosalita Sanchez), Lela Lee (Jody Chang), Dean Norris (W. D. Twitchell)

Based on Characters created by: S.S. Wilson, Brent Maddock, Ron Underwood; *Created by:* Brent Maddock, Nancy Roberts, S. S. Wilson; *Developed for television by:* S.S. Wilson, Brent Maddock, Nancy Roberts; *Executive Producers:* David Israel, Nancy Roberts, S.S. Wilson, Brent Maddock; *Co-Executive Producer:* John Schulian; *Supervising Producer:* Edward Ledding; *Producers:* Edward Ledding, P. J. Pesce, Michael Gross; *Associate Producer:* Aaron Staudinger; *Consulting Producer:* Babs Greyhosky; *Visual Effects Supervisor:* Gerard Black; *Directors of Photography:* Bradford May, Steven Shaw; *Writers included:* John Schulian, Christopher Silber, Babs Greyhosky, Brent Maddock, S. S. Wilson, Nancy Roberts; *Directors included:* Bradford May, Chuck Bowman, P. J. Pesce, Michael Shapiro, Ron Underwood, Whitney Ransick, Michael Grossman; *Guest Stars included:* Richard Biggs, Melinda Clarke, Sarah Rafferty, Armin Shimerman, Harrison Page, Vivica A. Fox, Joan McMurtrey, Michael Rooker, Rebecca McFarland, Jeffrey Johnson, Matt Malloy, J. D. Walsh (as Larry), Christopher Lloyd (as Cletus Poffenberger)

The Sci-Fi Channel/Universal Pictures/Stampede Entertainment; April 2003–August 2003; 60 minutes; 13 episodes

As you approach one small town in the Nevada desert, the first thing you see is a ragged sign with faded lettering: "Entering Perfection Valley. Extreme wildlife danger — stay on the pavement at all times." If you don't heed that warning and you venture onto the sand, you will end up the screaming prey of a giant worm with fangs. It will eat you alive. Actually, worm is the wrong word; it's a mutant that looks like a giant worm, and lives under the desert sand.

The series was based on the film *Tremors* (1990),

where townspeople were threatened by Graboid mutants, which are giant, leathery sandworms with long tentacles that shoot out from their throats. In the feature film, they were eventually blown to bits. Kevin Bacon, Fred Ward, Reba McEntire and Michael Gross were the stars and it paid homage to those 1950s B sci-fi films, where atomic-sized tarantulas or scorpions devoured unsuspecting characters. *Tremors* was a big hit and resulted in two sequels, both direct-to-video productions, *Tremors II: Aftershocks* (1996) and *Tremors 3: Back to Perfection* (2001). The Sci-Fi Channel expressed interest in a TV series. "The success of the *Tremors* films was essential to getting the series launched," notes co-creator S.S. Wilson. "It also contributed to getting the order for a full 13 episodes, uncommon in these times of more cautious TV executives. Creatively we tried to keep as many elements of the movies as possible."

Michael Gross enthusiastically signed on to continue his role as survival expert Burt Gummer. (When the first film was being cast, the producers felt Gross could never play an obnoxious guy like Gummer, until the actor surprised them with his audition.)

To cut costs, the series was filmed in Rosarito, Mexico, with an American-Mexican crew. The Sci-Fi Channel demanded that every week there had to be a monster, whether it was the giant Graboid worm or another creature.

In Perfection Valley (population 19), Burt, a divorced man with no sense of humor, constantly listens for sounds of the Graboid on his Geo-Phone radar scope, which picks up any underground movement. Low on cash and living in an underground bunker, the paranoid anti-government radical also runs "Burt Gummer's Survival School," where he teaches city folk how to survive in the wilderness.

Burt's life revolves around tracking the big worms' wiggles; Nancy, his closest friend, can't make any headway against his obsessions. "A man has got to know his terrain," he tells her. That effectively keeps their relationship as dry as the dustbowl they live in.

Much to his chagrin, Burt isn't allowed to kill the underground tunnelers because the Department of the Interior has proclaimed the mutant an endangered species. Agent W.D. Twitchell makes it clear to Burt: "If you shoot that Graboid, I'll hit you with a $50,000 fine!" So Burt and his friends must drive off the worm (nicknamed El Blanco) with non-lethal percussion grenades.

Other residents of Perfection include newcomer Victor Browne, a former NASCAR driver who has seen rough times. "I'm kind of in a pit stop," he says of his stalled life. But he soon shares Burt's passion for chasing sand monsters.

Rosalita is a pretty young Hispanic woman who runs the ranch her late uncle left to her. When she's scared or excited, she speaks Spanish really, really fast.

Nancy, an ex-hippie and the closest thing Burt has to a girlfriend, helps Jodi Chang run Walter Chang's Market, where food is served to the few tourists foolish enough to drop by.

Tremors: The Series is played tongue-in-cheek but people do die. In the first episode, a tourist runs screaming for his life across the desert. A Graboid snatches him with its tentacles and carries him away through the sand. In another episode, the blood-soaked skeletons of two missing geologists are found in the desert. Rather than feeling repulsion, the series' fans admired the skill of the makeup people for devising such disgusting dummies.

As Burt, Gross is the perfect control freak, a compulsive-obsessive man and a total narcissist. The actor was light years away from the bland Mr. Keaton in his previous series, *Family Ties*. "Michael brings talent, professionalism, a sense of humor, and great creativity to everything he does," notes Wilson. "On the series, he was the on-set anchor and often served as our voice on the set [since the producers were rarely able to make it to the Mexican location]. Michael helped the whole team get the tone right, in addition to being a father figure for the cast."

Fans of *Tremors* could be as obsessed as Burt. "One of my personal favorites was a fan asking what direction Burt's basement door faces," chuckles Wilson. "A lot of Burt's fans are very, very detail-oriented."

The other characters were fun too. Gladys Jimenez as Rosalie is funny and sexy. She tries to play with the action but when she says "Robert that!" over the walkie talkie, Burt can only roll his eyes and sigh, "That's Roger." Perfection Valley's residents are like rats trapped in a box, shack-led by their own neuroses. As one perceptive visitor says, "Man, you guys are all pretty much futureless here!"

Everyone wears seismic wristbands to monitor the Graboids' activity. Since El Blanco is a protected species, other monsters had to be blown up every week. This included El Blanco's mutated offspring, the Shriekers, bipedal critters with slavering jaws. Burt later discovered that an abandoned underground lab had created an assortment of monsters via a DNA splicing compound called MixMaster and these unlikely creatures perpetually lurked in the desert. These included a giant shrimp and monster insects that ate human flesh.

In "Flora or Fauna," Burt and Tyler befriend a striking red-headed scientist (Sarah Rafferty) who is searching for a killer plant that is melting her geologists with acid. When the plant reproduces hundreds of little plant pods, Tyler flies over them in a balloon and douses them with deadly chemicals.

In "Blast from the Past," two Las Vegas magicians need Burt's help to catch a flying lizard-like creature. This comes at an inopportune time for Burt, who is busy teaching his class vital survival life skills. ("Get your fire going and roast your lizards!" he tells his middle-aged pupils.) The flying lizard, a permutation of a Graboid, devours the top half of a truck driver (the bottom half of the man "crashes" his truck into a telephone pole). Examining the corpse, Burt says, "We have an ass blaster on the loose!" An ass blaster? "Because they kick your ass!"

What's worse, the lizard inhales volatile chemicals and farts these toxic chemicals over people. But despite Burt and Tyler's efforts, it's Nancy who saves the day by luring the lizard with its favorite cuisine, baked beef in sauce. When the lizard shows up, it's trapped in a macramé net and carried away.

Such fanciful storylines walked a perilous tightrope. Says Wilson, "The tightrope was there in the movies, too. For the TV show we leaned a bit more to the comedic, partly by design and partly through the influence of the new writers and directors brought in to staff it, along with the shows' creators. We found ourselves asking the new people to make things less funny and more scary. In *Tremors*, the laughs come out of playing the scary situations straight. We had very little difficulty with studio censorship. Indeed, the studio sometimes encouraged us to push the envelope more with shocks and violence."

P.J. Pesce, who directed four segments, agrees that balancing comedy and horror took some doing. "The way to deal with it was to play everything as real as possible. That brought out the absurdity of living with a murderous monster in your neighborhood." Pesce couldn't wait to work on the show because it was a serio-comedy. "It was a natural fit. I started as an actor and my background is in comedy and action, so *Tremors* was right up my alley."

The filming in Mexican valleys gave *Tremors* an authentic quality, but the remote locations meant cell phone contact was often lost between the crew and the writers in Los Angeles. The effects were fairly good by TV standards, but ate up the small budget. Whenever giant worms or their ilk got blasted, the gooey flying guts were actually nylon stockings filled with canned pumpkin.

"We don't have the fun anecdotes which come from being on a set since we, the core Stampede Entertainment production team, were not directing and producing in Mexico," says Wilson. "Our main challenge was trying to get the writing right, trying to make sure the show stayed true to what we felt fans of the movies would expect. It was mostly grueling — writing, casting, reading scripts, approving storyboards, costume, props, watching rough cuts. I remember that Babs Greyhosky brought in homemade desserts practically every week, which made staying on a diet a non-option. And we had a nice ongoing relationship with the building's late night janitor, a sci-fi fan and publisher of his own sci-fi magazine, since we were there most nights."

Pesce, however, was in the thick of location and recalls, "We found snakes all the time, but the weirdest animal we encountered was a mother dog and her pups. The boom operator and I adopted them and built a little hutch, because the torrential rains were just starting. The mother was completely emaciated except for her ... ummm ... bosom. It was an odd visual. The grips took to calling her, affectionately, 'Teats.' She and the pups became our mascot."

"We had a monsoon in early February," Pesce recalls. "The cast and crew were stuck on the set with no way to get out! The water was rising, and we were lucky to have the stunt coordinator drive a van across this stream and get most people out. Some people had to be carried on stuntmen's backs. We put a stick in the river with a mark on it that let us know, 'If the water rises above here, we're shutting down for the day.'

"The conditions were quite brutal. If it wasn't pouring rain, it was hot and dry. Getting equipment across the border could be tricky, especially guns. Having any weapons or ammo in your possession in Mexico, even blanks, is very serious. Of course, *Tremors* is like a Western, and we had to have lots of weapons in every script! Thank God we had a great prop guy who just said, 'Fuck it,' and put a whole cache of weapons in his trunk and drove across! If he had been caught, he'd no doubt still be in jail."

Despite the challenges, everybody pulled together. "We had a fantastic storyboard artist named Juan Leon, nicknamed Boom. He would stay up all night long in order to get some of the sequences finished. He and I and our first A.D., Carl Ludwig-Selig, were holed up in this shitty little trailer that had broken windows. The wind would just blow right through. Every day we were racing against the sun to shoot eight or ten pages plus action and effects. It was a total nightmare but we did it. The people were fantastic and we became a little family.

"Trying to find extras in Rosarito Beach, Mexico, who looked like Caucasians wasn't easy," Pesce says. "Sometimes we had to find featured extras who could actually act, and that was almost impossible. In one episode, we were trying to cast a featured extra and we didn't have the money to bring someone in from San Diego, so we were trying to cast a local. The line producer brings me over to this trailer and there's this guy there, he's around 25 years old, and he looks positively demented. He's been stuffed into a suit and has a tie strung around his neck. He's looking at me like I'm his ticket out of Rosarito and onto stardom. So I figure, all right, let me just give him a shot. So the producer reads the other lines in the audition scene. It's a scene where this character has to break down and admit he vandalized a bunch of stuff and this guy just mutters the scene in broken English and then looks at me. I'm like, 'Uh, okay, I don't think so.' But the producer says, 'No, no, no! Give him another chance! You've got to direct him in this audition!' So I say, in my broken Spanglish, 'Okay, fine. You need to give me some emotion here. You're breaking down and admitting your guilt. Do you understand?' He nods at me, they start the scene again, and the guy goes nuts, kind of a Captain Kirk–style acting moment. He throws himself on the ground and screams and yells, completely insane. And then he gets up and screams at the producer, as part of the scene, and grabs him by the shirt, and we were truly terrified that he was going to hit the producer! He really thought all this would get him the part."

For the record, it didn't.

When Michael Gross agreed to star in the last *Tremors* film, *Tremors 4: The Legend Begins* (a prequel set in 1889, with Gross playing Burt's great-grandfather), he had to be written out of the last three episodes of the series. Had the series continued, there was one storyline planned where Burt finds romance with a woman on the Internet only to learn that it's Nancy!

Tremors: The Series died after 13 episodes. "The ratings were the primary reason the show was dropped," explains Wilson. "We missed by a fraction the numbers Sci-Fi felt were needed to justify a second season."

In retrospect, he says, "The series' main strength was the unique blend of horror, sci-fi, and fun, which is *Tremors*. I'm proud of the episodes in which we got the blend right. That said, the production pace hurt the show. We had a hard-working cast and crew faced with shooting a very complex hour in seven days. TV shows much less difficult often have eight or nine. Performances were rushed. Creature effects were sometimes not shot well."

He also feels the wide variety of monsters hurt the show. "The monster-of-the-week concept, by adding a secret government lab to the Perfection Valley mythology, lessened the overall [credibility] of the show. It became inherently sillier, no matter how hard we tried to play it straight. Also, once it was learned that the DNA splicing compound MixMaster was going to keep creating new threats, why on Earth would these people keep living in Perfection Valley?"

Wilson says the fans are still out there. "I was moved, and continue to be moved, by the repeated eloquent calls to release the series on DVD. And I continue to be baffled by the studio's refusal to do so." In the meantime, if you're walking out in a quiet desert, keep your noise level down. El Blanco could be out there, listening and waiting.

Cast Notes

Michael Gross (Burt): The Chicago-born actor gained prominence as the star of *Family Ties* (1982–1989), where he and Meredith Baxter played former hippies who were raising a family. The focus was originally to be on them, until the actor playing their son (Michael J. Fox) shot to fame and became the star. Gross good-naturedly accepted being relinquished to supporting player. He later gained critical acclaim as a killer in the TV film *In the Line of Duty: The F.B.I. Murders* (1988). His TV guest shots include *The Outer Limits, ER* and *Ally McBeal.*

Victor Browne (Tyler): Born in Newfoundland, Canada, he spent his childhood traveling throughout the world as one of eight children in an Air Force family. He was a regular on daytime's *One Life to Live* (1996–1997) and had roles on *Lost, Sex and the City* and *Charmed.* His TV films include *Desolation Canyon* and *Found* (both 2005).

Marcia Strassman (Nancy): She began her career as a teen model and then starred in the off-Broadway musical *Best Foot Forward* in 1965, at the age of 15. She had a recurring role as a nurse on *M*A*S*H* (1972–1973) and hit real stardom as Mrs. Kotter on the series *Welcome Back, Kotter* (1975–1979). She also starred in the film *Honey, I Shrunk the Kids* (1989) and its sequel, *Honey, I Blew Up the Kid* (1992). Her later TV credits included *Providence* and *Third Watch.*

Gladise Jimenez (Rosalita): The striking Puerto Rican–born actress was a regular on the soap opera *The Bold and the Beautiful* (2000–2001) and began a regular role on *General Hospital* in 2004. Other TV credits include *Seven Days, Silk Stalkings, Renegade* and *Team Knight Rider.* She also co-starred in the feature film *East Side Story* (2005).

Lela Lee (Jody): This Los Angeles native has had a collection of her comic strip works, *Angry Little Asian Girl*, published. She's been seen in *Friends, Charmed* and *Profiler* and the film *Exposed* (2003).

Dean Norris (Twitchell): His TV credits stretch back to the 1980s (*Beauty and the Beast* and *The Equalizer*). He's also appeared in the films *Lethal Weapon 2* (1989), *Total Recall* (1990), and *American Gun* (2005).

Sources

McAvennie, Mike. "Hunter of the Worm." *Starlog* no. 313, August 2003.

The Twilight Zone

(2002–2003)

One of television's most recognizable science fiction–fantasy anthology series, its stories often featuring an ironic twist ending.

Host-Narrator: Forest Whitaker
Created by: Rod Serling; **Executive Producers:** Ira Steven Behr, Pen Densham, Mark Stern, John Watson; **Co-Executive Producers:** Brent V. Friedman, John P. Kousakis; **Producer:** Anthony Santa Croce; **Co-Producer and Associate Producer:** Anne Tabor; **Consulting Producers:** Frederick Rappaport, Ashley Miller; **Writers included:** Jill Blotevogel, James Crocker, Pen Densham, Bradley Thompson, David Weddle; **Directors included:** Jonathan Frakes, Debbie Allen, Lou Diamond Phillips, Tim Matheson, Brad Turner, John P. Kousakis, Winrich Kolbe, Bob Balaban; **Directors of Photography:** Rick Maguire, William Wages; **Production Designers:** Mark S. Freeborn, Craig Stearns, Ricardo Spinace; **Special Effects:** Stargate Digital; **Guest Stars included:** Jason Alexander, Shannon Elizabeth, Adrian Pasdar, Andrew McCarthy, Bill Mumy, Cloris Leachman, Lou Diamond Phillips, Elizabeth Berkley, Frank Whaley, Steve Bacic, Enid-Raye Adams, Jeffrey Combs, Sydney Tamia Poitier, Sean Patrick Flanery, Scott Hylands, Roger C. Cross, Jason Bateman, Keith Hamilton Cobb, Eriq LaSalle, Peter Williams, Don S. Davis, Colin Cunningham
UPN/Spirit Dance Entertainment/Trilogy Entertainment/New Line Television; 2002–2003; 60 minutes; 22 episodes; DVD status: Complete series

On the evening of September 18, 2002, anyone watching the UPN network heard once again, for the first time since 1988, one of the most famous main title themes in television history: a new reworking of Marius Constant's 1960 theme. Adapted and performed by Jonathan Davis of the rock group Korn, it's a musical composition that is instantly recognizable and hummable. This time, series host and narrator Forest Whitaker intoned the immortal words: "You're traveling in another dimension, a dimension not only of sight and sound but of mind, a journey into a wondrous land of the imagination ... you're entering the Twilight Zone...."

This is the fourth television incarnation of Rod Serling's classic series, but the title has taken off-

ramps into other formats such as a 1983 feature film and a 1994 TV-movie hosted by James Earl Jones ("The Lost Classics") which dramatized little-known Serling scripts.

Twilight Zone's return to television came about because executive producer-writer-director Pen Densham was such a fan that he spent three years, beginning in 1999, trying to convince Les Moonves, head of CBS, to revive the series.

"I had originally tried to create my own anthology series after having done *The Outer Limits*," says Densham. "But the argument against it was so stark from the networks—'Anthologies don't succeed!' I realized the only way to do it was to choose something like *Twilight Zone*, which CBS owned.

"I wrote a very long and involved thesis as to why it would entertain and I got a 'Yes' from Les, then he backed off, and he said, 'Anthologies don't work.' I wrote him a letter, 'Les, that's not true. You have two or three running on your network right now and one of them is your top-running show, it's called *60 Minutes*. The only reason they don't work is that nobody puts them on.'"

A year later, realizing that the original series was having its 40th anniversary, Densham resorted to an elaborate video presentation in pitching the show for a 21st century audience. When Moonves began overseeing the UPN network, Densham recognized an opportunity to put it back to back with *Star Trek: Enterprise* and attract the Trekkies. He wrote a letter to Moonves making that suggestion. The hook-up with *Enterprise* didn't happen but the show did get on the air.

"I was in his office within a week, and I was given 10 days to write the screenplay and we were shooting it like 15 days after that," says Densham. "They needed that hook."

The Twilight Zone debuted on UPN in the fall of 2002. Each of the 22 hour-long episodes were comprised of two half-hour stories. Densham says that New Line Television, UPN and the producers explored a range of options from "no host" to "the voice of God" for the narration duties of the show (handled on the original *TZ* by Rod

Serling). "We pushed for a host to bring a human face to put context on the stories," explained Densham. "But we felt it was really wrong to try and create a Rod Serling clone. We viewed ourselves as carrying the baton on a series that he started. Several people were considered. We advocated Forest Whitaker, because he had his own artistic integrity as both an actor and director. Forest had worked with us before on *Blown Away*. We knew he had a big heart and had championed other people's creativity on many occasions." *Cinescape*, a science fiction media magazine, wrote in response to this casting in 2002: "No review of the new *Twilight Zone* would be complete without a mention of the impeccably cast Forest Whitaker, who is about the only human being on Earth with enough class to walk in Rod Serling's shoes as *Zone*'s enigmatic narrator."

The *TZ* producers and writers concocted compelling, fantastic scenarios and then cast recognizable and talented "name" actors in the roles. Often, they went for offbeat casting choices, to give actors a chance to stretch.

In the first episode, Jeremy Piven was a telephone lineman, struck by lightning, who suddenly gained mind-reading powers. "The Lineman" was directed by Jonathan Frakes and written by Densham.

Other Hollywood talents who stepped into the Zone included Jason Alexander, playing "Death" to a dedicated doctor resident in "One Night at Mercy." Lou Diamond Phillips, the title character in "The Pool Guy," believed that he was being stalked by a killer. Shannon Elizabeth and *Mysterious Ways*' Adrian Pasdar shared an intimate relationship in "Dream Lover" and *Roswell*'s Katherine Heigl became a time traveler with an opportunity to kill Hitler as a baby in "Cradle of Darkness."

Singer and actress Jessica Simpson even walked through the twilight door as a babysitter who faced killer Barbie dolls. Screenwriter Kay Reindl recalls this idea came up in the writer's room. "There were several of us who were adamant that if we didn't do a killer doll episode, the show would be a complete failure!" she chuckles. "It's *The Twilight Zone*, and *Twilight Zone* needs killer dolls!"

In the story, a babysitter discovers that the young girls' Barbies are able to escape from their glass cabinet and move about the house with murderous intentions. "I like this episode," says Reindl. "I think it's the type of episode we should have done more of. One of the reasons the origi-

nal show worked so well is because the episodes were shot as plays. This episode was extremely self-contained and that was a real plus. The dolls, also, were fantastic. There was some talk about showing them move but we were convinced that they would be more frightening if they didn't. We really did get to tell the story we wanted to tell and it was fun."

Actors were even invited to write and direct episodes. Eriq LaSalle (one of the *E.R.* doctors) wrote and directed "Memphis," a story in which, via time travel, an attempt is made to prevent Martin Luther King's assassination.

"We had to have certain casting elements that UPN wanted, and since they were trying to be the urban network, they wanted to see more city environments and a variety of young minorities in the show," explained Densham. "We were excited to do that but it also meant we weren't allowed to use older people in some of the stories, that was a no-no. Those things limited us—like when we wanted to remake a Burgess Meredith episode [Serling's original 1959 story "Time Enough at Last"], which we thought was a gem, but that wasn't allowed to happen.

"We came under a concern from UPN not to make shows that featured characters that didn't relate in age to their target audience. The urban audience was young and UPN wanted to reflect that in the casting. Don't take this as a criticism. This is just the facts of the way the system worked. But it was exciting to us to do the show. It was the hardest thing we had ever done. We bonded together in the process, and we had fantastic writers, fantastic editing teams, and the creative team in Vancouver was great."

Executive producer-writer Ira Steven Behr wrote a story that has a very special place in his heart: the only sequel in the entire *Twilight Zone* mythos, "It's Still a Good Life," starring Bill Mumy and Cloris Leachman. They reprised roles originated in the series' 1960 episode, "It's a Good Life," inspired by a Jerome Bixby story.

In the original episode, six-year-old boy Anthony Fremont, who lives on a farm in Peaksville, Ohio, had an extraordinary, but very dangerous, mental ability of altering reality by the simple act of thinking about it. If people weren't nice to him, he would read their "bad thoughts," make them disappear, and "wish them into the cornfield." Everyone in his life, including his parents, was terrified of him and did everything they could to please him.

In the four decades since the episode was

filmed, this segment has played endlessly in syndication and has been released on VHS and DVD. In 1997 the staff at *TV Guide* and Nick at Nite cable assembled a list they called "The 100 Greatest TV Episodes of All Time" and this episode landed in the #31 slot.

In "It's Still a Good Life," we pick up the life of Anthony Fremont some 40 years later; now an adult, he has a six-year-old daughter named Audrey. He's still living in Peaksville, Ohio, with his mother and the few people who are still around in the town. The mother discovers that Audrey is beginning to exhibit similar mental powers as Anthony. What's going to happen when he finds out? How will the relationships change? Who will suffer as a result?

On the *Twilight Zone* set in Vancouver, Canada, Bill Mumy and Cloris Leachman reunited for this sequel. Also cast was Bill's daughter, Liliana; Allan Kroeker directed.

Mumy is most famous for playing Will Robinson on TV's *Lost in Space* (1965–1968), but he's also known for being a musician in rock bands and has written comic books. He even co-created a live-action children's television show with writer Peter David, *Space Cases*; the science fiction adventure show ran on Nickelodeon in 1996–97. Genre fans also know him as the Minibari aide Lennier on *Babylon 5*.

An avid SF convention guest, Mumy reported that in the years since he appeared in three of the original *TZ* episodes ("Long Distance Call," "In Praise of Pip," and of course the original "It's a Good Life"), fans talk to him as much about Anthony Fremont as they do Will Robinson. "Anthony is just one of those characters that won't go away," chuckles Mumy. "People have never stopped saying stuff to me like, 'Don't wish me into the cornfield!' or 'It's good that you wrote *Fish Heads*, it's real good.' I get that almost as much as 'Danger, Will Robinson!' Once at a comic book convention, some lunatic fan started ordering me to send him to the cornfield in a crowded elevator. I wasn't in the mood to perform for him at the time, and he literally started to strangle me, while screaming, 'Send me to the cornfield! Send me to the cornfield!' It was a very bizarre and not-so-cool moment. I'm not okay with strangers strangling me. Let's just say he almost got his wish. Literally."

Returning to Peaksville, Ohio, became a reality when the production staff talked to Ira Behr about remakes. He decided it would be more intriguing to attempt a sequel to an original *Twilight Zone* story. Behr was a friend of Mumy's and knew Mumy's daughter Liliana was an experienced child actor.

"Ira and I are friends and when he first accepted the gig of producing the new *Twilight Zone* series, he and I kicked around a handful of ideas," recalled Mumy. "I said, 'Wouldn't it be cool to see what Peaksville, Ohio, would be like 40 years later? It was almost hell then ... imagine how it would be now. Imagine what a 40-something Anthony Fremont would be like.'"

For the sequel to be made, the rights to the story had to be obtained from Jerome Bixby's estate. Bill and Liliana Mumy and Cloris Leachman were needed as the principal players. After a period of four months, the production managed to get all the pieces in place. Behr wrote the script in just two days.

"Once it was officially happening, Ira and I both wrote outlines for how we saw the story," says Mumy. "Ira's was definitely better than mine and we went with his. I loved the idea of Anthony having a daughter. That was Ira's. And he definitely wanted her to be played by Liliana, so that sold me 1000 percent right off the bat. Mine was a darker version of that possible reality. We incorporated some of my outline into Ira's. We met at his office and we beat out the pacing and the details of the show. Then Ira wrote it quickly and his first draft was really great and was basically what we filmed."

There were a number of story ideas that didn't make the final draft. In the original episode, there was a piano player named Dan (who became a "Jack in the Box"); one discarded idea was that Anthony kept Dan's rotting corpse and animated it to entertain him when he was in the mood for piano music. Says Mumy, "Can't you just see this skeleton in a Sears suit with a few chunks of rotting flesh left on it, waddling out from some corner to sit down and play the piano? I loved that. Anyway, it didn't end up in the episode, but it would've been very cool.

"Ira and I originally wanted the bowling alley scene to include mutants and people that [Anthony] had partially transformed into half creature-half human or taken away their mouths, things like that. Again, it was too hard to get it done properly within time and budget. We kicked around some other things that didn't fly. I think Anthony's wife was in Ira's original outline and we both decided we didn't need to see her."

Being reunited with Cloris Leachman was a joy for Mumy, who had played her son three times previously in other productions. "Cloris is a gift to work with," says Mumy. "She's one of the best actresses on the planet. She's a great talent and a fun, loving person to hang with. Her son, George Englund, and I were in a band together in the 1980s. I very much wanted her to be a part of this show from the second it was seriously discussed. Liliana and Cloris had a wonderful time together. They had great chemistry as actors and they got along wonderfully in between scenes. We went out to dinner together in Vancouver and it was very nice to be with her again. She's so good that she makes other actors who work with her better. She bumped my game up a notch and I loved that."

Before father and daughter could step before the cameras, it was first necessary to do a little research. Bill screened the original episode for Liliana a couple of times, "mostly to get [Anthony's] facial expressions down, when using [his] powers. Besides the eyes being wide and blank, there's also a nostril flare thing going on there. We worked to match what I'd done in the original. Liliana really helped me find

After a 41-year-break, actor Bill Mumy returned to a role he originated in the 1961 episode of *The Twilight Zone*. As an adult Anthony Fremont, Mumy starred in the sequel story "It's Still a Good Life," with his real-life daughter Liliana Mumy. She played Anthony's daughter Audrey (courtesy Eileen Mumy).

some buttons to push in my performance as well. It was great. And being away from home, isolated where we had nothing to think about but the show, was also a real good thing."

Mumy noted that the crew "seemed to relate to the fact that we were working on the sequel to something that has been called 'classic' by a lot of people over the years. Everybody went a little deeper to get it right. Ira was terrific. He allowed me to have a lot of creative input in the concept, the script, and even the set dressing and the music.

"I think it's a damn fine half-hour TV show. When shown back to back with the original, it holds its own. Ira and I both had hoped to see

it in black and white, but that was one battle we lost.

"I enjoyed every minute of it, and I think it came out good. Real good."

Paired up with this story in the same episode was an updated remake of a classic Rod Serling script, "The Monsters Are Due on Maple Street." In the original, a group of neighbors reacted with paranoia and fear to what they believed was an alien invasion.

In this modernized story, which starred Andrew McCarthy, the nature of the threat was different. In the Cold War of the 1960s, aliens from outer space (a metaphor for the "Russian Communists") were the obvious and easy target. In the 21st century, it's the more relevant theme of terrorism. And, curiously, the science fiction aspect of the story is almost non-existent. At the conclusion, it is revealed that terrorists were not involved — it was a military experiment, and the story is now an elaborate study in the paranoiac psychological reactions of a group of ordinary citizens, living together in a quiet suburban neighborhood. As a result of conflicting discussions and arguments among the individual neighbors, a house belonging to the "new arrival in the neighborhood" (whom we never see) ends up being burned to the ground.

"It's daunting to remake something as iconic as 'Monsters,'" says Kay Reindl, who co-wrote the episode with Erin Maher. "No matter how good your remake is, it will lack Serling's voice. The best way to go about it is to look at the message and find how it applies to what's happening today. We will always find something or someone to be afraid of, and that's why 'Monsters' works. That's why *Invasion of the Body Snatchers* can continually be remade, too. Once we found our metaphor — terrorism and a government experiment rather than aliens — the story pretty easily fell into place.

"One thing that we went back and forth on quite a bit was whether or not to show the new family. I think our decision to not show them was correct, because it really puts the audience in the characters' point of view. We wanted this to be a test for the audience as well as for the characters."

Enid-Raye Adams, a Canadian actress who played one of the eight paranoid neighbors, says, "What I found most interesting was the level of fear that we can all get wrapped up in. It's a choice to become fearful. The script showed what fear does, not in just a community but also globally — what it does to communities, to friendships and to families. It's crazy!

"These people [the neighbors] are really connected. They're all in the same boat, and [Serling] is showing what happens if you jump to fear, jump to judgment. What he's trying to convey is, 'Why is everyone running around like a bunch of paranoid freaks?' He's holding a mirror up to us, and asking, 'What do you see in the mirror?' And everyone looks in the mirror and sees something different."

Although Andrew McCarthy's character was the voice of reason, even his wife gets caught up with the tensions. Says Adams, "The point behind it all is to say, 'Look how ridiculous it all is, for a person to be torching another person's house on their own street.' I personally feel we judge other people because we're not connected to our own worth. Any time you look at someone else and you point the finger at them, you always have three fingers pointing back at you. I would like to think that while we see no changes being made to the lives of these characters, that people watching this would be able to look in the mirror and say, 'Yeah, I've judged someone for no good reason and got hysterical for no good reason and I need to check that.' So I don't know what happens to these characters but I can sure hope there's an effect and impact on those who watch the episode."

Reindl says she was impressed with what director Debbie Allen and the cast were able to create with her script. "I thought that for the most part, it turned out pretty well and the acting was strong," she says. "The actors seemed to really get into the story and the episode wouldn't have worked if they hadn't."

The series' short life echoes today's modern, fickle audience who are bombarded with many different technological distractions — Internet, 200 channels and video games. It's a jungle out there. In Densham's analysis, "The fan base didn't understand how lucky we were to get *Twilight Zone* on the air. Instead of helping us stay on the air and mature and giving an outlet for today's writers and directors and actors to do the show, there seemed to be a large, old-fashioned negative sense from the hard-core fan community. I wish we had them to support us because I think then we could have stayed on the air. And it was so close as to whether UPN kept us going or not. If there had been any groundswell of support, I think we would have stayed on. It was right down to the wire. But it was a tough show to do, trying to keep that level of quality up. It's astonishing to me that we were able to do that."

Densham explains that *Twilight Zone* represented "great storytelling and no limits to the environments or the surprises that the stories can encompass. They are just fascinating human stories. That's what Rod Serling found — you force humanity to reveal itself when you shine the light of a good supernatural or SF element on them. We're designed biologically to study survival. That's why we slow down at traffic accidents. It's bred into us to avoid doing the things that others have done that caused their demise. Which is why we'll watch *Jaws* or *Aliens* or a murder mystery thriller because the biological response in us is to try to understand how we can avoid that happening to us. So SF elevates that kind of behavior;

Enid-Raye Adams on the set of *Twilight Zone*'s "Monsters on Maple Street" with director Debbie Allen (courtesy Enid-Raye Adams).

there are cautionary tales or magical, mystical tales, which speak to morality. We like to see the heroes win, we don't like to see the villains rewarded. We like to see the male mate with the alpha female, and like to see the hero slay the thing that's feeding off the community. These stories are very simple but you dress them in a social and emotional context that makes them fresh and vibrant."

Bill Mumy offers a personal perspective: "To me, the anthology format is a great concept that was pulled off brilliantly in the original *Twilight Zone* series. New cast every episode. Never gets stale. Actors are always on their toes and doing their best work. Also, importantly, *Twilight Zone* was made when television was young and the talent pool was great. Wonderful character actors in those shows. Think about the level of talent in the cast of those episodes! Huge stars were doing them and future huge stars were doing them. *The Twilight Zone* is the unique vision and voice of *one* man. Rod Serling battled the network to maintain his vision and for the most part he was successful. Nowadays, sadly, there are often over a dozen producers on one half-hour television show! The networks insist on fiddling with projects constantly and the old saying 'Too many

cooks spoil the stew' is obviously true these days more often than not. Rod Serling was a tremendously gifted writer with a unique voice. His dialogue is as distinctive as Jimi Hendrix's guitar or Miles Davis' trumpet. You recognize his work right away as singular and special. No matter how many times *The Twilight Zone* gets redone in whatever format, it will never equal the original, for it can't without him. Also, in my opinion, black-and-white is a great arena for fantasy and sci-fi stories. It's easier to let your imagination take over when you're watching something in black-and-white. I'd love to see more shows experiment with black-and-white today. In a nutshell — *The Twilight Zone* succeeds because it's brilliantly and uniquely written and acted and filmed."

This 2002 incarnation of *Twilight Zone* was nominated for a Saturn Award, given out by the Academy of Science Fiction, Fantasy & Horror Films, for Best Network Series.

Summing up his thoughts on the opportunity to reopen that door once again, Pen Densham remarks, "I take great pride in that I convinced Les Moonves to put *Twilight Zone* back on the air. I feel I've taken two great American icons of the imagination [*Twilight Zone* and *The Outer Lim-*

its] and gave them both a shot to be on TV again. My genuine hope was to get a sanctuary built for the imagination, for those kinds of stories."

CAST NOTES

Forest Whitaker (Narrator-Host): In addition to being an actor, Whitaker is also a producer and director. He was discovered by talent agents while performing as an orderly in a student stage production of *Whose Life Is It Anyway?* One of his earliest roles was in *Fast Times at Ridgemont High* (1982); very quickly he landed more major feature roles: *The Color of Money* (1986, directed by Martin Scorsese), *Platoon* (1986, directed by

Oliver Stone), and *Bird* (1988, directed by Clint Eastwood as the jazz musician Charlie Parker); at the Cannes Film Festival, he won the Best Actor award for that role. In 2006 he joined the cast of FX's *The Shield* starring Michael Chiklis. In 2007 he received critical acclaim and won three Best Actor awards (the Golden Globe award, the SAG Award and the Academy Award) as the Ugandan president Idi Amin in *The Last King of Scotland*.

SOURCES

Wyatt, Chris. "The Twilight Zone: 'It's Still a Good Life / Monsters on Maple Street.'" Mania.com, February 19, 2003.

The Visitor

(1997–1998)

A U.S. pilot, abducted by aliens in 1947, returns to Earth with mysterious powers and a mission to save mankind from destruction. As he searches for his long-lost son, he's pursued by Col. James Vise, who is determined to kill him.

Cast: John Corbett (Adam MacArthur — The Visitor), Steve Railsback (Col. James Vise). **Created by:** Roland Emmerich, Dean Devlin; **Executive Producers:** Roland Emmerich, Dean Devlin, John Masius; **Co-Executive Producer:** Randy Zisk; **Supervising Producers:** Ute Emmerich, William Fay; **Producer:** Norman Morrill; **Co-Producers:** Monica Wyatt, Harker Wade; **Consulting Producer:** Thania St. John; **Writers included:** Valerie Mayhew, Vivian Mayhew, Hans Tobeason, Aya Marie Carrillo, Edward Gold, Samuel W. Gailey, Todd Adam Kessler; **Directors included:** Kevin Kerslake, Tony Bill, Timothy Van Patten, Allan Arkush, Davis Guggenheim, Tucker Gates; **Guest Stars:** Efrem Zimbalist Jr., Matt Clark, Ellen Bry, Mary Carver, Fred Pinkard, Brian Vaughn, Harry Shearer, Bill Morey, Jackie Debatin, Peter Carlin, Barbara Bain, Walter Olkewicz, Mary Mara, Courtney Peldon, Richard Ian Cox (Asst. Director Grushaw), Granville Ames (Sgt. Roberts), Grand L. Bush (Agent Wilcox), John Storey (Agent Van Patten), Leon Rippy (Agent LaRue), Adam Baldwin as Michael O'Ryan

Fox Network/20th Century–Fox Television/ Centropolis Television Production; September 1997–January 1998; 60 minutes; 13 episodes

Dean Devlin and Roland Emmerich felt *The Visitor* was destined for great things, at least commercially. They called their time slot "choice" (8 P.M. Fridays) and claimed that their show would make people feel good about themselves. An alienated man on the run has been a staple of SF TV since the 1970s — *The Immortal*, *The Phoenix*, *Starman*, *The Incredible Hulk*, *Logan's Run*, even a non–SF guy, *The Fugitive*. TV Guide noted, "Does TV really need another formulaic action-alien show?"

But when Fox purchased *The Visitor* in December 1996, they felt the well-fertilized idea was ripe for the 1990s. "There are definitely elements of *The Fugitive*," Devlin conceded. "But the science fiction aspect gives you an opportunity to talk about today's issues, out of their context, and put them into a fictional context."

John Corbett played an American pilot named MacArthur who disappears over the Bermuda Triangle in 1947. He's held hostage by aliens for the next fifty years. He escapes from his captors and crash-lands his alien pod in Utah. Showing no signs of aging after all of these years, and with mysterious powers that include healing, telepathy and speed reading, he sets out to find his son and to keep mankind safe from a future catastrophe. In hot pursuit is Col. James Vise of the ultra-secret National Security Agency, who wants him dead.

In the pilot, written by Devlin and directed by Kevin Kerslake, Col. Vise finds in the wreckage of MacArthur's ship a fingerprint which identifies the pilot as the missing airman from 1947. "We're chasing a ghost," cries a military man but Vise shrugs off the spookery, convinced this is an invader sent to destroy mankind.

MacArthur is given sanctuary by a stressed single mother, Nadine (Lucinda Jenney), and her boisterous, rebellious teenage son. As mystical as his behavior is, MacArthur is genuinely amazed by advances in human technology, marveling at the son's computer and a garbage disposal and, in a later show, crying "Eureka!" as he watches an electric can opener.

Kevin Kerslake was an offbeat choice to direct the pilot. He was selected because of his reputation for creating highly energetic music videos and commercials. "Dean and Roland had ambitions to bring some of the creative energy they saw in music videos to the world of television," says Kerslake, "That was of great interest to me. They were absolutely fearless in their defense of this idea, whereas the studio preferred to go with a more conventional choice for a director, one who was more predictably predictable. I was a total wild card."

Kerslake appreciated the pilot's depth. "With its obvious mythic parallels and seamless fusing of many genres, the heart of *The Visitor* was gushing with possibilities. It always comes down to story. Even in the supposed 'non-narrative' universe of music videos, story is more often than not the thrust of each video. It's one of the more baffling prejudices against music video directors, but, thankfully, it's a prejudice Dean and Roland didn't share."

The young director had his share of challenges while making the pilot. "We shot in the Salt Lake City area, but there was an early thaw that spring, so we had to go to higher elevations for the site of the plane crash, which was supposed to happen in a snow-covered forest. We found a spot just outside Heber, where temperatures were still hitting sub-freezing levels at night. [Actors] Grant Bush, Steve Railsback, John Storey and Leon Rippy did not take this into account when choosing their wardrobe, whereas everyone in the crew that night was walking around in Arctic gear, impervious to the cold. When we jumped in for a dialogue scene, we started hearing a strange sound, like a helicopter nearby. It finally clicked. It was the sound of teeth chattering. Every one of those actors was wearing thin-soled dress shoes with paper-thin socks, and no long underwear on underneath their clothes either, walking around in snow. They insisted on staying in character and not changing one item of clothing, even if it was out of frame. I told each of them to high-tail it to their trailer after their lines, but they each stood there for the other in an act of camaraderie. Talk about actors being there for other actors. Of course, we had to replace all their dialogue later!"

Most TV aliens have been immaculately groomed, but MacArthur looked like a hippie, with long, straggly hair. He could be either taken as a hip-looking Starman for the 1990s or a product of TV demographics, a vulnerable hunk for nurturing female viewers. Unlike Devlin and Emmerich's usual fare (they produced the blockbuster films *Independence Day* and *Godzilla*), visual effects in *The Visitor* was kept to a minimum. "We don't want to turn *The Visitor* into *Superman*," Devlin said in 1997. "The character is more about tapping into the potential of the human mind and body. What if we could use 100 percent of the brain? It's a wish list of what we could all achieve one day."

In the pilot, when MacArthur is shot down by the military outside Nadine's house and rushed to a hospital, he dies. A rejuvenating glow engulfs him and, like Jesus Christ, he rises from the dead. He bids the mother and son farewell and walks off into the sunset for another 12 adventures.

"I wanted to do this show because it was about human potential," says executive producer John Masius, who had created another feel-good show, *Touched By an Angel*. "It was about touching ordinary people's lives and getting them back on track. And while MacArthur has a lot of hope, he also has a lot of regret. It's a very complex situation he's dealing with."

To the show's credit, subsequent episodes kept the science fiction elements in focus. Whereas a previous TV fugitive like the Immortal once spent an episode harvesting tomatoes, and the fugitives of *Planet of the Apes* delivered a baby cow, the Visitor's adventures had a fantastic slant. In "Dreams," MacArthur tried to unravel a message he was receiving from deep space and in "Teufelsnacht," he encounters an alien (a recurring character, played by Adam Baldwin) who wants to take him back to the mothership.

As he hitchhiked across Oregon, South Dakota

and Florida, the Visitor dispensed quaint philosophies. "If you dream it, you can make it happen," he says to a depressed scientist. Or his advice to runaway kids: "It's tough facing your problems but things work out better if you do." And to a confused, pregnant woman: "All we have are the people that we love."

"Science fiction tends to be very cold," Devlin said during production. "It's either very spooky or very hardware-driven. We wanted this show to have heart. We did not want this to be about super-bad aliens trying to take over the world."

Kerslake says, "Adam MacArthur was the glue that held together all the various impulses of the show — sci-fi, drama, humor, suspense. He had so much humanity. I mean, come on! The guy is Jesus."

Another director, Tony Bill, felt Corbett had the perfect qualities as MacArthur, noting, "John had an inner strength and an aura of integrity that served the role very well."

The Visitor encountered "all types." When a scientist creates an anti-gravity device, he celebrates by running naked through a neighborhood. A 13-year-old boy latches onto the Visitor as a father figure and a wacky, over-the-top DJ pushes the envelope of annoyance as he freaks out over the landing of a UFO outside his studio.

We saw more of the Visitor's humanity via flashbacks of him, showing him getting into his plane back in 1947 as his young son Jason waves goodbye. He never locates his son in the series but a reliable psychic tells him, "One day you will find him."

MacArthur's exact mission to save humanity is kept ambiguous but it is made clear that mankind will perish unless he intervenes. John Corbett, a true believer in extraterrestrials, felt that the show's concept was believable. "I find it harder to believe that a big creature such as the Tyrannosaurus Rex once walked on the face of this planet than the possibility of life on other planets," he said during filming.

One of *The Visitor*'s most intriguing episodes was "Reunion," where MacArthur finds his now elderly wife (played by Barbara Bain) confined to a wheelchair in a retirement home, her mind lost in a fog. He can only stall her death. ("I can't cheat death," he deadpans. "We all die.") But he gives her a burst of energy that rejuvenates her mind long enough for her to recognize him as her long-lost husband. They share a tearful hug before she dies. Tony Bill (a former actor, and the Oscar-winning producer of *The Sting*) directed Valarie

and Vivian Mayhew's script. Bill's admiration for Dean Devlin's work, as well as a reading of the script, convinced him to direct the segment. "I liked how the episode had such a resonant emotional quotient. It addressed everyone's fantasy about going back in time, about making amends and seeing things clearly in retrospect."

Bain's performance is unforgettable, her face briefly lighting up with joy and recognition as she realizes this is her husband from 1947. "I really liked those scenes," says Bill. "Barbara Bain is a consummately skilled actress. She was unafraid to let her feelings show and I was moved to tears on the set by Barbara's performance. I did what any good director does with actors of that caliber — I got out of the way." There were other emotional issues to deal with during shooting. "Actor Leon Rippy [agent LaRue] heard one morning that his mother had died. Although he was very distressed, he carried on throughout the day like the pro he is. We got him onto a plane that night."

Col. Vise had his own mental baggage to cope with. "I pray you never have to make the choices I've had to make," he grumbles to a doctor. But Vise's menace is undermined by his weekly failure to catch the Visitor. "The nice thing about Col. Vise and the NSA is that they are not bad guys," noted Devlin. "They have a belief of who the Visitor is and what he's doing. They believe they're saving the world. That's what puts our hero into jeopardy."

In the last episode, "The Trial," an alien ship hovers above MacArthur and beams him aboard. He is put on trial inside the dark spaceship, surrounded by all kinds of past UFO abductees, ranging from old women to teenagers. The Visitor is charged with trying to change the destiny of mankind. Flashbacks from the previous episodes are used as part of his trial. Meanwhile, on Earth, Col. Vise is hospitalized when he develops a mysterious malady. The dying colonel gasps his philosophy: that anyone who is returned to Earth after a UFO abduction is either an alien or controlled by evil extraterrestrial forces and therefore must be destroyed. He bases this on his knowledge of what is inside top-secret UFO files. Despite ER doctors' frantic efforts, Vise dies on the operating table.

The alien elders rule in MacArthur's favor and release him. He appears beside the draped corpse of Col. Vise at the hospital, where he envelopes the colonel in a rejuvenating glow. As Vise is brought back to life, the Visitor tells him, "My mission is not over. But yours is. Stop following me." The last shot of the series shows MacArthur walking along a beach, to continue his quest for his son. Officially sanctioned by the alien elders, he will also keep a benevolent eye over mankind.

CAST NOTES

John Corbett (Adam): Born and raised in West Virginia, he and a couple of buddies drove to California where Corbett worked in a steel factory. When he decided to try for an acting career, he did local theater and landed his first TV commercial, for Samsung Electronics. From there he got a regular role on TV's *Northern Exposure* in the early 1990s. He auditioned to play Jeff Goldblum's role in *Independence Day* (1996) and co-starred as the groom in *My Big Fat Greek Wedding* (2002). In 2002 he received an Emmy nomination for his role as Sarah Jessica Parker's boyfriend on HBO's *Sex and the City*. A singer, he released a CD of his music in 2006.

Steve Railsback (Col. Vise): The Dallas-born actor appeared on Broadway in the late 1960s and early 1970s (Lee Strasberg was one of his acting teachers). It was his portrayal of Charles Manson in the mini-series *Helter Skelter* (1976) that brought him national fame (he had won the role over Walter Koenig, Chekov on *Star Trek*). He also starred in the films *The Stunt Man* (1980) and Tobe Hooper's space-vampire saga, *Lifeforce* (1985) and appeared on TV's *The X-Files* and *The Practice*. The actor said the 1960s version of *The Twilight Zone* was his favorite show and that he liked how *The Visitor* was evolving creatively in its brief life.

SOURCES

Fall preview. *TV Guide*, 1997.
Shapiro, Marc. "Visiting Hour — ID4 Creators Dean Devlin and Roland Emmerich Humanize Alien Encounters, Hosting The Visitor." *Starlog* no. 244, November 1997.

VR5

(1995)

A young telephone lineswoman enters virtual reality worlds by making phone calls to other people. She is recruited by a secret intelligence organization, The Committee, who use her talents on top-secret missions involving virtual reality.

Cast: Lori Singer (Sydney Bloom), Michael Easton (Duncan), David McCallum (Dr. Joseph Bloom), Louise Fletcher (Nora Bloom), Anthony Stewart Head (Oliver).

Created by: Thania St. John, Michael Katleman, Geoffrey Hemwall, Jeannine Renshaw, Adam Cherry; **Executive Producers:** Thania St. John, John Sacret Young; **Co-Executive Producers:** Eric Blakeney, Thania St. John; **Supervising Producers:** Michael Katleman, Jeannine Renshaw; **Producers:** Naomi Janzen, Mel Efros, Jack Clements; **Co-Producer:** Geoffrey Hemwall; **Director of Photography:** Brian R.R. Hebb; **Art Director:** Michael Southard; **Production Designer:** Nina Ruscio; **Visual Effects Supervisor:** Janet Muswell; **Writers included:** Toni Graphia, Jacquelyn Bain, Jeannine Renshaw, John Sacret Young, Thania St. John, Naomi Janzen; **Directors included:** Rob Bowman, D. J. Caruso, Jim Charles-

ton, Steve Dubin, Deborah Reinisch, Lorraine Senna, John Sacret Young, Michael Katleman; **Guest Stars included:** Dan O'Herlihy, Neal McDonough, Penn Jillette, Robert Davi, Markie Post, Turhan Bey, Frank Converse, Shirley Knight, Adam Baldwin, Robert Picardo, Janine Messersmith, Stephen Mills (as the Committee's Agent), Will Patten (as Dr. Frank Morgan), Tracey Needham (as Samantha Bloom)

Samoset Productions in association with Rysher Entertainment; Fox Channel/20th Century–Fox; March 1995–May 1995; 60 minutes; 13 episodes

When launched on the Fox network on Friday nights in 1995, *VR5*'s goal was to scare the daylight out of audiences.

It had state-of-the-art computer images and manipulated film with mismatched colors. For its first two weeks, the show had a robust 15 ratings share. But two months later, it was limping with an anemic 5–7 share and down to 84th place in the ratings. To cap it off, *People* magazine dismissed it as "the worst show of the tube" for 1995.

It is unfortunate that some shows, such as *Space: Above and Beyond* and *Firefly*, won't make it. Mainstream ratings firepower isn't there and cancellation is quick. But failure is truly bitter when a show begins as a hit, then abruptly fades. That is what happened to *VR5*.

The first episode opens in 1978 Pasadena as Dr. Joseph Bloom arrives home with a computer and raves that it has a 16K memory. "One day every home will have one of these," he predicts to his wife and two young daughters. "Maybe they'll even be all hooked up to each other!" But when a mysterious man from "The Committee" shows up at the door to deliver a message to Bloom, the kids are banished to the upstairs and they listen to their father and the man arguing. Later, Bloom is all smiles again, and drives them to get ice cream. But in the rainstorm, Bloom loses control, the car plunges over a cliff into a river and only Sydney manages to get free. Her father and sister Samantha drown.

Seventeen years later, Sydney is an introverted, frustrated telephone lineswoman. Her personality has been flattened by the residue of trauma of having grown up without a family. She has only one friend (Duncan, a semi-hippie) and a pet bird. A single woman with frizzy blonde hair and penetrating blue eyes, Sydney spends her off-time on the computer in a drab apartment. Her social life, even by cyberspace standards, is tragic. "You have zero messages," her computer announces when she comes home from work.

Wearing black goggles, she experiments on her computer with virtual reality. Strange things begin to happen. When she calls her nasty neighbor, Mr. Kravitz, she's swept into a nightmare VR world and watches Kravitz fall helplessly over a city, landing in front of a cement roller. He frantically tries to escape being squashed and runs into a bus, where the grinning driver has white (no pupils) eyes. A woman passenger spits flame and a strange dwarf takes off his shirt. Shaken, Sydney ends the VR experience by breaking the connection. This surrealistic tapestry is reminiscent of David Lynch's quirky *Twin Peaks* series.

The real Kravitz was not actually transported into the dream but Sydney realizes that by phoning someone, she can tap into that person's subconscious in the form of a VR adventure. It re-veals the person's guilts, fears and even past crimes to Sydney. "I've done something that's supposed to be impossible," she mutters.

She calls her mother, who resides in a nursing home. Once pretty, Mrs. Bloom is now bloated, old and uncommunicative. When a nurse hands the phone to the sick woman, another VR link is activated and Sydney is swept into her mother's subconscious.

But the defining VR experience is when she calls up co-worker Scott, and finds he's a serial rapist and murderer. Just as he's about to kill Sydney in the dream, she pulls the plug and seeks out Dr. Frank Morgan, who has been experimenting with VR. Morgan cautions that her VR travels could kill her for real. He cites an example of a man who had a VR experience of crashing a jet into the Earth from 40,000 feet. That man is now in a permanent coma. Sydney shrugs off his advice. To find out whether Scott is really a murderer or not, she invites Scott to a real late-night date on a mountain lookout. He suddenly turns violent, and chases her with a knife before knocking her out. She awakens to find him digging a grave, with the body of a prior victim's bony hand protruding from the dirt.

She hits Scott over the head with a shovel and he falls forward on his own knife. Just then, Dr. Morgan drives up. He's been hacking into Sydney's VR experiences and knew she was in danger. He explains that he works for The Committee, the secret security organization and they need her VR expertise. She and Morgan will now be working together.

This sets up the remaining 12 episodes. In addition to searching for her father's secret journal, she agrees to go missions for the Committee, such as using the VR to find a runaway teenage genius and saving hostages held in a traffic control center.

In "Love and Death," she learns there are rogue factions of The Committee, and one of them kills Dr. Morgan. In the next episode, "5D," Oliver Sampson (new regular Anthony Stewart Head) takes over as her permanent contact (and friend).

Each week Sydney visited weird, surrealistic VR worlds. "We wanted to create an environment that was new to our viewers," says visual effects supervisor Janet Muswell. "and convey an advanced placement of consciousness, with visuals that had never been seen before. I worked closely with Michael Southard, a wonderful artist who captured our wild dreams in vivid color. We used a film coloring technique called the CST System, used subsequently on films such as *Pleasantville*. There was approximately 20 minutes of VR scenes per episode, so we needed to produce an effect that was not only cost effective, but achievable in the time restrictions of weekly television. CST stripped our film to black and white and we used the contrast to dictate which colors we could use. I used a lot of color from the blue/purple pallet, a hue that isn't used much in nature. I tried to think what was relevant to the story, making them 'scary' colors or 'calm' colors. In one episode, I left the whole frame black and white, apart from the action the audience needed to concentrate on." She admits it was challenging. "I had a blast and never worked harder in my life. It was six-day weeks, 18-hour days."

One interesting *VR5* episode was "The Many Faces of Alex," which begins with Oliver and his colleague, Alex (Markie Post) unable to stop the assassination of the man they're escorting in East Germany in 1990. Alex vanishes and years later, Oliver, obsessed with finding her, enlists Sydney's help. Sydney learns the man who was shot was her father and he may have survived. Efforts to find Alex remain frustratingly elusive, since she always appears in various guises and even dies in a VR sequence. Oliver is anguished when Alex finally meets a tragic death in real life, just as he catches up with her.

Directed by John Sacret Young, this moody piece shows a vulnerable side to Oliver. Jacquelyn Blain scripted the episode and says, "One of my favorite things was to take a character as smug and ego-centric as Oliver and slowly unravel him, pull every plank he's standing on out from under him, and make him realize everything he believed to be true is actually a lie ... then watch him react."

Blain was just breaking into television writing when she joined the show as a researcher. She was already a big fan of Young's *China Beach* series. "To have the opportunity to learn from a man with that much experience and creativity was all I could have ever wanted as a beginning TV writer-producer," she says. "JSY [John Sacret Young] became my mentor."

He gave Blain a chance to select a story idea from the writers' board. "It was something like, 'Oliver's old love knows that Dr. Bloom and Samantha are alive.' That's provocative enough for any writer, but I saw it as a chance to write for Tony Head [Oliver]. I had never met him, but I watched the dailies and was terrifically impressed by how good he was. I'm also a sucker for tragic love stories, Hitchcock movies, and spy thrillers.

It turned out JSY also loved tragic love stories, Hitchcock, train stations and John le Carre, and he decided to direct it."

A scheduling change during Christmas forced Blain to write her script quickly. "I went into hyperdrive since I was leaving town for the holidays in two days. I wrote the teaser, which was all in a train station, and faxed it to John. He called me at my brother's house in Dallas the day after Christmas. 'It's great! I love it! It's gonna cost us ten million dollars to shoot, but I love it! Finish it.' I went into second stage hyperdrive, writing madly on the airplane home, and got it done in six days. Two days later, we were back in the office. John came tearing into my little cubicle. 'I love it. It needs to be darker and twister. Alex has to die!' She didn't die in my original draft — she got stuck in an institute because she went nuts. He had me work with Thania [St. John, executive producer] and gave me 24 hours to get the revision to him. I sat down with a writer friend of mine the next day. We tag teamed the typing and got the whole thing done in about eight hours."

The episode gave David McCallum a chance to return as Sydney's father. Blain recalls watching the filming as McCallum's character gets shot by a mysterious gunman. "We were shooting in the train station, and the weapons people fixed David McCallum up with the squibs. The guy handling the prop gun *also* played the guy with the gun, just for safety sake, and he went to rehearse with David. Now, David's an old hand at these kinds of make-believe mayhem. The prop guy said he was going point the gun slightly off to one side, so it wouldn't be pointing directly at David. That way, if there was a misfire with the quarter-load blank, David wouldn't get hurt. David told him to point it *at* him — it didn't worry him. But the prop guy was adamant and they shot it his way. I went to the prop guy later and asked him why he hadn't done as David had asked. He got this horrified look on his face. 'Are you kidding? What if something had happened? I'd be known as the man who killed Illya Kuryakin. No way.' He wandered off, shaking his head, muttering. That made David laugh when I told him later."

For a writer seeing one of her first scripts produced, it could get emotional. "We had been shooting for three days and had moved to the Union Station train depot. I had been incredibly busy and even overwhelmed by a couple of things. On this fourth day, I got to the station early and walked into the train station lobby. It was empty. Set dressing had already finished, and the place really looked like 1990 Eastern Germany, with the baggage carts, the old call board, the little flags. I knew the place was soon going to be filled with our cast and crew, four cameras, 100 extras, and blood squibs in just a few minutes, but for that moment, it looked real. And I realized that six weeks before, none of this had existed anywhere but in my head. None of this would be happening if I hadn't dreamed it all up and written it down. And I burst into tears. John's assistant Stacy caught me crying and made me tell her why. When I did, she told me I had to tell John. I was mortified. John's not one for emotional outbursts. But she insisted. So, eight hours later, John and I were walking alone together to check out the set and I told him the story. He got really quiet. I thought, 'Great. My career's over before it started.' So I said, 'Sorry, John. A momentary lapse of sanity. Won't happen again.' He put his hand on my shoulder, looked me square in the eye and said, 'Don't apologize. Those of us who are in this business need to be reminded once in a while of why we got into it in the first place." I started to tear up. 'Okay." Five hours later, he and I were screaming at each other about a shot. It was lovely."

She also praises Anthony Head for helping out during filming. "Tony is such a talented professional," she says. "He worked his butt off and went to emotional places that were very risky. He also stayed generous to the crew, even when he was exhausted. He was an incredible source of creative ideas and strength for both the episode and for me. I blew up one night at John Secret Young and stormed over to where everybody sat, and I scared poor David McCallum away! But Tony lit another cigarette and talked me through the story problem. He totally got what I was after, about dismantling the character of Oliver, and he went for it. I think it worked. And, of course, the last scene, when Alex and Oliver say hello and goodbye, is one of my favorites. I figured if John Secret Young wanted Alex to die, I wanted it to be damned tragic."

While Markie Post is known for her comedic work, such as on TVs *Night Court*, here she essayed a difficult role, under many disguises. "She brought a lot of enthusiasm, a sense of playfulness, and a willingness to go places emotionally that were really quite nice," says Blain. "Overall, the episode was very good and I'm terribly proud of it. It was one of the most character-driven episodes we did, and one of the best experiences of my TV career."

Film Comment Journal had reservations about the *VR5* series but praised "The Many Faces of Alex" as, "A striking episode about the fluidity of identity, a terrific pastiche of Hitchcockian themes and stylistic signatures, from *Vertigo, Strangers on a Train, Marnie, North by Northwest*, et al." However, they also labeled *VR5* as a series that, "too often suffers from the *Tron* Syndrome ... storylines drift through interesting stylistic environs, but lacks the push of passionate personality and clear turning points, and ultimately peter out into narrative limbo. [But] if it isn't yet a keeper, the series doesn't deserve to be a throwaway. Unfortunately, just as *VR.5* seemed to be picking up steam, character- and story-wise, Fox pulled the plug."

Blain concurs that the series was getting better. "The series got out there too early. If it had started a couple of years later, it would have done a lot better. Second, I'm not sure Lori created an empathetic enough character, but that's just me. Third, I think we were just beginning to find the show by the time we did mine (which was number nine). A lot of people weren't willing to wait until we got there."

Looking back on the series today, she says, "The show's biggest strength was its creativity and willingness to try stuff. I loved the idea of going into the subconscious, that played really well. The chemistry between the characters was strong for the most part and getting stronger. And I've worked on quite a few TV series since then, and I don't think I ever worked on one with better art direction and visual style. A great, great crew."

The character of Sydney did make progress in her quest — she discovers her father was a member of The Committee and bad men want Sydney's secret of how her brain connects via the computer and enter people's subconscious. If mastered by others, it would be a great weapon.

In the last episode, "Reunion," Sydney learns the car crash scenario she recalled as a youngster was all a VR illusion, manufactured by her father to protect her. Traitors in The Committee had actually abducted her Dad and sister, Samantha, years ago. Sydney finds Samantha and they search for their father, who is hunted by the lead traitor, Abernathy. His evil philosophy: "Power is no longer about accumulating territories and weapons — it's about accumulating minds." The episode ends with Sydney entering a VR maze in order to pull her mother out of her coma. Her mother awakens but as Samantha, Duncan and Oliver look on, Sydney collapses, her mind frozen in a VR fog. That was the last episode's cliffhanger.

The mental maze that Sydney urges her mother to walk out of looked like trees set against a cloudy sky. "It was hard to come up with something different," says Janet Muswell of that VR sequence. "I finally took a sped-up flight through trees and colorized it to look like we were zooming through a maze. At the end we pull back to see the maze pattern we had been alluding to all through the series— read into it what you will!"

VR5's juxtaposition of what's real and what's not may have confused audiences. Co-star Michael Easton, who played Sydney's friend Duncan, says, "The scripts were great. It was like *The Prisoner*, a very intelligent project. But those elements may have been hard for mainstream audiences to follow. It was *sort* of a SF show but also more of a cult thing."

Even criticism was mixed. "It's incoherent, it's overwrought, it's ridiculously obvious in its desire to become TVs next hip cult phenomenon," said Ken Tucker of *Entertainment Weekly*. "Yet *VR5* exerts its own uncanny pull ... Lori Singer is a good hero-hacker, her eyes are as blank as a dead computer screen, which enables her to come off as admirably restrained."

The characters also evolved. Sydney became more likable, Oliver became more of a rebel against the Committee and Duncan became more dimensional. Yet the concept and visuals took center stage.

"You needed a character that the audience relates too," Easton observes. "That's where SF is sometimes good, and sometimes where it's not so good. But I enjoyed the people I worked with and John Sacret Young was a brilliant guy. I wish the show had run four or five years."

Low ratings and high production costs ended *VR5*. Three of the show's episodes, "Send Me An Angel," "Sisters' and "Parallel Lives," never aired on Fox.

"*VR5* was a complex story to follow and that hurt it in the ratings," Janet Muswell observes. "You couldn't just drop into an episode and know what was going on. You had to follow the story from the beginning. It had the wrong slot at 8 P.M. It was a 9 P.M. or 10 P.M. show."

But she adds, "We pushed the envelope of what had been done for TV. That's what made it fun and interesting for me. It was a visually stimulating show. Not just the VFX, but the wonderful sets by Nina Ruscio and the excellent camera work. We had an incredible and unlikely team —

the executive producer, John Young, our writing team and a great cast."

And as with every SF series, there were the dedicated fans. They launched a letter campaign that resulted in European financing to make a concluding, two-hour movie. A script was drafted for production and it was to air in late 1995 on Fox. But the network changed its mind and the project was canceled. Sydney has been left in the VR dark ever since.

Cast Notes

Lori Singer (Sydney): Born in Corpus Christi, Texas, her father was a symphony conductor and her mother a concert pianist. Her first love was dancing and she later went to *Julliard Performing Arts School* in New York to major in music. She was also a model. Her brother, Marc Singer, was an actor (*V* and *Beastmaster*) and this inspired her to pursue acting. She starred in the first season (1982–1983) of the *Fame* TV series and won a starring role in the 1984 film, *Footloose*. Her *VR5* co-star Louise Fletcher loved Singer's dedication to the show. "She's very conscientious and works like a dog, which makes all of us work harder," she said during production. "She's very committed to the show and we work well together." Singer's recent credits include the films *Little Victim* (2005) and *I.R.A. King of Nothing* (2006).

Michael Easton (Duncan): He attended prep school in Ireland and England before going to the University of California to study English and history. He's also a screenwriter and book author. His other SF series was *Total Recall 2070* (1998–1999). He signed on as a regular on the daytime soap, *One Life to Live*, in 2003.

Anthony Stewart Head (Oliver): Born in London, England, he was a singer in a band called *Two Way* in the early 1980s. He became famous for his international TV coffee commercials (with Sharon Maughan) during the late 1980s. This led to a regular role on *Buffy: The Vampire Slayer* (1997–2002). He also appeared in the film, *Imagine You and Me* (2005).

David McCallum (Dr. Bloom): This Glasgow-born actor originally pursued a career in music. His early movie credits, *Billy Budd* (1962) and *The Great Escape* (1963) put him on the American radar map. He was cast as Illya Kuryakin in *The Man From U.N.C.L.E.* (1964–1968), which made him a TV superstar. He later starred in the series *The Invisible Man* (1975–1976) and the British series *Sapphire and Steel* (1979–1982). He went on to play the irascible coroner on TVs *Navy NCIS*, beginning in 2003.

Louise Fletcher (Mrs. Bloom): Born to deaf parents in Birmingham, Alabama, she was taught to speak by her Aunt. She moved to California and worked as a receptionist to make ends meet. Some of her early appearances in the late 1950s included *One Step Beyond* and *Perry Mason*. She hit major stardom when she received an Oscar for her role as the icy-cold Nurse Ratched in *One Flew Over the Cuckoo's Nest* (1978). She also had a recurring role on *Star Trek: Deep Space 9* as Kai Winn Adami (1993–1999). Her other TV credits include *Picket Fences, ER* and *Joan of Arcadia*.

SOURCES

Film Comment Journal, 1995.
People, 1995.
Spelling, Ian. "Virtual Veteran." *Starlog Explorer* no. 8, August 1995.

Welcome to Paradox
(1998)

An anthology of tales taking place in the futuristic city of Betaville, exploring themes of how society copes with, and uses, technology in positive and negative ways.

The Host: Michael Philip
Created by: Lewis B. Chesler; *Developed for Television by:* Jeremy Lipp; *Executive Producers:* Jeremy Lipp, Mary Sparacio, Lewis B. Chesler, David M. Perlmutter; *Line Producer:* Mary Guilfoyle; *Producer:* R.W. Vincent; *Associate Producer-Production Designer:* Michael Nemirsky; *Writers included:* Jeremy Lipp, William Harrison, Rick Drew, Miguel Tejada-Flores, Andrew McEvoy; *Directors included:* Charles Wilkinson, Jorge Montesi, Bruce MacDonald; *Director of Photography:* Philip Linzey; *Guest Stars included:* Henry Rollins, Steven Bauer, Ice-T, Mayim Balik, A. Martinez, Rachel Hayward, Alice Krige
Sci-Fi Channel/Chesler-Perlmutter Productions; 1998; 60 minutes; 13 episodes

In the city of Betaville, in the near future, the technology we developed controls us. But will our dreams of tomorrow be turned into a nightmare? Be careful what you wish for ... nothing is impossible any more...— The Host

Welcome to Paradox was a rare anthology series, made by a team of producers who seemed to understand and appreciate science fiction literature. They created 13 episodes adapting short stories by SF authors Alan Dean Foster ("Our Lady of the Machine"), A.E. Van Vogt ("Research Alpha"), Andrew Weiner ("News from D Street"), Greg Egan ("The Extra"), James Tiptree Jr. ("The Girl Who Was Plugged In"), Donald Westlake ("The Winner") and John Varley ("Blue Champagne" and "Options"), to name just a few.

Paradox takes place in Betaville, a megalopolis of the future, where technology interfaces, complicates and sometimes backfires on their lives.

According to its executive producer and creator, Lewis B. Chesler, *Paradox* was an attempt at creating Sci-Fi Channel's first anthology TV series. "I had a long history with the USA Network, I had done *The Hitchhiker*, which was considered quasi-fantasy," says Chesler, who partnered in a production company with David Perlmutter. "They were impressed with the quality of the work we had done. They needed an anthology series to launch the Sci-Fi Channel's commitment to drama programming."

With writer Jeremy Lipp, Chesler and Perlmutter "agreed on a concept that it would be an anthology series based on underlying literary material, from the SF genre," recalls Chesler. "I was knowledgeable and admiring of this material and felt a great deal of it would lend itself to dramatic construction. I also presented a thematic notion for the series, which was 'when science meets taboo.' The trio capitalized on this century's exponential growth in scientific discovery, inventions, and progress. While there were many positive values associated with this chronology, there were also concerns that we had crossed boundaries of human consciousness and human morality and behavior. I thought this was an exceptional thematic notion for scripted drama episodes. It would involve behavior that suggested both the promise and peril of science."

The stories on *The Hitchhiker* (1983–1991) were linked only by actor-narrator Page Fletcher. In a similar vein, *Paradox*'s stories were linked by the Host (Michael Philip). "I was a great fan of anthology, having been a fan of short story literature," says Chesler. "Today, networks want traditional series with continuing characters. But, at that time, they were open to it. Subsequently, management directors of the Sci-Fi Channel were not open to the idea of an anthology series."

Chesler assembled a staff of readers who scoured through known stories and hand-picked their favorites. "The show wasn't meant to be science fiction in a sense of something futuristic; it was more to be science fact. Because of the fantastic rate of scientific experimentation, progress, and discovery that we are witnessing today, we wanted to discuss ideas that were either presently achievable or within an imminent period of time. We looked for stories that were provocative, ones that challenged accepted conventions, or broke conventions and boundaries."

A sampling of *Paradox* storylines:

• Life inside a futuristic prison — where prisoners are held by biochips and no walls.
• What are the consequences when a girl's brain is plugged into a beautiful body grown just for her?
• Want to stay young? Hop into a series of cloned bodies and become immortal ... or so you hope.
• Psychotherapy by memory-wiping. Is this the best treatment?
• Learn how the other half lives. Swap genders at will.
• The future of law enforcement: Police vehicles that become judge, jury and executioner.
• Fall in love with a virtual reality megastar.
• Escape your failing marriage. Have an affair with a biologically enhanced robot.
• A detective is startled to discover he's living inside a cyber-reality.

Chesler says they went for "recognizable name" science fiction authors such as Foster, Varley and others. "These were not about visitors from other planets or from the beyond or about invasions or aliens of any sort. These were to be completely earthbound, in a universe the day after tomorrow and what had been historically enduring

human conflicts, human anxiety, human fear and human triumph, so there was a positive aspect to it as well."

Betaville was a landscape in which all these diverse stories could be played out. It would give the series a sense of continuity and coherence. For example, in "The Winner," there's a dialogue reference to "the feelies" which is a virtual reality entertainment device featured in another episode, "Blue Champagne." Connective tissue between episodes would be layered in either as dialogue, props or cityscape architecture and technology.

Paradox was filmed in Vancouver, Canada, and utilized name actors in the leading roles. The series was innovative and striking in three aspects: visual effects, costumes and production set design. To suggest a futuristic society, unusual costumes or "differently shaped" analogs of today's wardrobe were worn by the actors. Not having the budget for creating elaborate buildings or sets, production designer Michael Nemirsky simply "redressed" existing locations with futuristic objects or paraphernalia, suggesting a fictional universe; for example, transforming a modern-day Volkswagen Bug into a futuristic law enforcement vehicle for "In the Shop."

"I was a great fan of [French director] Jean-Luc Godard," says Chesler. "He had suggested a futuristic world that he had shot in the streets of Paris, simply by framing and cropping his camera on existing architecture and structures there, and so on, and in a distinct, aesthetic style. I incorporated that into the series. The camerawork was relatively consistent and the directors were very eager to create something that was framed differently than most television of the time. We did not have resources of CGI. At that time, special effects were still relatively costly. So we had limitations, but if we had more resources, we would have loved to have even more enhanced special effects. We tried to create something as compelling as possible, with an aesthetic, creative style. [Limited resources and budget] can be a spur to greater creativity. It was a universally positive experience, with exceptional, talented people."

When the series began airing in the summer of 1998, "[it] received exceptional critical response, very good reviews from most TV critics and very good response from the creative community, and had decent ratings numbers when we aired," says Chesler.

Reviewing the premiere episodes for Sci-Fi Weekly, an online webzine, Patrick Lee noted,

"The level of writing doesn't compare with *The Twilight Zone*, and the supporting characters tend to be caricatures. But the storylines are intriguing, and the acting in the first two episodes was uniformly on a high level.... The look of the show ... is deceptive: all muted jewel tones and bright blue skies— a counterpoint to the dark soul-searching at the core of the episodes. Perhaps a sign of *Paradox*'s modest budget, more effort appears to go into character interaction than into the sets, costumes or rudimentary special effect."

Commonweal's Frank McConnell raved in a December 1998 review, "It's a show that almost justifies the whole damn channel, maybe the real entry of SF at its best into the medium. The major networks could never make a profit out of a show this smart ... that just might be the first honest, canny, and responsible meeting of TV and SF at their mutual best."

But surprisingly, after just 13 episodes, Sci-Fi Channel didn't renew the series because, as so often happens, there was a change of executives in the boardroom. "There were some people within the Sci-Fi Channel who wanted to continue the show but the new management had come in and taken over," recalls Chesler. "It was regrettable. The ratings were very good at the time. Internet chatter was emerging too, with a huge volume of discussion about the show. It became kind of a cult show."

Sci-Fi Channel aired the series just once, without repeats. The show later aired in Canada.

Had the show continued, Chesler says that they would have been open to bringing back favorite characters who had appeared in individual segments. The show would have slipped somewhat from its anthological format, and we would have been able to delve deeper into the lives of those characters.

"I was saddened the show did not continue," says Chesler. "I was very proud. We did a very good job, given the resources given to us, because this was a time the Sci-Fi Channel did not have programming monies or licenses that were comparable to other networks. But there was a huge body of material available to us and we could have continued for many more years. It was about something. There was a philosophy to it."

CAST NOTES

Michael Philip (Host-Narrator): One of Philip's earliest roles was in the daytime soap *The Bold and the Beautiful* (1987). Later, he appeared in the *Friday the 13th* TV series (1990), *Street Justice* (1993), *Charmed* (1998), and *Angel* (2000). He's also appeared in the prime-time comedies *Frasier* (2001), and *Will & Grace* (2001).

SOURCES

Lee, Patrick. "Welcome to Paradox—The Sci-Fi Channel Tries to Transform Science Fiction Short Stories into Television Dramas with an Ambitious New Series." *Sci-Fi Weekly*, August 18, 1998.

McConnell, Frank. "Future Perfect: 'Welcome to Paradox.' Science-fiction Series on the Sci-Fi Channel." *Commonweal*, December 4, 1998.

The X-Files

(1993–2002)

Special agents Fox Mulder and Dana Scully investigate top-secret paranormal cases. Uncovered is a deranged world of government conspiracies, bizarre killers, extraterrestrial threats, flesh-eating insects, mutants, shapeshifters, biological weapons, killer clones, vampires, ghosts and monster reptiles.

Cast: David Duchovny (Fox Mulder) *Year 1–8*, Gillian Anderson (Dana Scully), Mitch Pileggi (Assistant FBI Director Walter Skinner), Robert Patrick (Special Agent John Doggett) *Year 8–9*, Annabeth Gish (Special Agent Monica Reyes) *Year 8–9*

Recurring Cast: William B. Davis (Cigarette Man), Jerry Hardin (Deep Throat), Steven Williams (Mr. X), Nicholas Lea (Agent Alex Krycek), John Neville (Well-Manicured Man). As the Lone Gunmen: Bruce Harwood (Byers), Dean Haglund (Langly), and Tom Braidwood (Frohike); ***Created***

by: Chris Carter; *Executive Producers:* Chris Carter, Howard Gordon *Year 3–4,* R. W. Goodwin *Year 4–5,* Frank Spotnitz *Year 7–9,* Vince Gilligan *Year 8–9,* John Shiban *Year 9;* *Co-Executive Producers:* Glen Morgan and James Wong *Year 1–2,* R. W. Goodwin *Year 1–3,* Howard Gordon *Year 3,* Vince Gilligan *Year 5–7,* Michael W. Watkins *Year 6–7,* Frank Spotnitz *Year 6–9,* Michelle MacLaren *Year 7–9,* John Shiban *Year 8,* Kim Manners *Year 8–9,* James Wong, David Greenwalt; *Supervising Producers:* Daniel Sackheim (pilot), Alex Gansa *Year 1,* Seth Green *Year 1,* R. W. Goodwin *Year 1–4,* Howard Gordon *Year 1–5,* Kim Manners *Year 7,* John Shiban *Year 7,* David Amann *Year 9,* Paul Rabwin *Year 9,* Vince Gilligan; *Producers:* Joseph Patrick Finn *Year 1–5,* David Nutter *Year 2,* Paul Brown *Year 2,* Kim Manners *Year 2–6,* Rob Bowman *Year 2–6,* Paul Rabwin *Year 5–8,* John Shiban *Year 6,* Bernadette Caulfield *Year 6–7,* Daniel Sackheim *Year 7,* David Amann *Year 8,* Harry V. Bring *Year 8–9,* Tony Wharmby *Year 9;* *Co-Producers included:* Paul Barber and Larry Barber *Year 1,* Paul Rabwin *Year 1–4,* Vince Gilligan *Year 4,* Frank Spotnitz *Year 4–5,* Lori Jo Nemhauser *Year 6,* David Amann *Year 7,* Mark R. Schilz, John Shiban, Timothy Silver; *Associate Producers included:* Crawford Hawkins, Suzanne Holmes, Gina Lamar, Lori Jo Nemhauser, Denise Pleune, Suzanne Welke; *Consulting Producers included:* Ken Horton, Glen Morgan, James Wong, Daniel Sackheim; *Writers included:* Howard Gordon, Glen Morgan, Chris Carter, James Wong, Darin Morgan, Vince Gilligan, Frank Spotnitz, David Duchovny, Gillian Anderson; *Directors included:* David Nutter, Daniel Sackheim, Jerrold Freedman, Rob Bowman, Kim Manners, R. W. Goodwin, David Duchovny, Gillian Anderson; *Special Makeup Effect Artists included:* Mark Alfrey, Toby Lindala; *Theme Music:* Mark Snow; *Directors of Photography included:* Bill Roe, John S. Bartley, Jon Joffin, Ron Stannett, Joel Ransom; *Guest Stars included:* Felicity Huffman, Peter Boyle, Darren McGavin, Burt Reynolds, Carrie Snodgress, Steve Railsback, Terry O'Quinn, Giovanni Ribisi, Lucy Liu, Charles Nelson Reilly, Patricia Dahlquist, Edward Asner, Dan Butler, Carrie Hamilton, Denise Crosby, Veronica Cartwright, Lucy Lawless, Cary Elwes, Jill Krop, M. Emmet Walsh, Piper Anderson, Morgan Woodward, John Milford, Jesse Ventura, Michael Berryman, John O'Hurley, Robert Clothier, Luke Wilson, Sheila Moore, Laura Harris, Lily Tomlin, Doc Harris, Donnelly Rhodes, James Sloyan, Henry Beckman, Andrew Robinson, Mimi Rogers, Lance Henriksen, Kim Darby, Patience Cleveland, Perla Walter, Kathy Griffin, Jack Black, Amanda Pays, Justina Vail, Kristen Lehman, Stefan Arngrim, Sebastian Spence, James Remar, Kellie Waymire, Adam Baldwin, William DeVane, Megan Follows, Judson Scott, Doug Hutchison (as Eugene Victor Tooms), Roy Thinnes (as Jeremiah Smith), Peter Donat (as William Mulder), Sheila Larken (as Margaret Scully)

Fox Network/Ten Thirteen Productions in Association with 20th Century–Fox Television; September 1993-2002.; 60 minutes; 202 episodes; DVD status: Complete series

"The truth is out there."— series tagline

"What were we all thinking?" Gareth Wigmore of *TV Zone* magazine asked after *The X-Files* went off. "Looking back, it's hard to think of *The X-Files'* phenomenal success as anything but an example of extraordinary popular delusion and the madness of crowds. Gillian Anderson a sex symbol? David Duchovny a film star? Half cocked, unfulfilling plots and an emphasis of style over substance?"

A surprising evaluation of a show often praised as groundbreaking. The mainstream world also embraced the moody series. *Saturday Night Live* spoofed it and *The Simpsons* did the takeoff *The Springfield Files*, with Duchovny and Anderson providing their voices. Mark Snow's haunting theme music was a hit. There was also merchandise — leather jackets (with "The Truth Is Out There" printed on them), jewelry, comic books, video games and paperbacks.

The X-Files sustained its appeal with carefully written stories and dimensional characters that resonated with audiences. But like a raging fever that had broken, once it peaked, *The X-Files* slipped off into a subdued world of reruns.

When the show debuted in 1993, critics were underwhelmed. "It's not quite sci-fi, not quite fantasy and yet not quite realistic," said Tom Shales of *The Washington Post* as the show struggled on Friday nights. "It ought to be an ex-series before too long." The Fox Network was confident that their other new show, *The Adventures of Brisco County Jr.,* would be the big hit of the 1993–1994 season. *Brisco* bombed.

When producer Joseph Patrick (J.P.) Finn signed up for *The X-Files,* "I asked, 'How many episodes did they order?' and they said 'Well ... 12.' That was June, so I calculated that would take me to Christmas! Little did I know!"

Duchovny and Anderson thought the show would only last a dozen episodes and the show failed to rank in the top 100 shows at the end of its first year. But it had the desired young audience and Fox, itself a struggling network that was seeking edgier material, could see its potential. Viewers appreciated the mix of science, the occult and horror, as well as conspiracy scenarios about how the existence of extraterrestrial life was being covered up by the government. The two humorless agents didn't camp it up, they took the show as seriously as their audience.

Agent Fox Mulder was a psychologist and criminal profiler and came to believe in aliens when he was 12 as he watched his sister levitated into a spacecraft and taken away. Mulder's sidekick Dana Scully was a medical doctor; she was assigned to keep an eye on Mulder, and to discredit his conspiracy research. The X-Files were secret government cases that Mulder was assigned to manage. Scully was a skeptic, trying to offer explanations for all of the flesh-eating insects, mutated killers and man-beasts they encountered that first year. Sometimes her penchant for explanations was redundant and annoying. When toads suddenly rain down on the agents, she's compelled to later interrupt Mulder with a dry, "The National Weather Service says tornadoes probably picked up the toads."

The series' first five years' worth of episodes were filmed in Vancouver, Canada, where the surrounding British Columbia landscape could simulate everything from the farm fields of Iowa to the urban cityscape of Washington, D.C. Canada also provided the misty woodlands that Mulder and Scully often found themselves walking through. The original plan was to film the show in Los Angeles but creator Chris Carter later quipped, "We couldn't find a good forest!" He considered Vancouver "one of the stars of the show" for providing an eerie ambiance.

Carter, former editor of *Surfing* magazine, grew up a fan of such shows as *The Invaders* (1966–68), *Rod Serling's Night Gallery* (1970–1973) and *Kolchak: The Night Stalker* (1974–75). His primary purpose was to make a show that scared people. He also wanted a male-female dynamic, inspired by his favorite show, *The Avengers*: two platonic loners who established a mutual respect and grew to care deeply about each other. Most significantly, the show's "Trust No One" line reflected Carter's distrust of the government. He wanted a paranoid series that underscored that feeling.

Carter pitched *The X-Files* to all of the networks and found no takers. Fox agreed to buy the series and vainly pressured Carter to make it more of a romantic mystery, with its leading characters reminiscent of the couple from the 1980s TV show, *Moonlighting*. Although Kevin Sorbo (*Hercules*) was considered as Mulder, it was David Duchovny, previously a transvestite character in David Lynch's series *Twin Peaks*, who turned out to be perfect as Fox Mulder, handsome yet vulnerable.

Gillian Anderson was a complete unknown. Unable to find feature film work, she was going to return to waitressing full-time. Carter prevailed on a reluctant network to hire her as Scully. Both young leads were soon receiving hundreds of fan letters per week.

"It was like making a feature film every week," notes Finn of that first year's production schedule. "We had T-shirts made up that said, 'Season 1, *The X-Files*— the best 10 years of my life.'"

"Darkness Falls," a year-one segment, had one of the creepiest teasers: Actor Ken Tremblett played a logger eaten alive by insects. "The story was about old growth trees being cut down," says Tremblett. "Glowing bugs come out of the centers of the trees and suck people dry and then leave them hanging in the trees, cocooned. I was a logger running through the forest, trying to escape the bugs and I trip and break my ankle. My buddy comes back to save me and I tell him I can't make it and 'Aghhhh!' I did my own stunts because I really wanted to. I had always wanted to be a stuntman so I was very happy. Even though I had a very small role, they treated me like a star. They treated all of us Canadian actors like true professionals. It was a great experience. And the episode was honored at the Environmental Media Awards."

During filming, Tremblett recalls there was much uncertainty over the series' future. "David Duchovny had no idea where the show was going to go. It ended up becoming one of the biggest TV shows in the world. Their budget was enormous but they also had great writing, great directing and a great crew and actors. It looked so creepy, dark and sinister — just wonderful. It always seemed to be shot in the rain, in the woods and in the dark. Many TV shows tried to hide from the weather, but *The X-Files* embraced it."

The X-Files started out with stand-alone adventures but the writers gradually developed the mythology tales of Mulder's obsessive hunt for his missing sister and his determination to uncover the government's secretive activities regarding aliens. The Cigarette Man became his archetypical nemesis. Progressively, a cast of semi-regular supporting players were added, representing both good and evil as Mulder and Scully explored the underbelly of the paranormal. The series also used the procedural approach, as its two leads went around talking to people of interest (a formula perfected on shows like *Law and Order).*

David Nutter has a reputation as a director who quickly identifies a show's strengths (his work includes *ER,* *The West Wing* and *Smallville).* When he was recruited to direct episode seven of *The X-Files,* "they were having difficulties with their schedule, going over budget, and they were having actor issues with Gillian Anderson," recalls Nutter. "I was given an amazing episode, 'Ice,' that Jim Wong and Glen Morgan had written. It was a great part for Gillian, where she could really stretch her wings and do some wonderful work. I had to do the show in eight days and up to that time, they hadn't done a show in eight days. I was used to shooting six- and seven-day schedules, so I was like, 'Sure, I can do this.'"

"Ice" had the agents investigating the deaths of an Arctic research team and uncovering an organism that intensifies human paranoia and rage. "It was basically a bottle show, with an entire ice station built on stage. I became fast friends with all of the crew. John Bartley, the director of photography, has been a friend for years. 'Ice' was an opportunity to do something different, because up to that point, the show's tone and visual sense was a bit staid. I wanted to shake it up and fortunately, I hit the right notes on the keyboard."

Another highlight for Nutter was "Beyond the Sea" (also written by Morgan and Wong), about a psychic convict named Luther Lee Boggs who helps the agents find a serial killer. Scully believes Luther's claims of talking to the dead when he seemingly communicates with her dead father. "Brad Dourif was probably the greatest actor I've ever worked with," marvels Nutter. "He played a death row inmate who was channeling Scully's thoughts and his performance was tremendous. It was a profound, effective and powerful episode."

As the series continued, Scully lost her trust in the government and realized there were truly strange things out there. (She had to—she would have looked ridiculous if she had continued to deny the existence of every creature they encountered.) The rough-looking Cigarette Man did everything he could to torment the agents during their investigations of UFOs. "Don't threaten me," he growls at Mulder in one show. "I've watched presidents die!" (alluding to his cantankerous dedication to political skullduggery). On another occasion, he remarks, "If people knew what I know, it would all fall apart."

"Here is a man whom everyone thought was evil, except the man himself," says William B. Davis of his scary character. "What would you do if your choice was to save a small corner of the human race or let them all die? How can one not be attracted to a character who seems to have so much power? Yet he was hollow inside. He had made so many compromises, he had to shut down almost all human feeling. Personal peace is an unlikely prospect." In "En Ami," one of Davis' favorite episodes, his character struggled with inner conflicts, revealing him as more than a one-dimensional villain, making him even scarier. Cigarette Man wanted Mulder silenced before he could uncover a web of government conspiracies but soon the agent was too high-profile to kill. His death could expose Cigarette Man's plans, so he tried to bribe Mulder over to his side, without luck.

Walter Skinner (Mitch Pileggi) was Mulder and Scully's boss, a man of integrity who was caught between loyalty to the duo and pressure from higher-ups.

For Mulder, deception was everywhere. To his horror, he couldn't even trust his parents. He learned his father had arranged to have Mulder's sister, Samantha, abducted by aliens. Other recurring characters included three nerdy conspiracy buffs called the Lone Gunmen, who exposed skullduggery through their newspaper. They believed rogue branches of the CIA had given refuge to extraterrestrials and provided Mulder with computer information and leads.

The agents endured their share of nightmares—Mulder's father was murdered, Scully battled cancer and had flashbacks of being artificially impregnated in a mysterious lab. A short-lived ally of Mulder's was Deep Throat, who insisted that space aliens had been amongst us for decades. When he's killed, his last gasp is, appropriately, "Trust no one!" This complicated tapestry drew either admiration from die-hard fans or headaches for viewers scrambling to keep a scorecard of every character's travails. Added to this were a lot of characters stepping out from the shadows: "The Well-Manicured Man," "Mr. X," "The Red-Haired Man," "Shadow Man," "Young Cigarette Smoking Man," "Toothpick Man," and "The Bounty Hunter." *TV Guide* reflected, "We could handle the truth, even if we didn't always understand it."

Anderson was stoic as Scully but she admitted the scripts genuinely frightened her and she never read them at night. Lee Bacchus of *The Vancouver Province* noted, "It's been a long time, since the days of *The Invaders* and *The Night Stalker,* that we've had a good TV series that really frightened us." And *TV Guide* claimed, "It's the most unsettling television series since *The Twilight Zone.*"

"I'm not interested in blood, guts and or gratuitous gunfire," Carter told the media. He felt the series capitalized on viewers' insecurity about progress. "We are living in a world where technological and medical advancements are making quantum leaps," he told *The Vancouver Sun* in 1996. "We don't quite know how to fathom these things and it gives us a feeling that we may not be in control."

A poll taken during the series revealed half of the American population believed that ETs had visited Earth. Many also believed that government conspiracies played a role in JFK's assassination and that a 1947 UFO crash at Roswell was covered up.

Dean Haglund, who played Lone Gunman Langly, recalls the first time in his life that he encountered *real,* sheer terror. "I was quite young and there was a TV commercial in Winnipeg for a clothing store," he recalls. "The commercial consisted of a series of shots of headless mannequins in a store window, floating in a black background with the cheesy '70s star-like sparkles. They played a Carpenters song over top of that and there was no voiceover, just these headless figures floating around as Karen Carpenter sang something likewise as creepy. These commercials played late at night, and they would send chills down my spine and made me pull a blanket over my head!"

Where did Langly's famous look, of long blonde hair and dark-rimmed glasses, come from? "The blond hair was mine," he says. "I've worn it that long since the fifth grade. I cut it only once, in 1986, for a play. The glasses were an afterthought from the props guy. He came up with a bag of glasses and said, 'Wear one of these.' If you look at the first few seasons you will notice that Langly wears different glasses each time because I kept throwing the glasses back in the bag and no one could remember what pair I had been wearing."

The three Lone Gunmen later had their own comedic-spy spin-off series (13 episodes in 2001). Haglund describes the three geeks as "computer hackers living outside the norm to fight the system. They were obsessed with social justice and wanted to find truth to bring down the structure that kept individuals from fulfilling their own destiny." The trio used their talents to hack into government computers.

Haglund found that audiences abroad particularly related to the show's paranoid philosophy. "Going overseas, my sense is that *The X-Files* expressed what foreign viewers were thinking, which is they didn't trust the American government either. For those who thought differently from the mainstream, this show made them realize they weren't alone in their thinking."

Other shows soon popped up, exuding a similar tone and style to *The X-Files—Dark Skies, Psi-Factor: Chronicles of the Paranormal, Strange World* and another Chris Carter creation, *Millennium.* But *The X-Files* had a unique flavor and became a monster hit. "*The X-Files* deserves its instant-legend status as a creepy and brainy plunge into ever-deepening mystery," raved *USA Today.* Novelists such as William Gibson and Stephen King wrote scripts for the series, and singer Cher admitted she was a huge fan. Duchovny's wife, actress Tea Leoni, appeared in the offbeat Duchovny-scripted episode "Hollywood AD," where a producer makes a movie based on the two agents' lives.

But the dangers were still out there — voodoo magic, living dolls, witches, invisible animals, a killer dog, werewolves, living shadows, and murderers who could squeeze through objects or astral-project through space. The show's flexibility also allowed mystery episodes such as "Sleepless," where the deaths of soldiers are linked to sleep-deprivation tests conducted during the Vietnam War.

"Clyde Bruckman's Final Repose" was another highlight. Darin Morgan's script dealt with a middle-aged psychic (Peter Boyle) who can predict death. "It was voted by *TV Guide* as one of the top 10 greatest TV episodes ever," says David Nutter, who directed this third-year episode after a hiatus from the series. "I had just finished reading all these terrible feature film scripts and when Chris Carter asked me to read the 'Clyde Bruckman' script, it was the best script I had ever read. It was so touching and funny. We fought to get Peter Boyle on the show. This was Peter's first foray into episodic television and he thought it would be a quick five-day thing. He wasn't expecting to be in Vancouver so long. He lived in New York, didn't know much about *The X-Files* and didn't want to be here."

Boyle made his displeasure known when he said to *TV Guide*, "I'm in Vancouver, it's a cold August day and I'm not smiling!" Boyle and Nutter got their signals crossed when the actor accidentally stepped into a scene earlier than Nutter wanted. "He was a little gruff with me after that, like, 'Don't mess this up again!'" says Nutter. "I suggested we meet on Sunday to talk about the next week's scenes. When I met him, he said, 'I didn't know I'd have to be here so long. My wife didn't want me to leave New York,' and he resented having to be here. I explained what a great script this was, and declared to him that he would win an Emmy for this role. And he did, which was wonderful. And the next week of filming was great, we had a lot of fun."

There were also several comedic episodes, including "The Post-Modern Prometheus," which received an Emmy nomination for best writing. The black-and-white segment featured a creature which mates with women in a small town whose citizens are Jerry Springer fans (Springer makes a cameo). Another bizarre fantasy was "How the Ghosts Stole Christmas," with Ed Asner and Lily Tomlin as two poltergeists who try to make the agents turn against each other in a haunted house. In "Drive," a takeoff of the film *Speed*, Mulder must drive a car at a fast rate to prevent his passenger's head from exploding from sinister low-frequency waves.

The show also had fun with casting. Jodie Foster was the voice of "Betty" in "Never Again," while David Duchovny's father appeared as an airline passenger, sitting behind Scully, in the first episode. Chris Carter made a cameo as an FBI agent in "Anasazi" while *Jeopardy!* game show host Alex Trebek appeared in "Jose Chung's from Outer Space." Duchovny's brother Daniel appeared in "The Unnatural" and Anderson's younger sister Zoe showed up as a young Scully in "A Christmas Carol."

While the FBI had been initially wary about the series, when Carter, Duchovny and Anderson visited the FBI offices, they were greeted warmly by agents.

Producer JP Finn had the greatest respect for Duchovny and Anderson. "David and Gillian were very young, excited, and inexperienced actors when they started but very hard-working. Because of the show's nature, one week they could be quite comedic, and the next week very dra-

matic, so they grew immensely as actors. I'd be dishonest if I didn't say they changed from being happy-go-lucky to taking their roles more seriously. That was a function of their trying to maintain the quality of the show and their acting."

"It was wonderful working with Gillian Anderson," says Nutter. "In particular, the 'Beyond the Sea' episode was really her show, with Scully's father dying. It was letting Gillian fly as an actress. I wanted to create an atmosphere where she knew she was being supported and she saw me as someone who wanted to help her do her best work. She hit it out of the park in that episode and from that day forward, we had a wonderful working relationship. She felt she could trust me, which is the most important role a director can take for an actor. She was such a talented actress and 'Ice' and 'Beyond the Sea' are the two episodes that gave her a foundation for her character. They also formed a basis for making Gillian Anderson one of the top actresses in television." Nutter also praises Duchovny. "He knew what I was doing from the first episode and he appreciated that. We became fast friends. I think he's going to have a real resurgence in the next few years because he's a fine, fine actor."

Director Jerrold Freedman adds, "Gillian is the hardest worker I've ever directed. She was new to the business then, and took nothing for granted. David was more laid-back, but very insightful about his character. He's very bright, with a great, dry sense of humor. Neither pulled rank, which was very refreshing."

"There were a lot of laughs on the set," says Haglund. "David and Gillian were especially funny. In fact, when David made some appearances on *The Garry Shandling Show* on HBO, that's closer to the way I knew him than his *X-Files* character."

The show was moved to Sunday nights from Fridays for its fourth year (Carter joked that it was being "abducted" to Sundays and expressed concern over its future). Continuing to prosper, it won a Peabody Award in 1996.

Despite *X-Files'* web of conspiratorial mysteries, William B. Davis says he *doesn't* really believe in ETs or government conspiracies. Indeed, in reality, civilized governments may be too well cocooned in labyrinth bureaucracy to sustain this kind of decades-old skullduggery. As for alien visitation, that evidence has lately been relegated to crop circles. It was here that the series received its most stinging criticism. During the show's heyday, psychologist Barry Beyerstein of Simon

Fraser University in Canada was quoted as saying, "It feeds a trend toward conspiratorial thinking and belief in magic. If that thinking really takes hold, it diverts people from the kind of tough analysis and hard work that we really need to tackle some of the problems facing us today." Today, Dr. Beyerstein says, "My worry wasn't so much that the show promoted belief in 'woo-hoo' stuff but that due to a phenomenon psychologists call 'source amnesia' we often remember things but forget how and when we learned them. As a result, rather disreputable sources can sometimes implant beliefs that are later given more credibility than they deserve. Fiction can be remembered as alleged fact."

Douglas Todd of *The Vancouver Sun* was troubled that the series "could be replacing flawed faiths with both bad science and bad religion."

Some *X-Files* writers didn't enjoy their stay with the show. "I didn't have fun working on the series," says Billy Brown, who (along with writing partner Dan Angel) provided the story for one episode, "All Souls." "There was an inner circle of writer-producers on *The X-Files*. Everyone else was treated rudely. They had our draft for months before they got around to giving us notes. They finally did give notes, on the last day before the Christmas holiday, expecting us to do the work then. We sent them a polite fax, saying we hoped they enjoyed their holiday with their families as we planned to do ourselves, and that we would address their notes after the New Year. They fired us, then ruined the episode with a rewrite, and then, for the first time in the history of the show, as punishment, I presume, they sent in the draft to the WGA, crediting us only with the story. We arbitrated and the WGA, unfairly I thought, ruled in their favor. That ruling has cost me thousands of dollars in residuals. I thought our draft was far more intriguing than what ended up being produced."

"All Souls" was about girls apparently killed by forces of Satanic evil. When Scully's daughter Emily is endangered, Mulder suspects a priest is the culprit. Frank Spotnitz and John Shiban are credited with the teleplay. "What was good about the episode came from our draft, mainly the four-faced, half human-half angel," says Brown. "But our [original] story had nothing to do with Satan. It was about an angel who defied God by impregnating a few human females, and God had sent an avenging angel to hunt down and destroy the offspring, who were abominations." As for Chris Carter, Brown notes, "He was a decent fellow, but

he was hidden from view by gatekeepers, all protective of their special status and fearful that someone might supplant them."

The show's popularity inspired an *X-Files* movie in 1998. Directed by series veteran Rob Bowman, its storyline sprang from one of the TV episodes, and had Mulder and Scully on the trail of an extraterrestrial virus, while coping with acts of domestic terrorism and conspiratorial strangers. Co-starring Martin Landau and Terry O'Quinn, the film had a disappointing domestic take of $85 million but attained a healthy worldwide gross of over $183 million. It was one of the few times in history that a feature film was made based on a current TV show (*Batman*, *McHale's Navy* and *The Munsters* also went the big-screen route in the 1960s).

In its sixth year (1998–99), *The X-Files* made a controversial and permanent move from rainy Vancouver to Los Angeles, prompted by Duchovny, who wanted to spend more time with Tea Leoni, his L.A.-based wife. "When they moved to L.A., the opening shot that year was of the sun as they panned down to Mulder," says guest actor Ken Tremblett. "It was like a slap in the face. Maybe it was an in-joke, but it indicated somebody really wanted to get out of Vancouver. It changed the feel of the show completely. It wasn't that dark, sinister, scary show any more. They did get back into it a *little* more, once they embraced their new home." The sunshine didn't hurt that sixth year; it finished in 12th place out of 150 shows in the ratings.

But the show had now peaked. The following year, *The X-Files* fell to 31st place, a descent that would continue. Duchovny, who had now settled a long-standing lawsuit against Fox, was interested in pursuing a film career, and cut back on his appearances during the eighth year. Scully and her new partner, agent John Doggett (Robert Patrick), searched for the missing Mulder as well as tackled new cases of the paranormal.

Patrick (best known as the liquid-metal killer robot from *Terminator 2*) played Doggett as a no-nonsense man who is skeptical of paranormal activity. The agent had his own personal quest, to find his missing son. Patrick, an excellent actor, respected the series and was hoping for a long run. He faced hostile Internet chat over *anyone* taking Mulder's place but his intense performance won fans over. Other actors considered for the Doggett role included Hart Bochner, Lou Diamond Phillips, Bruce Campbell and Chris Noth.

Ken Tucker of *Entertainment Weekly* noted

around this time, "Duchovny's and Anderson's boredom had been showing ... but there's no dust on *The X-Files* as it begins its eighth year. Robert Patrick is as hard-boiled and as effective as ever."

Annabeth Gish was also brought in during the eighth year as Special Agent Monica Reyes, a backup for the wearying Gillian Anderson, who wanted to leave the series.

Doggett and Reyes carried on for the ninth season, sometimes joined by Scully, who now had a baby with strange abilities. She strived to protect the child from sinister men. The agents also encountered a killer with X-ray vision and an adversary who could enter people's dreams.

Their most bizarre case was "Sunshine Days," where a crazed *Brady Bunch* fan sets up a deadly house based on the 1969–1974 TV sitcom. The production team recreated as closely as possible the Brady house interior, with actors cast to resemble the Brady clan.

But the magic and excitement of the show was gone. Duchovny said it best: "We have the kind of show that reaches further, in terms of story and execution, than any other show on television but we're going to get old, and the fans are going to be hip to our tricks."

So were critics. "Without Mulder and Scully, *The X-Files* is just another middling sci-fi anthology," said *New York Times* writer Joyce Millman. "The burnout has been painful to watch." In the tragic wake of 9/11's horrors, alien conspiracies now seemed archaic when real danger could strike any time from within America. Chris Carter decided to pull the plug at the end of year nine in 2002, while the stories were still good.

The two-hour finale, "The Truth," brought back a raving Mulder, who is under military arrest for murder. His resulting trial reveals that government men have corrupted alien biology and created a race of supermen to stave off a pending alien invasion. Sentenced to die, Mulder is sprung from military incarceration by his friends. He and Scully take off to the Indian Dunes where, to their surprise, they find a white-haired Cigarette Man in a cave. (Just episodes earlier, viewers had seen him fall down a stairway to his apparent death.) Smug as ever, he forecasts an alien invasion in 2012 and says the military wants him dead.

The convoluted plot has the Indian Dunes and Cigarette Man being destroyed by rogue helicopters. In the final scene of the final episode, Scully and Mulder lie together on a bed in the darkness of a dingy motel room in Roswell, looking back on the incredible events they've witnessed and the toll taken on their personal lives (at one point, Scully had lamented about giving up her super-baby, fueled by alien biology, which evil men wanted to corrupt). "We've sacrificed so much to uncover the truth," deadpans Mulder. And after nine long and eventful years, Scully and Mulder then clasp each other as the overhead camera slowly pulls back in a fade to black.

Don Kaplan of *The New York Post* noted, "Millions of fans said goodbye to the show last Sunday night but they still can't figure out whether they liked the ending." Nevertheless, those involved hold *The X-Files* in high regard.

"The show played on many different levels, appealing to paranoid fears, questions of the paranormal, suspense, mystery, and ultimately, our guy against the bad guys," says William B. Davis. "It came along at a time of deepening insecurity about the nature of the world. The world was feeling less tangible. A good place for weird things to happen."

J.P. Finn points to the show's perfect timing. "The Internet was becoming a social fabric of society and *The X-Files* embraced that. We were one of the earliest shows to do interviews on the Net and have a website. That's integral to the success of every episodic TV show today."

"It tapped into the cultural mistrust of the government," says Billy Brown. "It also had an intriguing and clear conflict between Mulder and Scully. It was fortunate to be a good show on an emerging network that didn't have enough product. Consequently, the show was allowed to stay on and find its audience. It dared to have a dark visual palette. The network let the creators do what they wanted. There was some fine writing, much of it attributable to Glen Morgan, James Wong and Howard Gordon."

"Chris Carter was adamant about putting quality first, which meant you shot the best show you could, often regardless of the budget or scheduling restraints," says director Jerrold Freedman. "He was far-sighted that way, proven by the incredible run of the series. The writing was excellent and the concept was unique and cool. It was a good combination of old-fashioned paranoia and new-age thinking. "

Dean Haglund cites examples of how the series impacted the real world. "I met many couples who had met through *X-Files* chat rooms and news groups. I also met many people who had gone through lengthy illnesses, using *The X-Files* as their only recuperation. The coolest thing was when I met a guy from NASA who was working on robotic satellites that circled the International Space Station to check for damage and air leaks. He said they renamed the unit Project X-Files and each one of the robots was named after a character in our show. So there is a space robot called Langly flying over our heads right now as you read this!"

TV Guide looked back in 2002 and said, "The murky depths of *The X-Files* were filled with a nightmarish brew of paranoia, suspense, off-kilter humor, mysticism, faith and aliens given to grisly mischief.... [I]t made us jump but it also made us think about the wonders of a very mysterious universe." They called it one of the greatest cult TV shows of all time, second only to *Star Trek*. The series had won a total of 16 Emmy Awards during its run, as well as a prestigious Peabody Award.

David Nutter recalls, "After I did *The X-Files*, I did a couple of SF things and people would say to me, 'Let's make it stranger and more weird and more crazy than *The X-Files*.' I would say, 'The secret to *The X-Files* was that it was a drama. It was based on real life, real people and real situations.' It was about making the world and characters as relatable as possible. That's what made it emotionally satisfying and successful. Don't just tweak the interest in their heads, get into their hearts too. As Jim Cameron once told me, 'It's not science fiction but science faction.' It was a real smart move on Chris Carter's part to have Mulder search for his missing sister. Audiences could relate to that family relationship and once you get them emotionally involved, they become vested in the paranormal stories and relate to the characters. You may not have always understood what Mulder and Scully were talking about, but you understood their passions and had compassion for what they were doing. *The X-Files* was also an intelligent science fiction show. SF audiences are the smartest audiences ever and *The X-Files* wrote up to the intelligence of that audience."

Six years after the series' cancellation in 2002, 20th Century–Fox gave Chris Carter an opportunity to catch up with the lives of Scully and Mulder in a second feature film titled *The X-Files: I Want to Believe* which was unveiled on July 24, 2008. A $35 million budgeted film, Carter directed and co-wrote it with Frank Spotnitz. Talking to the Canadian Press, Carter says, "We came here to do a TV pilot and we ended up staying five years," he said. "We stayed five years longer than we ever imagined staying, so it was time to go home. And now we're back and that's the lesson here. You can come home again."

Carter's goal was to create a "stand-alone X-File" that did not require prior knowledge of plots created during the TV series.

The film's story concerned the disappearance of a group of women in the winter plains of Virginia. A disgraced priest's psychic visions leads the FBI to the bodies' remains which indicated medical experiments. The dormant X-Files becomes reactivated, and Scully and Mulder are pulled in to help with the investigation. The featured guest stars were Billy Connolly as the disgraced Catholic priest and Amanda Peet as an FBI agent who recalls Mulder back into the FBI with Scully's help.

Filmed in British Columbia, *The X-Files 2* was not successful at the box office. The fans did not respond with the enthusiasm that was expected from their fierce loyalty. The take at the domestic opening weekend was just $10 million U.S. Barely a month later, it also reached just $51 million worldwide.

CAST NOTES

David Duchovny (Mulder): The New York–born actor decided to leave his doctoral studies at Yale and go into acting in 1987. His film debut was as a party guest in the movie *Working Girl* (1988). He gained attention playing a transvestite in three episodes of *Twin Peaks* (1991). He lived in Kitsilano (a suburb of Vancouver) during the making of *The X-Files*. In 1997, just before the series moved to Los Angeles, Duchovny made a ill-advised joke on Conan O'Brien's show: "It rains in Vancouver all the time," he told Conan. "It's a nice place to live if you like 400 inches of rainfall a day." The Vancouver media went crazy over Duchovny's apparent dislike for Vancouver and the bewildered actor was engulfed in a tidal wave of hostility from many locals, including radio DJs. "Ship his ass out of here!" an angry Langley resident snapped about Duchovny. "He's not that good of an actor anyway." One downtown night club put up a sign on its marquee, "David Duchovny is barred — go home." Duchovny was hurt when he drove past that sign, and spoke of angry strangers approaching him over his rainy Vancouver remark. But there were some supporters. "Duchovny has said he thinks Vancouver is a lovely city. Give him a break," said one. Another woman quipped, "I say he should stay and rust with the rest of us." Duchovny told *The Vancouver Province* in 2005 that his original comments on

Conan were in jest and taken out of context. "I had always been welcome [in Vancouver] and all of a sudden I was persona non grata. It was harmful. It's very ironic, because I actually enjoy that type of weather more than I like the sunny weather of L.A." His other films include *Kalifornia* (1993), *Evolution* (2001) and *The Secret* (2007).

Gillian Anderson (Scully): Born in Chicago, she lived in Puerto Rico and London as a child before her family settled in Michigan. She had wanted to be a marine biologist but acting in a theater play as a teenager convinced her to become an actress. Although she was not a science fiction fan, one of her favorite TV shows growing up was *The New Avengers* (1976–77). In high school, Anderson was voted "Most Bizarre Girl." Her major movie before *The X-Files* was *The Turning* (1992). She was a frequent late-night guest on Jay Leno and David Letterman during *The X-Files*' heyday and she won an Emmy Award in 1997 as Outstanding Lead Actress. She admitted that there were few parallels between her and her TV character. "Scully is not very spontaneous, I am," she told *Rolling Stone* in 1997. "She can live without personal relationships, I cannot. She's obscenely intelligent and I am not. She is at least five foot six and I am not." Her film credits include *The Last King of Scotland* (2006) and *Straightheads* (2007). Of *The X-Files*, she says today, "It gave me a tremendous opportunity to learn as an actress."

Mitch Pileggi (Skinner): He once worked in Iraq on defense contracts for the U.S. On a friend's recommendation, he did some acting in a movie about a killer dog called *Mongrel* (1982). His early TV credits include *Dallas*, *The A-Team* and *Alien Nation*. He also appeared in the film *Man in the Chair* (2006) and had a recurring role in *Stargate Atlantis* (as Col. Caldwell) beginning in 2005.

Robert Patrick (Doggett): In addition to playing the indestructible metal cop in *Terminator 2* (1991), this Georgia native also won acclaim as the space-age POW in the new *Outer Limits*' "A Quality of Mercy" (with Nicole deBoer). Patrick had read for Carter's *Harsh Realm* series (1999) but the role went to D.B. Sweeney. But Carter liked Patrick and remembered him for *The X-Files*. His other features films include *Die Hard 2* (1990), *Wayne's World* (1992), *Spy Kids* (2001), *Walk the Line* (2005) and *Lonely Street* (2006). He signed up as a regular on TV's *The Unit* in 2005.

Annabeth Gish (Monica Reyes): One of her earliest films was *Mystic Pizza* (1988). On *The X-Files*, she appeared in four episodes of season eight and was signed on as a regular for the final ninth season. The Albuquerque-born actress was disappointed that the series didn't carry on for a tenth season. She always felt her character of Monica Reyes was harboring a secret love for FBI man John Doggett. Gish admitted she had never seen a UFO but she did believe in ghosts. Her other TV work includes *West Wing*, *CSI Miami* and *Chicago Hope*.

William B. Davis (Cigarette Man): Although he was only a semi-regular on *The X-Files*, this Toronto-born actor made a permanent mark as the mysterious, sinister man with a dark past. For his role he had to constantly puff on a cigarette but since the actor had given up smoking in the 1970s (and was a spokesman for the Canadian Cancer Society) he smoked herbal, nicotine-free cigarettes. Before being cast in this role, he had read for the recurring part on *X-Files* of FBI agent Blevins. Davis was introduced to acting early, since his cousins ran a summer stock theater in Ontario. He also trained in England (working with people such as Laurence Olivier) and he opened the National Theater School in Vancouver. One of his earliest movie credits was Stephen King's *The Dead Zone* (1983). His other credits include *Stargate SG-1*, *Smallville*, *Andromeda*, and Stephen King's mini-series *Kingdom Hospital* (2004).

Sources

Clute, John. *Science Fiction: The Illustrated Encyclopedia*. New York: Dorling Kindersley, 1995.
Phillips, Mark. "100 Years of Classic TV and Films." *Starlog* Group, 1999.
Shales, Tom. *The X-Files* Review. "For the Circular 'Files.'" *Washington Post*, September 10, 1993.
Spaner, David. "Duchovny Excited to Return Here." *Vancouver Province*, May 2, 2005.
Strachan, Alex. "Secret of X-Files' Success is its Secrets." *Vancouver Sun*, July 25, 1996.
Todd, Douglas. "The X-Files: The Truth Isn't in There—The Trouble with The X-Files is it Could be Replacing Flawed Faiths with Both Bad Science and Bad Religion." *Vancouver Sun*, June 14, 1997.
Tucker, Ken. *Entertainment Weekly*, 2000.
TV Guide, 2002.
USA Today, 1996.
Warlick, Debra. "X-Files: Entering a 7th Season: Series Creator Chris Carter on Tying up the Loose Ends for the Show's Final Season." *Cinefantastique* 31:8, October 1999.
Wigmore, Gareth. "The Golden Age." *TV Zone* no. 193, 2005.

APPENDIX A:
WHO GOES THERE?

Additional memories from our interviewees.

Babylon 5

Guest star **Julie Caitlin Brown** (Na'Toth): "[Series creator-writer] Joe Straczynski was an extraordinary talent to have created such a detailed universe. He knows where the story is going. It's not, 'Oh, we've got 13 episodes, we'll figure out where to go from there...' He had to make adjustments because he ran into trouble after four seasons, not knowing if he was going to finish it. It was really a saga. A lot of episodic television meanders. They pull their storylines from the headlines, whereas Joe says, 'No, I have a story to tell and I believe you will enjoy it.'"

Battlestar Galactica

Actor **Aaron Douglas** (Chief Tyrol): "Chelan is one of our stand-ins and she's a beautiful, sweet, very shy girl. There's a scene where the president announces they've found the person responsible for leaving a hatch open, it's specialist Socinus. The A.D. was busy, so we asked Chelan to read the president's dialogue. Chelan had never seen Alonso's character's name, Socinus, written down before and she was very nervous. The hangar deck was filled with over 70 extras and so she reads out loud: 'Uh, the person responsible for leaving the hatch open has been found. He, um, has been taken into custody. Specialist Saucynuts.' The director yells cut, the whole place falls down in hysterics, and Chelan goes red like a tomato and runs off the set, realizing what she had done. She was mortified. She's fine now — after a year of therapy!"

Dark Angel

Executive producer **James Cameron**: "The minute I saw the first promo for the original *Star Trek*, of the spaceship flying past the camera, they had me. I waited with bated breath for the first episode to air in 1966. I was a very enthusiastic fan for the first year, then I lost interest. Maybe I got too hip for it, who knows? I didn't appreciate the series until years later, when I saw it in syndication. I realized just how good it really was."

Earth: Final Conflict

Producer-Production Designer **Stephen Roloff**: One of the key futuristic gadgets conjured up was the hand-held Global communicator. It was a device that could be held in one hand, and with a pull-out motion, a flat screen appeared with display graphics and a live image link of the person calling. A camera device on the Global simultaneously sent a live link of the user at the same time, making possible a lightweight, portable two-way videophone experience. (Thanks to MCI, as seen on the graphics.)

This technology suggested a flat, "rollable" screen that was opened and closed from a smaller receptacle. The use of the Global communicator allowed for the characters to exchange information (valuable plot and dialogue exposition!) anywhere and at any time. Operations were handled by the user's touching the flat-screen controls.

This communicator concept, created in 1997, predates emerging real-world technology, as Roloff explains: "I was contacted by a hi-tech research facility in the Netherlands. Someone had sent them a copy of the series and they came across the design of the Global which was exactly what they were building, they had a working prototype. It was a design that was vaguely clamshell-shaped. It opened the same way. It was all prefaced on the idea of having a flexible, flat rolling screen. The technology is breaking right now. The idea of having electronic paper has intrigued people for a long time. Many hi-tech corporations are working on it.

"It's a futuristic projection of today's world. Back then [at the time of filming] people were already walking around with cell phones. Not so much with PDAs, and personal communicators, but we thought, 'We'd better do our version of that.' Something that has an image screen on it. It has two different modes. A vertically oriented screen for communication and then it would fold out further, into a horizontal mode and 16 × 9 ratio for viewing media. That's exactly what they later came out with. I wish I had patented the design!"

First Wave

Holly Dale, an award-winning Canadian director of documentaries, on her desire to direct science fiction TV shows, including *Stargate: Atlantis* and *Tracker*: "I loved doing documentaries. I learned about directing and filming real people in real situations. But as a woman, I found it was hard to break into directing drama. I started doing feature films and movies of the week and then moved into episodic TV, which is all about coming in on time, on budget and making good shows. I had an agent who was the neighbor of a producer who was doing SF and he saw my work and that led to *First Wave*. In this business, if you do well in one genre, you get typecast in that genre. For example, in Toronto, I'm primarily known for doing dramatic series, and in Vancouver, I'm known as a science fiction director. The reason I'm one of the few women directing SF it is that guy producers and executives think of it as a man's genre. I've shown that it doesn't matter what sex you are. I have as much muscle in directing segments as any guy. SF is one of my favorite genres to work in, it's telling stories by pictures. It's wonderful how these SF shows have such longevity. Much of television is disposable but shows like *First Wave* and *Stargate* are probably going to run for years in reruns."

Guest star **Ken Tremblett** on his episode "The Apostles": "These guys were supposed to be a big, tough motorcycle gang but it was a real challenge for the stuntmen who had to ride them because the motorcycles kept breaking down. They would do their lines and then try to start the motorcycles and drive away but nothing would happen. 'Cut!' That challenged the director's patience!"

Jeremiah

Guest star **Alex Zahara** (Ezekiel) recalls auditioning for director Russell Mulcahy: "I'm supposed to have a really big knife and I'm sharpening a pencil. I was wearing a black hoodie, and you couldn't see my eyes. I did the audition. We stopped and Russell said, 'That's fucking perfect!' But then he said, 'Wait, wait! Hold on! Conference!' And they huddled together. He came back and said, 'Do it again but do it less crazy this time, just for the boys down south [the Los Angeles producers], to give them an option.' So I did. But that reaction from Russell, a director I respect the most, when he said, 'That was fucking perfect!' was it for me. I could have gone home and not gotten the job and been happy as hell...."

"I had Luke Perry down on the ground. He had smacked his head with a log and I'm checking him out. It was really snowing when we were shooting. I turned to run and I slipped, and I hit Luke in the head with my big army boots, *crack*, right in the noggin' and I ran off. Luke got up and said, 'Oowwww!' That was pretty funny....

"A stuntman almost lost an eye. We were racing out of an area as we were being shot at. [Actress] Kandyse McClure was in the back of the truck with co-star Malcolm [Jamal Warner], and Luke and there's a big firefight. My stunt double, Doug Chapman, drove the truck and one of the exploding pellets that simulates bullets, went through an open window, totally as an anomaly, and hit him right on the ridge of his nose and exploded. If it had hit in one of his eyes, he would have lost an eye. And this was just a rehearsal. I have a picture hanging on my refrigerator, of me going, 'Oh no!' and pointing at Doug's nose, and he's making a puffy face. That's why you've got stuntmen!"

Lexx

Star **Brian Downey** on being recognized as Stanley Tweedle: "I was in an airport and this guy standing in line said to me, 'Hey, there's this show I watch called *Lexx* and there's this really ugly, ugly guy named Tweedle. Man, I gotta say, you look just like him. You should watch it.' I said, 'Geez, I should. I'll have to look out for that show!'"

Guest star **Ellen Dubin**: "I'm so grateful to *Lexx* because I got to travel the world — Halifax, Berlin and Thailand. We also shot scenes in Studio Babelsberg, one of the oldest, most famous studios in the world, just outside of Berlin. It was where they filmed the movie *The Cabinet of Dr. Caligari* [1919]. *Lexx* also gave me the opportunity to play four different characters, so I was allowed to act crazy!"

Odyssey 5

Writer **Tracy Torme** about his inspiration for writing "Time Out of Mind": "One of my favorite *Twilight Zones* was 'And When the Sky Was Opened,' with Jim Hutton and Rod Taylor where, one by one, the astronauts are disappearing. It was three astronauts returning from a mission and suddenly there's only two. And then only one and only he remembers the other two. That was my motivation of this episode. It was my attempt to put some humor into the show....

"We originally wanted Harlan Ellison to fly up to Toronto and [play the part of an SF writer] for us. He's an old friend of mine. Showtime had a problem with him because of some fight they had previously and basically banned him from the show. He was going to do a reasonably sized part, which would have been a lot of fun, his playing a pompous, arrogant SF writer."

The Outer Limits

Writer **Alan Brennert** on the episode titled "Heart's Desire," shot on a Western town set previously used for the television series *Bordertown*: "The week we needed the *Bordertown* set, it was being used by Showtime for a movie called *Dead Man's Gun*. Trilogy and *Outer Limits* production managed to pull a few strings at Showtime and got them to shoot elsewhere for the time we needed the set. Ironically, Showtime aired *Dead Man's Gun* two nights after 'Heart's Desire'! So anyone watching Showtime would have seen this set on *Dead Man's Gun*, and they would have gone, 'Gee, this looks a little familiar...!' It defeated the purpose of having this great, unique location to give the episode an entirely different feel. Now it just looked like Showtime was being incredibly cheap! Apparently no one at the network even noticed. I mean, c'mon, when you have two films that were shot on the same location, you don't put them on, one after the other, for Pete's sake!"

Guest star **Garry Chalk** (Detective Barnett) on "Caught in the Act," in which he played a detective investigating strange murders: "It was a great concept of this alien creature that lands on the planet and infects women. If you were in *lust*, you got absorbed. If you were in *love*, you elevated the creature and sent him on his way. Everybody thought this was an AIDS/werewolf thing but it wasn't! It was an interesting message that love conquers everything."

Director **Mark Sobel** on working with Thora Birch, who played Aggie in "The Choice": "Thora Birch was such a delight, really bright and very talented. Her character, Aggie, was a little girl who's different. As a result, there are people who are afraid of her and want to kill her. The show is about intolerance and fear of people we don't fully understand. On a deeper level, 'The Choice' involves man's choosing whether to survive or not. Mankind was dying off, and Aggie's chromosome represented the next stage of man's evolutionary development. Man is so frightened by that, they're trying to kill off all these people. Ironically, what they're doing is killing off the future of mankind. So, we have a choice: be tolerant and not be afraid of what's inevitable, or we can kill ourselves. By killing off people like Aggie, effectively these groups were killing off man's next evolutionary step. It wasn't a script about technical stuff, it was a script about people. That's what made it unique. A lot of people have told me that it was one of their favorites. There was something very human about it."

Writer **Alan Brennert** on "The Refuge": "I set out to write a story that evoked some of the *Outer Limits* episodes that I grew up with — specifically, 'The Guests' and 'Don't Open Till Doomsday.' Both of those were set in gothic, musty old mansions, wherein various eccentric characters are trapped.

That's what I was going after, though with a modern twist: Instead of a mass of alien goo in the attic, it turns out the characters are all dreaming — a shared dream — in cryonic suspension. Sad to say, I didn't care much for how this episode turned out or for the direction, which was flat. I didn't care for some of the acting, which ranged from acceptable to painfully on the nose, particularly the characters of Justine and Angelique. Alas, several characters veered into caricature. The other thing I didn't really care for was a production decision. My original conception was this rambling old gothic mansion. The production team decided to change that to something that looked more like a hunting lodge. The set just looked kind of small and claustrophobic to me. And part of this is really my own damn fault. In the script I used the term 'gothic' to describe the staircase and mansion, but I should have come right out and said, 'I really would love for this to have a gothic feel to it.' But several people whose opinions I respect said they enjoyed the episode. Harlan Ellison called me the day after it was on and said, 'Hey, that was a good show!' So what do I know?"

Co-executive producer **Jonathan Glassner** on "Vanishing Act": 'This one had a very weird genesis. [Writer] Chris Dickie came to us and said, 'I have this cool idea.' It was about a guy who goes to work in the morning, has an automobile accident, wakes up and it's ten years later. He hasn't aged and he doesn't know why. That's all Chris had. We all thought, 'Cool! We haven't seen that before. Now what?' So we brought Chris and all the staff writers in and bounced every idea under the sun for a way to make that make sense. We went through every time machine thing you could imagine. Then, we looked at the only other way to lose time or gain time and that would be wormholes. So why would he go through wormholes? He's not an astronaut or anything. So we just kept bouncing until we came up with the idea that aliens were snatching poor Trevor McPhee on a regular basis to study and extract information from him. Each time they returned him, ten Earth years would have passed by. Over the course of the episode, six different time periods would be visited by the time-tripping (and very disoriented) McPhee. We saw slices of life from the 1940s to the 1990s. It was one of our weirdest concepts. We had Jon Cryer, who's a wonderful actor, playing a 1950s guy who wakes up in a different era and we picked *all* the fun eras."

Writer **Steven Barnes** on "The Heist": "When I originally pitched that idea, it was about an inner city gang that hijacks the truck. It was sort of *Boyz N the Hood* meets *Reservoir Dogs* meets *Alien*. I wasn't really thinking about [Howard Hawks' 1951 film] *The Thing from Another World*, but it came out that way. It was basically a bunch of people trapped in a big building among monsters, who were killing them off one at a time. That was kinda fun because I had never done it before! It came out looking very experimental, sort of 'guerrilla cinema' with hand-held cameras. It's not at the top of the list of the stuff I've done but it's not a loss, either. But I'm proud of all my children!"

Co-executive producer **Sam Egan**: "I really loved 'Jack,' which was a Jack the Ripper episode. We went to Victoria, B.C., and it was the most expensive *Outer Limits* ever to get the exteriors. The buildings. The streets. The back alleys. It's not an easy thing to find outside of London. Bringing the whole company out to Victoria was not cheap."

Co-executive producer **Jonathan Glassner**: "The beauty of an anthology show is we don't have that problem of, 'Captain Picard wouldn't say that!' Continuing TV series have that problem. But on an anthology show, it's new rules, new characters, new everything, every week. We have a tone to the show that we're very strict about sticking to. We have a lot of rules about credibility, and when and where it's set. [The story has] got to have a moral to it. Often writers will come in with a really cool story with absolutely no meaning to it and we usually won't buy a story like that. It's got to have a point to it. That's something writers bump into a lot, in addition to the, 'We've done that before' syndrome."

Prey

Director **William Corcoran**: "After the show was canceled, I received e-mails from all over the world from the *Prey* fan club and others, pleading with the network to put the show back on the air, but of course it was too late by then."

Psi-Factor: Chronicles of the Paranormal

Guest star **Kim Poirier** (Marisa): Sixteen years old, Poirier played the victim of a "gator-bear" monster in the episode "The Underneath": "I found it kinda funny, I had to be scared of this alligator-furry thingy. They tore up my dress and I had to lie there on the cold cement and die. They did some special effects on my legs and the blood they used, which tastes like cherries, stained my legs for a week. I remember lying there, giggling to myself in this pool of blood, and my screen-mother discovers me in all my glory and she was so good, she didn't break a smile. She was dramatic and emotionally affected, even though I was kinda chuckling at the whole thing. How unprofessional of me! From that point on, I swore I would always give it my all and stay in the moment, even if the camera was not on me. It was a fun experience and it was my first death. I've had many more since then."

Co-star **Barclay Hope** (Peter Axon): "Luc Chalifour was our first assistant director, he was French-Canadian. He talked with a French accent. And one day we had a friend of mine, Damir Andrei [as a guest star]. We had this whole town set up, and we were shooting at night. We had this immense crane with xenon lights shining up on this massive mirror that was bouncing the light back down to where we were shooting. It's two or three o'clock in the morning. Damir Andrei had finished his bit and Luc Chalifour came over the walkie-talkie and he said, 'Okay, that's it! Wrap Damir!' and they started to bring the mirror down. And he said, 'No, no! Wrap Damir! Not the mirror! *Damir!*' That's just funny. Stuff like that comes up all the time."

Quantum Leap

Guest star **Richard Herd** on his guest role in "Future Boy": "I read a lot of H.G. Wells and watched wonderful movies like *The Day the Earth Stood Still* and *Things to Come* as a young man, so I loved doing *Quantum Leap*. I played a TV host named Captain Galaxy and it remains my favorite television part — he was so vulnerable, so loving and so human. It was based on *Captain Video*, the TV show from the 1950s, which I watched occasionally in Boston. The episode was so successful there was talk of spinning Captain Galaxy into a series of its own. I would have loved to have done that."

Director **Gus Trikonis**: "The show was a lot like *Star Trek*, with rich characters. It could have gone on forever since it was dealing with history, where there are a million stories. During filming, my son asked me if I could get a cigar from Dean Stockwell and Dean even signed it! Dean and Scott Bakula were a joy to work with."

Space Above and Beyond

Director **Stephen Posey**: "[The series] was an interesting attempt to take duty and honor into deep space but I had a hard time relating to the characters. I also had a hard time not chuckling at the image of a drop-dead gorgeous actress leading a squad of Marines and firing rounds from an awesome automatic weapon. It was a great cartoon that probably took itself too seriously."

Actor **Tucker Smallwood** (Commodore Glen Van Ross): "As I moved through a major airport, I passed a military recruitment office. Hearing the sound of approaching footsteps, I turned to face an Army sergeant in dress greens, a healthy row of ribbons and decorations on his chest. He said to me, with great intensity, 'I watch your show every week! I make sure my son watches that show every week!' We shook hands and I went my way, but have never forgotten that encounter and cherish the approval from my peers who continue to acknowledge that we 'got it right!'"

Stargate SG-1

Guest star **Alex Zahara** on playing the fish-faced alien Xe'ls in the second-season episode "Spirits": "I got zapped out in a gurney in a medical ward, just lying there. It was like 38 degrees [Celsius] in the studio and 40 up in the rafters. It's hotter than hell. In between takes they put air conditioning up my skirt just to cool me down. It was so hot, I passed out. All I remember was Amanda Tapping, shaking my shoulder, 'Alex! Alex! You're snoring!' I was snoring between takes. My nose was sealed off [by the makeup]. That's hysterical.

"The most prevalent thing about having prosthetic makeup work is no one knows my face except for the makeup guys and the producers. Richard Dean Anderson never saw me without makeup. So when we finished lunch, I saw him standing across the studio, and I called out, 'Hey Richard! I'll see ya!' He looked at me, all perplexed, 'Who are you?' I went, 'Oh Richard, it's me!' I put one hand below my nose and the other above it, framing my eyes, and he went, 'Oh, Alex! Okay!' That's the only way he recognized me. I just blocked my face off and showed him my eyes! Probably 95 percent of the time he sees me in a mask."

Guest star **Peter Williams**, who made 20 appearances as the Goa'uld nemesis Apophis: "I was cast partially because of my physical resemblance to the actor Jaye Davidson, who played Ra in the movie. And I was assured that Apophis would be around, virtually in perpetually, as the nemesis to the SG-1 team. But every time he goes up against SG-1, he essentially loses. He has been killed once and has been brought back to life. I enjoy the fact that death is not necessarily the end for Apophis. I knew about the concept of the Sarcophagus, and the regenerative powers that it has, but I didn't realize it could be used so quite effectively. It was a pleasant surprise."

Starhunter

Star **Michael Pare** (Dante Montana): "I did *Starhunter* because it was supposed to be a western in outer space. Then they decided they didn't want to do a western in outer space. Fans have asked me, 'How come you never did any bounty hunting?' And I never did. We just picked up the bad guys and shipped them somewhere else."

Star Trek: Enterprise

Actor **Vaughn Armstrong** (Admiral Forrest): "*Star Trek* has a very hopeful theme. First, that we all live in peace. Second, that all beings unite in the quest for a better life for all, and third, that we will be able to accomplish this through steady progress in technology and understanding. Historically *Star Trek* has endeavored to touch on very contemporary and controversial themes. The shows have promoted unity in our society when others seemed hellbent on tearing it apart. It's a show that's inclusive of the rights of others. Although you may have this kind of forehead and I may have pointy ears, we're all in this together."

Star Trek: The Next Generation

Director **Cliff Bole** on the state of *Star Trek*: "Give it some breathing room. With *Enterprise*, it was a little too much, it got to be a little redundant. You begin running into a wall for awhile, even though you try to keep things interesting with new ideas."

Director **Winrich Kolbe**: "*The Next Generation* had one of the finest casts in television and excellent writing. Audiences didn't just watch it, they lived it."

Guest star **Ellen Bry** on the episode "The Quality of Life": "Memorizing the dialogue was like learning a foreign language. I had a wealth of technobabble to memorize. I felt proud about getting beyond the memorization to present a character. You can easily get hung up with the words."

Star Trek: Voyager

Director **Nancy Malone**: "TV has produced some extraordinary work but in some of today's episodic series, mostly everything and everybody looks the same. Everyone shoots the same, a lot of close-ups are used, a lot of hand-held, and very little variety in lighting styles. Where are the writers who can write people who are substantial? At their Playstations, I guess ... getting ideas."

Strange World

Star **Tim Guinee** on his strangest fan encounter: "A guy stopped me on the street in New York City. He said he loved the show and that it was especially meaningful to him because, he claimed, he was a clone. Well, what do you say to that? I told the clone I was glad he enjoyed the show and hurried down the street away from him!"

Guest star **Tony Alcantar**: "I thought *Strange World* would be a good show. However, the expectation of every new series is that it will peak right out of the box with record ratings numbers. If the same ridiculous standards were given to other TV shows, we'd never have known *Seinfeld*, *Cheers* or half of the Norman Lear sitcoms. On the other hand, what kept *Life With Jim* or *Becker* on the air?"

Total Recall 2070

Director **Mark Sobel** remembers working with character actor Henry Gibson in his episode "Bones Beneath My Skin": "Henry is one of the most underrated actors in Hollywood because everyone still thinks of him from *Rowan & Martin's Laugh-In* from the 1960s. Henry is just a wonderful actor with incredible range. We just had a great time. In fact, when I read the script, he was the first actor that came to mind. I said to [supervising producer] Jeff King, 'What about Henry Gibson?' and Jeff said, 'Well, let me put him on the list.' We had a list that would be sent to the executive producer. Jeff showed up the next day and said, 'They loved the idea of

Henry Gibson!' There was no one to sell. Everyone just thought it was a great idea.

"I have a memory of one lunch, I was sitting there. Karl [Pruner] was sitting there. And a young actress, who was just a day player on the show, I think she was the secretary. We were just chatting. Henry, out of paper, was making a little flower. As he got up, he handed her the paper flower. Smiled, and walked away. Karl turned to her and said, 'Do you know what it means to be handed a flower by Henry Gibson?' She was too young to remember him from *Rowan & Martin's Laugh-In*. She didn't get it. But both Karl and I thought, 'Wow!' It was a lot of fun. It's really interesting, as a student of film and TV, to be working with someone like that, who is a walking encyclopedia."

VR5

Writer **Jacqueline Blain**: "The pilot tape of *VR5* was dropped off at my house the night before my meeting with the producers. Frankly, in watching it, I thought the idea was better than the execution. The pilot was really over-saturated with color and not entirely convincing, but the premise was intriguing and I thought it might make an interesting show. The series' biggest strength was its creativity. I don't think I've worked on a show with better art direction or style. Had the series started a couple of years earlier, it would have done a lot better."

The X-Files

Actor **William B. Davis** (Cigarette Man) on fan recognition: "There was a person on an elevator and she suddenly noticed that she was alone with me. She nearly jumped out of her skin. When she calmed down, she said, 'You look like that scary guy on *The X-Files*!' When I said I was, she shrieked again and asked for pictures and autographs."

Director **Joe Napolitano**: "'Darkness Falls' was difficult because we had extreme weather problems. We were out in the middle of the woods and got rained out. There was a dam nearby and we were worried the dam was going to overflow or something and we would get trapped. The Parks Department actually forced us to leave. Those production problems messed the show up a bit, but I enjoyed working with Chris Carter and the crew was terrific."

Guest star (and former child actor on TV's *Land of the Giants*) **Stefan Arngrim** on his role as a prisoner in the two-parter "Terma" and "Tunguska": "You just saw my eyes as I conversed with David Duchovny's character in the cell of a gulag. It was an interesting acting challenge to convey my personality through my eyes. I really disappeared in that role and became someone else. People who have known me for years had no idea it was me. Working with creator Chris Carter was terrific. He's a brilliant writer who wrote our dialogue right there on set, which is very rare. I played a Russian prisoner and for background scenes, they found every Russian extra they could in Vancouver. These extras would speak to me in Russian, thinking I was a real Russian. I kept going, 'Uh, uh ... yeah, yeah ... sure, si!' They were shocked when I finally spoke English."

APPENDIX B:
LOOKING BACK AT
SCIENCE FICTION TELEVISION
SERIES, 1955–1989

These shows not only influenced later SF television but are cited by some contemporary creators and producers as personal favorites. As background material to this volume, here is a rundown of the previous decades of SFTV. These shows are covered in comprehensive detail in our previous McFarland volume, Science Fiction Television Series ... 1959–1989. *For more information, visit our website at: http://legacyweb.com/ scifibook*

Science Fiction Theater. 1955–1957. Syndicated. Host: Truman Bradley.

This anthology had stories about synthetic nutrients that extend human lives; aliens who are using the moon as a nuclear dumping ground, a boy who is cryogenically frozen so that his illness can one day be cured, etc., etc. Producer Ivan Tors later produced *Flipper* and *Daktari*. "Ivan would never accept junk like aliens attacking Earth or giant insects on the loose," said director Herbert L. Strock.

Men into Space. 1959–1960. CBS. Starring William Lundigan.

The first prime-time space series, dealing with the NASA-like adventures of Colonel Edward Mc-Cauley. He dealt with moonquakes, shuttle rides and visits to Mars. "Bill got pretty disgusted with the whole show," says his widow, Rena Lundigan. "He said he spent most of his time sitting in a space capsule, talking to himself!" The U.S. Defense Department grew concerned that stories could reveal military secrets. "A little man from Washington would arrive on set and demand to know where the writers were getting their ideas!" says Mrs. Lundigan.

World of Giants. 1959–1960. Syndicated. Starring Marshall Thompson, Arthur Franz.

"It was truly a ridiculous idea," says William Alland, who was brought aboard in midstream to pro-duce the faltering series. Mel Hunter was a six-inch-tall secret agent whose missions included exposing smugglers and stealing microfilm. Mel was also chased by giant cats, dogs and gophers. Alland credits Stan Horsley with creating the show's impressive special effects, but of the series says, "It would have great as a comic strip but as a TV series, it didn't fly."

The Twilight Zone. 1959–1964. CBS. Creator-Host: Rod Serling.

Twilight Zone allowed Serling to examine prejudice, conformity and political arenas without being browbeaten by nervous censors. He wrote many of the episodes and also hired prestigious writers such as Ray Bradbury, Richard Matheson, Earl Hamner Jr. and Charles Beaumont. "The show was about ordinary people who encountered fantasy," says producer Buck Houghton. "Fantasy or not, the scripts were damned good." Actress Jodie Foster said she would race home in the 1990s to watch *Twilight Zone* marathons on TV.

The Outer Limits. 1963–1965. ABC. The Control Voice: Vic Perrin.

Unusual monsters were its staple. It also had some unlikely fans. "Dick Van Dyke called me up after my episode 'The Man Who Was Never Born' aired and he just raved about the show," says actor Martin

Landau. "He loved it!" Joseph Stefano and Leslie Stevens produced the first year and Ben Brady took over for year two. While the early reviews were punishing ("It's powerful, although unintended, laugh medicine," said *The New York Herald-Tribune*), *Outer Limits* later became such a hit in syndication that ABC considered bringing it back in 1966. It would finally return to television in 1995 on Showtime. By then, the original was regarded as a classic show. Whether they be human or alien, characters always came away with new degrees of insight about their world.

Voyage to the Bottom of the Sea. 1964–1968. ABC. Starring Richard Basehart, David Hedison.

The early episodes were written by some of Hollywood's best TV writers, but things changed. Richard Basehart laughed when producer Irwin Allen excitedly described an upcoming show where the submarine *Seaview* battled a two-headed seaweed monster, until he realized Allen was serious. The monsters fed the ratings and by the third year the submariners were fighting leprechauns, mummies, killer toys, werewolves, ghosts and aliens. When Japanese tourists visited the set, a weary Basehart explained to them, "All I can tell you is that every Friday, someone flushes the toilet in Irwin Allen's office and the script ends up here."

Lost in Space. 1965–1968. CBS. Starring Guy Williams, June Lockhart, Mark Goddard, Jonathan Harris, Marta Kristen, Angela Cartwright, Bill Mumy.

A family is marooned on an uncharted planet, with their stowaway, Dr. Smith, getting them into trouble each week. The first year was fairly dramatic but Dr. Smith, young Will Robinson and the Robot took over in the comedic second year. In 1965, when someone pointed to a headline concerning America's first space walk to producer Irwin Allen, he snapped, "Who cares? That's only real life!" Composer John Williams provided much of the show's exciting music and Michael Rennie, Kurt Russell and Daniel J. Travanti were some of the guest stars. "*Lost in Space* was cancelled because Bill Paley, the head of CBS, hated the show," says writer Robert Hamner. "He never understood its appeal and wanted it off his network."

The Time Tunnel. 1966–1967. ABC. Starring James Darren, Robert Colbert, Lee Meriwether, Whit Bissell, John Zaremba.

Tony Newman and Doug Phillips were lost in time, materializing in hot spots of history. Some episodes had dimension — Tony crying over his dying father at Pearl Harbor in 1941 and Regis Toomey as a 20th century doctor, felled by ageism, who is transported to 1805 to work medical miracles. Ellen Burstyn, Dennis Hopper and Robert Duvall were some of the guest stars. The series' renewal for a second year was rescinded in favor of ABC's

ill-fated *Legend of Custer* series. Tom Hanks says *Time Tunnel* was his favorite TV show as a youngster.

Star Trek. 1966–1969. NBC. Starring William Shatner, Leonard Nimoy, DeForest Kelley, James Doohan, Nichelle Nichols, George Takei, Walter Koenig, Majel Barrett.

Cast chemistry and exciting, thought-provoking scripts gave this Gene Roddenberry series eternal life in syndication. William Shatner's heroic yet playful Captain Kirk and Leonard Nimoy's sensitive and believable Mr. Spock became iconic characters. The rushed filming schedule sometimes led to on-set snafus. Guest star Booker Bradshaw recalls slapping Mr. Spock in a sickbay sequence. "Leonard Nimoy told me to give him a real slap, so I slapped him and his Vulcan ears went flying off. Everyone collapsed in hysterics but Leonard was really pissed and he chased me around the set, yelling, 'I'm going to kill this guy!'"

The Invaders. 1966–1968. ABC. Starring Roy Thinnes.

An adult tale of one man's desperate battle against aliens who have assumed human form and infiltrated our society. When the aliens died, they emitted a spectacular red glow before turning to dust. Over the show's two years, architect David Vincent managed to convince 118 civilians of the invasion and later the U.S. Pentagon got involved. But the aliens were still among us when the show ended. The series was a cult phenomenon in France and in 1995 it was updated as a Fox mini-series starring Scott Bakula and Roy Thinnes.

The Champions. 1968. NBC. Starring Stuart Damon, Alexandra Bastedo, William Gaunt.

Three secret agents die in a plane crash in Tibet but a mystical old man revives them and gives them superpowers. The agents' missions were more Cold War than science fiction. Budget-deprived, the producers once chased a fire truck to get footage of a burning building, which they incorporated into the show. Hundreds of fans applauded when the three *Champions* stars reunited in 2006 at a U.K. convention.

The Prisoner. 1968. CBS. Starring Patrick McGoohan.

"I am not a number, I am a free man!" That was the weekly cry of a secret agent trapped in a village where "high security risk" people are confined for the rest of their lives. Number 6's mysterious captors want information which he refuses to divulge. His escape attempts were foiled by Rover, a giant bouncing ball. Patrick McGoohan co-created and produced the critically acclaimed series. "Creative people ran the asylum just for once," says writer Terence Feely. "We showed what a marvelous tool television is for surrealistic expression."

Land of the Giants. 1968–1970. ABC. Starring Gary Conway, Kurt Kasznar, Don Marshall, Deanna Lund, Don Matheson, Heather Young, Stefan Arngrim.

The Los Angeles Times and *Newsday* deemed this Irwin Allen series a winner and Frank Sinatra called it "one hell of a groovy series," but acerbic critic Rex Reed said, "It looks like it was written in 30 minutes over a pastrami sandwich." It was then the most expensive show in history, but its efforts to appeal to an adult audience sometimes backfired. ABC refused to broadcast a scene of human skeletons hanging in a giant spider's web. The crew members and passengers of a spaceflight struggled to survive on this giant, totalitarian world. Kurt Kasznar, who played Fitzhugh, celebrated the day *Giants* was cancelled. "It was an awful show!" he said.

The New People. 1969–1979. ABC. Starring Tiffany Bolling, David Moses, Jill Jaress, Peter Ratray.

A plane crashes on a mysterious island and its 40 survivors (college students) must now build their own society. It's a disparate bunch that includes a doctor, a bad girl, a pregnant girl, a rebel and a bully. Flashbacks provided the characterization while stories wrestled with issues of racism, women's rights and gun control. Rod Serling wrote the pilot (under a pseudonym) and Aaron Spelling was executive producer.

UFO. 1969–1970. Syndicated. Starring Ed Bishop, Michael Billington, George Sewell, Gabrielle Drake, Wanda Ventham.

SHADO was a military organization dedicated to battling hostile flying saucers, its headquarters hidden under a film studio. It controlled a fleet of submarines and a moonbase (where female operatives had purple hair). Despite the pulp-fiction premise, its stories were remarkably adult. Hugo award novelist David Gerrold says, "I enjoyed the series enormously. The episode where Commander Straker must choose between saving his son or continue his mission was my favorite. Straker's son dies and that was very bold storytelling."

The Immortal. 1970–1971. ABC. Starring Christopher George, Don Knight.

Ben Richards was a racecar driver who discovered he had "special blood" that doomed him to live forever. A rich businessman wanted Richards' blood and so the cross-country chase was on. ABC demanded the stories be rehashes of *The Fugitive* rather than SF, so Richards' exploits included working on a tomato farm and helping friendly Indians. The series was loosely based on the acclaimed novel *The Immortals* by James E. Gunn.

Rod Serling's Night Gallery. 1970–1973. NBC. Host: Rod Serling.

Each episode opened in a dark art gallery, as Serling introduced tales of horror and SF. Stories were varied — ranging from Burgess Meredith as a discredited doctor who uses a futuristic medical kit to cure sick people in ghettos to Lana Wood as a kindhearted android who leads a rebellion against humanity. There were also tales of earwigs that crawled into people's heads and mouse-like broaches that fed on blood. Serling enjoyed working on *Night Gallery*'s first year and said, "I think it will be a better show than *Twilight Zone*." But his creative control lessened and he was dismayed when the PTA accused the show of damaging kids' psyches.

The Starlost. 1973–1974. NBC. Starring Keir Dullea, Gay Rowan, Robin Ward.

Created by Harlan Ellison and filmed in Canada, *Starlost* had an ambitious premise: Three young people find their world is actually one of many domes on a giant spaceship carrying descendants of Earth. Hampered by an ultra-low budget, the protagonists' journeys were reduced to a few feet of corridor and static sets. "It was hurt by a tough schedule, with budgetary constraints," says main writer Norman Klenman. "But nobody should apologize for what they did. It was a damn good try."

The Six Million Dollar Man. 1974–1978. ABC. Starring Lee Majors, Richard Anderson.

"Pure crappo!" That's how novelist Martin Caidin, whose novel the series was based on, characterized the first two 90-minute episodes of this series. The producers initially wanted astronaut Steve Austin, the world's first bionic man, to be a globe-trotting James Bond type but that didn't work. Harve Bennett was brought in to produce the hour episodes and turned it into a hit series by making Austin a down-to-earth agent for the government.

Kolchak: The Night Stalker. 1974–1975. ABC. Starring Darren McGavin, Simon Oakland.

Based on two hugely successful TV movies, the series followed Chicago reporter Carl Kolchak as he chased zombies, werewolves, mummies, robots, aliens and even the Devil. Darren McGavin was perfect as Kolchak but while the show was a big hit with teenagers, older viewers stayed away. The show also endured production woes. "When *Night Stalker*'s cancellation was announced, the whole company stood up and applauded," says production manager Ralph Sariego.

Planet of the Apes. 1974. CBS. Starring Roddy McDowall, Ron Harper, James Naughton, Mark Lenard, Booth Colman.

CBS executives were sure this spin-off on the popular films would be a big hit. But it finished 67 out of 80 shows for the season. "That was incredibly disappointing," says star Ron Harper, who played one of the astronauts on the run from gorillas. "But the writing wasn't very imaginative. It boiled down to one of us being captured every week." Writer Arthur Brown contends, "The ape makeup factor killed the show, it was too expensive."

The Invisible Man. 1975–1976. NBC. Starring David McCallum, Melinda Fee, Craig Stevens.

A scientist turns himself invisible but can't reverse the process. The consequences are typical: He becomes a government agent! Instead of SF stories, plots revolved around bank robbers and crooked judges. "David McCallum got the blame for the show's demise, the network said he was too 'foreign' for viewers," says associate producer Richard Milton. "That was crap. The format of the show just never took off."

Space 1999. 1975–1977. Syndicated. Starring Martin Landau, Barbara Bain, Barry Morse (year 1).

Gerry Anderson's big-budgeted saga of the moon blasted into space, as residents of moonbase Alpha hold on tight as they encounter a hostile universe. There were good guests (Joan Collins, Christopher Lee, Peter Cushing) and lavish effects but it was often unintentionally funny ("We do not commit mindless violence!" Commander Koenig shouts woodenly). Year two became more juvenile, if easier to comprehend. "Had we stayed in the direction of the first year, we might have run for years," says Martin Landau.

The Bionic Woman. 1976–1978. ABC and NBC. Starring Lindsay Wagner, Richard Anderson.

Lindsay Wagner won an Emmy for her portrayal of former tennis champion Jaime Sommars, who gets bionic limbs after her parachute fails during a skydive. She reluctantly works for the government on spy missions. "It benefited greatly from Lindsay's warmth, charm, intelligence and sincerity," says writer Lionel Siegel. Director Larry Stewart agrees. "It was a fine series that humanized its premise to a great degree."

(The New, Original) Wonder Woman. 1976–1979. CBS. Starring Lynda Carter, Lyle Waggoner.

Developed for TV by *Batman* writer Stanley Ralph Ross, *Wonder Woman* starred Miss World USA, Lynda Carter. The first year, set during World War II, had the Amazon beauty fight Nazis but when the series was updated to the 1970s, she encountered aliens, leprechauns, deadly toys and time travelers.

The Gemini Man. 1976. NBC. Starring Ben Murphy, Katherine Crawford.

NBC made another stab at an invisible man, this time an adventurous secret agent whose wristwatch allows him to vanish for 15-minute intervals. But stale plots helped the show disappear after two months. "You're asking people to love someone who isn't there," laments executive producer Harve Bennett. "It also became very difficult to find inventive ways to use invisibility."

Future Cop. 1976–1978. ABC. Starring Ernest Borgnine, Michael Shannon, John Amos.

A rookie cop is actually an android and rides around with a veteran cop. A mix of drama and comedy, the premise was a little too old-hat. Novelists Ben Bova and Harlan Ellison successfully sued the series for copyright infringement, proving it was too similar to their story *Brillo* (published in 1970).

Fantastic Journey. 1977. NBC. Starring Jared Martin, Roddy McDowall, Katie Saylor, Ike Eisenmann, Carl Franklin.

Shipwrecked survivors travel across an island in the Bermuda Triangle, where different time zones project them into the past and future as they search for a portal back to their own time. "The scripts and characterizations were improving steadily," says story editor Dorothy C. Fontana. Jared Martin agreed. "It was a very dear series," he says. "It died because of the furious and merciless economics of television."

Man from Atlantis. 1977–78. NBC. Starring Patrick Duffy, Belinda J. Montgomery.

A humble water-breathing man washes ashore and becomes lead researcher aboard the submarine *Cetacean*. The first four TV movies were dramatic but the weekly series opted for fantasy as Mark Harris (Patrick Duffy) met elves, giant jellyfish, mermaids, a two-headed seahorse and a 19th century gunslinger. "A leading SF magazine wrote us a nasty, brutal letter — 'You have treated SF with disrespect!'" says writer Larry Alexander. "If people want to blame the witty, tongue-in-cheek approach for the show's failure, they can put it on my door completely."

Logan's Run. 1977–1978. CBS. Starring Gregory Harrison, Heather Menzies, Donald Moffat.

This series, based on the 1976 film *Logan's Run*, had scripts from writers such as Dorothy C. Fontana, Harlan Ellison and David Gerrold but its cold premise, of a world where people over 30 must die, turned off viewers. Logan, Jessica and the android Rem searched the post-apocalyptic countryside for a paradise called Sanctuary. "I would give the series an A for effort and a C for the show itself," says Gregory Harrison.

The Incredible Hulk. 1977–1982. CBS. Starring Bill Bixby, Lou Ferrigno, Jack Colvin.

Even Fred Rogers, of *Mr. Rogers' Neighborhood*, called it, "a fine show." When Kenneth Johnson translated the comic book hero to television, he took a human, sensitive approach, best evidenced by Mariette Hartley's Emmy award win as David Banner's fiancée. Themes of child abuse and drug addiction were also tackled. "I wanted to make it classy and classical — a show that adults could watch," says Johnson.

(The Amazing) Spiderman. 1978–1979. CBS. Starring Nicholas Hammond.

This series was briefly successful, but a time slot change felled it. Star Nicholas Hammond says, "The show was very popular with kids in the ghetto. I got mail from concerned parents who said, 'You are the only positive role model in my child's life. All he sees in this world are pimps, prostitutes and drug pushers." Fred Waugh did the incredible Spiderman stunts and creator Stan Lee served as a consultant.

Project UFO. 1978–1979. NBC. Starring William Jordan (year 1), Caskey Swaim, Edward Winter (year 2).

This Jack Webb production became an immediate top 20 hit, riding the *Close Encounters of the Third Kind* (1977) craze. Two Air Force men investigated UFO reports, debunking each one as a hoax or a natural phenomenon.

Battlestar Galactica. 1978–1979. ABC. Starring Lorne Greene, Richard Hatch, Dirk Benedict.

Its premiere made the covers of *Newsweek* and *TV Guide* but despite some good scripts, many stories were rehashes of *The Guns of Navarone*, *High Noon* and *The Towering Inferno*. It followed the space journey of humans (survivors of a robotic attack) who were looking for a mythical planet called Earth. Mainstream audiences abandoned the show but loyal fans remained, savoring the elements that weren't contaminated by derivative plotting. "The special effects were terrific and the acting was fine," says writer Donald P. Bellisario. "But it became too hung up on technology and not enough on the stories." The series was re-imagined by the Sci-Fi Network in 2003.

Salvage One. 1979. ABC. Starring Andy Griffith, Trish Stewart, Joel Higgins, Richard Jaeckel.

An enterprising junkman uses his homemade rocket ship to salvage junk on the surface of the moon. That was the pilot show. Other episodes had him assist trapped aliens, encounter ape-creatures, tow an iceberg and give refuge to a runaway robot. But later episodes collapsed into the mundane—helping drought-stricken farmers and corralling wild horses. "We couldn't top going to the moon," says executive producer Harve Bennett. "Where do you go from there?"

Cliffhangers: The Secret Empire. 1979. NBC. Starring Geoffrey Scott.

Created by Kenneth Johnson, this homage to the serials of yesteryear was comprised of three continuing segments: "The Secret Empire," "Stop Susan Williams" (Susan Anton as a reporter) and "Curse of Dracula" (starring Michael Nouri). "Secret Empire's" surface scenes were filmed in black-and-white, while the underground city was shot in color.

Buck Rogers in the 25th Century. 1979–1981. NBC. Starring Gil Gerard, Erin Gray, Tim O'Connor (year 1), Thom Christopher (year 2).

The comic strip character was given a high-energy camp treatment by Glen Larson and Leslie Stevens. Buck Rogers is an astronaut who awakens in the year 2491 and adjusts to a new world threatened by over-the-top villains. The second year dropped the humor and sent Buck out to explore the cosmos aboard the *Searcher*. The show had some vigorous detractors. "The National Organization of Women hated us because we dressed beautiful women in skimpy costumes," says producer John Gaynor. "That gave us a lot of laughs!"

Galactica 1980. 1980. ABC. Starring Lorne Greene, Kent McCord, Barry Van Dyke, Robyn Douglass.

This ill-advised sequel to *Battlestar* took place years later, as the *Galactica* locates present-day Earth. The crew makes reconnaissance missions as they prepare to colonize Earth. The series also featured a group of Galactican kids who monopolized the show as it progressed. It's early evening time slot made it subject to an FCC rule that called for the show to be kid friendly. "There had to be at least one educative message every act," says producer Jeff Freilich.

Beyond Westworld. 1980. CBS. Starring Jim McMullan, Connie Sellecca, William Jordan, James Wainwright.

A special agent fights androids who have infiltrated our society, controlled by nefarious genius Simon Quaid. It was based on the 1973 film *Westworld* but executive producer Fred Freiberger knew the show was doomed early on. "It was an impossible concept," he said.

The Greatest American Hero. 1981–1983. ABC. Starring William Katt, Robert Culp, Connie Sellecca.

A high school teacher is given an extraterrestrial suit that gives him amazing powers. Stephen J. Cannell stressed stories with human values, as well as humor, which the cast excelled at. Joey Scarbury, who sang the hit tune "Believe it or Not," admitted he never saw the show.

The Phoenix. 1982. ABC. Starring Judson Scott.

An alien, awakened from an ancient sarcophagus, goes on a search for his wife while being pursued by government agents. "The network wanted it to appeal to everyone but they didn't understand its nature," says co-creator Nancy Lawrence. "They wanted it to be more of a children's show."

V: The Series. 1984–1985. NBC. Starring Marc Singer, Michael Ironside, Faye Grant, Lane Smith and Jane Badler.

Resistance fighters battle The Visitors, alien lizards who have taken human form and now occupy the Earth. The series was based on the popular *V* miniseries. Action was a weekly staple, with good conflict between the two leads (characters played by Marc Singer and Michael Ironside). But when Ironside left, the series lost its momentum.

Powers of Matthew Star. 1982–1983. NBC. Starring Peter Barton, Lou Gossett Jr.

An alien teenager with superpowers seeks refuge from assassins by enrolling at an Earth high school. "It was the story of a teenager growing into manhood and accepting responsibility for himself and other people,' says Peter Barton. Because of poor ratings the premise was changed midway and Matthew became a secret agent for the government.

Voyagers. 1982–1983. NBC. Starring Jon-Erik Hexum, Meeno Peluce.

A time agent Phineas Bogg and 12-year-old orphan Jeffrey travel through time, correcting time anomalies. "It was a wonderful concept," says producer Jill Sherman, but there were disappointments. "A gentleman at Universal told us we couldn't do stories on Napoleon or Harriet Tubman because they didn't have a high enough TVQ recognition factor!"

Automan. 1983–1984. ABC. Starring Desi Arnaz Jr., Chuck Wagner.

A police computer expert creates a three-dimensional hologram that he dubs Automan and together they fight crime. "It was interesting because it was not only a superhero show but also a comedy," says Desi Arnaz Jr.

Otherworld. 1985. CBS. Starring Sam Groom, Gretchen Corbett.

A doorway in an Egyptian tomb propels an ordinary family into another dimension, where they travel from city to city to find a way home. The scene where the family gets lost in the tomb was based on a true-life experience of story editor Coleman Luck. "A guide took me and my family to the bottom of a pyramid in Cairo and then demanded more money. I refused, so he turned off his flashlight and ran off, leaving us in this dreary tomb. We struck matches and slowly made our way out!"

Misfits of Science. 1985–1986. NBC. Starring Dean Paul Martin, Courteney Cox, Kevin Peter Hall, Mark Thomas Miller.

NBC president Brandon Tartikoff wanted a superhero show but he disowned the series when he saw the result. "It makes me feel terrible when people call it a bad show because it wasn't a bad show," claims story editor Donald Todd. "It had a lot of human dimension and a great cast." Each misfit had different powers, and were under the guidance of eccentric Dr. Billy Hayes (Dean Paul Martin).

Amazing Stories. 1985–1987. NBC.

Steven Spielberg, a fan of the original *Twilight Zone* and *Outer Limits*, was given a 44-episode commitment to do a big budget anthology. He recruited a wide variety of actors (Sid Caesar, Danny DeVito, Hayley Mills), directors (Clint Eastwood, Burt Reynolds, Peter Hyams, Martin Scorsese, Joe Dante, Robert Zemeckis) and scripts by people such as Richard Matheson. But critics and audiences were underwhelmed. "The main reason why *Amazing Stories* didn't work for audiences is that they didn't know what to expect every week,' says director Mick Garris. "One week it would be a kid-oriented fantasy, the next week a dark thriller. But a third of the shows were terrific."

The Twilight Zone. 1985–1987. CBS. 1987–1988, Syndicated. Narrator Charles Aidman (year 1–2), Robin Ward (syndicated versions).

Philip DeGuere was given the task of updating the iconic series and while it never escaped Rod Serling's shadow, it did produce memorable stories. "Profile in Silver" was an ambitious story about a time traveler who successfully prevents President John Kennedy's assassination and the scenes of the traveler meeting with Kennedy aboard Air Force One afterward are chillingly authentic. "Her Pilgrim Soul" was a tour de force by Kristoffer Tabori as a scientist who falls in love with the hologram of a woman. After two years of tepid ratings on CBS, a third year was commissioned for syndication.

Starman. 1986–1987. ABC. Starring Robert Hays, Christopher Daniel Barnes.

Based on the 1984 feature film. Starman was an alien who assumed human form and traveled the country with his teenage son, Scott. As they try to locate Scott's human mother, they help people in need, as well as dodge perennially perplexed government agents. Producer Leon Tokatyan insisted on human tales. "Hard-edged stories wouldn't have worked," he says, "Nor did we feel we were doing an SF show, per se."

The Ray Bradbury Theater. 1986–1992. Host: Ray Bradbury.

A fantasy anthology that adapted Bradbury's fanciful short stories. "Out of 65 shows, only four were outright clinkers," says Bradbury. This Canadian-made show's reputation for quality attracted actors such as Gordon Pinsent, William Shatner, Drew Barrymore, Peter O'Toole, Jean Stapleton, Richard Kiley, Louise Fletcher and Robert Culp.

Max Headroom. 1987. ABC. Starring Matt Frewer, Amanda Pays.

An investigative reporter named Edison Carter is near death when he merges with an artificial intelligence program, creating the bizarre Max Headroom. Together, Edison and Max join forces for justice and higher ratings in a world dominated by TV images. "I think we were guilty of style over content," says star Matt Frewer. "As great as it was, it made the characters and stories suffer."

Captain Power and the Soldiers of the Future.
1987–1988. Syndicated.

Starring Tim Dunigan, Jessica Steen, Peter Mac-Neill, David Hemblen, Sven Thorson, Maurice Dean Wint, Bruce Gray.

This Canadian-filmed series, about human soldiers in 2147 A.D. battling mechanical opponents, was designed to sell toys, not drama. Still, creator Gary Goddard says, "Our goal was to do a quality SF show within our limitations."

Probe. 1988. ABC. Starring Parker Stevenson, Ashley Crow.

Did an anti-smoking cure turn people into zombies? Did a witch's curse really kill a TV host? Those were questions investigated by the brilliant (if obnoxious) head of Serendip, Austin James. Isaac Asimov and Michael Wagner created the show, which stressed real science.

War of the Worlds. 1988–1990. Syndicated. Starring Jared Martin, Lynda Mason Green, Richard Chaves (year 1), Adrian Paul (year 2).

This series was a continuation of George Pal's 1953 film, set 35 years later. The Martians return in their killing machines to attack Earth. A group of specialists battle the invaders.

Something Is Out There. 1988. NBC. Starring Joe Cortese, Maryam d'Abo.

The mini-series, about an alien woman hunting a shape-shifting creature, was a big hit but the weekly series had the female ET and a New York cop chase serial killers and bust drug rings. "I wish the show had worked," lamented Cortese years afterward. "But it didn't."

The Adventures of Superboy. 1988–1992. Syndicated. Starring John Haymes Newton (year 1), Gerard Christopher (year 2–4), Stacy Haiduk.

Superboy battles supervillains and crime while his alter-ego, Clark Kent, attends university as a journalism student.

Hard Time on Planet Earth. 1989. CBS. Starring Martin Kove.

An alien revolutionary, sentenced to serve out his time on planet Earth, does good deeds, such as reuniting a teen with her estranged family and convincing a rodeo star that life is worth living.

Alien Nation. 1989–1990. Fox. Starring Gary Graham, Eric Pierpoint, Michelle Scarabelli.

Aliens from the planet Tencton are acclimated into human society, where they face challenges as they adapt as the world's newest minority. Based on the 1988 feature film, this series gained a loyal audience. Although it was cancelled after a year, producer Kenneth Johnson reunited the cast for five *Alien Nation* movies in the 1990s.

INDEX

Main entries and their corresponding main entry page numbers are indicated in **bold**.